H A N D B O O K S

SOUTH
CAROLINA

JIM MOREKIS

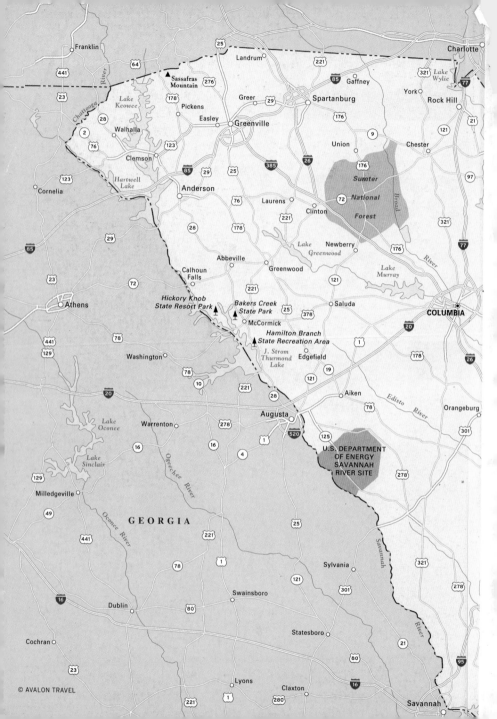

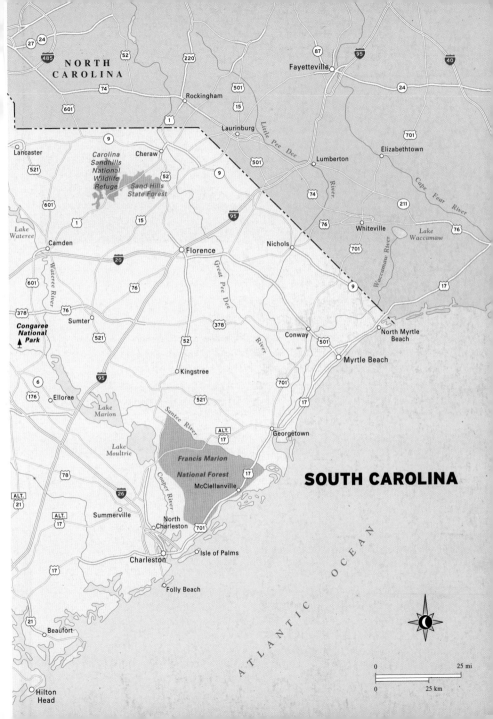

Contents

Discover South Carolina

Even by Southern standards, South Carolina is bathed in a certain mystique. I grew up right across the Savannah River in Georgia, and throughout my childhood the Palmetto State seemed to me an otherworldly locale, like something out of an old novel.

Who could resist the intrigue of the home of the Swamp Fox, a place where the first shots of the Civil War were fired, and rivers are named Ashepoo and Pee Dee? The Spanish moss hangs low, people catch their own seafood for dinner, and the creeks are like highways in the marsh.

As I got older, I discovered an important truth about South Carolina: Few states provide such a wealth of experience in such a small package. You can traverse its entire width in half a day, going from a beautiful white-sand beach to a stunning mountain overlook.

Along the way you'll experience a sampler of Southern culture encompassing the genteel remnants of the Lowcountry plantations, echoes of the old shag scene on the Grand Strand, and the very edge of Appalachia in the fast-growing Upstate region.

The common thread linking these disparate strands together is the people. Once here, you'll immediately tune in to a particularly South Carolinian vibe that's easygoing yet flamboyant, laid-back yet cocksure. This unique twist on proverbial Southern hospitality—a sort of assertive

niceness—is a product of the extraordinary resilience of South Carolinians, who have proudly maintained their identity despite centuries of war, strife, and natural disaster.

While history buffs flock to the region for its seemingly endless supply of colonial and Civil War sites, easily its most underrated attribute is the beauty of its environment and the scope of its outdoor recreation. You'll find the oldest cypress stands in the world, a wealth of mountain waterfalls, and some of the best fishing, kayaking, and white-water rafting in the country.

As for its essence, South Carolina has long been something of a paradox. Notorious as the cradle of secession during the Civil War, the state is today home to some of the nation's most patriotic citizens. Often caricatured as hopelessly retro, South Carolina's larger cities have quietly become magnets for high-tech jobs and foreign investment.

While the rest of the world tries to figure out what makes them tick, South Carolinians do what they've always done: make their way in the world, often too stubbornly, practicing their take on Southern hospitality and having as much fun as they can along the way.

Planning Your Trip

▶ WHERE TO GO

Charleston

One of America's oldest cities and an early national center of arts and culture, Charleston's legendary taste for the high life is matched by its forward-thinking outlook. The birthplace of the Civil War is not just a city of museums resting on its historic laurels. Situated on a hallowed spit of land known as "the peninsula," the Holy City is now a vibrant, creative hub of the New South.

Myrtle Beach and the Grand Strand

The 60-mile Grand Strand focuses on the resort and beach activity of Myrtle Beach and, to an increasing extent, North Myrtle Beach. Down the Strand are the more peaceful areas of Pawleys Island and Murrells Inlet, with the historic Georgetown area and its scenic plantations anchoring the bottom portion. Because of the Strand's long, skinny geography, always budget more time than you think you'll need to get around.

IF YOU HAVE . . .

Shopping on King Street in Charleston never disappoints.

- **A WEEKEND:** Make Charleston your home base. Include a jaunt down to the Beaufort and Hilton Head area, or north to Georgetown.
- **FIVE DAYS:** Add the heart of the Midlands: Columbia, Orangeburg, and Congaree National Park.
- **A WEEK:** Expand inland to Aiken's horse country and the Greenville and Spartanburg area, or back to the coast to Myrtle Beach and the Grand Strand.
- **10 DAYS:** Enough time to experience the whole state, including the Pee Dee and the Old English District.

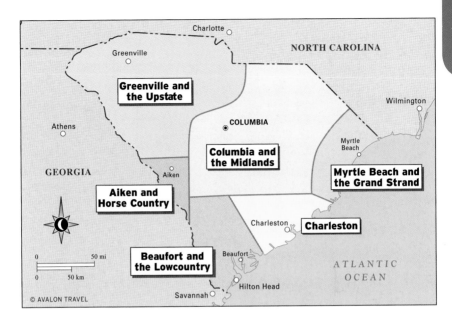

Beaufort and the Lowcountry

The Lowcountry's mossy, laid-back pace belies its former status as the heart of American plantation culture and the original cradle of secession. Today it is a mix of history (Beaufort and Bluffton), natural beauty (the ACE Basin), resort development (Hilton Head), military bases (Parris Island), and relaxed beaches (Edisto and Hunting Islands).

Columbia and the Midlands

The state capital and home of South Carolina's largest university, Columbia is still a very manageable, fun place. Visit the nationally known Riverbanks Zoo and Garden and the very good South Carolina State Museum, and enjoy the restaurants and nightlife of the Vista and Five Points neighborhoods. The surrounding area, the "real" South Carolina, offers a look at a small-town way of life usually seen in Norman Rockwell paintings.

Aiken and Horse Country

A resurgent polo scene is bringing affluent but accessible Aiken back to its full equestrian glory, and overall it remains one of the safest, friendliest, and most delightful little towns you'll ever visit. The nearby Savannah River valley contains rolling scenic farmland and charming towns steeped in history.

Greenville and the Upstate

Fast-growing Greenville can teach many other cities a lesson in tasteful, efficient renovation. Shopping is great, and Bob Jones University offers an excellent collection of religious art by old masters. A short drive away are the treats and treasures of South Carolina's Blue Ridge region—a more user-friendly, less expensive version of the trendy mountain towns over the border in North Carolina.

the strand along Myrtle Beach

▶ WHEN TO GO

Springtime is for lovers, and it's no coincidence that spring is when most love affairs with South Carolina begin. Unless you have severe pollen allergies, you should try to experience this area at its peak of natural beauty during the magical period from mid-March to mid-May. Not surprisingly, lodging is typically at a premium at that time.

The hardest time to get a room in Charleston is during Spoleto, Memorial Day to mid-June. Hilton Head's busiest time is during the RBC Heritage Classic Golf Tournament in mid-April.

For those interested in South Carolina's excellent state park system, be aware that there are minimum stays, usually one week, for cabin rentals during March-October. In the off-season, this doesn't apply.

June-October is hurricane season on the coast, with September in particular the time of highest risk.

In Myrtle Beach the high season is totally counterintuitive. Unlike the rest of the state, the absolute hottest months of summer are the big season—the better to enjoy the water, you see. Prices are higher and availability is lower during this time. Golfers, however, will tend to see bigger crowds on the links as the weather cools—though Myrtle Beach's oversupply of courses means there are usually tee times available and some good deals. In any case, starting about the middle of November you can find some very good prices on lodging in the entire Myrtle Beach area.

Under its metropolitan veneer, Columbia is still very much a college town. Fall means football, and that means the most festive time of year. It also means the most competition for lodging, especially when the Gamecocks are playing at home. Summer can get *really* slow in Columbia—and hot. As much as I like

The Upstate's many state parks offer relief from the heat in the rest of the state.

Columbia, I advise avoiding it during summer if possible.

Aiken has two big equestrian seasons. Most of March is taken up by the Triple Crown equestrian events, and October is big for tournament polo and steeplechase. Indirectly, April is also very competitive lodging-wise, largely because nearby Augusta, Georgia, hosts the insanely popular Masters golf tournament, with much spillover into Aiken.

The Upstate is great most any time of year. Spring is best weather-wise, and while summers can get quite hot, there's some real relief at night. Fall foliage scenery can be surprisingly glorious well into December.

While Columbia is Gamecock country, in the Upstate all things revolve around Clemson University Tiger football. During fall home games, lodging is more difficult to find in a wide radius around Clemson, and rooms sell out early.

My favorite time of year in South Carolina, though, is the middle of November, when the tourist crush subsides. Not only are the days delightful and the nights crisp (but not frigid), you can also get a room at a good price.

Explore South Carolina

▶ BEST SOUTH CAROLINA WEEKENDS

The Grand Strand

This long weekend gives you a taste of life in Myrtle Beach and the rest of the Grand Strand. The area is small enough to stay in one place for both nights, but so popular that travel along the 60-mile-long Strand can be slow. Be sure to leave enough time to get from place to place.

DAY 1

Begin the day at historic Hampton Plantation before taking a guided kayak tour around Winyah Bay or Hobcaw Barony. Have an early dinner on the waterfront in nearby Georgetown, then drive up to Myrtle Beach for the night. If you want to stay away from the resorts, camp at Huntington Beach State Park.

DAY 2

In the morning explore Brookgreen Gardens, one of the most unique sights in the Grand Strand. Spend the afternoon in Myrtle Beach: Shop at Broadway at the Beach. After dinner, go for a fun, cheesy round of miniature golf under the stars. Or perhaps take in a show at the Carolina Opry, or learn to dance the shag at old Ocean Drive Beach.

DAY 3

Spend the morning on the beach. After lunch visit one of the Ripley's attractions or take in a concert at the House of Blues in Barefoot Landing.

The Midlands

Sandwiched between the coast and the mountains, the Midlands are easily overlooked, but

Weston Lake, Congaree National Park

statue of Dizzy Gillespie in downtown Cheraw, by sculptor Ed Dwight

not for lack of attractions. This central section of the state is large and spread out. To fully experience the breadth of the area, bunk one night in Columbia and the next in Camden.

DAY 1

Devote a full day to touring South Carolina's capital, Columbia. Downtown sights include the South Carolina State Museum, the South Carolina State House, and the University of South Carolina. In addition, don't miss the Riverbanks Zoo and Garden. Have dinner in the trendy Vista area and finish with a nightcap in boisterous Five Points. Spend the night at the venerable Inn at USC.

DAY 2

Get up bright and early and drive out of town to Congaree National Park to walk along its primordial cypress swamp and old-growth forest. If you have time, go down to Orangeburg to see the Edisto Memorial Gardens. Head east and end the day in Camden. Explore the picturesque historic district with its many antiques shops.

DAY 3

Drive up U.S. 1 to Cheraw to see its charming historic district and visit the nearby Dizzy Gillespie home site and park. Then head down to Hartsville for lunch and a visit to Kalmia Gardens. Scoot over to Darlington and check out Darlington International Raceway, the grandfather of all stock car tracks. Spend the rest of the afternoon near Florence at Woods Bay State Natural Area, enjoying the well-preserved Carolina Bay.

Horse Country

You don't have to own a horse to enjoy a long weekend in Aiken and South Carolina's thoroughbred country. And since the area involved is so small, you can stay in the same hotel both nights. If you're here in spring, you can begin this trip on a Friday so you can see a polo match on Sunday.

CAROLINA FOR KIDS

Kids love the "lazy river" rides in Myrtle Beach.

Families with children will find plenty of fun and educational things to do in the Palmetto State, usually at very reasonable prices. Here are the highlights.

AROUND CHARLESTON

- Observe the many local marine habitats at the **South Carolina Aquarium** (page 41).
- Walk the flight deck of the USS *Yorktown* at **Patriots Point Naval and Maritime Museum** (page 67).
- Experience history on a restored explorer's sailing vessel at **Charles Towne Landing** (page 59).

- Do some serious shell collecting on **Edisto Island** (page 213).

MYRTLE BEACH

- Frolic amid the statuary at **Brookgreen Gardens** (page 167).
- Climb inside the "world's biggest boy" at **Children's Museum of South Carolina** (page 139).
- Get up close and personal with marine life at **Ripley's Aquarium** (page 137).
- Cater to the gators at **Alligator Adventure** (page 139).
- Putt-putt your butt off at **50 miniature golf courses** (page 155).
- And, of course, enjoy the beach itself!

AROUND COLUMBIA

- Learn about Palmetto State history at **South Carolina State Museum** (page 259).
- Enjoy kid-friendly exhibits at **EdVenture** (page 260).
- Visit **Riverbanks Zoo and Garden** (page 263), one of the country's best.
- Explore the old-growth forest at **Congaree National Park** (page 280).

THE UPSTATE

- See living Upstate history at **Historic Brattonsville** (page 414).
- Enjoy urban outdoor playtime at **Falls Park on the Reedy** (page 347).
- Pet the inhabitants of the **Greenville Zoo** (page 352).
- Tube the wild and scenic **Chattooga River** (page 377).

DAY 1

Explore Aiken's historic Winter Colony district and racetracks. After lunch, take a long relaxing hike in Hitchcock Woods before checking out the Carolina Bay Preserve. Head a little ways east to Montmorenci and check into Annie's B&B, or stay in Aiken at the classy Willcox or the old Aiken Hotel.

DAY 2

Get up bright and early to explore Aiken's Hitchcock Woods. If you're here in the fall and it's a Saturday, you might even catch a fox hunt. Then drive east to Blackville and its Healing Springs, stopping for lunch at Miller's Bread Basket in town. In the evening take in a movie at the Monetta Drive-In, one of only two functioning drive-in theaters in South Carolina.

DAY 3

In the morning, head west to Redcliffe Plantation State Historic Site and Riverview Park in North Augusta. If you're here in spring and it's a Sunday, after lunch return to Aiken in time for the afternoon polo match at Whitney Field.

The Upstate

This weekend trip highlights the best of the Upstate, from the beautiful natural setting to city life and early American history. Spend one night in the shadow of the Blue Ridge Mountains and another in cosmopolitan Greenville.

DAY 1

Begin at the South Carolina Botanical Garden in Clemson before heading over to little Pendleton and enjoying lunch on the Village Green. Head up to Walhalla in the afternoon and check out the unique Stumphouse Tunnel and Issaqueena Falls. Stay in a B&B or camp at Oconee State Park.

DAY 2

Spend the day in Greenville: enjoy Falls Park on the Reedy; do some shopping on restored Main Street; and maybe check out artworks by the great masters at the Bob Jones University Museum and Gallery. In the evening, take in a minor league baseball game at Fluor Field. Splurge for the night at the classy Westin Poinsett downtown.

DAY 3

Drive to Cowpens National Battlefield outside Spartanburg to learn about this pivotal Revolutionary War battle. After a classic greasy-spoon lunch at Spartanburg's Beacon Drive-In, head over to York County to check out Historic Brattonsville and its excellently restored upcountry homestead site, complete with living history demonstrations.

▶ MARSHES, SWAMPS, AND WHITE WATER

South Carolina packs a lot of habitat into a small area. Here's where to focus your environmental attention for maximum benefit.

Lowcountry

Kayak the inlet at Hunting Island State Park, where portions of *Forrest Gump* were filmed, then enjoy the scenic beach, concluding with a view from the top of the lighthouse.

Canoe in the ACE Basin, touring the Edisto River—the longest blackwater river in the world—on a guided trip. Head to Charleston and visit the South Carolina Aquarium to learn more about the entire state's vibrant water-oriented ecosystem.

North of Charleston, find the Sewee Visitor Center at the Cape Romain National Wildlife Refuge and see their family of rare red wolves. Then stop by Hobcaw Barony and

FOR SEAFOODIES

the docks of the Bluffton Oyster Company

South Carolina—especially the coastal region—is a paradise for seafood lovers. The state offers a wide range of epicurean pleasures, from the self-conscious high cuisine of Charleston's hot young chefs to rustic roadside seafood shacks. Here are some highlights you shouldn't miss.

SHRIMP AND GRITS

The most iconic South Carolina seafood dish combines surf (delectable shrimp) with turf (stoneground hominy) in a stunning yet deeply comforting taste combination. Enjoy this classic entrée in its most mouthwatering form at **Poogan's Porch** (page 110) and **Slightly North of Broad** (page 112) in Charleston.

LOWCOUNTRY BOIL

Also called Frogmore stew after the township on St. Helena Island where it originated, this deceptively simple dish, commonly found in family-style neighborhood restaurants, offers all the basic nutrients you need boiled together in one big pot: shrimp, sausage, potatoes, and corn on the cob, all with a spicy kick.

FRIED CATFISH

The lowly cat is a renowned freshwater fish in South Carolina, and fried up right it's a treat. This is what to order when you're inland and need a fresh-seafood fix.

MAY RIVER OYSTERS

While most of the great South Carolina stocks are long gone, the well-preserved May River at Bluffton still provides some of the best-quality oysters in the world. Buy them fresh at the **Bluffton Oyster Company** (page 239), which brings them in right off the boat during the season (Sept.-Apr.).

HAUTE CUISINE

Not everything is rustic in South Carolina. Fine dining spots, such as **McCrady's** (page 108) in Charleston or **Charlie's L'Etoile Verte** (page 235) in Hilton Head, serve seafood prepared with panache in a spirit of diverse experimentation.

kayaking the Chattooga River

take a guided kayak tour of the excellently preserved marsh.

Midlands

Visit the well-preserved Carolina Bay at the Woods Bay State Natural Area near Florence, right off I-95. Just outside the state's capital, Columbia, is the stunning Congaree National Park and its old-growth cypress swamp.

Enjoy some white-water rafting on the Broad and Saluda Rivers, which run through Columbia. Spend an afternoon at Columbia's nationally renowned Riverbanks Zoo and Garden.

Upstate

Head to the Upstate and choose between camping or a cabin at Devil's Fork State Park, which provides the only public access to beautiful Lake Jocassee at the base of the Blue Ridge.

Hike at Table Rock State Park in the Mountain Bridge Natural Wilderness Area or on the Foothills Trail along the Blue Ridge Escarpment.

Take the Cherokee Foothills Scenic Highway over to the wild and scenic Chattooga River for an equally wild and scenic day of white-water rafting.

▶ GULLAH AND AFRICAN AMERICAN HISTORY

There's no way to truly and completely understand South Carolina without a close look at its African American background, so integral to the state's history. Of particular interest is the story of the Gullah people, descendants of slaves whose culture survived in relative isolation on South Carolina's Sea Islands after the Civil War. This one-week journey takes you to all the key stops.

Day 1

From your base in Beaufort, explore the Gullah community of St. Helena Island, including the Penn Center, where Dr. Martin Luther King Jr. once organized civil rights activists. In the afternoon, pay your respects to African American Civil War hero Robert Smalls at his memorial at the Tabernacle Baptist Church, and see his former home on Prince Street. View the Berners Barnwell Sams House, where Harriet Tubman once worked as a nurse.

Day 2

Get up bright and early for a drive to Hilton Head Island to explore the remnants of African American history here, including the old Fort Mitchel and Mitchelville site where the first freedmen's community in the country once stood. Take the ferry to Daufuskie Island and spend the balance of the day relaxing and getting in touch with the substantial Gullah culture, including the Mary Field School, where author Pat Conroy once taught.

Day 3

Drive inland a little way to Walterboro, where you can pay your respects at the Tuskegee Airmen Memorial and browse the folk art at the South Carolina Artisans Center. Then head to Charleston to begin a two-day stay. On the way into town, stop at Drayton Hall along the Ashley River, a meticulously conserved plantation home. There's a program exploring African American life at the plantation as well as a slave cemetery.

Day 4

Spend the day exploring the well-preserved

grave of African American Civil War soldier in Hilton Head

Tuskegee Airmen Memorial at the Walterboro Airport

restored slave quarters at Boone Hall Plantation

African American history at the Aiken-Rhett House and visit the Old Slave Mart museum downtown. For a more intensive educational experience, pay a visit to the Avery Research Center for African American History and Culture at the College of Charleston. Randolph Hall and the historic "Cistern" on the campus hosted Barack Obama during a campaign rally in January 2008.

Day 5

Your last day in Charleston will be spent in and around the suburb of Mount Pleasant, visiting several key sites. With a stop along U.S. 17 to buy a sweetgrass basket from a roadside vendor, head to Boone Hall Plantation, which has 10 of the best-restored antebellum slave quarters in the country, with excellent interpretive programming. Just down the road is the Charles Pinckney National Historic Site, commemorating the life of the

early abolitionist and coauthor of the U.S. Constitution. End your day with a visit to relaxing Sullivan's Island and Fort Moultrie. Nearby, you'll find the "bench by the road," a monument to the million or so slaves who first arrived in America at Sullivan's Island, which was inspired by a line from a book by Toni Morrison.

Day 6

Drive up U.S. 17 to Georgetown, birthplace of comedian Chris Rock and once the main seaport for South Carolina's rice economy. Visit the Rice Museum to learn about the history and daily life of area plantations.

Day 7

This optional day takes you on a drive inland to the town of Cheraw, birthplace of the jazz great Dizzy Gillespie. Visit his home site, now a delightful park, and view his statue downtown.

GOLFERS' HEAVEN

Any attempt to definitively pick the top golf courses in links-mad South Carolina might easily lead to a very heated debate. Here's my shot at a list of the best courses open to the public, in alphabetical order:

· **Barefoot Resort and Golf Club, Fazio Course** (North Myrtle Beach): Strangely not as popular as the affiliated Love course, but many say it's way better (page 155).

· **Caledonia and True Blue** (Pawleys Island): These sister courses compete for the fierce affections of serious golfers; it's sublime (page 170).

· **Harbour Town** (Hilton Head): The host course of the RBC Heritage features a final three holes that are among the most challenging in the sport (page 231).

· **Kiawah Island Golf Resort, Ocean Course** (Kiawah Island): This Pete Dye design is considered the most wind-affected course outside the British Isles and possibly the most difficult resort course in the United States (page 98).

· **Legends at Parris Island:** Always considered one of the best military courses, a recent redesign of the 1957 original has been getting rave reviews (page 213).

· **Palmetto Dunes, Arthur Hills Course** (Hilton Head): Put away the drivers at this finesse course artfully situated in a residential area (page 231).

· **Wild Dunes, Links Course** (Charleston): This windy, winding beauty is the Holy City's most challenging course (page 98).

▶ CIVIL WAR SIGHTS

While most Civil War battles took place elsewhere, South Carolina was the cradle of secession and has many sites of great historical importance in the War Between the States, as it's sometimes called here.

The Birth and Death of the Confederacy

Little Abbeville in the Upstate is home to Secession Hill, where South Carolina first plotted its secession from the union. It is also where they announced their return to the union. Tour the Burt-Stark Mansion, where Jefferson Davis officially dissolved the Confederacy. Browse the Confederate-focused history books at the nearby Southern Patriot bookstore.

Battle Reenactments

In Aiken, a February reenactment marks the Battle of Aiken, one of the last Confederate victories of the war. Performed on a grand scale, over 10,000 visitors attend this two-day event.

Experience the reenactment of the Battle of Secessionville each November at Boone Hall Plantation in Charleston. While you're here, visit the restored brick slave cabins, a reminder of what the war left behind.

War Hospitals and Cemeteries

See St. Helena's Episcopal Church in Beaufort, used as a hospital by Union troops. Nearby is Beaufort National Cemetery, one of the few in the country where both Union and Confederate troops are interred.

Remnants of the War

Take the ferry out to Fort Sumter, target of Confederate batteries on the eve of war (ironically, none of the shots came from Charleston's Battery itself, as it was too far away).

Fort Sumter

See the newly raised CSS *Hunley* submarine on the old Navy base in North Charleston, and marvel at the bravery of the men on this suicide mission.

Visit historic Drayton Hall on the Ashley River, saved from torching by Union troops by a quick-thinking local who erected small-pox warning flags.

Monuments and Museums

In Columbia, tour the South Carolina State House and its numerous monuments to Civil War figures. Note the Yankee cannonball damage on the walls.

Visit the Confederate Museum on the second floor of Charleston's City Market to see its collection of military memorabilia.

BARBECUE!

Duke's Barbecue in Walterboro

The importance of barbecue in the South cannot be overstated. It's a noun down here, something you eat rather than a verb that you do. To the Southerner, barbecue is both delicacy and staple: one of life's greatest luxuries, but one without which a person cannot be said to be truly living.

South Carolina holds a rare distinction. It's the only state in the union that represents all known variants of barbecue sauce: vinegar and pepper, light tomato, heavy tomato, and the Palmetto State's own contribution, a hot, sweet mustard-based sauce. A culinary legacy of the German settlers who numbered heavily in that interior region, this indigenous mustard sauce is found mostly in the central Midlands portion of the state from Newberry almost to Charleston. The extreme Upstate leans toward the heavier tomato-based sauce, while a sweeter, ketchupy sauce is the trend along the Savannah River. The vinegar-and-pepper concoction—an eastern North Carolina transplant—holds sway everywhere else, especially east of the Wateree River in the Pee Dee region.

As for the meat itself, in all regions there's no question about what kind you mean when you say barbecue. It's always pork, period. And connoisseurs agree that if it isn't cooked whole over an open wood fire, it isn't authentic barbecue, merely a pale—if still tasty—imitation. Sides are important in South Carolina, especially the item known as hash, made from pork byproducts served over rice. In any genuine barbecue place you'll also encounter cracklin's (fried pork skin), whole loaves of white bread, and of course sweet iced tea (called simply "sweet tea").

Aficionados further insist that a real barbecue place is open only on Fridays and Saturdays (some generously extend the definition to include Thursdays), chops its own wood, and proffers its pig not à la carte but in a distinctive "all you care to eat" buffet style, which generally means one huge pass at the buffet line.

So where's the best 'cue joint in Carolina? I don't want to start a second Civil War, so I'll defer that question. Key purveyors of the culinary art form include:

- **Fiery Ron's Home Team BBQ,** Charleston (pages 117 and 119)
- **Carolina Bar-B-Que,** south of Aiken (page 337)
- **Henry's Smokehouse,** Greenville (page 361)
- **McCabe's Bar-B-Que,** Manning (page 308)
- **Po Pigs Bo-B-Q,** Edisto Island (page 216)
- **Sweatman's Bar-b-que,** outside of Holly Hill (page 307)
- **Duke's Barbecue,** Walterboro (page 245)

► ROMANCE IN CHARLESTON AND THE LOWCOUNTRY

Spanish moss, balmy beaches, good food— the Palmetto State is a great place for a romantic getaway. This trip centers on Charleston and the Lowcountry.

Day 1

Spend your first morning walking or biking around peaceful downtown Beaufort. In the afternoon, take a short drive to Hunting Island State Park and walk on the windswept beach. Then enjoy a tasty dinner at Saltus River Grill on the scenic waterfront. Spend the night at one of Beaufort's many classic B&Bs, such as the Beaufort Inn or the Rhett House Inn.

Day 2

Drive to Old Bluffton, walk down to the beautiful May River, and browse the many local art galleries around Calhoun Street. Visit the relaxing Pinckney Island National Wildlife Refuge before going into Hilton Head proper. Walk on the beach and enjoy live music and a great meal at The Jazz Corner. Head up to Charleston and check into a romantic room at the Vendue Inn or the Andrew Pinckney Inn.

Day 3

Drive out to Middleton Place and walk in the amazing formal gardens. Return to downtown Charleston to stroll along the Battery and Rainbow Row before doing some shopping on King Street. Take a late afternoon carriage ride through the French Quarter before dining at ultra-romantic Il Cortile del Re.

Day 4

After a relaxing morning, have a cozy brunch at Poogan's Porch downtown. Then take a drive to Sullivan's Island and enjoy some peaceful time on the beach. Have one last cocktail at warm and woody Poe's Tavern.

Many fun galleries can be found on Calhoun Street in Old Bluffton.

CHARLESTON

Charleston made news in 2011 when it unseated San Francisco for the first time ever in the annual *Condé Nast Traveler* Reader's Choice award for "Top U.S. City." That giant-killing win was quite a coup for this smallish, old-fashioned city in the Deep South. But the most revealing Charleston award is its perennial ranking at the top of the late Marjabelle Young Stewart's annual list for "Most Mannerly City in America." (Charleston has won the award so many times that Stewart's successor at the Charleston School of Protocol and Etiquette, Cindy Grosso, has retired the city from the competition.) This is a city that takes civic harmony so seriously that it boasts the country's only "Livability Court," a binding legal proceeding which meets regularly to enforce local quality-of-life ordinances.

Everyone who spends time in Charleston comes away with a story to tell about the locals' courtesy and hospitality. Mine came while walking through the French Quarter admiring a handsome old single house on Church Street, one of the few that survived the fire of 1775. To my surprise, the woman chatting with a friend nearby turned out to be the homeowner. Noticing my interest, she invited me, a total stranger, inside to check out the progress of her renovation.

To some eyes, Charleston's hospitable nature has bordered on licentiousness. From its earliest days, the city gained a reputation for vice.

© SOPHIA MOREKIS

HIGHLIGHTS

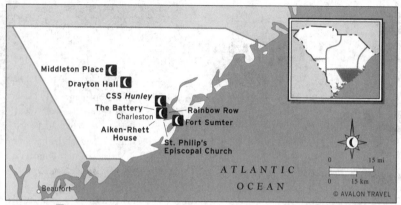

LOOK FOR **C** TO FIND RECOMMENDED SIGHTS, ACTIVITIES, DINING, AND LODGING.

C The Battery: Tranquil surroundings combine with beautiful views of Charleston Harbor, key historical points in the Civil War, and amazing mansions (page 32).

C Rainbow Row: Painted in warm pastels, these old merchant homes near the cobblestoned waterfront take you on a journey to Charleston's antebellum heyday (page 34).

C Fort Sumter: Take the ferry to this historic place where the Civil War began, and take in the gorgeous views along the way (page 42).

C St. Philip's Episcopal Church: A sublimely beautiful sanctuary and two historic graveyards await you in the heart of the evocative French Quarter (page 44).

C Aiken-Rhett House: There are certainly more ostentatious house museums in Charleston, but none that provide such a virtually intact glimpse into real antebellum life (page 54).

C Drayton Hall: Don't miss Charleston's oldest surviving plantation home and one of the country's best examples of professional historic preservation (page 60).

C Middleton Place: Wander in and marvel at one of the world's most beautifully landscaped gardens—and the first in North America (page 63).

C CSS Hunley: Newly ensconced for public viewing in its special preservation tank, the first submarine to sink a ship in battle is a moving example of bravery and sacrifice (page 66).

(The city's nickname, "The Holy City," derives from the skyline's abundance of church steeples rather than any excess of piety among its citizens.) The old drinking clubs are gone, and the yearly bacchanal of Race Week—in which personal fortunes were won or lost in seconds—is but a distant memory. But that hedonistic legacy is alive and well today in Charleston; the city is full of lovers of strong drink and serious foodies, with every weekend night finding downtown packed with partiers, diners, and show-goers.

Don't mistake the Holy City's charm and joie de vivre for weakness, however. That would be a mistake, for within Charleston's velvet glove has always been an iron fist. This is where the colonists scored their first clear victory over the British during the Revolution (another Charleston first). This is the place where the Civil War began, and which stoically endured one of the longest sieges in modern warfare during that conflict. This is the city that survived the East Coast's worst earthquake in 1886 and one of its worst hurricanes a century later.

Despite its fun-loving reputation, a martial spirit is never far from the surface in Charleston, from The Citadel military college along the Ashley River, to the aircraft carrier *Yorktown* moored at Patriots Point, to the cannonballs and mortars that children climb on at the Battery, and even to the occasional tour guide in Confederate garb.

Some of the nation's most progressive urban activity is going on in Charleston despite its reputation for conservatism, from the renovation of the old Navy Yard in North Charleston, to impressive green start-ups, to any number of sustainable residential developments. Charleston is a leader in conservation as well, with groups like the Lowcountry Open Land Trust and the Coastal Conservation League setting an example for the entire Southeast in how to bring environmental organizations and the business community together to preserve the area's beauty and ecosystem.

While many visitors come to see the Charleston of Rhett Butler and Pat Conroy—finding it and then some, of course—they leave impressed by the diversity of Charlestonian life. It's a surprisingly cosmopolitan mix of students, professionals, and longtime inhabitants—who discuss the finer points of Civil War history as if it were last year, party on Saturday night like there's no tomorrow, and go to church on Sunday morning dressed in their finest.

But don't be deceived by these history-minded people. Under the carefully honed tradition and the ever-present ancestor worship, Charleston possesses a vitality of vision that is irrepressibly practical and forward-looking.

HISTORY

Unlike so many of England's colonies in America that were based on freedom from religious persecution, Carolina was strictly a commercial venture from the beginning. The tenure of the Lords Proprietors—the eight English aristocrats who literally owned the colony—began in 1670 when the *Carolina* finished its journey to Albemarle Creek on the west bank of the Ashley River.

Those first colonists would set up a small fortification called Charles Towne, named for Charles II, the first monarch of the Restoration. In a year they'd be joined by colonists from the prosperous but overcrowded British colony of Barbados, who brought a Caribbean sensibility that exists in Charleston to this day.

Finding the first Charles Towne not very fertile and vulnerable to attack from Native Americans and the Spanish, they moved to the peninsula and down to "Oyster Point," what Charlestonians now call White Point Gardens. Just above Oyster Point they set up a walled town, bounded by modern-day Water Street to the south (then a marshy creek, as the name indicates), Meeting Street to the west, Cumberland Street to the north, and the Cooper River on the east.

Growing prosperous as a trading center for deerskin from the great American interior, Charles Towne came into its own after two nearly concurrent events in the early 1700s: the decisive victory of a combined force of Carolinians and Native American allies against the fierce Yamasee people, and the final eradication of the pirate threat in the deaths of Blackbeard and Stede Bonnet.

Flushed with a new spirit of independence, Charles Towne threw off the control of the anemic, disengaged Lords Proprietors, tore down the old defensive walls, and was reborn as an outward-looking, expansive, and increasingly cosmopolitan city that came to be called Charleston. With safety from hostile incursion came the time of the great rice and indigo plantations. Springing up all along the Ashley River soon after the introduction of the crops,

CHARLESTON

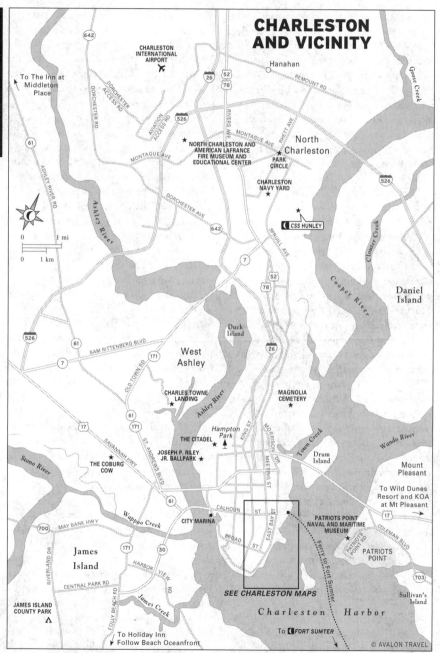

CHARLESTON AND VICINITY

To The Inn at Middleton Place

642

CHARLESTON INTERNATIONAL AIRPORT

Hanahan

26
52
78

REMOUNT RD

Goose Creek

DORCHESTER ACCESS RD

DORCHESTER RD

61

AVIATION ACCESS RD

526

RIVERS AVE

MONTAGUE AVE

RHETT AVE

North Charleston

MONTAGUE AVE

★ NORTH CHARLESTON AND AMERICAN LAFRANCE FIRE MUSEUM AND EDUCATIONAL CENTER

★ PARK CIRCLE

526

DORCHESTER AVE

Ashley River

642

SPRUILL AVE

CHARLESTON NAVY YARD ★

★ ▲ CSS HUNLEY

7

Clouter Creek

Cooper River

Daniel Island

52
78

526

61

SAM RITTENBERG BLVD

7

171

West Ashley

OLD TOWN RD

Duck Island

26

★ CHARLES TOWNE LANDING

Ashley River

MAGNOLIA CEMETERY ★

61
171

Wando River

17

SAVANNAH HWY

ST. ANDREWS BLVD

61

★ JOSEPH P. RILEY JR. BALLPARK ★

Hampton Park

★ THE CITADEL

KING ST

MEETING ST

MORRISON DR

Town Creek

Drum Island

Mount Pleasant

Stono River

★ THE COBURG COW

To Wild Dunes Resort and KOA at Mt Pleasant

Wappoo Creek

700
526

MAY BANK HWY

171

30

61

CALHOUN ST

ST

CITY MARINA ■

EAST BAY ST

BROAD ST

■ PATRIOTS POINT NAVAL AND MARITIME MUSEUM ★

COLEMAN BLVD

17

PATRIOTS POINT RD

PATRIOTS POINT

703

RIVERLAND DR

James Island

HARBOR VIEW RD

CENTRAL PARK RD

FOLLY BEACH RD

James Creek

Ferry to Fort Sumter

Sullivan's Island

JAMES ISLAND COUNTY PARK ▲

SEE CHARLESTON MAPS

Charleston   Harbor

→ To Holiday Inn Follow Beach Oceanfront

To ◖ FORT SUMTER

© AVALON TRAVEL

0   1 mi
0   1 km

CHARLESTON

© JIM MOREKIS

Charleston's nickname is "The Holy City" because of its numerous church steeples.

they turned the labor and expertise of imported Africans into enormous profit for their owners. However, the planters preferred the pleasures and sea breezes of Charleston, and gradually summer homes became year-round residences.

It was during this colonial era that the indelible Charlestonian character was stamped: a hedonistic aristocracy combining a love of carousing with a love of the arts; a code of chivalry meant both to reflect a genteel spirit and reinforce the social order; and, ominously, an ever-increasing reliance on slave labor.

As the storm clouds of civil war gathered in the early 1800s, the majority of Charleston's population was of African descent, and the city was the main importation point for the transatlantic slave trade. The worst fears of white Charlestonians seemed confirmed during the alleged plot by slave leader Denmark Vesey in the early 1820s to start a rebellion. The Lowcountry's reliance on slave labor put it front and center in the coming national confrontation

over abolition, which came to a head literally and figuratively in the bombardment of Fort Sumter in Charleston Harbor in April 1861.

By war's end, not only did the city lay in ruins—mostly from a disastrous fire in 1861, as well as from a 545-day Union siege—so did its way of life. Pillaged by Northern troops and freed slaves, the great plantations along the Ashley became the sites of the first strip mining in the United States, as poverty-stricken owners scraped away the layer of phosphate under the topsoil to sell—perhaps with a certain poetic justice—as fertilizer.

The Holy City didn't really wake up until the great "Charleston Renaissance" of the 1920s and 1930s, when the city rediscovered art, literature, and music in the form of jazz and the world-famous Charleston dance. This was also the time that the world rediscovered Charleston. In the 1920s George Gershwin read local author DuBose Heyward's novel *Porgy* and decided to write a score around the

NOT JUST A MATTER OF BLUE AND GRAY

While the Charleston area is most well known for its pivotal role in the Civil War, this is a drastic oversimplification. South Carolina may have been the "cradle of secession," but it also lost more men in the fight for American independence than any other colony. Here are some military history highlights from other eras:

In Charleston, go to **The Citadel** and enjoy the colorful weekly parade of cadets, the fabled "Thin Grey Line," at 3 P.M. most Fridays. In Mount Pleasant, eat lunch in the mess hall of the **USS Yorktown** at the **Patriot's Point Naval Museum.** Visit historic **Middleton Place,** home of one of the signers of the Declaration of Independence and where some scenes from Mel Gibson's The Patriot were filmed.

Further out of town at Santee National Wildlife Refuge on Lake Marion, see the remains of **Fort Watson**—itself built directly atop an an-cient Native American mound—which the great Francis Marion himself successfully took from the British during the Revolution. Climb to the top of the mound to enjoy the view.

Down in the Lowcountry, a visit to the **Tuskegee Airmen Memorial** in charming little Walterboro reveals a little-known chapter of World War II history. For an interesting combination of old and new, on Parris Island you can tour the iconic **Marine Corps Recruit Depot Parris Island** with its associated museum, and also see one of the oldest European archaeological sites in the United States, **Charlesfort,** located on post on what's now a golf course.

And of course a more lengthy jaunt deep into the Upstate takes you to **Cowpens National Battlefield,** site of one of the pivotal engagements of the Revolution.

story. Along with lyrics by Ira Gershwin, the three men's collaboration became the first American opera, *Porgy and Bess,* which debuted in New York in 1935. It was also during this time that a new appreciation for Charleston's history sprang up, as the local Preservation Society spearheaded the nation's first historic preservation ordinance.

World War II brought the same economic boom that came to much of the South then, most notably with an expansion of the Navy Yard and the addition of a military air base. By the 1950s, the automobile suburb and a thirst for "progress" claimed so many historic buildings that the inevitable backlash came with the formation of the Historic Charleston Foundation, which continues to lead the fight to keep intact the Holy City's architectural legacy.

Civil rights came to Charleston in earnest with a landmark suit to integrate the Charleston Municipal Golf Course in 1960. The biggest battle, however, would be the 100-day strike in 1969 against the Medical University of South Carolina, then, as now, a large employer of African Americans.

Charleston's next great renaissance—still ongoing today—came with the redevelopment of downtown and the fostering of the tourism industry under the nearly 40-year tenure of Mayor Joe Riley, during which so much of the current visitor-friendly infrastructure became part of daily life here. Today, Charleston is completing the transition away from a military and manufacturing base and attracting professionals and artists to town.

PLANNING YOUR TIME

Even if you're just going to confine yourself to the peninsula, I can't imagine spending less than two nights. You'll want half a day for shopping on King Street and a full day for seeing various attractions and museums. Keep in mind that one of Charleston's key sights, Fort Sumter, will take almost half a day to see once you factor in ticketing and boarding time for the ferry out to the fort and back; plan accordingly.

If you have a car, there are several great places

to visit off the peninsula—especially the plantations along the Ashley. None are very far away, and navigation in Charleston is a snap. The farthest site from downtown should take no more than 30 minutes, and because the plantations are roughly adjacent, you can visit all of them in a single day if you get an early start.

While a good time is never far away in Charleston, keep in mind that this is the South, and Sundays can get pretty slow. While the finely honed tourist infrastructure here means that there will always be something to do, the selection of open shops and restaurants dwindles on Sundays, though most other attractions keep working hours.

But for those of us who love the old city, there's nothing like a Sunday morning in Charleston—church bells ringing, families on their way to worship, a beguiling slowness in the air, perhaps spiced with the anticipation of a particular Charleston specialty—a hearty and delicious Sunday brunch.

The real issue for most visitors boils down to two questions: How much do you want to spend on accommodations, and in which part of town do you want to stay? Lodging is generally not cheap in Charleston, but because the price differential is not that much between staying on the peninsula and staying on the outskirts, I recommend the peninsula. You'll pay more, but not *that* much more, with the bonus of probably being able to walk to most places you want to see—which, after all, is the best way to enjoy the city.

ORIENTATION

Charleston occupies a peninsula bordered by the Ashley River to the west and the Cooper River to the east, which "come together to form the Atlantic Ocean," according to the haughty phrase once taught to generations of Charleston schoolchildren.

Although the lower tip of the peninsula actually points closer to southeast, that direction is regarded locally as due south, and anything toward the top of the peninsula is considered due north.

The peninsula is ringed by islands, many of which have become heavily populated suburbs. Clockwise from the top of the peninsula they are: Daniel Island, Mount Pleasant, Isle of Palms, Sullivan's Island, Morris Island, Folly Island, and James Island. The resort island of Kiawah and the much less-developed Edisto Island are farther south down the coast.

North Charleston is not only a separate municipality; it's also a different state of mind. A sprawling combination of malls, light industry, and low-income housing, it also boasts some of the more cutting-edge urban redesign activity in the area.

While Charlestonians would scoff, the truth is that Charleston proper has a surprising amount in common with Manhattan. Both are on long spits of land situated roughly north-south. Both were settled originally at the lower end in walled fortifications—Charleston's walls came down in 1718, while Manhattan still has its Wall Street as a reminder. Both cityscapes rely on age-old north-south streets that run nearly the whole length—Charleston's King and Meeting Streets, with only a block between them, and Manhattan's Broadway and Fifth Avenue. And like Manhattan, Charleston also has its own "Museum Mile" just off of a major green space, in Charleston's case up near Marion Square—though certainly its offerings are not as expansive as those a short walk from New York's Central Park.

Unfortunately, also like Manhattan, parking is at a premium in downtown Charleston. Luckily the city has many reasonably priced parking garages, which I recommend that you use. But cars should only be used when you have to. Charleston is best enjoyed on foot, both because of its small size and the cozy, meandering nature of its old streets, designed not for cars and tour buses but for boots, horseshoes, and carriage wheels.

Charleston is made up of many small neighborhoods, many of them quite old. The boundaries are confusing, so your best bet is to simply look at the street signs (signage in general is excellent in Charleston). If you're in a historic neighborhood, such as the French Quarter or Ansonborough, a smaller sign above the street name will indicate that.

Other key terms you'll hear are "the Crosstown," the portion of U.S. 17 that goes across the peninsula; "Savannah Highway," the portion of U.S. 17 that traverses "West Ashley," which is the suburb across the Ashley River; "East Cooper," the area across the Cooper River that includes Mount Pleasant, Isle of Palms, and Daniel and Sullivan's Islands; and "the Neck," up where the peninsula narrows. These are the terms that locals use, and hence what you'll see in this guide.

Sights

Though most key sights in Charleston do indeed have some tie to the city's rich history, house museums are only a subset of the attractions here. Charleston's sights are excellently integrated into its built environment, and often the enjoyment of nearby gardens or a lapping river is part of the fun.

SOUTH OF BROAD

As one of the oldest streets in Charleston, the east-west thoroughfare of Broad Street is not only a physical landmark, it's a mental one as well. The first area of the Charleston peninsula to be settled, the area south of Broad Street—often shortened to the mischievous acronym "SOB" by local wags—features older homes, meandering streets (many of them built on "made land" filling in former wharfs), and a distinctly genteel, laid-back feel.

As you'd expect, it also features more affluent residents, sometimes irreverently referred to as "SOB Snobs." This heavily residential area has no nightlife to speak of and gets almost eerily quiet after hours, but rest assured that plenty of people live here.

While I highly recommend just wandering among these narrow streets and marveling at the lovingly restored old homes, keep in mind that almost everything down here is in private hands. Don't wander into a garden or take photos inside a window unless you're invited to do so (and given Charleston's legendary hospitality, that can happen).

◖ The Battery

For many, the Battery (E. Battery St. and Murray Blvd., 843/724-7321, daily 24 hours, free) is the single most iconic Charleston spot, drenched in history and boasting dramatic views in all directions. A look to the south gives you the sweeping expanse of the Cooper River, with views of Fort Sumter, Castle Pinckney, Sullivan's Island, and, off to the north, the old carrier *Yorktown* moored at Mount Pleasant. A landward look gives you a view of the adjoining, peaceful **White Point Gardens,** the sumptuous mansions of the Battery, and a beguiling peek behind them into some of the oldest neighborhoods in Charleston.

But if you had been one of the first European visitors to this tip of the peninsula about 400 years ago, you'd have seen how it got its first name, Oyster Point: This entire area was once home to an enormous outcropping of oysters. Their shells glistened bright white in the harsh Southern sun as a ship approached from sea, hence its subsequent name, White Point. Although the oysters are long gone and much of the area you're walking on is actually reclaimed marsh, the Battery and White Point Gardens are still a balm for the soul.

Once the bustling (and sometimes seedy) heart of Charleston's maritime activity, the Battery was where pirate Stede Bonnet and 21 of his men were hanged in 1718. As you might imagine, the area got its name for hosting cannons during the

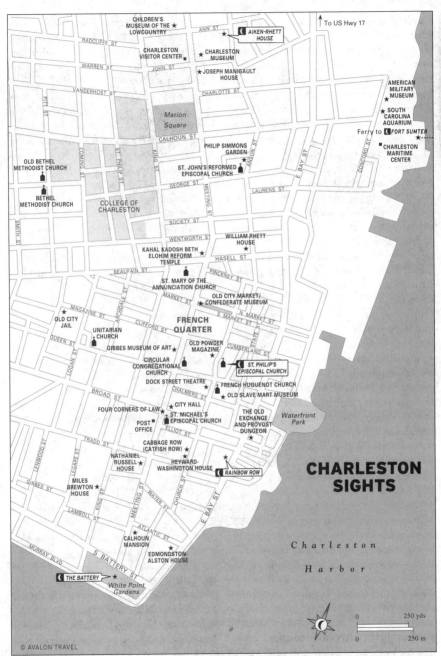

CHARLESTON

CHILDREN'S MUSEUM OF THE ★ LOWCOUNTRY

RADCLIFFE ST

ANN ST

★ AIKEN-RHETT HOUSE

To US Hwy 17

WARREN ST

JOHN ST

CHARLESTON VISITOR CENTER ■

★ CHARLESTON MUSEUM

VANDERHORST ST

★ JOSEPH MANIGAULT HOUSE

PITT ST

CHARLOTTE ST

Marion Square

AMERICAN MILITARY MUSEUM ★

SOUTH CAROLINA AQUARIUM ★

CALHOUN ST

Ferry to ☾ FORT SUMTER

COMING ST

ST PHILIP ST

KING ST

PHILIP SIMMONS GARDEN

ANSON ST

E BAY ST

CONCORD ST

■ CHARLESTON MARITIME CENTER

OLD BETHEL METHODIST CHURCH

ST. JOHN'S REFORMED EPISCOPAL CHURCH ★

BETHEL METHODIST CHURCH

GEORGE ST

MEETING ST

LAURENS ST

COLLEGE OF CHARLESTON

SMITH ST

SOCIETY ST

WENTWORTH ST

WILLIAM RHETT HOUSE ★

KAHAL KADOSH BETH ELOHIM REFORM TEMPLE ★

HASELL ST

BEAUFAIN ST

PINCKNEY ST

ARCHDALE ST

ST. MARY OF THE ANNUNCIATION CHURCH ★

MARKET ST

OLD CITY MARKET/ ★ CONFEDERATE MUSEUM

MAGAZINE ST

OLD CITY ★ JAIL

FRENCH QUARTER

S MARKET ST

N MARKET ST

STATE ST

CLIFFORD ST

UNITARIAN CHURCH †

GIBBES MUSEUM OF ART ★

QUEEN ST

LOGAN ST

OLD POWDER MAGAZINE ★

CUMBERLAND ST

CIRCULAR CONGREGATIONAL CHURCH †

★ ST. PHILIP'S EPISCOPAL CHURCH

DOCK STREET THEATRE ★

CHALMERS ST

★ FRENCH HUGUENOT CHURCH

★ OLD SLAVE MART MUSEUM

BROAD ST

★ CITY HALL

FOUR CORNERS OF LAW ★

ST. MICHAEL'S EPISCOPAL CHURCH †

POST ■ OFFICE

ELLIOT ST

THE OLD EXCHANGE AND PROVOST DUNGEON

Waterfront Park

TRADD ST

CABBAGE ROW (CATFISH ROW) ★

LENWOOD ST

LEGARE ST

KING ST

NATHANIEL RUSSELL ★ HOUSE

HEYWARD-WASHINGTON HOUSE ★

★ RAINBOW ROW

MEETING ST

WATER ST

CHURCH ST

E BAY ST

MILES BREWTON ★ HOUSE

CHARLESTON SIGHTS

GIBBES ST

LAMBOLL ST

ATLANTIC ST

CALHOUN MANSION ★

EDMONDSTON-ALSTON HOUSE

Charleston

MURRAY BLVD

S BATTERY ST

Harbor

☾ THE BATTERY ★

White Point Gardens

0   250 yds

0   250 m

© AVALON TRAVEL

War of 1812, with the current distinctive seawall structure built in the 1850s.

Contrary to popular belief, no guns fired from here on Fort Sumter, as they would have been out of range. However, many thankfully inoperable cannons, mortars, and piles of shot still reside here, much to the delight of kids of all ages. This is where Charlestonians gathered in a giddy, party-like atmosphere to watch the shelling of Fort Sumter in 1861, blissfully ignorant of the horrors to come. A short time later the North would return the favor, as the Battery and all of Charleston up to Broad Street would bear the brunt of shelling during the long siege of the city (the rest was out of reach of Union guns).

But now, the Battery is a place to relax, not fight. The relaxation starts with the fact that there's usually plenty of free parking all along Battery Street. A promenade all around the periphery is a great place to stroll or jog. Add the calming, almost constant sea breeze and the meditative influence of the wide, blue Cooper River and you'll see why this land's end—once so martial in nature—is now a favorite place for after-church family gatherings, travelers, love-struck couples, and weddings (about 200 a year at the gazebo in White Point Gardens).

Still, military history is never far away in Charleston, and one of the chief landmarks at the Battery is the USS *Hobson* Memorial, remembering the sacrifice of the men of that vessel when it sank after a collision with the carrier USS *Wasp* in 1952.

Look for the three-story private residence where East Battery curves northward. You won't be taking any tours of it, but you should be aware that it's the **DeSaussure House** (1 E. Battery St.), best known in Charleston history for hosting rowdy, celebratory crowds on the roof and the piazzas to watch the 34-hour shelling of Fort Sumter in 1861.

Edmondston-Alston House

The most noteworthy single attraction on the Battery is the 1825 Edmondston-Alston House (21 E. Battery St., 843/722-7171, www.middletonplace.org, Mon. 1-4:30 P.M., Tues.-Sat. 10 A.M.-4:30 P.M., Sun. 1:30-4:30 P.M., $10 adults, $8 students), the only Battery home open to the public for tours. This is one of the most unique and well-preserved historic homes in the United States, thanks to the ongoing efforts of the Alston family, who acquired the house from shipping merchant Charles Edmondston for $15,500 after the Panic of 1837 and still live on the third floor (tours only visit the first two stories).

Over 90 percent of the home's furnishings are original items from the Alston era, a percentage that's almost unheard of in the world of house museums. (Currently the House is owned and administered by the Middleton Place Foundation, best known for its stewardship of Middleton Place along the Ashley River.) You can still see the original paper bag used to store the house's deeds and mortgages. There's also a copy of the Ordinance of Secession and some interesting memorabilia from the golden days of Race Week, that time in February when all of Charleston society came out to bet on horses, carouse, and show off their finery. The Edmondston-Alston House has withstood storms, fires, earthquakes, and Yankee shelling, due in no small part to its sturdy construction; its masonry walls are two bricks thick, and it features both interior and exterior shutters. Originally built in the Federal style, second owner Charles Alston added several Greek Revival elements, notably the parapet, balcony, and piazza, where General Beauregard watched the attack on Fort Sumter.

◖ Rainbow Row

At 79-107 East Bay Street, between Tradd and Elliot Streets, is one of the most photographed sights in the United States: colorful Rainbow Row. The reason for its name becomes obvious when you see the array of pastel-colored

© JIM MOREKIS

Rainbow Row

mansions, all facing the Cooper River. The bright, historically accurate colors—nine of them, to be exact—are one of the many vestiges you'll see around town of Charleston's Caribbean heritage, a legacy of the English settlers from the colony of Barbados who were among the city's first citizens.

The homes are unusually old for this fire-, hurricane-, and earthquake-ravaged city, with most dating from 1730 to 1750. As you admire Rainbow Row from across East Battery, keep in mind you're actually walking on what used to be water. These houses were originally right on the Cooper River, their lower stories serving as storefronts on the wharf. The street was created later on top of landfill, or "made land" as it's called locally. Besides its grace and beauty, Rainbow Row is of vital importance to American historic preservation. These were the first Charleston homes to be renovated and brought back from early-20th-century seediness. The restoration projects on Rainbow Row directly inspired the creation of the Charleston Preservation Society, the first such group in the United States.

Continue walking up the High Battery past Rainbow Row and find Water Street. This aptly named little avenue was in fact a creek in the early days, acting as the southern border of the original walled city. The large brick building on the seaward side housing the Historic Charleston Foundation sits on the site of the old Granville bastion, a key defensive point in the wall.

Nathaniel Russell House

Considered one of Charleston's grandest homes despite being built by an outsider from Rhode Island, the Nathaniel Russell House (51 Meeting St., 843/724-8481, www.historiccharleston.org, Mon.-Sat. 10 A.M.-5 P.M., Sun. 2-5 P.M., last tour begins 4:30 P.M., $10 adults, $5 children) is now a National Historic Landmark and one of the country's best examples of neoclassicism. Built in 1808 for the then-princely sum of $80,000 by Nathaniel Russell,

CHARLESTON

KNOW YOUR CHARLESTON HOUSES

Charleston's homes boast not only a long pedigree but an interesting and unique one as well. Here are the basics of local architecture:

Single House: A legacy of the early Barbadians among the first settlers here, the Charleston single house is named for the fact that it's a single room wide. The phrase refers to layout, not style, which can range from Georgian to Federal to Greek Revival, or a combination. Furnished with full-length piazzas, or long verandas, on the south side to take advantage of southerly breezes, the single house is perhaps the nation's first sustainable house design. The house is lengthwise on the lot, with the entrance on the side of the house. This means the "backyard" is actually the side yard. They're everywhere in Charleston, but Church Street has great examples, including 90, 92, and 94 Church Street, and the oldest single house in town, the 1730 Robert Brewton House (71 Church St.).

Double House: This layout is two rooms wide with a central hallway and a porched facade facing the street. Double houses often had separate carriage houses. The Aiken-Rhett and Heyward-Washington houses are good examples.

Charleston Green: This uniquely Charlestonian color—extremely dark green that looks pitch black in low light—has its roots in the aftermath of the Civil War. The federal government distributed surplus black paint to contribute to reconstruction of the ravaged peninsula, but Charlestonians were too proud (and tasteful) to use as-is. So they added a tiny bit of yellow to each gallon, producing Charleston green.

Earthquake Bolt: Structural damage after the 1886 earthquake was so extensive that many buildings were retrofitted with one or more long iron rods running wall to wall to keep the house stable. The rod was capped at both ends by a "gib plate," often disguised with a decorative element such as a lion's head, an S or

X shape, or other design. Earthquake bolts can be seen all over town, but notable examples are at 235 Meeting Street, 198 East Bay Street, 407 King Street, and 51 East Battery (a rare star design); 190 East Bay Street is unusual for having both an X and an S plate on the same building.

Joggling Board: This long (10-15 feet) flexible plank of cypress, palm, or pine with a handle at each end served various recreational purposes for early Charlestonians. As babies, they might be bounced to sleep. As small children, they might use it as a trampoline. Later it was a method of courtship, whereby a couple would start out at opposite ends and bounce until they met in the middle.

Carolopolis Award: For over 50 years, the Preservation Society of Charleston has handed out these little black badges, to be mounted near the doorway of the winning home, to local homeowners who have renovated historic properties downtown. On the award you'll see "Carolopolis," the Latinized name of the city; "Condita A.D. 1670," the Latin word for founding with the date of Charleston's inception; and another date referring to when the award was given.

Ironwork: Before the mid-19th century, wrought iron was a widely used ornament. Charleston's best-known blacksmith, the late Philip Simmons, made a life's work of continuing the ancient craft of working in wrought iron, and his masterpieces are visible throughout the city, most notably at the Philip Simmons Garden (91 Anson St.), a gate for the Visitors Center (375 Meeting St.), and the Philip Simmons Children's Garden at Josiah Smith Tennent House (Blake St. and East Bay St.). *Chevaux-de-frise* are iron bars on top of a wall through which project some particularly menacing spikes. They became popular after the Denmark Vesey slave revolt conspiracy of 1822. The best example is on the wall of the Miles Brewton House (27 King St.).

a.k.a. "King of the Yankees," the home is furnished as accurately as possible to represent not only the lifestyle of the Russell family but the 18 African American servants who shared the premises. The house was eventually bought by the Allson family, who amid the poverty of Civil War and Reconstruction decided in 1870 to sell it to the Sisters of Charity of Our Lady of Mercy as a school for young Catholic women.

Restorationists have identified 22 layers of paint within the home, which barely survived a tornado in 1811, got away with only minimal damage in the 1886 earthquake, but was damaged extensively by Hurricane Hugo in 1989 (and was since repaired). As with fine antebellum homes throughout coastal South Carolina and Georgia, the use of faux finishing is prevalent throughout, mimicking surfaces such as marble, wood, and lapis lazuli. Visitors are often most impressed by the Nathaniel Russell House's magnificent "flying" spiral staircase, a work of such sublime carpentry and engineering that it needs no external support, twisting upward of its own volition.

When you visit, keep in mind that you're in the epicenter of not only Charleston's historic preservation movement but perhaps the nation's as well. In 1955, the Nathaniel Russell House was the first major project of the Historic Charleston Foundation, which raised $65,000 to purchase it. Two years later, admission fees from the house would support Historic Charleston's groundbreaking revolving fund for preservation, the prototype for many such successful programs. For an extra $6, you can gain admission to the Aiken-Rhett House farther uptown, also administered by the Historic Charleston Foundation.

Calhoun Mansion

The single largest of Charleston's surviving grand homes, the 1876 Calhoun Mansion (16 Meeting St., 843/722-8205, www.calhoun-mansion.net, tours daily 11 A.M.-5 P.M., $15) boasts 35 opulent rooms (with 23 fireplaces!) in a striking Italianate design taking up a whopping 24,000 square feet. The grounds feature some charming garden spaces. A new 90-minute "grand tour" is available for $50 pp; call for an appointment. Though the interiors at this privately run house are packed with antiques and furnishings, be aware that not all of them are accurate or period.

Miles Brewton House

A short distance from the Nathaniel Russell House but much less viewed by visitors, the circa-1769 Miles Brewton House (27 King St.), now a private residence, is maybe the best example of Georgian-Palladian architecture in the world. The almost medieval wrought-iron fencing, or chevaux-de-frise, was added in 1822 after rumors of a slave uprising spread through town. This imposing double house was the site of not one but two headquarters of occupying armies, British General Clinton in the Revolution and the federal garrison after the end of the Civil War. The great Susan Pringle Frost, principal founder of the Charleston Preservation Society and a Brewton descendant, grew up here.

Heyward-Washington House

The Heyward-Washington House (87 Church St., 843/722-0354, www.charlestonmuseum.org, Mon.-Sat. 10 A.M.-5 P.M., Sun. 1-5 P.M., $10 adults, $5 children, combo tickets to Charleston Museum and Manigault House available) takes the regional practice of naming a historic home for the two most significant names in its pedigree to its logical extreme. Built in 1772 by the father of Declaration of Independence signer Thomas Heyward Jr., the house also hosted George Washington during the president's visit to Charleston in 1791. It's now owned and operated by the Charleston Museum. The main attraction at the Heyward-Washington House is its masterful woodwork,

© JIM MOREKIS

the Miles Brewton House, host to two occupying army headquarters

exemplified by the cabinetry of legendary Charleston carpenter Thomas Elfe. You'll see his work all over the house, from the mantles to a Chippendale chair. Look for his signature, a figure eight with four diamonds.

Cabbage Row

You know these addresses, 89-91 Church Street, better as "Catfish Row" in Gershwin's opera *Porgy and Bess* (itself based on the book *Porgy* by the great Charleston author DuBose Heyward, who lived at 76 Church St.). Today this complex—which once housed 10 families—next to the Heyward-Washington House is certainly upgraded from years past, but the row still has the humble appeal of the tenement housing it once was, primarily for freed African American slaves after the Civil War. The house nearby at 94 Church Street was where John C. Calhoun and others drew up the infamous Nullification Acts that eventually led to the South's secession.

St. Michael's Episcopal Church

The oldest church in South Carolina, St. Michael's Episcopal Church (71 Broad St., 843/723-0603, services Sun. 8 A.M. and 10:30 A.M., tours available after services) is actually the second sanctuary on this spot. The first church here was made out of black cypress and was called St. Philip's, or "the English Church," which was later rebuilt on Church Street. Although the designer is not known, we do know that work on this sanctuary in the style of Christopher Wren began in 1752 as a response to the overflowing congregation at the rebuilt St. Philips, and it didn't finish until 1761. Other than a small addition on the southeast corner in 1883, the St. Michael's you see today is virtually unchanged, including the massive pulpit, outsized in the style of the time. Services here over the years hosted such luminaries as Marquis de Lafayette, George Washington, and Robert E. Lee, the latter two of whom are known to have sat in the "governor's pew."

Two signers of the U.S. Constitution, John Rutledge and Charles Cotesworth Pinckney, are buried in the sanctuary. The 186-foot steeple, painted black during the Revolution in a futile effort to disguise it from British guns, actually sank eight inches after the earthquake of 1886. Inside the tower, the famous "bells of St. Michael's" have an interesting story to tell, having made seven transatlantic voyages for a variety of reasons. They were forged in London's Whitechapel Foundry and sent over in 1764, only to be brought back as a war prize during the Revolution, after which they were returned to the church. Damaged during the Civil War, they were sent back to the foundry of their birth to be recast and returned to Charleston. In 1989 they were damaged by Hurricane Hugo, sent back to Whitechapel yet again, and returned to St. Michael's in 1993. Throughout the lifespan of the bells, the clock tower has continued to tell time, although the minute hand wasn't added until 1849.

St. Michael's offers informal, free guided tours to visitors after Sunday services; contact the greeter for more information.

Four Corners of Law

No guidebook is complete without a mention of the famous intersection of Broad and Meeting Streets, named Four Corners of Law for its confluence of federal law (the Post Office building), state law (the state courthouse), municipal law (City Hall), and God's law (St. Michael's Episcopal Church). That's all well and good, but no matter what the tour guides may tell you, the phrase "Four Corners of Law" was actually popularized by *Ripley's Believe It or Not!* Still, there's no doubt that this intersection has been key to Charleston from the beginning. Meeting Street was laid out around 1672 and takes its name from the White Meeting House of early Dissenters, meaning non-Anglicans. Broad Street was also referred to as Cooper Street in the early days. Right in the middle of the street

once stood the very first statue in the United States, a figure of William Pitt erected in 1766.

WATERFRONT

Charleston's waterfront is a place where tourism, history, and industry coexist in a largely seamless fashion. Another of the successful—if at one time controversial—developments spearheaded by Mayor Joe Riley, the centerpiece of the harbor area as far as visitors are concerned is Waterfront Park up toward the High Battery. Farther up the Cooper River is Aquarium Wharf, where you'll find the South Carolina Aquarium, the American Military Museum, the Fort Sumter Visitor Education Exhibit, and the dock where you take the various harbor ferries, whether to Fort Sumter or just a calming ride on the Cooper River.

The Old Exchange and Provost Dungeon

It's far from glamorous, but nonetheless the Old Exchange and Provost Dungeon (122 E. Bay St., 843/727-2165, www.oldexchange.com, daily 9 A.M.-5 P.M., $7 adults, $3.50 children and students) at the intersection of East Bay and Meeting Streets is brimming with history. It is known as one of the three most historically significant colonial buildings in the United States, along with Philadelphia's Independence Hall and Boston's Faneuil Hall. This is actually the old Royal Exchange and Custom House, with the cellar serving as a British prison, all built in 1771 over a portion of the old 1698 fortification wall, some of which you can see today. Three of Charleston's four signers of the Declaration of Independence did time downstairs for sedition against the crown. Later, happier times were experienced upstairs in the Exchange, as it was here that the state selected its delegates to the Continental Congress and ratified the U.S. Constitution, and it's where George Washington took a spin on the dance floor. Nearly a victim of early 20th-century

THE GREAT CHARLESTON EARTHQUAKE

The Charleston peninsula is bordered by three faults, almost like a picture frame: the Woodstock Fault above North Charleston, the Charleston Fault running along the east bank of the Cooper River, and the Ashley Fault to the west of the Ashley River. On August 31, 1886, one of them buckled, causing one of the most damaging earthquakes ever to hit the United States.

The earthquake of 1886 was actually signaled by several foreshocks earlier that week. Residents of the nearby town of Summerville, South Carolina, 20 miles up the Ashley River, felt a small earthquake after midnight on Friday, August 27. Most slept through it. But soon after dawn a larger shock came, complete with a loud bang, causing many to run outside their houses. That Saturday afternoon another tremor hit Summerville, breaking windows and throwing a bed against a wall in one home. Still, Charlestonians remained unconcerned. Then, that Tuesday at 9:50 P.M. came the big one. With an epicenter somewhere near the Middleton Place plantation, the Charleston earthquake is estimated to have measured about 7 on the Richter scale. Tremors were felt across half the country, with the ground shaking in Chicago and a church damaged in Indianapolis. A dam 120 miles away in Aiken, South Carolina, immediately gave way, washing a train right off the tracks. Cracks opened up parallel to the Ashley River, with part of the riverbank falling into the water. Thousands of chimneys all over the state either fell or were rendered useless. A Charleston minister at his summer home in Asheville, North Carolina, described a noise like the sound of wheels driving straight up the mountain, followed by the sound of many railroad cars going by. A moment later, one corner of his house lifted off the ground and slammed back down again. The quake brought a series of "sand blows," a particularly disturbing phenomenon whereby craters open up and spew sand and water up into the air like a small volcano. In Charleston's case, some of the craters were 20 feet wide, shooting debris another 20 feet into the air. The whole event lasted less than a minute.

In crowded Charleston, the damage was horrific: over 2,000 buildings destroyed, a quarter of the city's value gone, 27 killed immediately and almost 100 more to die from injuries and disease. Because of the large numbers of newly homeless, tent cities sprang up in every available park and green space. The American Red Cross's first field mission soon brought some relief, but the scarcity of food, and especially fresh water, made life difficult for everyone.

Almost every surviving building had experienced structural damage, in some cases severe, so a way had to be found to stabilize them. This led to the widespread use of the "earthquake bolt" now seen throughout older Charleston homes. Essentially acting as very long screws with a washer on each end, the idea of the earthquake bolt is simple: Poke a long iron rod through two walls that need stabilizing, and cap the ends. Charleston being Charleston, of course, the end caps were often decorated with a pattern or symbol.

The seismic activity of Charleston's earthquake was so intense that more than 300 aftershocks occurred in the 35 years after the event. In fact, geologists think that most seismic events measured in the region today—including a large event in December 2008, also centering near Summerville—are probably also aftershocks.

Earthquake bolts are a common sight in Charleston.

© JIM MOREKIS

shortsightedness—it was almost demolished for a gas station in 1913—the building now belongs to the Daughters of the American Revolution. Fans of kitsch will get a hoot out of the animatronic Hall of the Presidents-style figures. Kids might especially get a scary kick out of the basement dungeon, where the infamous pirate Stede Bonnet was imprisoned in 1718 before being hanged with his crew on the Battery.

Waterfront Park

Dubbing it "this generation's gift to the future," Mayor Joe Riley made this eight-acre project another part of his downtown renovation. Situated on Concord Street roughly between Exchange Street and Vendue Range, Waterfront Park (843/724-7327, daily dawn-dusk, free) was, like many waterfront locales in Charleston, built on what used to be marsh and water. This particularly massive chunk of "made land" juts about a football

field's length farther out than the old waterline. Visitors and locals alike enjoy the relaxing vista of Charleston Harbor, often from the many swinging benches arranged in an unusual front-to-back, single-file pattern all down the pier. On the end you can find viewing binoculars to see the various sights out on the Cooper River, chief among them the USS *Yorktown* at Patriot's Point and the big bridge to Mount Pleasant. Children will enjoy the large "Vendue" wading fountain at the Park's entrance off Vendue Range, while a bit farther south is the large and quite artful Pineapple Fountain with its surrounding wading pool. Contemporary art lovers of all ages will appreciate the nearby **Waterfront Park City Gallery** (34 Prioleau St., Mon.-Fri. noon-5 P.M., free).

South Carolina Aquarium

Honestly, if you've been to the more expansive aquariums in Monterey or Boston, you might

© JIM MOREKIS

the Pineapple Fountain at Waterfront Park

be disappointed at the breadth of offerings at the South Carolina Aquarium (100 Aquarium Wharf, 843/720-1990, www.scaquarium.org, March-Aug. daily 9 A.M.-5 P.M., Sept.-Feb. daily 9 A.M.-4 P.M., $20 adults, $13 children, combo tickets with Fort Sumter tour available). But nonetheless, it's clean and well done and is a great place for the whole family to have some fun while getting educated about the rich aquatic life off the coast and throughout this small but ecologically diverse state.

When you enter you're greeted with the 15,000-gallon Carolina Seas tank, with placid nurse sharks and vicious-looking moray eels. Other exhibits highlight the five key South Carolina ecosystems: beach, salt marsh, coastal plain, piedmont, and mountain forest. Another neat display is the Touch Tank, a hands-on collection of invertebrates found along the coast, such as sea urchins and horseshoe crabs. The pièce de résistance, however, is certainly the three-story Great Ocean Tank with literally hundreds of deeper-water marine creatures, including sharks, puffer fish, and sea turtles. Speaking of sea turtles: A key part of the aquarium's research and outreach efforts is the Turtle Hospital, which attempts to rehabilitate and save sick and injured specimens. The hospital has so far saved 20 sea turtles, the first one being a 270-pound female affectionately known as "Edisto Mama."

American Military Museum

Slightly out of place thematically with the Aquarium, the American Military Museum (360 Concord St., 843/577-7000, www.american-militarymuseum.org, Mon.-Sat. 10 A.M.-6 P.M., Sun. 1-5 P.M., $9 adults, $6 students) is one of those under-the-radar types of small museums that can be unexpectedly enriching. Certainly its location near the embarkation point for the Fort Sumter ferry hasn't hurt its profile. It's heavy on uniforms, with a wide range all the way from the Revolution to the modern day. My favorite

is the 1907 naval uniform from the cruiser USS *Charleston,* part of Teddy Roosevelt's Great White Fleet. There's also a good collection of rare military miniatures.

Fort Sumter

This is it: the place that brought about the beginning of the Civil War, a Troy for modern times. Though many historians insist the war would have happened regardless of President Lincoln's decision to keep Fort Sumter (843/883-3123, www.nps.gov/fosu, hours seasonal, free) in federal hands, nonetheless the stated *casus belli* was Major Robert Anderson's refusal to surrender the fort when requested to do so in the early morning hours of April 12, 1861. A few hours later came the first shot of the war, fired from Fort Johnson by Confederate Captain George James. That 10-inch mortar shell, a signal for the general bombardment to begin, exploded above Fort Sumter, and nothing in Charleston, or the South, or the United States, would ever be the same again. Notorious secessionist Edmund Ruffin gets credit for firing the first shot in anger, only moments after James's signal shell, from a battery at Cummings Point. Ruffin's 64-pound projectile scored a direct hit, smashing into the fort's southwest corner. The first return shot from Fort Sumter was fired by none other than Captain Abner Doubleday, the father of baseball. The first death of the Civil War also happened at Fort Sumter, not from the Confederate bombardment but on the day after. U.S. Army Private Daniel Hough died when the cannon he was loading, to be fired as part of a 100-gun surrender salute to the Stars and Stripes, exploded prematurely. Today the battered but still-standing Fort Sumter remains astride the entrance to Charleston Harbor on an artificial 70,000-ton sandbar. Sumter was part of the so-called Third System of fortifications ordered after the War of 1812. Interestingly, the fort was still not quite finished when the

MARY CHESNUT'S DIARY

I have always kept a journal after a fashion of my own, with dates and a line of poetry or prose, mere quotations, which I understood and no one else, and I have kept letters and extracts from the papers. From today forward I will tell the story in my own way.

                    Mary Boykin Chesnut

She was born in the middle of the state, but Mary Boykin Chesnut's seminal Civil War diary—originally titled *A Diary From Dixie* and first published in 1905—provides one of the most extraordinary eyewitness accounts of antebellum life in Charleston you'll ever read. By turns wise and witty, fiery and flirtatious, Chesnut's writing is a gripping, politically savvy, and dryly humorous chronicle of a life lived close to the innermost circles of Confederate decision-makers. Her husband, James Chesnut Jr., was a U.S. Senator until South Carolina seceded from the Union, whereupon he became a key aide to Confederate President Jefferson Davis and a general in the Confederate Army.

The diary runs from February 1861—three months before the firing on Fort Sumter, which she witnessed—to August 1865, after the Confederate surrender. Along the way the diary shifts to and from various locales, including Montgomery, Alabama; Richmond, Virginia; Columbia, South Carolina; and, of course, Charleston. A sample excerpt is typical of her high regard for the Holy City:

On the Battery with the Rutledges, Captain Hartstein was introduced to me. He has done some heroic things—brought home some ships and is a man of mark. Afterward he sent me a beautiful bouquet, not half so beautiful, however, as Mr. Robert Gourdin's, which already occupied the place of honor on my center table. What a dear, delightful place is Charleston!

Chesnut was a Southern patriot, and as you might imagine some of her observations are wildly politically incorrect by today's standards. But while supportive of slavery and suspicious of the motives of abolitionists—"People in those places expect more virtue from a plantation African than they can insure in practise among themselves with all their own high moral surroundings," she says of white Northern abolitionists—she does allow for a few nuanced looks at the lives of African Americans in the South, as in this observation about her own house servants after the fall of Fort Sumter:

You could not tell that they even heard the awful roar going on in the bay, though it has been dinning in their ears night and day. People talk before them as if they were chairs and tables. They make no sign. Are they stolidly stupid? or wiser than we are; silent and strong, biding their time?

While the diary begins on a confident note regarding the South's chances in the war, as the news from the battlefield gets worse we see how Southerners cope with the sure knowledge that they will lose:

I know how it feels to die. I have felt it again and again. For instance, some one calls out, "Albert Sidney Johnston is killed." My heart stands still. I feel no more. I am, for so many seconds, so many minutes, I know not how long, utterly without sensation of any kind—dead; and then, there is that great throb, that keen agony of physical pain, and the works are wound up again. The ticking of the clock begins, and I take up the burden of life once more.

Southern historian C. Vann Woodward compiled an annotated edition of the Chesnut diary in 1981, *Mary Chesnut's Civil War*, which won a Pulitzer Prize the following year. Her words came to even wider national exposure due to extensive quotations from her diary in Ken Burns's PBS miniseries *The Civil War*.

Confederate guns opened up on it 50 years later, and it never enjoyed its intended full complement of 135 big guns.

As you might expect, you can only visit by boat, specifically the approved concessionaire **Fort Sumter Tours** (843/881-7337, www.fortsumter-tours.com, $17 adults, $10 ages 6-11, $15 seniors). Once at the fort, there's no charge for admission. Ferries leave from Liberty Square at Aquarium Wharf on the peninsula three times a day during the high season (Apr.-Oct.); call or check the website for times. Make sure to arrive about 30 minutes before the ferry departs. You can also get to Fort Sumter by ferry from Patriot's Point at Mount Pleasant through the same concessionaire.

Budget at least 2.5 hours for the whole trip, including an hour at Fort Sumter. At Liberty Square on the peninsula is the **Fort Sumter Visitor Education Center** (340 Concord St., daily 8:30 A.M.-5 P.M., free), so you can learn more about where you're about to go. Once there, you can be enlightened by the regular ranger's talks on the fort's history and construction (generally at 11 A.M. and 2:30 P.M.), take in the interpretive exhibits throughout the site, and enjoy the view of the spires of the Holy City from afar. For many, though, the highlight is the boat trip itself, with beautiful views of Charleston Harbor and the islands of the Cooper River estuary. If you want to skip Sumter, you can still take an enjoyable 90-minute ferry ride around the harbor and past the fort on the affiliated **Spiritline Cruises** (800/789-3678, www.spiritlinecruises.com, $17 adults, $10 ages 6-11).

Some visitors are disappointed to find many of the fort's gun embrasures bricked over. This was done during the Spanish-American War, when the old fort was turned into an earthwork and the newer Battery Huger (pronounced "Huge-E") was built on top of it.

FRENCH QUARTER

Unlike the New Orleans version, Charleston's French Quarter is Protestant in origin and flavor. Though not actually given the name until a preservation effort in the 1970s, historically this area was indeed the main place of commerce for the city's population of French Huguenots, primarily a merchant class who fled religious persecution in their native country. Today the five-block area—roughly bounded by East Bay, Market Street, Meeting Street, and Broad Street—contains some of Charleston's most historic buildings, its most evocative old churches and graveyards, its most charming narrow streets, and its most tasteful art galleries.

◖ St. Philip's Episcopal Church

With a pedigree dating back to the colony's fledgling years, St. Philip's Episcopal Church (142 Church St., 843/722-7734, www.stphilipschurchsc.org, sanctuary Mon.-Fri. 10 A.M.-noon and 2-4 P.M., services Sun. 8:15 A.M.) is the oldest Anglican congregation south of Virginia. That pedigree gets a little complicated and downright tragic at times, but any connoisseur of Charleston history needs to be clear on the fine points: The first St. Philip's was built in 1680 at the corner of Meeting Street and Broad Street, the present site of St. Michael's Episcopal Church. That first St. Philip's was badly damaged by a hurricane in 1710, and the city fathers approved the building of a new sanctuary dedicated to the saint on Church Street. However, that building was nearly destroyed by yet another hurricane during construction. Fighting with local Native Americans further delayed rebuilding in 1721. Alas, that St. Philip's burned to the ground in 1835—a distressingly common fate for so many old buildings in this area. Construction immediately began on a replacement, and it's that building you see today. Heavily damaged by Hurricane Hugo in 1989, a $4.5 million renovation kept the church usable. So, to recap: St. Philip's was originally on the site of the present St. Michael's. And while St. Philip's is the oldest congregation in South Carolina, St.

Michael's has the oldest physical church building in the state. Are we clear?

South Carolina's great statesman John C. Calhoun—who ironically despised Charlestonians for what he saw as their loose morals—was originally buried across Church Street in the former "stranger's churchyard," or West Cemetery, after his death in 1850. (Charles Pinckney and Edward Rutledge are two other notable South Carolinians buried here.) But near the end of the Civil War, Calhoun's body was moved to an unmarked grave closer to the sanctuary in an attempt to hide its location from Union troops, who it was feared would go out of their way to wreak vengeance on the tomb of one of slavery's staunchest advocates and the man who invented the doctrine of nullification. In 1880, with Reconstruction in full swing, the state legislature directed and funded the building of the current large memorial in the West Cemetery.

French Huguenot Church

One of the oldest congregations in town, the French Huguenot Church (44 Queen St., 843/722-4385, www.frenchhuguenotchurch. org, liturgy Sun. 10:30 A.M.) also has the distinction of being the only remaining independent Huguenot Church in the country. Founded around 1681 by French Calvinists, the church had about 450 congregants by 1700. While refugees from religious persecution, they weren't destitute, as they had to pay for their passage to America. As is the case with so many historic churches in the area, the building you see isn't the original sanctuary. The first church was built on this site in 1687, and became known as the "Church of Tides" because at that time the Cooper River lapped at its property line. This sanctuary was deliberately destroyed as a firebreak during the great conflagration of 1796. The church was replaced in 1800, but that building was in turn

demolished in favor of the picturesque, stucco-coated Gothic Revival sanctuary you see today, which was completed in 1845 and subsequently survived Union shelling and the 1886 earthquake. Does the church look kind of Dutch to you? There's a good reason for that. In their diaspora, French Huguenots spent a lot of time in Holland and became influenced by the tidy sensibilities of the Dutch people. The history of the circa-1845 organ is interesting as well. A rare "tracker" organ, so named for its ultra-fast linkage between the keys and the pipe valves, it was built by famed organ builder Henry Erben. After the fall of Charleston in 1865, Union troops had begun dismantling the instrument for shipment to New York when the church organist, T. P. O'Neale, successfully pleaded with them to let it stay.

Sunday services are conducted in English now, but a single annual service in French is still celebrated in April. The unique Huguenot Cross of Languedoc, which you'll occasionally see ornamenting the church, is essentially a Maltese Cross, its eight points representing the eight beatitudes. Between the four arms of the cross are four fleurs-de-lis, the age-old French symbol of purity.

Dock Street Theatre

Fresh from an extensive multiyear renovation project, the Dock Street Theatre (135 Church St., 843/720-3968), right down the street from the Huguenot Church, is where any thespian or lover of the stage must pay homage to this incarnation of the first theater built in the Western Hemisphere. In a distressingly familiar Charleston story, the original 1736 Dock Street Theatre burned down. A second theater opened on the same site in 1754. That building was in turn demolished for a grander edifice in 1773, which, you guessed it, also burned down. The current building dates from 1809, when the Planter's Hotel was built near the site of the original Dock Street

FRENCH HUGUENOTS

A visitor can't spend a few hours in Charleston without coming across the many French-sounding names so prevalent in the region. Some are common surnames, such as Ravenel, Manigault ("MAN-i-go"), Gaillard, Laurens, or Huger ("huge-EE"). Some are street or place names, such as Mazyck or Legare ("Le-GREE"). Unlike the predominantly French Catholic presence in Louisiana and coastal Alabama, the Gallic influence in Charleston was strictly of the Calvinist Protestant variety. Known as Huguenots, these French immigrants—refugees from an increasingly intolerant Catholic regime in their mother country—were numerous enough in the settlement by the 1690s that they were granted full citizenship and property rights if they swore allegiance to the British crown.

The Huguenot's quick rise in Charleston was due to two factors. Unlike other colonies, Carolina never put much of a premium on religious conformity, a trait that exists to this day despite the area's overall conservatism. And unlike many who fled European monarchies to come to the New World, the French Huguenots were far from poverty-stricken. Most had to buy their own journeys across the Atlantic and arrived already well educated and skilled in one or more useful trades. In Charleston's early days, they were mostly farmers or tar burners (makers of tar and pitch for maritime use). In later times their pragmatism and work ethic would lead them to higher positions in local society, such

as lawyers, judges, and politicians. One of the wealthiest Charlestonians of all, the merchant Gabriel Manigault, was by some accounts the richest person in the American colonies during the early 1700s. South Carolina's most famous French Huguenot of all was Francis Marion, the "Swamp Fox" of Revolutionary War fame. Born on the Santee River, Marion grew up in Georgetown and is now interred near Moncks Corner.

During the 18th century a number of charitable aid organizations sprang up to serve various local groups, mostly along ethnoreligious lines. The wealthiest and most influential of them all was the South Carolina Society, founded in 1737 and first called "The Two Bit Club" because of the original weekly dues. The society still meets today at its building at 72 Meeting Street, designed in 1804 by none other than Manigault's grandson, also named Gabriel, who was Charleston's most celebrated amateur architect. Another aid organization, the **Huguenot Society of Carolina** (138 Logan St., 843/723-3235, www.huguenotsociety.org, Mon.-Fri. 9 A.M.-2 P.M.), was established in 1885. Their library is a great research tool for anyone interested in French Protestant history and genealogy.

To this day, the spiritual home of Charleston's Huguenots is the same as always: the French Huguenot Church on Church Street, one of the earliest congregations in the city. Though many of the old ways have gone, the church still holds one liturgy a year (in April) in French.

Theatre. To mark the theater's centennial, the hotel added a stage facility in 1835, and it's that building you see today. For the theater's second centennial, the Works Progress Administration completely refurbished Dock Street back into a working theater in time to distract Charlestonians from the pains of the Great Depression. In addition to a very active and well-regarded annual season from the resident Charleston Stage Company, the 464-seat venue has hosted umpteen events of the Spoleto Festival over the past three decades and since its renovation continues to do so.

Old Powder Magazine

The Old Powder Magazine (79 Cumberland St., 843/722-9350, www.powdermag.org, Mon.-Sat. 10 A.M.-4 P.M., Sun. 1-4 P.M., $2 adults, $1 children) may be small, but the building is quite historically significant. The 1713 edifice is the oldest public building in South Carolina and also the only one remaining from the days of the Lords Proprietors. As the name indicates, this was where the city's gunpowder was stored during the Revolution. The magazine is designed to implode rather than explode in the event of a direct hit.

© JIM MOREKIS

the newly restored Dock Street Theatre, one of America's oldest playhouses

This is another labor of love of the Historic Charleston Foundation, which has leased the building—which from a distance looks curiously like an ancient Byzantine church—from The Colonial Dames since 1993. It was opened to the public as an attraction in 1997. Now directly across the street from a huge parking garage, the site has continuing funding issues, so occasionally the hours for tours can be erratic. Inside, you'll see displays, a section of the original brick, and an exposed earthquake rod. Right next door is the privately owned, circa-1709 **Trott's Cottage,** the first brick dwelling in Charleston.

Old Slave Mart Museum

Slave auctions became big business in the South after 1808, when the United States banned the importation of slaves, thus increasing both price and demand. The auctions, with slaves forced to stand on display on long tables, generally took place in public buildings where everyone could watch the wrenching spectacle of families being torn apart and lives ruined. But in the 1850s, public auctions in Charleston were put to a stop when city leaders discovered that visitors from European nations—all of which had banned slavery outright years before—were horrified at the practice. The slave trade was moved indoors to "marts" near the Cooper River waterfront where the sales could be conducted out of the public eye. The last remaining such structure is the Old Slave Mart Museum (6 Chalmers St., 843/958-6467, www.charlestoncity.info, Mon.-Sat. 9 A.M.-5 P.M., $7 adults, $5 children, free under age 6). Built in 1859, and originally known as Ryan's Mart after the builder, it was only in service a short time before the outbreak of the Civil War. The last auction was held in November 1863. After the war, the Slave Mart became a tenement, and then in 1938 an African American history museum. The city of Charleston acquired the building in the 1980s and reopened it as a museum in late 2007. There are two main areas: the orientation area, where visitors learn about the transatlantic slave trade and the architectural history of the building itself; and the main exhibit area, where visitors can see documents, tools, and displays recreating what happened inside during this sordid chapter in local history and celebrating the resilience of the area's African American population.

NORTH OF BROAD

This tourist-heavy part of town is sometimes called the Market area because of its proximity to the Old City Market. We'll start east at the border of the French Quarter on Meeting Street and work our way west and north toward Francis Marion Square.

Circular Congregational Church

The historic Circular Congregational Church (150 Meeting St., 843/577-6400, www. circularchurch.org, services fall-spring Sun. 11 A.M., summer Sun. 10:15 A.M., tours Mon.-Fri. 10:30 A.M.) has one of the most interesting pedigrees of any house of worship in Charleston, which is saying a lot. Originally held on the site of the "White Meeting House," for which Meeting Street is named, services were held here beginning in 1681 for a polyglot mix of Congregationalists, Presbyterians, and Huguenots. For that reason it was often called the Church of Dissenters (*Dissenter* being the common term at the time for anyone not an Anglican). As with many structures in town, the 1886 earthquake necessitated a rebuild, and the current edifice dates from 1891. Ironically, in this municipality called "the Holy City" for its many high spires, the Circular Church has no steeple, and instead stays low to the ground in an almost medieval fashion. Look for the adjacent meeting house, which gave the street its name; a green-friendly addition

Circular Congregational Church

© JIM MOREKIS

houses the congregation's Christian outreach, has geothermal heating and cooling, and boasts Charleston's only vegetative roof.

Gibbes Museum of Art

The Gibbes Museum of Art (135 Meeting St., 843/722-2706, www.gibbesmuseum.org, Tues.-Sat. 10 A.M.-5 P.M., Sun. 1-5 P.M., $9 adults, $7 students, $5 ages 6-12) is one of those rare Southern museums that manages a good blend of the modern and the traditional, the local and the international. Beginning in 1905 as the Gibbes Art Gallery—the final wish of James Shoolbred Gibbes, who willed $100,000 for its construction—the complex has grown through the years in size and influence. The key addition to the original beaux arts building came in 1978 with the addition of the modern wing in the rear, which effectively doubled the museum's display space. Shortly thereafter the permanent collection and temporary exhibit space was also expanded. Serendipitously, these renovations enabled the Gibbes to become the key visual arts venue for the Spoleto Festival, begun about the same time. The influential Gibbes Art School in the early 20th century formed a close association with the Woodstock School in New York, bringing important ties and prestige to the fledgling institution. Georgia O'Keeffe, who taught college for a time in Columbia, South Carolina, brought an exhibit here in 1955. The first solo show by an African American artist came here in 1974 with an exhibit of the work of William H. Johnson. Don't miss the nice little garden and its centerpiece, the 1972 fountain and sculpture of Persephone by Marshall Fredericks.

Unitarian Church

In a town filled with cool old church cemeteries, the coolest belongs to the Unitarian Church (4 Archdale St., 843/723-4617, www.charlestonuu.org, services Sun. 11 A.M., free tours Fri.-Sat. 10 A.M.-1 P.M.). As a nod to the beauty and power of nature, vegetation and shrubbery in the cemetery have been allowed to take their natural course (walkways excepted). Virginia creeper wraps around 200-year-old grave markers, honeybees feed on wildflowers, and tree roots threaten to engulf entire headstones. The whole effect is oddly relaxing, making it one of my favorite places in Charleston. The church itself—the second-oldest such edifice in Charleston and the oldest Unitarian sanctuary in the South—is pretty nice too. Begun in 1776 because of overcrowding at the Circular Congregational Church, the brand-new building saw rough usage by British troops during the Revolution. In 1787 the church was repaired, though it was not officially chartered as a Unitarian church until 1839. An extensive modernization happened in 1852, during which the current English Perpendicular Gothic Revival walls were installed, along with the beautiful stained-glass windows. The church was spared in the fire of 1861, which destroyed the old Circular Church but stopped at the Unitarian Church's property line. Sadly, it was not so lucky during the 1886 earthquake, which toppled the original tower. The version you see today is a subsequent and less grand design.

Directly next door is **St. John's Lutheran Church** (5 Clifford St., 843/723-2426, www.stjohnscharleston.org, worship Sun. 8:30 A.M. and 11 A.M.), which had its origin in 1742 when Dr. Henry Melchior Muhlenberg stopped in town for a couple of days on his way to minister to the burgeoning Salzburger colony in Ebenezer, Georgia. He would later be known as the father of the Lutheran Church in America. To see the sanctuary at times other than Sunday mornings, go by the office next door Monday-Friday 9 A.M.-2 P.M. and they'll let you take a walk through the interior.

Old City Market

Part kitschy tourist trap, part glimpse into the old South, part community gathering place,

THE NEW CHARLESTON GREEN

Most people know "Charleston green" as a unique local color, the result of adding a few drops of yellow to post-Civil War surplus black paint. But these days the phrase might refer to all the environmentally friendly development in Charleston, which you might find surprising considering the city's location in one of the most conservative states in the country's most conservative region.

The most obvious example is the ambitious Navy Yard redevelopment, which seeks to re-purpose the closed-down facility. That project is part of a larger civic vision to reimagine the entire 3,000-acre historic Noisette community of North Charleston, with an accompanying wetlands protection conservancy. From its inception in 1902 at the command of President Theodore Roosevelt through the end of the Cold War, the Charleston Navy Yard was one of the city's biggest employers. Closed down in 1995 as part of a national base realignment plan, locals feared the worst. But a 340-acre section, the **Navy Yard at Noisette** (www.navyyardsc.com), now hosts an intriguing mix of green-friendly design firms, small nonprofits, and commercial maritime companies. The activity centers on the restoration of three huge former naval warehouses at 7, 10, and 11 Storehouse Row. Nearby, on the way to where the CSS *Hunley* is currently being restored, is the big Powerhouse, once the electrical station for the whole yard and now envisioned as the center of a future entertainment and retail district. In the meantime, the Navy Yard's no-frills retro look is so realistic that it has played host to scenes of the Lifetime TV series *Army Wives*. But the largest Navy Yard development is still to come. Clemson University—with the help of a massive federal grant, largest in the school's history—will oversee one of the world's largest wind turbine research facilities, to be built in Building 69. The project is expected to create hundreds of local jobs.

Also in North Charleston, local retail chain Half Moon Outfitters has a green-friendly warehouse facility in an old Piggly Wiggly grocery store. The first LEED (Leadership in Energy and Environmental Design) Platinum-certified building in South Carolina, the warehouse features solar panels, rainwater reservoirs, and locally harvested or salvaged interiors. There's also the LEED-certified North Charleston Elementary School as well as North Charleston's adoption of a "dark skies" ordinance to cut down on light pollution. On the peninsula, the historic meeting house of the Circular Congregation Church, which gave Meeting Street its name, has a green addition with geothermal heating and cooling, rainwater cisterns, and Charleston's first vegetative roof.

In addition to walking the historic byways of the Old Village of Mount Pleasant, architecture and design buffs might also want to check out the 243-acre **I'On** (www.ionvillage.com) "neo-traditional" planned community, a successful model for this type of pedestrian-friendly New Urbanist development. On adjacent Daniel Island, the developers of that island's 4,000-acre planned residential community have been certified as an "Audubon Cooperative Sanctuary" for using wildlife-friendly techniques on its golf and recreational grounds. Even ultra-upscale Kiawah Island has gone green in something other than golf—the fabled Kiawah bobcats are making a comeback, thanks to the efforts of the Kiawah Conservancy.

Why has Charleston proven so adept at moving forward? Locals chalk it up to two things: affluent, well-connected Charlestonians who want to maintain the area's quality of life, and the forward-thinking leadership of Mayor Joe Riley in Charleston and Mayor Keith Summey in North Charleston. For many Charlestonians, however, the green movement manifests in simpler things: the pedestrian and bike lanes on the new Ravenel Bridge over the Cooper River, the thriving city recycling program, or the Sustainable Seafood Initiative, a partnership of local restaurants, universities, and conservation groups that brings the freshest, most environmentally responsible dishes to your table when you dine out in Charleston.

the restored Old City Market

one stipulation was that no slaves were ever to be sold here—or else the property would immediately revert to the family's descendants. And judging by the prevalence of the Pinckney name in these parts to this day, there has never been a shortage of potential claimants should that stipulation have been violated. A recent multi-million-dollar renovation has prettified the bulk of City Market into a more big-city air-conditioned pedestrian shopping mall. It's not as shabbily charming as it once was, but certainly offers a more comfortable stroll during the warmer months.

Old City Market (Meeting St. and Market St., 843/973-7236, daily 6 A.M.-11:30 P.M.) remains Charleston's most reliable, if perhaps least flashy, attraction. It is certainly the practical center of the city's tourist trade, not least because so many tours originate nearby. Originally built on Daniel's Creek—claimed from the marsh in the early 1800s after the city's first marketplace at Broad and Meeting Streets burned in 1796—one of City Market's early features was a colony of vultures who hung around for scraps of meat from the many butcher stalls. Sensing that the carrion eaters would keep the area cleaner than any human could, city officials not only allowed the buzzards to hang around, they were protected by law, becoming known as "Charleston eagles" in tongue-in-cheek local jargon. No matter what anyone tries to tell you, Charleston's City Market never hosted a single slave auction. Indeed, when the Pinckney family donated this land to the city for a "Publick Market,"

Confederate Museum
Located on the second floor of City Market's iconic main building, Market Hall on Meeting Street, the small but spirited Confederate Museum (188 Meeting St., 843/723-1541, Tues.-Sat. 11 A.M.-3:30 P.M., $5 adults, $3 children, cash only) hosts an interesting collection of Civil War memorabilia, with an emphasis on the military side, and is also the local headquarters of the United Daughters of the Confederacy. Perhaps its best contribution, however, is its research library.

William Rhett House
The oldest standing residence in Charleston is the circa-1713 William Rhett House (54 Hasell St.), which once belonged to the colonel who captured the pirate Stede Bonnet. It's now a private residence, but you can admire this excellent prototypical example of a Charleston single house easily from the street and read the nearby historical marker.

St. Mary of the Annunciation Church
The oldest Roman Catholic church in the Carolinas and Georgia, St. Mary of the Annunciation (89 Hasell St., 843/722-7696, www.catholic-doc.org/saintmarys, mass Sun. 9:30 A.M.) traces its roots to 1789, when the Irish priest Father Matthew Ryan was sent to

begin the first Catholic parish in the colony. The original church was destroyed in the great Charleston fire of 1838, and the present sanctuary dates from immediately thereafter. While it did receive a direct hit from a Union shell during the siege of Charleston in the Civil War—taking out the organ—the handsome Greek Revival edifice has survived in fine form the 1886 earthquake, the great hurricane of 1893, and 1989's Hurricane Hugo. You can tour the interior most weekdays 9:30 A.M.-3:30 P.M.

Kahal Kadosh Beth Elohim Reform Temple

The birthplace of Reform Judaism in the United States and the oldest continuously active synagogue in the nation is Kahal Kadosh Beth Elohim Reform Temple (90 Hasell St., 843/723-1090, www.kkbe.org, services Sat. 11 A.M., tours Mon.-Fri. 10 A.M.-noon, Sun. 10 A.M.-4 P.M.). The congregation—Kahal Kadosh means "holy community" in Hebrew—was founded in 1749, with the current temple dating from 1840 and built in the Greek Revival style so popular at the time. The temple's Reform roots came about indirectly because of the great fire of 1838. In rebuilding, some congregants wanted to introduce musical instruments into the temple—previously a no-no—in the form of an organ. The Orthodox contingent lost the debate, and so the new building became the first home of Reform Judaism in the country, a fitting testament to Charleston's longstanding ecumenical spirit of religious tolerance and inclusiveness. Technically speaking, because the Holocaust destroyed all Reform temples in Europe, this is actually the oldest existing Reform synagogue in the world.

Old City Jail

If you made a movie called *Dracula Meets the Lord of the Rings,* the Old City Jail (21 Magazine St., 843/577-5245) might make a great set. Built in 1802 on a lot set aside for public use since 1680, the edifice was indeed the Charleston County lockup until 1939. It was once even more imposing, but the top story and a large octagonal tower fell victim to the 1886 earthquake. Its history is also the stuff from which movies are made. Some of the last pirates were jailed here in 1822 while awaiting hanging, as was slave rebellion leader Denmark Vesey. (As a response to the aborted Vesey uprising, Charleston for a while required that all black sailors in port be detained at the jail.) During the Civil War, prisoners of both armies were held here at various times.

The Old City Jail currently houses the American College of the Building Arts. Unless you're a student there, the only way to tour the Old Jail is through **Bulldog Tours** (40 N. Market St., 843/722-8687, www.bulldogtours. com). Their Haunted Jail Tour ($18 adults, $10 children) starts daily at 7 P.M., 8 P.M., 9 P.M., and 10 P.M.; meet at the jail.

UPPER KING AREA

For many visitors, the area around King Street north of Calhoun Street is the most happening area of Charleston, and not only because its proximity to the Visitors Center makes it the first part of town many see up close. On some days—Saturdays when the Farmers Market is open, for instance—this bustling, active area of town seems a galaxy away from the quiet grace of the older South of the Broad area. Its closeness to the beautiful College of Charleston campus means there's never a shortage of young people around to patronize the area's restaurants and bars and to add a youthful feel. And its closeness to the city's main shopping district, King Street, means there's never a shortage of happy shoppers toting bags of new merchandise.

Marion Square

While The Citadel moved lock, stock, and barrel almost a century ago, the college's old home, the South Carolina State Arsenal, still overlooks 6.5-acre Francis Marion Square (between King St. and Meeting St. at Calhoun St., 843/965-4104), a reminder of the former glory days when this was the institute's parade ground, the "Citadel Green" (the old Citadel is now a hotel). Interestingly, Marion Square can still be used as a parade ground, under agreement with the Washington Light Infantry and the Sumter Guard, which lease the square to the city. Seemingly refusing to give up on tradition—or perhaps just attracted by the many female College of Charleston students— uniformed cadets from The Citadel are still chockablock in Marion Square on any given weekend, a bit of local flavor that reminds you that you're definitely in Charleston. Marion Square is named for the "Swamp Fox" himself, Revolutionary War hero and father of modern guerrilla warfare Francis Marion, for whom the hotel at the square's southwest corner is also named. The newest feature of Marion Square is the Holocaust Memorial on Calhoun Street. However, the dominant monument is the towering memorial to John C. Calhoun. Its 1858 cornerstone includes one of the more interesting time capsules you'll encounter: $100 in Continental money, a lock of John Calhoun's hair, and a cannonball from the Fort Moultrie battle. Marion Square hosts many events, including the Farmers Market every Saturday mid-April-late December, the Food and Wine Festival, and, of course, some Spoleto events.

College of Charleston

The oldest college in South Carolina and the first municipal college in the country, the College of Charleston (66 George St., 843/805-5507, www.cofc.edu) boasts a fair share of history in addition to the way its 12,000-plus students bring a modern, youthful touch to so much of the city's public activities. While its services are no longer free, despite its historic moniker the College is now a full-blown state-supported university in its own right. Though the college has its share of modernistic buildings, a stroll around the campus will uncover some historic gems. The oldest building on this gorgeous campus, the Bishop Robert Smith House, dates from the year of the College's founding, 1770, and is now the president's house; find it on Glebe Street between Wentworth and George. The large Greek Revival building dominating the College's old quad off George and St. Philip's Streets is the magnificent Randolph Hall (1828), the oldest functioning college classroom in the country and now host to the president's office. The huge circular feature directly in front of it is "The Cistern," a historic reservoir that's a popular place for students to sit in the grass and enjoy the sun filtering through the live oaks. The cistern is also where then-candidate Barack Obama spoke at a rally in January 2008. Movies that have included scenes shot on campus include *Cold Mountain, The Patriot,* and *The Notebook.* If you have an iPhone or iPod Touch, you can download a neat self-guided tour, complete with video, from the Apple iTunes App Store (www.apple.com).

The College's main claims to academic fame are its outstanding Art History and Marine Biology departments and its performing arts program. The **Halsey Institute of Contemporary Art** (54 St. Philip St., 843/953-5680, www.halsey.cofc.edu, Mon.-Sat. 11 A.M.-4 P.M.) focuses on modern visual art and also offers film screenings and lectures. The groundbreaking **Avery Research Center for African American History and Culture** (843/953-7609, www.cofc.edu/avery, Mon.-Fri. 10 A.M.-5 P.M., Sat. noon-5 P.M.) features rotating exhibits from its permanent archive collection.

Charleston Museum

During its long history, the Charleston Museum (360 Meeting St., 843/722-2996, www.charlestonmuseum.org, Mon.-Sat.

9 A.M.-5 P.M., Sun. 1-5 P.M., $10 adults, $5 children, combo tickets to Heyward-Washington and Manigault Houses available) has moved literally all over town. It's currently housed in a noticeably modern building, but make no mistake: This is the nation's oldest museum, founded in 1773. It strives to stay as fresh and relevant as any new museum, with a rotating schedule of special exhibits in addition to its very eclectic permanent collection. For a long time this was the only place to get a glimpse of the CSS *Hunley,* albeit just a fanciful replica in front of the main entrance. (Now you can see the real thing at its conservation site in North Charleston, and it's even smaller than the replica would indicate.) Much of the Charleston Museum's collection focuses on aspects of everyday life of Charlestonians, from the aristocracy to slaves, including items such as utensils, clothing, and furniture. There are quirks as well, such as the Egyptian mummy and the fine lady's fan made out of turkey feathers. A particular and possibly surprising specialty includes work and research by noted regional naturalists like John James Audubon, André Michaux, and Mark Catesby. There are also numerous exhibits chronicling the local history of Native Americans and African Americans. There's something for children too in the hands-on interactive "Kidstory." The location is particularly convenient, being close not only to the excellent Charleston Visitors Center and its equally excellent parking garage but also to the Joseph Manigault House (which the museum runs), the Children's Museum of the Lowcountry, and the Gibbes Museum of Art.

Joseph Manigault House

Owned and operated by the nearby Charleston Museum, the Joseph Manigault House (350 Meeting St., 843/723-2926, www.charleston-museum.org, Mon.-Sat. 10 A.M.-5 P.M., Sun. 1-5 P.M., last tour 4:30 P.M., $10 adults, $5 children, combo tickets to Charleston Museum

and Heyward-Washington House available) is sometimes called the "Huguenot House." Its splendor is a good reminder of the fact that the French Protestants were far from poverty-stricken, unlike so many groups who came to America fleeing persecution. This circa-1803 National Historic Landmark was designed by wealthy merchant and investor Gabriel Manigault for his brother, Joseph, a rice planter of local repute and fortune. (Gabriel, quite the crackerjack dilettante architect, also designed Charleston City Hall.) The three-story brick town house is a great example of Adams, or Federal, architecture. The furnishings are top-notch examples of 19th-century handiwork, and the rooms have been restored as accurately as possible, down to the historically correct paint colors. The foundations of various outbuildings, including a privy and slaves' quarters, are clustered around the picturesque little Gate Temple to the rear of the main house in the large enclosed garden. Each December, the Manigault House offers visitors a special treat, as the Garden Club of Charleston decorates it in period seasonal fashion, using only flowers that would have been used in the 19th century.

◖ Aiken-Rhett House

One of my favorite spots in all of Charleston and a comparatively recent acquisition of the Historic Charleston Foundation, the poignant Aiken-Rhett House (48 Elizabeth St., 843/723-1159, www.historiccharleston.org, Mon.-Sat. 10 A.M.-5 P.M., Sun 2-5 P.M., last tour 4:15 P.M., $10 adults, $5 children) shows another side of that organization's mission. Whereas the Historic Charleston-run Nathaniel Russell House seeks to recreate a specific point in time, work at the Aiken-Rhett House emphasizes conservation and research. Built in 1818 and expanded by South Carolina Governor William Aiken Jr., after whom we know the house today, parts of this huge, rambling, almost Dickensian house remained sealed from 1918 until 1975

© JIM MOREKIS

the Aiken-Rhett House

when the family relinquished the property to the Charleston Museum, providing historians with a unique opportunity to study original documents from that period. As you walk the halls, staircases, and rooms—seeing the remains of original wallpaper and the various fixtures added through the years—you can really feel the impact of the people who lived within these walls and get a great sense of the full sweep of Charleston history. While the docents are very friendly and helpful, the main way to enjoy the Aiken-Rhett House is by way of a self-guided MP3 player audio tour—unique in Charleston. While you might think this isolates you from the others in your party, it's actually part of the fun—you can synchronize your players and move as a unit if you'd like.

Children's Museum of the Lowcountry

Yet another example of Charleston's savvy regarding the tourist industry is the Children's Museum of the Lowcountry (25 Ann St.,

843/853-8962, www.explorecml.org, Tues.-Sat. 9 A.M.-5 P.M., Sun. 1-5 P.M., $7, free under age 12 months). Recognizing that historic homes and Civil War memorabilia aren't enough to keep a family with young children in town for long, the city established this museum in 2005 specifically to give families with kids aged 3 months to 12 years a reason to spend more time (and money) downtown. A wide variety of hands-on activities—such as a 30-foot shrimp boat replica and a medieval castle—stretch the definition of *museum* to its limit. In truth, this is just as much an indoor playground as a museum, but no need to quibble. The Children's Museum has been getting rave reviews since it opened, and visiting parents and their children seem happy with the city's investment.

Philip Simmons Garden

Charleston's most beloved artisan is the late Philip Simmons. Born on nearby Daniel Island in 1912, Simmons went through

CHARLESTON

© JIM MOREKIS

ironwork at the Philip Simmons Garden

an apprenticeship to become one of the most sought-after decorative ironworkers in the United States. In 1982 the National Endowment for the Arts awarded him its National Heritage Fellowship. His work is on display at the National Museum of American History, the Smithsonian Institution, and the Museum of International Folk Art in Santa Fe, New Mexico, among many other places. In 1989, the congregation at Simmons's **St. John's Reformed Episcopal Church** (91 Anson St., 843/722-4241, www.stjohnsre.org) voted to make the church garden a commemoration of the life and work of this legendary African American artisan, who died in 2009 at age 97. Completed in two phases, the Bell Garden and the Heart Garden, the project is a delightful blend of Simmons's signature graceful, sinuous style and fragrant flowers.

Old Bethel United Methodist Church

The history of the Old Bethel United Methodist Church (222 Calhoun St., 843/722-3470), the third-oldest church building in Charleston, is a little confusing. Completed in 1807, the church once stood across Calhoun Street, until a schism formed in the black community over whether they should be limited to sitting in the galleries (in those days in the South, blacks and whites attended church together far more frequently than during the Jim Crow era). The entire black congregation wanted out, so in 1852 it was moved aside for the construction of a new church for whites, and then entirely across the street in 1880. Look across the street and sure enough you'll see the circa-1853 **Bethel Methodist Church** (57 Pitt St., 843/723-4587, worship Sun. 9 A.M. and 11:15 A.M.).

HAMPTON PARK AREA

Expansive Hampton Park is a favorite recreation spot for Charlestonians. The surrounding area near the east bank of the Ashley River has some of the earliest suburbs of Charleston, now in various states of restoration and hosting a diverse range of residents. Hampton Park is bordered by streets all around, which can be fairly heavily trafficked because this is the main way to get to The Citadel. But the park streets are closed to traffic Saturday mornings in the spring 8 A.M.-noon so neighborhood people, especially those with young children, can enjoy themselves without worrying about the traffic. This is also where the Charleston Police stable their Horse Patrol steeds.

The Citadel

Although for many its spiritual and historic center will always be at the old state Arsenal in Marion Square, The Citadel (171 Moultrie St., 843/953-3294, www.citadel.edu, grounds daily 8 A.M.-6 P.M.) has been at this 300-acre site farther up the peninsula along the Ashley River since 1922 and shows no signs of leaving. Getting there is a little tricky, in that the entrance to the college is situated behind beautiful Hampton Park off Rutledge Avenue, a main north-south artery on the western portion of the peninsula. The Citadel (technically its full name is The Citadel, The Military College of South Carolina) has entered popular consciousness through the works of graduate Pat Conroy, especially his novel *Lords of Discipline,* starring a thinly disguised "Carolina Military Institute." Other famous Bulldog alumni include construction magnate Charles Daniel (for whom the school library is named); Ernest "Fritz" Hollings, South Carolina governor and longtime U.S. senator; and current Charleston Mayor Joe Riley. You'll see The Citadel's living legacy all over Charleston in the person of the ubiquitous cadet, whose gray-and-white uniform, ramrod posture, and impeccable manners all hark back to the days of the Confederacy. But to best experience The Citadel, you should go to the campus itself.

© JIM MOREKIS

a peek inside the Citadel barracks

There's lots for visitors to see, including **The Citadel Museum** (843/953-6779, daily noon-5 P.M., free), on your right just as you enter campus; the "Citadel Murals" in the Daniel Library; "Indian Hill," the highest point in Charleston and former site of an Indian trader's home; and the grave of U.S. General Mark Clark of World War II fame, who was Citadel president from 1954 to 1966. Ringing vast Summerall Field—the huge open space where you enter campus—are the many castle-like cadet barracks. If you peek inside their gates, you'll see the distinctive checkerboard pattern on which the cadets line up. All around the field itself are various military items, such as a Sherman tank and an F-4 Phantom jet. The most interesting single experience for visitors to The Citadel is the colorful Friday afternoon dress parade on Summerall Field, in which cadets pass for review in full dress uniform (the fabled "long gray line") accompanied by a marching band and pipers. Often called "the best free show in Charleston," the parade happens almost every Friday at 3:45 P.M. during the school year; you might want to consult the website before your visit to confirm. Arrive well in advance to avoid parking problems.

The institute was born out of panic over the threat of a slave rebellion organized in 1822 by Denmark Vesey. The state legislature passed an act establishing the school to educate the strapping young men picked to protect Charleston from a slave revolt. Citadel folks will proudly tell you they actually fired the first shots of the Civil War, when on January 9, 1861, two cadets fired from a battery on Morris Island at the U.S. steamer *Star of the West* to keep it from supplying Fort Sumter. After slavery ended—and with it the school's original raison d'être—The Citadel continued, taking its current name in 1910 and moving to the Ashley River in 1922. While The Citadel is rightly famous for its pomp and circumstance—as well as its now-defunct no-lock "honor system,"

done away with after the Virginia Tech shootings—the little-known truth is that to be one of the 2,000 or so currently enrolled Citadel Bulldogs, you don't have to go through all that, or the infamous "Hell Week" either. You can just sign up for one of their many evening graduate school programs.

Joseph P. Riley Jr. Ballpark

When you hear Charlestonians talk about "The Joe" (360 Fishburne St., 843/577-3647, www.riverdogs.com), they're referring to this charming minor-league baseball stadium, home of the Charleston River Dogs, a New York Yankees affiliate playing April-August in the venerable South Atlantic League. It's also another part of the civic legacy of longtime Mayor Joe Riley, in this case in partnership with the adjacent Citadel. Inspired by the retro design of Baltimore's Camden Yards, The Joe opened in 1997 to rave reviews from locals and baseball connoisseurs all over the nation. From downtown, get there by taking Broad Street west until it turns into Lockwood Drive. Follow that north until you get to Brittlebank Park and The Joe, right next to The Citadel.

WEST ASHLEY

Ironically, Charleston's first postwar automobile suburb also has roots back to the first days of the colony's settlement and was the site of some of the antebellum era's grandest plantations. As the cost of housing on the peninsula continues to rise, this area on the west bank of the Ashley River is experiencing a newfound cachet today for hipsters and young families alike. For most visitors, though, the biggest draws are the ancient plantations and historic sites along the west bank of the river: Charles Towne Landing, Drayton Hall, Magnolia Plantation, and Middleton Place, farthest north. Getting to this area from Charleston proper is easy. Take U.S. 17 ("the Crosstown") west across the Ashley River to the junction

© JIM MOREKIS

Put yourself into the shoes of explorers at Charles Towne Landing.

with Highway 61 and take a right (north) onto Highway 61; veer right to get on Highway 7 for Charles Towne Landing, or stay left on Highway 61 for the plantations.

Charles Towne Landing

Any look at West Ashley must begin where everything began, with the 600-acre historic site Charles Towne Landing (1500 Old Towne Rd., 843/852-4200, www.charlestowne.org, daily 9 A.M.-5 P.M., $7.50 adults, $3.50 students, free under age 6). This is where Charleston's original settlers first arrived from Barbados and camped in 1670, remaining only a few years before eventually moving to the more defensible peninsula where the Holy City now resides. For many years the site was in disrepair and borderline neglect, useful mainly as a place to ship busloads of local schoolchildren on field trips. However, a recent long-overdue upgrade came to fruition with a grand "reopening" of sorts in 2006, which has been very well received and has given the

Landing a newfound sheen of respect. A beautiful and fully seaworthy replica of a settlers' ship is the main highlight, docked creek-side on the far side of the long and well-done exploration trail through the site. You can get on board, and a helpful ranger will explain aspects of the ship as well as the original settlement. Another highlight is the archaeological remnant of the original palisade wall (there's a reconstructed palisade to show what it looked like). Ranger-guided programs are available Wednesday-Friday at 10 A.M.; call ahead for reservations.

Not just a historic site, this is also a great place to bring the family. It has Charleston's only zoo, the "Animal Forest," featuring otters, bears, cougars, and buffalo, and 80 acres of beautiful gardens to relax in, many featuring fabulously ancient live oaks and highlighting other indigenous flora the settlers would have been familiar with. A new audio tour has been instituted, where you can rent an MP3 player ($5), but the self-guided approach

Drayton Hall

works just fine, and you can get a nice map from the front desk to help you around. The outdoor highlights of Charles Towne Landing are obvious, but don't miss the fantastic exhibits inside the visitors center, which are particularly well done and give a comprehensive and informative look back at the time of the original settlers.

◖ Drayton Hall

A mecca for historic preservationists all over the country, Drayton Hall (3380 Ashley River Rd., 843/769-2600, www.draytonhall.org, daily 9 A.M.-4 P.M., $18 adults, $8 ages 12-18, $6 ages 6-11, grounds only $8) is remarkable not only for its pedigree but for the way in which it has been preserved. This stately redbrick Georgian-Palladian building, the oldest plantation home in the country that is open to the public, has been literally historically preserved—as in no electricity, heat, or running water. Since its construction in 1738

by John Drayton, son of Magnolia Plantation founder Thomas, Drayton Hall has survived almost completely intact through the ups and downs of Lowcountry history. Drayton died while fleeing the British in 1779; subsequently his house served as the headquarters of British General Clinton and later General Cornwallis. In 1782, however, American General "Mad Anthony" Wayne claimed the house as his own headquarters. During the Civil War, Drayton Hall escaped the depredations of the conquering Union Army, one of only three area plantation homes to survive. Three schools of thought have emerged to explain why it was spared the fate of so many other plantation homes: (1) A slave told the troops it was owned by "a Union Man," Drayton cousin Percival, who served alongside Admiral David Farragut of "damn the torpedoes" fame; (2) General William Sherman was in love with one of the Drayton women; and (3) one of the Draytons, a doctor, craftily posted smallpox warning flags at the

© JIM MOREKIS

outskirts of the property. Of the three scenarios, the last is considered most likely.

Visitors expecting the more typical approach to house museums, i.e. subjective renovation with period furnishings that may or may not have any connection with the actual house, might be disappointed. But for others the experience at Drayton Hall is quietly exhilarating, almost in a Zen-like way. Planes are routed around the house so that no rattles will endanger its structural integrity. There's no furniture to speak of, only bare rooms, decorated with original paint, no matter how little remains. It can be jarring at first, but after you get into it you might wonder why anyone does things any differently.

Another way the experience is different is in the almost military professionalism of the National Trust for Historic Preservation, which has owned and administered Drayton Hall since 1974. The guides hold degrees in the field, and a tour of the house—offered punctually at the top of the hour, except for the last tour of the day, which starts on the half-hour—takes every bit of 50 minutes, about twice as long as most house tours. A separate 45-minute program is "Connections: From Africa to America," which chronicles the diaspora of the slaves who originally worked this plantation, from their capture to their eventual freedom. "Connections" is given at 11:15 A.M., 1:15 P.M., and 3:15 P.M.

The site comprises not only the main house but two self-guided walking trails, one along the peaceful Ashley River and another along the marsh. Note also the foundations of the two "flankers," or guest wings, at each side of the main house. They survived the Yankees only for one to fall victim to the 1886 earthquake and the other to the 1893 hurricane. Also on-site is an African American cemetery with at least 33 known graves. It's kept deliberately untended and unlandscaped to honor the final wish of Richmond Bowens (1908-1998), the seventh-generation descendant of some of Drayton Hall's original slaves.

Magnolia Plantation and Gardens

A different legacy of the Drayton family is Magnolia Plantation and Gardens (3550 Ashley Rd., 843/571-1266, www.magnoliaplantation. com, Mar.-Oct. daily 9 A.M.-4:30 P.M., call for winter hours, $15 adults, $10 children, free under age 6). It claims not only the first garden in the United States, dating back to the 1680s, but also the first public garden, dating to 1872. Magnolia's history spans back two full centuries before that, however, when Thomas Drayton Jr.—scion of Norman aristocracy, son of a wealthy Barbadian planter—came from the Caribbean to build his own fortune. He immediately married the daughter of Stephen Fox, who began this plantation in 1676. Through wars, fevers, depressions, earthquakes, and hurricanes, Magnolia has stayed in the possession of an unbroken line of Drayton descendants to this very day.

As a privately run attraction, Magnolia has little of the academic veneer of other plantation sites in the area, most of which have long passed out of private hands. There's a slightly kitschy feel here, the opposite of the quiet dignity of Drayton Hall. And unlike Middleton Place a few miles down the road, the gardens here are anything but manicured, with a wild, almost playful feel. That said, Magnolia can claim fame to being one of the earliest bona fide tourist attractions in the United States and the beginning of Charleston's now-booming tourist industry. It happened after the Civil War, when John Grimke Drayton, reduced to near-poverty, sold off most of his property, including the original Magnolia Plantation, just to stay afloat. (In a common practice at the time, as a condition of inheriting the plantation, Mr. Grimke, who married into the family, was required to legally change his name to Drayton.) The original plantation home was burned during the war—either by Union troops or freed slaves—so Drayton barged a colonial-era summer house in Summerville, South Carolina, down the Ashley River to this site and built the modern Magnolia

© JIM MOREKIS

the maze at Magnolia Plantation and Gardens

Plantation around it specifically as an attraction. Before long, tourists regularly came here by crowded boat from Charleston (a wreck of one such ferry is still on-site). Magnolia's reputation became so exalted that at one point Baedecker's listed it as one of the three main attractions in America, alongside the Grand Canyon and Niagara Falls. The family took things to the next level in the 1970s, when John Drayton Hastie bought out his brother and set about marketing Magnolia Plantation and Gardens as a modern tourist destination, adding more varieties of flowers so that something would always be blooming nearly year-round. While spring remains the best—and also the most crowded—time to come, a huge variety of camellias blooms in early winter, a time marked by a yearly Winter Camellia Festival.

Today Magnolia is a place to bring the whole family, picnic under the massive old live oaks, and wander the lush, almost overgrown grounds. Children will enjoy finding their way

through "The Maze" of manicured camellia and holly bushes, complete with a viewing stand to look within the giant puzzle. Plant lovers will enjoy the themed gardens such as the Biblical Garden, the Barbados Tropical Garden, and the Audubon Swamp Garden, complete with alligators and named after John James Audubon, who visited here in 1851. Hundreds of varieties of camellias, clearly labeled, line the narrow walkways. House tours, the 45-minute Nature Train tour, the 45-minute Nature Boat tour, and a visit to the Audubon Swamp Garden run about $8 pp extra for each offering.

Of particular interest is the poignant old Drayton Tomb, along the Ashley River, which housed many members of the family until being heavily damaged in the 1886 earthquake. Look closely at the nose of one of the cherubs on the tomb; it was shot off by a vengeful Union soldier. Nearby you'll find a nice walking and biking trail along the Ashley among the old paddy fields.

© JIM MOREKIS

Middleton Place

◖ Middleton Place

Not only the first landscaped garden in America but still one of the most magnificent in the world, Middleton Place (4300 Ashley River Rd., 843/556-6020, www.middletonplace.org, daily 9 A.M.-5 P.M., $25 adults, $15 students, $10 children, guided house tour $12 extra) is a sublime, unforgettable combination of history and sheer natural beauty. Nestled along a quiet bend in the Ashley River, the grounds contain a historic restored home, working stables, and 60 acres of breathtaking gardens, all manicured to perfection. A stunning piece of modern architecture, the Inn at Middleton Place completes the package in surprisingly harmonic fashion. First granted in 1675, Middleton Place is the culmination of the Lowcountry rice plantation aesthetic. That sensibility is most immediate in the graceful Butterfly Lakes at the foot of the green landscaped terrace leading up to the Middleton Place House itself, the only surviving remnant of the vengeful Union occupation.

The two wing-shaped lakes, 10 years in construction, seem to echo the low paddy fields that once dotted this entire landscape. In 1741 the plantation became the family seat of the Middletons, one of the most notable surnames in U.S. history. The first head of the household was Henry Middleton, president of the First Continental Congress, who began work on the meticulously planned and maintained gardens. The plantation passed to his son Arthur, a signer of the Declaration of Independence; then on to Arthur's son Henry, governor of South Carolina; and then down to Henry's son Williams Middleton, a signer of the Ordinance of Secession. It was then that things turned sour, both for the family and for the grounds themselves. As the Civil War wound down, on February 22, 1865, the 56th New York Volunteers burned the main house and destroyed the gardens, leaving only the circa-1755 guest wing, which today is the Middleton Place House Museum. The great earthquake of 1886 added insult to injury by wrecking the Butterfly Lakes. It wasn't until 1916 that renovation began, when heir J. J. Pringle Smith took on the project as his own. No one can say he wasn't successful. At the garden's bicentennial in 1941, the Garden Club of America awarded its prestigious Bulkley Medal to Middleton Place. In 1971 Middleton Place was named a National Historic Landmark, and 20 years later the International Committee on Monuments and Sites named Middleton Place one of six U.S. gardens of international importance. In 1974, Smith's heirs established the nonprofit Middleton Place Foundation, which now owns and operates the entire site.

All that's left of the great house are the remains of the foundation, still majestic in ruin. Today visitors can tour the excellently restored **Middleton Place House Museum** (4300 Ashley River Rd., 843/556-6020, www.middletonplace.org, guided tours Mon. 1:30-4:30 P.M., Tues.-Sun. 10 A.M.-4:30 P.M., $12)—actually the only remaining "flanker" building—and see furniture, silverware, china, and books belonging to the Middletons as well as family portraits by Thomas Sully and Benjamin West.

A short walk takes you to the Plantation Stableyards, where costumed craftspeople still work using historically authentic tools and methods, surrounded by a happy family of domestic animals. The newest addition to the Stableyards is a pair of magnificent male water buffalo. Henry Middleton originally brought a pair in to work the rice fields—the first in North America—but today they're just there to relax and add atmosphere. They bear the Turkish names of Adem (the brown one) and Berk (the white one), or "Earth" and "Solid." Meet the fellas daily 9 A.M.-5 P.M. If you're like most folks, however, you'll best enjoy simply wandering and marveling at the gardens. "Meandering" is not the right word to describe them, since they're systematically laid out. "Intricate" is the word I prefer, and

that sums up the attention to detail that characterizes all the garden's portions, each with a distinct personality and landscape design template. To get a real feel for how things used to be here, for an extra $15 pp you can take a 45-minute carriage ride through the bamboo forest to an abandoned rice field. Rides start around 10 A.M. and run every hour or so, weather permitting.

The 53-room **Inn at Middleton Place,** besides being a wholly gratifying lodging experience, is also a quite self-conscious and largely successful experiment. Its bold Frank Lloyd Wright-influenced modern design, comprising four units joined by walkways, is modern. But both inside and outside it manages to blend quite well with the surrounding fields, trees, and riverbanks. The Inn also offers kayak tours and instruction—a particularly nice way to enjoy the grounds from the waters of the Ashley—and features its own organic garden and labyrinth, intriguing modern counterpoints to the formal gardens of the plantation itself.

They still grow the exquisite Carolina Gold rice in a field at Middleton Place, harvested in the old style each September. You can sample some of it in many dishes at the **Middleton Place Restaurant** (843/556-6020, www.middletonplace.org, lunch daily 11 A.M.-3 P.M., dinner Tues.-Thurs. 6-8 P.M., Fri.-Sat. 6-9 P.M., Sun. 6-8 P.M., $15-25). Hint: You can tour the gardens for free if you arrive for a dinner reservation at 5:30 P.M. or later.

The Coburg Cow

The entire stretch of U.S. 17 (Savannah Highway) heading into Charleston from the west is redolent of a particularly Southern brand of retro Americana. The chief example is the famous Coburg Cow, a large, rotating dairy cow accompanied by a bottle of chocolate milk. The current installation dates from 1959, though a version of it was on this site as far back as the early 1930s when this area was open countryside. During Hurricane Hugo the Coburg Cow was moved to a safe location. In 2001 the attached dairy closed down, and the city threatened to have the cow moved or demolished. But community outcry preserved the delightful landmark, which is visible today on the south side of U.S. 17 in the 900 block. You can't miss it—it's a big cow on the side of the road!

NORTH CHARLESTON

For years synonymous with crime, blight, and sprawl, North Charleston—actually a separate municipality—was for the longest time considered a necessary evil by most Charlestonians, who generally ventured there only to shop at a mall or see a show at its concert venue, the Coliseum. But as the cost of real estate continues to rise on the peninsula in Charleston proper, more and more artists and young professionals are choosing to live here. Make no mistake: North Charleston still has its share of crime and squalor, but some of the most exciting things going on in the metro area are taking place right here. While many insisted that the closing of the U.S. Navy Yard in the 1990s would be the economic death of the whole city, the free market stepped in and is transforming the former military facility into a hip mixed-use shopping and residential area. This is also where to go if you want to see the raised submarine CSS *Hunley,* now in a research area on the grounds of the old Navy Yard. In short, North Charleston offers a lot for the more adventurous traveler and will no doubt only become more and more important to the local tourist industry as the years go by. And as they're fond of pointing out up here, there aren't any parking meters.

Magnolia Cemetery

Although not technically in North Charleston, historic Magnolia Cemetery (70 Cunnington Ave., 843/722-8638, Sept.-May daily 8 A.M.-5 P.M., Jun.-Aug. daily 8 A.M.-6 P.M.) is on the way, well north of the downtown tourist district in the area called "The Neck." This historic burial ground, while not quite the aesthetic equal of Savannah's Bonaventure, is still a stirring site for its natural beauty and ornate memorials as well as for its historic aspects. Here are buried the crewmen who died aboard the CSS *Hunley,* reinterred after their retrieval from Charleston Harbor. In all, over 2,000 Civil War dead are buried here, including five Confederate generals and 84 rebels who fell at Gettysburg and were moved here.

Charleston Navy Yard

A vast postindustrial wasteland to some and a fascinating outdoor museum to others, the Charleston Navy Yard is in the baby steps of rehabilitation from one of the Cold War era's major military centers to the largest single urban redevelopment project in the United States. The Navy's gone now, forced off the site during a phase of base realignment in the mid-1990s. But a 340-acre section, the **Navy Yard at Noisette** (1360 Truxtun Ave., 843/302-2100, www.navyyardsc.com, daily 24 hours), now hosts an intriguing mix of homes, green design firms, nonprofits, and commercial maritime companies and was named the country's sixth-greenest neighborhood by *Natural Home* magazine in 2008. It has even played host to some scenes of the Lifetime TV series *Army Wives.* Enter on Spruill Avenue and you'll find yourself on wide streets lined with huge, boarded-up warehouse facilities, old machine shops, and dormant power stations. A notable project is the restoration of **10 Storehouse Row** (2120 Noisette Blvd., 843/302-2100, Mon.-Fri. 9 A.M.-5 P.M.), which now hosts the American College of Building Arts along with design firms, galleries, and a small café. Nearby, Clemson University will soon be administering one of the world's largest wind turbine research facilities. At the north end lies the new **Riverfront**

Park (843/745-1087, daily dawn-dusk) in the old Chicora Gardens military residential area. There's a nifty little fishing pier on the Cooper River, an excellent naval-themed band shell, and many sleekly designed modernist sculptures paying tribute to the sailors and ships that made history here. From Charleston you get to the Navy Yard by taking I-26 north to exit 216B (you can reach the I-26 junction by just going north on Meeting Street). After exiting, take a left onto Spruill Avenue and a right onto McMillan Avenue, which takes you straight in.

CSS *Hunley*

For the longest time, the only glimpse of the ill-fated Confederate submarine was a not-quite-accurate replica outside the Charleston Museum. But after maritime novelist and adventurer Clive Cussler and his team finally found the *Hunley* in 1995 off Sullivan's Island, the tantalizing dream became a reality: We'd

finally find out what it looked like, and perhaps even be lucky enough to bring it to the surface. That moment came on August 8, 2000, when a team comprising the nonprofit **Friends of the Hunley** (Warren Lasch Conservation Center, 1250 Supply St., Bldg. 255, 866/866-9938, www.hunley.org, Sat. 10 A.M.-5 P.M., Sun. noon-5 P.M., $12, free under age 5), the federal government, and private partners successfully implemented a plan to safely raise the vessel. It was recently moved to its new home in the old Navy Yard, named after Warren Lasch, chairman of the Friends of the Hunley. You can now view the sub in a 90,000-gallon conservation tank on the grounds of the old Navy Yard, see the life-size model from the TNT movie *The Hunley,* and look at artifacts such as the "lucky" gold piece of the commander. You can even see facial reconstructions of some of the eight sailors who died on board the sub that fateful February day in 1864,

replica of the CSS *Hunley* outside the Charleston Museum

© JIM MOREKIS

when it mysteriously sank right after successfully destroying the USS *Housatonic* with the torpedo attached to its bow. So that research and conservation can be performed during the week, tours only happen on Saturday-Sunday. Because of this limited window of opportunity and the popularity of the site, I strongly recommend reserving tickets ahead of time. The sub itself is completely submerged in an electrolyte formula to better preserve it, and photography is strictly forbidden. (The remains of the crew lie in Magnolia Cemetery, where they were buried in 2004 with full military honors.) To get to the Warren Lasch Center from Charleston, take I-26 north to exit 216B. Take a left onto Spruill Avenue and a right onto McMillan Avenue. Once in the Navy Yard, take a right on Hobson Avenue, and after about one mile take a left onto Supply Street. The Lasch Center is the low white building on the left.

Park Circle

The focus of restoration in North Charleston is the old Park Circle neighborhood (intersection of Rhett Ave. and Montague Ave., www.parkcircle.net). The adjacent **Olde North Charleston** development has a number of quality shops, bars, and restaurants.

Fire Museum

It's got a mouthful of a name, but the **North Charleston and American LaFrance Fire Museum and Educational Center** (4975 Centre Pointe Dr., 843/740-5550, www.legacyofheroes.org, Mon.-Sat. 10 A.M.-5 P.M., Sun. 1-5 P.M., last ticket 4 P.M., $6 adults, free under age 14), right next to the huge Tanger Outlet Mall, does what it does with a lot of chutzpah—which is fitting considering that it pays tribute to firefighters and the tools of their dangerous trade. The museum, which opened in 2007 and shares a huge 25,000-square-foot space with the North Charleston Convention and Visitors Bureau, is primarily dedicated to

maintaining and increasing its collection of antique American LaFrance firefighting vehicles and equipment. The 18 fire engines here date from 1857 to 1969. The museum's exhibits have taken on greater poignancy in the wake of the tragic loss of nine Charleston firefighters killed trying to extinguish a warehouse blaze on U.S. 17 in summer 2007—second only to the 9/11 attacks as the largest single loss of life for a U.S. firefighting department.

EAST COOPER

The main destination in this area on the east bank of the Cooper River is the island of Mount Pleasant, primarily known as a peaceful, fairly affluent suburb of Charleston—a role it has played for about 300 years now. Although few old-timers (called "hungry necks" in local lingo) remain, Mount Pleasant does have several key attractions well worth visiting—the old words of former Charleston mayor John Grace notwithstanding: "Mount Pleasant is neither a mount, nor is it pleasant." Through Mount Pleasant is also the only land route to access Sullivan's Island, Isle of Palms, and historic Fort Moultrie. Shem Creek, which bisects Mount Pleasant, was once the center of the local shrimping industry, and while there aren't near as many shrimp boats as there once were, you can still see them docked or on their way to and from a trawling run. (Needless to say, there are a lot of good seafood restaurants around here as well.) The most common route for visitors is by way of U.S. 17 over the massive Arthur Ravenel Jr. Bridge.

Patriots Point Naval and Maritime Museum

Directly across Charleston Harbor from the old city lies the Patriots Point Naval and Maritime Museum complex (40 Patriots Point Rd., 843/884-2727, www.patriotspoint.org, daily 9 A.M.-6:30 P.M., $18 adults, $11 ages 6-11, free for active-duty military), one of the first

RAISING THE *HUNLEY*

The amazing, unlikely raising of the Confederate submarine CSS *Hunley* from the muck of Charleston harbor sounds like the plot of an adventure novel—which makes sense considering that the major player is an adventure novelist. For 15 years, the undersea diver and best-selling author Clive Cussler looked for the final resting place of the *Hunley*. The sub was mysteriously lost at sea after sinking the USS *Housatonic* on February 17, 1864, with the high-explosive "torpedo" mounted on a long spar on its bow. It marked the first time a sub ever sank a ship in battle.

For over a century before Cussler, treasure-seekers had searched for the sub, with P.T. Barnum even offering $100,000 to the first person to find it. But on May 3, 1995, a magnetometer operated by Cussler and his group, the National Underwater Marine Agency, discovered the *Hunley*'s final resting place—in 30 feet of water and under three feet of sediment about four miles off Sullivan's Island at the mouth of the harbor. Using a specially designed truss to lift the entire sub, a 19-person dive crew and a team of archaeologists began a process that would result in raising the vessel on August 8, 2000. But before the sub could be brought up, a dilemma had to be solved: For 136 years the saltwater of the Atlantic had permeated its metallic skin. Exposure to air would rapidly disintegrate the entire thing. So the conservation team, with input from the U.S. Navy, came up with a plan to keep the vessel submerged in a special solution indefinitely at the specially constructed **Warren Lasch Conservation Center** (1250 Supply St., Bldg. 255, 866/866-9938, www.hunley.org, Sat. 10 A.M.-5 P.M., Sun.

noon-5 P.M., $12, free under age 5) in the old Navy Yard while research and conservation was performed on it piece by piece.

And that's how you see the *Hunley* today, submerged in its special conservation tank, still largely covered in sediment. Upon seeing the almost unbelievably tiny, cramped vessel—much smaller than most experts imagined it would be—visitors are often visibly moved at the bravery and sacrifice of the nine-man Confederate crew, who no doubt would have known that the *Hunley*'s two previous crews had drowned at sea in training accidents. Theirs was, in effect, a suicide mission. That the crew surely realized this only makes the modern visitor's experience even more poignant.

The Warren Lasch Center, operated under the auspices of Clemson University, is only open to the public on weekends. Archaeology continues apace during the week—inch by painstaking inch, muck and tiny artifacts removed millimeter by millimeter. The process is so thorough that archaeologists have even identified an individual eyelash from one of the crewmembers. Other interesting artifacts include a three-fold wallet with a leather strap, owner unknown; seven canteens; and a wooden cask in one of the ballast tanks, maybe used to hold water or liquor or even used as a chamber pot.

The very first order of business once the sub was brought up, however, was properly burying those brave sailors. In 2004, Charleston came to a stop as a ceremonial funeral procession took the remains of the nine to historic Magnolia Cemetery, where they were buried with full military honors.

chapters in Charleston's tourism renaissance. The project began in 1975 with what is still its main attraction, the World War II aircraft carrier **USS Yorktown,** named in honor of the carrier lost at the Battle of Midway. Much of "The Fighting Lady" is open to the public, and kids and nautical buffs will thrill to walk the decks and explore the many stations below

deck on this massive 900-foot vessel, a veritable floating city. You can even have a full meal in the CPO Mess Hall just like the crew once did (except you'll have to pay $8.50 pp). And if you really want to get up close and personal, try the Navy Flight Simulator for a small additional fee. Speaking of planes, aviation buffs will be overjoyed to see that the *Yorktown* flight

COURTESY OF CHARLESTONCVB.COM

the USS *Yorktown* at Patriots Point

deck (the top of the ship) and the hangar deck (right below) are packed with authentic warplanes, not only from World War II but from subsequent conflicts the ship participated in. You'll see an F6F Hellcat, an FG-1D Corsair, and an SBD Dauntless like those that fought the Japanese, on up to an F-4F Phantom and an F-14 Tomcat from the jet era.

Patriots Point's newest exhibit is also on the *Yorktown:* the **Medal of Honor Memorial Museum,** which opened in 2007 by hosting a live broadcast of the *NBC Nightly News.* Included in the cost of admission, the Medal of Honor museum is an interactive experience documenting the exploits of the medal's honorees from the Civil War through today. Other ships moored beside the *Yorktown* and open for tours are the Coast Guard cutter USCG *Ingham,* the submarine USS *Clamagore,* and the destroyer USS *Laffey,* which survived being hit by three Japanese bombs and five kamikaze attacks—all within an hour. The Vietnam era

is represented by a replica of an entire Naval Support Base Camp, featuring a river patrol boat and several helicopters.

A big plus is the free 90-minute guided tour. If you really want to make a family history day out of it, you can also hop on the ferry from Patriots Point to Fort Sumter and back.

Old Village

It won't blow you away if you've seen Charleston, Savannah, or Beaufort, but Mount Pleasant's old town has its share of fine colonial and antebellum homes and historic churches. Indeed, Mount Pleasant's history is almost as old as Charleston's. First settled for farming in 1680, it soon acquired cachet as a great place for planters to spend the hot summers away from the mosquitoes inland. The main drag is Pitt Street, where you can shop and meander among plenty of shops and restaurants (try an ice cream soda at the historic Pitt Street Pharmacy). The huge meeting hall on the waterfront, Alhambra Hall, was the old ferry terminal.

Boone Hall Plantation

Visitors who've also been to Savannah's Wormsloe Plantation will see the similarity in the majestic, live oak-lined entrance avenue to Boone Hall Plantation (1235 Long Point Rd., 843/884-4371, www.boonehallplantation.com, mid-Mar.-Labor Day Mon.-Sat. 8:30 A.M.-6:30 P.M., Sun. noon-5 P.M., Labor Day-Nov. Mon.-Sat. 9 A.M.-5 P.M., Sun. 1-4 P.M., Dec.-mid-Mar. Mon.-Sat. 9 A.M.-5 P.M., Sun. noon-5 P.M., $19.50 adults, $9.50 children). But this site is about half a century older, dating back to a grant to Major John Boone in the 1680s (the oaks of the entranceway were planted in 1743). Unusually in this area, where fortunes were originally made mostly on rice, Boone Hall's main claim to fame was as a cotton plantation as well as a noted brick-making plant. Boone Hall takes the phrase "living history" to its extreme, as it's not only an active agricultural facility but lets visitors go on "u-pick" walks through its fields, which boast succulent strawberries, peaches, tomatoes, and even pumpkins in October—as well as free hayrides. Currently owned by the McRae family, which first opened it to the public in 1959, Boone Hall is called "the most photographed plantation in America." And photogenic it certainly is, with natural beauty to spare in its scenic location on the Wando River and its adorable Butterfly Garden. But as you're clicking away with your camera, do keep in mind that the plantation's "big house" is not original; it's a 1935 reconstruction. While Boone Hall's most genuine historic buildings include the big Cotton Gin House (1853) and the 1750 Smokehouse, to me the most poignant and educational structures by far are the nine humble brick slave cabins from the 1790s, expertly restored and most fitted with interpretive displays. The cabins are the center of Boone Hall's educational programs, including an exploration of Gullah culture at the outdoor "Gullah Theatre" on the unfortunately named Slave Street. Summers see some serious Civil War reenacting going on. In all, three different tours are available: a 30-minute house tour, a tour of Slave Street, and a garden tour.

Charles Pinckney National Historic Site

This is one of my favorite sights in Charleston, for its uplifting, well-explored subject matter as well as its tastefully maintained house and grounds. Though "Constitution Charlie's" old Snee Farm is down to only 28 acres from its original magnificent 700, the Charles Pinckney National Historic Site (1240 Long Point Rd., 843/881-5516, www.nps.gov/chpi, daily 9 A.M.-5 P.M., free) that encompasses it is still an important repository of local and national history. Sometimes called "the forgotten Founder," Charles Pinckney was not only a hero of the American Revolution and a notable early abolitionist but one of the main authors of the U.S. Constitution. His great aunt Eliza Lucas Pinckney was the first woman agriculturalist in the United States, responsible for opening up the indigo trade. Her son Charles Cotesworth Pinckney was one of the signers of the Constitution. The current main house, doubling as the visitors center, dates from 1828, 11 years after Pinckney sold Snee Farm to pay off debts. That said, it's still a great example of Lowcountry architecture, replacing Pinckney's original home, where President George Washington slept and had breakfast under a nearby oak tree in 1791 while touring the south. Another highlight at this National Park Service-administered site is the 0.5-mile self-guided walk around the site, some of it on boardwalks over the marsh. No matter what anyone tells you, no one is buried underneath the tombstone in the grove of oak trees bearing the name of Constitution Charlie's father, Colonel Charles Pinckney. The marker incorrectly states the elder Pinckney's age, so it was put here only as a monument. A memorial to the colonel is in the churchyard of the 1840s-era Christ Church about one mile down Long Point Road.

Isle of Palms

This primarily residential area of about 5,000 people received the state's first "Blue Wave" designation from the Clean Beaches Council for its well-managed and preserved beaches. Like adjacent Sullivan's Island, there are pockets of great wealth here, but also a laid-back, windswept beach-town vibe. You get here from Mount Pleasant by taking the Isle of Palms Connector off U.S. 17 (Johnnie Dodds/Chuck Dawley Blvd.). Aside from just enjoying the whole scene, the main self-contained attraction here is **Isle of Palms County Park** (14th Ave., 843/886-3863, www.ccprc.com, May-Labor Day daily 9 A.M.-7 P.M., Mar.-Apr. and Sept.-Oct. daily 10 A.M.-6 P.M., Nov.-Feb. daily 10 A.M.-5 P.M., $7 per vehicle, free for pedestrians and cyclists), with its ocean-front beach, complete with umbrella rental, a volleyball court, a playground, and lifeguards. Get here by taking the Isle of Palms Connector (Hwy. 517) from Mount Pleasant, going through the light at Palm Boulevard, and taking the next left at the gate. The island's other claim to fame is the excellent (and surprisingly affordable) **Wild Dunes Resort** (5757 Palm Blvd., 888/778-1876, www.wilddunes.com), with its two Fazio golf courses and 17 clay tennis courts. Breach Inlet, between Isle of Palms and Sullivan's Island, is where the Confederate sub *Hunley* sortied to do battle with the USS *Housatonic*. During 1989's Hurricane Hugo, the entire island was submerged.

Sullivan's Island

Part funky beach town, part ritzy getaway, Sullivan's Island has a certain timeless quality. While much of it was rebuilt after Hurricane Hugo's devastation, plenty of local character remains, as evidenced by some cool little bars in its tiny "business district" on the main drag of Middle Street. There's a ton of history on Sullivan's, but you can also just while the day away on the quiet, windswept beach on the Atlantic, or ride a bike all over the island and back. Unless you have a boat, you can only get here from Mount Pleasant. From U.S. 17, follow the signs for Highway 703 and Sullivan's Island. Cross the Ben Sawyer Bridge, and then turn right onto Middle Street; continue for about 1.5 miles.

FORT MOULTRIE

While Fort Sumter gets the vast bulk of the media, the older Fort Moultrie (1214 Middle St., 843/883-3123, www.nps.gov/fosu, daily 9 A.M.-5 P.M., $3 adults, free under age 16) on Sullivan's Island actually has a much more sweeping history. Furthering the irony, Major Robert Anderson's detachment at Fort Sumter at the opening of the Civil War was actually the Fort Moultrie garrison, reassigned to Sumter because Moultrie was thought too vulnerable from the landward side. Indeed, Moultrie's first incarnation, a perimeter of felled palm trees, didn't even have a name when it was unsuccessfully attacked by the British in the summer of 1776, the first victory by the colonists in the Revolution. The redcoat cannonballs bounced off those soft, flexible trunks, and thus was born South Carolina's nickname, "The Palmetto State." The hero of the battle, Sergeant William Jasper, would gain immortality for putting the blue and white regimental banner—forerunner to the modern blue and white state flag—on a makeshift staff after the first one was shot away. Subsequently named for the commander at the time, William Moultrie, the fort was captured by the British in a later engagement. That first fort fell into decay and a new one was built over it in 1798 but was soon destroyed by a hurricane. In 1809 a brick fort was built here;

© JIM MOREKIS

Fort Moultrie on Sullivan's Island

it soon gained notoriety as the place where the great chief Osceola was detained soon after his capture, posing for the famous portrait by George Catlin. His captors got more than they bargained for when they jokingly asked the old guerrilla soldier for a rendition of the Seminole battle cry. According to accounts, Osceola's realistic performance scared some bystanders half to death. The chief died here in 1838, and his modest grave site is still on-site, in front of the fort on the landward side. Other famous people to have trod on Sullivan's Island include Edgar Allan Poe, who was inspired by Sullivan's lonely, evocative environment to write *The Gold Bug* and other works. There's a Gold Bug Avenue and a Poe Avenue here today, and the local library is named after him as well. A young Lieutenant William Tecumseh Sherman was also stationed here during his Charleston stint in the 1830s before his encounter with history in the Civil War. Moultrie's main Civil War role was as a target for Union shot during the long siege of Charleston. It was pounded so hard and for so long that its walls fell below a nearby sand hill and were finally unable to be hit anymore. A full military upgrade happened in the late 1800s, extending over most of Sullivan's Island (some private owners have even bought some of the old batteries and converted them into homes). It's the series of later forts that you'll visit on your trip to the Moultrie site, which is technically part of the Fort Sumter National Monument and administered by the National Park Service.

Most of the outdoor tours are self-guided, but ranger programs typically happen Memorial Day-Labor Day daily at 11 A.M. and 2:30 P.M. There's a bookstore and visitors center across the street, offering a 20-minute video on the hour and half-hour 9 A.M.-4:30 P.M. Keep in mind there's no regular ferry to Fort Sumter from Fort Moultrie; the closest ferry to Sumter leaves from Patriots Point on Mount Pleasant.

© JIM MOREKIS

a view of Folly Beach from the pier

BENCH BY THE ROAD
Scholars say that about half of all African Americans alive today had an ancestor who once set foot on Sullivan's Island. As the first point of entry for at least half of all slaves imported to the United States, the island's "pest houses" acted as quarantine areas so slaves could be checked for communicable diseases before going to auction in Charleston proper. But few people seem to know this. In a 1989 magazine interview, African American author and Nobel laureate Toni Morrison said about historic sites concerning slavery, "There is no suitable memorial, or plaque, or wreath or wall, or park or skyscraper lobby. There's no 300-foot tower, there's no small bench by the road." In 2008, that last item became a reality, as the first of several planned "benches by the road" was installed on Sullivan's Island to mark the sacrifice of enslaved African Americans. It's a simple black steel bench, with an attached marker and a nearby plaque.

The Bench by the Road is at the Fort Moultrie visitors center.

FOLLY BEACH
A large percentage of the town of Folly Beach was destroyed by Hurricane Hugo in 1989, and erosion since then has increased and hit the beach itself pretty hard. All that said, enough of Folly's funky charm is left to make it worth visiting. Called "The Edge of America" during its heyday from the 1930s through the 1950s as a swinging resort getaway, Folly Beach is now a slightly beaten but enjoyable little getaway on this barrier island. As with all areas of Charleston, the cost of living here is rapidly increasing, but Folly Beach still reminds locals of a time that once was: a time of soda fountains, poodle skirts, stylish one-piece bathing suits, and growling hot rods. Folly's main claim to larger historic fame is playing host to George Gershwin, who stayed at a cottage on West Arctic Avenue to write the score for

Porgy and Bess, set across the harbor in downtown Charleston. (Ironically, Gershwin's opera couldn't be performed in its original setting until 1970 because of segregationist Jim Crow laws.) Original *Porgy* author DuBose Heyward stayed around the corner at a summer cottage on West Ashley Avenue that he dubbed "Follywood."

Called Folly Road until it gets to the beach, Center Street is the main drag here, dividing the beach into east and west. In this area you'll find the **Folly Beach Fishing Pier** (101 E. Arctic Ave., 843/588-3474, Apr.-Oct. daily 6 A.M.-11 P.M., Nov. and Mar. daily 7 A.M.-7 P.M., Dec.-Feb. daily 8 A.M.-5 P.M., $7 parking, $8 fishing fee), which replaced the grand old wooden pier-and-pavilion structure that tragically burned down in 1960.

Back in the day, restaurants, bars, and amusement areas with rides lined the way up to the old pavilion. As the premier musical venue in the region, the pavilion hosted legends like Tommy and Jimmy Dorsey, Benny Goodman, and Count Basie. The new fishing pier, while not as grand as the old one, is worth visiting—a massive, well-built edifice jutting over 1,000 feet into the Atlantic with a large diamond-shaped pavilion at the end. Fishing-rod holders and cleaning stations line the entire thing. Out on the "front beach," daytime activities once included boxing matches and extralegal drag races. In the old days, the "Washout" section on the far west end was where you went to go crabbing or fly-fishing or maybe even steal a kiss from your sweetie. Today, though, the Washout is known as the prime surfing area in the Carolinas, with a dedicated group of diehards.

To get to Folly Beach from Charleston, go west on Calhoun Street and take the James Island Connector. Take a left on Folly Road (Hwy. 171), which becomes Center Street on into Folly Beach.

At the far east end of Folly Island, about 300 yards offshore, you'll see the **Morris Island Lighthouse,** an 1876 beacon that was once surrounded by lush green landscape, now completely surrounded by water as the land has eroded around it. Now privately owned, there's an extensive effort to save and preserve the lighthouse (www.savethelight.org). There's also an effort to keep high-dollar condo development off of beautiful bird-friendly Morris Island itself (www.morrisisland.org). To get there while there's still something left to enjoy, take East Ashley Street until it dead-ends. Park in the lot and take a 0.25-mile walk to the beach.

TOURS

Because of the city's small, fairly centralized layout, the best way to experience Charleston is on foot—either yours or via hooves of equine nature. Thankfully, there's a wide variety of walking and carriage tours for you to choose from. The sheer number and breadth of tour options in Charleston is beyond the scope of this section. For a full selection of available tours, visit the **Charleston Visitor Reception and Transportation Center** (375 Meeting St., 800/774-0006, www.charlestoncvb.com, Mon.-Fri. 8:30 A.M.-5 P.M.), where they have entire walls of brochures for all the latest tours, with local tourism experts on-site. Here are some notable highlights.

Walking Tours

If you find yourself walking around downtown soon after dark, you'll almost invariably come across a walking tour in progress, with a small cluster of people gathered around a tour guide. There are too many walking tours to list them all, but here are the best.

For more than 10 years, **Ed Grimball's Walking Tours** (306 Yates Ave., 843/762-0056, www.edgrimballtours.com, $16 adults, $8 children) has run two-hour tours on Friday-Saturday mornings, courtesy of the knowledgeable and still-sprightly Ed himself, a native Charlestonian. All of Ed's walks start from the big Pineapple Fountain in Waterfront Park, and reservations are a must. **Original Charleston**

DOIN' THE CHARLESTON

It has been called the biggest song and dance craze of the 20th century. It first entered the American public consciousness via New York City in a 1923 Harlem musical called *Runnin' Wild,* but the roots of the dance soon to be known as the Charleston were indeed in the Holy City. No one is quite sure of the day and date, but local lore assures us that members of Charleston's legendary Jenkins Orphanage Band were the first to start dancing that crazy "Geechie step," a development that soon became part of the band's act. The Jenkins Orphanage was started in 1891 by the African American Baptist minister Reverend D. J. Jenkins and was originally housed in the Old Marine Hospital at 20 Franklin Street (which you can see today, although it's not open to the public). To raise money, Reverend Jenkins acquired donated instruments and started a band comprising talented orphans from the house. The orphans traveled as far away as London, where they were a hit with the locals but not with the constabulary, who unceremoniously fined them for stopping traffic.

A Charleston attorney who happened to be in London at the time, Augustine Smyth, paid their way back home, becoming a lifelong supporter of the orphanage in the process.

From then on, playing in donated old Citadel uniforms, the Jenkins Orphanage Band frequently took its act on the road. They played at the St. Louis and Buffalo expositions, and even at President Taft's inauguration. They also frequently played in New York, and it was there that African American pianist and composer James P. Johnson heard the Charlestonians play and dance to their Gullah rhythms, considered exotic at the time. Johnson would incorporate what he heard into the tune "Charleston," one of many songs in the revue *Runnin' Wild.* The catchy song and its accompanying loose-limbed dance seemed tailor-made for the Roaring '20s and its liberated, hedonistic spirit. Before long the Charleston had swept the nation, becoming a staple of jazz clubs and speakeasies across the country, and indeed, the world.

Walks (45 Broad St., 800/729-3420, www.charlestonwalks.com, daily 8:30 A.M.-9:30 P.M., $18.50 adults, $10.50 children) has received much national TV exposure. They leave from the corner of Market and State Streets and have a full slate of tours, including a popular adults-only pub crawl. **Charleston Strolls Walk with History** (843/766-2080, www.charlestonstrolls.com, $18 adults, $10 children) is another popular tour good for a historical overview and tidbits. They have three daily embarkation points: Charleston Place (9:30 A.M.), the Days Inn (9:40 A.M.), and the Mills House (10 A.M.). **Architectural Walking Tours** (173 Meeting St., 800/931-7761, www.architecturalwalkingtoursofcharleston.com, $20) offers an 18th-century tour Monday and Wednesday-Saturday at 10 A.M. and a 19th-century tour at 2 P.M., which are geared more toward historic preservation. They leave from the Meeting Street Inn (173 Meeting St.). A relatively new

special interest tour is **Charleston Art Tours** (53 Broad St., 843/860-3327, www.charlestonarttours.com, $49). The brainchild of local artists Karen Hagan and Martha Sharp, this tour is led by a professional artist guide and includes refreshments and a gift bag from one of the featured galleries. The Fine Art Tour ($50) runs 2-4 P.M. and leaves from 27½ State Street. They also run a Charleston Renaissance tour ($55), which includes a visit to the Gibbes Museum of Art (Tues.-Sat. 10 A.M.) and a "Gibbes Museum Plus" tour (Thurs. and Sat. 1:30 P.M.)

Ghost tours are very popular in Charleston. **Bulldog Tours** (40 N. Market St., 843/722-8687, www.bulldogtours.com) has exclusive access to the Old City Jail, which features prominently in most of their tours. Their most popular tour, the Haunted Jail Tour ($18 adults, $10 children) leaves daily at 7 P.M., 8 P.M., 9 P.M., and 10 P.M.; meet at the Old City Jail (21 Magazine St.). The Ghosts and

Dungeons tour ($18) leaves March-November Tuesday-Saturday at 7 P.M. and 9 P.M. from 40 North Market Street. Other tours include the Ghosts and Graveyard Tour (7:30 P.M. and 9:30 P.M., $18) and the adults-only Dark Side of Charleston (daily 8 P.M. and 10 P.M., $18). **Tour Charleston** (184 E. Bay St., 843/723-1670, www.tourcharleston.com, $18) offers two paranormal tours, Ghosts of Charleston I, which leaves daily at 5:30 P.M., 7:30 P.M., and 9:30 P.M. from Waterfront Park, and Ghosts of Charleston II, which leaves at 7 P.M. and 9 P.M. from Marion Square.

Carriage Tours

The city strictly regulates the treatment and up-keep of carriage horses and mules, so there's not a heck of a lot of difference in service or price among the various tour companies. Typically, rides take 1-1.5 hours and hover around $20 per adult, about half that per child. Tours sometimes book up early, so call ahead. The oldest service in town is **Palmetto Carriage Works** (40 N. Market St., 843/723-8145, www.carriagetour.com), which offers free parking at its "red barn" base near City Market. Another popular tour is **Old South Carriage Company** (14 Anson St., 843/723-9712, www.oldsouthcarriage.com) with its Confederate-clad drivers. **Carolina Polo & Carriage Company** (16 Hayne St., 843/577-6767, www.cpcc.com) leaves from several spots, including the Doubletree Hotel and their Hayne Street stables.

Motorized Tours

Leaving from Charleston Visitor Reception and Transportation Center (375 Meeting St.), **Adventure Sightseeing** (843/762-0088, www.touringcharleston.com, $20 adults, $11 children) offers several comfortable 1.5-2 hour rides, including the only motorized tour to the Citadel area. Tour times are daily at 9:30 A.M., 10 A.M., 10:30 A.M., 10:45 A.M., 11:30 A.M., 12:20 P.M., 1:30 P.M., and 2:45 P.M. You can make a day

of it with **Charleston's Finest Historic Tours** (843/577-3311, www.historictoursofcharleston.com, $19 adults, $9.50 children), which has a basic two-hour city tour each day at 10:30 A.M. and offers some much longer tours to outlying plantations. They offer free downtown pickup from most lodgings. The old faithful **Gray Line of Charleston** (843/722-4444, www.graylineofcharleston.com, $20 adults, $12 children) offers a 90-minute tour departing from the Visitors Center March-November daily every 30 minutes 9:30 A.M.-3 P.M. (hotel pickup by reservation). The last tour leaves at 2 P.M. during the off-season.

African American History Tours

Charleston is rich in African American history, and a couple of operators specializing in this area are worth mentioning: Al Miller's **Sites & Insights Tours** (843/762-0051, www.sitesandinsightstours.com, $13-18) has several packages, including a Black History and Porgy & Bess Tour as well as a good combo city and island tour, all departing from the Visitors Center. Alphonso Brown's **Gullah Tours** (843/763-7551, www.gullahtours.com, $18), featuring stories told in the Gullah dialect, all leave from the African American Art Gallery (43 John St.) near the Visitors Center Monday-Friday at 11 A.M. and 1 P.M. and Saturday at 11 A.M., 1 P.M., and 3 P.M.

Water Tours

The best all-around tour of Charleston Harbor is the 90-minute ride offered by **Spiritline Cruises** (800/789-3678, www.spiritlinecruises.com, $17 adults, $10 ages 6-11), which leaves from either Aquarium Wharf or Patriots Point. Allow about 30 minutes for ticketing and boarding. They also have a three-hour dinner cruise in the evening leaving from Patriots Point (about $50 pp) and a cruise to Fort Sumter. **Sandlapper Water Tours** (843/849-8687, www.sandlappertours.com, $20-27) offers many types of evening and dolphin cruises on a 45-foot catamaran. They also offer Charleston's only waterborne ghost tour. Most of their tours leave from the Maritime Center near East Bay and Calhoun Streets.

Ecotours

This aspect of Charleston's tourism scene is very well represented. The best operators include: **Barrier Island Eco Tours** (50 41st Ave., 843/886-5000, www.nature-tours.com, from $38), taking you up to the Cape Romain Refuge out of Isle of Palms; **Coastal Expeditions** (514-B Mill St., 843/884-7684, www.coastalexpeditions.com, prices vary), with a base on Shem Creek in Mount Pleasant, offering several different-length sea kayak adventures; and **PaddleFish Kayaking** (843/330-9777, www.paddlefishkayaking.com, from $45), offering several kinds of kayaking tours (no experience necessary) from downtown, Kiawah Island, and Seabrook Island.

Entertainment and Events

Charleston practically invented the idea of diversion and culture in the United States, so it's no surprise that there's plenty to do here, from museums to festivals and a brisk nightlife scene.

NIGHTLIFE

Unlike the locals-versus-tourists divide you find so often in other destination cities, in Charleston it's nothing for a couple of visitors to find themselves at a table next to four or five college students enjoying themselves in true Charlestonian fashion: loudly and with lots of good food and strong drink nearby. Indeed, the Holy City is downright ecumenical in its partying. The smokiest dives also have some of the best brunches. The toniest restaurants also have some of the most hopping bar scenes. Tourist hot spots written up in all the guidebooks also have their share of local regulars. But through it all, one constant remains: Charleston's finely honed ability to seek out and enjoy the good life. It's a trait that comes naturally and traditionally, going back to the days of the earliest Charleston drinking and gambling clubs, like the Fancy Society, the Meddlers Laughing Club, and the Fort Jolly Volunteers. Bars close in Charleston at 2 A.M. The old days of the "mini-bottle"—in which no free pour was allowed and all drinks had to be made from the little airline bottles—are gone, and it seems that local bartenders have finally figured out how to mix a decent cocktail. At the retail level, all hard-liquor sales stop at 7 P.M., with none at all on Sundays. You can buy beer and wine in grocery stores 24-7.

Pubs and Bars

In a nod to the city's perpetual focus on well-prepared food, it's difficult to find a Charleston watering hole that *doesn't* offer really good food in addition to a well-stocked bar. One of Charleston's favorite neighborhood spots is **Moe's Crosstown Tavern** (714 Rutledge Ave., 843/722-3287, daily 11 A.M.-2 A.M.) at Rutledge and Francis in the Wagener Terrace/Hampton Square area. A newer location, **Moe's Downtown Tavern** (5 Cumberland St., 843/577-8500, daily 11 A.M.-2 A.M.) offers a similar vibe and menu, but the original, and best, Moe's experience is at the Crosstown.

Nipping on Moe's heels for best pub food in town is **A.C.'s Bar and Grill** (467 King St., 843/577-6742, daily 11 A.M.-2 A.M.). Though this dark, quirky watering hole might seem out of place in the increasingly tony Upper King area, this only adds to its appeal. A.C.'s at its best is all things to all people: Charleston's favorite late-night bar, a great place to get a burger basket, and also one of the best (and certainly most unlikely) Sunday brunches in town, featuring chicken and waffles.

The action gets going late at **Social Wine Bar** (188 E. Bay St., 843/577-5665, daily 4 P.M.-2 A.M.), a hopping hangout near the French Quarter. While the hot and cold tapas are tasty—I like the special sashimi—the real action here, as you'd expect, is the wine. They offer at least 50 wines by the glass and literally hundreds by the bottle. My favorite thing to do here is partake of the popular "flights," triple tastes of kindred spirits, as it were. If the pricing on the menu seems confusing, ask your server to help you out.

Johnson's Pub (12 Cumberland St., 843/958-0662, daily noon-2 A.M.), a quirky but popular downtown spot, offers seven varieties of burger, all incredible, plus great pizza; it's also well known for its Caesar salad. Oh, yeah, and they keep the drinks coming too.

The Guinness flows freely at **Tommy Condon's Irish Pub** (160 Church St., 843/577-3818, www.tommycondons.com, Sun.-Thurs. 11 A.M.-2 A.M., dinner until 10 P.M., Fri.-Sat. 11 A.M.-2 A.M., dinner until 11 P.M.)—after the obligatory and traditional slow-pour, that is—as do the patriotic Irish songs performed live most nights. You have three sections to choose from in this large, low building right near City Market: the big outdoor deck, the cozy pub itself, and the back dining room with classic wainscoting.

If it's a nice day out, a good place to relax and enjoy happy hour outside is **Vickery's Bar and Grill** (15 Beaufain St., 843/577-5300, www.vickerysbarandgrill.com, Mon.-Sat. 11:30 A.M.-2 A.M., Sun. 11 A.M.-1 A.M., kitchen closes 1 A.M.), actually part of a small regional chain based in Atlanta. Start with the oyster bisque, and maybe try the turkey and brie sandwich or crab cakes for your entrée.

Because of its commercial nature, Broad Street can get quiet when the sun goes down and the office workers disperse back to the burbs. But a warm little oasis can be found a few steps off Broad Street in the **Blind Tiger** (36-38 Broad St., 843/577-0088, daily 11:30 A.M.-2 A.M., kitchen closes Mon.-Thurs. 10 P.M., Fri.-Sun. 9 P.M.), which takes its name from the local Prohibition-era nickname for a speakeasy. Wood panels, Guinness and Bass on tap, and some good bar-food items make this a good stop off the beaten path if you find yourself in the area. A patio out back often features live music.

Located not too far over the Ashley River on U.S. 17, Charleston institution **Gene's Haufbrau** (17 Savannah Hwy., 843/225-4363, www.geneshaufbrau.com, daily 11:30 A.M.-2 A.M.) is worth making a special trip into West Ashley. Boasting the largest beer selection in Charleston—from the Butte Creek Organic Ale from California to a can of PBR—Gene's also claims to be the oldest bar in town, established in 1952.

Though Sullivan's Island has a lot of high-dollar homes, it still has friendly watering holes like **Dunleavy's Pub** (2213-B Middle St., 843/883-9646, Sun.-Thurs. 11:30 A.M.-1 A.M., Fri.-Sat. 11:30 A.M.-2 A.M.). Inside is a great bar festooned with memorabilia, or you can enjoy a patio table. The other Sullivan's watering hole of note is **Poe's Tavern** (2210 Middle St., 843/883-0083, daily 11 A.M.-2 A.M., kitchen closes 10 P.M.) across the street, a nod to Edgar Allan Poe and his service on the island as a clerk in the U.S. Army. It's a lively, mostly-locals scene, set within a fun but suitably dark interior (though you might opt for one of the outdoor tables on the raised patio). Simply put, no trip to Sullivan's is complete without a stop at one (or possibly both) of these two local landmarks, each within a stone's throw of the other.

If you're in Folly Beach, enjoy the great views and the great cocktails at **Blu Restaurant and Bar** (1 Center St., 843/588-6658, www.blu-follybeach.com, $10-20) inside the Holiday Inn Folly Beach Oceanfront. There's nothing

© JIM MOREKIS

Poe's Tavern is a great hangout on Sullivan's Island.

like a Spiked Lemonade on a hot Charleston day at the beach. Another notable Folly Beach watering hole is the **Sand Dollar Social Club** (7 Center St., 843/588-9498, Sun.-Fri. noon-1 A.M., Sat. noon-2 A.M.), the kind of cash-only, mostly local, and thoroughly enjoyable dive you often find in little beach towns. You have to pony up for a "membership" to this private club, but it's only a buck. There's a catch, though: You can't get in until your 24-hour "waiting period" is over.

If you find yourself up in North Charleston, by all means stop by **Madra Rua Irish Pub** (1034 E. Montague Ave., 843/554-2522, daily 11 A.M.-1 A.M.), an authentic watering hole with a better-than-average pub food menu that's also a great place to watch a soccer game.

Live Music

Charleston's music scene is best described as hit-and-miss. There's no distinct "Charleston sound" to speak of (especially now that the heyday of Hootie and the Blowfish is long past), and there's no one place where you're assured of finding a great band any night of the week. The scene is currently in even more of a state of flux because the city's best-regarded live rock club, Cumberland's on King Street, closed in 2007 after 15 years in business. The best place to find up-to-date music listings is the local free weekly *Charleston City Paper* (www. charlestoncitypaper.com).

These days the hippest music spot in town is out on James Island at **The Pour House** (1977 Maybank Hwy., 843/571-4343, www.charlestonpourhouse.com, 9 P.M.-2 A.M. on nights with music scheduled, call for info), where the local characters are sometimes just as entertaining as the acts onstage. The venerable **Music Farm** (32 Ann St., 843/722-8904, www.musicfarm. com) on Upper King isn't much to look at from the outside, but inside the cavernous space has played host to all sorts of bands over the past two decades. Recent concerts have included G. Love and Special Sauce, Third Eye Blind, Galactic, Modest Mouse, and Drive-By Truckers.

For jazz, check out **Mistral** (99 S. Market St., 843/722-5708, Sun.-Thurs. 11 A.M.-11 P.M., Fri.-Sat. 11 A.M.-midnight). There's a constant stream of great performers from a variety of traditions, including Dixieland, every night of the week—not to mention some awesome food. Another great jazz place—and, like Mistral, a very good restaurant to boot—is **Mercato** (102 N. Market St., 843/722-6393, www.mercatocharleston.com, bar 4 P.M.-2 A.M., late-night food menu until 1 A.M.). Italian in menu and feel, the live jazz and R&B (Wed.-Sat.) at this establishment—owned by the same company that owns the five-star Peninsula Grill—is definitely all-American. The late kitchen hours are a great bonus.

Lounges

Across the street from Gene's Haufbrau, the retro-chic **Voodoo Lounge** (15 Magnolia Lane, 843/769-0228, Mon.-Fri. 4 P.M.-2 A.M., Sat.-Sun. 5:30 P.M.-2 A.M., kitchen until 1 A.M.) is another very popular West Ashley hangout. It has a wide selection of trendy cocktails and killer gourmet tacos.

The aptly named **Rooftop Bar and Restaurant** (23 Vendue Range, 843/723-0485, Tues.-Sat. 6 P.M.-2 A.M.) at the Library Restaurant in the Vendue Inn is a very popular waterfront happy-hour spot from which to enjoy the sunset over the Charleston skyline. It's also a hot late-night hangout with a respectable menu.

Located in a 200-year-old building and suitably right above a cigar store, **Club Habana** (177 Meeting St., 843/853-5900, Mon.-Sat. 5 P.M.-1 A.M., Sun. 6 P.M.-midnight) is the perfect place to sink down into a big couch, warm yourself by the fireplace, sip a martini (or port, or single-malt scotch), and enjoy a good smoke in the dim light. Probably the last, best vestige of the cigar-bar trend in Charleston, Club Habana remains popular. You get your cigars downstairs in Tinderbox Internationale, which

features a range of rare "Legal Cuban" smokes, rolled from preembargo tobacco that has been warehoused for decades in Tampa, Florida.

Dance Clubs

The **Trio Club** (139 Calhoun St., 843/965-5333, Thurs.-Sat. 9 P.M.-2 A.M.), right off Marion Square, is a favorite place to make the scene. There's a relaxing outdoor area with piped-in music, an intimate sofa-filled upstairs bar for dancing and chilling, and the dark candlelit downstairs with frequent live music. Without a doubt Charleston's best dance club is **Club Pantheon** (28 Ann St., 843/577-2582, Fri.-Sun. 10 P.M.-2 A.M.).

Gay and Lesbian

Charleston is very tolerant by typical Deep South standards, and this tolerance extends to gays and lesbians as well. Most gay- and lesbian-oriented nightlife centers in the Upper King area. Charleston's hottest and hippest dance spot of any type, gay or straight, is **Club Pantheon** (28 Ann St., 843/577-2582, Fri.-Sun. 10 P.M.-2 A.M.) on Upper King on the lower level of the parking garage across from the Visitors Center (375 Meeting St.). Pantheon is not cheap—cover charges are routinely well over $10—but it's worth it for the great DJs, the dancing, and the people-watching, not to mention the drag cabaret on Friday and Sunday nights. Just down the street from Club Pantheon—and owned by the same people—is a totally different kind of gay bar, **Dudley's** (42 Ann St., 843/577-6779, daily 4 P.M.-2 A.M.). Mellower and more appropriate for conversation or a friendly game of pool, Dudley is a nice contrast to the thumping Pantheon a few doors down.

Though **Vickery's Bar and Grill** (15 Beaufain St., 843/577-5300, www.vickerysbarand-grill.com, Mon.-Sat. 11:30 A.M.-2 A.M., Sun. 11 A.M.-1 A.M., kitchen closes 1 A.M.) does not market itself as a gay and lesbian establishment, it has nonetheless become quite popular with

CHARLESTON NATIVES

In addition to the long list of historic figures, some notable modern personalities born in Charleston or closely associated with the city include:

- Counterculture artist Shepard Fairey, who designed the iconic "Hope" campaign poster for Barack Obama
- Actress Mabel King (*The Wiz*)
- Actress-model Lauren Hutton
- Author Nancy Friday
- Actor Thomas Gibson (*Criminal Minds*)
- Author-lyricist DuBose Heyward
- Author Josephine Humphreys
- Author Sue Monk Kidd (*The Secret Life of Bees*)
- Actress Vanessa Minnillo (attended high school)
- Actor Will Patton (*Remember the Titans*)
- Author Alexandra Ripley
- Musician Darius Rucker (singer for Hootie & the Blowfish, now a solo country artist)
- Comedian Andy Dick
- Comedian Stephen Colbert

Thomas Otway's *The Orphan*. The play's success led to the building of the Dock Street Theatre on what is now Queen Street. On February 12, 1736, it hosted its first production, *The Recruiting Officer,* a popular play for actresses of the time because it calls for some female characters to wear tight-fitting British army uniforms. Live theater became a staple of Charleston social life, with notable thespians including both Edwin and Junius Booth (brothers of Lincoln's assassin John Wilkes) and Edgar Allan Poe's mother Eliza performing here. Several high-quality troupes continue to keep that proud old tradition alive, chief among them being **Charleston Stage** (843/577-7183, www.charlestonstage.com), the resident company of the Dock Street Theatre. In addition to its well-received regular season of classics and modern staples, Charleston Stage has debuted more than 30 original scripts over the years, most recently *Gershwin at Folly,* recounting the composer's time at Folly Beach working on *Porgy and Bess.*

The city's most unusual players are **The Have Nots!** (843/853-6687, www.thehavenots.com), with a total ensemble of 35 comedians who typically perform their brand of edgy improv every Friday night at Theatre 99 (280 Meeting St.). The players of **PURE Theatre** (843/723-4444, www.puretheatre.org) perform at the Circular Congregation Church's Lance Hall (150 Meeting St.). Their shows emphasize compelling, mature drama, beautifully performed. This is where to catch less-glitzy, more-gritty productions like *Rabbit Hole, American Buffalo,* and *Cold Tectonics,* a hit at Piccolo Spoleto. **The Footlight Players** (843/722-4487, www.footlightplayers.net) are the oldest continuously active company in town (since 1931). This community-based amateur company performs a mix of crowd-pleasers (*The Full Monty*) and cutting-edge drama (*This War is Live*) at their space at 20 Queen Street.

that population—not least because of the good reputation its parent tavern in Atlanta has with that city's large and influential gay community.

PERFORMING ARTS
Theater

Unlike the more puritanical (literally) colonies farther up the American coast, Charleston was from the beginning an arts-friendly settlement. The first theatrical production in the western hemisphere happened in Charleston in January 1735, when a nomadic troupe rented a space at Church and Broad Streets to perform

STEPHEN COLBERT, NATIVE SON

A purist would insist that Charlestonians are born, not made. While it's true that Comedy Central star Stephen Colbert was actually born in Washington DC, he did spend most of his young life in the Charleston suburb of James Island, attending the Porter-Gaud School. And regardless of his literal birthplace, few would dispute that Colbert is the best-known Charlestonian in American pop culture today.

While it's commonly assumed that Colbert's surname is a link to Charleston's French Huguenot heritage, the truth is that it's really an Irish name. To further burst the bubble, Colbert's father, a vice president at Charleston's Medical University of South Carolina, adopted the current French pronunciation himself—historically his family pronounced the *t* at the end. That being said, Colbert returns quite often to Charleston, as he did in a December 2007 performance at the Sottile Theater, *I am Charleston—and So Can You!*, a play on the title of his recent book.

In 2007, Colbert cooperated with Ben & Jer-ry's Ice Cream to create a new flavor, "Americone Dream" (vanilla with fudge-covered waffle cone pieces and caramel swirl), proceeds from which went to the Coastal Community Foundation of South Carolina. To unveil the flavor, Colbert appeared at "The Joe" and threw out the first pitch at a Charleston River Dogs minor league game. Soon after, Colbert told *Charleston* magazine that he and wife Evelyn "went to the Pig and bought eight pints"—a reference to the ubiquitous Southern grocery chain Piggly Wiggly, a.k.a. "the Pig."

Later that year, Colbert embarked on an ill-fated tongue-in-cheek bid to get on the South Carolina presidential primary ballot, which never materialized. In a video message to the South Carolina Agricultural Summit in November he cried mock tears and said, "I wanted to be president of South Carolina so bad. I was going to be sworn in on a sack of pork ribs and I was going to institute the death penalty for eating Chinese shrimp."

Music

The forerunner to the **Charleston Symphony Orchestra** (CSO, 843/554-6060, www.charlestonsymphony.com) performed for the first time on December 28, 1936, at the Hibernian Hall on Meeting Street. During that first season the CSO accompanied *The Recruiting Officer,* the inaugural show at the renovated Dock Street Theatre. For seven decades, the CSO continued to provide world-class orchestral music, gaining "Metropolitan" status in the 1970s, when they accompanied the first-ever local performance of *Porgy and Bess,* which despite its Charleston setting couldn't be performed locally before then due to segregation laws. Due to financial difficulty, the CSO cancelled its 2010-2011 season. They are making quite the comeback of late, however, and I suggest checking the website for upcoming concerts.

The separate group **Chamber Music Charleston** (843/763-4941, www.chamber-musiccharleston.org), which relies on many core CSO musicians, continues to perform around town, including at Piccolo Spoleto. They play a wide variety of picturesque historic venues, including the Old Exchange (120 E. Bay St.), the Calhoun Mansion (16 Meeting St.), and the Footlight Players Theatre (20 Queen St.). They can also be found at private house concerts, which sell out quickly.

The excellent music department at the College of Charleston sponsors the annual **Charleston Music Fest** (www.charlestonmusicfest.com), a series of chamber music concerts at various venues around the beautiful campus, featuring many faculty members of the college as well as visiting guest artists. Other college musical offerings include: The **College of Charleston Concert Choir** (www.cofc.edu/music), which performs at various venues, usually churches, around town during the fall; the **College of Charleston Opera,** which performs at least one full-length production during the school year and often performs at Piccolo Spoleto; and the popular **Yuletide Madrigal Singers,** who sing in early December at a series of concerts in historic Randolph Hall.

Dance

The premier company in town is the 20-year-old **Charleston Ballet Theatre** (477 King St., 843/723-7334, www.charlestonballet.org). Its 18 full-time dancers perform a great mix of classics, modern pieces, and, of course, a yuletide *Nutcracker* at the Gaillard Municipal Auditorium. Most performances are at the Sottile Theatre (44 George St., just off King St.) and in the Black Box Theatre at their home office on Upper King Street.

CINEMA

The most interesting art house and indie venue in town is currently **The Terrace** (1956 Maybank Hwy., 843/762-9494, www.terrace-theater.com), and not only because they offer beer and wine, which you can enjoy at your seat. Shows before 5 P.M. are $7. It's west of Charleston on James Island; get there by taking U.S. 17 west from Charleston and go south on Highway 171, then take a right on Maybank Highway (Hwy. 700).

For a generic but good multiplex experience, go over to Mount Pleasant to the **Palmetto Grande** (1319 Theater Dr., 843/216-8696).

FESTIVALS AND EVENTS

Charleston is a festival-mad city, especially in the spring and early fall. And new festivals are being added every year, further enhancing the hedonistic flavor of this city that has also mastered the art of hospitality. Here's a look through the calendar at all the key festivals in the area.

January

Held on a Sunday in late January at historic Boone Hall Plantation on Mount Pleasant, the

Lowcountry Oyster Festival (www.charlestonlowcountry.com, 11 A.M.-5 P.M., $8, food additional) features literally truckloads of the sweet shellfish for your enjoyment. Gates open at 10:30 A.M., and there's plenty of parking. Oysters are sold by the bucket and served with crackers and cocktail sauce. Bring your own shucking knife or glove, or buy them on-site.

February

One of the more unique events in town is the **Southeastern Wildlife Exposition** (various venues, 843/723-1748, www.sewe.com, $12.50 per day, $30 for 3 days, free under age 13). For the last quarter century, the Wildlife Expo has brought together hundreds of artists and exhibitors to showcase just about any kind of naturally themed art you can think of, in over a dozen galleries and venues all over downtown. Kids will enjoy the live animals on hand as well.

March

Generally straddling late February and the first days of March, the four-day **Charleston Food & Wine Festival** (www.charlestonfoodandwine.com, various venues and admission) is a glorious celebration of one of the Holy City's premier draws: its amazing culinary community. While the emphasis is on Lowcountry gurus like Donald Barickman of Magnolia's and Robert Carter of the Peninsula Grill, guest chefs from as far away as New York, New Orleans, and Los Angeles routinely come to show off their skills. Oenophiles, especially of domestic wines, will be in heaven as well. Tickets aren't cheap—an all-event pass is over $500 pp—but then again, this is one of the nation's great food cities, so you might find it worth every penny.

Immediately before the Festival of Houses and Gardens is the **Charleston International Antiques Show** (40 E. Bay St., 843/722-3405, www.historiccharleston.org, admission varies), held at Historic Charleston's headquarters at the Missroon House on the High Battery. It features over 30 of the nation's best-regarded dealers and offers lectures and tours.

Mid-March-April, the perennial favorite **Festival of Houses and Gardens** (843/722-3405, www.historiccharleston.org, admission varies) is sponsored by the Historic Charleston Foundation and is held at the very peak of the spring blooming season for maximum effect. In all, the Festival goes into a dozen historic neighborhoods to see about 150 homes. Each day sees a different three-hour tour of a different area, at about $45 pp. This is a fantastic opportunity to peek inside some amazing old privately owned properties that are inaccessible to visitors at all other times. A highlight is a big oyster roast and picnic at Drayton Hall.

Not to be confused with the above festival, the **Garden Club of Charleston House and Garden Tours** (843/530-5164, www.thegardenclubofcharleston.com, $35) are held over a weekend in late March. Highlights include the Heyward-Washington House and the private garden of the late great Charleston horticulturalist Emily Whaley.

One of Charleston's newest and most fun events, the five-night **Charleston Fashion Week** (www.fashionweek.charlestonmag.com, admission varies) is sponsored by *Charleston* magazine and benefits a local women's charity. Mimicking New York's Fashion Week events under tenting in Bryant Park, Charleston's version features runway action under big tents in Marion Square—and, yes, past guests have included former contestants on *Project Runway.*

April

The annual **Cooper River Bridge Run** (www.bridgerun.com) happens the first Saturday in April (unless that's Easter weekend, in which case it runs the week before) and features a six-mile jaunt across the massive new Arthur Ravenel Bridge over the Cooper River, the longest cable span in the western hemisphere.

It's not for those with a fear of heights, but it's still one of Charleston's best-attended events—with well over 30,000 participants. The whole crazy idea started when Dr. Marcus Newberry of the Medical University of South Carolina in Charleston was inspired by an office fitness trail in his native state of Ohio to do something similar in Charleston to promote fitness. Participants can walk the course if they choose, and many do. Signaled with the traditional cannon shot, the race still begins in Mount Pleasant and ends downtown, but over the years the course has changed to accommodate growth—not only in the event itself but in the city. Auto traffic, of course, is rerouted from the night before the race. The Bridge Run remains the only elite-level track and field event in South Carolina, with runners from Kenya typically dominating year after year. Each participant in the Bridge Run now must wear a transponder chip; new "Bones in Motion" technology allows you to track a favorite runner's exact position in real time during the race. The 2006 Run had wheelchair participants for the first time. There's now a Kid's Run in Hampton Square the Friday before, which also allows strollers.

From 1973 to 2000—except for 1976, when it was in Florida—the **Family Circle Cup** (161 Seven Farms Dr., Daniel Island, 843/856-7900, www.familycirclecup.com, admission varies) was held at Sea Pines Plantation on Hilton Head Island. But the popular Tier 1 Women's tennis tournament in 2001 moved to Daniel Island's brand-new Family Circle Tennis Center, specifically built for the event through a partnership of *Family Circle* magazine and the city of Charleston. (The Tennis Center is also open to the public and hosts many community events as well.)

Mount Pleasant is the home of Charleston's shrimping fleet, and each April sees all the boats parade by the Alhambra Hall and Park for the **Blessing of the Fleet** (843/884-8517, www.

townofmountpleasant.com). Family events and lots and lots of seafood are also on tap.

May

Free admission and free parking are not the only draws at the outdoor **North Charleston Arts Festival** (5000 Coliseum Dr., www.northcharleston.org), but let's face it, that's important. Held beside North Charleston's Performing Arts Center and Convention Center, the festival features music, dance, theater, multicultural performers, and storytellers. There are a lot of kids' events as well.

Held over three days at the Holy Trinity Greek Orthodox Church up toward the Neck, the **Charleston Greek Festival** (30 Race St., 843/577-2063, www.greekorthodoxchs.org, $3) offers a plethora of live entertainment, dancing, Greek wares, and, of course, fantastic Greek cuisine cooked by the congregation. Parking is not a problem, and there's even a shuttle to the church from the lot.

One of Charleston's newest annual events is the **Charleston International Film Festival** (843/817-1617, www.charlestoniff.com, various venues and prices). Despite being a relative latecomer to the film-festival circuit, the event is pulled off with Charleston's usual aplomb.

Indisputably Charleston's single biggest and most important event, **Spoleto Festival USA** (843/579-3100, www.spoletousa.org, admission varies) has come a long way since it was a sparkle in the eye of the late Gian Carlo Menotti three decades ago. Though Spoleto long ago broke ties with its founder, his vision remains indelibly stamped on the event from start to finish. There's plenty of music, to be sure, in genres that include orchestral, opera, jazz, and avant-garde, but you'll find something in every other performing art, such as dance, drama, and spoken word, in traditions from Western to African to Southeast Asian. For 17 days from Memorial Day weekend through early June, Charleston hops and hums nearly

24 hours a day to the energy of this vibrant, cutting-edge, yet accessible artistic celebration, which dominates everything and every conversation for those three weeks. Events happen in historic venues and churches all over downtown and as far as Middleton Place, which hosts the grand finale under the stars. If you want to come to Charleston during Spoleto—and everyone should, at least once—book your accommodations and your tickets far in advance. Tickets usually go on sale in early January for that summer's festival.

As if all the hubbub around Spoleto didn't give you enough to do, there's also **Piccolo Spoleto** (843/724-7305, www.piccolospoleto.com, various venues and admission), literally "little Spoleto," running concurrently. The intent of Piccolo Spoleto—begun just a couple of years after the larger festival came to town and run by the city's Office of Cultural Affairs—is to give local and regional performers a time to shine, sharing some of that larger spotlight on the national and international performers at the main event. Of particular interest to visiting families will be Piccolo's children's events, a good counter to some of the decidedly more adult fare at Spoleto USA.

June

Technically part of Piccolo Spoleto but gathering its own following, the **Sweetgrass Cultural Arts Festival** (www.sweetgrassfestival.org) is held the first week in June in Mount Pleasant at the Laing Middle School (2213 U.S. 17 N.). The event celebrates the traditional sweetgrass basket-making skills of African Americans in the historical Christ Church Parish area of Mount Pleasant. If you want to buy some sweetgrass baskets made by the world's foremost experts in the field, this would be the time.

The free, weekend-long, outdoor **Charleston Harbor Fest** (www.charlestonharborfest.org, free) at the Maritime Center on the waterfront is without a doubt one of the coolest events in

A MAN, A PLAN: SPOLETO!

Sadly, Gian Carlo Menotti is no longer with us, having died in 2007 at the age of 95. But the overwhelming success of the composer's brainchild and labor of love, **Spoleto Festival USA,** lives on, enriching the cultural and social life of Charleston and serving as the city's chief calling card to the world at large.

Menotti began writing music at age seven in his native Italy. As a young man he moved to Philadelphia to study music, where he shared classes—and lifelong connections—with Leonard Bernstein and Samuel Barber. His first full-length opera, *The Consul,* would garner him the Pulitzer Prize, as would 1955's *The Saint of Bleecker Street.* But by far Menotti's best-known work is the beloved Christmas opera *Amahl and the Night Visitors,* composed especially for NBC television in 1951. At the height of his fame in 1958, the charismatic and mercurial genius—fluent and witty in five languages—founded the "Festival of Two Worlds" in Spoleto, Italy, specifically as a forum for young American artists in Europe. But it wasn't until nearly two decades later, in 1977, that Menotti was able to make his long-imagined dream of an American counterpart a reality.

Attracted to Charleston because of its longstanding support of the arts, its undeniable good taste, and its small size—ensuring that his festival would always be the number-one activity in town while it was going on—Menotti worked closely with the man who was to become the other key part of the equation: Charleston Mayor Joe Riley, then in his first term in office. Since then, the city has built on Spoleto's success by founding its own local version, **Piccolo Spoleto**—literally, "little Spoleto"—which focuses exclusively on local and regional talent.

Things haven't always gone smoothly. Menotti and the stateside festival parted ways in 1993, when he took over the Rome Opera. Making matters more uneasy, the Italian festival—run by Menotti's longtime partner (and later adopted son) Chip—also became estranged from what was intended to be its soul mate in South Carolina. (Chip was later replaced by the Italian Culture Ministry.) But perhaps this kind of creative tension is what Menotti intended all along. Indeed, each spring brings a Spoleto USA that seems to thrive on the inherent conflict between the festival's often cutting-edge offerings and the very traditional city that hosts it. Unlike so many of the increasingly generic arts "festivals" across the nation, Spoleto still challenges its audiences, just as Menotti intended it to. Depending on the critic and the audience member, that modern opera debut you see may be groundbreaking or gratuitous. The drama you check out may be exhilarating or tiresome.

Still, the crowds keep coming, attracted just as much to Charleston's many charms as to the art itself. Each year, a total of about 500,000 people attend both Spoleto and Piccolo Spoleto. (Despite the weak economy, the 2009 edition actually broke a five-day ticket sales record.) Nearly one-third of the attendees are Charleston residents—the final proof that when it comes to supporting the arts, Charleston puts its money where its mouth is.

town for the whole family. You can see and tour working tall ships, and watch master boatbuilders at work building new ones. There are free sailboat rides into the harbor, and the U.S. Navy provides displays. As if all that weren't enough, you get to witness the start of the 777-mile annual Charleston-to-Bermuda race.

July

Each year over 30,000 people come to see the **Patriots Point Fourth of July Blast** (866/831-1720), featuring a hefty barrage of fireworks shot off the deck of the USS *Yorktown* moored on the Cooper River in the Patriots Point complex. Food, live entertainment, and kids' activities are also featured.

September

From late September into the first week of October, the city-sponsored **MOJA Arts**

sweetgrass baskets, celebrated at June's Sweetgrass Cultural Arts Festival

residences and is the nearly 90-year-old organization's biggest fund-raiser. Tickets typically go on sale the previous June, and they tend to sell out very quickly.

October
Another great food event in this great food city, on a weekend in October, the **Taste of Charleston** (1235 Long Point Rd., 843/577-4030, www.charlestonrestaurantassociation. com, 11 A.M.-5 P.M., $12) is held at Boone Hall Plantation in Mount Pleasant and sponsored by the Greater Charleston Restaurant Association. Over 50 area chefs and restaurants come together so you can sample their wares, including a wine and food pairing, with proceeds going to charity.

November
Plantation Days at Middleton Place (4300 Ashley River Rd., 843/556-6020, www.middletonplace.org, daily 9 A.M.-5 P.M., last tour 4:30 P.M., guided tour $10) happen each Saturday in November, giving visitors a chance to wander the grounds and see artisans at work practicing authentic crafts, as they would have done in antebellum days, with a special emphasis on the contributions of African Americans. A special treat comes on Thanksgiving, when a full meal is offered on the grounds at the Middleton Place restaurant (843/556-6020, www.middletonplace. org, reservations strongly recommended).

Though the **Battle of Secessionville** actually took place in June 1862 much farther south, November is the time the battle is re-enacted at Boone Plantation (1235 Long Point Rd., 843/884-4371, www.boonehallplantation. com, $17.50 adults, $7.50 children) on Mount Pleasant. Call for specific dates and times.

December
A yuletide in the Holy City is an experience you'll never forget, as the **Christmas in Charleston** (843/724-3705, www.charlestoncity.info) events clustered around the first

Festival (843/724-7305, www.mojafestival. com, various venues and admission) highlights the cultural contributions of African Americans and people from the Caribbean with dance, visual art, poetry, cuisine, crafts, and music in genres that include gospel, jazz, reggae, and classical. In existence since 1984, MOJA's name comes from the Swahili word for "one," and its incredibly diverse range of offerings in so many media have made it one of the Southeast's premier events. Highlights include a Reggae Block Party and the always-fun Caribbean Parade. Some events are ticketed, while others, such as the kids' activities and many of the dance and film events, are free.

For five weeks from the last week of September into October, the Preservation Society of Charleston hosts the much-anticipated **Fall Tours of Homes & Gardens** (843/722-4630, www.preservationsociety.org, $45). The tour takes you into over a dozen local

week of the month prove. For some reason—whether it's the old architecture, the friendly people, the churches, the carriages, or all of the above—Charleston feels right at home during Christmas. The festivities begin with Mayor Joe Riley lighting the city's 60-foot Tree of Lights in Marion Square, followed by a parade of brightly lit boats from Mount Pleasant all the way around Charleston up the Ashley River. The key event is the Sunday Christmas Parade through downtown, featuring bands, floats, and performers in the holiday spirit. The Saturday Farmers Market in the square continues through the middle of the month with a focus on holiday items.

Shopping

For a relatively small city, Charleston has an impressive amount of big-name, big-city stores to go along with its charming one-of-a-kind locally owned shops. I've never known anyone to leave Charleston without bundles of good stuff.

KING STREET

Without a doubt, King Street is by far the main shopping thoroughfare in the area. It's unique not only for the fact that so many national name stores are lined up so close to each other but because there are so many great restaurants of so many different types scattered in and among the retail outlets, ideally positioned for when you need to take a break to rest and refuel. Though I don't necessarily recommend doing so—Charleston has so much more to offer—a visitor could easily spend an entire weekend doing nothing but shopping, eating, and carousing up and down King Street from early morning to the wee hours of the following morning. King Street has three distinct areas with three distinct types of merchandise: Lower King is primarily top-of-the-line antiques stores (most are closed Sundays, so plan your trip accordingly); Middle King is where you'll find upscale name-brand outlets such as Banana Republic and American Apparel as well as some excellent shoe stores; and Upper King, north of Calhoun Street, is where you'll find funky housewares shops, generally locally owned.

Antiques

A relatively new addition to Lower King's cluster of antique shops, **Alexandra AD** (156 King St., 843/722-4897, Mon.-Sat. 10 A.M.-5 P.M.) features great chandeliers, lamps, and fabrics. As the name implies, **English Patina** (179 King St., 843/853-0380, Mon.-Sat. 10 A.M.-5 P.M.) specializes in European furniture, brought to its big James Island warehouse three times a year in shipping containers. Since 1929, **George C. Birlant & Co.** (191 King St., 843/722-3842, Mon.-Sat. 9 A.M.-5:30 P.M.) has been importing 18th- and 19th-century furniture, silver, china, and crystal, and also deals in the famous "Charleston Battery Bench." On the 200 block, **A'riga IV** (204 King St., 843/577-3075, Mon.-Sat. 10:30 A.M.-4:30 P.M.) deals in a quirky mix of 19th-century decorative arts, including rare apothecary items. **Carlton Daily Antiques** (208 King St., 843/853-2299, Mon.-Sat. 10 A.M.-5:30 P.M.) intrigues with its unusual focus on art deco and modernist pieces and furnishings.

Art Galleries

Ever since native son Joseph Allen Smith began one of the country's first art collections in Charleston in the late 1700s, the Holy City has been fertile ground for visual artists. For most visitors, the center of visual arts activity is in the French Quarter between South Market and Tradd Streets. Thirty galleries reside here within short walking distance,

King Street is the center of shopping in Charleston.

including: **Charleston Renaissance Gallery** (103 Church St., 843/723-0025, www.fineartsouth.com, Mon.-Sat. 10 A.M.-5 P.M.), specializing in 19th- and 20th-century oils and sculpture, featuring artists from the American South, including some splendid pieces from the Charleston Renaissance; the city-funded **City Gallery at Waterfront** (34 Prioleau St., 843/958-6484, Tues.-Fri. 11 A.M.-6 P.M., Sat.-Sun. noon-5 P.M.); the **Pink House Gallery** (17 Chalmers St., 843/723-3608, http://pinkhousegallery.tripod.com, Mon.-Sat. 10 A.M.-5 P.M.), in the oldest tavern building in the South, circa 1694; **Helena Fox Fine Art** (106-A Church St., 843/723-0073, www.helenafoxfineart.com, Mon.-Sat. 10 A.M.-5 P.M.), dealing in 20th-century representational art; the **Anne Worsham Richardson Birds Eye View Gallery** (119-A Church St., 843/723-1276, www.anneworshamrichardson.com, Mon.-Sat. 10 A.M.-5 P.M.), home of South Carolina's official painter of the state flower and state bird;

and the more modern-oriented **Robert Lange Studios** (2 Queen St., 843/805-8052, www.robertlangestudios.com, daily 11 A.M.-5 P.M.). The best way to experience the area is to go on one of the popular and free **French Quarter ArtWalks** (843/724-3424, www.frenchquarterarts.com), held the first Friday of March, May, October, and December 5-8 P.M. and featuring lots of wine, food, and, of course, art. You can download a map at the website.

One of the most important single venues, the nonprofit **Redux Contemporary Art Center** (136 St. Philip St., 843/722-0697, www.reduxstudios.org, Tues.-Thurs. noon-8 P.M., Fri.-Sat. noon-5 P.M.) features modernistic work in a variety of media, including illustration, video installation, blueprints, performance art, and graffiti. Outreach is hugely important to this venture and includes lecture series, classes, workshops, and internships. For a more modern take from local artists, check out the **Sylvan Gallery** (171 King St., 843/722-2172, www.

MAYOR JOE'S LEGACY

Few cities anywhere have been as greatly influenced by one mayor as Charleston has by Joseph P. "Joe" Riley, reelected in November 2011 to his 10th four-year term (he swears this will be his last). "Mayor Joe," or just "Joe," as he's usually called, is not only responsible for instigating the vast majority of redevelopment in the city, he continues to set the bar for its award-winning tourism industry—always a key component in his long-term plans.

Riley won his first mayoral race at the age of 32, the second Irish American mayor of the city. The first was John Grace, elected in 1911 and eventually defeated by the allegedly anti-Catholic Thomas P. Stoney. Legend has it that soon after winning his first mayoral election in 1975, Riley was handed an old envelope written decades before by the Bishop of Charleston, addressed to "The Next Irish Mayor." Inside was a note with a simple message: "Get the Stoneys."

The well-regarded lawyer, Citadel grad, and former member of the state legislature had a clear vision for his administration: It would bring unprecedented numbers of women and minorities into city government, rejuvenate then-seedy King Street, and enlarge the city's tax base by annexing surrounding areas (during Riley's tenure the city has grown from 16.7 square miles to over 100). But in order to make any of that happen, one thing had to happen first—Charleston's epidemic street crime had to be brought under control. Enter a vital partner in Riley's effort to remake Charleston: Chief of Police Reuben Greenberg. From 1982 to 2005, Greenberg—who intrigued locals and the national media not only for his dominant personality but because he was that comparative rarity, an African American Jew—turned old ideas of law enforcement in Charleston upside down through his introduction of "community policing." Charleston cops would have to have a college degree. Graffiti would not be tolerated. And for the first time in recent memory, they would have to walk beats instead of stay in their cars. With Greenberg's help, Riley was able to keep together the unusual coalition of predominantly white business and corporate interests and African American voters that brought him into office in the first place.

It hasn't all been rosy. Riley was put on the spot in 2007 after the tragic deaths of the "Charleston 9" firefighters, an episode which seemed to expose serious policy and equipment flaws in the city's fire department. And he's often been accused of being too easily infatuated with high-dollar development projects instead of paying attention to the needs of regular Charlestonians, such as perennial flooding problems.

Here's only a partial list of the major projects and events Mayor Joe has made happen in Charleston that visitors are likely to enjoy:

- Charleston Maritime Center
- Charleston Place
- Children's Museum of the Lowcountry
- Hampton Park rehabilitation
- King Street-Market Street retail district
- Mayor Joseph P. Riley Ballpark (named after the mayor at the insistence of city council, over his objections)
- MOJA Arts Festival
- Piccolo Spoleto
- The South Carolina Aquarium
- Spoleto USA
- Waterfront Park
- West Ashley Bikeway & Greenway

thesylvangallery.com, Mon.-Fri. 9 A.M.-5 P.M., Sat. 10 A.M.-5 P.M., Sun. 11 A.M.-4 P.M.), which specializes in 20th- and 21st-century art and sculpture. Right up the street and incorporating works from the estate of Charleston legend Elizabeth O'Neill Verner is **Ann Long Fine Art** (177 King St., 843/577-0447, www.annlongfineart.com, Mon.-Sat. 11 A.M.-5 P.M.), which seeks to combine the painterly aesthetic of the Old World with the edgy vision of the New. Farther up King and specializing in original Audubon prints and antique botanical prints is **The Audubon Gallery** (190 King St., 843/853-1100, www.audubonart. com, Mon.-Sat. 10 A.M.-5 P.M.), the sister store of the Joel Oppenheimer Gallery in Chicago. In the Upper King area is **Gallery Chuma** (43 John St., 843/722-7568, www.gallerychuma. com, Mon.-Sat. 10 A.M.-6 P.M.), which specializes in the art of the Gullah people of the South Carolina coast. They do lots of cultural and educational events about Gullah culture as well as display art on the subject.

Charleston's favorite art supply store is **Artist & Craftsman Supply** (434 King St., 843/579-0077, www.artistcraftsman.com, Mon.-Sat. 10 A.M.-7 P.M., Sun. noon-5 P.M.), part of a well-regarded Maine-based chain. They cater to the pro as well as the dabbler and have a fun children's art section as well.

Books and Music

It's easy to overlook at the far southern end of retail development on King, but the excellent

Preservation Society of Charleston Book and Gift Shop (147 King St., 843/722-4630, Mon.-Sat. 10 A.M.-5 P.M.) is perhaps the best place in town to pick up books on Charleston lore and history as well as locally themed gift items. The charming **Pauline Books and Media** (243 King St., 843/577-0175, Mon.-Sat. 10 A.M.-6 P.M.) is run by the Daughters of Saint Paul and carries Christian books, Bibles, rosaries, and images from a Roman Catholic perspective. Housed in an extremely long and narrow storefront on Upper King, Jonathan Sanchez's funky and friendly **Blue Bicycle Books** (420 King St., 843/722-2666, www.bluebicyclebooks.com, Mon.-Sat. 10 A.M.-6 P.M., Sun. 1-6 P.M.) deals primarily in used books and has a particularly nice stock of local and regional books, art books, and fiction.

Clothes

Cynics may scoff at the proliferation of high-end national retail chains on Middle King,

© JIM MOREKIS

Blue Bicycle Books on Upper King Street

but rarely will a shopper find so many so conveniently located, and in such a pleasant environment. The biggies are: **The Gap** (269 King St., 843/577-2498, Mon.-Thurs. 10 A.M.-7 P.M., Fri.-Sat. 10 A.M.-8 P.M., Sun. 11 A.M.-7 P.M.); **Banana Republic** (247 King St., 843/722-6681, Mon.-Fri. 10 A.M.-7 P.M., Sat. 10 A.M.-8 P.M., Sun. noon-6 P.M.); **J.Crew** (264 King St., 843/534-1640, Mon.-Thurs. 10 A.M.-6 P.M., Fri.-Sat. 10 A.M.-8 P.M., Sun. noon-6 P.M.); and **American Apparel** (348 King St., 843/853-7220, Mon.-Sat. 10 A.M.-8 P.M., Sun. noon-7 P.M.). Of particular note is the massive **Forever 21** (211 King St., 843/937-5087, www.forever21.com, Sun.-Wed. 10 A.M.-8 P.M., Thurs.-Sat. 10 A.M.-9 P.M.), housed in what was formerly Saks Fifth Avenue. This edition of the well-known tween mecca goes well beyond what you're probably used to in other markets and features clothes for (slightly) older women as well as a small men's section.

For a locally owned clothing shop, try the innovative **Worthwhile** (268 King St., 843/723-4418, www.shopworthwhile.com, Mon.-Sat. 10 A.M.-6 P.M., Sun. noon-5 P.M.), which has lots of organic fashion. Big companies' losses are your gain at **Oops!** (326 King St., 843/722-7768, Mon.-Fri. 10 A.M.-6 P.M., Sat. 10 A.M.-7 P.M., Sun. noon-6 P.M.), which buys factory mistakes and discontinued lines from major brands at a discount, passing along the savings to you. The range here tends toward colorful and preppy. If hats are your thing, make sure you visit **Magar Hatworks** (57 Cannon St., 843/577-7740, leighmagar@ aol.com, www.magarhatworks.com), where Leigh Magar makes and sells her whimsical, all-natural hats, some of which she designs for Barneys New York. Another notable locally owned clothing store on King Street is the classy **Berlins Men's and Women's** (114-120 King St., 843/722-1665, Mon.-Sat. 9:30 A.M.-6 P.M.), dating from 1883.

Health and Beauty

The Euro-style window display of **Stella Nova** (292 King St., 843/722-9797, Mon.-Sat. 10 A.M.-7 P.M., Sun. 1-5 P.M.) beckons at the corner of King and Society. Inside this locally owned cosmetics store and studio you'll find a wide selection of high-end makeup and beauty products. There's also a Stella Nova day spa (78 Society St., 843/723-0909, Mon.-Sat. 9 A.M.-6 P.M., Sun. noon-5 P.M.).

Inside the Francis Marion Hotel near Marion Square is **Spa Adagio** (387 King St., 843/577-2444, Mon.-Sat. 10 A.M.-7 P.M., Sun. by appointment only), offering massage, waxing, and skin and nail care. On Upper King you'll find **Allure Salon** (415 King St., 843/722-8689, Tues. and Thurs. 10 A.M.-7 P.M., Wed. and Fri. 9 A.M.-5 P.M., Sat. 10 A.M.-3 P.M.) for stylish haircuts.

Home, Garden, and Sporting Goods

With retail locations in Charleston and Savannah and a new cutting-edge, green-friendly warehouse in North Charleston, **Half Moon Outfitters** (280 King St., 843/853-0990, www.halfmoonoutfitters.com, Mon.-Sat. 10 A.M.-7 P.M., Sun. noon-6 P.M.) is something of a local legend. Here you can find not only top-of-the-line camping and outdoor gear and good tips on local recreation but some really stylish outdoorsy apparel as well. A couple of good home and garden stores are worth mentioning on Upper King: **Charleston Gardens** (650 King St., 866/469-0118, www.charlestongardens.com, Mon.-Sat. 9 A.M.-5 P.M.) for furniture and accessories; and **Haute Design Studio** (489 King St., 843/577-9886, www.hautedesign.com, Mon.-Fri. 9 A.M.-5:30 P.M.) for upper-end furnishings with an edgy feel.

Jewelry

Joint Venture Estate Jewelers (185 King St., 843/722-6730, www.jventure.com, Mon.-Sat.

10 A.M.-5:30 P.M.) specializes in antique, vintage, and modern estate jewelry as well as pre-owned watches, including Rolex, Patek Philippe, and Cartier. Since 1919, **Croghan's Jewel Box** (308 King St., 843/723-3594, www.croghansjewelbox.com, Mon.-Fri. 9:30 A.M.-5:30 P.M., Sat. 10 A.M.-5 P.M.) has offered amazing locally crafted diamonds, silver, and designer pieces to generations of Charlestonians. An expansion in the late 1990s tripled the size of the historic location. **Art Jewelry by Mikhail Smolkin** (312 King St., 843/722-3634, www.fineartjewelry.com, Mon.-Sat. 10 A.M.-5 P.M.) features one-of-a-kind pieces by this St. Petersburg, Russia, native.

Shoes

Rangoni of Florence (270 King St., 843/577-9554, Mon.-Sat. 9:30 A.M.-6 P.M., Sun. 12:30-5:30 P.M.) imports the best women's shoes from Italy, with a few men's designs as well. **Copper Penny Shooz** (317 King St., 843/723-3838, Mon.-Sat. 10 A.M.-7 P.M., Sun. noon-6 P.M.) combines hip and upscale fashion. Funky and fun **Phillips Shoes** (320 King St., 843/965-5270, Mon.-Sat. 10 A.M.-6 P.M.) deals in Dansko for men, women, and kids (don't miss the awesome painting above the register of Elvis fitting a customer). **Mephisto** (322 King St., 843/722-4666, www.mepcomfort.com, Mon.-Sat. 10 A.M.-6 P.M.) deals in that incredibly comfortable, durable brand. A famous locally owed place for footwear is **Bob Ellis Shoe Store** (332 King St., 843/722-2515, www.bobellisshoes.com, Mon.-Sat. 10 A.M.-6 P.M.), which has served Charleston's elite with high-end shoes since 1950.

CHARLESTON PLACE

Charleston Place (130 Market St., 843/722-4900, www.charlestonplaceshops.com, Mon.-Wed. 10 A.M.-6 P.M., Thurs.-Sat. 10 A.M.-8 P.M., Sun. noon-5 P.M.), a combined retail-hotel development begun to much controversy in the late 1970s, was the first big downtown redevelopment project of Mayor Riley's tenure. While naysayers said people would never come downtown to shop for boutique items, Riley proved them wrong, and 30 years later The Shops at Charleston Place and the Riviera (the entire complex has itself been renovated through the years) remains a big shopping draw for locals and visitors alike. Highlights inside the large, stylish space include Gucci, Talbots, Louis Vuitton, Yves Delorme, Everything But Water, and Godiva.

NORTH OF BROAD

In addition to the myriad of tourist-oriented shops in the Old City Market itself, there are a few gems in the surrounding area that also appeal to locals. For years dominated by a flea market vibe, **Old City Market** (Meeting St. and Market St., 843/973-7236, daily 6 A.M.-11:30 P.M.) was recently upgraded and is now chockablock with boutique retail all along its lengthy interior. The more humble crafts tables are toward the back. If you must have one of the handcrafted sweetgrass baskets, try out your haggling skills—the prices have wiggle room built in.

Women come from throughout the region to shop at the incredible consignment store **The Trunk Show** (281 Meeting St., 843/722-0442, Mon.-Sat. 10 A.M.-6 P.M.). You can find one-of-a-kind vintage and designer wear and accessories. Some finds are bargains, some not so much, but there's no denying the quality and breadth of the offerings. For a more budget-conscious and countercultural vintage shop, walk a few feet next door to **Factor Five** (283 Meeting St., 843/965-5559), which has retro clothes, rare CDs, and assorted paraphernalia. **Indigo** (4 Vendue Range, 800/549-2513, Sun.-Thurs. 10 A.M.-6 P.M., Fri.-Sat. 10 A.M.-7 P.M.), a favorite home accessories store, has plenty of one-of-a-kind pieces, many of them by regional artists and rustic in flavor, almost like outsider

The Trunk Show on Meeting Street

art. Affiliated with the hip local restaurant chain Maverick Kitchens, **Charleston Cooks!** (194 East Bay St., 843/722-1212, www.charlestoncooks.com, Mon.-Sat. 10 A.M.-9 P.M., Sun. 11 A.M.-6 P.M.) has an almost overwhelming array of gourmet items and kitchenware, and even offers cooking classes.

OFF THE PENINSULA

Though the best shopping is in Charleston proper, there are some noteworthy independent stores in the surrounding areas. Mount Pleasant boasts a fun antiques and auction spot, **Page's Thieves Market** (1460 Ben Sawyer Blvd., 843/884-9672, www.pagesthievesmarket.com, Mon.-Fri. 9 A.M.-5:30 P.M., Sat. 9 A.M.-5 P.M.). The biggest music store in the region is **The Guitar Center** (7620 Rivers Ave., 843/572-9063, Mon.-Fri. 11 A.M.-7 P.M., Sat. 10 A.M.-7 P.M., Sun. noon-6 P.M.) in North Charleston across from Northwood Mall. With just about everything a musician might want or

need, it's part of a chain that has been around since the late 1950s, but the Charleston location is relatively new. Probably Charleston's best-regarded home goods store is the nationally recognized **ESD, Elizabeth Stuart Design** (422 Savannah Hwy./U.S. 17, 843/225-6282, www. esdcharleston.com, Mon.-Sat. 10 A.M.-6 P.M.), with a wide range of antique and new furnishings, art, lighting, jewelry, and more.

SHOPPING CENTERS

The newest and most pleasant mall in the area is the retro-themed, pedestrian-friendly **Mount Pleasant Towne Center** (1600 Palmetto Grande Dr., 843/216-9900, www.mtpleasanttownecentre. com, Mon.-Sat. 10 A.M.-9 P.M., Sun. noon-6 P.M.), which opened in 1999 to serve the growing population of East Cooper residents tired of having to cross a bridge to get to a big mall. In addition to national chains you'll find a few cool local stores in here, like Stella Nova spa and day salon, Shooz by Copper Penny, and the men's store Jos. A. Banks.

You'll find the **Northwoods Mall** (2150 Northwoods Blvd., North Charleston, 843/797-3060, www.shopnorthwoodsmall.com, Mon.-Sat. 10 A.M.-9 P.M., Sun. noon-6 P.M.) up in North Charleston. Anchor stores include Dillard's, Belk, Sears, and J. C. Penney. North Charleston also hosts the **Tanger Outlet** (4840 Tanger Outlet Blvd., 843/529-3095, www.tangeroutlet.com, Mon.-Sat. 10 A.M.-9 P.M., Sun. 11 A.M.-6 P.M.). Get factory-priced bargains from stores such as Adidas, Banana Republic, Brooks Brothers, CorningWare, Old Navy, Timberland, and more.

Citadel Mall (2070 Sam Rittenberg Blvd., 843/766-8511, www.shopcitadel-mall.com, Mon.-Sat. 10 A.M.-9 P.M., Sun. noon-6 P.M.) is in West Ashley (and curiously not at all close to the actual Citadel college). Anchors here are Dillard's, Parisian, Target, Belk, and Sears.

Sports and Recreation

Because of the generally great weather in Charleston, helped immensely by the steady, soft sea breeze, outdoor activities are always popular and available. Though it's not much of a spectator sports town, there are plenty of things to do on your own, such as golf, tennis, walking, hiking, boating, and fishing.

ON THE WATER
Beaches

In addition to the charming town of Folly Beach itself, there's the modest county-run **Folly Beach County Park** (1100 W. Ashley Ave., Folly Beach, 843/588-2426, www.ccprc.com, May-Feb. daily 10 A.M.-dark, Mar.-Apr. daily 9 A.M.-dark, $7 per vehicle, free for pedestrians and cyclists) at the far west end of Folly Island. It has a picnic area, restrooms, outdoor showers, and beach chair and umbrella rentals. Get here by taking Highway 171 (Folly Rd.) until it turns into Center Street, and then take a right on West Ashley Avenue.

On Isle of Palms you'll find **Isle of Palms County Park** (14th Ave., Isle of Palms, 843/886-3863, www.ccprc.com, fall-spring daily 10 A.M.-dark, summer daily 9 A.M.-dark, $5 per vehicle, free for pedestrians and cyclists), which has restrooms, showers, a picnic area, a beach volleyball area, and beach chair and umbrella rentals. Get there by taking the Isle of Palms Connector (Hwy. 517) to the island, go through the light at Palm Boulevard, and take the next left at the park gate. There's good public beach access near the Pavilion Shoppes on Ocean Boulevard, accessed via J C Long Boulevard.

On the west end of Kiawah Island to the south of Charleston is **Kiawah Island Beachwalker Park** (843/768-2395, www.ccprc.com, Mar.-Apr. and Oct. Sat.-Sun. only 10 A.M.-6 P.M., May-Aug. daily 9 A.M.-7 P.M., Sept. daily 10 A.M.-6 P.M., Nov.-Feb. closed, $7 per vehicle, free for pedestrians and cyclists), the only public facility on this mostly private resort island. It has restrooms, showers, a picnic area with grills, and beach chair and umbrella rentals. Get there from downtown by taking Lockwood Avenue onto the Highway 30 Connector bridge over the Ashley River. Turn right onto Folly Road, then take a left onto Maybank Highway. After about 20 minutes you'll take another left onto Bohicket Road, which leads you to Kiawah in 14 miles. Turn left from Bohicket Road onto the Kiawah Island Parkway. Just before the security gate, turn right on Beachwalker Drive and follow the signs to the park.

For a totally go-it-alone type of beach day, go to the three-mile-long beach on the Atlantic Ocean at **Sullivan's Island.** There are no facilities, no lifeguards, strong offshore currents, and

CHARLESTON

no parking lots on this residential island (park on the side of the street). There's also a lot of dog-walking on this beach, since no leash is required November-February. Get there from downtown by crossing the Ravenel Bridge over the Cooper River and bearing right onto Coleman Boulevard, which turns into Ben Sawyer Boulevard. Take the Ben Sawyer Bridge onto Sullivan's Island. Beach access is plentiful and marked.

Kayaking

An excellent outfit for guided kayak tours is **Coastal Expeditions** (654 Serotina Court, 843/881-4582, www.coastalexpeditions.com), which also runs the only approved ferry service to the Cape Romain National Wildlife Refuge. They'll rent you a kayak for roughly $50 per day. Coastal Expeditions also sells an outstanding kayaking, boating, and fishing map of the area (about $12). **Barrier Island Eco Tours** (50 41st Ave., 843/886-5000, www.nature-tours. com) takes you up to the Cape Romain refuge out of Isle of Palms. **PaddleFish Kayaking** (843/330-9777, www.paddlefishkayaking.com) offers several kinds of kayaking tours (no experience necessary) and is quite accommodating in terms of scheduling them. Another good tour operator is **Nature Adventures Outfitters** (1900 Iron Swamp Rd., McClellanville, 800/673-0679) out of Awendaw Island. Closer to town, many kayakers put in at the **Shem Creek Marina** (526 Mill St., 843/884-3211, www.shemcreekmarina.com) or the public **Shem Creek Landing** in Mount Pleasant. From here it's a safe, easy paddle—sometimes with appearances by dolphins or manatee— to the Intracoastal Waterway. Some kayakers like to go from Shem Creek straight out into Charleston Harbor to **Crab Bank Heritage Preserve,** a prime birding island. Another good place to put in is at **Isle of Palms Marina** (50 41st Ave., 843/886-0209) behind the Wild

Folly Beach County Park

Dunes Resort on Morgan Creek, which empties into the Intracoastal Waterway. Local company **Half Moon Outfitters** (280 King St., 843/853-0990; 425 Coleman Blvd., 843/881-9472, www.halfmoonoutfitters.com, Mon.-Sat. 10 A.M.-7 P.M., Sun. noon-6 P.M.) sponsors an annual six-mile Giant Kayak Race at Isle of Palms Marina in late October, benefiting the Coastal Conservation League.

Behind Folly Beach is an extensive network of waterways, including lots of areas that are great for camping and fishing. The Folly River Landing is just over the bridge to the island. On Folly Island, a good tour operator and rental house is **OceanAir Sea Kayak** (520 Folly Rd., 800/698-8718, www.seakayaksc.com).

Fishing and Boating

For casual fishing off a pier, try the well-equipped new **Folly Beach Fishing Pier** (101 E. Arctic Ave., Folly Beach, 843/588-3474, $5 parking, $8 fishing fee, rod rentals available) on Folly Beach or the **North Charleston Riverfront Park** (843/745-1087, www.north-charleston.org, daily dawn-dusk) along the Cooper River on the grounds of the old Navy Yard. Get onto the Navy Yard grounds by taking I-26 north to exit 216B. Take a left onto Spruill Avenue and a right onto McMillan Avenue.

Key local marinas include **Shem Creek Marina** (526 Mill St., 843/884-3211, www.shemcreekmarina.com), **Charleston Harbor Marina** (24 Patriots Point Rd., 843/284-7062, www.charlestonharbormarina.com), **Charleston City Marina** (17 Lockwood Dr., 843/722-4968), **Charleston Maritime Center** (10 Wharfside St., 843/853-3625, www.cmcevents.com), and the **Cooper River Marina** (1010 Juneau Ave., 843/554-0790, www.ccprc.com).

Good fishing charter outfits include **Barrier Island Eco Tours** (50 41st Ave., 843/886-5000, www.nature-tours.com, about $80) out of Isle of Palms; **Bohicket Boat Adventure & Tour Co.** (2789 Cherry Point Rd., 843/559-3525, www.bohicketboat.com) out of the Edisto River; and **Reel Fish Finder Charters** (315 Yellow Jasmine Court, Moncks Corner, 843/697-2081). Captain James picks up clients at many different marinas in the area. For a list of all public landings in Charleston County, go to www.ccprc.com.

Diving

Diving here can be challenging because of the fast currents, and visibility can be low. But as you'd expect in this historic area, there are plenty of wrecks, fossils, and artifacts. In fact, there's an entire Cooper River Underwater Heritage Trail with the key sites marked for divers. Offshore diving centers on the network of offshore artificial reefs (see www.dnr.sc.gov for a list and locations), particularly the "Charleston 60" sunken barge and the new and very popular "Train Wreck," comprising 50 deliberately sunk New York City subway cars. The longtime popular dive spot known as the "Anchor Wreck" was recently identified as the Norwegian steamer *Leif Erikkson*, which sank in 1905 after a collision with another vessel. In addition to being fun dive sites, these artificial reefs have proven to be important feeding and spawning grounds for marine life.

Probably Charleston's best-regarded outfitter and charter operator is **Charleston Scuba** (335 Savannah Hwy., 843/763-3483, www.charlestonscuba.com) in West Ashley. You also might want to check out **Cooper River Scuba** (843/572-0459, www.cooperriverdiving.com) and **Atlantic Coast Dive Center** (209 Scott St., 843/884-1500).

Surfing and Boarding

The surfing at the famous **Washout** area on the eastside of Folly Beach isn't what it used to be due to storm activity and beach erosion. But the diehards still gather at this area when the swell hits—generally about 3-5 feet (occasionally with dolphins). Check out the conditions yourself from the three views of the Folly Surfcam (www.follysurfcam.com).

The best local surf shop is undoubtedly the historic **McKevlin's Surf Shop** (8 Center St., Folly Beach, 843/588-2247, www.mckevlins. com) on Folly Beach, one of the first surf shops on the East Coast, dating to 1965 (check out an employee's "No Pop-Outs" blog at http:// mckevlins.blogspot.com). Other shops include **Barrier Island Surf Shop** (2013 Folly Rd., Folly Beach, 843/795-4545) and **The Point Break** (369 King St., 843/722-4161) on the peninsula. For lessons, **Folly Beach Shaka Surf School** (843/607-9911, www.shakasurfschool. com) offers private and group sessions at Folly; you might also try **Sol Surfers Surf Camp** (843/881-6700, www.solsurfers.net) in Mount Pleasant. Kiteboarders might want to contact **Air** (1313 Long Grove Dr., Mount Pleasant, 843/388-9300, www.catchsomeair.us), which offers several levels of lessons.

Water Parks

During the summer months, Charleston County operates three water parks, though none are on the peninsula: **Splash Island Waterpark** (444 Needlerush Pkwy., Mount Pleasant, 843/884-0832); **Whirlin' Waters Adventure Waterpark** (University Blvd., North Charleston, 843/572-7275); and **Splash Zone Waterpark at James Island County Park** (871 Riverland Dr., 843/795-7275), on James Island west of town. Admission runs about $10 pp. Go to www.ccprc.com for more information.

ON LAND
Golf

The country's first golf course was constructed in Charleston in 1786. The term "green fee" is alleged to have evolved from the maintenance fees charged to members of the South Carolina Golf Club and Harleston Green in what's now downtown Charleston. So, as you'd expect, there's some great golfing in the area, generally on the outlying islands. Here are some of the highlights; fees are averages and subject to season and time of day.

The folks at the nonprofit **Charleston Golf, Inc.** (423 King St., 843/958-3629, www. charlestongolfguide.com) are your best one-stop resource for tee times and packages. The main public course is the 18-hole **Charleston Municipal Golf Course** (2110 Maybank Hwy., 843/795-6517, www.charlestoncity.info, $40). To get here from the peninsula, take U.S. 17 south over the Ashley River, take Highway 171 (Folly Rd.) south, and then take a right onto Maybank Highway. Probably the most renowned area facilities are at the acclaimed **Kiawah Island Golf Resort** (12 Kiawah Beach Dr., Kiawah Island, 800/654-2924, www.kiawahgolf.com), about 20 miles from Charleston. The resort has five courses in all, the best-known of which is the **Kiawah Island Ocean Course,** site of the famous "War by the Shore" 1991 Ryder Cup. This 2.5-mile course, which is walking-only until noon each day, hosted the Senior PGA Championship in 2007 and will host the 2012 PGA Championship. The Resort offers a golf academy and private lessons galore. These are public courses, but be aware that tee times are limited for golfers who aren't guests at the resort.

Two excellent resort-style public courses are at **Wild Dunes Resort Golf** (5757 Palm Blvd., Isle of Palms, 888/845-8932, www.wilddunes. com, $165) on Isle of Palms. The 18-hole **Patriots Point Links** (1 Patriots Point Rd., Mount Pleasant, 843/881-0042, www.patriotspointlinks.com, $100) on the Charleston Harbor right over the Ravenel Bridge is one of the most convenient courses in the area, and it boasts some phenomenal views. Also on Mount Pleasant is perhaps the best course in the area for the money, the award-winning **Rivertowne Golf Course** (1700 Rivertowne Country Club Dr., Mount Pleasant, 843/856-9808, www. rivertownecountryclub.com, $150) at the

Rivertowne Country Club. Opened in 2002, the course was designed by Arnold Palmer.

Tennis

Tennis fans are in for a treat at the new **Family Circle Tennis Center** (161 Seven Farms Dr., 800/677-2293, www.familycirclecup.com, Mon.-Thurs. 8 A.M.-8 P.M., Fri. 8 A.M.-7 P.M., Sat. 8 A.M.-5 P.M., Sun. 9 A.M.-5 P.M., $15 per hour) on Daniel Island. This multimillion-dollar facility is owned by the city of Charleston and was built in 2001 specifically to host the annual Family Circle Cup women's competition, which was previously held in Hilton Head for many years. But it's also open to the public year-round (except when the Cup is on) with 17 courts.

The best resort tennis activity is at the **Kiawah Island Golf Resort** (12 Kiawah Beach Dr., Kiawah Island, 800/654-2924, www.kiawahgolf.com), with a total of 28 courts. There are four free, public, city-funded facilities on the peninsula: **Moultrie Playground** (Broad St. and Ashley Ave., 843/769-8258, www.charlestoncity.info, six lighted hard courts), **Jack Adams Tennis Center** (290 Congress St., six lighted hard courts), **Hazel Parker Playground** (70 East Bay St., on the Cooper River, one hard court), and **Corrine Jones Playground** (Marlowe St. and Peachtree St., two hard courts). Over in West Ashley, the city also runs the public **Charleston Tennis Center** (19 Farmfield Rd., 843/769-8258, www.charlestoncity.info, 15 lighted courts).

Hiking and Biking

If you're like me, you'll walk your legs off just making your way around the sights on the peninsula. Early risers will especially enjoy the beauty of dawn breaking over the Cooper River as they walk or jog along the Battery or a little farther north at Waterfront Park. Charleston-area beaches are perfect for a leisurely bike ride on the sand. Sullivan's Island is a particular favorite, and you might be surprised at how long you can ride in one direction on these beaches. Those desiring a more demanding use of their legs can walk or ride their bike in the dedicated pedestrian and bike lane on the massive **Arthur Ravenel Jr. Bridge** over the Cooper River, the longest cable-stayed bridge in the western hemisphere. The extra lanes are a huge advantage over the old span on the same site, and a real example for other cities to follow in sustainable transportation solutions. There's public parking on both sides of the bridge, on the Charleston side off Meeting Street and on the Mount Pleasant side on the road to Patriots Point. **Bike the Bridge Rentals** (360 Concord St., 843/853-2453, www.bikethebridgerentals.com) offers self-guided tours over the Ravenel Bridge and back on a Raleigh Comfort bike, and also rents road bikes for lengthier excursions. In West Ashley, there's an urban walking and biking trail, the **West Ashley Greenway,** built on a former rail bed. The 10-mile trail runs parallel to U.S. 17 and passes parks, schools, and the Clemson Experimental Farm, ending near John Island. To get to the trailhead from downtown, drive west on U.S. 17. About 0.5 miles after you cross the bridge, turn left onto Folly Road (Hwy. 171). At the second light, turn right into South Windermere Shopping Center; the trail is behind the center on the right.

The most ambitious trail in South Carolina is the **Palmetto Trail** (www.palmettoconservation.org), begun in 1997 and eventually covering 425 miles from the Atlantic to the Appalachians. The coastal terminus near Charleston, the seven-mile Awendaw Passage through the Francis Marion National Forest, begins at the trailhead at the Buck Hall Recreational Area (843/887-3257, $5 vehicle fee), which has parking and restroom facilities. Get there by taking U.S. 17 north from Charleston about 20 miles and through the Francis Marion National Forest and then Awendaw. Take a right onto Buck Hall Landing Road.

Another good nature hike outside town is

on the eight miles of scenic and educational trails at **Caw Caw Interpretive Center** (5200 Savannah Hwy., Ravenel, 843/889-8898, www.ccprc.com, Wed.-Fri. 9 A.M.-3 P.M., Sat.-Sun. 9 A.M.-5 P.M., $1) on an old rice plantation.

One of the best outfitters in town is **Half Moon Outfitters** (280 King St., 843/853-0990, www.halfmoonoutfitters.com, Mon.-Sat. 10 A.M.-7 P.M., Sun. noon-6 P.M.). They have a Mount Pleasant location (425 Coleman Blvd., 843/881-9472) as well, and it has better parking.

Bird-Watching

Right in Charleston Harbor is the little **Crab Bank Heritage Preserve** (803/734-3886), where thousands of migratory birds can be seen, depending on the season. October-April you can either kayak there yourself or take a charter with **Nature Adventures Outfitters** (1900 Iron Swamp Rd., Awendaw Island, 800/673-0679). On James Island southwest of Charleston is **Legare Farms** (2620 Hanscombe Point Rd., 843/559-0763, www.legarefarms.com), which holds migratory bird walks ($6 adults, $3 children) in the fall each Saturday at 8:30 A.M.

Ice-Skating

Ice-skating in South Carolina? Yep, 100,000 square feet of it, year-round at the two NHL-size rinks of the **Carolina Ice Palace** (7665 Northwoods Blvd., North Charleston, 843/572-2717, www.carolinaicepalace.com, $7 adults, $6 children). This is also the practice facility for the local hockey team, the Stingrays, as well as where the Citadel hockey team plays.

SPECTATOR SPORTS
Charleston River Dogs

A New York Yankees farm team playing in the South Atlantic League, the Charleston River Dogs (www.riverdogs.com, $5 general admission) play April-August at Joseph P. Riley Jr. Park, a.k.a. "The Joe" (360 Fishburne St.). The park is great, and there are a lot of fun promotions to keep things interesting should the play on the field be less than stimulating (as minor league ball often can be). Because of the intimate, retro design of the park, there are no bad seats, so you might as well save a few bucks and go for the general admission ticket. From downtown, get to The Joe by taking Broad Street west until it turns into Lockwood Drive. Follow that north until you get to Brittlebank Park and The Joe, next to the Citadel. Expect to pay $3-5 for parking.

Family Circle Cup

Moved to Daniel Island in 2001 from its longtime home in Hilton Head, the prestigious Family Circle Cup women's tennis tournament is held each April at the **Family Circle Tennis Center** (161 Seven Farms Dr., Daniel Island, 843/856-7900, www.familycirclecup.com, admission varies). Almost 100,000 people attend the multiple-week event. Individual session tickets go on sale the preceding January.

Charleston Battery

The professional A-League soccer team Charleston Battery (843/971-4625, www.charlestonbattery.com, about $10) play April-July at Blackbaud Stadium (1990 Daniel Island Dr.) on Daniel Island, north of Charleston. To get here from downtown, take I-26 north and then I-526 to Mount Pleasant. Take exit 23A, Clements Ferry Road, and then a left on St. Thomas Island Drive. Blackbaud Stadium is about one mile along on the left.

South Carolina Stingrays

The ECHL professional hockey team the South Carolina Stingrays (843/744-2248, www.stingrayshockey.com, $15) get a good crowd out to their rink at the North Charleston Coliseum (5001 Coliseum Dr., North Charleston), playing October-April.

Citadel Bulldogs

The Citadel (171 Moultrie St., 843/953-3294, www.citadelsports.com) plays Southern

Conference football home games at Johnson-Hagood Stadium, next to the campus on the Ashley River near Hampton Park. The basketball team plays home games at McAlister Field House on campus. The school's hockey team skates home games at the Carolina Ice Palace (7665 Northwoods Blvd., North Charleston).

Accommodations

As one of the country's key national and international destination cities, Charleston has a very well-developed infrastructure for housing visitors—a task made much easier by the city's longstanding tradition of hospitality. Because the bar is set so high, few visitors experience a truly bad stay in town. Hotels and bed-and-breakfasts are generally well maintained and have a high level of service, ranging from very good to excellent. There's a 12.5 percent tax on hotel rooms in Charleston.

SOUTH OF BROAD
$150-300

On the south side of Broad Street is a great old Charleston lodging, **€ Governor's House Inn** (117 Broad St., 843/720-2070, www.governorshouse.com, $285-585). This circa-1760 building, a National Historic Landmark, is associated with Edward Rutledge, signer of the Declaration of Independence. Though most of its 11 guest rooms—all with four-poster beds, period furnishings, and high ceilings—go for around $300, some of the smaller guest rooms can be had for closer to $200 in the off-season.

The nine guest rooms of **€ Two Meeting Street Inn** (2 Meeting St., 843/723-7322, www.twomeetingstreet.com, $220-435) down by the Battery are individually appointed, with themes like "The Music Room" and the "The Spell Room." The decor in this 1892 Queen Anne bed-and-breakfast is very traditional, with lots of floral patterns and hunt club-style pieces and artwork. It's considered by many to be the most romantic lodging in town, and you won't soon forget the experience of sitting on the veranda enjoying the sights, sounds, and breezes. Three of the guest rooms—the Canton, Granite, and Roberts—can be had for not much over $200.

WATERFRONT AND FRENCH QUARTER
$150-300

About as close to the Cooper River as a hotel gets, the **Harbourview Inn** (2 Vendue Range, 843/853-8439, www.harbourviewcharleston.com, $259) comprises a "historic wing" and a larger, newer, but still tastefully done main building. For the best of those eponymous harbor views, try to get a room on the third floor or you might have some obstructions. It's the little touches that keep guests happy here, with wine, cheese, coffee, tea, and cookies galore and an emphasis on smiling, personalized service. The guest rooms are quite spacious, with big baths and 14-foot ceilings. You can take your complimentary breakfast—good but not great—in your room or eat it on the nice rooftop terrace.

Over $300

The guest rooms and the thoroughly hospitable service are the focus at the nearby **€ Vendue Inn** (19 Vendue Range, 843/577-7970, www.vendueinn.com, $359). With a range of decor from colonial to French Provincial, all guest rooms are sumptuously appointed in that boutique style, with lots of warm, rich fabrics, unique pieces, and high-end bath amenities. That said, the public spaces are cool as well,

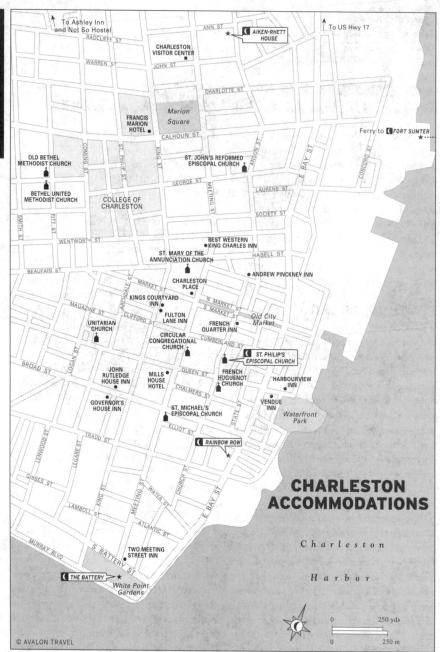

CHARLESTON

To Ashley Inn and Not So Hostel
RADCLIFFE ST
WARREN ST
ANN ST
CHARLESTON VISITOR CENTER
JOHN ST
AIKEN-RHETT HOUSE
To US Hwy 17
CHARLOTTE ST
Marion Square
FRANCIS MARION HOTEL
CALHOUN ST
Ferry to FORT SUMTER
OLD BETHEL METHODIST CHURCH
COMING ST
ST. PHILIP ST
KING ST
MEETING ST
ANSON ST
E BAY ST
CONCORD ST
ST. JOHN'S REFORMED EPISCOPAL CHURCH
GEORGE ST
BETHEL UNITED METHODIST CHURCH
COLLEGE OF CHARLESTON
LAURENS ST
SOCIETY ST
PITT ST
ST. PHILIP ST
WENTWORTH ST
BEST WESTERN KING CHARLES INN
BEAUFAIN ST
ST. MARY OF THE ANNUNCIATION CHURCH
HASELL ST
ANDREW PINCKNEY INN
MARKET ST
ARCHDALE ST
MAGAZINE ST
CHARLESTON PLACE
KINGS COURTYARD INN
CLIFFORD ST
FULTON LANE INN
N. MARKET ST
S. MARKET ST
Old City Market
UNITARIAN CHURCH
FRENCH QUARTER INN
CIRCULAR CONGREGATIONAL CHURCH
CUMBERLAND ST
LOGAN ST
BROAD ST
ST. PHILIP'S EPISCOPAL CHURCH
JOHN RUTLEDGE HOUSE INN
MILLS HOUSE HOTEL
QUEEN ST
FRENCH HUGUENOT CHURCH
HARBOURVIEW INN
GOVERNOR'S HOUSE INN
CHALMERS ST
STATE ST
VENDUE INN
ST. MICHAEL'S EPISCOPAL CHURCH
ELLIOT ST
Waterfront Park
LENWOOD ST
LEGARE ST
TRADD ST
CHURCH ST
E BAY ST
RAINBOW ROW
GIBBES ST
KING ST
MEETING ST
WATER ST
CHARLESTON ACCOMMODATIONS
LAMBOLL ST
ATLANTIC ST
Charleston
MURRAY BLVD
S BATTERY ST
TWO MEETING STREET INN
Harbor
THE BATTERY
White Point Gardens

© AVALON TRAVEL

0   250 yds
0   250 m

with a cozy den area with chess and checkers and a nice area in which to enjoy your excellent, made-to-order hot breakfast (complimentary!). They have a row of bikes out front for guests to use, free of charge, to roam around the city. The inn gets a lot of traffic in the evenings because of the popular Library restaurant and its hopping Rooftop Bar, which has amazing views.

Another great place in this part of town is the **French Quarter Inn** (166 Church St., 843/722-1900, www.fqicharleston.com, $359). The decor in the 50 surprisingly spacious guest rooms is suitably high-period French, with low-style noncanopied beds and crisp fresh linens. Many guest rooms feature fireplaces, whirlpool baths, and private balconies. One of Charleston's hottest restaurants, Tristan, is on the ground floor. You're treated to champagne on your arrival, and goodies are available all day, with wine and cheese served every night at 5 P.M.

NORTH OF BROAD
$150-300

It calls itself a boutique hotel, perhaps because each room is totally different and sumptuously appointed. But the charming ◀ **Andrew Pinckney Inn** (199 Church St., 843/937-8800, www.andrewpinckneyinn.com, $200-290) is very nearly in a class by itself in Charleston not only for its great rates but for its casual West Indies-style decor, charming courtyard, gorgeous three-story atrium, and rooftop terrace on which you can enjoy your complimentary (and delicious) breakfast. For the money and the amenities, it's possibly the single best lodging package in town.

Free parking, a great location, friendly staff, and reasonable prices are the highlights of the **Best Western King Charles Inn** (237 Meeting St., 843/723-7451, www.kingcharlesinn.com, $200-250). It's not where you'd want to spend your honeymoon, but it's plenty nice enough, and frequent visitors to town swear by it.

If you plan on some serious shopping, you might want to stay right on the city's main shopping thoroughfare at the **Kings Courtyard Inn** (198 King St., 866/720-2949, www.kingscourtyardinn.com, $240-270). This 1853 Greek Revival building houses a lot more guest rooms—more than 40—than meets the eye, and it can get a little crowded at times. Still, its charming courtyard and awesome location on King Street are big bonuses, as is the convenient but cramped parking lot right next door (about $12 per day, a bargain for this part of town), with free in-and-out privileges.

Although it is a newer building by Charleston standards, the **Mills House Hotel** (115 Meeting St., 843/577-2400, www.ichotelsgroup.com, $285-380) boasts an important pedigree and still tries hard to maintain the old tradition of impeccable Southern service at this historic location. An extensive round of renovations completed in 2007 has been well received. Dating to 1853, the first incarnation was a grand edifice that hosted luminaries such as Robert E. Lee. Through the years, fire and restoration wrought their changes, and the modern version basically dates from an extensive renovation in the 1970s. Because of its healthy banquet and event schedule—much of it centering on the very good restaurant and lounge inside—the Mills House isn't the place to go for peace and quiet. Rather, this Holiday Inn-affiliated property is where you go to feel the bustle of downtown Charleston and to be conveniently close to its main sightseeing and shopping attractions. Some of the upper floors of this seven-story building offer spectacular views.

Over $300

Considered Charleston's premier hotel, ◀ **Charleston Place** (205 Meeting St., 843/722-4900, www.charlestonplace.com, $419-590) maintains a surprisingly high level of service and decor considering its massive 440-room size. Now owned by the London-based

© JIM MOREKIS

Charleston Place is considered Charleston's premier hotel.

Orient-Express Hotels, Charleston Place is routinely rated as one of the best hotels in North America by *Condé Nast Traveler* and other publications. The guest rooms aren't especially large, but they are well appointed, featuring Italian marble baths, high-speed Internet, and voice messaging—and, of course, there's a pool available. A series of suite offerings—Junior, Junior Executive, Parlor, and the 800-square-foot Senior—feature enlarged living areas and multiple TVs and phones. A Manager's Suite on the Private Club level up top comprises 1,200 square feet of total luxury that will set you back at least $1,600 per night. It's the additional offerings that make Charleston Place closer to a lifestyle decision than a lodging decision. The on-site spa (843/937-8522) offers all kinds of massages, including couples and "mommy to be" sessions. Diners and tipplers have three fine options to choose from: the famous **Charleston Grill** (843/577-4522, dinner daily from 6 P.M.) for fine

dining; the breakfast, lunch, and brunch hot spot **Palmetto Cafe** (843/722-4900, breakfast daily 6:30-11 A.M., lunch daily 11:30 A.M.-3 P.M.); and the **Thoroughbred Club** (daily 11 A.M.-midnight) for cocktails and afternoon tea.

On the north side of Broad Street, the magnificent ◖ **John Rutledge House Inn** (116 Broad St., 843/723-7999, www.johnrutledgehouseinn.com, $300-442) is very close to the old South of Broad neighborhood not only in geography but in feel. Known as "America's most historic inn," the Rutledge House boasts a fine old pedigree indeed: Built for Constitution signer John Rutledge in 1763, it's one of only 15 homes belonging to the original signers to survive. George Washington breakfasted here with Mrs. Rutledge in 1791. The interior is stunning: Italian marble fireplaces, original plaster moldings, and masterful ironwork abound in the public spaces. The inn's 19 guest rooms are divided among the original mansion and two carriage houses. All have antique furnishings and canopy beds, and some suites have fireplaces and whirlpool baths. A friendly and knowledgeable concierge will give you all kinds of tips and make reservations for you.

Affiliated with the Kings Courtyard—and right next door, in fact—is the smaller, cozier **Fulton Lane Inn** (202 King St., 866/720-2940, www.fultonlaneinn.com, $300), with its lobby entrance on tiny Fulton Lane between the two inns. Small, simple guest rooms—some with fireplaces—have comfortable beds and spacious baths. This is the kind of place for active people who plan to spend most of their days out and about but want a cozy place to come back to at night. You mark down your continental breakfast order at night, leave it on your doorknob, and it shows up at the *exact* time you requested the next morning. Then when you're ready to shop and walk, just go down the stairs and take the exit right out onto busy King Street. Also nice is the $12-per-day parking with free in-and-out privileges.

UPPER KING AREA
Under $150

Stretching the bounds of the "Upper King" definition, we come to the **Ashley Inn** (201 Ashley Ave., 843/723-1848, www.charleston-sc-inns.com, $100-125) well northwest of Marion Square, almost in the Citadel area. Although it's too far to walk from here to most any historic attraction in Charleston, the Ashley Inn does provide free bikes to its guests as well as free off-street parking, a particularly nice touch. It also deserves a special mention not only because of the romantic, well-appointed nature of its six guest rooms, suite, and carriage house but for its outstanding breakfasts. You get to pick a main dish, such as Carolina sausage pie, stuffed waffles, or cheese blintzes.

$150-300

In a renovated 1924 building overlooking beautiful Marion Square, the **Francis Marion Hotel** (387 King St., 843/722-0600, www.francismarioncharleston.com, $200-300) offers quality accommodation in the hippest, most bustling area of the peninsula—but be aware that it's quite a walk down to the Battery from here. The guest rooms are plush and big, though the baths can be cramped. The hotel's parking garage costs a reasonable $12 per day, with valet parking available until about 8 P.M. A Starbucks in the lobby pleases many a guest on their way out or in. Most rooms hover around $300, but some are a real steal.

HAMPTON PARK AREA
Under $150

Charleston's least-expensive lodging is also its most unique, the **◖ Not So Hostel** (156 Spring St., 843/722-8383, www.notsohostel.com, $21 dorm, $60 private). The already-reasonable prices also include a make-your-own bagel breakfast, off-street parking, bikes, high-speed Internet access in the common room, and even an airport, train, and bus shuttle. The inn

actually comprises three 1840s Charleston single houses, all with the obligatory piazzas to catch the breeze. (However, unlike some hostels, there's air-conditioning in all the rooms.) Because the free bike usage makes up for its off-the-beaten-path location, a stay at the Not So Hostel is a fantastic way to enjoy the Holy City on a budget, while having the opportunity to meet cool people from all over the world who are also staying here. One caveat: While they offer private rooms in addition to dorm-style accommodation, keep in mind this is still a hostel, despite the Charleston-style hospitality and perks. In other words, if there's a problem at 3 A.M., you may not be able to get anyone to help you in a hurry.

WEST ASHLEY
$150-300

Looking like Frank Lloyd Wright parachuted into a 300-year-old plantation and got to work, **◖ The Inn at Middleton Place** (4290 Ashley River Rd., 843/556-0500, www.theinnatmiddletonplace.com, $215-285) is one of Charleston's most unique lodgings—and not only because it's on the grounds of the historic and beautiful Middleton Place Plantation. The four connected buildings, comprising over 50 guest rooms, are modern yet deliberately blend in with the forested, neutral-colored surroundings. The spacious guest rooms have that same woody minimalism, with excellent fireplaces, spacious Euro-style baths, and huge floor-to-ceiling windows overlooking the grounds and the river. Guests also have full access to the rest of the gorgeous Middleton grounds. The only downside is that you're a lengthy drive from the peninsula and all its attractions, restaurants, and nightlife. While those who need constant stimulation will be disappointed in the deep quietude here, nature-lovers and those in search of peace and quiet will find this almost paradise. And don't worry about food—the excellent Middleton Place Restaurant is open for lunch and dinner.

ISLE OF PALMS
$150-300

One of the more accessible and enjoyable resort-type stays in the Charleston area is on the Isle of Palms at **Wild Dunes Resort** (5757 Palm Blvd., 888/778-1876, www.wilddunes.com, $254-320). This is the place to go for relaxing, beach-oriented vacation fun, either in a traditional hotel room, a house, or a villa. Bustling Mount Pleasant is only a couple of minutes away, and Charleston proper not much farther.

FOLLY BEACH
$150-300

The upbeat but still cozy renovation of the **Holiday Inn Folly Beach Oceanfront** (1 Center St., 843/588-6464, $250-270) has locals raving. If you're going to stay on Folly Beach, this hotel—with its combination of attentive staff and great oceanfront views—is the place to be.

CAMPING

Charleston County runs a family-friendly, fairly boisterous campground at **James Island County Park** (871 Riverland Dr., 843/795-7275, www.ccprc.com, $31 tent site, $37 pull-through site). A neat feature here is the $5-pp round-trip shuttle to the Visitors Center downtown, Folly Beach Pier, and Folly Beach County Park. The Park also has 10 furnished cottages (843/795-4386, $138) for rental, sleeping up to eight people. Reservations are recommended. For more commercial camping in Mount Pleasant, try the **KOA of Mt. Pleasant** (3157 U.S. 17 N., 843/849-5177, www.koa.com, from $30 tent sites, from $50 pull-through sites).

Food

If you count the premier food cities in the United States on one hand, Charleston has to be one of the fingers. Its long history of good taste and livability combines with an affluent and sophisticated population to attract some of the brightest chefs and restaurateurs in the country. Kitchens here eschew fickle trends, instead emphasizing quality, professionalism, and most of all, freshness of ingredients. In a sort of Southern Zen, the typical Charleston chef seems to take pride in making a melt-in-your-mouth masterpiece out of the culinary commonplace—in not fixing what ain't broke, as they say down here. (I've heard Charleston's cuisine described as "competent classics," which also isn't far off the mark.) Unlike Savannah, its more drink-oriented neighbor to the south, even Charleston's bars have great food. So don't assume you have to make reservations at a formal restaurant to fully enjoy the cuisine here. An entire volume could easily be written about Charleston restaurants,

but here's a baseline from which to start your epicurean odyssey. You'll note a high percentage of **C** recommendations in the list; there's a good reason for that.

SOUTH OF BROAD
Classic Southern

The only bona fide restaurant in the quiet old South of Broad area is also one of Charleston's best and oldest: **C Carolina's** (10 Exchange St., 843/724-3800, Sun.-Thurs. 5-10 P.M., Fri.-Sat. 5-11 P.M., $18-30). There's a new chef in town, Jeremiah Bacon, a Charleston native who spent the last seven years honing his craft in New York City. His Lowcountry take on European classics includes grilled salmon with potato gnocchi, tagliatelle with Lowcountry prosciutto, and pan-roasted diver scallops, with as many fresh ingredients as possible from the nearby Kensington Plantation. A tried-and-true favorite that predates Bacon's tenure, however, is Perdita's *fruit de mer*—a recipe that goes back

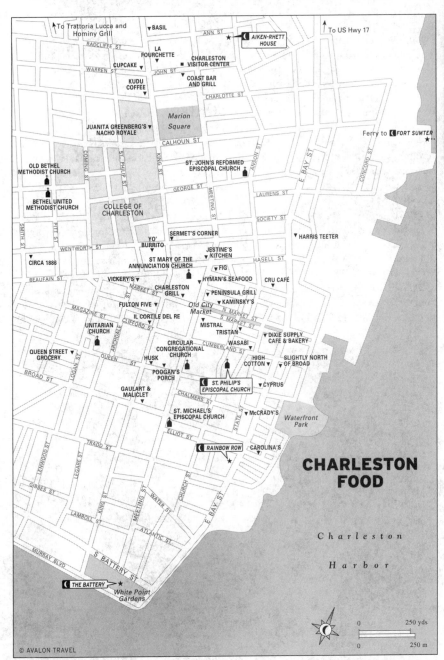

To Trattoria Lucca and Hominy Grill

▼ BASIL

ANN ST

★ ◖ AIKEN-RHETT HOUSE

↑ To US Hwy 17

RADCLIFFE ST

LA FOURCHETTE ▼

CHARLESTON VISITOR CENTER ■

CUPCAKE ▼

WARREN ST

JOHN ST

KUDU COFFEE

COAST BAR AND GRILL

CHARLOTTE ST

Marion Square

JUANITA GREENBERG'S ▼ NACHO ROYALE

CALHOUN ST

Ferry to ◖ FORT SUMTER ★ --

OLD BETHEL METHODIST CHURCH ✚

ST. JOHN'S REFORMED EPISCOPAL CHURCH ✚

BETHEL UNITED METHODIST CHURCH ✚

GEORGE ST

LAURENS ST

COLLEGE OF CHARLESTON

SOCIETY ST

COMING ST
ST. PHILIP ST
KING ST
MEETING ST
ANSON ST
E BAY ST
CONCORD ST

SMITH ST
PITT ST

SERMET'S CORNER ▼

▼ HARRIS TEETER

WENTWORTH ST

YO' BURRITO ▼

JESTINE'S KITCHEN ▼

▼ CIRCA 1886

ST MARY OF THE ANNUNCIATION CHURCH ✚

HASELL ST

▼ FIG

BEAUFAIN ST

VICKERY'S ▼

CHARLESTON GRILL ▼

▼ HYMAN'S SEAFOOD

CRU CAFÉ

MARKET ST

▼ PENINSULA GRILL

FULTON FIVE ▼

▼ KAMINSKY'S

MAGAZINE ST

IL CORTILE DEL RE

Old City Market

N MARKET ST
S MARKET ST

CLIFFORD ST

UNITARIAN CHURCH ✚

MISTRAL

ARCHDALE ST

TRISTAN ▼

▼ DIXIE SUPPLY CAFE & BAKERY

QUEEN STREET GROCERY

LOGAN ST

QUEEN ST

CIRCULAR CONGREGATIONAL CHURCH ✚

CUMBERLAND ST

WASABI ▼

BROAD ST

HUSK

HIGH COTTON ▼

SLIGHTLY NORTH OF BROAD

POOGAN'S PORCH

★ ◖ ST. PHILIP'S EPISCOPAL CHURCH

▼ CYPRUS

GAULART & MALICLET ▼

CHALMERS ST

ST. MICHAEL'S ✚ EPISCOPAL CHURCH

▼ McCRADY'S

Waterfront Park

ELLIOT ST

TRADD ST

STATE ST

◖ RAINBOW ROW ★

CAROLINA'S ▼

LENWOOD ST
LEGARE ST
GIBBES ST

CHARLESTON FOOD

Charleston

LAMBOLL ST

KING ST
WATER ST
CHURCH ST
MEETING ST
E BAY ST

Harbor

ATLANTIC ST

MURRAY BLVD

S BATTERY ST

◖ THE BATTERY ★

White Point Gardens

0   250 yds

0   250 m

© AVALON TRAVEL

to the restaurant's 1950s predecessor, Perdita's, which is commonly regarded as Charleston's first fine-dining restaurant. If you can get the whole table to agree, try the $49-pp Perdita's four-course tasting menu (wine flights extra). A recent renovation of this Revolutionary War-era building—once the legendary Sailor's Tavern—hasn't negatively affected the romantic ambience of the three themed areas: Perdita's Room (the oldest dining area), the Sidewalk Room, and the Bar Room. Free valet parking is a nice plus.

French

If you find yourself in lodging near the Broad Street area—or if you just love crepes—you will want to acquaint yourself with the **Queen Street Grocery** (133 Queen St., 843/723-4121, www.queenstreetgrocerycafe.com, Mon.-Sat. 8 A.M.-8:30 P.M., kitchen Mon.-Sat. 10 A.M.-5 P.M., Sun. 11 A.M.-3 P.M., $7-10). The kind of place frequented almost exclusively by locals, this corner store is where you can load up on light groceries, beer, wine, and cigarettes—as well as some of the tastiest made-to-order crepes this side of France.

WATERFRONT
New Southern

Few restaurants in Charleston inspire such impassioned vocal advocates as ◖ **McCrady's** (2 Unity Alley, 843/577-0025, www.mccradysrestaurant.com, Sun.-Thurs. 5:30-10 P.M., Fri.-Sat. 5:30-11 P.M., $28-40). Housed in Charleston's oldest tavern building (circa 1788), McCrady's is also known as Charleston's best-kept secret, since despite its high quality it has managed to avoid the siege of tourists common at many local fine-dining spots. But their loss can be your gain as you enjoy the prodigious talents of Chef Sean Brock, whose *sous vide,* or vacuum cooking, is spoken of in hushed tones by his

Get a great crepe at the Queen Street Grocery.

© JIM MOREKIS

clientele. McCrady's is not the place to gorge on usual Lowcountry fare. Portions here are small and dynamic, based on a rotating seasonal menu. Many diners find the seven-course Chef's Tasting ($90), in which you get whatever floats Chef Brock's boat that night, a near-religious experience. For an extra $75, master sommelier Clint Sloan provides paired wine selections. Or you can just go with a three-course ($45) or four-course ($60) dinner where you pick your courses. You may read complaints in online reviews about the prices at McCrady's. Let me set the record straight: (a) They're not really that high at all when you break them down per item, and (b) the perfect blending of flavors you will enjoy with any dish on the menu is worth every penny and then some. Quite simply, McCrady's is a world-class restaurant that, were it in just about any other city in the world, would actually set you back quite a bit more. Just go.

While not as flashy as some other local chefs, Craig Deihl has, over the past decade, brought **Cypress** (167 E. Bay St., 843/727-0111, www.magnolias-blossom-cypress.com, Sun.-Thurs. 5:30-10 P.M., Fri.-Sat. 5:30-11 P.M., $20-40) to the forefront of the local foodie movement. From aged beef from a local farm to sustainably caught wreckfish, the menu reflects a deep commitment to locavore sensibilities. Any meat or seafood entrée is a can't-lose proposition here. They also offer table-side service of chateaubriand or rack of lamb for two.

FRENCH QUARTER
New Southern

With an art deco-style vibe that's a refreshing change from the usual Charleston restaurant decor, **Tristan** (55 Market St., 843/534-2155, www.tristandining.com, Mon.-Thurs. 11:30 A.M.-10 P.M., Fri.-Sat. 11:30 A.M.-11 P.M., Sun. 11 A.M.-10 P.M., $18-32) inside the French Quarter Inn draws raves for its globally influenced cuisine. At last count, the copious wine list boasted over 400 labels. The real scene here is for the à la carte Sunday brunch, with crab cake benedicts, corned beef hash, frittatas, live jazz, and Bloody Marys galore. Save room for the ridiculously good fried chocolate doughnut dessert.

NORTH OF BROAD
Asian

For whatever reason, the Asian influence is not prevalent in Charleston cuisine. But **Wasabi** (61 State St., 843/577-5222, Mon.-Thurs. 11 A.M.-9:30 P.M., Fri.-Sat. 11 A.M.-11 P.M., Sun. noon-9 P.M., $10-15) has made quite a name for itself as a great place for sushi downtown, though its hibachi work is impressive as well. The bar gets hopping after dinner.

Breakfast and Brunch

You can sit inside the crowded, noisy diner, or outside literally in the parking lot of a strip mall; either way you're doing the right thing at **☾ Dixie Supply Cafe and Bakery** (62 State St., 843/722-5650, www.dixiecafecharleston.com, daily 8 A.M.-2:30 P.M., $8-10), certainly one of the humblest but no doubt tastiest places in Charleston and perhaps the entire South. Dixie Supply has gained a certain amount of cachet lately with the filming of a *Diners, Drive-ins and Dives* episode, but don't let the trendiness keep you away. What you get at this simple old-school eatery is some of the best comfort food you'll ever taste, with a focus on breakfast and brunch items. A case could be made that their signature Tomato Pie—melted cheese over a perfect tomato slice with a delicious crust on the bottom, served with a hunk of sweet potato cornbread—is the single best dish in Charleston. However, you could make the same case for their Shrimp 'n' Grits or, for that matter their "stuffed" french toast. You place your order at the front counter, the cooks a few feet away. When your plate is ready, they call you, and you just come up and get your food and take it back to your table. It can get crowded, but just brave the lines and go. And while they do take plastic, they appreciate cash.

Classic Southern

Walk through the gaslit courtyard of the Planter's Inn at Market and Meeting Streets into the stately yet surprisingly intimate dining room of the **⟨ Peninsula Grill** (112 N. Market St., 843/723-0700, www.peninsulagrill.com, daily from 5:30 P.M., $28-35) and begin an epicurean journey you'll not soon forget. Known far and wide for impeccable service as well as the mastery of Chef Robert Carter, Peninsula Grill is perhaps Charleston's quintessential purveyor of high-style Lowcountry cuisine and the odds-on favorite as best restaurant in town. From the lobster skillet cake and crab cake appetizer to the bourbon-grilled jumbo shrimp to the benne-crusted rack of lamb to sides like wild mushroom grits and hoppin' John, the menu reads like a "greatest hits" of regional cooking. You'll almost certainly want to start with the sampler trio of soups and finish with Carter's legendary coconut cake, a family recipe. Whatever you choose in between those bookends is almost guaranteed to be excellent. Choose from 20 wines by the glass or from over 300 bottles. Four stars from the Mobil Travel Club, four diamonds from AAA, and countless other accolades have come this restaurant's way. Needless to say, reservations are strongly recommended.

Named for a now-deceased beloved dog who once greeted guests, **Poogan's Porch** (72 Queen St., 843/577-2337, www.poogansporch. com, lunch Mon.-Fri. 11:30 A.M.-2:30 P.M., dinner daily 5-9:30 P.M., brunch Sat.-Sun. 9 A.M.-3 P.M., $12-20) is the prototype of a classic Charleston restaurant: lovingly restored old home, professional but unpretentious service, great fried green tomatoes, and rich, calorie-laden Lowcountry classics. I can't decide which entrée I like best, the crab cakes or the shrimp

and grits. Some swear that even the biscuits at Poogan's—flaky, fresh-baked, and moist—are better than some entrées around town, although that's a stretch. Brunch is the big thing here, a bustling affair with big portions, Bloody Marys, mimosas, and soft sunlight bathing what were, after all, living and dining rooms where people once lived.

Executive chef Sean Brock of McCrady's fame already has a healthy reputation as one of Charleston's—indeed, the country's—leading purveyors of the farm-to-table fine dining aesthetic, and one with a particularly Southern panache. He cements that reputation with the opening of **⟨ Husk** (76 Queen St., 843/577-2500, www.huskrestaurant.com, lunch Mon.-Sat. 11:30 A.M.-2 P.M., dinner Sun.-Thurs. 5:30-10 P.M., Fri.-Sat. 5:30-11 P.M., brunch Sun. 10 A.M.-2:30 P.M., $25), voted "Best New Restaurant in the U.S." by *Bon Appétit* magazine soon after its 2011 opening. While the hype is a little overdone, Husk is still firmly in the top tier of local restaurants. Upon entering the cleanly restored interior of the multistory historic home this once was, you'll see a blackboard with the origins of the day's ingredients—the farms and their location, never more than a day's drive away. Understandably, the spare, focused menu—"If it doesn't come from the South, it's not coming through the door," Brock says of his ingredients—is constantly changing with the seasons. On a recent lunch visit my party enjoyed two types of catfish (a fried catfish BLT on Texas toast and a lightly cornmeal-dusted broiled catfish with local vegetables), Husk's signature cheeseburger, and—wait for it—lamb barbecue. We finished with a sweet potato pie dessert to die for. The emphasis on the freshest of ingredients means a subtle, unpretentious palette of flavors. Unlike many of today's trendy chefs, Brock doesn't overseason the food, so you taste it the way nature intended. Husk is literally right next door to Poogan's Porch, and as with Poogan's, reservations are recommended.

For many visitors to Charleston, there comes a point when they just get tired of stuffing themselves with seafood. If you find yourself in that situation, the perfect antidote is **High Cotton** (199 E. Bay St., 843/724-3815, www.mavericksouthernkitchens.com, Mon.-Thurs. 5:30-10 P.M., Fri. 5:30-11 P.M., Sat. 11:30 A.M.-2:30 P.M. and 5:30-11 P.M., Sun. 10 A.M.-2 P.M. and 5:30-10 P.M., $20-44), a meat-lovers paradise offering some of the best steaks in town as well as a creative menu of assorted lamb and pork dishes. Chef Anthony Gray places heavy emphasis on using fresh local ingredients, both veggies or game, and the rotating menu always reflects that. None of this comes particularly cheap, but splurges rarely do. In the woody (and popular) bar area there's usually a solo live pianist or sax player after 6 P.M.

The long lines at Wentworth and Meeting Streets across from the fire station are waiting to follow Rachael Ray's lead and get into

© JIM MOREKIS
Il Cortile del Re

Jestine's Kitchen (251 Meeting St., 843/722-7224, Tues.-Thurs. 11 A.M.-9:30 P.M., Fri.-Sat. 11 A.M.-10 P.M., $8-15) to enjoy a simple, Southern take on such meat-and-three comfort food classics as meatloaf, pecan-fried fish, and fried green tomatoes. Most of the recipes are handed down from the restaurant's namesake, Jestine Matthews, the African American woman who raised owner Dana Berlin.

French

On the north side of Broad Street itself you'll find **Gaulart & Maliclet** (98 Broad St., 843/577-9797, www.fastandfrench.org, Mon. 8 A.M.-4 P.M., Tues.-Thurs. 8 A.M.-10 P.M., Fri.-Sat. 8 A.M.-10:30 P.M., $12-15), subtitled "Fast and French." This is a gourmet bistro with a strong takeout component. Prices are especially reasonable for this area of town, with great lunch specials under $10 and Thursday-night "fondue for two" coming in at just over $20.

Mediterranean

One of the most romantic restaurants in Charleston—which is saying a lot—is **Il Cortile del Re** (193A King St., 843/853-1888, Mon.-Sat. 5-10:30 P.M., $18-30) is amid the antiques stores on Lower King. Thankfully the Italian owners don't overdo the old country sentimentality, either in atmosphere or in menu. Sure, the tablecloths are white and the interior is warm, dark, and decorated with opera prints. But the piped-in music is long on cool jazz and short on over-the-top tenors, and the skinny wine bar in the front room is a favorite destination all its own. Portions here manage to be simultaneously large and light, as in the overtopped mussel plate in a delightfully thin and spicy tomato sauce, or the big spinach salad with goat cheese croutons sprinkled with a subtle vinaigrette. The entrées emphasize the Tuscan countryside, focusing both on slow-roasted meats and sublime takes on traditional pasta dishes. My favorite is the perfect roasted lamb in a dark juniper and rosemary sauce, served on a bed of what are likely to be the best mashed potatoes in the world. Save room for the gelato dessert, served swimming in a pool of dark espresso.

Literally right around the corner from Il Cortile del Re is the other in Charleston's one-two Italian punch, **Fulton Five** (5 Fulton St., 843/853-5555, Mon.-Sat. from 5:30 P.M., $15-32). The cuisine of northern Italy comes alive in this bustling, dimly lit room, from the *bresaola* salad of spinach and thin dried beef to the caper-encrusted tuna on a bed of sweet pea risotto. It's not cheap, and the portions aren't necessarily the largest, but with these tasty, non-tomato-based dishes and this romantic, gusto-filled atmosphere, you'll be satiated with life itself.

One of Charleston's original hip people-watching spots and still a personal favorite is **Sermet's Corner** (276 King St., 843/853-7775, lunch daily 11 A.M.-3 P.M., dinner Sun.-Thurs. 4-10 P.M., Fri.-Sat. 4-11 P.M., $9-16), at the bustling intersection of King and Wentworth Streets. Charismatic chef and owner Sermet Aslan—who also painted most of the artwork on the walls of this charming, high-ceilinged space—dishes up large, inexpensive portions of Mediterranean-style goodies like panini, pastas, pestos, calamari, and inventive meat dishes.

Mexican

If you find yourself craving Mexican while shopping on King Street, duck about a block down Wentworth Street to find the cavernous, delightful **Yo' Burrito** (86 Wentworth St., 843/853-3287, www.yoburrito.com, Sun.-Thurs. 11 A.M.-10 P.M., Fri.-Sat. 11 A.M.-11 P.M., $5-8), a local legend in its own right. Order at the counter from a variety of overstuffed specialty burritos, tasty quesadillas, and stacked nachos, and take a seat at one of the large communal-style tables, perhaps enjoying a freshly squeezed lemonade while you wait. But the real kicker is the condiment bar of homemade salsas.

New Southern

Don't be put off by the initials of **Slightly North of Broad** (192 East Bay St., 843/723-3424, www.mavericksouthernkitchens.com, lunch Mon.-Fri. 11:30 A.M.-3 P.M., dinner daily 5:30-11 P.M., $15-35). Its acronym, "SNOB," is an ironic play on the often pejorative reference to the insular South of Broad neighborhood. This hot spot, routinely voted best restaurant in town in such contests, is anything but snobby. Hopping with happy foodies for lunch and dinner, the fun is enhanced by the long open kitchen with its own counter area. The dynamic but comforting menu here is practically a bible of the new wave of Lowcountry cuisine, with dishes like beef tenderloin, jumbo lump crab cakes, grilled barbecue tuna—and of course the sinful Wednesday night dinner special: deviled crab-stuffed flounder. An interesting twist at SNOB is the selection of "medium plates," i.e., dishes a little more generous than an appetizer but with the same adventurous spirit.

Just across the street from Hyman's Seafood is that establishment's diametrical opposite, the intimate bistro and stylish bar **FIG** (232 Meeting St., 843/805-5900, www.eatatfig. com, Mon.-Thurs. 6-11 P.M., Fri.-Sat. 6 P.M.-midnight, $20-25)—but the two do share one key thing: a passion for fresh, simple ingredients. While Hyman's packs in the tourists, FIG—short for "Food Is Good"—attracts young professional scenesters as well as the diehard foodies. Chef Mike Lata won James Beard's Best Chef of the Southeast award in 2009. FIG is one of Charleston's great champions of the Sustainable Seafood Initiative, and the kitchen staff strives to work as closely as possible with local farmers and anglers in determining its seasonal menu.

Inside the plush Charleston Place Hotel you'll find **Charleston Grill** (224 King St., 843/577-4522, www.charlestongrill.com, dinner daily from 6 P.M., $27-50), one of the city's favorite (and priciest) fine-dining spots for locals and visitors alike. Veteran executive

© JIM MOREKIS

the oyster bar at Hyman's Seafood

chef Bob Waggoner was recently replaced by his longtime sous chef Michelle Weaver, but the menu still specializes in French-influenced Lowcountry cuisine like a niçoise vegetable tart. There are a lot of great fusion dishes as well, such as the tuna and *hamachi* sashimi topped with pomegranate molasses and lemongrass oil. Reservations are a must.

A new hit with local foodies, **Cru Café** (18 Pinckney St., 843/534-2434, lunch Tues.-Sat. 11 A.M.-3 P.M., dinner Tues.-Thurs. 5-10 P.M., Fri.-Sat. 5-11 P.M., $20-24) boasts an adventurous menu within a traditional-looking Charleston single house, with a choice of interior or exterior seating. Sample entrées include Poblano and Mozzarella Fried Chicken and Seared Maple Leaf Duck Breast.

The hard-to-define **Mistral** (99 S. Market St., 843/722-5708, Sun.-Thurs. 11 A.M.-11 P.M., Fri.-Sat. 11 A.M.-midnight, $10-25) is part seafood restaurant, part sexy French bistro, part Lowcountry living. With live, serious jazz

blowing it hot Monday-Saturday nights and some of the best mussels and shrimp in the area served up fresh, all you really need to do is enjoy. If you're not a shellfish fan, try the sweetbreads or their excellent veal.

Seafood

Hyman's Seafood (215 Meeting St., 843/723-6000, www.hymanseafood.com, Mon.-Thurs. 11 A.M.-9 P.M., Fri.-Sun. 11 A.M.-11 P.M., $14-25) is thought by many locals to border on a tourist trap. That said, this is a genuine tradition—rest assured that some member of the same family that began Hyman's in 1890 will be on the premises any time it's open for business. To keep things manageable, Hyman's offers the same menu and prices for both lunch and dinner. After asking for some complimentary fresh boiled peanuts in lieu of bread, start with the Carolina Delight, a delicious appetizer (also available as an entrée) involving a lightly fried cake of grits topped with your choice of delectable seafood, or maybe a half dozen oysters from the Half Shell oyster bar. In any case, definitely try the she-crab soup, some of the best you'll find anywhere. As for entrées, the ubiquitous Lowcountry crispy scored flounder is always a good bet. Alas, this establishment, popular with locals and visitors as well as the occasional movie star, doesn't take reservations, so budget your time accordingly. Lunch crowds are generally lighter, although that's a relative term.

UPPER KING AREA
Asian

There's usually a long wait to get a table at the great Thai place **Basil** (460 King St., 843/724-3490, www.basilthairestaurant.com, lunch Mon.-Thurs. 11:30 A.M.-2:30 P.M., dinner Mon.-Thurs. 5-10:30 P.M., Fri.-Sat. 5-11 P.M., Sun. 5-10 P.M., $15-23) on Upper King, since they don't take reservations. But Basil also has one of the hippest, most happening bar scenes in the area, so you won't necessarily mind. (Tip: Basil calls your cell phone when your table is ready, so a lot of people go across the street to Chai's to have a drink while they wait.) Basil is a long, loud room with big open windows for people-watching. But most of the action takes place inside, as revelers down cosmos and diners enjoy fresh, succulent takes on Thai classics like cashew chicken and pad thai, all cooked by Asian chefs. The signature dish, as you might imagine, is the basil duck.

French

A taste of the Left Bank on Upper King, the intimate bistro ◖ **La Fourchette** (432 King St., 843/722-6261, Mon.-Sat. from 6 P.M., $15-20) is regarded as the best French restaurant in town and, *naturellement,* one of the most romantic. You'll be pleasantly surprised by the reasonable prices as well. Cassoulet, the French national dish, is front and center among Chef Perig Goulet's concoctions, arriving in its own casserole dish on a trivet. Whatever you do,

make sure you start with the *pommes frites* double-fried in duck fat. Your arteries may not thank you, but your taste buds will.

Mexican

The best quesadilla I've ever had was at **Juanita Greenberg's Nacho Royale** (439 King St., 843/723-6224, www.juanitagreenbergs.com, daily 11 A.M.-11 P.M., $6-8)—perfectly packed with jack cheese but not overly so, full of spicy sausage, and finished with a delightful *pico de gallo.* This modest Mexican joint on Upper King caters primarily to a college crowd, as you can tell from the reasonable prices, the large patio out back, the extensive tequila list, and the bar that stays open until 2 A.M. on weekends.

Seafood

Many say the cashew-encrusted seared rare tuna on a bed of crabmeat and buckwheat noodles at **COAST Bar and Grill** (39D John St., 843/722-8838, www.coastbarandgrill.com, daily from 5:30 P.M., $18-30) is the single best dish in Charleston. I wouldn't go that far, but it's certainly up there. COAST makes the most of its loud, hip former warehouse setting. Beautifully textured Lowcountry-themed paintings and kitschy faux-Polynesian items ring the walls, as the clanging silverware competes with the boisterous conversation. While the fun-loving decor in the dining room will suck you in, what keeps you happy is what goes on in the kitchen—specifically on its one-of-a-kind hickory-and-oak grill, which cooks up some of the freshest seafood in town. The raw bar is also satisfying, with a particularly nice take on and selection of seviche. COAST is a strong local advocate of the Sustainable Seafood Initiative, whereby restaurants work directly with the local fishing industry to make the most of the area's stock while making sure it thrives for future generations. Getting here is a little tricky: find Rue de Jean on John Street and then duck about 100 feet down the alley beside it.

LOWCOUNTRY LOCAVORES

It might seem strange that a Deep South city founded in 1670 would be on the country's cutting edge of the sustainable food movement, but that's the case with Charleston. Perhaps more seamlessly than any other community in the United States, Charleston has managed to merge its own indigenous and abiding culinary tradition with the "new" idea that you should grow your food as naturally as possible and purchase it as close to home as you can. From bacon to snapper to sweet potatoes, the typical Charleston dish of today is much like it was before the days of processed factory food and back to its soulful Southern roots.

Spurred in part by an influx of trained chefs after the establishment of the Spoleto Festival in the 1970s, the locavore movement in Charleston came about less from market demand than from the efforts of a diehard cadre of epicureans committed to sustainability and the principles of community-supported agriculture (CSA). Spearheaded by visionaries like the James Beard Award-winning Mike Lata of the bistro FIG and McCrady's Sean Brock, a multitude of sustainable food initiatives have sprung up in Charleston and the Lowcountry, such as the South Carolina Aquarium's Sustainable Seafood Initiative (http://scaquarium.org), partnering with local restaurants to assure a sustainable wild-caught harvest; Certified South Carolina (www.certifiedsc.com), guaranteeing that the food you eat was grown in the Palmetto State; a local chapter of the Slow Food Movement (http://slowfoodcharleston.org); and Cypress Artisan Meat Share (www.magnolias-blossom-cypress.com), in which a group of highly regarded restaurants makes their fine locally sourced meats available to the public.

The list of Holy City restaurants relying almost exclusively on local and sustainable sources is too long to replicate in this space, but here are a few notable examples:

- Husk (76 Queen St., 843/577-2500, www.huskrestaurant.com)
- McCrady's (2 Unity Alley, 843/577-0025, www.mccradysrestaurant.com)
- Cypress (167 E. Bay St., 843/727-0111, www.magnolias-blossom-cypress.com)
- Charleston Grill (224 King St., 843/577-4522, www.charlestongrill.com)
- High Cotton (199 E. Bay St., 843/724-3815, www.mavericksouthernkitchens.com)
- FIG (232 Meeting St., 843/805-5900, www.eatatfig.com)
- Al Di La (25 Magnolia Rd., 843/571-2321)
- Queen Street Grocery (133 Queen St., 843/723-4121)
- Carolina's (10 Exchange St., 843/724-3800)
- Middleton Place Restaurant (4300 Ashley River Rd., 843/556-6020, www.middletonplace.org)
- Circa 1886 (149 Wentworth St., 843/853-7828, www.circa1886.com)
- COAST Bar and Grill (39D John St., 843/722-8838, www.coastbarandgrill.com)
- Cru Café (18 Pinckney St., 843/534-2434)
- Hominy Grill (207 Rutledge Ave., 912/937-0930)
- Il Cortile del Re (193A King St., 843/853-1888)
- Peninsula Grill (112 N. Market St., 843/723-0700, www.peninsulagrill.com)
- Tristan (55 Market St., 843/534-2155, www.tristandining.com)

COLLEGE OF CHARLESTON AREA
New Southern

Focusing on purely seasonal offerings that never stay on the menu longer than three months, **Circa 1886** (149 Wentworth St., 843/853-7828, www.circa1886.com, Mon.-Sat. 5:30-9:30 P.M., $23-32) combines the best Old World tradition of Charleston with the vibrancy of its more adventurous kitchens. The restaurant—surprisingly little-known despite its four-star Mobil rating—is located in the former carriage house of the grand Wentworth Mansion B&B just west of the main College of Charleston campus. It is now the playground of Chef Marc Collins, who delivers entrées like a robust beef au poivre and a shrimp-and-crab stuffed flounder, to name two recent offerings. The service here is impeccable and friendly, the ambience classy and warm, and the wine list impressive. Be sure to check the daily prix fixe offerings; those can be some great deals.

HAMPTON PARK AREA
Classic Southern

Moe's Crosstown Tavern (714 Rutledge Ave., 843/722-3287, Mon.-Sat. 11 A.M.-midnight, bar until 2 A.M., $10-15) is not only one of the classic Southern dives but has one of the best kitchens on this side of town, known for hand-cut fries, great wings, and, most of all, excellent burgers. On Tuesdays, the burgers are half price at happy hour—one of Charleston's best deals.

With a motto like "Grits are good for you," you know what you're in store for at **Hominy Grill** (207 Rutledge Ave., 912/937-0930, breakfast Mon.-Fri. 7:30-11:30 A.M., lunch and dinner daily 11:30 A.M.-8:30 P.M., brunch Sat.-Sun. 9 A.M.-3 P.M., $10-20), set in a renovated barbershop at Rutledge Avenue and Cannon Street near the Medical University of South Carolina. Primarily revered for his Sunday brunch, Chef Robert Stehling has fun—almost mischievously so—breathing new life into American and Southern classics. Because this is largely a locals' place, you can impress your friends back home by saying you had the rare pleasure of the Hominy's sautéed shad roe with bacon and mushrooms—when the shad are running, that is.

Italian

A new rave of Charleston foodies is the Tuscan-inspired fare of Chef Ken Vedrinski at **Trattoria Lucca** (41 Bogard St., 843/973-3323, www.trattorialuccadining.com, Tues.-Thurs. 6-10 P.M., Fri.-Sat. 6-11 P.M., Sun. 5-8 P.M., $20-23). The menu is simple but perfectly focused, featuring handmade pasta and signature items like the pork chop or the fresh cheese plate. You'll be surprised at how much food your money gets you here. Sunday evenings see a family-style prix fixe communal dinner.

WEST ASHLEY
American

The kitchen at **Gene's Haufbrau** (17 Savannah Hwy., 843/225-4363, www.geneshaufbrau.com, daily 11:30 A.M.-1 A.M., $6-10) complements its fairly typical bar-food menu with some good wraps. Start with the "Drunken Trio" (beer-battered cheese sticks, mushrooms, and onion rings) and follow with a portobello wrap or a good old-fashioned crawfish po'boy. One of the best meals for the money in town is Gene's rotating $6.95 blue plate special, offered Monday-Friday 11:30 A.M.-4:30 P.M. The late-night kitchen hours, until 1 A.M., are a big plus.

Barbecue

For connoisseurs, **Bessinger's** (1602 Savannah Hwy., 843/556-1354, www.bessingersbbq.com) is worth the trip over to West Ashley for its Carolina-style mustard-based wizardry. There are two scenes at Bessinger's, the sit-down Southern buffet (Thurs. 5-8 P.M., Fri.-Sat. 5-9 P.M., Sun. noon-8 P.M., $11.50 adults, $6 children)—Friday is fried catfish

© JIM MOREKIS

Make sure you try Fiery Ron's ribs and pulled pork.

night—and the Sandwich Shop (Mon.-Sat. 10:30 A.M.-9:30 P.M., $6.35 for a "Big Joe" basket) for quick takeout. In old-school tradition, Bessinger's is a dry joint that doesn't sell alcohol. (To clarify: Bessinger's in Charleston was founded by the brother of Maurice Bessinger, who started the Columbia-based "Maurice's Gourmet BBQ" chain, famous for its ultra-right-wing neo-Confederate sensibilities. You may safely patronize Bessinger's in Charleston without worrying that you are supporting anything you may have objections to.)

However, another West Ashley joint, **Fiery Ron's Home Team BBQ** (1205 Ashley River Rd., 843/225-7427, www.hometeambbq.com, Mon.-Sat. 11 A.M.-9 P.M., Sun. 11:30 A.M.-9 P.M., $7-20) is even better than Bessinger's. I cannot say enough about both the pulled pork and the ribs, which rank with the best I've had anywhere in the country. Even the sides are amazing here, including perfect collards and tasty mac-and-cheese. Chef Madison Ruckel provides an array of table-side sauces, including hot sauce, indigenous South Carolina mustard sauce, and his own "Alabama white," a light and delicious mayonnaise-based sauce. As if that weren't enough, the owners' close ties to the regional jam-band community means there's great live blues and indie rock after 10 P.M. most nights (Thursday is bluegrass night) to spice up the bar action, which goes until 2 A.M.

Classic Southern

Tucked away on the grounds of the Middleton Place Plantation is the romantic **Middleton Place Restaurant** (843/556-6020, www.middletonplace.org, lunch daily 11 A.M.-3 P.M., dinner Tues.-Thurs. 6-8 P.M., Fri.-Sat. 6-9 P.M., Sun. 6-8 P.M., $15-25). Theirs is a respectful take on traditional plantation fare like hoppin' John, gumbo, she-crab soup, and collards. The special annual Thanksgiving buffet is a real treat. Reservations are required for dinner.

A nice plus is being able to wander the gorgeous landscaped gardens before dusk if you arrive at 5:30 P.M. or later with a dinner reservation.

Mediterranean

Anything on this northern Italian-themed menu is good, but the risotto—a legacy of original chef John Marshall—is the specialty dish at **Al Di La** (25 Magnolia Rd., 843/571-2321, www.aldilarestaurant.com, Tues.-Sat. 6-10 P.M., $13-20), a very popular West Ashley fine dining spot. Reservations are recommended.

New Southern

One of the more unassuming advocates of farm-to-table dining, **⚫ Glass Onion** (1219 Savannah Hwy., 843/225-1717, www.ilovethe-glassonion.com, Mon.-Thurs. 11 A.M.-9 P.M., Fri. 11 A.M.-10 P.M., Sat. 4-10 P.M., brunch Sat. 10 A.M.-3 P.M., $15) is also in an unassuming location, on U.S. 17 (Savannah Hwy.) on the western approaches to town. That said, their food is right in the thick of the sustainable food movement, and is also incredibly tasty to boot (not to mention more parking than downtown). The interior says "diner," and indeed the emphasis here is on Southern soul and comfort food classics. A recent trip saw a duck leg with pork belly as a special entrée, and a chicken and andouille gumbo that was zesty without being overspiced, thick without being pasty. There are occasional "all-you-can-eat quail" nights, and every Tuesday is Fried Chicken Dinner night, offering what many insist is the best fried chicken in Charleston. The Glass Onion also boasts a good variety of specialty craft brews to wash it all down with. Another plus: In this town full of Sunday brunches, Glass Onion's specialty is a Saturday brunch!

MOUNT PLEASANT

Most restaurant action in Mount Pleasant centers on the picturesque shrimping village of Shem Creek, which is dotted on both banks with bars and restaurants, most dealing in fresh local seafood. As with Murrells Inlet up the coast, some spots on Shem Creek border on tourist traps. Don't be afraid to go where the lines aren't.

Seafood

A well-regarded spot on Shem Creek is **Water's Edge** (1407 Shrimp Boat Lane, 843/884-4074, daily 11 A.M.-11 P.M., $20-30), which consistently takes home a *Wine Spectator* Award of Excellence for its great selection of vintages. Native Charlestonian Jimmy Purcell concentrates on fresh seafood with a slightly more upscale flair than many Shem Creek places.

Right down the road from Water's Edge is another popular spot, especially for a younger crowd: **Vickery's Shem Creek Bar and Grill** (1313 Shrimp Boat Lane, 843/884-4440, daily 11:30 A.M.-1 A.M., $11-16). With a similar menu to its partner location on the peninsula, this Vickery's has the pleasant added bonus of a beautiful view overlooking the Creek. You'll get more of the Vickery's Cuban flair here, with a great black bean soup and an awesome Cuban sandwich.

If you find yourself thirsty and hungry in Mount Pleasant after dark, you might want to stop in the **Reddrum Gastropub** (803 Coleman Blvd., 843/849-0313, www.red-drumpub.com, Mon.-Tues. 5:30-9 P.M., Wed.-Sat. 5:30-10 P.M.), so named because the food here is just as important as the drink. While you're likely to need reservations for the dining room, where you can enjoy Lowcountry-Tex-Mex fusion-style cuisine with a typically Mount Pleasant-like emphasis on seafood, the bar scene is very hopping and fun, with live music every Wednesday-Thursday night.

Vegetarian

For a vegetarian-friendly change of pace from seafood, go to the **Mustard Seed** (1026 Chuck Dawley Blvd., 843/849-0050, Mon.-Sat. 11 A.M.-2:30 P.M. and 5-9:30 P.M., $14-18). The pad thai is probably the best thing on

New York-trained chef Sal Parco's creative and dynamic menu, but you might also get a kick out of the sweet potato ravioli.

For a real change of pace, try **The Sprout Cafe** (629 Johnnie Dodds Blvd., 843/849-8554, www.thehealthysprout.com, Mon.-Fri. 6 A.M.-8 P.M., Sat. 9 A.M.-3 P.M., Sun. 11 A.M.-3 P.M., $3-10) on U.S. 17. Dealing totally in raw foods, the obvious emphasis here is on health and freshness of ingredients. You might be surprised at the inventiveness of their breakfast-through-dinner seasonal menu—memorably described by the staff as "grab and go"—which might include a tasty crepe topped with a pear-and-nut puree and maple syrup, or a raw squash and zucchini "pasta" dish topped with walnut "meatballs."

SULLIVAN'S ISLAND

A new location of ◖ **Fiery Ron's Home Team BBQ** (2209 Middle St., 843/883-3131, www.hometeambbq.com, kitchen Mon.-Sat. 11 A.M.-11 P.M., Sun. 11:30 A.M.-11 P.M., $8-14) provides the same incredible melt-in-your-mouth pork and ribs made famous by the original West Ashley location. For a friendly bite and an adult beverage or two, go straight to **Poe's Tavern** (2210 Middle St., 843/883-0083, daily 11 A.M.-2 A.M., kitchen until 10 P.M.), a nod to Edgar Allan Poe's stint at nearby Fort Moultrie. **Atlanticville** (2063 Middle St., 843/883-9452, www.atlanticville.net, daily 5:30-10 P.M., brunch Sun. 10 A.M.-2 P.M., $25) is where to go for classic fine dining on Sullivan's. If you just want to pick up some healthy goodies for picnicking on the beach, head to the little **Green Heron Grocery** (2019 Middle St., 843/883-0751).

FOLLY BEACH
Breakfast and Brunch

The closest thing to a taste of old Folly is the **Lost Dog Café** (106 W. Huron St., 843/588-9669, daily 6:30 A.M.-3 P.M., $5-7), so named for its bulletin board stacked with alerts about lost pets, pets for adoption, and newborns for sale or giveaway. They open early, the better to offer a tasty, healthy breakfast to the surfing crowd. It's a great place to pick up a quick, inexpensive, and tasty meal while you're near the beach.

Mexican

Taco Boy (15 Center St., 843/588-9761, Sun.-Thurs. 11 A.M.-10 P.M., Fri.-Sat. 11 A.M.-11 P.M., $5-15) is a fun place to get a fish taco, have a margarita, and take a walk on the nearby beach afterward. Though no one is under any illusions that this is an authentic Mexican restaurant, the fresh guacamole is particularly rave-worthy, and there's a good selection of tequilas and beers *hecho en México,* with the bar staying open until 2 A.M. on weekends.

Seafood

Fans of the legendary ◖ **Bowens Island Restaurant** (1870 Bowens Island Rd., 843/795-2757, Tues.-Sat. 5-10 P.M., $5-15, cash only), on James Island just before you get to Folly, went into mourning when it burned to the ground in 2006. But you can't keep a good oysterman down, and owner Robert Barber rebuilt. Regulars insist that this institution, which began in the 1940s as a fishing camp, remains as old-school as ever. A universe removed from the Lexus-and-khaki scene downtown, Bowens Island isn't the place for the uptight. This is the place to go when you want shovels of oysters literally thrown onto your table, freshly steamed and delicious and all-you-can-eat. The fried shrimp, flounder, and hush puppies are incredible too. The understated setting—a nondescript building with little to no signage—only adds to the authenticity of the whole experience. To get there from the peninsula, take Calhoun Street west onto the James Island Connector (Hwy. 30). Take exit 3 onto Highway 171 south and look for Bowens Island Road on the right. The restaurant will be on the left in a short while, after passing by several ritzy McMansions that in no way resemble the restaurant you're about to experience.

NORTH CHARLESTON

If you have a hankering for pizza in North Charleston, don't miss **EVO Pizzeria** (1075 E. Montague Ave., 843/225-1796, www.evopizza. com, lunch Tues.-Fri. 11 A.M.-2:30 P.M., dinner Tues.-Fri. 5-10 P.M., Sat. 6-10 P.M., $10-15) in the Olde North Charleston area at Park Circle. They specialize in a small but rich menu of unusual gourmet pizza toppings, like pistachio pesto.

COFFEE, TEA, AND SWEETS

By common consensus, the best java joint in Charleston is **Kudu Coffee** (4 Vanderhorst Ave., 843/853-7186, Mon.-Sat. 6:30 A.M.-7 P.M., Sun. 9 A.M.-6 P.M.) in the Upper King area. A kudu is an African antelope, and the Africa theme extends to the beans, which all have an African pedigree. Poetry readings and occasional live music add to the mix. A lot of green-friendly, left-of-center community activism goes on here as well; a recent discussion group was titled "How to Survive the Bible Belt but Still Find God." The adjacent African art store is owned by the coffeehouse.

If you find yourself needing a quick pick-me-up while shopping on King Street, avoid the lines at the two Starbucks on the avenue and instead turn east on Market Street and duck inside **City Lights Coffeehouse** (141 Market St., 843/853-7067, Mon.-Thurs. 7 A.M.-9 P.M., Fri.-Sat. 7 A.M.-10 P.M., Sun. 8 A.M.-6 P.M.). The sweet goodies are delectable in this cozy little Euro-style place, and the Counter Culture organic coffee is to die for. If you're really lucky, they'll have some of their Ethiopian Sidamo brewed.

A unique Charleston phenomenon on Upper King by Marion Square is the aptly named **Cupcake** (433 King St., 843/853-8181, www.freshcupcakes.com, Mon.-Sat. 10 A.M.-7 P.M.). Their eponymous specialty compels Charlestonians to form lines onto the sidewalk, waiting to enjoy one or more of the 30 flavors of little cakes. Routinely voted as having the best desserts in the city, the cakes alone at **Kaminsky's** (78 N. Market St., 843/853-8270, daily noon-2 A.M.) are worth the trip to the City Market area. The fresh fruit torte, the red velvet, and the "Mountain of Chocolate" are the three best sellers. There's also a Mount Pleasant location (1028 Johnnie Dodds Blvd., 843/971-7437).

MARKETS AND GROCERIES

A fun and favorite local fixture April-mid-December, the **Charleston Farmers Market** (843/724-7309, www.charlestoncity.info, Sat. 8 A.M.-2 P.M.) rings beautiful Marion Square with stalls of local produce, street eats, local arts and crafts, and kids' activities. Running April-October, East Cooper has its own version in the **Mount Pleasant Farmers Market** (843/884-8517, http://townofmountpleasant. com, Tues. 3 P.M.-dark) at the Moultrie Middle School on Coleman Boulevard.

For organic groceries or a quick healthy bite while you're in Mount Pleasant, check out **Whole Foods** (923 Houston Northcutt Blvd., 843/971-7240, daily 8 A.M.-9 P.M.). The biggest and best supermarket near the downtown area is the regional chain **Harris Teeter** (290 E. Bay St., 843/722-6821, daily 24 hours). There are other Harris Teeter stores in Mount Pleasant (920 Houston Northcutt Blvd. and 620 Long Point Rd., 843/881-4448) and Folly Beach (675 Folly Rd., 843/406-8977). For a charming grocery shopping experience, try **King Street Grocery** (435 King St., 843/958-8004, daily 8 A.M.-midnight) on Upper King. If you're down closer to the Battery, go to the delightful **Queen Street Grocery** (133 Queen St., 843/723-4121, Mon.-Sat. 8 A.M.-8:30 P.M., kitchen Mon.-Sat. 10 A.M.-5 P.M., Sun. 11 A.M.-3 P.M.). Need groceries at 4 A.M. on Folly Beach? Go to **Bert's Market** (202 E. Ashley Ave., 843/588-9449, daily 24 hours).

Information and Services

VISITORS CENTERS

I highly recommend a stop at the **Charleston Visitor Reception and Transportation Center** (375 Meeting St., 800/774-0006, www.charlestoncvb.com, Mon.-Fri. 8:30 A.M.-5 P.M.). Housed in a modern building with an inviting, open design, the Center has several high-tech interactive exhibits, including an amazing model of the city under glass. Wall after wall of well-stocked, well-organized brochures will keep you informed on everything a visitor would ever want to know about or see in the city. A particularly welcoming touch is the inclusion of the work of local artists all around the center. I recommend using the attached parking garage not only for your stop at the Center but also anytime you want to see the many sights this part of town has to offer, such as the Charleston Museum, the Manigault and Aiken-Rhett Houses, and the Children's Museum. The big selling point at the center is the friendliness of the smiling and courteous staff, who welcome you in true Charleston fashion and are there to book rooms and tours and find tickets for shows and attractions. If for no other reason, you should go to the center to take advantage of the great deal offered by the **Charleston Heritage Passport** (www.heritagefederation.org), which gives you 40 percent off admission to all of Charleston's key historic homes, the Charleston Museum, and the two awesome plantation sites on the Ashley River: Drayton Hall and Middleton Place. You can get the Heritage Passport *only* at the Charleston Visitor Reception and Transportation Center on Meeting Street.

Other area visitors centers include the **Mt. Pleasant-Isle of Palms Visitors Center** (Johnnie Dodds Blvd., 843/853-8000, daily 9 A.M.-5 P.M.) and the new **North Charleston Visitors Center** (4975B Centre Pointe Dr., 843/853-8000, Mon.-Sat. 10 A.M.-5 P.M.).

HOSPITALS

If there's a silver lining in getting sick or injured in Charleston, it's that there are plenty of high-quality medical facilities available. The premier institution is the **Medical University of South Carolina** (171 Ashley Ave., 843/792-2300, www.muschealth.com) in the northwest part of the peninsula. Two notable facilities are near each other downtown: **Roper Hospital** (316 Calhoun St., 843/402-2273, www.roperhospital.com) and **Charleston Memorial Hospital** (326 Calhoun St., 843/792-2300). In Mount Pleasant there's **East Cooper Regional Medical Center** (1200 Johnnie Dodds Blvd., www.eastcoopermedctr.com). In West Ashley there's **Bon Secours St. Francis Hospital** (2095 Henry Tecklenburg Ave., 843/402-2273, www.ropersaintfrancis.com).

POLICE

For nonemergencies in Charleston, West Ashley, and James Island, contact the **Charleston Police Department** (843/577-7434, www.charlestoncity.info). You can also contact the police department in Mount Pleasant (843/884-4176). North Charleston is a separate municipality with its own police department (843/308-4718, www.northcharleston.org). Of course, for emergencies always call **911.**

MEDIA
Newspapers

The daily newspaper of record is the *Post and Courier* (www.charleston.net). Its entertainment insert, *Preview,* comes out on Thursdays. The free alternative weekly is the *Charleston City Paper* (www.charlestoncitypaper.com), which comes out on Wednesdays and is the best place to find local music and arts listings. A particularly well-done and lively metro glossy is *Charleston* magazine (www.charlestonmag.com), which comes out once a month.

Radio and Television

The National Public Radio affiliate is the South Carolina ETV radio station WSCI at 89.3 FM. South Carolina ETV is on television at WITV. The local NBC affiliate is WCBD, the CBS affiliate is WCSC, the ABC affiliate is WCIV, and the Fox affiliate is WTAT.

LIBRARIES

The main branch of the **Charleston County Public Library** (68 Calhoun St., 843/805-6801, www.ccpl.org, Mon.-Thurs. 9 A.M.-9 P.M., Fri.-Sat. 9 A.M.-6 P.M., Sun. 2-5 P.M.) has been at its current site since 1998. Named for Sullivan's Island's most famous visitor, the **Edgar Allan Poe** (1921 I'on Ave., 843/883-3914, www.ccpl.org, Mon. and Fri. 2-6 P.M., Tues., Thurs., and Sat. 10 A.M.-2 P.M.) has been housed in Battery Gadsden, a former Spanish-American War gun emplacement, since 1977.

The College of Charleston's main library is the **Marlene and Nathan Addlestone Library** (205 Calhoun St., 843/953-5530, www.cofc.edu), home to special collections, the Center for Student Learning, the main computer lab, the media collection, and even a café. The college's **Avery Research Center for African American History and Culture** (125 Bull St., 843/953-7609, www.cofc.edu/avery, Mon.-Fri. 10 A.M.-5 P.M., Sat. noon-5 P.M.) houses documents relating to the history and culture of African Americans in the Lowcountry.

For other historical research on the area, check out the collections of the **South Carolina Historical Society** (100 Meeting St., 843/723-3225, www.southcarolinahistoricalsociety.org, Mon.-Fri. 9 A.M.-4 P.M., Sat. 9 A.M.-2 P.M.). There's a $5 research fee for nonmembers.

GAY AND LESBIAN RESOURCES

Contrary to many media portrayals of the region, Charleston is quite open to gays and lesbians, who play a major role in arts, culture, and business. As with any other place in the South, however, it's generally expected that people—straights as well—will keep personal matters and politics to themselves in public settings. A key local advocacy group is the **Alliance for Full Acceptance** (29 Leinbach Dr., Suite D-3, 843/883-0343, www.affa-sc.org). The **Lowcountry Gay and Lesbian Alliance** (843/720-8088) holds a potluck the last Sunday of each month. For the most up-to-date happenings, try the Gay Charleston blog (http://gaycharleston.ccpblogs.com), part of the *Charleston City Paper.*

Getting There and Around

BY AIR

Way up in North Charleston is **Charleston International Airport** (CHS, 5500 International Blvd., 843/767-1100, www.chs-airport.com), served by AirTran (www.airtran.com), American Airlines (www.aa.com), Continental Airlines (www.continental.com), Delta (www.delta.com), United Airlines (www.ual.com), and US Airways (www.usairways.com). As in most cities, taxi service from the airport is regulated. This translates to about $30 for two people from the airport to Charleston Place downtown.

BY CAR

There are two main routes into Charleston, I-26 from the west-northwest (which dead-ends downtown) and U.S. 17 from the west (called Savannah Highway when it gets close to Charleston proper), which continues on over the Ravenel Bridge into Mount Pleasant and beyond. There's a fairly new perimeter highway, I-526 (Mark Clark Expressway), which loops around the city from West Ashley to North Charleston to Daniel Island and into Mount Pleasant. It's accessible both from I-26 and U.S.

17. Keep in mind that I-95, while certainly a gateway to the region, is actually a good ways out of Charleston, about 30 miles west of the city.

Car Rentals

Charleston International Airport has rental kiosks for **Avis** (843/767-7031), **Budget** (843/767-7051), **Dollar** (843/767-1130), **Enterprise** (843/767-1109), **Hertz** (843/767-4550), **National** (843/767-3078), and **Thrifty** (843/647-4389). There are a couple of rental locations downtown: **Budget** (390 Meeting St., 843/577-5195) and **Enterprise** (398 Meeting St., 843/723-6215). **Hertz** has a location in West Ashley (3025 Ashley Town Center Dr., 843/573-2147), as does **Enterprise** (2004 Savannah Hwy., 843/556-7889).

BY BUS

Public transportation by **Charleston Area Regional Transit Authority** (CARTA, 843/724-7420, www.ridecarta.com) is a convenient and inexpensive way to enjoy Charleston without the more structured nature of an organized tour. There's a wide variety of routes, but most visitors will limit their acquaintance to the tidy, trolley-like **DASH** (Downtown Area Shuttle) buses run by CARTA primarily for visitors. Each ride is $1.75 pp ($0.85 seniors). The best deal is the $6 one-day pass, which you get at the Charleston Visitors Center (375 Meeting St.). Keep in mind that DASH only stops at designated places. DASH has three routes: the 210, which runs a northerly circuit from the Aquarium to the College of Charleston; the 211, running up and down the parallel Meeting and King Streets from Marion Square down to the Battery; and the 212 Market/Waterfront shuttle from the Aquarium area down to Waterfront Park.

BY TAXI

The South is generally not big on taxis, and Charleston is no exception. The best bet is simply to call rather than try to flag one down. Charleston's most fun service is **Charleston Black Cabs** (843/216-2627, www.charleston-blackcabcompany.com), using Americanized versions of the classic British taxi. A one-way ride anywhere on the peninsula below the bridges is about $10 pp, and rates go up from there. They're very popular, so call as far ahead as you can or try to get one at their stand at Charleston Place. Two other good services are **Safety Cab** (843/722-4066) and **Yellow Cab** (843/577-6565).

You can also try a human-powered taxi service from **Charleston Rickshaw** (843/723-5685). A cheerful (and energetic) young cyclist will pull you and a friend to most points on the lower peninsula for about $10-15. Call 'em or find one by City Market. They work late on Friday and Saturday nights too.

PARKING

As you'll quickly see, parking is at a premium in downtown Charleston. An exception seems to be the large number of free spaces all along the Battery, but unless you're an exceptionally strong walker, that's too far south to use as a reliable base from which to explore the whole peninsula. Most metered parking downtown is on and around Calhoun Street, Meeting Street, King Street, Market Street, and East Bay Street. That may not sound like a lot, but it constitutes the bulk of the area that most visitors visit. Most meters have three-hour limits, but you'll come across some as short as 30 minutes. Technically you're not supposed to "feed the meter" in Charleston, as city personnel put little chalk marks on your tires to make sure people aren't overstaying their welcome. Metered parking is free 6 P.M.-6 A.M. and all day Sunday. On Saturdays, expect to pay.

The city has several conveniently located and comparatively inexpensive parking garages. I strongly suggest that you make use of them. They're located at: The Aquarium, Camden and Exchange Streets, Charleston

Place, Concord and Cumberland Streets, East Bay and Prioleau Streets, Marion Square, Gaillard Auditorium, Liberty and St. Philip Streets, Majestic Square, the Charleston Visitor Reception and Transportation Center, and Wentworth Street. There are several private parking garages as well, primarily clustered in the City Market area. They're convenient, but many have parking spaces that are often too small for some vehicles. The city's website (www.charlestoncity.info) has a good interactive map of parking.

Greater Charleston

Although one could easily spend a lifetime enjoying the history and attractions of Charleston itself, there are many unique experiences to be had in the less-developed areas surrounding the city. Generally there are two types of vibes: isolated close-knit communities with little overt development (although that's changing), or private resort-style communities amid stunning natural beauty.

SUMMERVILLE AND VICINITY

The Dorchester County town of Summerville, population 30,000, is gaining a reputation as a friendly, scenic, and upscale suburb north of Charleston. That's funny, since that's basically what Summerville has always been. Founded as Pineland Village in 1785, Summerville made its reputation as a place for plantation owners and their families to escape the insects and heat of the swampier areas of the Lowcountry. While the plantation system disintegrated with the South's loss in the Civil War, Summerville got a second wind at the turn of the 20th century, when it was recommended by doctors all over the world as a great place to recover from tuberculosis (supposedly all the turpentine fumes in the air from the pine trees were a big help). Summerville is about 30 minutes from downtown Charleston; take I-26 north.

Sights

Due to its longstanding popularity as a getaway for wealthy planters and then as a spa town, Summerville boasts a whopping 700 buildings on the National Register of Historic Places. For a walking tour of the historic district, download the map at www.visitsummerville.com or pick up a hard copy at the **Summerville Visitors Center** (402 N. Main St., 843/873-8535). Alas, the grand old Pine Forest Inn, perhaps the greatest of all Summerville landmarks, Winter White House for presidents William Taft and Theodore Roosevelt, was torn down after World War II, a victim of the Florida vacation craze. Much visitor activity in Summerville centers on **Azalea Park** (S. Main St. and W. 5th St. S., daily dusk-dawn, free), rather obviously named for its most scenic inhabitants. Several fun yearly events take place here, most notably the **Flowertown Festival** (www.flowertownfestival.com, free) each April, a three-day affair heralding the coming of spring and the blooming of the flowers. One of the biggest festivals in South Carolina, 250,000 people usually attend. Another event, **Sculpture in the South** (www.sculptureinthe-south.com) in May, takes advantage of the extensive public sculpture in the park.

To learn more about Summerville's interesting history, go just off Main Street to the **Summerville-Dorchester Museum** (100 E. Doty Ave., 843/875-9666, www.sum-mervilledorchestermuseum.org, Mon.-Sat. 9 A.M.-2 P.M., donation). Located in the former town police station, the museum has a wealth of good exhibits and boasts a new curator, Chris Ohm, with wide local experience, including at Middleton Place and with the CSS *Hunley* project in North Charleston.

Just south of Summerville on the way back to Charleston is the interesting **Colonial Dorchester State Historic Site** (300 State Park Rd., 843/873-1740, www.southcarolinaparks.com, daily 9 A.M.-6 P.M., $2 adults, free under age 16), chronicling a virtually unknown segment of Carolina history. Turns out a contingent of Massachusetts Puritans ("Congregationalists" in the parlance of the time) were given special dispensation in 1697 to form a settlement of their own specifically to enhance commercial activity on the Ashley River, which they did in fine form. Today little is left of old Dorchester but the tabby walls of the 1757 fort overlooking the Ashley. Don't miss the unspectacular but still historically vital remains of the wooden wharf on the walking trail along the river, once the epicenter of a thriving port. Other sites include restorations of the palisade wall and a community house-turned-butterfly garden. The most-photographed thing on-site is the bell tower of the Anglican church of St. George—which actually wasn't where the original settlers worshiped and was in fact quite resented by them since they were forced to pay for its construction. The dispute with the Anglican Church became tense enough to cause many Congregationalists to leave and settle little Midway, Georgia, where many became key figures in the movement for American independence. The resulting Revolutionary War would be the downfall of Dorchester itself, abandoned during the upheaval.

Accommodations and Food

The renowned **Woodlands Resort & Inn** (125 Parsons Rd., 843/875-2600, $325-650) is one of a handful of inns in United States with a five-star rating both for lodging and dining. Its 18 guest rooms within the 1906 great house are decorated in a mix of old-fashioned plantation high-style and contemporary designer aesthetics, with modern, luxurious baths. There's also a freestanding guest cottage ($850) that seeks

to replicate a hunting-lodge type of vibe. As you'd expect, there's a full day spa on the premises; a one-hour massage, the most basic offering, will run you $110. The pool is outside, but it's heated for year-round enjoyment, at least theoretically. Woodlands is making a big play for the growing pet-friendly market and eagerly pampers your dog or cat while you stay. You might not want to leave the grounds, but you should take advantage of their complimentary bikes to tour around historic Summerville. Within Woodlands is its award-winning world-class restaurant, simply called **The Dining Room** (Mon.-Sat. 11 A.M.-2 P.M. and 6-9 P.M., brunch Sun. 11:30 A.M.-2 P.M., $25-40). It will come as no surprise to find out that the 900-entry wine list and sommelier are collectively awesome, as are the desserts. Jackets are required, and reservations are strongly advised.

In Summerville proper, try **Mustard Seed** (101 N. Main St., 843/821-7101, lunch Mon.-Sat. 11 A.M.-2:30 P.M., dinner Mon.-Thurs. 5-9 P.M., Fri.-Sat. 5-10 P.M., $8-10), a health-food restaurant that doesn't skimp on the taste. For a more down-home-style pancakes-and-sandwich place that's popular with the locals at all hours of the day, try **Flowertown Restaurant** (120 E. 5th N. St., 843/871-3202, daily 24 hours, $8).

Another popular local landmark is **Guerin's Pharmacy** (140 S. Main St., 843/873-2531, Mon.-Fri. 9 A.M.-6 P.M., Sat. 9 A.M.-5 P.M.), which claims to be the State's oldest pharmacy. Complete with an old-fashioned soda fountain, they offer malted milkshakes and lemonade.

AWENDAW AND POINTS NORTH

This area just north of Charleston along U.S. 17—named for the Sewee Indian village originally located here, and known to the world chiefly as the place where Hurricane Hugo made landfall in 1989—is seeing some new growth, but still hews to its primarily rural, nature-loving roots.

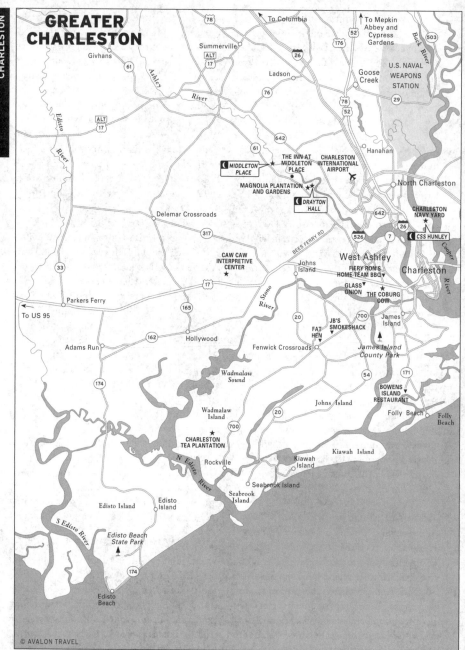

GREATER CHARLESTON

To Columbia

To Mepkin Abbey and Cypress Gardens

U.S. NAVAL WEAPONS STATION

Givhans

Summerville

Ladson

Goose Creek

North Charleston

Delemar Crossroads

MIDDLETON PLACE

THE INN AT MIDDLETON PLACE

CHARLESTON INTERNATIONAL AIRPORT

MAGNOLIA PLANTATION AND GARDENS

DRAYTON HALL

CHARLESTON NAVY YARD

CSS HUNLEY

CAW CAW INTERPRETIVE CENTER

West Ashley

Johns Island

FIERY RON'S HOME TEAM BBQ

GLASS ONION

THE COBURG COW

Charleston

Parkers Ferry

To US 95

JB'S SMOKESHACK

James Island

Adams Run

FAT HEN

Hollywood

Fenwick Crossroads

James Island County Park

Wadmalaw Sound

BOWENS ISLAND RESTAURANT

Johns Island

Folly Beach

Wadmalaw Island

CHARLESTON TEA PLANTATION

Kiawah Island

Rockville

Kiawah Island

Seabrook Island

Edisto Island

Edisto Island

Seabrook Island

Edisto Beach State Park

Edisto Beach

Ashley River

Edisto River

Stono River

Cooper River

Back River

N Edisto River

S Edisto River

Hanahan

© AVALON TRAVEL

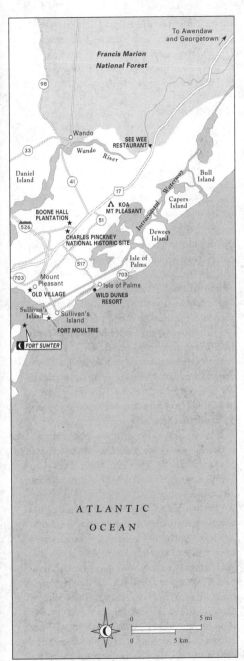

Sewee Visitor and Environmental Education Center

Twenty miles north of Charleston you'll find the Sewee Visitor and Environmental Education Center (5821 U.S. 17, 843/928-3368, www.fws.gov/seweecenter, Tues.-Sat. 9 A.M.-5 P.M., free). Besides being a gateway of sorts for the almost entirely aquatic Cape Romain National Wildlife Refuge, Sewee is primarily known for its population of rare red wolves, who were part of a unique release program on nearby Bull Island begun in the late 1970s.

Cape Romain National Wildlife Refuge

One of the best natural experiences in the area is north of Charleston at Cape Romain National Wildlife Refuge (5801 U.S. 17 N., 843/928-3264, www.fws.gov/caperomain, year-round daily dawn-dusk). Essentially comprising four barrier islands, the 66,000-acre refuge—almost all of which is marsh—provides a lot of great paddling opportunities, chief among them **Bull Island** (no overnight camping). A fairly lengthy trek from where you put in lies famous Boneyard Beach, where hundreds of downed trees lie on the sand, bleached by sun and salt. Slightly to the south within the refuge, **Capers Island Heritage Preserve** (843/953-9300, www.dnr.sc.gov, daily dawn-dusk, free) is still a popular camping locale despite heavy damage from 1989's Hurricane Hugo. Get permits in advance by calling the South Carolina Department of Natural Resources. You can kayak to the refuge yourself or take the only approved ferry service from **Coastal Expeditions** (514B Mill St., Mount Pleasant, 843/881-4582, www.coastalexpeditions.com). **Barrier Island Eco Tours** (50 41st Ave., Isle of Palms, 843/886-5000, www.nature-tours.com) on Isle of Palms also runs trips to the area.

I'on Swamp Trail

Once part of a rice plantation, the I'on Swamp

Trail (843/928-3368, www.fs.fed.us, daily dawn-dusk, free) is one of the premier bird-watching sites in South Carolina, particularly during spring and fall migrations. The rare Bachman's warbler, commonly considered one of the most elusive birds in North America, has been seen here. To get here, head about 15 miles north of Mount Pleasant and take a left onto I'on Swamp Road (Forest Service Rd. 228). The parking area is 2.5 miles ahead on the left.

Food

A must-stop roadside diner in the Awendaw area is **🄲 See Wee Restaurant** (4808 U.S. 17 N., 843/928-3609, Mon.-Thurs. 11 A.M.-8:30 P.M., Fri.-Sat. 11 A.M.-9:30 P.M., Sun. 11 A.M.-8 P.M., $10-23), located about 20 minutes' drive north of Charleston in a humble former general store on the west side of U.S. 17 (the restrooms are still outside). Folks come from Charleston and as far away as Myrtle Beach to enjoy signature menu items like the grouper and the unreal she-crab soup, considered by some epicures to be the best in the world; you can't miss with any of their seafood entrées. Occasionally the crowds can get thick, but rest assured it's worth any wait.

POINTS WEST AND SOUTHWEST
Caw Caw Interpretive Center

Just west of Charleston on U.S. 17 you'll find the unique Caw Caw Interpretive Center (5200 Savannah Hwy., Ravenel, 843/889-8898, www.ccprc.com, Wed.-Sun. 9 A.M.-5 P.M., $1), a treasure trove for history buffs and naturalists wanting to learn more about the old rice culture of the South. With a particular emphasis on the expertise of those who worked on the rice plantations using techniques they brought with them from Africa, the county-run facility comprises 650 acres of land on an actual former rice plantation built on a cypress swamp, eight miles of interpretive trails, an educational center with exhibits, and a wildlife sanctuary with seven different habitats. Most Wednesday and Saturday mornings, guided bird walks are held at 8:30 A.M. ($5 pp). You can put in your own canoe for $10 October-April on Saturdays and Sundays. Bikes and dogs aren't allowed on the grounds.

Johns Island

The outlying community of Johns Island is where you'll find **Angel Oak Park** (3688 Angel Oak Rd., Mon.-Sat. 9 A.M.-5 P.M., Sun. 1-5 P.M.), home of a massive live oak, 65 feet in circumference, that's well over 1,000 years old and commonly considered the oldest tree east of the Mississippi River. The tree and the park are owned by the city of Charleston, and the grounds are often used for weddings and special events. Get here from Charleston by taking U.S. 17 over the Ashley River, then Highway 171 to Maybank Highway. Take a left onto Bohicket Road near the Piggly Wiggly, and then look for signs on the right.

Here is also where you'll find **Legare Farms** (2620 Hanscombe Point Rd., 843/559-0763, www.legarefarms.com), open to the public for various activities, including its annual pumpkin patch in October, its "sweet corn" festival in June, and bird walks (Sat. 8:30 A.M., $6 adults, $3 children) in fall.

If you find your tummy growling on Johns Island, don't miss **🄲 Fat Hen** (3140 Maybank Hwy., 843/559-9090, Tues.-Sat. 11:30 A.M.-3 P.M. and 5:30-10 P.M., Sun. 10 A.M.-3 P.M., $15-20), a self-styled "country French bistro" begun by a couple of old Charleston restaurant hands. The fried oysters are a particular specialty. There's also a bar menu for late-night hours (10 P.M.-2 A.M.).

If barbecue is more your thing, head straight to **🄲 JB's Smokeshack** (3406 Maybank Hwy., 843/557-0426, www.jbssmokeshack.com, Wed.-Sat. 11 A.M.-8:30 P.M., $8), one of the best 'cue joints in the Lowcountry. They offer a buffet for $8.88 pp ($5 under age 11), or you can opt for a barbecue plate, including hash, rice, and two sides. In a nice twist, the plates include a three-meat option: pork, chicken, ribs, or brisket.

Wadmalaw Island

Like Johns Island, Wadmalaw Island is one of those lazy, scenic areas gradually becoming subsumed within Charleston's growth. That said, there's plenty of meandering, laid-back beauty to enjoy, and a couple of interesting sights.

Currently owned by the R. C. Bigelow Tea corporation, the **Charleston Tea Plantation** (6617 Maybank Hwy., 843/559-0383, www.charlestonteaplantation.com, Mon.-Sat. 10 A.M.-4 P.M., Sun. noon-4 P.M., free) is no cute living history exhibit: It's a big, working tea plantation—the only one in the U.S.—with acre after acre of *Camellia sinensis* being worked by modern farm machinery. Visitors get to see a sample of how the tea is made, "from the field to the cup." Factory tours are free, and a trolley tour of the "Back 40" is $10. And, of course, there's a gift shop where you can sample and buy all types of teas and tea-related products. Unlike many agricultural sites in the area, the 127-acre Charleston Tea Plantation was never actually a plantation. It was first planted at the relatively late date of 1960, when the Lipton tea company moved some plants from Summerville, South Carolina, to its research facility on Wadmalaw Island. Lipton decided the climate and high labor costs of the American South weren't conducive to making money, so they sold the land to two employees, Mack Fleming and Bill Hall, in 1987. The two held onto the plantation until 2003, when R. C. Bigelow won it at auction for $1.28 million. Growing season is from April through October. The tea bushes, direct descendants of plants brought over in the 1800s from India and China, "flush up" 2-3 inches every few weeks during growing season. To get here from Charleston, take the Ashley River Bridge, stay left to Folly Road (Hwy. 171), turn right onto Maybank Highway for 18 miles, and look for the sign on the left.

The muscadine grape is the only varietal that dependably grows in South Carolina. That said, the state has several good wineries, among them Wadmalaw's own **Irvin House Vineyard** (6775 Bears Bluff Rd., 843/559-6867, www.charlestonwine.com, Thurs.-Sat. 10 A.M.-5 P.M.), the Charleston area's only vineyard. Jim Irvin, a Kentucky boy, and his wife, Anne, a Johns Island native, make several varieties of muscadine wine here, with tastings and a gift shop. They also give free tours of the 50-acre grounds every Saturday at 2 P.M. There's a Grape-stomping Festival at the end of each August ($5 per car). Also on the Irvin Vineyard grounds you'll find **Firefly Distillery** (6775 Bears Bluff Rd., 843/559-6867, www.fireflyvodka.com), home of their signature Firefly Sweet Tea Vodka. They offer tastings (Feb.-Dec. Wed.-Sat. 11 A.M.-5 P.M., $6 per tasting). To get here from Charleston, go west on Maybank Highway about 10 miles to Bears Bluff Road, veering right. The vineyard entrance is on the left after about eight miles.

Kiawah Island

Only one facility for the general public exists on beautiful Kiawah Island, the **Kiawah Island Beachwalker Park** (843/768-2395, www.ccprc.com, Mar.-Apr. and Sept. daily 10 A.M.-6 P.M., May-Labor Day daily 9 A.M.-7 P.M., Oct. Mon.-Fri. 9 A.M.-5 P.M., Sat.-Sun. 10 A.M.-6 P.M., Nov.-Feb. daily 10 A.M.-5 P.M., $7 per vehicle, free for pedestrians and cyclists). Get here from downtown Charleston by taking Lockwood Drive onto the Highway 30 Connector bridge over the Ashley River. Turn right onto Folly Road, then a left onto Maybank Highway. After about 20 minutes, take a left onto Bohicket Road, which leads to Kiawah in 14 miles. Turn left from Bohicket Road onto the Kiawah Island Parkway. Just before the security gate, turn right on Beachwalker Drive and follow the signs to the park.

The island's other main attraction is the

Kiawah Island Golf Resort (12 Kiawah Beach Dr., 800/654-2924, www.kiawahgolf.com), which is a key location for PGA tournaments. Several smaller private, family-friendly resorts exist on Kiawah, with fully furnished homes and villas and every amenity you could ask for and then some, giving you full access to the island's 10 miles of beautiful beach. Go to www.explorekiawah.com for a full range of options or call 800/877-0837.

Through the efforts of the **Kiawah Island Conservancy** (23 Beachwalker Dr., 843/768-2029, www.kiawahconservancy.org), over 300 acres of the island have been kept as an undeveloped nature preserve. The island's famous bobcat population has made quite a comeback, with somewhere between 24 and 36 animals currently active. The bobcats are vital to the island ecosystem, since as top predator they help cull what would otherwise become untenably large populations of deer and rabbit. As a side note, while you're enjoying the beautiful scenery of the islands on the Carolina coast, it's always important to remember that most, including Kiawah, were logged or farmed extensively in the past. While they're certainly gorgeous now, it would be incorrect to call them "pristine."

Seabrook Island

Like its neighbor Kiawah, Seabrook Island is also a private resort-dominated island. In addition to offering miles of beautiful beaches, on its 2,200 acres are a wide variety of golfing, tennis, equestrian, and swimming facilities as well as extensive dining and shopping options. There are also a lot of kids' activities as well. For information on lodging options and packages, go to www.seabrook.com or call 866/249-9934.

MYRTLE BEACH AND THE GRAND STRAND

The West has Las Vegas, Florida has Orlando, and South Carolina has Myrtle Beach. There's no Bellagio Resort or Magic Kingdom here, but Myrtle Beach remains the number one travel destination in the state, with even more visitors than Charleston. Unlike Charleston, you'll find little history here. With several theme parks, 100 golf courses, 50 miniature golf courses, over 2,000 restaurants—not to mention miles of beautiful shoreline—Myrtle Beach is built for all-out vacation enjoyment.

The hot, hazy height of the summer also marks the busy season on the Strand. Its long main drag, Kings Highway (a.k.a. Business U.S. 17), is packed full of families on the go eager for more swimming, more shopping, more eating, and just plain more.

While to many people the name Myrtle Beach conjures an image of tacky, downscale people doing tacky, downscale things, that's an outmoded stereotype. Tacky is certainly still in vogue here, but an influx of higher-quality development, both in accommodations and entertainment value, has lifted the bar significantly. Rather than slumming in a beat-up motel, quaffing PBR on the beach, and loading up on $2 T-shirts like in the "good old days," a typical Myrtle Beach vacation now involves a stay in a large condo apartment with flat-screen TVs, a full kitchen, and a sumptuous palmetto-lined

© JIM MOREKIS

MYRTLE BEACH

HIGHLIGHTS

(Broadway at the Beach: You'll find good cheesy fun along with tons of interesting shops, theme restaurants, and, of course, miniature golf (page 136).

(Barefoot Landing: North Myrtle Beach's answer to Broadway at the Beach, with the Alabama Theatre and the House of Blues nearby (page 139).

(Ocean Drive Beach: The still-beating, still-shuffling heart of the Grand Strand is also the center of shag dancing culture (page 141).

(Carolina Opry: This popular show offers corny but quality family entertainment in an intimate, friendly setting (page 144).

(Brookgreen Gardens: Enjoy the country's largest collection of outdoor sculptures, set amid a fine collection of formal gardens (page 167).

(Huntington Beach State Park: The scenic beach combines with one-of-a-kind Atalaya Castle to make for a unique getaway (page 168).

(Hampton Plantation: This historic Georgian mansion on the scenic Wambaw Creek inspired a South Carolina poet laureate to give it to the state for posterity (page 178).

LOOK FOR (TO FIND RECOMMENDED SIGHTS, ACTIVITIES, DINING, AND LODGING.

pool; dining at the House of Blues; having drinks at the Hard Rock Café; stops at high-profile attractions like Ripley's Aquarium; and shopping at trendy retailers like Anthropologie and Abercrombie & Fitch.

The Grand Strand on which Myrtle Beach sits—a long, sandy peninsula stretching 60 miles from Winyah Bay to the North Carolina border—has also been a vacation playground for generations of South Carolinians. Unlike Hilton Head, where New York and Midwestern accents are more common than Lowcountry drawls, Myrtle Beach and the Grand Strand remain largely homegrown passions, with many visitors living within a few hours' drive. Despite

the steady increase of money and high-dollar development in the area, its strongly regional nature works to your advantage in that prices are generally lower than in Vegas or Orlando.

To the south of Myrtle proper lies the understated, affluent, and relaxing Pawleys Island, with nearby Murrells Inlet and its great seafood restaurants. Unique, eclectic Brookgreen Gardens hosts the largest collection of outdoor sculpture in the country, with one-of-a-kind Huntington Beach State Park literally right across the street.

Even farther south, in the northern quarter of the Lowcountry proper, you'll find a totally different scene: the remnants of the Carolina rice culture in quaint old Georgetown, and the

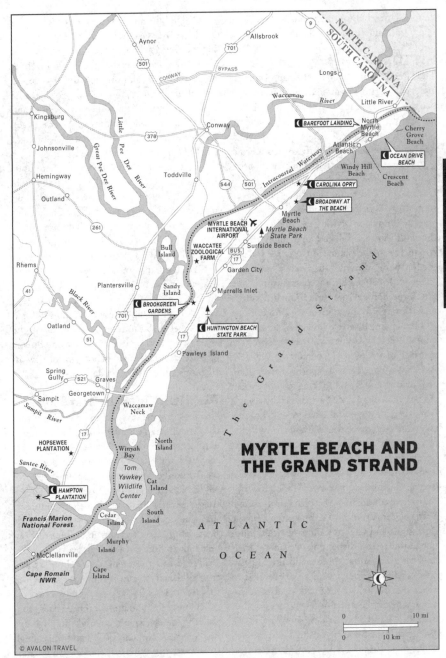

MYRTLE BEACH

NORTH CAROLINA
SOUTH CAROLINA

Aynor
Allsbrook
Longs
Little River
Kingsburg
Johnsonville
Conway
CONWAY
BYPASS
Waccamaw River
BAREFOOT LANDING
North Myrtle Beach
Atlantic Beach
Cherry Grove Beach
OCEAN DRIVE BEACH
Windy Hill Beach
Crescent Beach
Hemingway
Toddville
Intracoastal Waterway
CAROLINA OPRY
BROADWAY AT THE BEACH
Outland
MYRTLE BEACH INTERNATIONAL AIRPORT
Myrtle Beach
Myrtle Beach State Park
Surfside Beach
WACCATEE ZOOLOGICAL FARM
Bull Island
Garden City
Rhems
Plantersville
Sandy Island
Murrells Inlet
BROOKGREEN GARDENS
Oatland
HUNTINGTON BEACH STATE PARK
Pawleys Island
Spring Gully
Graves
Georgetown
Waccamaw Neck
Sampit
Winyah Bay
North Island
HOPSEWEE PLANTATION
Tom Yawkey Wildlife Center
Cat Island
Santee River
HAMPTON PLANTATION
Francis Marion National Forest
Cedar Island
South Island
McClellanville
Murphy Island
Cape Romain NWR
Cape Island

MYRTLE BEACH AND THE GRAND STRAND

The Grand Strand

A T L A N T I C

O C E A N

Great Pee Dee River
Little Pee Dee River
Black River
Sampit River

0   10 mi
0   10 km

© AVALON TRAVEL

haunting antebellum mansions at Hampton Plantation and Hopsewee Plantation.

HISTORY

The Grand Strand was once the happy hunting and shellfish-gathering grounds of the Waccamaw people, whose legacy is still felt today in the name of the dominant river in the region and the Strand's main drag itself, Kings Highway, which is actually built on an old Native American trail.

The southern portion of the Strand, especially Georgetown and Pawleys Island, rapidly became home to a number of rice plantations soon after the area was colonized. However, the area now known as Myrtle Beach didn't share in the wealth since its soil and topography weren't conducive to the plantation system. Indeed, the northern portion of the Grand Strand was largely uninhabited during colonial times, and hurricane damage prevented much development through the first half of the 19th century.

That changed after the Civil War with the boom of nearby Conway to the west, now the seat of Horry County (pronounced "OR-ee"). As Conway's lumber and export economy grew, a railroad spur was built to bring in lumber from the coast, much of which was owned by a single firm, the Conway Lumber Company. Lumber company employees began using the rail lines to take vacation time on the Strand, in effect becoming the first of millions of tourists to the area. At this time it was simply called "New Town," in contrast to Conway's "Old Town."

In the second half of the 19th century, Civil War veteran Franklin G. Burroughs, of the Burroughs and Collins Company, which supplied lumber and turpentine to Conway business interests, sought to expand the tourism profitability of the coastal area. He died in 1897, but his heirs continued his dream, inaugurated by the opening of the Seaside Inn in 1901. The first bona fide resort came in the 1920s with the building of the Arcady resort, which included the first golf course in the area.

In 1938 Burroughs's widow, Adeline, known locally as "Miss Addie," was credited with giving the town its modern name, after the locally abundant wax myrtle shrub. During this time, locals on the Strand originated the shagging subculture, built around the dance of the same name and celebrated at numerous pavilions and "beach clubs." The building of Myrtle Beach Air Force Base in 1940—now closed—brought further growth and jobs to the area.

Tourism, especially, grew apace here until Hurricane Hazel virtually wiped the slate clean in 1954. In typical Carolinian fashion, residents and landowners made lemonade out of lemons, using the hurricane's devastation as an excuse to build even bigger resort developments, including a plethora of golf courses.

Since then, the Strand has grown to encompass about 250,000 permanent residents, with about 10 million visitors on top of that each year. A huge influx of money in the 1990s led to a higher-dollar form of development on the coast, sadly leading to the demolition of many of the old beach pavilions in favor of new attractions and massive condo high-rises.

PLANNING YOUR TIME

The most important thing to remember is that the Grand Strand is *long*—60 miles from one end to the other. This has real-world effects that need to be taken into account. For example, while the separate municipality of North Myrtle Beach (actually a fairly recent aggregation of several small beachside communities) may sound like it is right next door to Myrtle Beach proper, getting from one to the other can take half an hour even in light traffic.

Due to this geographical stretching, as well as to all the attractions, it is impossible to cover this area in a single day, and even two days is a ridiculously short amount of time. That's probably the main reason many folks indulge in a weekly rental. Not only does it give you enough time to see everything, it enables you to relax, slow down, and enjoy the beaches and the general laid-back attitude.

In May, Memorial Day weekend and Bike Week have traditionally signaled the beginning of the tourism season in Myrtle Beach. The busy season exactly corresponds with the hottest months of the year, July and August. This is when crowds are at their peak, restaurants are most crowded, and the two spurs of U.S. 17 are at their most gridlocked.

Springtime in Myrtle Beach is quite nice, but keep in mind that water temperatures are still chilly through April. There is almost always one last cold snap in March that augurs the spring.

Personally, I recommend hitting Myrtle Beach just as the busy season wanes, right after Labor Day. Rooms are significantly cheaper, but most everything is still fully open and adequately staffed, with the added benefit of the biggest crush of visitors being absent.

Winter on the Grand Strand is very slow, as befitting this very seasonal locale. Many restaurants, especially down the Strand near Murrells Inlet, close entirely through February.

ORIENTATION

Don't get too hung up on place names around here. This part of the Strand comprises several different municipalities, from Surfside Beach to the south up to Little River near the North Carolina border, but for all intents and purposes it's one big place all its own. As a general rule,

development (read: money) is moving more quickly to the North Myrtle Beach area rather than the older Myrtle Beach proper to the south.

North Myrtle is actually a recent aggregation of several historic beachfront communities: Windy Hill, Crescent Beach, Cherry Grove, and Ocean Drive. You'll see numerous signs announcing the entrance or exit into or out of these communities, but keep in mind you're still technically in North Myrtle Beach.

The Grand Strand grid is based on a system of east-west avenues beginning just north of Myrtle Beach State Park. Confusingly, these are separated into "North" and "South" avenues. Perhaps even more confusing, North Myrtle Beach also uses its own distinct north-and-south avenue system, also for roads running east-west. Got it? It goes like this: Myrtle Beach starts with 29th Avenue South at the Myrtle Beach International Airport and goes up to 1st Avenue South just past Family Kingdom Amusement Park. From here, the avenues are labeled as "North" from 1st Avenue North up to 82nd Avenue North, which concludes Myrtle Beach proper. North Myrtle Beach begins at 48th Avenue South near Barefoot Landing and goes up to Main Street (the center of the shag culture). It continues with 1st Avenue North, goes up to 24th Avenue North (Cherry Grove Beach), and finally concludes at 61st Avenue North, near the North Carolina state line.

Sights

MYRTLE BEACH

◖ BROADWAY AT THE BEACH

Love it or hate it, Broadway at the Beach (1325 Celebrity Circle, 800/386-4662, www.broadwayatthebeach.com, summer daily 10 A.M.-11 P.M., winter daily 11 A.M.-6 P.M.), between 21st and 29th Avenues, is one of Myrtle's biggest and flashiest attractions—which is saying a lot. First opened over 15 years ago and added onto significantly since then, this collection of three hotels, over two dozen restaurants, about 50 shops, and a dozen kid-oriented activities sprawls over 350 acres with several other major attractions, restaurants, and clubs (such as the Hard Rock Café and Planet Hollywood) on its periphery.

Just like the Magic Kingdom that many of Myrtle's attractions seek to emulate, Broadway at the Beach has at its center a large lagoon, around which everything else is situated. Needless to say there's also a massive parking lot. Activity goes on all day and well into the wee hours, with the weekly Tuesday-night fireworks a big draw. While there's plenty to do, what with the great shops, tasty treats, and fun piped-in music following you everywhere, it's also fun just to walk around.

The main complaint about Broadway at the Beach has to do with the price of the various attractions within the park, some of which are fairly small-scale. Indeed, the quality of the attractions within Broadway at the Beach varies, and much depends on what floats your boat, but you can still find plenty to enjoy as long as you know the scoop ahead of time. Here's a quick guide to the specific attractions.

The biggest new attraction at Broadway—and it's really big—is **Wonderworks** (1313 Celebrity Circle, 843/626-9962, www.wonderworksonline.com, $23 adults, $15 children). You can't miss it—look for the thing that looks exactly like a massive, life-size, crumbling, upside-down creepy mansion. Inside you'll find a wide and quite varied assortment of interactive experiences designed to let you know what it's like to be upside down, or on a bed of nails, or in a hurricane, or freezing after the *Titanic* sank, and things of that nature. Think Ripley's Believe It or Not updated for a modern age, complete with laser tag.

Harry Potter fans will likely enjoy **MagiQuest** (1185 Celebrity Circle, 843/913-9460, www.magiquest.com, $26-40), which takes you on a 90-minute journey to find clues that lead to hidden treasure. Folks of an older generation will find it a surprisingly high-tech experience for something dealing with the ancient arts of wizardry—including an orientation session and the programmable wands that are indispensable to the quest. But don't worry; the young ones will get it.

MagiQuest has a certain addictive quality, and many people opt to go back for more (additional quests cost less) after their usually confusing, full-price first experience. Note that there's an intro game you can play online, which might help you get acquainted. Like many attractions at Myrtle Beach, this one can get very crowded, which is certain to impede the quality of your experience (Whose wand uncovered the clue? Who knows?). Try to go right when it opens.

Similarly medieval—and right nearby—is **Medieval Times** (2904 Fantasy Way, 843/236-4635, www.medievaltimes.com, $51 adults, $31 ages 3-12), a combination dinner theater and medieval tournament reenactment.

Now that almost all of the old-fashioned amusement parks at Myrtle Beach are gone, victims of "modernization," you can find a facsimile of sorts at **Pavilion Nostalgia Park** (843/913-9400, www.pavilionnostalgiapark.com, summer daily 11 A.M.-11 P.M., hours vary in other seasons, rides $4 each), which seeks to simulate the days of Myrtle gone by.

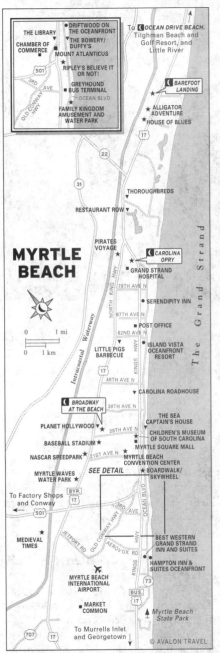

MYRTLE BEACH

THE LIBRARY
CHAMBER OF COMMERCE
DRIFTWOOD ON THE OCEANFRONT
THE BOWERY/ DUFFY'S
MOUNT ATLANTICUS
RIPLEY'S BELIEVE IT OR NOT!
GREYHOUND BUS TERMINAL
OCEAN BLVD
FAMILY KINGDOM AMUSEMENT AND WATER PARK
501
3RD AVE
OLD CONWAY HWY

To OCEAN DRIVE BEACH, Tilghman Beach and Golf Resort, and Little River

BAREFOOT LANDING
ALLIGATOR ADVENTURE
HOUSE OF BLUES
17

22
31

THOROUGHBREDS
RESTAURANT ROW
PIRATES VOYAGE
CAROLINA OPRY
GRAND STRAND HOSPITAL
79TH AVE N
SERENDIPITY INN
67TH AVE N
POST OFFICE
62ND AVE N
LITTLE PIGS BARBECUE
ISLAND VISTA OCEANFRONT RESORT
17
48TH AVE N
CAROLINA ROADHOUSE
38TH AVE N
BROADWAY AT THE BEACH
THE SEA CAPTAIN'S HOUSE
PLANET HOLLYWOOD
28TH AVE N
CHILDREN'S MUSEUM OF SOUTH CAROLINA
BASEBALL STADIUM
MYRTLE SQUARE MALL
NASCAR SPEEDPARK
21ST AVE N
MYRTLE BEACH CONVENTION CENTER
MYRTLE WAVES WATER PARK
SEE DETAIL
BOARDWALK/ SKYWHEEL
BYP.
17
To Factory Shops and Conway
501
3RD AVE
OCEAN BLVD
MEDIEVAL TIMES
BEST WESTERN GRAND STRAND INN AND SUITES
JETPORT RD
OLD CONWAY HWY
AEROVOX RD
KINGS HWY
HAMPTON INN & SUITES OCEANFRONT
MYRTLE BEACH INTERNATIONAL AIRPORT
73
MARKET COMMON
BUS. 17
Myrtle Beach State Park
707
17
To Murrells Inlet and Georgetown
© AVALON TRAVEL

The Grand Strand
Intracoastal Waterway
NORTH KING HWY
KINGS HWY

0   1 mi
0   1 km

MYRTLE BEACH

Of course nowhere in Myrtle is really complete without miniature golf, and Broadway at the Beach's version is **Dragon's Lair Fantasy Golf** (1197 Celebrity Circle, 843/913-9301, $9), with two medieval-themed 18-hole courses boasting a fire-breathing dragon.

Ripley's Aquarium

If you've been to Boston's New England Aquarium, don't expect something similar at Ripley's Aquarium (1110 Celebrity Circle, 800/734-8888, www.ripleysaquarium.com, Sun.-Thurs. 9 A.M.-8 P.M., Fri.-Sat. 9 A.M.-9 P.M., $22 adults, $11 ages 6-11, $4 ages 2-5, free under age 2) at Broadway at the Beach. This is a smaller but quite delightful aquarium built primarily for entertainment purposes rather than education. Calming music plays throughout, and a moving sidewalk takes you around and under a huge main tank filled with various marine creatures. There's even the requisite stingray-petting touch tank.

You'll no doubt see the garish billboards for the Aquarium up and down U.S. 17, featuring massive sharks baring rows of scary teeth. But don't expect an over-the-top shark exhibit—the truth is that most of the sharks in the aquarium are smaller and much more peaceful.

NASCAR SpeedPark

Just outside Broadway at the Beach you'll find the NASCAR SpeedPark (1820 21st Ave. N., 843/918-8725, www.nascarspeedpark.com, summer daily 10 A.M.-11 P.M., shorter hours in other seasons, from $30), where can you speed around at 50 mph in a fairly decent replica of an actual NASCAR track. Because there are several different tracks to choose from, based on age and difficulty, there's something here for adults and kids alike.

The serious track, Thunder Road, is open only to drivers age 16 and over; it allows drivers to get into half-size versions of Nextel Cup cars. Pint-size drivers 48, 40, and 36 inches

MYRTLE BEACH

© JIM MOREKIS

Ripley's Aquarium

tall can take part in racing on the Champions, Qualifier, and Kiddie Speedway courses, respectively. As if all that's not enough, there are water-based racing courses and, this being Myrtle Beach, NASCAR-themed miniature golf.

If you're worried about metal-shearing, flame-spewing, multiple-car pileups like in a real NASCAR race, don't. Safety is a paramount concern at this national chain of parks, and the likelihood of an accident at the SpeedPark is far less than on crowded U.S. 17, a stone's throw away.

Myrtle Waves Water Park

Billed as South Carolina's largest water park, Myrtle Waves Water Park (U.S. 17 Bypass and 10th Ave. N., 843/913-9260, www.myrtle-waves.com, summer daily 10 A.M.-6 P.M., hours vary in other seasons, $28 age 7 and over, $22 ages 3-6, free under age 3) is right across the street from Broadway at the Beach, covers 20 acres, and features all kinds of safe fun "rides,"

such as the Ocean in Motion Wave Pool, the Layzee River, and the Saturation Station, wherein a huge water volcano absolutely soaks everybody in proximity every five minutes or so. That's just to name a few.

As you would expect, there are plenty of lifeguards on hand at all the rides. Food is plentiful if unremarkable, and there are shaded areas for the less adventurous to chill while the kids splash around. With one admission price covering all rides all day, this is one of the better deals in Myrtle Beach, which has more than its share of confusingly (and occasionally exorbitantly) priced attractions.

MYRTLE BEACH BOARDWALK AND PROMENADE

The new pride of old Myrtle, the Boardwalk (www.visitmyrtlebeach.com, daily 24 hours, free) is a fun, meandering 1.2-mile jaunt from 2nd Avenue Pier to the 14th Avenue Pier. Built in three different and distinct sections, the point of the Boardwalk is not only to take you through the more commercial areas of the beachfront area but to provide easy pedestrian beach access. One section provides a nice peaceful walking experience amid the dune-scape.

Unveiled in 2010, the Boardwalk has been a very important civic and morale improvement in the wake of the loss of the old pavilion nearby, now mostly a grassy field.

Skywheel

You can't miss spotting the new Skywheel (1110 N. Ocean Blvd., 843/839-9200, myrtlebeachs-kywheel.com, summer daily noon-midnight, $13 adults, $9 children), a huge Ferris wheel dominating the skyline at the new Boardwalk. The cars are family-size, fully enclosed, and offer a great view of the ocean and surrounding area during the approximately 10-minute, three-rotation trip.

© JIM MOREKIS

the new Skywheel at the Boardwalk

◖ BAREFOOT LANDING

Before the arrival of Broadway at the Beach was the Strand's original high-concept retail and dining complex, Barefoot Landing (4898 U.S. 17 S., 843/272-8349, www.bflanding.com, hours vary). It's less flashy on the surface and certainly more tasteful, but trust me, it's just as commercial.

The centerpiece of the two-decade-old entertainment and shopping complex is **The Alabama Theatre** (4750 U.S. 17 S., 843/272-5758, www.alabama-theatre.com, ticket prices vary), a project of the famed country-and-western band of the same name, who despite their eponymous roots actually got their start gigging in juke joints in the Grand Strand. A stone's throw away is the **House of Blues** (4640 U.S. 17 S., 843/272-3000, www.hob.com), bringing in name acts on an almost nightly basis as well as diners to its excellent restaurant. On some nights you can pose for a picture with a real live tiger cub on your lap at **T.I.G.E.R.S. Preservation Station** (843/361-4552, www.ti-gerfriends.com, hours vary). Shopping is mostly the name of the game here, though.

Alligator Adventure

One of the most popular attractions within Barefoot Landing is Alligator Adventure (www.alligatoradventure.com, $18 adults, $12 ages 4-12, free under age 4). They have hundreds of alligators, yes, but also plenty of turtles, tortoises, snakes, and birds. The otters are a big hit as well. The highlight, though, comes during the daily alligator feedings, when you get a chance to see the real power and barely controlled aggression of these magnificent indigenous beasts. Keep in mind that due to the cold-blooded reptiles' dormant winter nature, the feedings are not held in the colder months.

CHILDREN'S MUSEUM OF SOUTH CAROLINA

A less-expensive form of entertainment with an added educational component at Myrtle

Alligator Adventure

is the Children's Museum of South Carolina (2501 N. Kings Hwy., 843/946-9469, www. cmsckids.org, summer Mon.-Sat. 9 A.M.-4 P.M., $8). This facility tries hard to compete with the splashier attractions in town but still manages to keep a reasonably strong educational focus with programs like "Crime Lab Chemistry," "World of Art," and "Space Adventures."

FAMILY KINGDOM AMUSEMENT AND WATER PARK

For a taste of old-time beachfront amusement park fun, try the Family Kingdom (300 4th Ave. S., 843/626-3471, www.family-kingdom. com, free admission, cost of rides varies) overlooking the Atlantic Ocean. It boasts several good old-school rides, such as the Sling Shot, the Yo-Yo, and everyone's favorite, the wooden Swamp Fox roller coaster with a crazy 110-foot free fall. The attached Water Park, though not a match to the one at Broadway at the Beach, is

a lot of fun, with the requisite slides and a long "lazy river" floating ride.

As Family Kingdom's marketing is quick to point out, one of the big attractions here is the fact that you can look out over the beach itself. I think one of the best things is that there is no admission charge—you pay by the ride (although all-inclusive wristbands are available starting at $24.50). This means parents and grandparents without the stomach for the rides don't have to pay through the nose just to chauffeur the little ones who do.

RIPLEY'S BELIEVE IT OR NOT!

Distinct in all but name from Ripley's Aquarium at Broadway at the Beach, this combo attraction down in the older area of Myrtle Beach—but very close to the brand-new Boardwalk—features several separate, though more or less adjacent, offerings from the venerable Ripley's franchise.

The **Ripley's Believe It or Not! Odditorium** (901 N. Ocean Blvd., 843/448-2331, www.ripleys. com, Sun.-Thurs. 10 A.M.-10 P.M., Fri.-Sat. 10 A.M.-11 P.M., $15 adults, $8 ages 6-11, free under age 6) is your typical Ripley's repository of strange artifacts from around the world, updated with video and computer graphics for the new generation.

Ripley's Haunted Adventure (915 N. Ocean Blvd., 843/448-2331, www.ripleys.com, Sun.-Thurs. noon-10 P.M., Fri.-Sat. noon-11 P.M., $14 adults, $8 ages 6-11, free under age 6) is a sort of scaled-down version of Disney's famous Haunted House ride, with live actors scaring you through three floors.

Ripley's Moving Theater (917 N. Ocean Blvd., 843/448-2331, www.ripleys.com, Sun.-Thurs. 10 A.M.-10 P.M., Fri.-Sat. 10 A.M.-11 P.M., $14 adults, $8 ages 6-11, free under age 6) is a combined ride and movie theater featuring two motion-oriented films screened on a self-contained human conveyor belt, with a sort of kinetic IMAX effect.

WACCATEE ZOOLOGICAL FARM

The closest thing to a bona fide zoo in Myrtle is Waccatee Zoological Farm (8500 Enterprise Rd., 843/650-8500, www.waccateezoo.com,

© JIM MOREKIS

Ripley's Believe It or Not!

daily 10 A.M.-5 P.M., $9 adults, $4 ages 1-12). A humble affair by comparison to the state's premier zoo in Columbia, Waccatee is a totally private venture on 500 acres of land about 15 minutes' drive out of town. There are buffalo, zebras, kangaroos, and emus, many of which the kids will enjoy feeding for a few bucks per bag.

Animal activists be forewarned: Many of the animals are kept in enclosed spaces, and there is a noticeable lack of professionally trained staff.

◖ OCEAN DRIVE BEACH

Less an actual place than a state of mind, the "OD" up in North Myrtle Beach is notable for its role in spawning one of America's great musical genres, beach music. Don't confuse beach music with the Beach Boys or Dick Dale— that's surf music. Beach music, simply put, is music to dance the shag to. Think the Drifters, the Platters, and the Swingin' Medallions.

To experience the OD, go to the intersection of Ocean Boulevard and Main Street and take in the vibe. There's still major shag action going on up here, specifically at several clubs specializing in the genre. If you don't want to shag, don't worry—this is still a charming, laid-back area that's a lot of fun simply to stroll around and enjoy a hot dog or ice cream cone.

CHERRY GROVE PIER

One of the few grand old pavilions left on the southeast coast, North Myrtle's Cherry Grove Pier (3500 N. Ocean Blvd., 843/249-1625, www.cherrygrovepier.com, Sun.-Thurs. 6 A.M.-midnight, 6 A.M.-2 A.M. Fri.-Sat.) was built in the 1950s. Despite remodeling in the late 1990s, it still retains that nostalgic feel, with anglers casting into the waters and kids eating ice cream cones. There's a neat two-story observation deck, and on a clear day you can see North Carolina.

Unusually, this is a privately owned pier. It's particularly popular with anglers, who have their state licensing needs covered by the pier.

Get bait or rent a fishing rod ($20 per day plus refundable $50 deposit) at the **Tackle and Gift Shop** (843/249-1625). They'll also sell you a crab net to cast off the pier ($6, with licenses and permits included).

LA BELLE AMIE VINEYARD

The only vineyard on the Strand, the peaceful and scenic La Belle Amie Vineyard (1120 St. Joseph Rd., 843/399-9463, www.labelleamie. com, Mon.-Sat. 10 A.M.-6 P.M.) in Little River is owned by two sisters, Vicki Weigle and June Bayman, who are descended from this old tobacco plantation's owners (in French the vineyard's name means "beautiful friend," but it's also a play on the family name, Bellamy). You can purchase wine for your own enjoyment or for gifts, or you can just visit the tasting room (Mon.-Sat. 10 A.M.-4:30 P.M.), where a mere $5 pp gets you a sampling of any five wines. Coupons for discounted purchase are available at the tasting room.

TOURS

The number of tours offered in Myrtle Beach is nothing compared to Charleston, this being much more of a "doing" place than a "seeing" place. The most fun and comprehensive tour in the area is **Coastal Safari Jeep Tours** (843/497-5330, www.carolina-safari.com, $38 adults, $20 children), which takes you on a guided tour in a super-size jeep (holding 12-14 people). You'll go well off the commercial path to see such sights on the Waccamaw Neck as old plantations, Civil War sites, and slave cabins as well as hear lots of ghost stories. They'll pick you up at most area hotels.

Entertainment and Events

NIGHTLIFE

Any discussion of Myrtle Beach nightlife must begin with a nod to **The Bowery** (110 9th Ave. N., 843/626-3445, www.thebowerybar.com, 11 A.M.-2 A.M. daily), a country-and-western and Southern-rock spot right off the beach, which has survived several hurricanes since opening in 1944. Its roadhouse-style decor hasn't changed a whole lot since then, other than some cheesy marketing to play up its role in history as the place where the country band Alabama got its start playing for tips in 1973 under the name Wildcountry. They were still playing gigs here when their first hit, "Tennessee River," hit the charts in 1980.

Bands usually crank up here around 9 P.M., and there is a nominal cover charge. There's only one type of draft beer served at The Bowery, at $2.50 per mug, and there is no real dance floor to speak of. If the proud display of Confederate flags doesn't bother you, it's usually a lot of fun.

Once overlooking the now-razed historic Myrtle Beach Pavilion, as of this writing The Bowery is fronted by an empty lot that will presumably be filled by a more modern attraction; if history is any guide, The Bowery will probably outlive it as well. Right next door is The Bowery's "sister bar," **Duffy's** (110 9th Ave. N., 843/626-3445), owned by the same folks and with a similarly down-home vibe, except without the live music.

For a more upscale if definitely less personal and unique experience, Broadway at the Beach hosts the high-profile (some say overrated) national clubs **Planet Hollywood** (2915 Hollywood Dr., 843/448-7827, www.planethollywood.com, hours vary by season) and the **Hard Rock Cafe** (1322 Celebrity Circle, 843/946-0007, www.hardrock.com, Mon.-Sun. 11 A.M.-midnight).

You don't have to be a Parrothead to enjoy **Jimmy Buffett's Margaritaville** (1114

© JIM MOREKIS

The Bowery, where country band Alabama got its start

Celebrity Circle, 843/448-5455, www.margaritaville.com, daily 11 A.M.-midnight) at Broadway at the Beach, actually a pretty enjoyable experience considering it's a national chain. The eponymous margaritas are, of course, the beverage highlight, but they also serve Jimmy's signature LandShark Lager on tap for the beer lovers.

Nearby is the techno- and house music-oriented **Club Kryptonite** (2925 Hollywood Dr., 843/839-9200, www.club-kryptonite.com), more of a full-on nightclub with DJs in both the main room and in the more intimate Cherry Martini Lounge. Hours can be erratic during the off-season.

In addition to its attached live performance space, the **House of Blues** (4640 U.S. 17, 843/272-3000, www.hob.com) at Barefoot Landing features a hopping bar in its dining area, situated amid a plethora of folk art reminiscent of the Mississippi Delta. Most nights feature live entertainment on a small stage starting at about 10 P.M.

SHAG DANCING

North Myrtle Beach is the nexus of that Carolina-based dance known as the shag. There are several clubs in town that have made a name for themselves as the unofficial "shag clubs" of South Carolina. The two main ones are **Duck's** (229 Main St., 843/249-3858, www.ducksatoceandrive.com) and **Fat Harold's** (210 Main St., 843/249-5779, www.fatharolds.com). There's also **The Pirate's Cove** (205 Main St., 843/249-8942).

Another fondly regarded spot is the **OD Pavilion** (91 S. Ocean Blvd., 843/280-0715), a.k.a. the Sunset Grill or "Pam's Palace," on the same site as the old Roberts Pavilion that was destroyed by 1954's Hurricane Hazel. Legend has it this was where the shag was born. Also in North Myrtle, the **Ocean Drive Beach Club** (100 S. Ocean Blvd., 843/249-6460), a.k.a. "the OD Lounge," inside the Ocean Drive Beach and Golf Resort, specializes in shag dancing most days after 4 P.M. The resort is a focal point of local shag conventions and is even home to the **Shaggers Hall of Fame.** Also inside the Ocean Drive Resort is another popular shag club, **The Spanish Galleon** (100 N. Ocean Blvd., 843/249-1047), a.k.a. "The Galleon."

Key local shag events, which are quite well attended, include the **National Shag Dance Championships** (www.shagnationals.com, Jan.-Mar.), the **Spring Safari** (www.shagdance.com, Apr.), and the **Fall Migration** (www.shagdance.com, mid-Sept.).

THE ARTS
◖ Carolina Opry

Nothing can duplicate the experience of the Grand Ole Opry in Nashville, but don't snicker at Myrtle's Carolina Opry (8901-A Business U.S. 17, 800/843-6779, www.thecarolinaopry.com, showtimes and ticket prices vary). Since 1986 this well-respected stage show, begun by legendary promoter Calvin Gilmore, has packed 'em in at the Grand Strand. It is a hoot for country music fans and city slickers alike.

The main focus is the regular Opry show, done in the classic, free-wheeling, fast-moving variety format known to generations of old-school country fans from the original Opry. Some of the humor is corny, and the brief but open displays of patriotic and faith-based music aren't necessarily for everyone and might be slightly confusing given the emphasis on sexy and accomplished female dancers. But there's no arguing the high energy and vocal and instrumental abilities of these very professional singers, instrumentalists, and dancers, who gamely take on hits through the generations ranging from bluegrass to Motown, pop, and modern country.

The Carolina Opry augments its regular music, comedy, and dance show with a seasonal Christmas special, which is highly popular and sells out even faster than the regular shows, often six or more months in advance. There is generally one other bit of specialty programming each year, such as the recent *Good Vibrations* pop hits revue.

The 2,200-seat Carolina Opry theater, while no match for Nashville's classic Ryman Auditorium, is pretty classy for a venue only built in 1992.

Legends in Concert

Way down in Surfside Beach, where the big buildup on the Strand begins, you'll find *Legends in Concert* (301 Business U.S. 17, 843/238-7827, www.legendsinconcert.com, prices vary), a popular rotating show of celebrity impersonators from Elvis to Barbra Streisand. As cheesy as that sounds, the resemblances can be quite uncanny, and the shows are quite entertaining.

House of Blues

Besides being a great place for dinner, on the other side of the restaurant is the stage for the House of Blues (4640 U.S. 17 S., 843/272-3000, www.hob.com, prices vary) at Barefoot Landing in North Myrtle Beach. They bring some pretty happening names in R&B, straight blues, and rock-and-roll to this fun venue dedicated to preserving old-school music and live performance.

Medieval Times

Oh, come on—what's not to like about bountiful feasts, juggling jesters, skillful falconers, fetching maidens, and brave jousting knights? At Medieval Times (2904 Fantasy Way, 843/236-4635, www.medievaltimes.com, $51 adults, $31 under age 13) you'll get all that and more. The kitsch quotient is high at this Renaissance Faire on steroids, a live-action story line featuring plenty of stage combat, music, and a steady stream of culinary items for your enjoyment (and yes, there's a full bar for those of drinking age). But there's an honest-to-goodness educational element as well: You'll be eating everything with your hands—no utensils in the 11th century—and most of the action and history is roughly authentic. The price may seem high at first glance, but keep in mind you're getting a hearty full dinner plus a two-hour stage show.

THE STORY OF THE SHAG

Judy's House of Oldies deals in rare shag music recordings.

In South Carolina, the shag is neither a type of rug nor what Austin Powers does in his spare time. It's a dance—a smooth, laid-back, happy dance done to that equally smooth, laid-back, happy kind of rhythm-and-blues called beach music (not to be confused with surf music such as the Beach Boys). The boys twirl the girls while their feet kick and slide around with a minimum of upper-body movement—the better to stay cool in the Carolina heat.

Descended from the Charleston, another indigenous Palmetto State dance, the shag originated on the Strand sometime in the 1930s, when the popular Collegiate Shag was slowed down to the subgenre now called the Carolina Shag. While shag scholars differ as to the exact spawning ground, there's a consensus that North Myrtle Beach's Ocean Drive, or "OD" in local patois, became the home of the modern shag sometime in the mid-1940s.

Legend has it that the real shag was born when white teenagers, "jumping the Jim Crow rope" by watching dancers at black nightclubs in the segregated South, brought those moves back to the beach and added their own twists.

Indeed, while the shag has always been primarily practiced by white people, many of the leading beach music bands were (and still are) African American.

By the mid-late 1950s the shag, often called simply "the basic" or "the fas' dance," was all the rage with the Strand's young people, who gathered at beachfront pavilions and in local juke joints called beach clubs, courting each other to the sounds of early beach music greats like the Drifters, the Clovers, and Maurice Williams and the Zodiacs. This is the time period most fondly remembered by today's shaggers, a time of penny loafers (no socks!), poodle skirts, and 45-rpm records, when the sea breeze was the only air-conditioning.

The shag is practiced today by a graying but devoted cadre of older fans, with a vanguard of younger practitioners keeping the art form alive. A coterie of North Myrtle clubs specializes in the dance, while the area hosts several large-scale gatherings of shag aficionados each year.

To immerse yourself in shag culture, head on up to Ocean Drive Beach in North Myrtle at the intersection of Ocean Boulevard and Main Street and look down at the platters in the sidewalk marking the **Shaggers Walk of Fame.** Walk a couple of blocks up to the corner of Main Street and Hillside Drive and visit the mecca of beach music stores, **Judy's House of Oldies** (300 Main St., 843/249-8649, www.judyshouseofoldies.com, Mon.-Sat. 9 A.M.-6 P.M.). They also sell instructional DVDs.

To get a taste of the dance itself, stop by the **OD Pavilion** (91 S. Ocean Blvd., 843/280-0715), **Duck's** (229 Main St., 843/249-3858, www.ducksatoceandrive.com), or **Fat Harolds** (210 Main St., 843/249-5779, www.fatharolds.com), or visit **The Spanish Galleon** (100 N. Ocean Blvd., 843/249-1047) inside the Ocean Drive Beach Resort. If you're interested, don't be shy. Shaggers are notoriously gregarious and eager to show off their stock-in-trade. It's easy to learn, it's family-friendly, and there will be no shortage of pleasant young-at-heart shaggers around who will be happy to teach you the steps.

Carolina Opry

© JIM MOREKIS

Pirate's Voyage

Sharing a parking lot with the Carolina Opry is Pirate's Voyage (8901-B N. Kings Hwy., 843/497-9700, www.piratesvoyage.com, $42 adults, $22 ages 4-11), the newest entertainment attraction to hit Myrtle Beach. Affiliated with Dolly Parton's entertainment empire—her "Dixie Stampede" originally occupied this building—Pirate's Voyage takes you on a rollicking two-hour trip into the world of buccaneers, with fighting, lost treasure, dancing, acrobatics, mermaids, and assorted high-seas drama, all with photographers on hand to document your experience...for a price, me hearties. Like Medieval Times, this is essentially dinner theater with three shows a day in the high season of late summer, offering a variety of suitably swashbuckling menu items like chicken, pork, and fried shrimp. OK, so you don't come here for the food.

The Alabama Theatre

The Alabama Theatre (4750 U.S. 17, 843/272-5758, www.alabama-theatre.com, ticket prices vary) at Barefoot Landing in North Myrtle Beach focuses on the long-running song-and-dance revue *One: The Show* as well as big-name acts who may be past their prime but are still able to fill seats, such as the Oakridge Boys, George Jones, Kenny Rogers, and, of course, the eponymous troubadours Alabama, who got their big break while playing at Myrtle Beach. It's not all country, though—Motown and beach music acts like the Temptations and the Platters are often featured as well. As with the Carolina Opry, Barefoot Landing has its own Christmas special, and as with the Opry's offering, this one sells out well in advance.

Palace Theatre

The Palace Theatre (1420 Celebrity Circle, 800/905-4228, www.palacetheatremyrtle-beach.com, ticket prices vary) at Broadway at the Beach offers a variety of toned-down Vegas-style entertainment. The most recent show was *Le*

Grande Cirque, a family-friendly version of the kind of show made famous by Cirque du Soleil.

CINEMA

At Broadway on the Beach, there's a multiplex, Carmike's **Broadway Cinema 16** (843/445-1600, www.carmike.com). Other movie theaters include the **Cinemark** (2100 Coastal Grand Circle, 843/839-3221, www.cinemark.com) at the Coastal Grand Mall and the massive new **Grand 14 at the Market Common** (4002 Deville St., 843/282-0550) at the multiuse Market Common, actually a repurposed Air Force base.

FESTIVALS AND EVENTS

Interestingly, most events in Myrtle Beach don't happen during the three-month high season of June-August, mostly because it's so darn hot that all anyone wants to do is get in the water.

Winter

The Grand Strand is the birthplace of the dance called the shag, and each winter for the last 25 years the **National Shag Dance Championships** (2000 N. Kings Hwy., 843/497-7369, www.shagnationals.com, from $15 per night) have been the pinnacle of the art form. Beginning with preliminaries in January, contestants in five age ranges compete for a variety of awards, culminating in the finals the first week in March. The level of professionalism might amaze you—for such a lazy-looking dance, these are serious competitors.

Spring

You might not automatically associate our colder neighbor to the north with Myrtle Beach, but **Canadian American Days** (various venues, www.myrtlebeachinfo.com, free), or "Can Am," brings tens of thousands of visitors of both nationalities to sites all over the Strand each March to enjoy a variety of musical and cultural events. Always on top of marketing opportunities, the Myrtle Beach Chamber

© JIM MOREKIS

MYRTLE BEACH

House of Blues at Barefoot Landing

of Commerce makes sure this happens during Ontario's spring holidays to ensure maximum north-of-the-border attendance. While most of the events have little or nothing to do with Canada itself, this is basically a great excuse for Canucks to get some Carolina sunshine.

The **Spring Games and Kite Flying Contest** (843/448-7881, free) brings an exciting array of airborne craft to the Strand in front of Broadway on the Beach on an April weekend as the springtime winds peak.

Also in April is the area's second-largest shag event, the **Society of Stranders Spring Safari** (www.shagdance.com). Several clubs in North Myrtle Beach participate in hosting shag dancers from all over for a week of, well, shagging.

The biggest single event in Myrtle Beach happens in May with the **Spring Bike Rally** (various venues, www.myrtlebeachbikeweek.com, free), always known simply as "Bike Week." In this nearly 70-year-old event, over 250,000 Harley-Davidson riders and their

MYRTLE BEACH

MOTORCYCLE MADNESS

Growling engines? Spinning tires? Patriotic colors? Polished chrome? Bikini car washes? Erotic bull-riding contests? That is the spectacle known as Myrtle Beach Bike Week, one of the largest gatherings of Harley-Davidson enthusiasts on the East Coast and one of the oldest, at about 65 years.

The event has historically happened each May on the weekend before Memorial Day weekend, bringing over 250,000 motorcyclists and their entourages to town for 10 days of riding, bragging, and carousing. South Carolina's lack of a helmet law is a particular draw to these freedom-cherishing motorcyclists. A few days later, on Memorial Day weekend, there's another bike rally, this one simply called Black Bike Week. Nearly as large as the regular Bike Week, the focus is on African American riders and their machines.

Contrary to stereotype, there's not much of an increase in crime during either Bike Week. Regardless, they are widely known as a particularly bad time to bring families to the area, and therein lies the controversy. Joining other municipalities around the nation in discourag-

ing motorcycle rallies, the city of Myrtle Beach has enacted tough measures to force the bike rallies to leave town and make the area more family-friendly during that time. Most controversial among recent measures was a municipal helmet law, enforceable only within Myrtle Beach city limits, that was later struck down by the South Carolina Supreme Court. Other, still-standing measures include stringent noise ordinances designed to include the roaring, rattling tailpipes of pretty much every Harley ever made. The separate municipality of North Myrtle Beach, however, has made it clear that bikers are welcome there even if they're non grata a few miles to the south.

As of now, it seems that the rallies will remain on the Strand rather than gun their collective throttle and head elsewhere, as they occasionally threaten to do when relations with local municipalities and police departments get too tense. The upshot for the nonmotorcyclist visitor? Bikers are somewhat less of a factor than in years past, and certainly local police are taking them more seriously. But the time around Memorial Day is still as crowded as ever.

---

entourages gather to cruise around the place, admire each other's custom rides, and generally party their patooties off. While the typical Harley dude these days is getting on in years and is probably a mild-mannered store manager in regular life, young or old they all do their best to let their hair down at this festive event. Dozens of related events go on throughout the week at venues all over the Strand, from tough-man contests to "foxy boxing" matches to wet T-shirt contests. You get the picture—it's not for the politically correct or for young children.

Summer

Right after the Spring Bike Rally is the **Atlantic Beach Bikefest** (various venues), on Memorial Day weekend, much more commonly referred

to as "Black Bike Week." This event started in the 1980s and is spiritually based in Atlantic Beach, formerly the area's "black beach" during the days of segregation. It sees over 200,000 African American motorcycle enthusiasts gather in Myrtle Beach for a similar menu of partying, bikini contests, cruising, and the like. While the existence of separate events often reminds some people of the state's unfortunate history of segregation, supporters of both Bike Week and Black Bike Week insist it's not a big deal, and that bikers of either race are welcome at either event.

Kicking off with a festive parade, the 50-year-old **Sun Fun Festival** (various venues, www.grandstrandevents.com), generally held the weekend after Memorial Day weekend, signals the real beginning of the summer season with bikini contests, Jet Ski races, parades, air shows, and concerts galore.

The **City of Myrtle Beach Independence Day Celebration** (www.cityofmyrtlebeach. com, free) each July 4 weekend is when the largest number of visitors is in Myrtle Beach. It's fun, it's hot, there's fireworks aplenty, and boy, is it crowded.

Fall

For a week in mid-September, North Myrtle Beach hosts one of the world's largest shag dancing celebrations, the **Society of Stranders Fall Migration** (www.shagdance.com, free). Head up to the intersection of Ocean Drive and Main Street to hear the sounds of this unique genre, and party with the shaggers at various local clubs. If you don't know the steps, don't worry—instructors are usually on hand.

There's another, smaller Harley riders' rally the first week in October, the **Fall Motorcycle Rally** (various venues, www.myrtlebeachbike-week.com, free).

Thanksgiving Day weekend, when the beaches are much less crowded and the hotels much cheaper, is the **South Carolina Bluegrass Festival** (2101 N. Oak St., 706/864-7203, www.aandabluegrass.com, $30 adults, $20 ages 6-13, free under age 6), a delightful and well-attended event at the Myrtle Beach Convention Center, celebrating the Appalachian music tradition in a coastal setting with some of the biggest names in the genre.

Shopping

Shopping on the Grand Strand is strongly destination-oriented. You tend to find shops of similar price points and merchandise types clustered together in convenient locations: Upscale shops are in one place and discount and outlet stores in another. Here's a rundown of the main retail areas on the Strand with some of the standout shops.

BROADWAY AT THE BEACH

The sprawling Broadway at the Beach complex (U.S. 17 Bypass and 21st Ave. N., www. broadwayatthebeach.com, hours vary) has scads of stores, some of which are quite interesting and rise well beyond tourist schlock. There are maps and directories of the site available at various kiosks around the area.

One of my favorite shops is **Retroactive** (843/916-1218, www.shopretroactive.com), a shop specializing in '70s and '80s styles and kitsch, with some of the best (and wittiest) pop-culture T-shirts I've seen. The owners are frank about their continuing obsession with '80s hair bands. Another awesome T-shirt and trinket shop that the kids and teens will particularly enjoy is **Stupid Factory** (843/448-1100). There are lots of mediocre sports apparel stores out there, but **Sports Fanatics** (843/445-2585) has an amazing collection of jerseys, shirts, and lids, primarily focused on pro teams. The kids—and those with a sweet tooth—will go crazy in the aptly named **It'SUGAR** (843/916-1300, www.itsugar.com), a store dedicated to just about any kind of candy and candy-themed merchandise you can think of, from modern brands to retro favorites. If the packaged or bulk varieties don't float your boat, you can design your own massive chocolate bar. And, of course, this being Myrtle Beach, there's a **Harley Davidson** (843/293-5555) gift store with Hog-oriented merch galore.

The bottom line on Broadway at the Beach, though, is that it's made for walking around and browsing. Just bring your walking shoes—the place is huge—and keep in mind that there's not a lot of shade.

© JIM MOREKIS

a typical storefront at Broadway at the Beach

BAREFOOT LANDING

There are over 100 shops at Barefoot Landing (4898 U.S. 17 S., 843/272-8349, www.bfland-ing.com, hours vary) in North Myrtle Beach—as well as one cool old-fashioned carousel—but perhaps the most unique spot is **T.I.G.E.R.S. Preservation Station** (843/361-4552, www.tigerfriends.com, hours vary), where you get the opportunity to have your picture taken with a live tiger or lion cub. This is the fund-raising arm of a local organization for conservation of the big cats as well as gorillas and monkeys, so the service isn't cheap. Portraits begin at about $60 to pose with a single critter and go up from there depending on the number of animals you want to pose with. However, you don't pay per person, so the whole family can get in the shot for the same price as a child. It may sound like a lot of money, but this is truly a once-in-a-life-time experience. An attendant takes the animal of your choice out of a spacious holding area, places it on your lap, and a photographer takes

the shot. Sometimes you can hold a milk bottle to the cub's mouth. If you don't want to spring for a photo, you can just watch the frolicking (or more often, slumbering) cubs up close from behind a transparent wall. They're unbelievably cute, as you can imagine.

Just relocated to the Strand from their grape yards in Chester, South Carolina, is **Carolina Vineyards Winery** (843/361-9181, www.carolinavineyards.com). Buy wine as a gift, or taste any seven of their labels for only $3.

There are magic shops, and then there are *magic shops.* **Conley's House of Magic** (843/272-4227, http://conleyshouseofmagic.com) is definitely the latter. Packed in this relatively small space is just about every legendary trick and trick deck known to the magician's art, along with a cool variety of magic books teaching you, in deadly serious fashion, the innermost secrets of the trade. **Toys & Co.** (843/663-0748, www.toysandco.com) carries a wide range of toys and games, with an emphasis

© JIM MOREKIS

Meet a tiger cub at Barefoot Landing.

on way-cool European-style brands you won't see at the local Wal-Mart.

THE MARKET COMMON

One of the most hotly anticipated and cutting-edge things to hit Myrtle Beach in years, The Market Common (4017 Deville St., www.marketcommonmb.com, hours vary) is an ambitious residential-retail mixed-use development opened for business on the site of the decommissioned Myrtle Beach Air Force Base. While its location near the Myrtle Beach International Airport means it's not exactly amid the sun-and-fun action (possibly a good thing, depending on the season), the very pedestrian-friendly development style and tasteful shops might provide a refreshing change of pace.

There are three dozen (and counting) stores, including Anthropologie, Williams-Sonoma, Copper Penny, Chico's, Brooks Brothers, Fossil, Banana Republic, Barnes & Noble, and Jake and Company ("Life Is Good"). There are plenty of restaurants, including Ultimate California Pizza and P. F. Chang's, and a large multiplex movie theater.

For those interested in how the sprawling old base was closed in the 1990s and repurposed so completely, there's interpretive signage all around the pedestrian mall and along the roadways leading to it. At the Market Common's entrance is Warbird Park, a well-done veterans memorial featuring an Air Force A-10 attack aircraft, an F-100 Super Sabre, and a Corsair II.

MALLS

The premier mall in the area is **Coastal Grand Mall** (2000 Coastal Grand Circle, 843/839-9100, www.coastalgrand.com, Mon.-Sat. 10 A.M.-9 P.M., Sun. noon-6 P.M.) at the U.S. 17 Bypass and U.S. 501. It's anchored by Belk, J. C. Penney, Sears, Dillard's, and Dick's Sporting Goods.

Your basic meat-and-potatoes mall, **Myrtle Beach Mall** (10177 N. Kings Hwy., 843/272-4040, http://shopmyrtlebeachmall.com,

The Market Common's innovative repurposing of the old Myrtle Beach Air Force Base

whalesnauticalgifts.com), **Wing's Beachwear** (www.wingsbeachwear.com), and **Bargain Beachwear (www.bargainbeachwear.com)** These are the kinds of places to get assorted bric-a-brac and items for your beach visit. The quality isn't that bad, and the prices are uniformly low.

OUTLET MALLS

There are two massive **Tanger Outlets** (www.tangeroutlet.com) at Myrtle Beach: **Tanger Outlet North** (10835 Kings Rd., 843/449-0491) off Kings Road/U.S. 17, and **Tanger Outlet South** (4635 Factory Stores Blvd., 843/236-5100) off U.S. 501. Both offer over 100 factory outlet stores of almost every imaginable segment, from Fossil to Disney, OshKosh B'Gosh to Timberland. Full food courts are available, and many folks easily spend an entire day here.

For years, busloads of hard-core shoppers from throughout the South have taken organized trips to the Grand Strand specifically to shop at **Waccamaw Factory Shoppes** (3071 Waccamaw Blvd., 843/236-8200). Their passion hasn't abated, as new generations of shopaholics get the fever to come here and browse the often deeply discounted offerings at row after row of outlet stores. There are actually two locations, the Factory Shoppes themselves and the nearby **Waccamaw Pottery** (3200 Pottery Dr., 843/236-6152). Bring your walking shoes (or buy some new ones at one of the many shoe stores), but don't worry about getting from one mall to the other—there's a free shuttle.

Mon.-Sat. 10 A.M.-9 P.M., Sun. noon-6 P.M.) is anchored by Belk, J. C. Penney, and Bass Pro Shops.

DISCOUNT BEACHWEAR

Literally dozens of cavernous, tacky, deep-discount T-shirt-and-towel type places are spread up and down Kings Highway like mushrooms after a rain. The vast majority of them belong to one of several well-established chains: **Eagles Beachwear** (www.eaglesbeachwear.net), **Whales** (www.

Sports and Recreation

Myrtle Beach's middle name might as well be recreation. While some of the local variety tends toward overkill—I personally loathe Jet Skis, for example—there's no denying that if it involves outdoor activity, it's probably offered here. For general info, visit www.grandstrandevents.com. For municipal recreation info, visit www.cityofmyrtlebeach.com.

ON THE WATER
Beaches
The center of activity is on the Strand itself: miles of user-friendly beaches. They're not the most beautiful in the world, but they're nice enough, and access is certainly no problem. In Myrtle Beach and North Myrtle Beach, you'll find clearly designated public access points off Ocean Boulevard, some with parking and some without. Both municipalities run well-marked public parking lots at various points, some of which are free during the off-season.

Dog owners will be pleased to know that May 15-September 15, dogs are allowed on the beach before 9 A.M. and after 5 P.M. September 15-May 15, dogs are allowed on the beach at any time of day.

Restrict your swimming to within 150 feet of shore. Surfside Beach to the south is a no-smoking beach with access points at 16th Avenue North, 6th Avenue North, 3rd Avenue North, Surfside Pier, 3rd Avenue South, 4th Avenue South, 13th Avenue South, and Melody Lane.

Surfing
There's a steady, if low-key, surf scene in Myrtle Beach despite the fact that the surfing is not really that good and the sport is restricted to certain areas of the beach during the busy summer season. The rules are a little complicated. In Myrtle Beach proper, surfing is only allowed April 15-September 15 daily 10 A.M.-5 P.M. in the following zones:

- 29th Avenue South to the southern city limits
- 37th Avenue North to 47th Avenue North
- 62nd Avenue North to 68th Avenue North
- 82nd Avenue North to northern city limits

Up in North Myrtle Beach, surfers must stay in the following zones May 15-September 15 daily 9 A.M.-4 P.M.:

- Cherry Grove Pier
- 6th Avenue North
- 13th Avenue South
- 28th Avenue South
- 38th Avenue South

Down at Surfside Beach, surfing is restricted to the following zones, year-round daily 10 A.M.-5 P.M.:

- 12th Avenue North to 14th Avenue North
- Melody Lane to 13th Avenue South

The oldest surf shop in the area, south of Myrtle in Garden City Beach, is the **Village Surf Shoppe** (500 Atlantic Ave., 843/651-6396, www.villagesurf.com), which has catered to the Strand's growing surf scene since 1969. Nearly as old is the **Surf City Surf Shop** (1758 U.S. 17 S., 843/272-1090; 3001 N. Kings Hwy., 843/626-5412, www.surfcitysurfshop.com) franchise in Myrtle proper.

Diving
Diving is popular on the Strand. As with fishing, many trips depart from Little River just above North Myrtle Beach. Offshore features include many historic wrecks, including the post-Civil War wreck of the USS *Sherman* offshore of Little River, and artificial reefs such as the famed "Barracuda Alley," teeming with marine life, off Myrtle Beach.

Coastal Scuba (1901 U.S. 17 S., 843/361-3323, www.coastalscuba.com) in North Myrtle is a large operator, offering several different dive tours.

Parasailing, Windsurfing, and Jet Skis

Ocean Watersports (405 S. Ocean Blvd., 843/445-7777, www.parasailmyrtlebeach.com) takes groups up to six on well-supervised, well-equipped parasailing adventures (about $50 pp), with tandem and triple flights available. Observers can go out on the boat for about $20. They also rent Jet Skis and offer "banana boat" rides ($15) in which a long—yes, banana-shaped—raft, straddled by several riders, is towed by a boat up and down the beach.

Downwind Watersports (2915 S. Ocean Blvd., 843/448-7245, www.downwindsailsmyrtlebeach.com) has similar offerings, with the addition of good old-fashioned sailboat lessons and rentals ($16). Parasailing is about $65 pp single ride, banana boats are $16 for 20 minutes, and Jet Ski rentals about $100 per hour.

Farther up the Strand in North Myrtle, between Cherry Grove Beach and Little River, you'll find **Thomas Outdoors Watersports** (2200 Little River Neck Rd., 843/280-2448, www.mbjetski.com), which rents kayaks in addition to Jet Skis and pontoon boats. They offer several Jet Ski tours ($75-125), including a dolphin-watching trip, as well as all-day kayak rental ($45 pp).

Fishing

Most fishing on the Strand is saltwater, with charters, most based in Little River, taking anglers well into Atlantic waters. Tuna, wahoo, mackerel, and dolphin (not the mammal!) are big in the hot months, while snapper and grouper are caught year-round but are best in the colder months.

A good operator up in Little River is **Longway Fishing Charters** (843/249-7813, www.longwaycharters.com), which specializes in offshore fishing. Another in the same area is **Capt. Smiley's Inshore Fishing** (843/361-7445, www.captainsmileyfishingcharters.com). **Fish Hook Charters** (2200 Little River Neck Rd., 843/283-7692, www.fishhookcharters.com) takes a 34-foot boat out from North Myrtle Beach.

For surf fishing on the beach, you do not need a license of any type. All other types of fishing require a valid South Carolina fishing license, available for a nominal fee online (http://dnr.sc.gov) or at any tackle shop and most grocery stores.

Cruises

Except in the winter months, there are plenty of places to cruise in the Strand, from Little River down to Murrells Inlet, from the Waccamaw River to the Intracoastal Waterway. The **Great American Riverboat Company** (8496 Enterprise Rd., 843/650-6600, www.mbriverboat.com) offers sightseeing and dinner cruises along the Intracoastal Waterway. **Island Song Charters** (4374 Landing Rd., 843/467-7088, www.islandsongcharters.com) out of Little River takes you on sunset and dolphin cruises on the 32-foot sailboat *Island Song*.

Up in North Myrtle, **Getaway Adventures** (843/663-1100, www.myrtlebeachboatcruises.com) specializes in dolphin tours. Also in North Myrtle, **Thomas Outdoors Watersports** (2200 Little River Neck Rd., 843/280-2448, www.mbjetski.com) runs dolphin cruises.

ON LAND
Golf

The Grand Strand in general, and Myrtle Beach in particular, is world golf central. There are over 120 courses in this comparatively small area, and if golfers can't find something they like here, they need to sell their clubs. While the number of truly great courses is few—the best courses are farther down the Strand near Pawleys Island—the quality overall is still quite high.

A great bonus is affordability. Partially because of dramatically increased competition due to the glut of courses, and partially because of savvy regional marketing, green fees here are significantly lower than you might expect, in many cases under $100. For even more savings, finding a golf-lodging package deal in Myrtle

Beach is like finding sand on the beach—almost too easy. Check with your hotel to see if they offer any golf packages. At any time of year, some good one-stop shops on the Internet are at www.mbn.com and www.myrtlebeachgolf.com.

Some highlights of area golf include the Davis Love III-designed course at **Barefoot Resort** (4980 Barefoot Resort Ridge Rd., 843/390-3200, www.barefootgolf.com, $105-185) in North Myrtle, maybe the best in the Strand outside Pawleys Island. Or would that be the Greg Norman course, or the Tom Fazio course, or the Pete Dye course, all also at Barefoot? You get the picture.

Also up near North Myrtle is a favorite with visitors and locals alike, the challenging **Glen Dornoch Golf Club** (4840 Glen Dornoch Way, 800/717-8784, www.glensgolfgroup.com, from $100), on 260 beautiful acres. Affiliated with Glen Dornoch are the 27 holes at Little River's **Heather Glen** (4650 Heather Glen Way, 800/868-4536, www.glensgolfgroup.com), which are divided into Red, White, and Blue courses. They combine for what's consistently rated one of the best public courses in the United States.

And no list of area golf is complete without a nod to **Myrtle Beach National** (4900 National Dr., 843/347-4298, www.mbn.com, from $80). With three distinct courses—King's North, West, and South Creek, with its South Carolina-shaped sand trap at hole 3—the National is one of the state's legendary courses, not to mention a heck of a deal.

Miniature Golf

Don't scoff—miniature golf, or "putt-putt" to an older generation, is a big deal in Myrtle Beach. If you thought there were a lot of regular golf courses here, the 50 miniature golf courses will also blow your mind. Sadly, almost all of the classic old-school miniature golf courses are no more, victims of the demand for increased production values and modernized gimmick

holes. But here are some of the standouts, including the best of the North Myrtle courses as well; prices listed are for 18 holes.

The most garishly wonderful course is the completely over-the-top **Mount Atlanticus Minotaur Goff** (707 N. Kings Hwy., 843/444-1008, www.mountatlanticus.com, $10) down near the older section of Myrtle. And yes, that's how it's spelled—get it? Legend has it that this one course cost $3 million to build. Literally the stuff of dreams—or maybe hallucinations—this sprawling course mixes the mythological with the nautical to wonderful effect. You don't actually encounter the Minotaur until the bonus 19th hole, a fiendish water trap. If you get a hole in one, you get free golf here for life.

Hawaiian Rumble (3210 U.S. 17, 843/458-2585, www.prominigolf.com) in North Myrtle is not only a heck of a fun, attractive course, it's also the headquarters of the official training center for the U.S. Professional Miniature Golf Association (the folks who generally get a hole in one on every hole). The Rumble's sister course is **Hawaiian Village** (4205 U.S. 17, 843/361-9629, www.prominigolf.com) in North Myrtle, which is also the home of serious professional miniature golf competitions.

For a bit of retro action, try **Rainbow Falls** (9550 Kings Hwy., 843/497-2557). It's not as garish as some of the newer courses, but fans of old-school putt-putt will love it.

While at Broadway at the Beach, you might want to try the popular medieval-themed **Dragon's Lair** (1197 Celebrity Circle, 843/913-9301, hours vary by season). Yep, it has a 30-foot fire-breathing dragon, Sir Alfred, that you have to make your way around. While the dinosaur craze has cooled somewhat, the golf at **Jurassic Golf** (445 29th Ave., 843/448-2116), festooned with dozens of velociraptors and the like, certainly has stayed hot. There is a similarly themed site in North Myrtle, the new **Dinosaur Adventure** (700 7th Ave., 843/272-8041).

Tennis

There are over 200 tennis courts in the Myrtle Beach area. The main municipal site is the **Myrtle Beach Tennis Center** (3302 Robert Grissom Pkwy., 843/918-2440, www.myrtlebeachtennis.com, $2 pp per hour), which has 10 courts, eight of them lighted. The city also runs six lighted courts at **Midway Park** (U.S. 17 and 19th Ave. S.).

The privately owned **Kingston Plantation** (843/497-2444, www.kingstonplantation.com) specializes in tennis vacations, and you don't even have to be a guest. They have a pro on staff and offer lessons. Down in Pawleys Island, the **Litchfield Beach and Golf Resort** (14276 Ocean Hwy., 866/538-0187, www.litchfieldbeach.com) has two dozen nice courts.

Cycling

In Myrtle Beach, when they say "biker," they mean a Harley dude. Bicycling—or safe bicycling, anyway—is largely limited to fat-tire riding along the beach and easy pedaling through the quiet residential neighborhoods near Little River. There is a bike lane on North Ocean Boulevard from about 29th Avenue North to about 82nd Avenue North. Riding on the sidewalk is strictly prohibited.

As for bike rentals, a good operator is **Beach Bike Shop** (711 Broadway St., 843/448-5335, www.beachbikeshop.com). In North Myrtle, try **Wheel Fun Rentals** (91 S. Ocean Blvd., 843/280-7900, www.wheelfunrentals.com).

Horseback Riding

A horse ride along the surf is a nearly iconic image of South Carolina, combining two of the state's chief pursuits: equestrian sports and hanging out on the beach. A great way to enjoy a horseback ride along the Grand Strand without having to bring your own equine is to check out **Horseback Riding of Myrtle Beach** (843/294-1712, www.myrtlebeachhorserides.com). They offer a variety of group rides, each with a guide, going to nature-preserve or beach locales. While they'll take you out any day of the week, advance reservations are required. Ninety minutes on a nature preserve costs about $50 pp, while a 90-minute ride on the beach is about $75 pp.

You can go horseback riding on Myrtle Beach from the third Saturday in November until the end of February, with these conditions: You must access the beach from Myrtle Beach State Park, you cannot ride over sand dunes in any way, and you must clean up after your horse.

SPECTATOR SPORTS

Playing April-early September in a large new stadium near Broadway at the Beach are the **Myrtle Beach Pelicans** (1251 21st Ave. N., 843/918-6000, www.myrtlebeachpelicans.com, $8-11), a single-A affiliate of the Atlanta Braves playing in the Carolina League.

NASCAR fans already know of the **Myrtle Beach Speedway** (455 Hospitality Lane, www.myrtlebeachspeedway.com, $12, free under age 10) off U.S. 501, one of the more vintage tracks in the country, dating back to 1958 (it was actually a dirt track well into the 1970s). Currently the main draw are the NASCAR Whelen All-American Series races (Apr.-Nov. Sat. 7:30 P.M.).

Other spectator sports in the area tend to revolve around the Chanticleer teams of **Coastal Carolina University** (132 Chanticleer Dr. W., 843/347-8499, www.goccusports.com) just inland from Myrtle Beach in Conway. They play football in the Big South Conference. By the way, *chanticleer* is an old name for a rooster, and in this case is a self-conscious derivative of the mascot of the University of South Carolina, the gamecock.

Accommodations

There is no dearth of lodging in the Myrtle Beach area, from the typical high-rise "resorts" (think condos on steroids) to chain hotels, vacation villas, house rentals, and camping. Because of the plethora of options, prices are generally reasonable, and competition to provide more and more on-site amenities—free breakfasts, "lazy river" pools, washers and dryers, hot tubs, poolside grills, and so on—has only increased. You are the beneficiary, so you might as well take advantage of it.

Note that the stated price range may be very broad because so many Myrtle Beach lodgings offer several room options, from one-bed guest rooms to full three-bedroom suites. Here are a few general tips to consider when booking a room:

- The larger suites are generally "condo apartments," meaning they're privately owned. While they're usually immaculately clean for your arrival, it means that housekeeping is minimal and you won't get lots of complimentary goodies whenever you call the front desk.

- The entire Myrtle Beach area is undergoing growth, and that includes the accommodations. This means that many properties have older sections and newer ones. Ask beforehand which section you're being booked in.

- Check www.myrtlebeachhotels.com for last-minute deals and specials at 11 well-run local resorts.

- By the end of September, prices drop dramatically.

- Almost all area lodgings, especially the highrises, feature on-site pools galore, lounge chairs and tables are at a premium and go very quickly during high season when the sun's out.

- Always keep in mind that summer is the high season here, unlike the rest of South Carolina, and guest rooms, especially at beachfront places, get snapped up very early.

UNDER $150

For 75 years, **◖Driftwood on the Oceanfront** (1600 N. Ocean Blvd., 843/448-1544, www.

driftwoodlodge.com, $100-120) has been a favorite place to stay. Upgraded over the years, but not *too* upgraded, this low five-story 90-room complex is family-owned and takes pride in delivering personalized service that is simply impossible to attain in the larger high-rises nearby. As you'd expect, the guest rooms and suites are a bit on the small side by modern Myrtle Beach standards—with none of the increasingly popular three-bedroom suites available—but most everyone is impressed by the value.

Probably the best-regarded bed-and-breakfast in Myrtle Beach (yes, there are a precious few) is the **◖ Serendipity Inn** (407 71st Ave. N., 843/449-5268, www.serendipityinn.com, $90-150). A short walk from the beach but sometimes seemingly light years away from the typical Myrtle sprawl, this 15-room gem features a simple but elegant pool, an attractive courtyard, and sumptuous guest rooms. The full breakfast is simple but hearty. There's free Wi-Fi throughout the property.

If you're looking for a basic, inexpensive, one-bed hotel experience on the beach, ask for a room at the new oceanfront section of the **Best Western Grand Strand Inn and Suites** (1804 S. Ocean Blvd., 843/448-1461, $80-140), a smallish but clean and attentively run chain hotel. The property's other buildings are significantly older and are located across busy Ocean Boulevard, and the walk across the street to the beach can be difficult, especially if you have small kids. That said, this is a great value and a quality property.

If water park-style entertainment is your thing, try **Dunes Village Resort** (5200 N. Ocean Blvd., 877/828-2237, www.dunesvillage.com, $140-300), also one of the better values in Myrtle. Its huge indoor water park has copious waterslides, including several for adults, and various other aquatic diversions.

© JIM MOREKIS

Poolside relaxation is everywhere in Myrtle Beach.

The buildings themselves—the property comprises two high-rise towers—are new and well-equipped, although since this is a time-share-style property, housekeeping is minimal.

$150-300

My favorite place to stay at Myrtle Beach is the **Island Vista Oceanfront Resort** (6000 N. Ocean Blvd., 888/733-7581, www.islandvista. com). While not the flashiest or heaviest in amenities by any means, Island Vista's location in a quiet residential area overlooking a mile of the Strand's best and least-traveled beach makes it a standout alternative to the often crowded and logistically challenging environment you'll find in the more built-up high-rise blocks farther south on the beach. In the high season you'll be paying about $300 for a one-bedroom suite, but the prices on the spacious and very well-equipped two- and three-bedroom suites are competitive. They have the usual multiple-pool option, including an indoor heated pool

area. A big plus is the fact that the in-house fine-dining restaurant, the **Cypress Room,** is a definite cut above most area hotel kitchens.

Consistently one of the best-regarded properties in Myrtle proper, the **Hampton Inn & Suites Oceanfront** (1803 S. Ocean Blvd., 843/946-6400, www.hamptoninnoceanfront. com, $169-259) has been made even better by a recent and thorough upgrade. This is a classic beachfront high-rise (not to be confused with the Hampton Inn at Broadway at the Beach), clean inside and out, with elegant tasteful guest rooms in various sizes (yes, flat-screen TVs were part of the makeover). Guest rooms range from typical one-bed, one-bath hotel-style rooms to larger condo-style suites with a fridge.

Situated more toward North Myrtle and hence closer to those attractions, the **Sea Watch Resort** (161 Sea Watch Blvd., $171-395) is a good choice for those who want the full-on condo high-rise Myrtle Beach experience but not necessarily the crowds that usually go with it. The guest rooms are clean and well-equipped, and by edging north a little on the beach, you can actually spread out and enjoy some breathing room.

An oldie but a goodie, the beachfront **Carolina Winds** (200 76th Ave. N., 843/497-5648, www.carolinawinds.com, $150-300) remains one of the better overall condo-style vacation spots in Myrtle. Unlike many of the newer monolithic high-rises, Carolina Winds almost has a retro Miami Beach feel to it, both in architecture and attitude. A two-night minimum stay is required during the high season.

One of the better-quality stays for the price in Myrtle is the **Roxanne Towers** (1604 N. Ocean Blvd., 843/839-1016, www.theroxanne.com, $150-250). Known for attentive service, this is a busy property in a busy area. Parking is historically something of a problem. Keep in mind that room size is capped at two bedrooms, so there are none of the sprawling three-bedroom suites that many other local places have.

For a quality stay in the heart of Myrtle's beach bustle, go for the **Sandy Beach Resort** (201 S. Ocean Blvd., 800/844-6534, www.beachtrips.com, $200-300). The guest rooms are top-notch, and the service professional. As is the case with many local properties, there is a newer section, the Palmetto Tower, and an "old" section, the venerable Magnolia Tower. There are one-, two-, and three-bedroom units available, the latter a particularly good value.

Considered one of the major remaining centers of the shag subculture on the Strand, the **Ocean Drive Beach and Golf Resort** (98 N. Ocean Blvd., $200-350) up in North Myrtle Beach hosts many events surrounding the notable regional dance, including the Shaggers Hall of Fame. Its on-site lounge, **The Spanish Galleon,** specializes in beach music. It's also just a great place to stay, with amenities such as a "lazy river," a whirlpool, full galley-style kitchens, and, of course, extreme proximity to the beach. A remodel in 2007 has made it even plusher inside and out.

Also up in North Myrtle is the new ◖ **Tilghman Beach and Golf Resort** (1819 Ocean Blvd., 843/280-0913, www.tilghmanresort.com, $200-350), owned by the same company as the Ocean Drive Beach Resort. It's not directly on the beach, but since the buildings in front of it are pretty low, you can still get awesome ocean views. Even the views from the back of the building aren't bad, since they overlook a golf course. But you don't have to be a duffer to enjoy the Tilghman—the pool scene is great, the balconies are roomy, and the suites are huge and well enough equipped (a flat-screen TV in every room) to make you feel right at home.

VACATION RENTALS

There are hundreds, probably thousands, of privately rented condo-style lodgings at Myrtle Beach, in all shapes and forms. Most, however, do a great job of catering to what vacationers here really seem to want: space, convenience, and a working kitchen. All rental agencies basically work with the same listings, so looking for and finding a rental is easier than you might think.

Some of the key brokers are **Myrtle Beach Vacation Rentals** (800/845-0833, www.mb-vacationrentals.com), **Beach Vacations** (866/453-4818, www.beachvacationsmb.com), **Barefoot Vacations** (800/845-0837, www.barefootvacations.info), **Elliott Realty and Beach Rentals** (www.elliottrealty.com), and **Atlantic Dunes Vacation Rentals** (866/544-2568, www.atlanticdunesvacations.com).

CAMPING

Let's start off with what should be obvious by now: Myrtle Beach is not where you go for a pristine quiet camping experience. For that, I suggest Huntington State Park down near Murrells Inlet. However, there is plenty of camping, almost all of it heavily RV-oriented, if you want it. For more info, visit www.campmyrtlebeach.com.

The closest thing to a real live campground

is good old **Myrtle Beach State Park** (4401 S. Kings Hwy., 843/238-5325, www.southcaro-linaparks.com, daily 6 A.M.-10 P.M., $4 adults, $1.50 ages 6-15, free under age 6), which despite being only a short drive from the rest of the beachfront sprawl is still a fairly relaxing place to stay, complete with its own scenic fishing pier (daily fishing fee $4.50). There's even a nature center with a little aquarium and exhibits.

The charming and educational atmosphere is largely due to the fact that this is one of the 17 Civilian Conservation Corps parks, built during the Great Depression and still lovingly maintained by the state of South Carolina. There are four cabins ($54-125) available, all fully furnished and about 200 yards from the beach. The main campground is about 300 yards from the beach and comprises 300 sites

with electricity and water ($23-25) and a 45-site tent and overflow campground ($17-19), which is only open during the summer high season.

The **Myrtle Beach KOA** (613 6th Ave. S., 800/562-7790, www.myrtlebeach-koa.com), though not at all cheap ($40-50 even for tenters), offers the usual safe, dependable amenities of that well-known chain, including rental "kabins" and activities for kids.

Willow Tree RV Resort and Campground (520 Southern Sights Dr., 843/756-4334, www.willowtreervr.com) is set inland on a well-wooded 300-acre tract with large sites well away from the sprawl and offers lakeside fishing and bike trails. In the summer high season, basic sites are $50-82, and the one- and two-bedroom cabins range $120-190.

Food

There are about 2,000 restaurants in the Myrtle Beach area, not counting hotel room service and buffets. You can find any dining option that floats your boat at almost any price level. Seafood, of course, is big and is heartily recommended. But there are steak houses, rib joints, pizza places, and vegetarian restaurants galore as well. We can only explore a small fraction here, but following is a breakdown of some of the more unique and tasty experiences on this bustling part of the Grand Strand.

BREAKFAST
Pancakes are big on the Strand, with many flap-jack places open daily 24 hours to accommodate partiers and night owls. If you've got a hanker-ing, just drive up and down Kings Highway/U.S. 17 long enough and you're bound to find a place. A prime purveyor of pancakes is **Harry's Breakfast Pancakes** (2306 N. Kings Hwy., 843/448-8013, www.harryspancake.com, daily 5:30 A.M.-2 P.M., $4-10). They're not open all

day, but there's enough time to enjoy their fluffy stacks and rich omelets.

BARBECUE, BURGERS, AND STEAKS
The best barbecue in town—and a delight-fully low-key experience in this often too-flashy area—is at **◖ Little Pigs Barbecue** (6102 Frontage Rd., 843/692-9774, Mon.-Sat. 11 A.M.-8 P.M., $8-12). This is a local-heavy place dealing in no-frills pulled pork, piled high at the counter and reasonably priced with a selection of sauces. The lack of atmosphere *is* the atmo-sphere, and they prefer to let the barbecue (and the hushpuppies and onion rings) do the talking.

Since opening 20 years ago, **◖ Thoroughbreds** (9706 N. Kings Hwy., 843/497-2636, www.thoroughbredsrestau-rant.com, Sun.-Thurs. 5-10 P.M., Fri.-Sat. 5-11 P.M., $20), on the old Restaurant Row, has been considered the premier fine-dining place in Myrtle Beach, dealing in the kind of wood-heavy, clubby, Old World-meets-New World ambience you'd expect to see in Palm Beach, Florida. That said, the prices are definitely more Myrtle Beach; you can easily have a romantic dinner for two for under $100. The menu is a carnivore's delight: Beef includes the signature prime rib, a great steak au poivre, and a nod to cowboy machismo, the 22-ounce bone-in rib eye. The veal, pork chops, and rack of lamb are also topflight. A special treat is the exquisite chateaubriand for two, a steal at $75. However, seafood lovers shouldn't entirely skip Thoroughbreds, as the crab cakes and the shrimp and grits stack up to most any you'll find in the Carolinas.

The new darling of the steak-loving set is **Rioz Brazilian Steakhouse** (2920 Hollywood Dr., 843/839-0777, www.rioz.com, daily 4-10 P.M., $20-40). It's not cheap—the recommended 15-item meat sampler is about $35 pp—but then again, an experience this awesome shouldn't be cheap (a big plus is that kids under age 7 eat for free). The meats are fresh and vibrant, slow-cooked over a wood fire in the simple but succulent style typical of the gaucho *churrascaria* tradition. The service is widely considered to be the best in the area. But the biggest surprise may turn out to be the salad and seafood bar, which even has sushi.

There is no dearth of places to nosh at Barefoot Landing, but meat lovers (not to mention golfers) will probably enjoy **Greg Norman's Australian Grille** (4930 Kings Hwy. S., 843/361-0000, www.gregnormansaustraliangrille.com, lunch daily 11 A.M.-3 P.M., dinner daily 5-10 P.M., $20-30), which, despite the chain-sounding name, is the only restaurant of its kind. With the dark clubby ambience you'd expect at a place named for a golf pro, this is not necessarily where you want to take the kids. Instead, it's the place to enjoy a cocktail by the lake and a premium entrée like the lobster-crusted swordfish, the rack of lamb, or the prime rib.

For a less pricey but still very tasty experience, try **Liberty Tap Room and Grill** (7651 N. Kings Hwy., 843/839-4677, www.libertytaproom.com, daily 11 A.M.-11 P.M., $15-20). This regional chain not only boasts high-quality steaks and burgers in a casual atmosphere but has some good pizza and even seafood as well.

You wouldn't expect a place with the name **Carolina Roadhouse** (4617 N. Kings Hwy., 843/497-9911, Sun.-Thurs. 11 A.M.-10 P.M., Fri.-Sat. 11 A.M.-11 P.M., $10-28) to have excellent croissant appetizers, but that kind of twist is what makes this a cut above the usual steak-and-ribs joint. Virtually anything on the menu is very good, but since you're likely to be waiting for a table, you may as well go for the incredible ribs.

I normally shy away from mentioning national chain-type places because of the cheese factor, but I'll make an exception for Myrtle Beach, where you expect things to be a little cheesy. **Jimmy Buffett's Margaritaville** (1114 Celebrity Circle, 843/448-5455, www.margaritavillemyrtlebeach.com, Sun.-Thurs. 11 A.M.-10 P.M., Fri.-Sat. 11 A.M.-midnight, $13-22) at Broadway at the Beach is widely regarded as the best single location of the national chain. The signature Cheeseburger in Paradise is the obvious big hit. You get a lot of entertainment for your money as well, with balloon-twisting performers coming to your table and a bizarre whirling "hurricane" that acts up in the main dining area every now and then. As you'd expect, the margaritas are good, if expensive.

Many locals insist the better burger is at another Buffett-owned chain, the succinctly titled **Cheeseburger in Paradise** (7211 N. Kings Hwy., 843/497-3891, www.cheeseburgerinparadise.com, Sun.-Thurs. 11:30 A.M.-11 P.M., Fri.-Sat. 11:30 A.M.-midnight, $10-15), which offers a range of burgers on the menu with sweet potato chips on the side, all served up in a less flashy but still very boisterous atmosphere than the flagship restaurant.

CLASSIC SOUTHERN

If you've got a hankering for some spicy Cajun-creole food, go no farther than **The House of Blues** (4640 U.S. 17 S., 843/272-3000, www.hob.com, Mon.-Fri. 4-9 P.M., Sat. 8 A.M.-9 P.M., Sun. 9 A.M.-2 P.M. and 3-9 P.M., $10-25) at Barefoot Landing in North Myrtle Beach. With 17 similarly themed locations around North America, this particular venue deals in the same kind of retro Delta vibe, with specially commissioned folk art festooning the walls and live music cranking up at about 9 P.M. At your table, a gregarious server will walk you through the limited but intense menu, which includes such tasty bits as Buffalo Tenders (actually boneless chicken wings in a perfectly spicy sauce) and a couple of excellent jambalaya-type dishes. All portions are enormous and richly spiced. It's a loud, clanging room, so keep in mind that this is less a romantic experience than an exuberant earthy one.

A special experience at House of Blues is the weekly Gospel Brunch (9 A.M.-2 P.M. Sun., $20 adults, $10 ages 6-12), an opportunity not only to enjoy some tasty Southern-style brunch treats like cheese grits, jambalaya, and catfish tenders but to enjoy some really rather outstanding gospel entertainment at the same time. The Gospel Brunch is served in seatings, and reservations are recommended.

CONTINENTAL

In Myrtle Beach it can be difficult to find a good meal that's not fried or smothered or both. For a highbrow change of pace, try **The Library** (1212 N. Kings Hwy., 843/448-4527, www.thelibraryrestaurantsc.com, Mon.-Sat. 5-10 P.M., $20-50), which is hands-down the most romantic dining experience in Myrtle proper. It's not cheap, but then again, nothing about this place is pedestrian, from the very attentive European-style service to the savvy wine list and the signature dishes (many of them prepared tableside), like she-crab soup, Caesar salads, Steak Diane, and the ultimate splurge, steak and lobster.

Like art? Like food? Try the **Collector's Café** (7726 N. Kings Hwy., 843/449-9370, www.collectorscafeandgallery.com, $10-20), which, as the name implies, is a combined gallery and dining space. Don't be daunted by the strip mall setting—inside is a totally different ball game with a trendy open kitchen and plush, eclectic furniture awaiting you amid the original artwork. As for the menu, you may as well go for what's widely regarded as the best single dish, the scallop cakes. Make sure you save room for dessert.

ITALIAN

The best-regarded Italian place in Myrtle Beach—though it could just as easily go in the *Steaks* category, since that's its specialty—is **Angelo's** (2011 S. Kings Hwy., 843/626-2800, www.angelosteakandpasta.com, Sun.-Thurs. 4-8:30 P.M., Fri.-Sat. 4-9 P.M., $12-25). The signature dishes are intriguingly spiced cuts of steak (request beforehand if you don't want them seasoned), cooked medium and under for an exquisite tenderness. You can get spaghetti as a side with the steaks, or just go with the classic baked potato. Don't forget to check out the Italian buffet, including lasagna, Italian sausage, chicken cacciatore, ravioli, and, of course, pizza.

A particularly well-run franchise of a national chain, **Ultimate California Pizza** (2500 N. Kings Hwy., 843/626-8900, www.ultimate-californiapizza.com, daily 11 A.M.-11 P.M., $7-18) delivers the goods in Barefoot Landing in North Myrtle. They offer an almost bewildering variety of specialty pizzas, including a surf-and-turf pizza, one topped with filet mignon, and various interesting veggie styles. Many folks simply opt to build their own pie, however, with toppings such as apples and goat cheese and an incredibly diverse range of sauces.

WHAT'S A CALABASH?

In Myrtle Beach you'll no doubt see garish restaurant signs boasting of "Calabash Cooking" or a "Calabash Buffet." Named for a seaside shrimping and fishing village just over the border in North Carolina, Calabash cooking basically means fresh seafood that's fried in spiced corn meal soon after it's caught.

In usual practice, Calabash seafood is served in huge buffets, and to most people on the Strand the phrase really just refers to the sheer volume of food. Shrimp is the dominant motif, though flounder is big too. By all means enjoy Calabash cooking while you're on the Strand, but don't expect the catch to be fresh. Connoisseurs insist you need to go to Calabash, North Carolina, for that.

SEAFOOD

The grandest old Calabash seafood joint in town, **Original Benjamin's** (9593 N. Kings Hwy., 843/449-0821, daily 3:30-10 P.M., buffet $25 adults, $12 children) on the old Restaurant Row is one of the more unique dining experiences in Myrtle Beach. With themed rooms overlooking the Intracoastal Waterway, including the concisely named Bus Room—yes, it has an old school bus in it—you'll find yourself in the mood to devour copious amounts of fresh seafood at its humongous 170-item buffet line. That's not a misprint—170 items, including mounds of shrimp prepared in every style; all

kinds of tuna, salmon, and catfish; a variety of crabmeat dishes; and nonseafood stuff like chicken and barbecue.

Closer to Broadway on the Beach, try **George's** (1401 29th Ave. N., 843/916-2278, www.captaingeorges.com, Mon.-Sat. 3-10 P.M., Sun. noon-9 P.M., buffet $31, $16 ages 5-12). Despite the usual kitschy nautical decor, this is the kind of place even locals will admit going to for the enormous seafood buffet, widely considered a cut above the norm.

With old reliables like crab cakes and sea scallops as well as signature house dishes like pecan-encrusted grouper and stuffed flounder, you can't go wrong at **The Sea Captain's House** (3002 N. Ocean Blvd., 843/448-8082, daily 6-10:30 A.M., 11:30 A.M.-2:30 P.M., and 5-10 P.M., $10-20), one of Myrtle Beach's better seafood restaurants. This opinion is widely held, however, so prepare to wait—often up to two hours. Luckily, you can sip a cocktail and gaze out over the Atlantic Ocean as you do so. Old hands will tell you it's not as good as back in the day, but it's still a cut above.

When you're at Ocean Drive Beach up in North Myrtle, check out another venerable old name, the **Duffy Street Seafood Shack** (202 Main St., 843/281-9840, www.duffyst.com, daily noon-10 P.M., $10). This is a humble unkempt roadside affair dealing in the kind of down-home treats Myrtle Beach seems to love ("pigskin" shrimp, fried pickles, and the like). Overall, it's a good place to get a tasty bite and soak in the flavor of this Cherry Grove neighborhood at the heart of the old shag culture.

MYRTLE BEACH

Information and Services

The main visitors center for Myrtle Beach is the **Myrtle Beach Area Chamber of Commerce and Visitor Center** (1200 N. Oak St., 843/626-7444, www.visitmybeach.com, Mon.-Fri. 8:30 A.M.-5 P.M., Sat. 10 A.M.-2 P.M.). There's an **airport welcome center** (1180 Jetport Rd., 843/626-7444) as well, and a visitors center in North Myrtle Beach, the **North Myrtle Beach Chamber of Commerce and Convention & Visitors Bureau** (270 U.S. 17 N., 843/281-2662, www.northmyrtlebeachchamber.com).

The main health care facility in the Myrtle Beach area is **Grand Strand Regional Medical Center** (809 82nd Pkwy., 843/692-1000, www.grandstrandmed.com). Myrtle Beach is served by the **Myrtle Beach Police Department** (1101 N. Oak St., 843/918-1382, www.cityof-myrtlebeach.com). The separate municipality of North Myrtle Beach is served by the **North Myrtle Beach Police Department** (843/280-5555, www.nmb.us).

The newspaper of record for Myrtle Beach is **The Sun News** (www.myrtlebeachonline.com). For a look at the grittier side of Myrtle Beach music and nightlife, look for a copy of **The Weekly Surge** (www.weeklysurge.com).

In Myrtle Beach, you can choose between the main **U.S. Post Office** (505 N. Kings Hwy., 800/275-8777, Mon.-Fri. 8:30 A.M.-5 P.M., Sat. 9 A.M.-1 P.M.) or the other convenient location (820 67th Ave. N., 800/275-8777, Mon.-Fri. 9 A.M.-4:30 P.M., Sat. 11 A.M.-1 P.M.). In North Myrtle beach, try the main post office (621 6th Ave. S., 800/275-8777, Mon.-Fri. 8:30 A.M.-5 P.M., Sat. 9 A.M.-noon) or the other convenient location in Cherry Grove Beach (227 Sea Mountain Hwy., 800/275-8777, Mon.-Fri. 8:30 A.M.-5 P.M.).

Getting There and Around

GETTING THERE

The Myrtle Beach area is served by the fast-growing **Myrtle Beach International Airport** (MYR, 1100 Jetport Rd., 843/448-1589, www.flymyrtlebeach.com), which hosts Delta, Northwest, Southern Skyways, Spirit, U.S. Airways, and United.

Unusually for South Carolina, a state that is exceptionally well-served by the interstate highway system, the main route into the area is the smaller U.S. 17, which runs north-south, with a parallel business spur, from Georgetown up to the North Carolina border. The approach from the west is by U.S. 501, called Black Skimmer Trail as it approaches Myrtle Beach.

The local **Greyhound Bus terminal** (511 7th Ave. N., 843/231-2222) is in "downtown" Myrtle Beach.

GETTING AROUND

In practice, the Myrtle Beach municipalities blend and blur into each other in one long sprawl parallel to the main north-south route, U.S. 17. However, always keep this in mind: Just south of Murrells Inlet, U.S. 17 divides into two distinct portions. There's the U.S. 17 Bypass, which continues to the west of much of the coastal growth, and there's Business U.S. 17, also known as Kings Highway, the main drag along which most key attractions and places of interest are located.

The other key north-south route, Ocean Boulevard, runs along the beach. This is a two-lane road that can get pretty congested in the summer, especially when it's used for cruising by younger visitors or during one of the several motorcycle rallies throughout the year.

Thankfully, area planners have provided a great safety valve for some of this often horrendous traffic. Highway 31, the Carolina Bays Parkway, begins inland from Myrtle Beach at about 16th Avenue. This wide new highway roughly parallels the Intracoastal Waterway and takes you on a straight shot, with a 65 mph speed limit, all the way to Highway 22 (the Conway Bypass) or all the way to Highway 9 at Cherry Grove Beach, the farthest extent of North Myrtle Beach. The bottom line is that if time is of the essence, you should use Highway 31 whenever possible.

Rental Car, Taxi, and Bus

You will need a vehicle to make the most of this area. Rental cars are available at the airport. Rental options outside the airport include **Enterprise** (1377 U.S. 501, 843/626-4277; 3401 U.S. 17 S., 843/361-4410, www.enterprise.com), **Hertz** (851 Jason Blvd., 843/839-9530, www.hertz.com), and the unique **Rent-a-Wreck** (901 3rd Ave. S., 843/626-9393).

Taxi service on the Strand is plentiful but fairly expensive. Look in the local Yellow Pages for full listings; a couple of good services are **Yellow Cab** (917 Oak St., 843/448-5555) and **Beach Checker Cab** (843/272-6212) in North Myrtle.

The area is served by the **Coastal Rapid Public Transit Authority** (1418 3rd Ave., 843/248-7277), which runs several routes up and down the Strand. Ask at a visitors center or call for a schedule.

By Bicycle

Bicyclists in Myrtle Beach can take advantage of some completed segments of the South Carolina portion of the **East Coast Greenway** (www.greenway.org), which generally speaking is Ocean Boulevard. In Myrtle Beach there's a bike lane on North Ocean Boulevard from about 82nd Avenue North down to 29th Avenue North. You can actually ride Ocean Boulevard all the way from 82nd Avenue North down to the southern city limit, if you like. Inland, a portion of the Greenway is on Grissom Parkway, which takes you by Broadway at the Beach.

In North Myrtle Beach, from Sea Mountain Highway in Cherry Grove, you can bike Ocean Boulevard clear down to 46th Avenue South, with a detour from 28th to 33rd Avenues. A right on 46th Avenue South takes you to Barefoot Landing. And, of course, for a scenic ride, you can pedal on the beach itself for miles. But remember: Bicycling on the sidewalk is strictly prohibited.

As for bike rentals, try **Beach Bike Shop** (711 Broadway St., 843/448-5335, www.beachbikeshop.com). In North Myrtle, try **Wheel Fun Rentals** (91 S. Ocean Blvd., 843/280-7900, www.wheelfunrentals.com).

MYRTLE BEACH

Points Inland

CONWAY

A nice day trip west of Myrtle Beach—and a nice change from that area's intense development—is to the charming town of Conway, just northwest of Myrtle Beach on U.S. 501 and the Waccamaw River. Founded in 1733 with the name Kingston, it originally marked the frontier of the colony. It was later renamed Conwayborough, soon shortened to Conway, in honor of local leader Robert Conway, and now serves as the seat of Horry County.

Conway's heyday was during Reconstruction, when it became a major trade center for timber products and naval stores from the interior. The railroad came through town in 1887 (later being extended to Myrtle Beach), and most remaining buildings date from this period or later. The most notable Conway native is perhaps an unexpected name: William Gibson, originator of the cyberpunk genre of science fiction, was born here in 1948.

Conway is small and easily explored. Make your first stop at the **Conway Visitors Center** (903 3rd Ave., 843/248-1700, www.cityofconway.com, Mon.-Fri. 9 A.M.-5 P.M.), where you can pick up maps. It also offers guided tours ($2 pp) that depart from City Hall (3rd Ave. and Main St.); call for a schedule. You can also visit the **Conway Chamber of Commerce** (203 Main St.) for maps and information.

Sights

Conway's chief attraction is the 850-foot **Riverwalk** (843/248-2273, www.conwayscchamber.com, daily dawn-dusk) along the blackwater Waccamaw River, a calming location with shops and restaurants nearby. Waterborne tours on the *Kingston Lady* leave from the Conway Marina at the end of the Riverwalk.

Another key stop is the **Horry County Museum** (428 Main St., 843/248-1542, www.horrycountymuseum.org, Tues.-Sat. 9 A.M.-4 P.M., free), which tells the story of this rather large South Carolina county from prehistory to the present. It holds an annual Quilt Gala in February, which features some great regional examples of the art.

Across from the campus of Coastal Carolina University is the circa-1972 Traveler's Chapel, a.k.a. **The Littlest Church in South Carolina** (U.S. 501 and Cox Ferry Rd.). At 12 by 24 feet, it seats no more than a dozen people. Weddings are held here throughout the year. Admission is free, but donations are accepted.

Accommodations

The best stay in town is at the four-star **Cypress Inn** (16 Elm St., 843/248-8199, www.acypressinn.com, $145-235), a beautiful and well-appointed 12-room B&B right on the Waccamaw River.

LEWIS OCEAN BAY HERITAGE PRESERVE

The humongous (over 9,000 acres) Lewis Ocean Bay Heritage Preserve (803/734-3886, www.dnr.sc.gov, daily dawn-dusk, free) is one of the more impressive phenomena in the Palmetto State, from a naturalist's viewpoint, made all the more special by its location a short drive from heavily developed Myrtle Beach. Managed by the state, it contains an amazing 23 Carolina bays, by far the largest concentration in South Carolina. These elliptical depressions, scattered throughout the Carolinas and all oriented in a northwest-southeast direction, are typified by a cypress-tupelo bog environment. The nearby Highway 31 is named the Carolina Bays Parkway in a nod to its neighbors. As if that weren't enough, the preserve boasts other unique aspects as well. It has the largest concentration of Venus flytraps in the state, and it is also said to be the only place in eastern South Carolina where black bears still live in the wild. Clemson University is conducting a study on their habits and so far has concluded that they roam back and forth between here and North Carolina. The bird-watching is extra-special too, with a good number of bald eagles and endangered red-cockaded woodpeckers in the area. Several miles of trails take you through a variety of habitats.

Keep in mind that despite its great natural beauty, the preserve is not pristine. As with most of Horry County, heavy logging and turpentine operations took place throughout the preserve's acreage during the 1800s and early 1900s. As with most South Carolina heritage preserves, hunting is allowed, and there are no facilities.

To get here from Myrtle Beach, take U.S. 501 north to Highway 90 and head east. After about seven miles, turn east on the unpaved International Drive across from the Wild Horse subdivision. After about 1.5 miles on International Drive, veer left onto Old Kingston Road. The preserve is shortly ahead on both sides of the road; park along the shoulder.

The Lower Grand Strand

Pawleys Island, Murrells Inlet, and the rest of the so-called Waccamaw Neck are the lower portion of the Grand Strand. While a certain amount of Myrtle Beach-style development is encroaching southward, this area is still far away in spirit and generally much more relaxed.

Tiny Pawleys Island (year-round population about 200) likes to call itself "America's first resort" because of its early role in the late 1700s as a place for planters to go with their families to escape the mosquito-infested rice and cotton fields; George Washington visited in 1791. It's still a vacation getaway and still has a certain elite understatement, an attitude the locals call "arrogantly shabby." Beach access is correspondingly more difficult than farther up the Strand near Myrtle Beach. While you can visit casually, most people who enjoy the famous Pawleys Island beaches do so from one of the many vacation rental properties. Shabby arrogance does have its upside, however—there is a ban on further commercial development in the community, allowing Pawleys to remain indefinitely slow and peaceful. The maximum speed limit throughout town is a suitably lazy 25 mph. For generations, Pawleys was famous for its cypress cottages, many on stilts. Sadly, 1989's Hurricane Hugo destroyed a great many of these iconic structures—27 out of 29 on the south end alone, most of which have been replaced by far less aesthetically pleasing homes.

Directly adjacent to Pawleys, Litchfield Beach offers similar low-key enjoyment along with a world-class golf resort. While several key attractions in the Grand Strand are technically in Murrells Inlet, that's more for post office convenience than anything else. Murrells Inlet is chiefly known for a single block of seafood restaurants on its eponymous waterway.

SIGHTS
◖ Brookgreen Gardens

One of the most unique—and unlikely—sights in the developed Grand Strand area is bucolic Brookgreen Gardens (1931 Brookgreen Dr., 843/235-6000, www.brookgreen.org, May-Mar. daily 9:30 A.M.-5 P.M., Apr. 9:30 A.M.-8 P.M., $14 adults, $7 ages 6-12, free under age 6), directly across U.S. 17 from Huntington Beach State Park. An eclectic compilation of sorts, Brookgreen combines scenic manicured gardens, copious amounts of outdoor sculpture by a host of artists, and a low-key but worthwhile nature center with live animals.

Once one of several massive contiguous plantations in the Pawleys Island area, the modern Brookgreen is a result of the charity and passion of Archer Milton Huntington and his wife, Anna Hyatt. Seeking to preserve the area's

© SONJA WALLEN

Brookgreen Gardens, America's largest outdoor sculpture collection flora and fauna and celebrate American sculpture at the same time, the couple turned the entire place into a nonprofit in 1931. Quite the sculptor in her own right, Anna Huntington saw to it that Brookgreen's 9,000 acres would host by far the largest single collection of outdoor sculpture in the United States.

Designed and added onto over the past century, the sculpture gardens themselves are a sprawling collection of tastefully themed, colorfully planted gardens that are generally built around a key sculpture or two. As you're walking, don't forget to examine the various nooks, crannies, and corners inside and outside the walls where you'll find hundreds of smaller sculptures, generally along natural or mythological themes. The sculptures don't stop there—you'll see plenty of them out in the fields, overlooking lakes, and tucked into bushes all around the site. In all, there are over 1,200 works by more than 300 artists. While most sculptures tend toward a certain style—thick, robust, and often depicting some form of struggle—some are more whimsical and even downright charming, such as the one near the visitors center, which depicts several kids pledging allegiance to the flag. To learn more, visit the on-site **Carroll A. Campbell Jr. Center for American Sculpture,** which offers seminars and workshops throughout the year.

Botanists and green thumbs will find plenty to enjoy as well. At least 2,000 species of plants have been planted at Brookgreen, with something always guaranteed to be in bloom regardless of the season. A special treat is the stunning Oak Allee section, where some of the live oaks are 250 years old. One huge and ancient specimen, the Constitution Oak, has been designated a "living witness" to the signing of the U.S. Constitution.

On the other end of the grounds opposite the gardens is the **E. Craig Wall Jr. Lowcountry Nature Center,** which includes a small enclosed cypress swamp with a boardwalk, herons and egrets, and an absolutely delightful river otter exhibit, where you can see the playful critters swim and frolic. Other animals include alligators and several species of raptors. Almost all the animals have been treated for injuries that render them unfit to return to life in the wild.

To add an extra layer of enjoyment to your visit, you can explore this massive preserve much more deeply by taking one of several tours offered on Brookgreen's pontoon boat ($7 adults, $4 children on top of regular admission); check the website for a schedule.

◖ Huntington Beach State Park

Right across the street from Brookgreen is Huntington Beach State Park (16148 Ocean Hwy., 843/237-4440, www.southcarolinaparks.com, daily 6 A.M.-10 P.M., $5 adults, $3 ages 6-15, free under age 6), probably the best of South Carolina's state parks not built by the Civilian Conservation Corps. Once a part of the same vast parcel of land owned by Archer Huntington and his wife, Anna Hyatt, the state has leased it from the trustees of their estate since the 1960s.

You can tour the "castle" on the beach, Atalaya, former home of the Huntingtons and now the yearly site of the Atalaya Arts and Crafts Festival. This evocative Moorish-style National Historic Landmark is open to the public for free guided tours (Memorial Day-end of Sept. daily noon-1 P.M., Oct. 1-31 Tues.-Sat. noon-2 P.M., Sun.-Mon. noon-1 P.M.).

Today, a walk through the park is a delightful and convenient way to enjoy the Grand Strand's natural legacy. A great variety of birds use Huntington Beach as a migratory stopover. You can stroll three miles of beach, view birds and wildlife from several boardwalks into the marsh, hike several nature trails, and visit the well-done **Environmental Education Center** (843/235-8755, Tues.-Sun. 10 A.M.-5 P.M.), which features a saltwater touch tank and a baby alligator. In all, it's a great experience for the whole family, or a very romantic outing for a couple.

© JIM MOREKIS

Weston House in the Pawleys Island Historic District

Pawleys Island Historic District

Although many of the island's homes were leveled by Hurricane Hugo, the Pawleys Island Historic District (843/237-1698, www.townof-pawleysisland.com) in the central portion of the island still has a dozen contributing structures, almost all on Myrtle Avenue. Among them are the **Weston House** (506 Myrtle Ave.), or Pelican Inn, and the **Ward House** (520 Myrtle Ave.), or Liberty Lodge. As you view the structures, many with their own historic markers, note the architecture. Because these were intended to be lived in May-November, they resemble open and airy Caribbean homes, with extensive porches and plenty of windows.

EVENTS

The highlight of the lower Grand Strand calendar is the annual **Atalaya Arts and Crafts Festival** (www.atalayafestival.com, $6 adults, free under age 16), which takes place on the grounds of Huntington Beach State Park each September. Like the park itself, the festival, now nearing its 40th year, is a philanthropic legacy of Archer Huntington and his wife, Anna Hyatt. There's music, food, and about 100 vendors who show their art and wares within the exotic Atalaya home. Admission to the park is free during the festival.

Also in September is the **Pawleys Island Festival of Music and Art** (www.pawleys-music.com, prices vary), which happens outdoors, across U.S. 17 under the stars in Brookgreen Gardens, with a few performances at nearby Litchfield Plantation.

A main event in Murrells Inlet is the annual **Fourth of July Boat Parade** (843/651-0900, free), which celebrates American independence with a patriotically themed procession of all kinds of streamer- and flag-bedecked watercraft down the inlet. It begins at about 6 P.M. and ends, of course, with a big fireworks display.

Another big deal in Murrells Inlet is the annual **Blessing of the Inlet** (843/651-5099, www.belinumc.org), always held the first Saturday in May and sponsored by a local Methodist church. Enjoy food vendors, goods baked by local women, and a great family atmosphere.

SHOPPING

The shopping scene revolves around the famous Pawleys Island hammock, a beautiful and practical bit of local handiwork sold primarily at the **Hammock Shops Village** (10880 Ocean Hwy., 843/237-8448, Mon.-Sat. 10 A.M.-6 P.M., Sun. 1-5 P.M.). This is actually a collection of 25 shops and restaurants, the closest thing to a mall environment you'll find in the area.

To purchase a Pawleys Island hammock, go to **The Original Hammock Shop** (843/237-9122, www.thehammockshop.com), housed in a century-old cottage. Next door is the affiliated **Hammock Shop General Store,** which, as the name implies, sells a variety of other goods such as beachwear, books, and a notable style of local fudge. The actual hammocks are hand-crafted in the shed next door, the way they have been since 1889.

SPORTS AND RECREATION
Beaches
First, the good news: The beaches are pristine and beautiful. The bad news: Public access is very limited. Simply put, that means the best way to enjoy the beach is to rent one of the many private beach homes for a week or so. Although it's only a short distance from Myrtle Beach, the beaches at Pawleys and vicinity are infinitely more peaceful and easygoing.

Beach access with parking at Pawleys Island includes a fairly large lot at the south end of the island and parking areas off Atlantic Avenue at Hazard, 1st, Pearce, 2nd, and 3rd Streets, and Shell Road.

Kayaking and Canoeing
The Waccamaw River and associated inlets and creeks are peaceful and scenic places to kayak, with plenty of bird-watching opportunities to boot. For a two-hour guided tour of the area salt marsh, reserve a spot on the kayak trips sponsored by the **Environmental Education Center** (Huntington Beach State Park, 843/235-8755, office Tues.-Sun. 10 A.M.-5 P.M., $30 pp). Call for tour days and times. Or you can put in yourself at Oyster Landing, about one mile from the entrance to the state park.

Ecotours
The most popular and extensive dolphin tour in the area is the **Blue Wave Adventures Dolphin Watch** (843/651-3676, www.bluewaveadventures.com, $29 adults, $19 under age 13) on the waterfront in Murrells Inlet. The basic 90-minute tour leaves every day and takes you to the waters where the area pods, as well known as any local resident, tend to congregate. Call for tour times; morning tours are the best for finding dolphins.

Fishing
A good all-around charter operator in Murrells Inlet, **Capt. Dicks** (4123 Business U.S. 17, 843/651-3676, www.captdicks.com, prices vary), runs a variety of trips, from deep-sea sportfishing to more casual inshore adventures. Dicks also offers nonfishing trips, such as a dolphin tours and a popular marsh ecotour. It's in the same building as Spuds restaurant.

Golf
Home to some of the best links in the Carolinas, the lower part of the Grand Strand recently organized its courses under the umbrella moniker **Waccamaw Golf Trail** (www.waccamawgolftrail.com), chiefly for marketing purposes. No matter, the courses are still as superb as ever, if generally pricier than their counterparts up the coast.

The best course, hands down, in the area, and one of the best in the country, is the **Caledonia Golf and Fish Club** (369 Caledonia Dr., 843/237-3675, www.fishclub.com, $195). While the course itself is almost ridiculously young—it opened in 1995—this masterpiece is built, as so many area courses are, on the grounds of a former rice plantation. The clubhouse, in fact, dates from before the Civil War. Besides its signature 18th hole, other hallmarks of Caledonia are its copious amount of very old live oaks and its refusal to allow homes or condos to be built on the grounds. Packages are available (800/449-4005, www.myrtlebeachcondorentals.com). Affiliated with Caledonia is the fine **True Blue Golf Club** (900 Blue Stem Dr., 843/235-0900, www.fishclub.com, $100), considered perhaps the most challenging single course on the Strand.

Another excellent Pawleys course, and one with a significantly longer pedigree, is the **Litchfield Country Club** (U.S. 17 and Magnolia Dr., 843/237-3411, www.litchcc.com, $60), one of the Grand Strand's oldest courses and the first in Pawleys Island. The facilities are self-consciously dated—this is a country club, after all—setting it apart from the flashier, newer courses sprouting like mushrooms farther up the Strand. It's a deceptive course that's short on yards but heavy on doglegs.

The Jack Nicklaus-designed **Pawleys Plantation Golf and Country Club** (70 Tanglewood Dr., 843/237-6100, www.pawleysplantation.com, $150) has set a tough example for the last 20 years. Beautiful but challenging, it has a Jekyll-and-Hyde nature. The front nine is a traditional layout, while the back nine melts into the marsh.

ACCOMMODATIONS
Under $150

Similarly named but definitely not to be confused with Litchfield Plantation is the nearby **Litchfield Beach and Golf Resort** (14276 Ocean Hwy., 866/538-0187, www.litchfieldbeach.com, $100-170). In typical Grand Strand fashion, this property delivers a lot of service for a surprisingly low price. Also typical for the area, it offers a wide range of lodging choices, from a basic room at the Seaside Inn on the low end to four-bedroom villas ($230, still a great deal). Though not all units are right on the beach, a regular free shuttle takes you to the sand pretty much whenever you want. There are also lots of water activities right on the premises, including a ubiquitous "lazy river" tube course.

$150-300

The premier B&B-style lodging on the entire Grand Strand is ⟨ **Litchfield Plantation** (Kings River Rd., 843/237-9121, www.litchfieldplantation.com, $230-275) on Pawleys Island, built, as you've probably come to expect by now, on an old plantation. There is a host of lodging choices, all of them absolutely splendid. The Plantation House has four sumptuous suites, all impeccably decorated. The humbly named Guest House—actually an old mansion—has six bedrooms, and the entire second floor is an executive suite. Lastly, the newer outparcel Villas contain an assortment

of two- and three-bedroom suites. Amenities include a complimentary full plantation breakfast each morning and a three-story beach club for use only by guests. If you visit in the winter, you can get a room for as little as $150, a heck of a deal regardless of the temperature outside.

Vacation Rentals

Many who enjoy the Pawleys area do so using a vacation rental as a home base rather than a traditional hotel or B&B. **Pawleys Island Realty** (88 N. Causeway Rd., 800/937-7352, www.pawleysislandrealty.com) can hook you up.

Camping

For great camping in this area, go no farther than **Huntington Beach State Park** (16148 Ocean Hwy., 843/237-4440, www.southcarolinaparks.com, daily 6 A.M.-10 P.M., $5 adults, $3 ages 6-15, free under age 6). The beach is beautiful, there are trails and an education center, and the bird-watching is known as some of the best on the East Coast. While there are 131 RV-suitable sites ($23-28), tenters should go to one of the six walk-in tent sites ($17-19).

FOOD
Breakfast and Brunch

The high-end strip mall setting isn't the most romantic, but by broad consensus the best breakfast on the entire Strand is at **Applewood House of Pancakes** (14361 Ocean Hwy., 843/979-1022, daily 6 A.M.-2 P.M., $5-10) in Pawleys. Eggs Benedict, specialty omelets, crepes, waffles, and pancakes abound in this roomy, unpretentious dining room. Do it; you won't regret it.

Seafood

The Pawleys-Litchfield-Murrells Inlet area has some good seafood places, although the long lines during high season at some of the better-known, more touristy places are not necessarily a sign of quality. A visit in the fall or winter brings a culinary treat to help take the chill off: fresh local oysters. Do keep in mind that many restaurants keep substantially shorter hours in the winter, and some close completely.

Murrells Inlet has several good places clustered together along the marsh on U.S. 17. The best is **Lee's Inlet Kitchen** (4460 Business U.S. 17, 843/651-2881, www.leesinletkitchen.com, Mar.-Nov. Mon.-Sat. 4:30-10 P.M., $20-40), which is the only original Murrells Inlet joint still in the original family—in this case the Lee family, who started the place in the mid-1940s. The seafood is simply but delectably prepared (your choice of fried or broiled), with particular pride taken in its freshness. Their sole drawback is that they close down December-February.

Along similar lines and almost as recommendable is **Flo's Place Restaurant** (3797 Business U.S. 17, 843/651-7222, www.flosplace.com, daily 11 A.M.-10 P.M., $15-25). Flo is sadly no longer with us, but her place still eschews schlock for a more humble, down-home feel. Everything is fresh, hot, and tasty, from the fried green tomatoes to the crab cakes and the alligator nuggets—yes, it's real alligator meat; they like to say it tastes like a cross between chicken and veal. But the signature dish is the legendary Dunkin' Pot—a big kettle filled with oysters, clams, shrimp, potatoes, sausage, and seasonal shellfish. As if that weren't enough, it's topped with snow crab legs. Do save room for some fried pickles.

On the other end of the spectrum style-wise is **Divine Fish House** (3993 Business U.S. 17, 843/651-5800, www.divinefishhouse.com, daily 5-10 P.M., $20-33), which offers more adventurous high-end cuisine like the fine San Antonio Salmon (smothered with pepper-jack cheese and bacon) and the Asian-flavored Banana Leaf Mangrove Grouper.

Just down the road at Pawleys is **Hanser House** (14360 Ocean Hwy., 843/235-3021, www.hanserhouse.com, daily 4-10 P.M., $19), which offers succulent seafood dishes like its signature crabmeat-stuffed flounder or king crab legs, but also offers some crackerjack steaks. Check out their frequent oyster roasts October-February.

Coffee, Tea, and Sweets

A favorite is **Kudzu Bakery** (221 Willbrook Blvd., 843/235-8560, www.kudzubakery.com, Mon.-Fri. 9 A.M.-6 P.M., Sat. 9 A.M.-3 P.M.), recognizable from its popular original spot in Georgetown and similarly renowned for delectable fresh-baked goodies.

INFORMATION AND SERVICES

On Pawleys Island is the **Georgetown County Visitors Bureau** (95-A Centermarsh Lane, 843/235-6595, www.visitgeorgetowncountysc.com). The **Myrtle Beach Area Chamber of Commerce** (3401 U.S. 17, 843/651-1010, www.visitmybeach.com) and the new **Waccamaw Community Hospital** (4070 U.S. 17 Bypass, 843/652-1000, www.georgetownhospital-system.org) are in Murrells Inlet. Pawleys Island is served by the **Pawleys Island Police Department** (321 Myrtle Ave., 843/237-3008, www.townofpawleysisland.com).

Pawleys Island has a small newspaper, the *Coastal Observer* (www.coastalobserver.com). Pawleys Island has a **U.S. Post Office** (10993 Ocean Hwy., 800/275-8777, Mon.-Fri. 8 A.M.-4:30 P.M., Sat. 10 A.M.-noon), as does Murrells Inlet (654 Bellamy Ave., 800/275-8777, Mon.-Fri. 8:30 A.M.-5 P.M., Sat. 9 A.M.-noon).

Georgetown and Vicinity

Think of Georgetown as Beaufort's lesser-known cousin. Like Beaufort, it's an hour away from Charleston, except to the north rather than to the south. Like Beaufort, it boasts a tidy historic downtown that can be walked from end to end in an afternoon. And like Beaufort, it was once a major center of Lowcountry plantation culture.

However, Georgetown gets significantly less attention and less traffic. Unlike Beaufort, no movies are shot, and no rambling Southern memoirs were penned here. Certainly the fact that the entrance to town is dominated by the sprawling ominous-looking Georgetown Steel mill on one side of the road and the massive smelly International Paper plant on the other has something to do with it. Make no mistake; industry is a way of life here. An important seaport for most of its history, Georgetown today boasts South Carolina's second busiest port after Charleston. But when you take a quick turn to the east and go down to the waterfront, you'll see the charm of old Georgetown: bright, attractive, historical homes, cute shops and cafés, and the peaceful Sampit River flowing by.

There are several enjoyable and educational places a short way north on U.S. 17. Chief among them are Hobcaw Barony, former playground of the rich turned environmental education center, and Hampton Plantation, a well-preserved look back into antebellum elegance and rice-culture history. Indeed, the coastal stretch from Georgetown down to the Charleston suburb of Mt. Pleasant is an inexplicably underrated microcosm of the Lowcountry that's easy to travel, relatively rustic, yet close enough to "civilization" that you never really have to leave your comfort zone.

One particularly delightful aspect is the fact that the massive Francis Marion National Forest is your constant companion on the west side of U.S. 17—helping to keep at bay much of the egregious overdevelopment that is taking place elsewhere on the South Carolina coast. The forest also provides plenty of hiking, biking, and bird-watching opportunities.

HISTORY

The third-oldest city in South Carolina, after Charleston and Beaufort, Georgetown was founded in 1729 on a four- by eight-block grid, most of which still exists today, complete with original street names.

Georgetown's influence was acute during the American Revolution, with the father-son team of Palmetto State signers of the Declaration of Independence Thomas Lynch and Thomas Lynch Jr. both hailing from here. The Revolutionary War hero Francis Marion, the "Swamp Fox," was born in nearby Berkeley County and conducted operations in and around the area during the entire war, including an unsuccessful assault on British forces holding Georgetown.

The biggest boom was still ahead for Georgetown. While Charleston-area plantations get most of the attention, the truth is that by 1840 about 150 rice plantations on the Sampit and Little Pee Dee Rivers were producing half of the entire national output of the staple crop. Indeed, Georgetown held fast to rice even as most Southern planters switched to growing cotton after the invention of the cotton gin.

After the Civil War, the collapse of the slave-based economy (at its height, 90 percent of Georgetown's population was slaves) meant the relative collapse of the rice economy as well. Although the plantations stayed in operation, their output was much smaller, and the coming of the boll weevil infestation in the early 1900s merely brought it to a merciful end.

In 1905 Bernard Baruch—native South Carolinian, Wall Street mover and shaker, and

THE SPANISH AT WINYAH BAY

The Georgetown area is best known for its Anglophile tendencies in history, character, and architecture. But before the English came the Spanish.

Beautiful Winyah Bay outside Georgetown—estuary of the Sampit, Pee Dee, Black, and Waccamaw Rivers—was the site of one of the first landfalls by Europeans in the New World. It happened in 1526 when six Spanish ships, commanded by Lucas Vázquez de Ayllón, came to establish a colony in the area.

The wealthy heir to a sugar-planting fortune on Hispaniola in the Caribbean, Ayllón was also a master of PR. On a previous scouting trip, he had captured an Indian and brought him back to Spain. Upon hearing the captive's proud descriptions of his homeland, King Charles V promptly gave Ayllón permission to settle the area, just as Ayllón had hoped. The king was pretty crafty himself; he insisted that Ayllón mount the expedition at his own expense.

Upon arrival with his 500 colonists, Ayllón's reluctant Indian passengers—including his only interpreter, the same man he'd brought before the king—vanished into the maritime forest, never to be found. Even worse for the Spanish, one of Ayllón's ships, the *Capitana*, sank in Winyah Bay with most of the expedition's supplies. It remains there to this day, though no one knows quite where it is or what is left of it.

Ayllón would finally get his colony, though not in South Carolina. Finding the local soil too acidic for crops and the local Native Americans too scarce in number to provide dependable slave labor, he decamped and headed down the coast to the area of St. Catherine's Sound in modern-day Georgia. His settlement there, San Miguel de Gualdape, lasted only a few months until falling victim to disease, poor nutrition, and Indian attack. But it was indeed the first European colony in what would become the United States—preceding the Spanish settlement at St. Augustine, Florida, by nearly 40 years and the first English colony at Jamestown, Virginia, by almost a century.

adviser to presidents—came to town, purchasing Hobcaw Barony, a former plantation. It became his winter residence and hunting ground, and his legacy of conservation lives on there today in an education center on the site.

The Depression was particularly hard on Georgetown, with virtually the entire city being unemployed at one point. But in 1936, the opening of a massive paper mill turned things around, with economic effects that you can see (and olfactory effects that you can smell, unfortunately) to this day.

Today, Georgetown is a quiet place where most people either make their living working at the port, the steel mill, or the paper plant, with a good smattering of tourism-related businesses in the historic district. On the national level it's perhaps best known for being the hometown of comedian Chris Rock; although he moved away long ago, many members of his family continue to live here, and he usually pays a visit at Christmas.

SIGHTS
Kaminski House

The city of Georgetown owns and operates the historic Kaminski House (1003 Front St., 843/546-7706, www.cityofgeorgetownsc.com, Mon.-Sat. 9 A.M.-5 P.M., Sun. 1-4 P.M., $7 adults, $3 ages 6-12, free under age 6). Built in 1769, it was home to several city mayors, including Harold Kaminski, who ran the city from 1931 to 1935. "Stately" pretty much describes the elegant exterior of this two-story masterpiece, but the real goods are inside. It's furnished with a particularly exquisite and copious selection of 18th- and 19th-century antiques. The grounds are beautiful as well, overlooking the Sampit River and lined with Spanish moss-covered oaks.

The only way to see the inside of the house is to take the free 45-minute guided tour. Fortunately, they're quite frequent, generally departing every hour on the hour

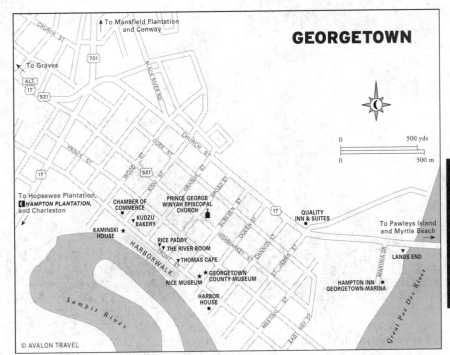

Monday-Saturday 10 A.M.-4 P.M. and Sunday 1-4 P.M.; call ahead to confirm tour times.

Rice Museum

The succinctly named Rice Museum (633 Front St., 843/546-7423, www.ricemuseum.org, Mon.-Sat. 10 A.M.-4:30 P.M., $7 adults, $3 ages 6-21, free under age 6) is just that: A look back at the all-important staple crop and its massive effects on Georgetown, which at one point accounted for half of the country's rice production.

There are actually two parts of the museum: The Old Market building, often simply called "The Town Clock" because of its 1842 timepiece, hosts the bulk of the archival information on the impact of rice growing on the region's history and economy; the adjacent Kaminski Hardware building includes a 17-minute video on the rice industry, a good Gullah-Geechee cultural exhibit, and a gift shop. However, its main claim to fame is the collection of regional maritime history, including the remains of the oldest colonial boat in North America, the 50-foot *Brown's Ferry Vessel,* built in 1710.

Several key exhibits in the Rice Museum trace the fundamental but generally reluctant role in the rice industry of African Americans, almost all of whom were slaves and who comprised nearly 90 percent of the local population during the height of the rice industry. You'll learn the story of Joseph Rainey, the first African American elected to the U.S. House of Representatives, who once worked in the fields around Georgetown. You'll learn about Miss Ruby Forsythe, who spent her life teaching African American children in a one-room school on Pawleys Island.

Most visitors to the Rice Museum take a one-hour guided tour, included in the price of admission.

MYRTLE BEACH

© JIM MOREKIS

Rice Museum

Georgetown County Museum

For a more complete look at all aspects of local history, check out the Georgetown County Museum (632 Prince St., 843/545-7020, Tues.-Fri. 10 A.M.-5 P.M., Sat. 10 A.M.-3 P.M., $4 adults, $2 ages 6-18, free under age 6). The highlight is a recently discovered letter written by Francis Marion.

Prince George Winyah Episcopal Church

It has seen better days—the British partially burned it during the Revolution—but Prince George Winyah Episcopal Church (301 Broad St., 843/546-4358, www.pgwinyah.org, Mon.-Fri. 11:30 A.M.-4:30 P.M., services Sun. 8 A.M., 9 A.M., and 11 A.M.) is still a fine example of the Anglican tradition of the Lowcountry rice culture. First built in 1750 out of ballast stones (the parish itself dates from substantially earlier, 1721), the sanctuary features classic box pews, expert stained glass, and ornate woodwork on the inside. The bell tower dates from 1824.

One of the oldest churches in continuous use in North America, Prince George is certainly worth preserving. The parish has formed its own nonprofit group, the Preservation Trust for Historic Prince George Winyah Church (843/546-4358), to raise funds and direct conservation efforts.

Hopsewee Plantation

Beautiful in an understated way, Hopsewee Plantation (494 Hopsewee Rd., 843/546-7891, www.hopsewee.com, Feb.-Nov. Tues.-Fri. 10 A.M.-4 P.M., Sat. noon-4 P.M., Dec.-Jan. by appointment only, $17.50 adults, $10.50 ages 12-17, $7.50 ages 5-11) on the Santee River 12 miles south of Georgetown was the birthplace of Thomas Lynch Jr., one of South Carolina's signers of the Declaration of Independence. Some key archaeological work is going on at the former slave village on this old indigo plantation; you can visit two of the original slave cabins on the tour.

THE SWAMP FOX AND THE COMING OF GUERRILLA WARFARE

I have it from good authority, that this great soldier, at his birth, was not larger than a New England lobster, and might easily enough have been put into a quart pot.

Peter Horry,
who fought with Francis Marion

Short, bowlegged, and moody, Francis Marion was as far away from the template of the dashing war hero as his tactics were from the storybook exploits of military literature. The father of modern guerrilla warfare was born an unimpressively small and sickly baby, the youngest of seven, somewhere in Berkeley County, South Carolina, in 1732 to hardworking French Huguenot parents. Soon his family would move near Georgetown on the coast, and the teenage Marion became enamored with the sea. While his infatuation with maritime life lasted exactly one voyage—a whale rammed and sank his ship—a taste for adventure remained.

During the French and Indian War, Marion fought local Cherokees, and revisionist historians would later revile the enthusiasm he showed in this venture. But Marion's own words show a more conflicted character, as shown by his reaction to an order to burn Cherokees out of their homes.

Some of our men seemed to enjoy this cruel work, laughing very heartily at the curling flames, as they mounted loud crackling over the tops of the huts. But to me it appeared a shocking sight. Poor creatures! thought I, we surely need not grudge you such miserable habitations.

While the irregular tactics Marion learned fighting the Cherokee would come in handy during the Revolution, his first experience in that conflict was in more textbook engagements, such as the defenses of Fort Moultrie and Fort Sullivan and the siege of Savannah. But with the fall of Charleston in 1780, a vengeful Marion and his ragged band of volunteer fighters—who, unusually for the time, included African Americans—vanished into the bogs of the Pee Dee and took up a different way of warfare: ambush and retreat, harass and vanish. In a foreshadowing of the revolutionary movements of the 20th century, "Marion's Men" provisioned themselves with food and supplies from a sympathetic local populace, offering receipts for reimbursement after the war.

Astride small agile mounts called Marsh Tackies, descendants of horses originally left by the Spanish, the Patriots rode where bigger British cavalry horses balked. Marion's nocturnal cunning and his superior intelligence network frustrated the British army and their Loyalist supporters to no end, leading to his nickname, "The Swamp Fox."

British Colonel Banastre Tarleton, himself known as "The Butcher" for atrocities on civilians, was dispatched to neutralize Marion. The savage cat-and-mouse game between the two formed the basis for the storyline of Mel Gibson's 2000 film *The Patriot* (Gibson's character was reportedly a composite of Marion and several other South Carolina irregulars). Filmed entirely in South Carolina—including at Middleton Plantation, Cypress Gardens, and Historic Brattonsville—*The Patriot* is far from an exact chronicle, but it does accurately portray the nature of the war in the Southern theater, in which quarter was rarely asked or given, and little distinction was made between combatant and civilian.

While certainly the most famous, the Swamp Fox was merely first among equals in a veritable menagerie of hit-and-run fighters. Thomas Sumter, a Virginian by birth, became known as "The Carolina Gamecock" for his ferocity on the battlefield. Andrew Pickens, "The Wizard Owl," and his militiamen played a key role in the Battle of Cowpens in the Upstate.

After the war, Marion served in elected office, married, and settled down at his Pine Bluff Plantation, now submerged under the lake that bears his name. He died in 1795 at the age of 63, peaceful at last.

MYRTLE BEACH

While not as grand as many other Lowcountry plantation homes, the 1740 main house is a masterpiece of colonial architecture, and all the more impressive because it's very nearly original, with the black cypress exterior largely intact. The focus here is on preservation, not restoration.

The home and its surrounding plantation were owned by the wealthy planter Thomas Lynch, one of South Carolina's original delegates to the First Continental Congress. While deliberating in Philadelphia in 1776, Lynch suffered a severe stroke. His son, Thomas Jr., asked for leave from the South Carolina militia in order to tend to his ailing father. The request was denied, but the state legislature intervened and named the 26-year-old a delegate to the Continental Congress so he could join his father. And that's how the Lynches became the only father-son team of signers of the Declaration of Independence—in spirit,

anyway: There's an empty signature line on the original Declaration between South Carolina's Edward Rutledge and the younger Lynch; the elder Lynch, who would die shortly afterward, was physically unable to sign his name.

Unusually, this home remains in private hands, and as such it has a more lived-in feel than other house museums of its type. There's a fairly active calendar of events throughout the year, including sweetgrass basket-weaving classes in the basement. Check the website for info on specific events.

Hampton Plantation

Tucked away three miles off U.S. 17 on the South Santee River is Hampton Plantation State Historic Site (1950 Rutledge Rd., 843/546-9361, www.southcarolinaparks. com, grounds open daily, call for hours, free, house tours $7.50 adults, $3.50 ages 6-15). This Georgian gem, one of the grandest of the

Hampton Plantation

© JIM MOREKIS

antebellum Lowcountry homes, hosted George Washington in 1791. It was also the home of South Carolina poet laureate Archibald Rutledge, who sold it to the state in 1971. Because it's now a state-run project, admission fees are significantly lower than at most of the private plantation homes in the area.

Hampton's pedigree is a virtual who's who of great South Carolina family names. In addition to the Rutledges, the Pinckneys and the Horries also called it home at one time or another.

The imposing antebellum main house, circa 1735, is magnificent both inside and out, with some of the rooms remaining unfurnished to better explain the architecture. The grounds are gorgeous as well, overflowing with live oaks, azaleas, and camellias. If you want to skip the house tour, visiting the grounds is free. A two-mile nature trail takes you around one of the original rice fields on Wambaw Creek.

St. James-Santee Episcopal Church

This redbrick church doesn't look that old, but the sanctuary of St. James-Santee Episcopal Church (Old Georgetown Rd., 843/887-4386), south of Georgetown near Hampton Plantation State Historic Site, dates from before the Revolutionary War. While it suffered damage from Union troops during and after the Civil War, much of it is intact.

A registered National Historic Landmark and known simply as "the brick church" to differentiate it from a church in nearby McClellanville that more often hosts the present congregation, it dates from 1768, but the St. James-Santee parish it serves was actually the second in the colony after St. Michael's in Charleston. The parish was notable for incorporating large numbers of French Huguenots.

The interior is nearly as Spartan as the exterior, featuring the rare sight of old-fashioned family pews. While the brick was imported from Britain, the columns are made of cypress. Look for original plasterwork on the ceiling.

Today, only one official service is held each year in the old brick church, during Easter.

McClellanville

The tiny and almost unbearably cute little fishing village of McClellanville is nestled among the woods of Francis Marion National Forest and is known mostly for the annual **Lowcountry Shrimp Festival and Blessing of the Fleet** (http://lowcountryshrimpfestival.com) held on the waterfront in early May. This is the place to go for any kind of delectable fresh shrimp dish you might want, from fried shrimp to shrimp kebabs and shrimp tacos. The event culminates with the colorful and touching Blessing of the Fleet ceremony.

Hobcaw Barony

Once a plantation, then a winter home for a Wall Street investor, and now an environmental education center, Hobcaw Barony (22 Hobcaw Rd., 843/546-4623, www.hobcawbarony.org, hours and prices vary) is one of the more unusual stories of the Lowcountry. Its name comes from a Native American word meaning "between the waters," an allusion to its location on the Waccamaw Neck, the beginnings of the Grand Strand itself. By 1718 the surrounding land comprised various rice plantations, among South Carolina's earliest, which stayed in operation through the end of the 1800s.

Hobcaw entered its modern period when 11 of the former plantations were purchased en masse in 1905 by Wall Street investor Bernard Baruch, a South Carolina native who wanted a winter residence to escape the brutal Manhattan winters. Presidents and prime ministers came to hunt and relax on its nearly 18,000 acres.

Fifty years later, Baruch died, and his progressive-minded daughter Belle took over, immediately wanting to open the grounds for university and scientific research. Still privately owned by the Belle W. Baruch Foundation, much of Hobcaw Barony is open only to researchers, but the **Hobcaw Barony Discovery Center** (843/546-4623, www.hobcawbarony. org, Mon.-Fri. 9 A.M.-5 P.M., free) has various exhibits on local history and culture, including Native American artifacts and a modest but fun aquarium with a touch tank.

To experience the rest of Hobcaw Barony, you must take one of the various themed guided tours (call for days and times). The basic Hobcaw tour ($20) takes you on a three-hour van ride all around the grounds, including the main Hobcaw House, historic stables, and the old slave quarters, with an emphasis on the natural as well as human history of the area. Other special tours include Birding on the Barony ($30), Christmas in the Quarters ($20), and a catch-and-release fly-fishing tour ($250) of local waters.

Georgetown Lighthouse

While you can't access the state-owned Georgetown Lighthouse, you can indeed take a trip to the beach on North Island, where the lighthouse stands. The 1811 structure, repaired after heavy damage in the Civil War, is still an active beacon, now entirely automated.

North Island was part of lands bequeathed to the state by former Boston Red Sox owner Tom Yawkey. North Island is now part of a wildlife preserve bearing Yawkey's name. In 2001, the Georgetown Lighthouse was added to the preserve, and it is also on the National Register of Historic Places.

Tours and Cruises

One of the most sought-after tour tickets in the Georgetown area is for the annual **Plantation Home Tour** (843/545-8291). Sponsored by the Episcopal Church Women of Prince George Winyah Parish, this event, generally happening the first week in April, brings visitors onto many local private antebellum estates that are not open to the public at any other time. Each ticket is for either the Friday or Saturday tour,

both of which feature a different set of homes. Tickets include tea at the Winyah Indigo Society Hall each afternoon.

For a standard downtown tour, get on one of the blue-and-white trams of **Swamp Fox Historic District Tours** (1001 Front St., 843/527-6469, $10 pp), which leave daily on the hour starting at 10 A.M. near the Harborwalk.

The best walking tour of Georgetown is **Miss Nell's Tours** (843/546-3975, Tues. and Thurs. 10:30 A.M. and 2:30 P.M., other times by appointment, $7-24 depending on tour length chosen). Leaving from the Harborwalk Bookstore (723 Front St.), Miss Nell, who's been doing this for over 20 years, takes you on a delightful trek through Georgetown's charming downtown waterfront.

Water dominates life in this region, and that may just be the best way to enjoy it. One of the more interesting local waterborne tours is on board the *Jolly Rover* and *Carolina Rover* (735 Front St., 843/546-8822, www.rovertours. com, Mon.-Sat., times and prices vary). The *Jolly Rover* is an honest-to-goodness tall ship that takes you on a two-hour tour of beautiful Winyah Bay and the Intracoastal Waterway, all with a crew in period dress. The *Carolina Rover* takes you on a three-hour ecotour to nearby North Island, site of the historic Georgetown Lighthouse. You can't tour the lighthouse itself, but you can get pretty darn close to it on this tour. The always-entertaining **Cap'n Sandy's Tours** (343 Ida Dr., 843/527-4106) also takes you to North Island in the shadow of the Lighthouse; call for times and rates.

For a more intense maritime ecotourism experience, contact **Black River Outdoors Center and Expeditions** (21 Garden Ave., 843/546-4840, www.blackriveroutdoors.com). Their stock-in-trade is a nice half-day kayak tour ($55 adults, $35 under age 13), generally including creeks in and around Huntington Beach and through the fascinating matrix of blackwater and cypress swamps that once

BROAD STREET TO WALL STREET: THE STORY OF BERNARD BARUCH

He became one of the country's most influential men and a world-famous adviser to presidents during both world wars, but Bernard Baruch never strayed far in spirit from his South Carolina home.

Born to German-Jewish parents in the town of Camden, near Columbia, Baruch was born a mere five years after the end of the Civil War. Ironically, his father emigrated from Prussia to avoid the draft, but soon after arriving in the United States, he found himself a surgeon on Robert E. Lee's staff.

Educated in New York City, Baruch gained a love of finance and a taste for the high life. By age 30 he had become so wealthy playing the market that he was able to buy a seat on the New York Stock Exchange. It was during this phase of his life that he purchased the 18,000-acre Hobcaw Barony near Georgetown, a conglomeration of several former rice plantations that became his hunting retreat, a hallowed place of solitude where no phones were allowed.

Baruch's prowess in the realm of high finance led him to a post as adviser to President Woodrow Wilson; perhaps influencing the selection was the whopping $50,000 contribution Baruch gave to Wilson's 1914 campaign, an enormous sum for that time. Required to divest his funds and give up his stock-exchange seat, Baruch turned his aggressive financier's mind to a larger playing field. A sort of economic czar for the Wilson administration, he would play a key role in mobilizing American industry for the war effort, turning what had been a largely agrarian rural society into a modern manufacturing juggernaut.

Under President Franklin D. Roosevelt, Baruch was a key member of the New Deal's National Recovery Administration and favored a centralized (some said heavy-handed) approach to organizing the national economy. While this served him well during the New Deal and World War II, his often idealistic approach—which envisioned a key role of the United States as an enforcer of nuclear nonproliferation—fell out of favor with the Truman administration's realpolitik. Still, Baruch would leave his mark on the postwar era as well: He was the first to coin the phrase *Cold War*, in a speech in 1947.

Indeed, Baruch was always a colorful and succinct communicator, no doubt a legacy of his Southern boyhood. He is said to have originated the witticism "If all you have is a hammer, everything looks like a nail." Other great one-liners of his include "Millions saw the apple fall, but only Newton asked why," and "Old age is always 15 years older than I am."

Baruch died in New York City in June 1965, but he spent all that May down in South Carolina at Hobcaw Barony. By that time his daughter Belle had purchased most of Hobcaw and would eventually deed it to a foundation in her name, administered by the University of South Carolina and Clemson University.

Baruch's boyhood home in Camden is no more, but it is commemorated with a marker on Broad Street. You can also enjoy the beauty and tranquility of **Hobcaw Barony** (22 Hobcaw Rd., 843/546-4623, www.hobcawbarony.org, hours and prices vary) for yourself.

hosted the rice kingdom of Georgetown and vicinity. They also offer a harbor tour ($35 pp).

For a much simpler, less nature-oriented water tour, try **Cap'n Rod's Lowcountry Tours** (843/477-0287, www.lowcountrytours.com). Rod's pontoon boat is on the Harborwalk just behind the Rice Museum. A three-hour Plantation River Tour (Mon.-Sat. 10 A.M.) costs about $25 adults, $20 children.

ENTERTAINMENT AND EVENTS

The **Winyah Bay Heritage Festival** (632 Prince St., 843/833-9919, www.winyahbay.org, free) happens each January at various venues and benefits the local historical society. The focus is on wooden decoys and waterfowl paintings, similar to Charleston's well-known Southeast Wildlife Exposition.

Each October brings the delightful **Wooden**

Boat Show (843/545-0015, www.woodenboatshow.com, free) to the waterfront, a 20-year-old celebration of, you guessed it, wooden boats. These aren't toys but the real thing—sleek, classic, and beautiful in the water. There are kid's activities, canoe-making demonstrations, a boat contest, and the highlight, a boatbuilding challenge involving two teams working to build a skiff in four hours.

SHOPPING

As you might expect, the bulk of shopping opportunities in Georgetown are down on the waterfront, chiefly at **The Shoppes on Front Street** (717-A Front St., 843/527-0066), the umbrella name for an association of downtown merchants. Highlights include **Harborwalk Books** (723 Front St., 843/546-8212, www.harborwalkbooks.com) and the children's boutique **Doodlebugs** (721 Front St., 843/546-6858).

SPORTS AND RECREATION
Kayaking and Canoeing

Kayakers and canoeists will find a lot to do in the Georgetown area, the confluence of five rivers and the Atlantic Ocean.

A good trip for more advanced paddlers is to go out **Winyah Bay** to undeveloped North Island. With advance permission from the state's Department of Natural Resources (803/734-3888), you can camp here. Any paddling in Winyah Bay is pleasant, whether you camp or not.

Another long trip is on the nine-mile blackwater **Wambaw Creek Wilderness Canoe Trail** in the Francis Marion National Forest, which takes you through some beautiful cypress and tupelo habitats. Launch sites are at the Wambaw Creek Boat Ramp and a bridge landing. Other good trips in the national forest are on the Santee River and Echaw Creek.

For rentals and guided tours, contact **Nature Adventures Outfitters** (800/673-0679), which runs daylong paddles (about $85 pp), and **Black**

River Outdoors Center and Expeditions (21 Garden Ave., 843/546-4840, www.blackriveroutdoors.com), which runs a good half-day tour ($55 adults, $35 under age 13). For those who want to explore the intricate matrix of creeks and tidal canals that made up the Georgetown rice plantation empire, a guided tour is essential.

Occasional kayak ecotours leave from the **Hobcaw Barony Discovery Center** (843/546-4623, www.hobcawbarony.org, Mon.-Fri. 9 A.M.-5 P.M., $50) under the auspices of the **North Inlet Winyah Bay National Estuarine Research Reserve** (843/546-6219, www.northinlet.sc.edu).

Fishing

Inshore saltwater fishing is big here, mostly for red drum and sea trout. For the full-on Georgetown fishing experience, contact **Delta Guide Service** (843/546-3645, www.deltaguideservice.com), which charges about $350 per day for a fishing charter along the coast.

Hiking

The **Francis Marion National Forest** (www.fs.fed.us) hosts a number of great hiking opportunities, chief among them the Swamp Fox passage of the **Palmetto Trail** (www.palmettoconservation.org). This 47-mile route winds through longleaf pine forests, cypress swamps, bottomland hardwood swamps, and various bogs, much of the way along an old logging rail bed. The main entrance to the trail is near Steed Creek Road off U.S. 17; the entrance is clearly marked on the west side of the highway.

Another way to access the Swamp Fox passage is at **Buck Hall Recreation Area** (843/887-3257) on the Intracoastal Waterway. This actually marks the trailhead of the Awendaw Connector of that part of the Palmetto Trail, a more maritime environment. Another trailhead from which to explore Francis Marion hiking trails is farther down U.S. 17 at the **Sewee Visitor**

Center (5821 U.S. 17, 843/928-3368, www.fws. gov/seweecenter, Tues.-Sat. 9 A.M.-5 P.M.).

Golf

The closest really good links to Georgetown are the courses of the **Waccamaw Golf Trail** (www.waccamawgolftrail.com), a short drive north on U.S. 17. The best public course close to Georgetown is the **Wedgefield Plantation Golf Club** (129 Clubhouse Lane, 843/546-8587, www.wedgefield.com, $69), on the grounds of an old rice plantation on the Black River about four miles west of town. A famous local ghost story revolves around Wedgefield; allegedly the ghost of a British soldier, beheaded with a single slash from one of Francis Marion's men, still wanders the grounds.

ACCOMMODATIONS
Under $150

Close to the historic district is **Quality Inn & Suites** (210 Church St., 843/546-5656, www. qualityinn.com, $90-140), which has an outdoor pool and an included breakfast. On the north side of town on U.S. 17 you'll find the **Hampton Inn Georgetown-Marina** (420 Marina Dr., 843/545-5000, www.hamptoninn. com, $140-170), which also offers a pool and complimentary breakfast.

$150-300

By far the most impressive lodging near Georgetown—and indeed among the most impressive in the Southeast—is **(Mansfield Plantation** (1776 Mansfield Rd., 843/546-6961, www.mansfieldplantation.com, $150-200), a bona fide antebellum estate dating from a 1718 king's grant. It is so evocative and so authentic that Mel Gibson shot part of his film *The Patriot* here, and renovation was recently completed on a historic slave chapel and cabin. As is typical of the Georgetown area, you will find the prices almost ridiculously low for this unique experience on this historic 1,000-acre

tract, with gardens, trails, and free use of bicycles. Pets can even stay for an extra $20 per day. As for you, you can stay in one of nine guest rooms situated in three guesthouses on the grounds, each within easy walking distance of the public areas in the main house, which include a 16-seat dining room.

With the closing of the longtime favorite B&B, the Dupre House, it's left to another B&B, the **Harbor House** (15 Cannon St., 843/546-6532, www.harborhousebb.com, $159-189), to carry on the tradition. Its four riverfront suites are perhaps slightly more modernized than you'd expect in this Georgian home, with eight fireplaces and heart-pine floors. But step into either the living room or the dining room, where the sumptuous breakfasts are served, and it's like 1850 again.

FOOD

Don't be fooled by Georgetown's small size—there's often a wait for tables at the better restaurants.

Breakfast and Brunch

The *Southern Living*-recommended **Thomas Cafe** (703 Front St., 843/546-7776, www.thomascafe. net, Mon.-Fri. 7 A.M.-2 P.M., Sat. 7 A.M.-1 P.M., $5-9) offers awesome omelets and pancakes in addition to more Lowcountry-flavored lunch dishes like crab-cake sandwiches and fried green tomatoes.

Classic Southern

Georgetown's best-known fine-dining establishment is **The Rice Paddy** (732 Front St., 843/546-2021, www.ricepaddyrestaurant.com, lunch Mon.-Sat. 11:30 A.M.-2 P.M., dinner Mon.-Sat. 6-10 P.M., $20-30), with the name implying not an Asian menu but rather a nod to the town's Lowcountry culture. Set inside a former bank building, the interior is a bit more modern than you might expect. The seafood is strong, but they do a mean veal scaloppine and rack of lamb as well. Reservations are strongly recommended.

Coffee, Tea, and Sweets

A perennial favorite is **(Kudzu Bakery** (120

MYRTLE BEACH

King St., 843/546-1847, Mon.-Fri. 9 A.M.-5:30 P.M., Sat. 9 A.M.-2 P.M.), renowned for its fresh-baked goodies such as delectable breakfast muffins, velvety chocolate cakes, and seasonal pies with fresh ingredients like strawberries, peaches, and pecans.

Seafood

Find the best shrimp and grits in town at **The River Room** (801 Front St., 843/527-4110, www.riverroomgeorgetown.com, Mon.-Sat. 11:30 A.M.-2:30 P.M. and 5-10 P.M., $15-25), which combines a gourmet attitude in the kitchen with a casual attitude on the floor. However, dishes like the herb-encrusted grouper or the signature crab cakes taste like fine dining all the way. Reservations are not accepted, and dress is casual. Literally right on the waterfront, the dining room in this former hardware store extends 50 feet over the Sampit River, adjacent to a public dock where many diners arrive by boat. There's even a large aquarium inside to complete the atmosphere.

Over at the Georgetown Marina, with great views of the river, is **Lands End** (444 Marina Dr., 843/527-1376, Mon.-Fri. 11 A.M.-2:30 P.M. and 5-9:30 P.M., Sat. 5-9:30 P.M., Sun. 11 A.M.-2:30 P.M., $15-25), which serves good Southern-style seafood and prime rib in a relaxing atmosphere.

INFORMATION AND SERVICES

In the historic waterfront area, you'll find the **Georgetown County Chamber of Commerce and Visitor Center** (531 Front St., 843/546-8436, www.georgetownchamber.com). **Georgetown Memorial Hospital** (606 Black River Rd., 843/527-7000, www.georgetown-hospitalsystem.org) is the main medical center in the area; this 131-bed institution is in the middle of a proposed expansion and relocation. If you need law enforcement help, call the **Georgetown Police** (2222 Highmarket St., 843/545-4300, www.cityofgeorgetownsc.com). In emergencies call 911.

The newspaper of record in Georgetown is the **Georgetown Times** (www.gtowntimes.com). An unofficial visitors' guide to the town is **Harborwalk** (www.theharborwalk.com), a monthly newsletter geared toward visitors. For your postal needs, visit Georgetown's main **U.S. Post Office** (1101 Charlotte St., 800/275-8777, Mon.-Fri. 9 A.M.-5 P.M., Sat. 10 A.M.-noon).

GETTING THERE AND AROUND

Georgetown is at the extreme southern tip of the Grand Strand, accessible by U.S. 17 from the east and south and U.S. 521 (called Highmarket St. in town) from the west. Very centrally located for a tour of the coast, it's about an hour north of Charleston and slightly less than an hour from Myrtle Beach.

Though there's no public transportation to speak of in Georgetown, its small size makes touring fairly simple. Metered parking is available downtown.

BEAUFORT AND THE LOWCOUNTRY

For many people around the world, the Lowcountry is the first image that comes to mind when they think of the American South. For the people that live here, the Lowcountry is altogether unique, but it does embody many of the region's most noteworthy qualities: an emphasis on manners, a constant look back into the past, and a slow and leisurely pace (embodied in the joking but largely accurate nickname "Slowcountry").

History hangs in the humid air where first the Spanish came to interrupt the native tribes' ancient reverie, then the French, followed by the English. Although time, erosion, and development have erased most traces of these various occupants, you can almost hear their ghosts in the rustle of the branches in a sudden sea breeze, or in the piercing call of a heron over the marsh.

Artists and arts lovers the world over are drawn here to paint, photograph, or otherwise be inspired by some of the most gorgeous wetlands in the United States, so vast that human habitation appears fleeting and intermittent. Sprawling between Beaufort and Charleston is the huge ACE (Ashley, Combahee, Edisto) Basin, a beautiful and important estuary and a national model for good conservation practices. In all, the defining characteristic of the Lowcountry is its liquid nature—not only literally, in the creeks and waterway that dominate every vista and the seafood cooked in all manner of ways, but figuratively too, in the slow

© JIM MOREKIS

HIGHLIGHTS

◖ **Henry C. Chambers Waterfront Park:** Walk the dog or while away the time on a porch swing at this clean and inviting gathering place on the serene Beaufort River (page 191).

◖ **St. Helena's Episcopal Church:** To walk through this Beaufort sanctuary and its walled graveyard is to walk through Lowcountry history (page 193).

◖ **Penn Center:** Not only the center of modern Gullah culture and education, this is a key site in the history of the civil rights movement as well (page 203).

◖ **Hunting Island State Park:** One of the most peaceful natural getaways on the East Coast but only minutes away from the more civilized temptations of Beaufort (page 209).

◖ **ACE Basin:** It can take a lifetime to learn your way around this massive, marshy estuary—or just a few hours soaking in its lush beauty (page 210).

◖ **Edisto Beach State Park:** Relax at this quiet, friendly, and relatively undeveloped Sea Island, a mecca for shell collectors (page 214).

◖ **Pinckney Island National Wildlife Refuge:** This well-maintained sanctuary is a major birding location and a great getaway from nearby Hilton Head (page 220).

◖ **Coastal Discovery Museum at Honey Horn:** This beautifully repurposed plantation house and spacious grounds near the island's entrance are a great way to learn about Hilton Head history, both human and natural (page 221).

◖ **Old Bluffton:** Gossipy and gorgeous by turns, this charming village on the May River centers on a thriving artists colony (page 237).

◖ **South Carolina Artisans Center:** Visual artists and fine craftspeople from all over the state contribute work to this high-quality collective in Walterboro (page 243).

LOOK FOR ◖ TO FIND RECOMMENDED SIGHTS, ACTIVITIES, DINING, AND LODGING.

but deep quality of life here. Once outside what passes for urban areas, you'll find yourself taking a look back through the decades to a time of roadside produce stands, shade-tree mechanics, and men fishing and crabbing on tidal creeks—not for sport but for the family dinner. Indeed, not so very long ago, before the influx of resort development, retirement subdivisions, and tourism, much of the Lowcountry was like a flatter,

more humid Appalachia—poverty-stricken and desperately underserved. While the archetypal South has been marketed in any number of ways to the rest of the world, here you get a sense that this is the real thing—timeless, endlessly alluring, but somehow very familiar.

South of Beaufort is the historically significant Port Royal area and the East Coast Marine Recruit Depot of Parris Island. East of Beaufort

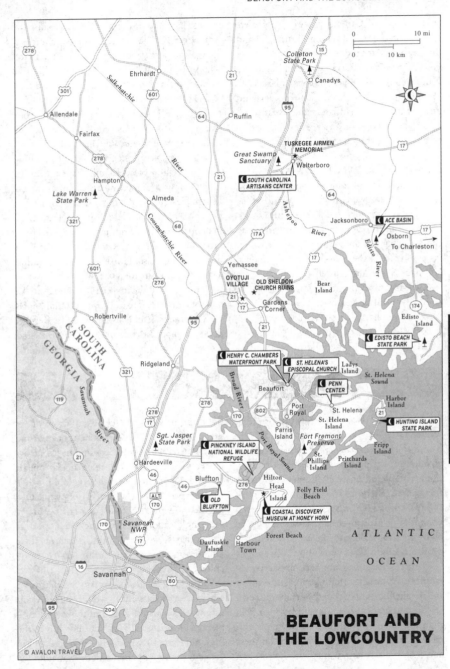

BEAUFORT

BEAUFORT AND THE LOWCOUNTRY

© AVALON TRAVEL

is the center of Gullah culture, St. Helena Island, and the scenic gem of Hunting Island. To the south is the scenic but entirely developed golf and tennis mecca, Hilton Head Island, and Hilton Head's close neighbor but diametrical opposite in every other way, Daufuskie Island, another important Gullah center. Nestled between is the close-knit and gossipy little village of Bluffton on the gossamer May River.

PLANNING YOUR TIME

The small scale and comparative lack of traffic in most of the Lowcountry are its more charming aspects. Don't let that fool you into thinking you can knock everything out in a day, though. That would defeat the purpose, which is not only to see the sights but to fully enjoy its laid-back, slow, and leisurely pace.

A common-sense game plan is to use the centrally located Beaufort as a home base. Take at least half a day of leisure to walk all over Beaufort. Another full day should go to St. Helena's Penn Center and on to Hunting Island. If you're in the mood for a road trip, dedicate a full day to tour the surrounding area to the north and northeast, with perhaps a jaunt to the ACE Basin National Wildlife Refuge, and a stop at the Old Sheldon Church Ruins in the late afternoon on your way back to Beaufort. If you have extra time, split it between Port Royal and a tour of the historic and military sites of interest on Parris Island.

While the New York accents fly fast and furious on Hilton Head Island, that's no reason for you to rush. Certainly a casual visitor can do Hilton Head in a day, but its natural attractions beg for a more considered sort of enjoyment. Plan on at least half a day just to enjoy the fine, broad beaches alone. I recommend another half day to tour the island itself, maybe including a stop in Sea Pines for a late lunch or dinner.

While most of the marketing materials make scant mention of it, nature lovers shouldn't miss the Pinckney Island National Wildlife Refuge, gorgeous enough to be a must-see but small and convenient enough to fully enjoy in a few hours.

Beaufort

Sandwiched halfway between the prouder, louder cities of Charleston and Savannah, Beaufort is in many ways a more authentic slice of life from the past than either of those two. Long a staple of movie crews seeking to portray some archetypal aspect of the old South (*The Prince of Tides, The Great Santini, Forrest Gump*) or just to film beautiful scenery for its own sake (*Jungle Book, Last Dance*), Beaufort—pronounced "BYOO-fert," by the way, not "BO-fort"—features many well-preserved examples of Southern architecture, most all of them in idyllic, family-friendly neighborhoods.

The pace in Beaufort is languid, slower even than the waving Spanish moss in the massive old live oak trees. The line between business and pleasure is a blurry one here. As you can tell from the signs you see on storefront doors saying things like "Back in an hour or so," time is an entirely negotiable commodity. The architecture combines the relaxed Caribbean flavor of Charleston with the Anglophilic dignity of Savannah. In fact, plenty of people prefer the individualistic old homes of Beaufort, seemingly tailor-made for the exact spot on which they sit, to the historic districts of either Charleston or Savannah in terms of sheer architectural delight.

While you'll run into plenty of charming and gracious locals during your time here, you might be surprised at the number of transplanted Northerners. That's due not only to the high volume of retirees who've moved to the area but the active presence of three major U.S.

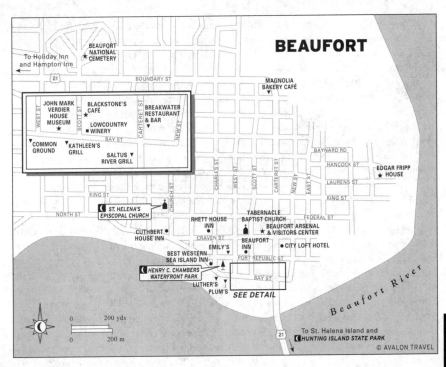

BEAUFORT

To Holiday Inn and Hampton Inn ← 21

BOUNDARY ST

BEAUFORT NATIONAL CEMETERY

MAGNOLIA BAKERY CAFÉ ▼

JOHN MARK VERDIER HOUSE MUSEUM ★

BLACKSTONE'S CAFÉ ★

BREAKWATER RESTAURANT & BAR ▼

LOWCOUNTRY WINERY ■

COMMON GROUND ▼

KATHLEEN'S GRILL ▼

BAY ST

SALTUS ▼ RIVER GRILL

WEST ST   SCOTT ST   CARTERET ST   NEW ST

BAYNARD RD

HANCOCK ST

EDGAR FRIPP HOUSE ★

CHARLES ST   WEST ST   SCOTT ST   CARTERET ST   NEW ST   EAST ST

LAURENS ST

KING ST

KING ST

NORTH ST

CHURCH ST

ST. HELENA'S EPISCOPAL CHURCH ☾

TABERNACLE BAPTIST CHURCH

FEDERAL ST

RHETT HOUSE INN

BEAUFORT ARSENAL ★ & VISITORS CENTER

CUTHBERT HOUSE INN ●

CRAVEN ST

BEAUFORT INN ●

CITY LOFT HOTEL ●

EMILY'S ▼

BEST WESTERN SEA ISLAND INN

PORT REPUBLIC ST

HENRY C. CHAMBERS ☾ WATERFRONT PARK

BAY ST

LUTHER'S ▼

PLUM'S ▼   *SEE DETAIL*

Beaufort River

0   200 yds
0   200 m

To St. Helena Island and ☾HUNTING ISLAND STATE PARK   21

© AVALON TRAVEL

BEAUFORT

Navy facilities: the Marine Corps Air Station Beaufort, the Marine Corps Recruit Depot on nearby Parris Island, and the Beaufort Naval Hospital. Many is the time a former sailor or Marine has decided to put down roots in the area after being stationed here, the most famous example being author Pat Conroy's father, a.k.a. "The Great Santini."

HISTORY

Though little known to most Americans, the Port Royal Sound area is not only one of the largest natural harbors on the East Coast, it's one of the nation's most historic places, a fact made all the more maddening in how little of that history remains.

This was the site of the second landing by the Spanish on the North American continent, the expedition of Captain Pedro de Salazar in 1514 (Ponce de León's more famous landing at St. Augustine was but a year earlier). A Spanish slaver made a brief stop in 1521, long enough to name the area Santa Elena—one of the oldest European place-names in the United States. Port Royal Sound didn't get its modern name until the first serious attempt at a permanent settlement, Jean Ribault's exploration in 1562. Though ultimately disastrous, Ribault's base of Charlesfort was the first French settlement in America. Ribault returned to France for reinforcements to find his country in an all-out religious civil war. He sought safety in England only to be clapped in the Tower of London. Meanwhile his soldiers at Charlesfort became restive and revolted against their absentee commander, with most moving to the French settlement Fort Caroline near present-day Jacksonville, Florida. In a twist straight out of Hollywood, in 1565 Fort Caroline bought food and a ship to return to France from a passing vessel, which turned out to be commanded by the infamous English privateer John Hawkins. While the French waited for a favorable wind for the trip home, who should arrive but Jean Ribault himself, fresh out of prison and at the head of 600 French soldiers and settlers sent to rescue his colony. In yet another unlikely development, a Spanish fleet soon appeared, intent on driving the French out for good. Ribault went on the offensive, intending to mount a preemptive attack on the Spanish base at St. Augustine. However, a storm wrecked the French ships, and Ribault was washed ashore near St. Augustine and killed by waiting Spanish troops. As if the whole story couldn't get any stranger, back at Charlesfort things had become so desperate for the 27 original colonists who stayed behind that they decided to build a ship to sail back home to France—technically the first ship built in America for a transatlantic crossing. The vessel made it across the Atlantic, but not without paying a price; running out of food, the French soldiers began eating shoe leather before moving on, so the accounts say, to eating each other. Twenty survivors were rescued in the English Channel.

After the French faded from the scene, Spaniards came to garrison Santa Elena. But steady Indian attacks and Francis Drake's attack on St. Augustine forced the Spanish to abandon the area in 1587. Within the next generation, British indigo planters had established a firm presence in the Port Royal area, chief among them John "Tuscarora Jack" Barnwell of Port Royal Island and Thomas Nairn of St. Helena. These men would go on to found the town of Beaufort, named for Henry Somerset, Duke of Beaufort, and it was chartered in 1711 as part of the original Carolina colony. In 1776, Beaufort planter Thomas Heyward Jr. signed the Declaration of Independence. After independence was gained, Lowcountry planters turned to cotton as the main cash crop, since England had been their prime customer for

indigo. The gambit paid off, and Beaufort soon became one of the wealthiest towns in the new nation. The so-called "golden age" of Sea Island cotton saw storm clouds gather on the horizon as the Lowcountry became the hotbed of secession, with the very first Ordinance of Secession being drawn up in Beaufort's Milton Maxey House. Only seven months after secessionists fired on Fort Sumter in nearby Charleston in 1861, a huge Union fleet sailed into Port Royal and occupied Hilton Head, Beaufort, and the rest of the Lowcountry for the duration of the war—a relatively uneventful occupation that ensured that many of the classic homes would survive.

Gradually developing their own distinct dialect and culture, much of it linked to their West African roots, isolated Lowcountry African Americans became known as the Gullah. Evolving from an effort by abolitionist missionaries early in the Civil War, in 1864 the Penn School was formed on St. Helena Island specifically to teach the children of the Gullah communities. Now known as the Penn Center, the facility has been a beacon for the study of this aspect of African American culture ever since.

The 20th century ushered in a time of increased dependence on military spending, with the opening of a training facility on Parris Island in the 1880s (the Marines didn't begin training recruits there until 1915). The Lowcountry got a further boost from wartime spending in the 1940s. Parris Island, already thriving as a Marine hub, was joined by the Marine Corps Naval Air Station in nearby Beaufort in 1942. In 1949, the Naval Hospital opened.

Today, the tourism industry has joined the military as a major economic driver in the Lowcountry. Hollywood discovered its charms as well, in a series of critical and box-office hits like *The Big Chill, The Prince of Tides,* and *Forrest Gump.*

ORIENTATION

Don't be discouraged by the big-box sprawl that assaults you on the approaches to Beaufort on

Boundary Street, lined with the usual discount megastores, fast food outlets, and budget motels. This is a popular area for relocation as well as for visitors, and when you add to the mix the presence of several bustling military facilities, you have a recipe for gridlock and architectural ugliness. But after you make the big 90-degree bend where Boundary turns into Carteret Street—known locally as the "Bellamy Curve"—it's like entering a whole new world of slow-paced, Spanish moss-lined avenues, friendly people, gentle breezes, and inviting storefronts. While you can make your way to downtown by taking Carteret Street all the way to Bay Street—don't continue over the big bridge unless you want to go straight to Lady's Island and St. Helena Island—I suggest availing yourself of one of the "Downtown Access" signs before you get that far. Because Carteret Street is the only way to that bridge, it can get backed up at rush hour. By taking a quick right and then a left all the way to Bay Street, you can come into town from the other, quieter end, with your first glimpse of downtown proper being its timelessly beguiling views of the Beaufort River.

Once there, try to park your car slightly outside the town center and simply walk everywhere you want to go. Conversely, you can park in the long-term metered spaces at the marina. Unlike Charleston or Savannah, any visitor in reasonably good shape can walk the entire length and breadth of Beaufort's 300-acre downtown with little trouble. In fact, that's by far the best way to experience it.

SIGHTS
◖ Henry C. Chambers Waterfront Park

Before you get busy shopping, dining, and admiring Beaufort's fine old homes, go straight to the town's pride and joy since 1980, the Henry C. Chambers Waterfront Park (843/525-7054, www.cityofbeaufort.org, daily 24 hours), stretching for hundreds of feet directly on the Beaufort River. A tastefully designed, well-maintained, and user-friendly mix of walkways, bandstands, and patios, Waterfront Park is a favorite gathering place for locals and visitors alike, beckoning one and all with its open green space and wonderful marsh-front views. My favorite part is the long row of swinging benches on which to peacefully sit and while away the time looking out over the marsh. Kids will especially enjoy the park not only because there's so much room to run around but for the charming playground at the east end near the bridge, complete with a jungle gym in the form of a Victorian home. The clean, well-appointed public restrooms are a particularly welcome feature.

John Mark Verdier House Museum

A smallish but stately Federalist building on the busiest downtown corner, the Verdier House Museum (801 Bay St., 843/379-6335, www.historicbeaufort.org, Mon.-Sat. 10 A.M.-4 P.M., $5) is the only historic Beaufort home open to regular tours. Built in 1805 for the wealthy planter John Mark Verdier, its main claim to fame was acting as the Union headquarters during the long occupation of Beaufort during the Civil War. However, perhaps its most intriguing link to history—a link it shares with Savannah's Owens-Thomas House—is its connection to the Revolutionary War hero the Marquis de Lafayette, who stayed at the Verdier House on the Beaufort leg of his 1825 U.S. tour. Despite the late hour of his arrival, a crowd gathered at the corner of Bay and Scott Streets, and Lafayette finally had to come to the entranceway to satisfy their desire for a speech. When the Verdier House was faced with demolition in the 1940s, the Historic Beaufort Foundation purchased the house and renovated it to its current state, reflective of the early 1800s.

Beaufort Arsenal and Visitors Center

The imposing yellow-gray tabby facade of the 1852 Beaufort Arsenal (713 Craven St.) once

PAT CONROY'S LOWCOUNTRY

I was always your best subject, son.
Your career took a nose dive after
The Great Santini came out.

Colonel Donald Conroy, to his son Pat

Although born in Georgia, no other person is as closely associated with the South Carolina Lowcountry as author Pat Conroy. After moving around as a child in a military family, he began high school in Beaufort. His painful teen years there formed the basis of his first novel, a brutal portrait of his domineering Marine pilot father, Colonel Donald Conroy, a.k.a. Colonel Bull Meecham of *The Great Santini* (1976). Many scenes from the 1979 film adaptation were filmed at the famous Tidalholm, the Edgar Fripp House (1 Laurens St.) in Beaufort. (The house was also front and center in *The Big Chill*.)

Conroy's pattern of thinly veiled autobiography actually began with his first book, the self-published *The Boo*, a tribute to a teacher at The Citadel in Charleston while Conroy was still a student there. His second work, *The Water is Wide* (1972), is a chronicle of his experiences teaching in a one-room African American school on Daufuskie Island. Though ostensibly a straightforward first-person journalistic effort, Conroy changed the location to the fictional Yamacraw Island, supposedly to protect Daufuskie's fragile culture from curious outsiders. The 1974 film adaptation starring Jon Voight was titled *Conrack* after the way his students mispronounced his name. You can visit that same two-room school today on Daufuskie. Known as the Mary Field School, the building is now a local community center.

Conroy also wrote the foreword to the cookbook *Gullah Home Cooking the Daufuskie Way: Smokin' Joe Butter Beans, Ol' 'Fuskie Fried Crab Rice, Sticky-Bush Blackberry Dumpling,* *and Other Sea Island Favorites* by Daufuskie native and current Savannah resident Sallie Ann Robinson. Conroy would go on to publish in 1980 *The Lords of Discipline*, a reading of his real-life experience with the often-savage environment faced by cadets at The Citadel—though Conroy would change the name, calling it the Carolina Military Institute. Still, when it came time to make a film adaptation in 1983, The Citadel refused to allow it to be shot there, so the "Carolina Military Institute" was filmed in England instead.

For many of his fans, Conroy's *The Prince of Tides* is his ultimate homage to the Lowcountry. Surely, the 1991 film version starring Barbra Streisand and Nick Nolte—shot on location and awash in gorgeous shots of the Beaufort River marsh—did much to implant an idyllic image of the area with audiences around the world. According to local legend, Streisand originally didn't intend to make the film in Beaufort, but a behind-the-scenes lobbying effort allegedly coordinated by Conroy himself, and including a stay at the Rhett House Inn, convinced her.

The Bay Street Inn (601 Bay St.) in Beaufort was seen in the film, as was the football field at the old Beaufort High School. The beach scenes were shot on nearby Fripp Island. Interestingly, some scenes set in a Manhattan apartment were actually shot within the old Beaufort Arsenal (713 Craven St.), now a visitors center. Similarly, the Beaufort Naval Hospital doubled as New York's Bellevue.

Despite the many personal tribulations he faced in the area, Conroy has never given up on the Lowcountry and still makes his home here with his family on Fripp Island. As for the "Great Santini" himself, you can visit the final resting place of Colonel Conroy in the Beaufort National Cemetery—Section 62, Grave 182.

© JIM MOREKIS

Henry C. Chambers Waterfront Park

housed the Beaufort Museum, which sadly closed due to financial issues. The historic building currently houses the relocated offices of the Beaufort Chamber of Commerce and Convention and Visitors Bureau (843/986-5400, www.beaufortsc.org, daily 9 A.M.-5:30 P.M.), and you can find plenty of visitor information and gifts inside; there are also public restrooms.

St. Helena's Episcopal Church

Nestled within the confines of a low brick wall surrounding this historic church and cemetery, St. Helena's Episcopal Church (505 Church St., 843/522-1712, Tues.-Fri. 10 A.M.-4 P.M., Sat. 10 A.M.-1 P.M.) has witnessed some of Beaufort's most compelling tales. Built in 1724, this was the parish church of Thomas Heyward, one of South Carolina's signers of the Declaration of Independence. John "Tuscarora Jack" Barnwell, an early Indian fighter and one of Beaufort's founders, is buried on the grounds.

The balcony upstairs in the sanctuary was intended for black parishioners; as was typical throughout the region before the Civil War, both races attended the same church services. After the entire congregation fled with the Union occupation, Federal troops decked over the second floor and used St. Helena's as a hospital—with surgeons using tombstones as operating tables. The wooden altar was carved by the crew of the USS *New Hampshire* while the warship was docked in the harbor during Reconstruction.

While the cemetery and sanctuary interior are likely to be your focus, take a close look at the church exterior—many of the bricks are actually ships' ballast stones. Also be aware that you're not looking at the church's original footprint; the building has been expanded several times since its construction (a hurricane in 1896 destroyed the entire east end). A nearly $3 million restoration, mostly for structural repairs, was completed in 2000.

Tabernacle Baptist Church

Built in 1845, this handsome sanctuary (911

© JIM MOREKIS

The visitors center is in the old Beaufort Arsenal.

Craven St., 843/524-0376) had a congregation of over 3,000 before the Civil War. Slaves made up most of the congregation, though the vast majority of slaves generally worshipped separately on plantation ground. During the war, freed slaves purchased the church for their own use. A congregant was the war hero Robert Smalls, who kidnapped the Confederate steamer he was forced to serve on and delivered it to Union forces. He is buried in the church cemetery and has a nice memorial dedicated to him there, proudly facing the street.

Beaufort National Cemetery

It's not nearly as poignantly ornate as Savannah's Victorian cemeteries, but Beaufort National Cemetery (1601 Boundary St., daily 8 A.M.-sunset) is worth a stop, as you enter or leave Beaufort, for its history. Begun by order of Abraham Lincoln in 1863, this is one of the few cemeteries containing the graves of both Union and Confederate troops, mostly the

former. National Cemetery is where 19 soldiers of the all-black Massachusetts 54th and 55th Infantries were reinterred with full military honors after being found on Folly Island near Charleston. Sergeant Joseph Simmons, Buffalo Soldier and veteran of both world wars, is buried here, as is none other than "The Great Santini" himself, novelist Pat Conroy's father, Donald.

A Walking Tour of Beaufort Homes

One of the more unique aspects of the Lowcountry is the large number of historic homes in private hands. When buyers purchase one of these fine old homes, they generally know what's in store: a historical marker of some sort might be nearby, organized tours will periodically swing by their home, and production companies will sometimes approach them about using the home as a film set. It's a trade-off most homeowners are only too glad to accept.

Here's a walking tour of some of Beaufort's fine historic homes in private hands. You won't be taking any tours of the interiors, but these homes are part of the legacy of the area and are locally valued as such. Be sure to respect the privacy of the inhabitants by keeping the noise level down and not trespassing on private property to take photos. And be amazed at the fine old live oaks all around.

- **Thomas Fuller House:** Begin at the corner of Harrington and Bay Streets and view the 1796 Thomas Fuller House (1211 Bay St.), one of the oldest in Beaufort and even more unique in that much of the building material is tabby (hence the home's other name, the Tabby Manse).

- **Milton Maxcy House:** Walk east on Bay Street one block and take a left on Church Street; walk up to the corner of Church and Craven Streets. Otherwise known as the Secession House (113 Craven St.), this 1813 home was built on a tabby foundation dating from 1743. In 1860, when it was the residence of attorney Edmund Rhett, the first Ordinance of Secession was signed here, and the rest, as they say, is history.

- **Lewis Reeve Sams House:** Pick up the walking tour on the other side of the historic district, at the foot of the bridge in the old neighborhood simply called "The Point." The beautiful Lewis Reeve Sams House (601 Bay St.) at the corner of Bay and New Streets, with its double-decker veranda, dates from 1852 and like many Beaufort mansions served as a Union hospital during the Civil War.

- **Berners Barnwell Sams House:** Continue up New Street, where shortly ahead on the left you'll find the 1818 Berners Barnwell Sams House (310 New St.), which served as the African American hospital during the Union occupation. Harriet Tubman of Underground Railroad fame worked here for a time as a nurse.

- **Joseph Johnson House:** Continue up New Street and take a right on Craven Street. Cross East Street to find the 1850 Joseph Johnson House (411 Craven St.), with the massive live oak in the front yard. Legend has it that when the Yankees occupied Hilton Head, Mr. Johnson buried his valuables under an outhouse. After the war he returned to find his home for sale due to unpaid back taxes. He dug up his valuables, paid the taxes, and resumed living in the home. You might recognize the home from the film *Forces of Nature*.

- **Marshlands:** Backtrack to East Street, walk north to Federal Street, and go to the end. Built by James R. Verdier, Marshlands (501 Pinckney St.) was used as a hospital during the Civil War, as many Beaufort homes were, and is now a National Historic Landmark. It was the setting of Francis Griswold's 1931 novel *A Sea Island Lady*.

- **The Oaks:** Walk up to King Street and take a right. Soon after you pass a large open park on the left, King Street dead-ends at the Short Street. The Oaks (100 Laurens St.) at this corner was owned by the Hamilton family, who lost a son who served with General Wade Hampton's cavalry in the Civil War. After the conflict, the family couldn't afford the back taxes, and neighbors paid the debts and returned the deed to the Hamiltons.

- **Edgar Fripp House:** Continue east on Laurens Street toward the water to find this handsome Lowcountry mansion, sometimes called Tidalholm (1 Laurens St.). Built in 1856 by the wealthy planter for whom nearby Fripp Island is named, this house was a key setting in *The Big Chill* and *The Great Santini*.

- **Francis Hext House:** Go back to Short Street, walk north to Hancock Street, and take a left. A short way ahead on the right, the handsome red-roofed estate known as Riverview (207 Hancock St.) is one of the oldest structures in Beaufort; it was built in 1720.

- **Robert Smalls House:** Continue west on Hancock Street, take a short left on East Street, and then a quick right on Prince Street. The 1834 Robert Smalls House (511 Prince St.) was the birthplace of Robert Smalls, a former slave and Beaufort native who stole the Confederate ship *Planter* from Charleston Harbor while serving as helmsman and delivered it to Union troops in Hilton Head. Smalls and a few compatriots commandeered the ship while the officers were at a party at Fort Sumter. Smalls used the bounty for the act of bravery to buy his boyhood home. After the war, Smalls was a longtime U.S. congressman.

Organized Tours

Colorful character Jon Sharp runs the popular **Jon Sharp's Walking History Tour** (843/575-5775, www.jonswalkinghistory.com, Tues.-Sat. 11 A.M., $20), taking a break during the summer months. The two-hour jaunt begins and ends at the Downtown Marina and takes you all through the downtown area. **The Spirit of Old Beaufort** (103 West St. Extension, 843/525-0459, www.thespiritofoldbeaufort.com, Mon.-Sat. 10:30 A.M., 2 P.M., and 7 P.M., $13 adults, $8 children) runs a year-round series of good walking tours, roughly two hours long, with guides usually in period dress. If you don't want to walk, you can hire one of their guides to join you in your own vehicle (from $50).

As you might expect, few things could be more Lowcountry than an easygoing carriage ride through the historic neighborhoods. **Southurn Rose Buggy Tours** (843/524-2900, www.southurnrose.com, daily 10 A.M.-5 P.M., $18 adults, $7 children)—yes, that's how they spell it—offers 50-minute narrated carriage rides of the entire Old Point, including movie locations, embarking and disembarking near the Downtown Marina about every 40 minutes.

An important specialty bus tour in the area is **Gullah-N-Geechie Man Tours** (843/838-7516, www.gullahngeechietours.net, $20 adults, $18 children), focusing on the rich Gullah history and culture of the St. Helena Island area, including the historic Penn Center. Call for pickup information.

ENTERTAINMENT AND EVENTS
Nightlife

Those looking for a rowdy time will be happier

seeking it in the notorious party towns of Charleston or Savannah. However, a few notable places in downtown Beaufort do double duty as dining havens and neighborhood watering holes. Sadly, the well-regarded restaurant within the Beaufort Inn on Port Republic Street closed for good in 2007. But several establishments tucked together on Bay Street, all with café seating out back facing the waterfront, can also show you a good time.

The convivial **Kathleen's Grill** (822 Bay St., 843/524-2500, daily 11 A.M.-2 A.M.) features live music by a variety of regional artists. Weekend tunes crank up about 10 P.M. **Plum's** (904½ Bay St., 843/525-1946, daily 5 P.M.-2 A.M.) offers not only a tasty menu but some fun at 10 P.M. when the kitchen closes down and the focus turns to its great beer selection. Close by is **Luther's Rare & Well Done** (910 Bay St., 843/521-1888, daily 5 P.M.-midnight, $15), which offers a late-night appetizer menu to go with its rock-oriented live music on weekends.

Performing Arts

Beaufort's fine arts scene is small but professional in outlook. Most performances are based in the nice new Performing Arts Center on the oak-lined campus of the University of South Carolina Beaufort (USCB, 801 Carteret St., 843/521-4100). A prime mover of the local performing arts scene is **Beaufort Performing Arts Inc.** (www.uscb.edu), formed by a mayoral task force in 2003 specifically to encourage arts and cultural development within the area. The most recent season, with performances at USCB's Performing Arts Center, included performances by Celtic fiddler Natalie MacMaster, the Claremont Trio, and the Bee Gees. Ticket prices typically range $12-40.

Perhaps surprisingly for such a small place, Beaufort boasts its own full orchestra, the **Beaufort Orchestra** (1106 Carteret St., 843/986-5400, www.beaufortorchestra.org), which plays in the Performing Arts Center.

A recent season included Paganini's Violin Concerto in D, Tchaikovsky's "Pathétique" Symphony No. 6, and *Beaufort Goes to Broadway.*

Cinema

One of only two functional drive-ins in the state, the **Highway 21 Drive In** (55 Parker Dr., 843/846-4500, www.hwy21drivein.com) has two screens, great sound, and awesome concessions that include Angus beef hamburgers. All you need to provide is the car and the company. The best multiplex in the area is the cool **Sea Turtle Cinemas** (106 Buckwalter Pkwy., 843/706-2888, www.seaturtlecinemas.com) in the Berkeley Place shopping center.

Festivals and Events

Surprisingly for a town so prominent in so many films, Beaufort didn't have its own film festival until 2007. The **Beaufort Film Festival** (843/986-5400, www.beaufortfilmfestival. com) is held in February. It's small in scale—the inaugural festival was only two days, at a now-defunct theater—but boasts a diverse range of high-quality, cutting-edge entries, including shorts and animation.

Foodies will also enjoy **A Taste of Beaufort** (www.downtownbeaufort.com), usually held the first Saturday in May, which features the offerings of two dozen or so local restaurants with live music, all along historic Bay Street.

Now over 20 years old, the **Gullah Festival of South Carolina** celebrates Gullah history and culture on Memorial Day weekend at various locations throughout town, mostly focusing on Waterfront Park.

By far the biggest single event on the local festival calendar is the over 50-year-old **Beaufort Water Festival** (www.bftwaterfestival.com), held over two weeks in June or July each year, centering on the Waterfront Park area. One of the most eclectic and idiosyncratic events of its kind in a region already known for quirky hyperlocal festivals, the Beaufort Water Festival features events as diverse as a raft race, badminton, boccie, billiards, croquet, and golf tournaments, a children's toad fishing tournament, a ski show, a bed race, a street dance, and all sorts of live music and local art exhibits. The signature events are the Saturday-morning two-hour Grand Parade and a blessing and parade of the shrimp fleet on the closing Sunday.

Fall in the Lowcountry means shrimping season, and early October brings the **Beaufort Shrimp Festival** (www.beaufortsc.org). Highlights include an evening concert with specially lighted shrimp boats docked along the river, a 5K run over the Woods Memorial Bridge, and a more laid-back 5K walk through the historic district. Various cooking competitions are held, obviously centering around the versatile crustaceans that are the raison d'être of the shrimp fleet.

St. Helena Island hosts the three-day **Penn Center Heritage Days** (www.penncenter.com) each November, without a doubt the Beaufort area's second-biggest celebration after the Water Festival. Focusing on Gullah culture, history, and delicious food, Heritage Days does a great job of combining fun with education. The event culminates in a colorful Saturday-morning parade, featuring lots of traditional Gullah garb, from St. Helena Elementary School to the Penn Center Historic District.

SHOPPING

The Beaufort area's shopping allure comes from the rich variety of independently owned shops, most of which keep a pretty high standard and don't deal too much in touristy schlock. The main drag in town, Bay Street, is also the shopping hub. Note that in Beaufort's shops as well as most everything else in town, hours of operation are loose guidelines and not rigidly observed.

My favorite shop in Beaufort is **The Bay Street Trading Company** (808 Bay St., 843/524-2000, www.baystreettrading.com, Mon.-Fri. 10 A.M.-5:30 P.M., Sat. 10 A.M.-5 P.M.,

BEAUFORT

Sun. noon-5 P.M.), sometimes known simply as "The Book Shop," which has a very friendly staff and the best collection of Lowcountry-themed books I've seen in one place.

Across the street, the recently renovated Old Bay Marketplace, with a facade so bright red you can't miss it, hosts a few cute shops, most notably the stylish **Lulu Burgess** (917 Bay St., 843/524-5858, Mon.-Sat. 10 A.M.-6 P.M., Sun. noon-5 P.M.), an eclectic store that brings a rich, quirky sense of humor to its otherwise tasteful assortment of gift items for the whole family.

A unique gift item, as well as something you can enjoy on your own travels, can be found at **Lowcountry Winery** (705 Bay St., 843/379-3010, Mon.-Sat. 10 A.M.-5 P.M.). Not only can you purchase bottles of their various red and white offerings, they host tastings daily in the tasting room (because of state law, they must charge a fee for the tasting, but it's only $1 pp).

Just off the Waterfront Park and right across the walk from Common Grounds coffee shop is the delightful **Lollipop Shop** (103 West St. Extension, 843/379-POPS—843/379-7677, www.thelollipopshop.net, Mon.-Thurs. 10 A.M.-5 P.M., Fri.-Sat. 10 A.M.-9 P.M., Sun. 1-5 P.M.). Part of a regional franchise chain, the Lollipop Shop offers a wide range of treats from jelly beans to M&Ms in custom colors as well as wind-up toys and stuff-them-yourself teddy bears.

Art Galleries

As you'd expect in such a visually stirring locale, there's a plethora of great art galleries in the Beaufort-St. Helena area. While most are clustered on Bay Street, there are gems scattered all over. Almost all are worth a look, but here are a few highlights.

My favorite gallery in town is the simply named **The Gallery** (802 Bay St., 843/470-9994, www.thegallery-beaufort.com, Mon.-Sat. 11 A.M.-5 P.M.). Deanna Bowdish brings in the most cutting-edge regional contemporary artists in a large, friendly, loftlike space. The

Beaufort Art Association Gallery (1001 Bay St., 843/379-2222, www.beaufortartassociation.com, Mon.-Sat. 10 A.M.-5 P.M.) hosts rotating exhibits by member artists in the stately and historic Elliott House. A complete art experience blending the traditional with the cutting-edge is at the **I. Pinckney Simons Art Gallery** (711 Bay St., 843/379-4774, www.ipinckneysimonsgallery.com, Tues.-Fri. 11 A.M.-5 P.M., Sat. 11 A.M.-3 P.M.), which is pronounced "Simmons" despite the spelling. There you will find not only paintings but compelling photography, sculpture, and jewelry as well, all by local and regional artists of renown.

Right on the water is a fun local favorite, the **Longo Gallery** (103 Charles St., 843/522-8933, Mon.-Sat. 11 A.M.-5 P.M.). Owners Suzanne and Eric Longo provide a whimsical assortment of less traditional art than you might find in the more touristy waterfront area. Take Charles Street as it works its way toward the waterfront, and the gallery is right behind a storefront on the corner of Charles and Bay Streets.

You'll find perhaps the area's best-known gallery over the bridge on St. Helena Island. Known regionally as one of the best places to find Gullah folk art, **Red Piano Too** (870 Sea Island Parkway, 843/838-2241, www.redpianotoo.com, Mon.-Sat. 10 A.M.-5 P.M.) is on the corner before you turn onto the road to the historic Penn Center. Over 150 artists from a diverse range of traditions and styles are represented in this charming little 1940 building with the red tin awning, historically significant in its own right because it once hosted a produce cooperative that was the first store in the area to pay African Americans with cash rather than barter for goods.

SPORTS AND RECREATION

Beaufort County comprises over 60 islands, so it's no surprise that nearly all recreation in the area revolves around the water, which dominates so many aspects of life in the Lowcountry.

The closer to the ocean you get, the more it's a salt marsh environment. But as you explore more inland, in the sprawling ACE Basin, you'll encounter primarily blackwater.

Kayaking

The Lowcountry is tailor-made for kayaking. Most kayakers put in at the public landings in nearby Port Royal (1 Port Royal Landing Dr., 843/525-6664) or Lady's Island (73 Sea Island Pkwy., 843/522-0430), across the river from downtown Beaufort. The catch here, as with all of the Lowcountry, is to know your way around if you choose to leave the main waterways. It's easy to get lost because of the sheer number of creeks, and they all seem to look the same once you get into them a good ways. If you don't feel comfortable with your navigation skills, it's a good idea to contact Kim and David at **Beaufort Kayak Tours** (843/525-0810, www.beaufortkayaktours.com), who rent kayaks and can guide you on a number of excellent tours of all three key areas. They charge about $40 for adults and $30 for children for a two-hour trip. A tour with Beaufort Kayak Tours is also the best (and nearly the only) way to access the historically significant ruins of the early British tabby Fort Frederick, now located on the grounds of the Beaufort Naval Hospital and inaccessible by car.

Fishing and Boating

Key marinas in the area are the **Downtown Marina** (1006 Bay St., 843/524-4422) in Beaufort, the **Lady's Island Marina** (73 Sea Island Pkwy., 843/522-0430), and the **Port Royal Landing Marina** (1 Port Royal Landing Dr., 843/525-6664). Hunting Island has a popular 1,000-foot fishing pier at the south end. A good local fishing charter service is Captain Josh Utsey's **Lowcountry Guide Service** (843/812-4919, www.beaufortscfishing.com). Captain Ed Hardee (843/441-6880) offers good inshore charters.

The ACE Basin is a very popular fishing, crabbing, and shrimping area. It has about two dozen public boat ramps, with colorful names like Cuckold's Creek and Steamboat Landing. There's a useful map of them all at www.acebasin.net, or look for the brown signs along the highway.

Hiking and Biking

Despite the Lowcountry's, well, lowness, biking opportunities abound. It might not get your heart rate up like a ride in the Rockies, but the area lends itself to laid-back two-wheeled enjoyment. Many local B&Bs provide bikes free for guests, and you can rent your own just across the river from Beaufort in Lady's Island at **Lowcountry Bikes** (102 Sea Island Pkwy., 843/524-9585, Mon.-Tues. and Thurs.-Fri. 10 A.M.-6 P.M., Wed. 10 A.M.-1 P.M., Sat. 10 A.M.-3 P.M., about $5 per hour). They can also hook you up with some good routes around the area.

Bicycling around Beaufort is a delight for its paucity of traffic as well as its beauty. Port Royal is close enough that you can easily make a circuit to that little town. To get to Port Royal from Beaufort, take Bay Street west to Ribaut Road (U.S. 21) and veer left onto Paris Avenue into downtown Port Royal, where the biking is easy, breezy, and fun.

For a visually delightful ride, the bridge over the Beaufort River also features a pedestrian and bike lane with some awesome views. You can either turn back at the base of the bridge and go back into Beaufort or push on to Lady's Island and St. Helena Island, although the traffic on U.S. 21 can get daunting.

ACCOMMODATIONS

Beaufort's historic district is blessed with an abundance of high-quality accommodations that blend well with their surroundings. There are plenty of budget-minded chain places, some of them acceptable, in the sprawl of Boundary Street outside of downtown, but here are some

BEAUFORT

suggestions within bicycling distance of the Historic District. (That's not a hypothetical, as most inns offer free bicycles to use as you please during your stay.)

Under $150

The **Best Western Sea Island Inn** (1015 Bay St., 843/522-2090, www.bestwestern. com, $135-170) is a good value for those for whom the B&B experience is not paramount. Anchoring the southern end of the historic district in a tasteful low brick building, the Best Western offers decent service, basic amenities, and surprisingly attractive rates for the location on Beaufort's busiest street.

$150-300

Any list of upscale Beaufort lodging must highlight the **❰ Beaufort Inn** (809 Port Republic St., 843/379-4667, www.beaufortinn.com, $152-425), consistently voted one of the best B&Bs in the nation. It's sort of a hybrid in that it comprises not only the 1897 historic central home but also a cluster of freestanding historical cottages, each with a charming little porch and rocking chairs. With everything connected by gardens and pathways, you could almost call it a campus. Still, for its sprawling nature—44 guest rooms in total—the Beaufort Inn experience is intimate, with attentive service and top-flight amenities such as wet bars, large baths, and sumptuous king beds. Within or outside the main building, each suite has a character all its own, whether it's the 1,500-square-foot Loft Apartment (complete with a guest bedroom and a full kitchen) or one of the cozier (and more affordable) Choice Rooms with a queen-sized bed.

The 18-room, circa-1820 **Rhett House Inn** (1009 Craven St., 843/524-9030, www. rhetthouseinn.com, $175-320) is the local vacation getaway for the stars. Such arts and entertainment luminaries as Robert Redford, Julia Roberts, Ben Affleck, Barbra Streisand, Dennis Quaid, and Demi Moore have all stayed here at one time or another. Owner Steve Harrison is also a local realtor and no doubt has helped many a guest relocate to town after they've fallen in love with it while staying at his inn. As if Beaufort's great restaurants weren't caloric enough, you can put on a few pounds just staying at the Rhett House. Of course you get the requisite full Southern breakfast, but you'll also be treated to afternoon tea and pastries, more munchies at cocktail hour, and homemade late-night desserts.

There's nothing like enjoying the view of the Beaufort River from the expansive porches of the **❰ Cuthbert House Inn** (1203 Bay St., 843/521-1315, www.cuthberthouseinn.com, $205-250), possibly the most romantic place to stay in Beaufort. This grand old circa-1790 Federal mansion was once the home of the wealthy Cuthbert family of rice and indigo planters and is now on the National Register of Historic Places. General Sherman spent a night here in 1865. Some of the king rooms have fireplaces and claw-foot tubs. Of course you get a full Southern breakfast, in addition to sunset hors d'oeuvres on the veranda.

While a stay at a B&B is the classic way to enjoy Beaufort, many travelers swear by the new **City Loft Hotel** (301 Carteret St., 843/379-5638, www.citylofthotel.com, $200). Housed in a former motel, City Loft is a total modernist makeover, gleaming from stem to stern with chrome and various art deco touches. While the stay is definitely "boutique," the prices aren't.

FOOD
Breakfast and Brunch

One of the best breakfasts I've had anywhere was a humble two-egg plate for five bucks at Beaufort's most popular morning hangout, **❰ Blackstone's Café** (205 Scott St., 843/524-4330, Mon.-Sat. 7:30 A.M.-2:30 P.M., Sun. 7:30 A.M.-2 P.M., under $10), complete with tasty hash browns, a comparative rarity in this part of the country, where grits rule as the breakfast

LOWCOUNTRY BOIL OR FROGMORE STEW?

Near Beaufort it's called Frogmore stew after the township (now named St. Helena) just over the river. Closer to Savannah it's simply called Lowcountry boil. Supposedly the first pot of this delectable, hearty concoction was made by Richard Gay of the Gay Fish Company. As with any vernacular dish, dozens of local and family variants abound. The key ingredient that makes Lowcountry boil/Frogmore stew what it is—a well-blended mélange with a character all its own rather than just a bunch of stuff thrown together in a pot of boiling water—is some type of crab-boil seasoning. You'll find Zatarain's seasoning suggested on a lot of websites, but Old Bay is far more common in the eponymous Lowcountry where the dish originated.

In any case, here's a simple six-serving recipe to get you started. The only downside is that it's pretty much impossible to make it for just a few people. The dish is intended for large gatherings, whether a football tailgate party on a Saturday or a family afternoon after church on Sunday. Note the typical ratio of one ear of corn and 0.5 pounds each of meat and shrimp per person.

- 6 ears fresh corn on the cob, cut into 3-inch sections
- 3 pounds smoked pork sausage, cut into 3-inch sections
- 3 pounds fresh shrimp, shells on
- 5 pounds new potatoes
- 6 ounces Old Bay Seasoning

Put the sausage and potato pieces, along with half of the Old Bay, in two gallons of boiling water. When the potatoes are about halfway done, about 15 minutes in, add the corn and boil for about half that time, seven minutes. Add the shrimp and boil for another three minutes, until they just turn pink. Do not overcook the shrimp. Take the pot off the heat and drain; serve immediately. If you cook the shrimp just right, the oil from the sausage will cause those shells to slip right off.

This is but one of dozens of recipes. Some cooks add some lemon juice and beer in the water as it's coming to a boil; others add onion, garlic, or green peppers.

starch of choice. Tucked on a side street just off busy Bay Street, Blackstone's roomy but inviting interior—festooned with various collegiate, nautical, and military motifs and a checkerboard floor—has more than enough room for you to spread out and relax before continuing on with your travels (there's even free Wi-Fi).

Burgers and Sandwiches

Another longtime lunch favorite is **Magnolia Bakery Café** (703 Congress St., 843/524-1961, Mon.-Sat. 9 A.M.-5 P.M., under $10). It's a little ways north of the usual tourist area but well worth going out of your way for (Beaufort is pretty small, after all). Lump crab cakes are a particular specialty item, but you can't go wrong with any of the lunch sandwiches. They even offer a serviceable crepe. Vegetarian

diners are particularly well taken care of with a large selection of black-bean burger plates. As the name indicates, the range of desserts here is tantalizing, to say the least, with the added bonus of a serious espresso bar.

Coffeehouses

The charming and popular **Common Ground** (102 West St., 843/524-2326, daily 7:30 A.M.-10 P.M.) coffeehouse in the Waterfront Park area is not only a great place for a light sandwich or sweet treat; the java is a cut above most such places, featuring a wide selection of excellent fair-trade "Dancing Goat" brews.

New Southern

The stylishly appointed **Wren Bistro, Bar and Market** (210 Carteret St., 843/524-9463,

$15-25) is known for any of its chicken dishes. While the food is great, the interior is particularly well-done, simultaneously warm and classy. As seems to be typical of Beaufort, the lunches are as good as the dinners.

Seafood

The hottest dinner table in town is at the **Saltus River Grill** (802 Bay St., 843/379-3474, Sun.-Thurs. 5-9 P.M., Fri.-Sat. 5-10 P.M., $10-39). Executive chef Jim Spratling has made this fairly new restaurant, housed in a historic tabby building on the waterfront, famous throughout the state for its raw bar menu featuring oysters from Nova Scotia, Chesapeake Bay, Oregon, and British Columbia. Sushi lovers can also get a fix here, whether it's a basic California roll or great sashimi. Other specialties include she-crab bisque, lump crab cakes, flounder fillet, and, of course, the ubiquitous shrimp and grits. The Saltus River Grill is more upscale in feel and in price than most Lowcountry places, with a very see-and-be-seen attitude and a hopping bar. Reservations are recommended.

Sharing an owner with the Saltus River Grill is **Plum's** (904½ Bay St., 843/525-1946, lunch daily 11 A.M.-4 P.M., dinner daily 5-10 P.M., $15-25). The short and focused menu keys in on entrées highlighting local ingredients, such as the shrimp penne *al'amatriciana* and fresh black mussel pasta. Because of the outstanding microbrew selection, Plum's is a big nightlife hangout as well; be aware that after 10 P.M., when food service ends but the bar remains open until 2 A.M., it's no longer smoke-free, although there's a friendly porch where you can get some fresh air and feed the resident cat.

An up-and-comer downtown is **Breakwater Restaurant & Bar** (203 Carteret St., 843/379-0052, www.breakwater-restaurant.com, dinner Thurs.-Sat. 6-9:30 P.M., bar until 2 A.M., $10-20). The concise menu makes up in good taste what it lacks in comprehensiveness, with an emphasis on seafood, of course. An especially enticing marine-oriented tapas plate is the diver scallops in a vanilla cognac sauce. (This restaurant recently moved from a West Street location.)

Steaks

Luther's Rare & Well Done (910 Bay St., 843/521-1888, daily 10 A.M.-midnight, from $8) on the waterfront is the kind of meat-lover's place where even the french onion soup has a morsel of rib eye in it. While the patented succulent rubbed steaks are a no-brainer here, the handcrafted specialty pizzas are also quite popular. If a steak is too rich for your blood but you still crave some protein, their hamburgers are awesome too. Housed in a historic pharmacy building, Luther's is also a great place for late eats after many other places in this quiet town have rolled up the sidewalk. A limited menu of appetizers and bar food to nosh on at the inviting and popular bar is available after 10 P.M.

Tapas

Right around the corner from Breakwater is **Emily's** (906 Port Republic St., 843/522-1866, www.emilysrestaurantandtapasbar.com, dinner Mon.-Sat. 4-10 P.M., bar until 2 A.M., $10-20), a very popular fine dining spot that specializes in a more traditional brand of rich, tasty tapas (available 4-5 P.M.) and is known for its active bar scene.

INFORMATION AND SERVICES

The **Beaufort Visitors Information Center** (713 Craven St., 843/986-5400, www.beaufortsc.org, daily 9 A.M.-5:30 P.M.), the headquarters of the Beaufort Chamber of Commerce and Convention and Visitors Bureau, has relocated from its old Carteret Street location and can now be found within the Beaufort Arsenal, once home to the now-closed Beaufort Museum.

The U.S. Postal Service has a **post office** (501 Charles St., 843/525-9085) in downtown Beaufort.

The daily newspaper of record in Beaufort is the *Beaufort Gazette* (www.beaufortgazette.

com). An alternative weekly focusing mostly on the arts is *Lowcountry Weekly* (www.lcweekly. com), published every Wednesday.

GETTING THERE AND AROUND

While the Marines can fly their F-18s directly into Beaufort Naval Air Station, you won't have that luxury. The closest major airport to Beaufort is the **Savannah/Hilton Head International Airport** (SAV, 400 Airways Ave., 912/964-0514, www.savannahairport.com) off I-95 outside Savannah. If you're not going into Savannah for any reason, the easiest route to the Beaufort area from the airport is to take I-95's exit 8, and from there to take U.S. 278 east to Highway 170.

Alternately, you could fly into the **Charleston International Airport** (CHS, 5500 International Blvd., www.chs-airport.com), but because that facility is on the far north side of Charleston, it actually might take you longer to get to Beaufort. From the Charleston Airport the best route south to Beaufort is U.S. 17 south, exiting onto U.S. 21 at Gardens Corner and then into Beaufort.

If you're coming into the region by car, I-95 will be your likely primary route, with your main point of entry being exit 8 off I-95 connecting to U.S. 278.

There's no public transportation to speak of in Beaufort, but that's OK—the historic section is quite small and can be traversed in an afternoon. A favorite mode of transport is by bicycle, often complimentary to bed-and-breakfast guests. Rent one at **Lowcountry Bikes** (102 Sea Island Pkwy., 843/524-9585, Mon.-Tues. and Thurs.-Fri. 10 A.M.-6 P.M., Wed. 10 A.M.-1 P.M., Sat. 10 A.M.-3 P.M., about $5 per hour) in Lady's Island just over the bridge.

OUTSIDE BEAUFORT

The areas outside tourist-traveled Beaufort can take you even further back into sepia-toned Americana, into a time of sharecropper homesteads, sturdy oystermen, and an altogether variable and subjective sense of time.

Lady's Island

Directly across the Beaufort River is Lady's Island, now a predominantly residential area with a bigger variety of national shopping and grocery outlets than you'll find in Beaufort proper. However, there are a few places to eat here that are worth mentioning. Cuisine options include the casual **Steamer Oyster and Steak House** (168 Sea Island Pkwy., 843/522-0210, daily 11 A.M.-9:30 P.M., $15-20). The big hit here is the Frogmore stew, a.k.a. Lowcountry boil. For vegan and vegetarian soups, salads, and sandwiches, try **It's Only Natural** (45 Factory Creek Court, 843/986-9595, Mon.-Fri. 8 A.M.-6 P.M., Sat. 9 A.M.-4:30 P.M., $5), which also offers a range of health-food items and produce. It's visible right off the main road, the Sea Island Parkway (U.S. 21). For excellent seafood in the Southern tradition try **Factory Creek Fish Company** (71 Sea Island Pkwy., 843/379-3288, www.factorycreekfish-company.com, Mon.-Sat. 11 A.M.-10 P.M., Sun. 11 A.M.-9 P.M., $15-20). The shrimp and grits as well as fried catfish are particular favorites.

◖ Penn Center

By going across the Richard V. Woods Memorial Bridge over the Beaufort River on the Sea Island Parkway (which turns into U.S. 21), you'll pass through Lady's Island and reach St. Helena Island. Known to old-timers as Frogmore, the area took back its old Spanish-derived place name in the 1980s. Today St. Helena Island is most famous for the Penn Center (16 Martin Luther King Jr. Dr., 843/838-2474, www.penncenter.com, Mon.-Sat. 11 A.M.-4 P.M., $4 adults, $2 seniors and children), the spiritual home of Gullah culture and history. When you visit here among the live oaks and humble but well-preserved buildings, you'll instantly see

© JIM MOREKIS

the Penn Center on St. Helena Island

why Martin Luther King Jr. chose this as one of his major retreat and planning sites during the civil rights era. The dream began as early as 1862, when a group of abolitionist Quakers from Philadelphia came during the Union occupation with the goal of teaching recently freed slave children. They were soon joined by African American educator Charlotte Forten. After Reconstruction, the Penn School continued its mission by offering teaching as well as agricultural and industrial trade curricula. In the late 1960s, the Southern Christian Leadership Conference used the school as a retreat and planning site, with both the Peace Corps and the Conscientious Objector Programs training here. The Penn Center continues to serve an important civil rights role by providing legal counsel to African American homeowners in St. Helena. Because clear title is difficult to acquire in the area due to the fact that so much of the land has stayed in the families of former slaves, developers are constantly making shady offers so that ancestral land can be opened up to upscale development.

The beautiful 50-acre campus of the Penn Center is part of the Penn School Historic District, a National Historic Landmark comprising 19 buildings, most of key historical significance, including Darrah Hall, the oldest building on the campus; the old "Brick Church" right across MLK Jr. Drive; and Gantt Cottage, where Dr. King himself stayed periodically in the 1963-1967 period. Another building, the Retreat House, was intended for Dr. King to continue his strategy meetings, but he was assassinated before being able to stay there. The museum and bookshop are housed in the Cope Building, now called the York W. Bailey Museum, situated right along MLK Jr. Drive. A self-guided nature trail takes you all around the campus. The key public event here happens each November with the Penn Center Heritage Days, in which the entire St. Helena community comes together to celebrate and enjoy entertainment such as the world-famous, locally based Hallelujah Singers.

To get to the Penn Center from Beaufort, proceed over the bridge until you get to St. Helena Island. Take a right onto MLK Jr. Drive when you see the Red Piano Too Art Gallery. The Penn Center is a few hundred yards down on your right. If you drive past the Penn Center and continue a few hundred yards down MLK Jr. Drive, look for the ancient tabby ruins on the left side of the road. This is the **Chapel of Ease,** the remnant of a 1740 church destroyed by forest fire in the late 1800s.

If you get hungry, just before you take a right to get to the Penn Center on St. Helena Island is **Gullah Grub** (877 Sea Island Pkwy., 843/838-3841, Mon.-Thurs. 11:30 A.M.-7 P.M., under $20), an unpretentious, one-room lunch spot focusing on down-home Southern specialties with a Lowcountry touch, such as hushpuppies, collard greens, and shrimp-'n'-shark.

Fort Fremont Preserve

Military historians and sightseers of a particularly adventurous type will want to drive several miles past the Penn Center on St. Helena Island to visit **Fort Fremont** (Lands End Rd., www.fortfremont.org), daily 9 A.M.-dusk, free). Two artillery batteries remain of this Spanish-American War-era coastal defense fort (an adjacent private residence is actually the old army hospital.) The big guns defending Port Royal Sound are long gone, but the concrete emplacements—along with many very dark tunnels and small rooms—are still here. I enjoy touring the labyrinthine bowels of the fort, but bring a flashlight and be aware that there is graffiti and evidence of frequent visitation by young partiers. Also be warned that, fascinating as this county-maintained site is, there are no facilities of any kind, including lights and safety guardrails. It's fun to climb all over the gun emplacements, but a fall would be disastrous. When at Fort Fremont,

don't miss the opportunity to go down to the small "beach" area on the sound and enjoy the scintillating view.

Old Sheldon Church Ruins

A short ways north of Beaufort are the poignantly desolate ruins of the once-magnificent Old Sheldon Church (Old Sheldon Church Rd., off U.S. 17 just past Gardens Corner, daily dawn-dusk, free). Set a couple of miles off the highway on a narrow road, the serene, oak-lined grounds containing this massive empty edifice give little hint of the violence so intrinsic to its history. One of the first Greek Revival structures in the United States, the house of worship held its first service in 1757 as Prince William's Parish Church. The sanctuary was first burned by the British in 1779, mainly because of reports that the Patriots were using it to store gunpowder captured from a British ship. After being rebuilt in 1826, the sanctuary survived until General Sherman's arrival in 1865, whereupon Union troops razed it once more. Nothing remains now but these towering walls and columns, made of red brick instead of the tabby often seen in similar ruins on the coast. It's now owned by the nearby St. Helena's Episcopal Church in Beaufort, which holds outdoor services here the second Sunday after Easter. In all, it's an almost painfully compelling bit of history set amid stunning natural beauty, and well worth the short drive.

Oyotunji Village

Continuing north of the Sheldon Church a short way, the more adventurous can find a quirky Lowcountry attraction, Oyotunji Village (56 Bryant Lane, 843/846-8900, www.oyotunjiafricanvillage.org, daily 10 A.M.-dusk, $10). Built in 1970 by self-proclaimed "King" Ofuntola Oseijeman Adelabu Adefunmi I, a former used car dealer with an interesting past, Oyotunji claims to be North America's only authentic

THE LOST ART OF TABBY

Let's clear up a couple of misconceptions about tabby, that unique construction technique combining oyster shells, lime, water, and sand found along the South Carolina and Georgia coast.

First, it did not originate with Native Americans. The confusion is due to the fact that the native population left behind many middens, or trash heaps, of oyster shells. While these middens indeed provided the bulk of the shells for tabby buildings to come, Native Americans had little else to do with it.

Second, although the Spanish were responsible for the first use of tabby in the Americas, contrary to lore almost all remaining tabby in the area dates from later English settlement. The British first fell in love with tabby after the siege of Spanish-held St. Augustine, Florida, and quickly began building with it in their colonies to the north.

Scholars are divided as to whether tabby was invented by West Africans or its use spread to Africa from Spain and Portugal, circuitously coming to the United States through the knowledge of imported slaves. The origin of the word itself is also unclear, as similar words exist in Spanish, Portuguese, Gullah, and Arabic to describe various types of wall.

We do know for sure how tabby is made: The primary technique was to burn alternating layers of oyster shells and logs in a deep hole in the ground, thus creating lime. The lime was then mixed with oyster shells, sand, and freshwater and poured into wooden molds, or "forms," to dry and then be used as building blocks, much like large bricks. Tabby walls were usually plastered with stucco. Tabby is remarkably strong and resilient, able to survive the hurricanes that often batter the area. It also stays cool in the summer and is insect-resistant, two enormous advantages down here.

Following are some great examples of true tabby you can see today on the South Carolina and Georgia coasts, from north to south:

- **Dorchester State Historic Site** in Summerville, north of Charleston, contains a well-preserved tabby fort.

- Several younger tabby buildings still exist in downtown Beaufort: the **Barnwell-Gough House** (705 Washington St.); the Thomas Fuller House, or **"Tabby Manse"** (1211 Bay St.); and the **Saltus House** (800 block of Bay St.), perhaps the tallest surviving tabby structure.

- The **Chapel of Ease** on St. Helena Island dates from the 1740s. If someone tells you Sherman burned it down, don't believe it; the culprit was a forest fire.

- The **Stoney-Baynard Ruins** in Sea Pines Plantation on Hilton Head are all that's left of the home of the old Braddock's Point Plantation. Foundations of a slave quarters are nearby.

- **Wormsloe Plantation** near Savannah has the remains of Noble Jones's fortification of the Skidaway Narrows.

- **St. Cyprian's Episcopal Church** in Darien is one of the largest tabby structures still in use.

- **Fort Frederica** on St. Simons Island has not only the remains of a tabby fort but many foundations of tabby houses in the surrounding settlement.

- The remarkably intact walls of the **Horton-DuBignon House** on Jekyll Island, Georgia, date from 1738, and the house was occupied into the 1850s.

African village, with 5-10 families residing on its 30 acres. It also claims to be a separate kingdom and not a part of the United States—though I'm sure the State Department begs to differ.

With a mission to preserve the religious and cultural aspects of the Yoruba Orisa culture of West Africa, each spring the village hosts an annual Warrior's Festival, celebrating traditional male rites of passage. Truth is, there's not much to see here but a few poorly built "monuments." But connoisseurs of roadside Americana will be pleased.

© JIM MOREKIS

Old Sheldon Church ruins

Yemassee

Going still farther north on U.S. 17 you'll come to the small, friendly town of Yemassee. Its main claim to fame is nearby **Auldbrass,** designed by Frank Lloyd Wright in 1939. The home is privately owned by Hollywood producer Joel Silver, but rare, much-sought-after tours happen every other year in November through the auspices of the Beaufort County Open Land Trust. To find out about the next tour and to get on the list, email your mailing address to bcolt2@islc.net or call 843/521-2175 to receive ticket information the summer before.

The Amtrak train depot in downtown Yemassee actually is historically important as one of the oldest continuously used train stations in the region. From 1914 to 1964 it was the point of embarkation for Marine recruits headed for boot camp at Parris Island. Under the auspices of the Yemassee Revitalization Corporation, plans are afoot to restore the historic depot to a nostalgic 1940s ambience.

Port Royal

This sleepy hamlet between Beaufort and Parris Island touts itself as a leader in "small-town New Urbanism," with an emphasis on livability, retro-themed shopping areas, and relaxing walking trails. However, Port Royal is still pretty sleepy—but not without very real charms, not the least of which is the fact that everything is within easy walking distance of everything else. The highlight of the year is the annual Soft Shell Crab Festival, held each April to mark the short-lived harvesting season for that favorite crustacean.

While much of the tiny historic district has a scrubbed, tidy feel, the main historic structure is the charming little **Union Church** (11th St., 843/524-4333, Mon.-Fri. 10 A.M.-4 P.M., donation), one of the oldest buildings in town, with guided docent tours.

Don't miss the new boardwalk and observation tower at **The Sands** municipal beach and boat ramp. The 50-foot-tall structure provides a commanding view of Battery Creek. To get to The Sands, go to 7th Street and then turn onto Sands Beach Road.

Another environmentally oriented point of pride is the **Lowcountry Estuarium** (1402 Paris

Ave., 843/524-6600, www.lowcountryestuarium. org, Wed.-Sat. 10 A.M.-5 P.M., feedings 11:30 A.M. and 3 P.M., $5 adults, $3 children). The point of the facility is to give hands-on opportunities to learn more about the flora and fauna of the various ecosystems of the Lowcountry, such as salt marshes, beaches, and estuaries.

If you get hungry in Port Royal, try the waterfront seafood haven **11th Street Dockside** (1699 11th St., 843/524-7433, daily 4:30-10 P.M., $17-27). The Dockside Dinner is a great sampler plate with lobster tail, scallops, crab legs, and shrimp. The views of the waterfront and the adjoining shrimp-boat docks are relaxing and beautiful.

Parris Island

Though more commonly known as the home of the legendary **Marine Corps Recruit Depot Parris Island** (283 Blvd. de France, 843/228-3650, www.mcrdpi.usmc.mil, free), the island is also of historic significance as the site of some of the earliest European presence in the New World. The U.S. Marine Corps began its association with Parris Island in 1891, though the island's naval roots actually go back to its use as a coaling station during the long Union occupation. By the outbreak of World War I, a full-blown military town had sprung up, now with its own presence on the National Register of Historic Places. In November 1915, Parris Island went into business as a recruit depot, and today it's where all female Marine recruits and all male recruits east of the Mississippi River go through the grueling 13-week boot camp. Almost every Friday during the year marks the graduation of a company of newly minted Marines. That's why you might notice an influx of visitors to the area each Thursday, a.k.a. "Family Day," with the requisite amount of celebration on Fridays after that morning's ceremony.

You don't have to be a U.S. Marine to get something out of a trip to Parris Island.

Unlike many military facilities in the post-9/11 era, Parris Island still hosts plenty of visitors, about 120,000 a year. It's easy to get onto the Depot. Just check in with the friendly sentry at the gate and show your valid driver's license, registration, and proof of insurance. Rental car drivers must show a copy of the rental agreement. On your way to the Depot proper, there are a couple of beautiful picnic areas. Because this is a military base and therefore immune to the rampant residential development that has come to the Lowcountry, you will see some incredible ancient live oak trees in this part of the facility. Once inside, stop first at the **Douglas Visitor Center** (Bldg. 283, Blvd. de France, 843/228-3650, Mon. 7:30 A.M.-noon, Tues.-Wed. 7:30 A.M.-4:30 P.M., Thurs. 6:30 A.M.-7 P.M., Fri. 7:30 A.M.-3 P.M.), a great place to find maps and touring information. As you go by the big parade ground, or "deck," be sure to check out the beautiful sculpture recreating the famous photo of Marines raising the flag on Iwo Jima. A short ways ahead is the **Parris Island Museum** (Bldg. 111, 111 Panama St., 843/228-2951, daily 8:30 A.M.-4:30 P.M., free) a little ways in from the museum, which not only lovingly details the entire U.S. military experience in the area but also features a good exhibit on the area's earliest colonial history. Be sure to check out the second floor for a particularly detailed and well-done series of exhibits on Marine campaigns through the centuries.

The Spanish built Santa Elena directly on top of the original French settlement, Charlesfort. They then built two other settlements, San Felipe and San Marcos. The Santa Elena-Charlesfort site (http://santaelena.us), now on the circa-1950s depot golf course, is now a National Historic Landmark. Many artifacts are viewable at the nearby **clubhouse-interpretive center** (daily 7 A.M.-5 P.M., free). You can take a self-guided tour; to get to the site from the museum, continue on Panama Street and take a right on Cuba Street. Follow the signs to the golf course and continue through the main parking lot of the course.

Do not use your cell phone while driving. While Parris Island kindly welcomes visitors, be aware that all traffic rules within the camp are strictly enforced, and your vehicle is subject to inspection at any time.

◖ Hunting Island State Park

Rumored to be a hideaway for Blackbeard himself, the aptly named Hunting Island was indeed for many years a notable hunting preserve, and its abundance of wildlife remains to this day. The island is one of the East Coast's best birding spots and also hosts dolphins, loggerheads, alligators, and deer. Thanks to preservation efforts by President Franklin Roosevelt and the Civilian Conservation Corps, however, the island is no longer for hunting but for sheer enjoyment. And enjoy it people do, to the tune of one million visitors per year. A true family-friendly outdoor adventure spot, Hunting Island State Park (2555 Sea Island Pkwy., 866/345-7275, www.huntingisland.com, winter daily 6 A.M.-6 P.M., during daylight saving time daily 6 A.M.-9 P.M., $5 adults, $3 children) has something for everyone—kids, parents, and newlyweds. Yet it still retains a certain sense of lush wildness—so much so that it doubled as Vietnam in the movie *Forrest Gump.*

At the north end past the campground is the island's main landmark, the historic **Hunting Island Light,** which dates from 1875. Although the lighthouse ceased operations in 1933, a rotating light—not strong enough to serve as an actual navigational aid—is turned on at night. While the 167-step trek to the top (donation $2 pp) is quite strenuous, the view from the little observation area at the top of the lighthouse is stunning, a complete panorama of Hunting Island and much of the Lowcountry coast.

At the south end of the island is a marsh walk, nature trail, and a fishing pier complete with a cute little nature center. Hunting

Island's three miles of beautiful beaches also serve as a major center of loggerhead turtle nesting and hatching, a process that begins around June as the mothers lay their eggs and culminates in late summer and early fall, when the hatchlings make their daring dash to the sea. At all phases the turtles are strictly protected, and while there are organized events to witness the hatching of the eggs, it is strictly forbidden to touch or otherwise disturb the turtles or their nests. Contact the park ranger for more detailed information. The tropical-looking inlet running through the park is a great place to kayak or canoe.

Getting to Hunting Island couldn't be easier—just take the Sea Island Parkway (U.S. 21) about 20 minutes beyond Beaufort and you'll run right into it.

Fripp Island

If you keep driving past Hunting Island, you'll reach Fripp Island, one of South Carolina's private developed barrier islands. Unlike its more egalitarian neighbor, Fripp only welcomes visitors who are guests of the **Fripp Island Golf and Beach Resort** (800/845-4100, www.frippislandresort.com), which offers a range of lodging from oceanfront homes to villas to golf cottages. Family-friendly recreation abounds, not only in 36 holes of high-caliber golf but in over three miles of uncrowded beach. A major allure is Camp Fripp, providing activities for kids.

◖ ACE Basin

Occupying pretty much the entire area between Beaufort and Charleston, the ACE Basin—the acronym signifies its role as the collective estuary of the Ashepoo, Combahee, and Edisto Rivers—is one of the most enriching natural experiences the country has to offer. The Basin's three core rivers, the Edisto being

the Grove Plantation House at the Ernest F. Hollings ACE Basin National Wildlife Refuge

© JIM MOREKIS

the largest, are the framework for a matrix of waterways crisscrossing its approximately 350,000 acres of salt marsh. It's this intimate relationship with the tides that makes the area so enjoyable, and also what attracted so many plantations throughout its history (canals and dikes from the old paddy fields are still visible throughout). Other uses have included tobacco, corn, and lumbering. While the ACE Basin can in no way be called "pristine," it's a testament to the power of nature that after 6,000 years of human presence and often intense cultivation, the Basin manages to retain much of its untamed feel.

The ACE Basin is so big that it is actually divided into several parts for management purposes under the umbrella of the ACE Basin Project (www.acebasin.net), a task force begun in 1988 by the state of South Carolina, the U.S. Fish and Wildlife Service, and various private firms and conservation groups. The project is now considered a model for responsible watershed preservation techniques in a time of often rampant coastal development. A host of species, both common and endangered, thrive in the area, including wood storks, alligators, sturgeon, loggerheads, teals, and bald eagles.

About 12,000 acres of the ACE Basin Project comprise the **Ernest F. Hollings ACE Basin National Wildlife Refuge** (8675 Willtown Rd., 843/889-3084, www.fws.gov/acebasin, grounds year-round daily dawn-dusk, office Mon.-Fri. 7:30 A.M.-4 P.M., free), run by the U.S. Fish and Wildlife Service. The historic 1828 **Grove Plantation House** is in this portion of the Basin and houses the refuge's headquarters. Sometimes featured on local tours of homes, it's one of only three antebellum homes left in the ACE Basin. Surrounded by lush, ancient oak trees, it's really a sight in and of itself.

This section of the Refuge, the **Edisto Unit,** is almost entirely composed of impounded paddy fields from the area's role as a rice plantation before the Civil War. Restored rice

trunks—the tidal gates used to manage water flow into the paddies—are still used to maintain the amount of water in the impounded areas, which are now rife with birds since the refuge is along the Atlantic Flyway. You may not always see them, but you'll definitely hear their calls echoing over the miles of marsh. (Speaking of miles, there are literally miles of walking and biking trails throughout the Edisto Unit, through both wetlands and forest.) To get to the Edisto Unit of the Hollings/ACE Basin National Wildlife Refuge, take U.S. 17 to Highway 174 (going all the way down this route takes you to Edisto Island) and turn right onto Willtown Road. The unpaved entrance road is about two miles ahead on the left. There are restrooms and a few picnic tables, but no other facilities of note.

You can also visit the two parts of the **Combahee Unit** of the refuge, which offers a similar scene of trails among impounded wetlands along the Combahee River, with parking; it's farther west near Yemassee. Get here by taking a left off U.S. 17 onto Highway 33. The larger portion of the Combahee Unit is very soon after the turnoff, and the smaller, more northerly portion is about five miles up the road.

About 135,000 acres of the entire ACE Basin falls under the protection of the South Carolina Department of Natural Resources (DNR) as part of the **National Estuarine Research Reserve System** (www.nerrs.noaa.gov/acebasin). The DNR also runs two Wildlife Management Areas (WMAs), **Donnelly WMA** (843/844-8957, www.dnr.sc.gov, year-round Mon.-Sat. 8 A.M.-5 P.M.) and **Bear Island WMA** (843/844-8957, www.dnr.sc.gov, Feb. 1-Oct. 14 Mon.-Sat. dawn-dusk), both of which provide rich opportunities for birding and wildlife observation.

Over 128,000 acres of the ACE Basin Project are permanently protected through conservation easements, management agreements, and fee title purchases. While traditional uses such as farming, fishing, and hunting do indeed continue in the ACE Basin, the area is off-limits to the gated communities, which are sprouting like mildew all along the Carolina coast. Because it is so well defended, the ACE Basin also functions like a huge outdoor laboratory for the coastal scientific community, with constant research going on in botany, zoology, microbiology, and marine science.

Recreation
KAYAKING

A 10-minute drive away from Beaufort in little Port Royal is **The Sands** public boat ramp into Battery Creek. You can also put in at the ramp at the **Lady's Island Marina** (73 Sea Island Pkwy., 843/522-0430) just across the bridge from Beaufort. **Hunting Island State Park** (2555 Sea Island Pkwy., 866/345-7275, www.huntingisland.com, winter daily 6 A.M.-6 P.M., during daylight saving time daily 6 A.M.-9 P.M., $5 adults, $3 children) has a wonderful inlet that is very popular with kayakers.

North and northeast of Beaufort lies the ACE Basin region, with about two dozen public ramps indicated by brown signs. Comprising hundreds of miles of creeks and tributaries in addition to its three rivers, the ACE Basin also features a fun paddling bonus: canals from the old rice plantations. A good service for rental and knowledgeable guided tours of the Basin is **Outpost Moe's** (843/844-2514, www.geocities.ws/outpostmoe), where the basic 2.5-hour tour costs $40 pp, and an all-day extravaganza through the Basin is $80. Moe's provides lunch for most of its tours. Another premier local outfitter for ACE Basin tours is **Carolina Heritage Outfitters** (U.S. 15 in Canadys, 843/563-5051, www.canoesc.com), which focuses on the Edisto River trail. In addition to guided tours ($30) and rentals, you can camp overnight in their cute tree houses ($125) along the kayak routes. They load you up with your gear and drive you 22 miles upriver; then you paddle downriver to the tree house for the evening.

The next day, you paddle yourself the rest of the way downriver back to home base.

To have a drier experience of the ACE Basin from the deck of a larger vessel, try **ACE Basin Tours** (1 Coosaw River Dr., Beaufort, 843/521-3099, www.acebasintours.com, Mar.-Nov. Wed. and Sat. 10 A.M., $35 adults, $15 children), which will take you on a three-hour tour in the 40-passenger *Dixie Lady*. To get to their dock, take Carteret Street over the bridge to St. Helena Island, and then take a left on Highway 802 east (Sam's Point Rd.). Continue until you cross Lucy Point Creek; the ACE Basin Tours marina is on your immediate left after you cross the bridge.

If you prefer self-guided paddling, keep in mind that you can spend a lifetime learning your way around the ACE Basin. The state of South Carolina has conveniently gathered some of the best self-guided kayak trips at www.acebasin.net/canoe.html.

BIRD-WATCHING

Because of its abundance of both saltwater and freshwater environments and its relatively low human density, the Lowcountry offers a stunning glimpse into the diversity and majesty of the Southeast's bird population, both regional and migratory. Serious birders swear by **Hunting Island State Park** (2555 Sea Island Pkwy., 866/345-7275, www.huntingisland.com, winter daily 6 A.M.-6 P.M., during daylight saving time daily 6 A.M.-9 P.M., $5 adults, $3 children), which—thanks to its undeveloped state and its spot on key migratory routes—is a great place to see brown pelicans, loons, herons, falcons, plovers, and egrets of all types. Park naturalists conduct frequent guided walks.

The tall observation tower at Port Royal's The Sands, where Battery Creek joins the Beaufort River, is a convenient vantage point from which to see any number of local bird species. The **ACE Basin** (8675 Willtown Rd., 843/889-3084, www.fws.gov/acebasin, grounds year-round dawn-dusk, office Mon.-Fri.

7:30 A.M.-4 P.M.) hosts at least 19 species of waterfowl and 13 species of wading birds.

At the northeast corner of the ACE Basin is the **Bear Island Wildlife Management Area** (843/844-8957, www.dnr.sc.gov, Feb.-Oct. Mon.-Sat. dawn-dusk), considered one of the best birding spots in South Carolina. To get here, take U.S. 21 north of Beaufort to U.S. 17 north. Take a right on Bennett's Point Road and continue south about 13 miles. The entrance is about one mile along, on the left, after crossing the Ashepoo River.

BIKING

Bikes can be rented in Lady's Island at **Lowcountry Bikes** (102 Sea Island Pkwy., 843/524-9585, Mon.-Tues. and Thurs.-Fri. 10 A.M.-6 P.M., Wed. 10 A.M.-1 P.M., Sat. 10 A.M.-3 P.M., about $5 per hour).

GOLF

Golf is much bigger in Hilton Head than in the Beaufort area, but here are some local highlights. The best-regarded public course in the area, and indeed one of the best military courses in the world, is **Legends at Parris Island** (Bldg. 299, Parris Island, 843/228-2240, www.mccssc.com, $30). You have to call in advance for a tee time before you can come on Parris Island to golf.

Another popular public course is **South Carolina National Golf Club** (8 Waveland Ave., Cat Island, 843/524-0300, www.scnational. com, $70). Get to secluded Cat Island by taking the Sea Island Parkway onto Lady's Island and continuing south as it turns into Lady's Island Drive. Turn onto Island Causeway and continue for about three miles.

CAMPING

Hunting Island State Park (2555 Sea Island Pkwy., 866/345-7275, www.huntingisland. com, winter daily 6 A.M.-6 P.M., during daylight saving time daily 6 A.M.-9 P.M., $5 adults, $3 children, $25 campsites, $87-172 cabins) has 200 campsites on the north end of the island, with individual water and electric hookups. Most are available by reservation only, but 20 are available on a first-come, first-served basis. (There used to be plenty of cabins for rent, but beach erosion has sadly made the ones near the water uninhabitable. One cabin near the lighthouse is still available for rent.)

Another neat place to camp is **Tuck in De Wood** (22 Tuc In De Wood Lane, St. Helena, 843/838-2267, $25), a very well-maintained 74-site private campground just past the Penn Center on St. Helena Island.

Edisto Island

One of the last truly unspoiled places in the Lowcountry, Edisto Island has been highly regarded as a getaway spot since the Edisto people first started coming here for shellfish. (Proof of their patronage is in the huge shell midden, or debris pile, at the state park.) In fact, locals here swear that the island was settled by English-speaking colonists even before Charleston was settled in 1670. In any case, we do know that the Spanish established a short-lived mission on St. Pierre's Creek. Then, in 1674, the island was purchased from the Edistos for a few trinkets by the perhaps appropriately named Earl of Shaftesbury. For most of its modern history, cotton plantations specializing in the top-of-the-line Sea Island strain were Edisto Island's main claim to fame—it was called McConkey's Island for most of that time—and after the Civil War fishing became the primary occupation. Because of several hurricanes in the mid-20th century, little remains from previous eras. Now this barrier island, for the moment unthreatened by the encroachment of planned communities and private resorts so endemic to the Carolina coast, is a nice getaway for area residents in addition to being a great—if a little isolated—place to live for its 800 or so full-time residents. The beaches are quiet and beautiful, the shells are plentiful, the walks are romantic, the people are friendly, and the food is good but casual. The residents operate on "Edisto Time," with a *mañana* philosophy (i.e., it'll get done when it gets done) that results in a mellow pace of life out in these parts.

ORIENTATION

Edisto Island is basically halfway between Beaufort and Charleston. There's one main land route here, south on Highway 174 off U.S. 17. It's a long way down to Edisto, but the 20-30-minute drive is scenic and enjoyable.

Most activity on the island centers on the township of Edisto Beach, which voted to align itself with Colleton County for its lower taxes (the rest of Edisto Island is part of Charleston County). Once in town, there are two main routes to keep in mind. Palmetto Boulevard runs parallel to the beach and is noteworthy for the lack of high-rise development so common in other beach areas of South Carolina. Jungle Road runs parallel to Palmetto Boulevard several blocks inland and contains the tiny business district.

◖ EDISTO BEACH STATE PARK

Edisto Beach State Park (8377 State Cabin Rd., 843/869-2156, www.southcarolinaparks.com, Nov.-mid-Mar. daily 8 A.M.-6 P.M., mid-Mar.-Oct. daily 6 A.M.-10 P.M., $4 adults, $1.50 children, free under age 6) is one of the world's foremost destinations for shell collectors. Largely because of fresh loads of silt from the adjacent ACE Basin, there are always

The beach at Edisto Island is remarkably free of overdevelopment.

© SOPHIA MOREKIS

new specimens, many of them fossils, washing ashore. The park stretches almost three miles and features the state's longest system of fully accessible hiking and biking trails, including one leading to the 4,000-year-old shell midden, now much eroded from past millennia. The new and particularly well-done **interpretive center** (Tues.-Sat. 9 A.M.-4 P.M.) has plenty of interesting exhibits about the nature and history of the park as well as the surrounding ACE Basin. Don't let the kids miss it.

Like many state recreational facilities in the South, Edisto Beach State Park was developed by the Civilian Conservation Corps (CCC), one of President Franklin D. Roosevelt's New Deal programs during the Great Depression, which had the doubly beneficial effect of employing large numbers of people while establishing much of the conservation infrastructure we enjoy today.

OTHER SIGHTS

The charming **Edisto Museum** (8123 Chisolm Plantation Rd., 843/869-1954, www.edistomuseum.org, Tues.-Sat. 1-4 P.M., $4 adults, $2 children, free under age 10), a project of the Edisto Island Historic Preservation Society, is in the middle of a major expansion that will incorporate a nearby slave cabin. Its well-done exhibits of local lore and history are complemented by a good gift shop. The Edisto Museum is before you get to the main part of the island, off Highway 174.

The **Botany Bay Wildlife Management Area** (www.preserveedisto.org, Wed.-Mon. dawn-dusk, closed on hunt days, free) is a great way to enjoy the unspoiled nature of Edisto Island. On the grounds of two former rice and indigo plantations comprising 4,000 acres, Botany Bay features several historic remains of the old plantations and a small, wonderful beach. There are no facilities to speak of, so pack and plan accordingly.

Opened in 1999 by local snake-hunters the Clamp brothers, the **Edisto Island**

Serpentarium (1374 Hwy. 174, 843/869-1171, www.edistoserpentarium.com, hours vary, $13 adults, $10 ages 6-12, $6 ages 4-5, free under ages 3) is educational and fun, taking you up close and personal with a variety of reptilian creatures native to the area. The Serpentarium is on the main route into Edisto before you get to the beach area. Keep in mind they usually close Labor Day-April 30.

TOURS

Edisto has many beautiful plantation homes, relics of the island's longtime role as host to cotton plantations. While all are in private hands and therefore off limits to the public, an exception is offered through **Edisto Island Tours & T'ings** (843/869-9092, $20 adults, $10 under age 13). You'll take a van tour around Edisto's beautiful churches and old plantations. The only other way to see the homes is during the annual **Tour of Homes** (843/869-1954, www.edistomuseum.org) the second weekend in October, run by the Edisto Island Historic Preservation Society. Tickets sell out very early.

SHOPPING

Not only a convenient place to pick up odds and ends, the **Edistonian Gift Shop & Gallery** (406 Hwy. 174, 843/869-4466, daily 9 A.M.-7 P.M.) is also an important landmark, as the main supply point before you get into the main part of town. Think of a really nice convenience store with an attached gift shop and you'll get the picture. For various ocean gear, try the **Edisto Surf Shop** (145 Jungle Rd., 843/869-9283, daily 9 A.M.-5 P.M.). You can find whimsical Lowcountry-themed art for enjoyment or purchase at **Fish or Cut Bait Gallery** (142 Jungle Rd., 843/869-2511, www.fishorcutbaitgallery.com, Tues.-Sat. 10 A.M.-5 P.M.).

If you need some groceries, there's always the **Piggly Wiggly** (104 Jungle Rd., 843/869-0055, Sun.-Thurs. 7 A.M.-9 P.M., Fri.-Sat. 7 A.M.-10 P.M.) grocery store, a.k.a. "The Pig." For

BEAUFORT

fresh seafood, try **Flowers Seafood Company** (1914 Hwy. 174, 843/869-0033, Mon.-Sat. 9 A.M.-7 P.M., Sun. 9 A.M.-5 P.M.).

SPORTS AND RECREATION

As the largest river of the ACE (Ashepoo, Combahee, Edisto) Basin complex, the Edisto River figures large in the lifestyle of residents and visitors. A good public landing is at Steamboat Creek off Highway 174 on the way down to the island. Take Steamboat Landing Road (Hwy. 968) from Highway 174 near the James Edwards School. Live Oak Landing is farther up Big Bay Creek near the Interpretive Center at the State Park. The **Edisto Marina** (3702 Docksite Rd., 843/869-3504) is on the far west side of the island.

Captain Ron Elliott of **Edisto Island Tours** (843/869-1937) offers various ecotours and fishing trips as well as canoe and kayak rentals for about $25 per day. A typical kayak tour runs about $35 pp for a 1.5-2-hour trip, and he offers a "beach-combing" trip for $15 pp. **Ugly Ducklin'** (843/869-1580) offers creek and inshore fishing charters. You can get gear as well as reserve boat and kayak tours of the entire area, including into the ACE Basin, at **Edisto Watersports & Tackle** (3731 Docksite Rd., 843/869-0663, www.edistowatersports.com). Their guided tours run about $30 pp, with a two-hour rental running about $20.

Riding a bike on Edisto Beach and all around the island is a great relaxing way to get some exercise and enjoy its scenic, laid-back beauty. The best place to rent a bike—or a kayak or canoe, for that matter—is **Island Bikes and Outfitters** (140 Jungle Rd., 843/869-4444, Mon.-Sat. 9 A.M.-4 P.M.). Bike rentals run about $16 per day; single kayaks are about $60 per day.

There's one golf course on the island, the 18-hole **Plantation Course at Edisto** (21 Fairway Dr., 843/869-1111, $60), finished in 2006.

ACCOMMODATIONS

A great thing about Edisto Island is the total absence of ugly chain lodging or beachfront condo development. My recommended option is staying at the **Edisto Beach State Park** (843/869-2156, www.southcarolinaparks.com, $25 tent sites, $75-100 cabins) itself, either at a campsite on the Atlantic side or in a marsh-front cabin on the northern edge. During high season (Apr.-Nov.), there's a minimum weeklong stay in the cabins; during the off-season, the minimum stay is two days. You can book cabins up to 11 months in advance, and I strongly recommend doing so as they go very quickly.

If you want something a little more plush, there are rental homes galore on Edisto Island. Because of the aforementioned lack of hotels, this is the most popular option for most vacationers here—indeed, it's just about the only option. Contact **Edisto Sales and Rentals Realty** (1405 Palmetto Blvd., 800/868-5398, www.edistorealty.com).

FOOD

One of the all-time great barbecue places in South Carolina is on Edisto, **❰ Po Pigs Bo-B-Q** (2410 Hwy. 174, 843/869-9003, Wed.-Sat. 11:30 A.M.-9 P.M., $4-10) on the way into town. This is the real thing, the full pig cooked in all its many ways: white meat, dark meat, cracklin's, and hash, served in the local style of "all you care to eat." Unlike many BBQ spots, they do serve beer and wine.

Another popular joint on the island is **Whaley's** (2801 Myrtle St., 843/869-2161, Tues.-Sat. 11:30 A.M.-2 P.M. and 5-9 P.M., bar daily 5 P.M.-2 A.M., $5-15), a down-home place in an old gas station a few blocks off the beach. This is a good place for casual seafood like boiled shrimp, washed down with a lot of beer. The bar is open seven days a week.

Although it was closed in recent years, the legendary **❰ Old Post Office** (1442 Hwy. 174, 843/869-2339, www.theoldpostofficerestaurant.com, Tues.-Sun. 5:30-10 P.M., $20), a Lowcountry-style fine-dining spot, kept a devoted clientele for 20 years. It recently reopened with a bang and thankfully kept its old-school mystique intact. Specialties include fine crab cakes drizzled with mousseline sauce, the pecan-encrusted Veal Edistonian, and a Carolina rib eye topped with a pimiento cheese sauce, something of a state culinary tradition.

McConkey's Jungle Shack (108 Jungle Rd., 843/869-0097, Mon.-Fri. 11 A.M.-8 P.M., Sat.-Sun. 8 A.M.-8 P.M., $4-10) on the eastern end of the beach is known for its fish-and-chips basket and great burgers.

Hilton Head Island

Literally the prototype of the modern planned resort community, Hilton Head Island is also a case study in how utterly a landscape can change when enough money is introduced. From Reconstruction until the post-World War II era, the island consisted almost entirely of African Americans with deep historic roots in the area. In the mid-1950s Hilton Head began its transformation into an almost all-white, upscale golf, tennis, and shopping mecca populated largely by Northern transplants and retirees. As you can imagine, the flavor here is now quite different from surrounding areas of the Lowcountry, to say the least, with an emphasis on material excellence, top prices, get-it-done-yesterday punctuality, and the attendant aggressive traffic. Giving credit where it's due, however, Hilton Head knows what its target audience is and delivers the goods in a thoroughly professional manner. While it's easy to dismiss it as a sort of Disney World for the elite—a disjointed collection of gated communities that take up 70 percent of its land—the truth is that millions of visitors, not all of them elite by any stretch, not only enjoy what Hilton Head has to offer, they swear by it. The attraction is quality, whether in the stunning beaches, outstanding cultural offerings, plush accommodations, attentive service, or copious merchandise. You won't see any litter, and you're unlikely to experience any crime. Certainly that's to Hilton Head's credit and no small reason for its continued success.

One of the unsung positive aspects of modern Hilton Head is its dedication to sustainable living. With the support of voters, the town routinely buys large tracts of land to preserve as open space. Hilton Head was the first municipality in the country to mandate the burying of all power lines, and one of the first to regularly use covenants and deed restrictions. All new development must conform to rigid guidelines on setbacks and tree canopy. It has one of the most comprehensive signage ordinances in the country as well, which means no garish commercial displays will disrupt your views of the night sky. If those are "elite" values, then certainly we might do well in making them more mainstream.

HISTORY

The second-largest barrier island on the East Coast, Hilton Head Island was inhabited by Native Americans at least 10,000 years ago. It was named in 1663 by adventurer Sir William Hilton, who thoughtfully named the island—with its notable headland or "Head"—after himself. Hilton, who was from the British colony of Barbados, like many of Charleston's original settlers, was purposely trying to drum up interest in the island as a commercial venture, famously describing his new namesake as having "sweet water" and "clear sweet air." Though Hilton Head wasn't the first foothold of English colonization in Carolina, it did acquire commercial status first as the home of rice and indigo plantations. Later it gained fame as the first location of the legendary "Sea Island Cotton," a long-grain variety which, following its introduction in 1790 by William Elliott II

BEAUFORT

HILTON HEAD ISLAND

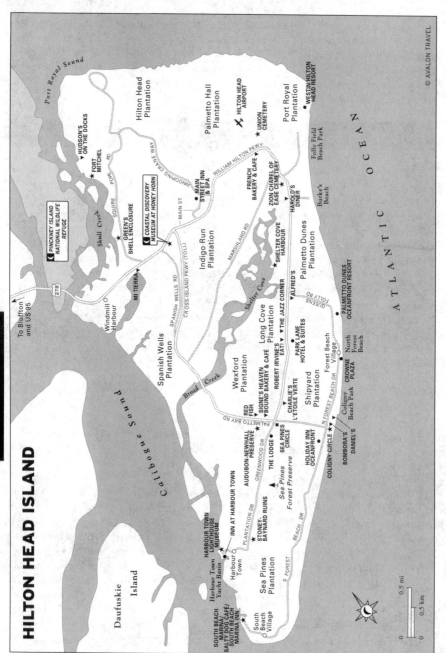

© AVALON TRAVEL

Port Royal Sound

Hilton Head Plantation

Palmetto Hall Plantation

HILTON HEAD AIRPORT

UNION CEMETERY

Port Royal Plantation

WESTIN HILTON HEAD RESORT

ATLANTIC OCEAN

HUDSON'S ON THE DOCKS
FORT MITCHEL

Skull Creek

PINCKNEY ISLAND NATIONAL WILDLIFE REFUGE

GREEN'S SHELL ENCLOSURE

COASTAL DISCOVERY MUSEUM AT HONEY HORN

MAIN STREET INN & SPA

FRENCH BAKERY & CAFÉ

ZION CHAPEL OF EASE CEMETERY

HAROLD'S DINER

Burke's Beach

Folly Field Beach Park

SQUIRE POPE RD

JARVIS CREEK LANE WAY

MAIN ST

WILLIAM HILTON PKWY

MI TIERRA

Windmill Harbour

278

To Bluffton and US 95

SPANISH WELLS RD

CROSS ISLAND PKWY (TOLL)

Indigo Run Plantation

MARSHLAND RD

Shelter Cove

SHELTER COVE HARBOUR

Palmetto Dunes Plantation

ALFRED'S

THE JAZZ CORNER

PALMETTO DUNES OCEANFRONT RESORT

QUEENS FOLLY RD

GREENS FOLLY RD

Spanish Wells Plantation

Calibogue Sound

Broad Creek

Wexford Plantation

Long Cove Plantation

ROBERT IRVINE'S EAT!

SIGNE'S HEAVEN BOUND BAKERY & CAFÉ

PARK LANE HOTEL & SUITES

Forest Beach Village

North Forest Beach

PALMETTO BAY RD

RED FISH

CHARLIE'S L'ÉTOILE VERTE

Shipyard Plantation

CROWNE PLAZA

Coligny Beach Park

N FOREST BEACH RD

AUDUBON-NEWHALL PRESERVE

GREENWOOD DR

THE LODGE

SEA PINES CIRCLE

HOLIDAY INN OCEANFRONT

COLIGNY CIRCLE

BOMBORA'S

DANIEL'S

Daufuskie Island

SOUTH BEACH MARINA CAFÉ/
SALTY DOG CAFÉ/
SOUTH BEACH MARINA INN

South Beach Village

HARBOUR TOWN LIGHTHOUSE MUSEUM

INN AT HARBOUR TOWN

Harbour Town Yacht Basin

Harbour Town

PLANTATION DR

STONEY-BAYNARD RUINS

Sea Pines Forest Preserve

Sea Pines Plantation

BEACH DR

S FOREST BEACH DR

ATLANTIC OCEAN

0   0.5 mi
0   0.5 km

BEAUFORT

of the Myrtle Bank Plantation, would soon be the dominant version of the cash crop.

Hilton Head planters were outspoken in the cause of American independence. The chief pattern in the Lowcountry during that conflict involved the British raiding Hilton Head and surrounding areas from their stronghold on Daufuskie Island, burning plantations and capturing slaves to be resold in Caribbean colonies. As a reminder of the savage guerrilla nature of the conflict in the South, British hit-and-run raids on Hilton Head continued for weeks after Cornwallis surrendered.

Nearby Bluffton was settled by planters from Hilton Head Island and the surrounding area in the early 1800s as a summer retreat. Though Charleston likes to claim the label today, Bluffton was actually the genuine "cradle of secession." Indeed, locals still joke that the town motto is "Divided We Stand." Fort Walker, a Confederate installation on the site of the modern Port Royal Plantation development on Hilton Head, was the target of the largest fleet ever assembled in North America at the time, when a massive Union force sailed into Port Royal Sound in October 1861. A month later, the fort—and effectively the entire area—had fallen, though by that time most white residents had long since fled. During the Civil War, Bluffton was also evacuated and, like Hilton Head, escaped serious action. However, in June 1863, Union troops destroyed most of the town except for about a dozen homes and two churches.

Though it seems unlikely given the island's modern demographics, Hilton Head was almost entirely African American through much of the 20th century. When Union troops occupied the island at the outbreak of the Civil War, freed and escaped slaves flocked to the island, and most of the dwindling number of African Americans on the island today are descendants of this original Gullah population.

For the first half of the 20th century, logging was Hilton Head's main commercial pursuit. Things didn't take their modern shape until the 1950s, when the Fraser family bought 19,000 of the island's 25,000 acres with the intent to continue forestry on them. But in 1956—not at all coincidentally the same year the first bridge to the island was built—Charles Fraser convinced his father to sell him the southern tip of Hilton Head. Fraser's brainchild and decades-long labor of love—some said his obsession—Sea Pines Plantation was the prototype of the golf-oriented resort community so common today on both U.S. coasts. Fraser himself was killed in a boating accident in 2002, but he survived to see Sea Pines encompass much of Hilton Head's economic activity, including Harbour Town, and to see the Town of Hilton Head incorporated in 1983. Fraser is buried under the famous Liberty Oak in Harbour Town, which he personally made sure wasn't harmed during the development of the area.

ORIENTATION

Hilton Head Islanders have long referred to their island as the "shoe" and speak of driving to the toe or going to the heel. If you take a look at a map, you'll see why: Hilton Head bears an uncanny resemblance to a running shoe pointed toward the southeast, with the aptly named Broad Creek forming a near facsimile of the Nike "swoosh" symbol. Running the length and circumference of the shoe is the undisputed main drag, U.S. 278 Business (William Hilton Parkway), which crosses onto Hilton Head right at the "tongue" of the shoe, a relatively undeveloped area where there are still a few old African American communities. The new Cross Island Parkway toll route (U.S. 278), beginning up toward the ankle as you first get on the island, is a quicker, more convenient route straight to the toe near Sea Pines. While it is technically the business spur, when locals say "278" they're talking about the William Hilton Parkway. It takes you along the entire sole of the shoe, including the beaches, and on down to the toe, where you'll find a confusing, crazy British-style roundabout called Sea Pines Circle. It's also the site of the Harbour Town Marina and the island's oldest planned development, Sea Pines Plantation.

There's no "town center" per se, but activity here tends to revolve around just a few places: the Shelter Cove shopping and residential development near the entrance to the island; Coligny Plaza, an older, more casual shopping center near the main beach entrance; Sea Pines Circle, a center of nightlife; and two spots within Sea Pines itself, Harbour Town and South Beach—the former a blend of upscale and family attractions, and the latter catering a bit more to the beach crowd.

While making your way around the island, always keep in mind that the bulk of it consists of private developments, and local law

enforcement frowns on people who aimlessly wander among the condos and villas.

SIGHTS

Contrary to what many think, there are quite a few things to do on Hilton Head that don't involve swinging a club at a little white ball or shopping for designer labels but instead celebrate the area's rich history and natural setting. The following are some of those attractions, arranged in geographical order from where you first access the island.

◖ Pinckney Island National Wildlife Refuge

Actually consisting of many islands and hammocks, Pinckney Island National Wildlife Refuge (912/652-4415, daily dawn-dusk, free) is the only part of this small but very well-managed 4,000-acre refuge that's open to the public. Almost 70 percent of the former rice

© JIM MOREKIS

Pinckney Island National Wildlife Refuge

plantation is salt marsh and tidal creeks, making it a perfect microcosm for the Lowcountry as a whole, as well as a great place to kayak or canoe. Native Americans liked the area as well, with a 10,000-year presence and over 100 archaeological sites being identified to date. Like many coastal refuges, it was a private game preserve for much of the 20th century. Some of the state's richest birding opportunities abound here, with observers able to spot gorgeous white ibis, rare wood storks, herons, egrets, eagles, and ospreys with little trouble from its miles of trails. Getting here is easy: On U.S. 278 east to Hilton Head, the refuge entrance is right between the two bridges onto the island.

Green's Shell Enclosure

Less known than the larger Native American shell ring farther south at Sea Pines, the Green's Shell Enclosure (803/734-3886, daily dawn-dusk) is certainly easier to find, and you don't have to pay $5 to enter the area, as with Sea Pines. This three-acre Heritage Preserve dates back to at least the 1300s.

The heart of the site comprises a low embankment, part of the original fortified village. Don't expect to be wowed—shell rings are a subtle pleasure. As is the case with most shell rings, the shells themselves are underneath a layer of dirt; don't disturb them.

To get here, take a left at the intersection of U.S. 278 and Squire Pope Road. Turn left into Greens Park, pass the office on the left, and park. The entrance to the shell enclosure is on the left behind a fence. You'll see a small community cemetery that has nothing to do with the shell ring; veer to your right to get to the short trail entrance. Camping is not allowed.

C Coastal Discovery Museum at Honey Horn

With the acquisition of Honey Horn's 70-acre spread of historic plantation land, Hilton Head finally has a full-fledged museum worthy of the

name, and the magnificent Coastal Discovery Museum (70 Honey Horn Dr., 843/689-6767, www.coastaldiscovery.org, Mon.-Sat. 9 A.M.-4:30 P.M., Sun. 11 A.M.-3 P.M., free) is an absolute must-see, even for those who came to the island mostly to golf and soak up sun. (The name "Honey Horn" is supposedly based on a mispronunciation by field hands of one of the plantation's owning families, the Hannahans.)

The facility centers on the expertly restored Discovery House, the only antebellum house still existing on Hilton Head. But instead of being a Charleston- or Savannah-style house museum, the Discovery House now hosts a real museum, with exhibits and displays devoted to the history of the island, from the early Spanish explorers to the Sea Island cotton plantations to the modern day. The Museum is also a great one-stop place to sign up for a variety of specialty on-site and off-site guided tours, such as birding and Gullah history tours. The cost for most on-site tours is a very reasonable $10 adults and $5 children. The museum is also a partner with the state of South Carolina in a sea turtle protection program, which you can learn a lot more about once you're here.

But the real draw here is the 0.5-mile trail through the Honey Horn grounds, including several boardwalk viewpoints over the marsh, a neat little butterfly habitat, a few gardens, and a stable and pasture that host Honey Horn May and Tadpole, the museum's two Marsh Tackies—short, tough little ponies descended from Spanish horses and used to great effect by Francis "Swamp Fox" Marion and his freedom fighters in the American Revolution. The trail even features a replica of an ancient Native American shell ring of oyster shells, but do be aware that it is not a genuine shell ring (you can find the real thing at Green's Shell Enclosure a bit farther west on Highway 278 and in Sea Pines at the south end of the island).

While a glance at a map and area signage might convince you that you must pay the

$1.25 toll on the Cross Island Parkway to get to Honey Horn, that isn't so. The exit to Honey Horn on the Parkway is actually before you get to the toll plaza, therefore access is free.

Union Cemetery

A modest but key aspect of African American history on Hilton Head is at Union Cemetery (Union Cemetery Rd.), a small burial ground featuring several graves of black Union Army troops (you can tell by the designation "USCI" on the tombstone, for "United States Colored Infantry"). Also of interest are the charming, hand-carved cement tombstones of nonveterans. To get here, turn north off of William Hilton Parkway onto Union Cemetery Road. The cemetery is a short way ahead on the left. There is no signage or site interpretation.

Fort Mitchel and Mitchelville

There's not much left of the old Union

© JIM MOREKIS

Audubon-Newhall Preserve

encampment at Fort Mitchel, nor of the freedman community, Mitchelville, which grew up alongside it. You can see the earthworks, a couple of cannons, and a historical marker on the grounds of the Hilton Head Plantation, a gated development. Tell the security guard you'd like to see Fort Mitchel. Once inside Hilton Head Plantation, take a left onto Seabrook Drive and then a right onto Skull Creek Drive. Fort Mitchel is a short way ahead on the left. It's not a well-maintained site, but it's an important part of local history.

At the intersection of Bay Gall and Beach City Roads is a marker for the site of Mitchelville, founded in 1862 as the first freedman settlement in the United States. Also on Beach City Road is a fenced-in area with what's left of Fort Howell, a Union encampment built by African American troops.

Zion Chapel of Ease Cemetery

More like one of the gloriously desolate scenes common to the rest of the Lowcountry, this little cemetery in full view of the William Hilton Parkway at Folly Field Road is all that remains of one of the "Chapels of Ease," a string of chapels set up in the 1700s. The Zion Chapel of Ease Cemetery (daily dawn-dusk, free) is said to be haunted by the ghost of William Baynard, whose final resting place is in a mausoleum on the site (the remains of his ancestral home are farther south at Sea Pines Plantation).

Audubon-Newhall Preserve

Plant lovers shouldn't miss this small but very well-maintained 50-acre wooded tract in the south-central part of the island on Palmetto Bay Road between the Cross Island Parkway and Sea Pines circle. Almost all plant life, even that in the water, is helpfully marked and identified. But if all you want to do is just enjoy, that's fine too, because the preserve has two miles of nature trails. Unusually, there's a well-preserved bog environment (*pocosin* to the indigenous people here). The preserve (year-round dawn-dusk, free) is open to the public, but you can't camp here. For more information, call the Hilton Head Audubon Society (843/842-9246).

Sea Pines Plantation

This private residential resort development at the extreme west end of the island—first on Hilton Head and the prototype of every other such development in the country—hosts several attractions that collectively are well worth the $5 per vehicle "road use" fee, which you pay at the main entrance gate.

HARBOUR TOWN

It's not particularly historic and not all that natural, but Harbour Town is still pretty cool. The dominant element is the squat, colorful **Harbour Town Lighthouse Museum** (149 Lighthouse Rd., 843/671-2810, www.harbour-townlighthouse.com, daily 10 A.M.-dusk, $3), which has never really helped a ship navigate its way near the island. The 90-foot structure was built in 1970 purely to give visitors a little atmosphere, and that it does, as kids especially love climbing the stairs to the top ($2 pp) and looking out over the island's expanse. This being Hilton Head, of course, there's a gift shop too. The other attractions here are the boisterous café and shopping scene around the marina and the nearby park area.

STONEY-BAYNARD RUINS

These tabby ruins (Plantation Dr., dawn-dusk, free) in a residential neighborhood are what remains of the circa-1790 central building of the old Braddock's Point Plantation, first owned by Patriot and raconteur Captain "Saucy Jack" Stoney and then the Baynard family. Active during the island's heyday as a cotton center, the plantation was destroyed after the Civil War. Site interpretation here is barebones, but suffice it to say that this is a great remaining example of colonial tabby architecture. Two other foundations are nearby, one for slave quarters and one whose use is still unknown. Note that there is a $5 fee to enter Sea Pines.

SEA PINES FOREST PRESERVE

The Sea Pines Forest Preserve (175 Greenwood Dr., 843/363-4530, free) is set amid the Sea Pines Plantation golf resort development, but you don't need a bag of clubs to enjoy this 600-acre preserve, which is built on the site of an old rice plantation (dikes and logging trails are still visible). Here you can ride a horse, fish, or just take a walk on the eight miles of trails (dawn-dusk) and enjoy the natural beauty around you. No bike riding is allowed on the trails, however.

In addition to the Native American shell ring farther north off Squire Pope Road, the Sea Pines Forest Preserve also boasts a shell ring set within a canopy of tall pines, forming a natural cathedral of sorts. A combination ceremonial area and communal common space, the shell ring today is actually a series of low rings made of discarded oyster shells covered with earth. The rewards here are contemplative in nature, since the vast bulk of the actual oyster shells are beneath layers of soil. Scientists date the ring itself to about 1450 B.C., although human habitation on the island goes as far back as 8000 B.C.

Tours and Cruises

Most guided tours on Hilton Head focus on the water. **Harbour Town Cruises** (843/363-9023, www.vagabondcruise.com) offers several sightseeing tours as well as excursions to Daufuskie and Savannah. They also offer a tour on a former America's Cup racing yacht.

"Dolphin tours" are extremely popular on Hilton Head, and there is no shortage of operators. **Dolphin Watch Nature Cruises** (843/785-4558, $25 adults, $10 children) departs from Shelter Cove, as does **Lowcountry Nature Tours** (843/683-0187, www.lowcountrynaturetours.com, $40 adults, $35 children, free under age 3). The *Gypsy* (843/363-2900,

BEAUFORT

www.bitemybait.com, $15 adults, $7 children) sails out of South Beach Marina, taking you all around peaceful Calibogue Sound. Two dolphin tours are based on Broad Creek, the large body of water which almost bisects the island through the middle. "Captain Jim" runs **Island Explorer Tours** (843/785-2100, www.dolphintourshiltonhead.com, two-hour tour $45 pp) from a dock behind the old Oyster Factory on Marshland Road. Not to be outdone, "Captain Dave" leads tours at **Dolphin Discoveries** (843/681-1911, two-hour tour $40 adults, $30 under age 13), leaving out of Simmons Landing next to the Broad Creek Marina on Marshland Road. **Outside Hilton Head** (843/686-6996, www.outsidehiltonhead.com) runs a variety of water ecotours and dolphin tours as well as a guided day-trip excursion to Daufuskie, complete with golf cart rental.

There is a notable land-based tour by **Gullah Heritage Trail Tours** (leaves from Coastal Discovery Museum at Honey Horn, 843/681-7066, www.gullahheritage.com, $32 adults, $15 children) delving into the island's rich, if poorly preserved, African American history, from slavery through the time of the freedmen.

ENTERTAINMENT AND EVENTS
Nightlife

The most high-quality live entertainment on the island is at **The Jazz Corner** (1000 William Hilton Pkwy., 843/842-8620, www.thejazzcorner.com, dinner daily 6-9 P.M., late-night menu after 9 P.M.), which brings in the best names in the country—and outstanding regulars like Bob Masteller and Howard Paul—to perform in this space in the somewhat unlikely setting of a boutique mall, the Village at Wexford. The dinners are actually quite good, but the attraction is definitely the music. Reservations are recommended. Live music starts around 7 P.M.

For years islanders have jokingly referred to the "Barmuda Triangle," an area named

for the preponderance of bars within walking distance of Sea Pines Circle. While some of the names have changed over the years, the longtime anchor of the Barmuda Triangle is the **Tiki Hut** (1 S. Forest Beach Dr., 843/785-5126, Sun.-Thurs. 11 A.M.-8 P.M., Fri.-Sat. 11 A.M.-10 P.M., bar until 2 A.M.), actually part of the Holiday Inn Oceanfront Hotel at the entrance to Sea Pines. This popular watering hole is the only beachfront bar on the island, which technically makes it the only place you can legally drink alcohol on a Hilton Head beach. Another Barmuda Triangle staple is **Hilton Head Brewing Company** (7 Greenwood Dr., 843/785-3900, daily 11 A.M.-2 A.M.), the only brewpub on the island and indeed South Carolina's first microbrewery since Prohibition. They offer a wide range of handcrafted brews, from a Blueberry Wheat to a Mocha Porter. Another longtime Triangle fave is **The Lodge** (7 Greenwood Dr., 843/842-8966, www.hiltonheadlodge.com). After the martini and cigar craze waned, this popular spot successfully remade itself into a beer-centric place with 36 rotating taps. They still mix a mean martini, though. Also nearby is **Murphy's Irish Pub** (81 Pope Ave., 843/842-3448, Mon. 5-10 P.M., Tues.-Thurs. 3 P.M.-midnight, Fri.-Sat. noon-4 A.M., Sun. 11 A.M.-10 P.M.), where the name pretty much says it all (unlike most pubs with made-up Irish names, this one's actually run by a guy named Murphy). There is great bangers and mash in this frequent rugby players' hangout.

Despite its location in the upscale strip mall of the Village at Wexford, the **British Open Pub** (1000 William Hilton Pkwy./Hwy. 278, 843/686-6736) offers a fairly convincing English vibe with, as the name suggests, a heavy golf theme. The fish-and-chips and shepherd's pie are both magnificent.

Inside Sea Pines is the **Quarterdeck Lounge and Patio** (843/842-1999, www.seapines.com, Sun.-Thurs. 5:30-10 P.M., Fri.-Sat.

5:30 P.M.-midnight) at the base of the Harbour Town Lighthouse. This is where the party's at after a long day on the fairways during the Heritage golf tournament. Within Sea Pines at the South Beach marina is also where you'll find **The Salty Dog Cafe** (232 S. Sea Pines Dr., 843/671-2233, www.saltydog.com, lunch daily 11 A.M.-3 P.M., dinner daily 5-10 P.M., bar daily until 2 A.M.), one of the area's most popular institutions (some might even call it a tourist trap) and something akin to an island empire, with popular T-shirts, a gift shop, books, and an ice cream shop, all overlooking the marina. My suggestion, however, is to make the short walk to the affiliated **Wreck of the Salty Dog** (843/671-7327, daily until 2 A.M.) where the marsh views are better and the atmosphere not quite so tacky.

There's only one bona fide gay club on Hilton Head, **Vibe** (32 Palmetto Bay Rd., 843/341-6933, www.vibehhi.com, Mon.-Fri. 8 P.M.-3 A.M., Sat. 8 P.M.-2 A.M.). Wednesday is karaoke night, and Thursdays bring an amateur drag revue.

Performing Arts

Because so many residents migrated here from art-savvy metropolitan areas in the Northeast, Hilton Head maintains a very high standard of top-quality entertainment. Much of the activity centers on the multimillion-dollar **Arts Center of Coastal Carolina** (14 Shelter Cove Lane, 843/842-2787, www.artshhi.com), which hosts touring shows, resident companies, musical concerts, dance performances, and visual arts exhibits.

Now over a quarter-century old and under the direction of maestro John Morris Russell, the **Hilton Head Symphony Orchestra** (843/842-2055, www.hhso.org) performs a year-round season of masterworks and pops programs at various venues, primarily the First Presbyterian Church (540 William Hilton Pkwy./Hwy. 278). They also take their show on the road with several concerts in Bluffton and even perform several "Symphony Under the Stars" programs at Shelter Cove. **Chamber Music Hilton Head** (www.cmhh.org) performs throughout the year with selections ranging from Brahms to Smetana at All Saints Episcopal Church (3001 Meeting St.).

The **South Carolina Repertory Company** (136 Beach City Rd., 843/342-2057, www.hiltonheadtheatre.com) performs an eclectic, challenging season, including musicals, cutting-edge drama, and the avant-garde.

Cinema

There's an art house on Hilton Head, the charming **Coligny Theatre** (843/686-3500, www.colignytheatre.com) in the Coligny Plaza shopping center before you get to Sea Pines. For years this was the only movie theater for miles around, but it has reincarnated as a primarily indie film venue. Look for the entertaining murals by local artist Ralph Sutton. Showtimes are Monday 11:30 A.M. and 4 P.M., Tuesday and Friday 11:30 A.M., 4 P.M., and 7 P.M., Wednesday-Thursday and Saturday-Sunday 4 P.M. and 7 P.M.

The main multiplex on Hilton Head is **Northridge Cinema 10** (Hwy. 278 and Mathews Dr., 843/342-3800, www.southeastcinemas.com) in the Northridge Plaza shopping center. Off the island is the way-cool new **Sea Turtle Cinemas** (106 Buckwalter Pkwy., 843/706-2888, www.seaturtlecinemas.com) in the Berkeley Place shopping center. To get here, take the William Hilton Parkway (U.S. 278) west off Hilton Head for about 10 miles. Turn left at Buckwalter Parkway. Sea Turtle Cinemas is 0.5 miles farther on the right.

Festivals and Events

Late February-early March brings the **Hilton Head Wine and Food Festival** (www.hiltonheadhospitality.org), culminating in what they call "The East Coast's Largest Outdoor Public Tasting and Auction," which is generally held at the Coastal Discovery Museum at Honey Horn. Some events charge admission.

BEAUFORT

the Coligny Theatre

Hilton Head's premier event is the **RBC Heritage Classic Golf Tournament** (843/671-2248, http://theheritagegolfsc.com), held each April (usually the week after the Master's) at the Harbour Town Golf Links on Sea Pines Plantation. Formerly known as the Verizon Heritage Classic, the event is South Carolina's only PGA Tour event and brings thousands of visitors to town yearly.

A fun and fondly anticipated yearly event is the **Kiwanis Club Chili Cookoff** (www.hilton-headkiwanis.org), held each October at Honey Horn on the south end. A low admission price gets you all the chili you can eat plus free antacids. All funds go to charity, and all excess chili goes to a local food bank.

Every November brings Hilton Head's second-largest event, the **Hilton Head Concours d'Elegance & Motoring Festival** (www.hhiconcours.com), a multiday event bringing together vintage car clubs from throughout the nation and culminating in a prestigious "Best of Show" competition. It started as a fundraiser for the Hilton Head Symphony, but now people come from all over the country to see these fine vintage cars in a beautiful setting.

SHOPPING

As you'd expect, Hilton Head is a shopper's delight, with an emphasis on upscale stores and prices to match. Keep in mind that hours may be shortened in the off-season (Nov.-Mar.). Here's a rundown of the main island shopping areas in the order you'll encounter them as you enter the island.

Shelter Cove

As of this writing, the Mall at Shelter Cove is being completely repurposed, with plans for boutique retail centered around a Belk anchor store. The other two shopping entities at this shopping area on Broad Creek right off the William Hilton Parkway are the **Plaza at Shelter Cove** and the dockside **Shelter**

Cove Harbour. The most interesting store at the Plaza is the flagship location of **Outside Hilton Head** (843/686-6996, www.outside-hiltonhead.com, Mon.-Sat. 10 A.M.-5:30 P.M., Sun. 11 A.M.-5:30 P.M.), a complete outdoor outfitter with a thoroughly knowledgeable staff. Whatever outdoor gear you need and whatever tour you want to take, they can most likely hook you up. Shelter Cove Harbour hosts a few cute shops hewing to its overall nautical-vacation theme, such as the clothing stores **Camp Hilton Head** (843/842-3666, Mon.-Sat. 10 A.M.-9 P.M., Sun. noon-5 P.M.) and the marine supplier **Ship's Store** (843/842-7001, Mon.-Sat. 7:30 A.M.-5 P.M., Sun. 7:30 A.M.-4 P.M.).

Village at Wexford

Easily my favorite place to shop on Hilton Head, this well-shaded shopping center on William Hilton Parkway (Hwy. 278) hosts plenty of well-tended shops, including the foodie equipment store **Le Cookery** (843/785-7171, Mon.-Sat. 10 A.M.-6 P.M.), the Lily Pulitzer signature women's store **S.M. Bradford Co.** (843/686-6161, Mon.-Sat. 10 A.M.-6 P.M.) and the aromatic **Scents of Hilton Head** (843/842-7866, Mon.-Fri. 10 A.M.-6 P.M., Sat. 10 A.M.-5 P.M.).

My favorite shop on all Hilton Head is at Wexford, **The Oilerie** (843/681-2722, www.oilerie.com, Mon.-Sat. 10 A.M.-7 P.M., Sun. noon-5 P.M.). This franchise provides free samples of all its high-quality Italian olive oils and vinegars. After you taste around awhile, you pick what you want and the friendly staff bottles it for you in souvenir-quality glassware. They also have a selection of spices, soaps, and other goodies.

Coligny Circle

This is the closest Hilton Head comes to funkier beach towns like Tybee Island or Folly Beach, although it doesn't really come that close. You'll find dozens of delightful and somewhat quirky stores here, many keeping long hours in the summer, like the self-explanatory **Coligny Kite & Flag Co.** (843/785-5483, Mon.-Sat. 10 A.M.-9 P.M., Sun. 11 A.M.-6 P.M.), the hippie-fashion **Loose Lucy's** (843/785-8093, Mon.-Sat. 10 A.M.-6 P.M., Sun. 11 A.M.-5 P.M.), and the Caribbean-flavored **Jamaican Me Crazy** (843/785-9006, daily 10 A.M.-10 P.M.). Kids will love both **The Shell Shop** (843/785-4900, Mon.-Sat. 10 A.M.-9 P.M., Sun. noon-9 P.M.) and **Black Market Minerals** (843/785-7090, Mon.-Sat. 10 A.M.-10 P.M., Sun. 11 A.M.-8 P.M.).

Harbour Town

The Shoppes at Harbour Town (www.seapines.com) are a collection of about 20 mostly boutique stores along Lighthouse Road in Sea Pines Plantation. At **Planet Hilton Head** (843/363-5177, www.planethiltonhead.com, daily 10 A.M.-9 P.M.) you'll find some cute, eclectic gifts and home goods. Other clothing highlights include **Knickers Men's Store** (843/671-2291, daily 10 A.M.-9 P.M.) and **Radiance** (843/363-5176), a very cute and fashion-forward women's store.

The **Top of the Lighthouse Shoppe** (843/671-2810, www.harbourtownlighthouse.com, daily 10 A.M.-9 P.M.) is where many a climbing visitor has been coaxed to part with some of their disposable income. And, of course, as you'd expect being near the legendary Harbour Town links, there's the **Harbour Town Pro Shop** (843/671-4485), routinely voted one of the best pro shops in the nation.

South Beach Marina

On South Sea Pines Drive at the Marina you'll find several worthwhile shops, including a good ship's store and all-around grocery dealer **South Beach General Store** (843/671-6784, daily 8 A.M.-10 P.M.). I like to stop in the **Blue Water Bait and Tackle** (843/671-3060, daily 7 A.M.-8 P.M.) and check out the cool nautical stuff. They can also hook you up with a variety of kayak trips and fishing charters. And, of course, right on the water there's the ever-popular **Salty Dog Cafe** (843/671-2233, www.saltydog.com, lunch daily 11 A.M.-3 P.M., dinner daily 5-10 P.M.), whose ubiquitous T-shirts seem to adorn every other person on the island.

Thrift Shops

Don't scoff: Every thrift store connoisseur knows the best place to shop secondhand is in an affluent area like Hilton Head, where the locals try hard to stay in style and their castoffs are first-class. Key stops here are **The Bargain Box** (546 William Hilton Pkwy., 843/681-4305, Mon., Wed., and Fri. 1-4 P.M., Thurs. 2-5 P.M., Sat. 9:15 A.M.-12:15 P.M.) and **St. Francis Thrift Store** (2 Southwood Dr., 843/689-6563, Wed.-Sat. 10 A.M.-3 P.M.) right off the William Hilton Parkway.

Art Galleries

Despite the abundant wealth apparent in some quarters here, there's no freestanding art museum in the area, that role being filled by independent galleries. A good representative example is **Morris & Whiteside Galleries** (220 Cordillo Pkwy., 843/842-4433, www.morris-whiteside.com, Mon.-Fri. 9 A.M.-5 P.M., Sat. 10 A.M.-4 P.M.), located in the historic Red Piano Art Gallery building, which features a variety of paintings and sculpture, heavy on landscapes but also showing some fine figurative work. The nonprofit **Art League of Hilton Head** (14 Shelter Cove Lane, 843/681-5060, Mon.-Sat. 10 A.M.-6 P.M.) is located in the Walter Greer Art Gallery within the Arts Center of Coastal Carolina and displays work by member artists in all media. The **Nash Gallery** (13 Harbourside Lane, 843/785-6424, Mon.-Fri. 10 A.M.-9 P.M., Sat. 10 A.M.-8 P.M., Sun. 11 A.M.-5 P.M.) in Shelter Cove Harbour deals more in North American craft styles. Hilton Head art isn't exactly known for its avant-garde nature, but you can find some whimsical stuff at **Picture**

This (78D Arrow Rd., 843/842-5299, Mon.-Fri. 9:30 A.M.-5:30 P.M., Sat. 9:30 A.M.-12:30 P.M.), including a selection of Gullah craft items. A wide range of regional painters, sculptors, and glass artists is featured at **Endangered Arts** (841 William Hilton Pkwy., 843/785-5075, www.endangeredarts.com).

SPORTS AND RECREATION
Beaches

First, the good news: Hilton Head Island has 12 miles of some of the most beautiful safe beaches you'll find anywhere. The bad news is that there are only a few ways to gain access, generally at locations referred to as "beach parks." Don't just drive into a residential neighborhood and think you'll be able to park and find your way to the beach; for better or worse, Hilton Head is not set up for that kind of casual access.

Driessen Beach Park has 207 long-term parking spaces, costing $0.25 for 30 minutes. There's free parking but fewer spaces at the Coligny Beach Park entrance and at Fish Haul Creek Park. Also, there are 22 metered spaces at Alder Lane Beach Access, 51 at Folly Field Beach Park, and 13 at Burkes Beach Road. Most other beach parks are for permit parking only. Clean, well-maintained public restrooms are available at all the beach parks. You can find beach information at 843/342-4580 and www.hiltonhead-islandsc.gov. Beach Park hours vary: Coligny Beach Park is open daily 24 hours; all other beach parks are open March-September daily 6 A.M.-8 P.M. and October-February daily 6 A.M.-5 P.M.

Alcohol is strictly prohibited on Hilton Head's beaches. This may cut down on your vacation fun, but the plus side is the ban makes the beaches very friendly for families. There are lifeguards on all the beaches during the summer, but be aware that the worst undertow is on the northern stretches. Also remember to leave the sand dollars where they are; their population is dwindling due to souvenir hunting.

Kayaking

Kayakers will enjoy Hilton Head Island,

© JIM MOREKIS

The beach at Hilton Head is particularly well suited for bicycles.

which offers several gorgeous routes, including Calibogue Sound to the south and west and Port Royal Sound to the north. For particularly good views of life on the salt marsh, try Broad Creek, which nearly bisects Hilton Head Island, and Skull Creek, which separates Hilton Head from the natural beauty of Pinckney Island. Broad Creek Marina is a good place to put in. There are also two public landings, Haigh Landing and Buckingham Landing, on Mackay Creek at the entrance to the island, one on either side of the bridge.

If you want a guided tour, there are plenty of great kayak tour outfits to choose from in the area. Chief among them is certainly **Outside Hilton Head** (32 Shelter Cove Lane, 800/686-6996, www.outsidehiltonhead.com). They offer a wide range of guided trips, including "The Outback," in which you're first boated to a private island and then taken on a tour of tidal creeks, and five- or seven-hour "Ultimate Lowcountry Day" trips to Daufuskie, Bluffton,

or Bull Creek. Other good places to book a tour or just rent a kayak are **Water-Dog Outfitters** (Broad Creek Marina, 843/686-3554) and **Kayak Hilton Head** (Broad Creek Marina, 843/684-1910). Leaving out of the Harbour Town Yacht Basin is **H2O Sports** (843/671-4386, www.h2osportsonline.com), which offers 90-minute guided kayak tours ($30) and rents kayaks for about $20 per hour. Within Palmetto Dunes Oceanfront Resort (4 Queens Folly Rd., 800/827-3006, www.palmetto-dunes.com) is **Palmetto Dunes Outfitters** (843/785-2449, www.pdoutfitters.com, daily 9 A.M.-5 P.M.), which rents kayaks and canoes and offers lessons on the resort's 11-mile lagoon.

Fishing and Boating

As you'd expect, anglers and boaters love the Hilton Head-Bluffton area, which offers all kinds of saltwater, freshwater, and fly-fishing opportunities. Captain Brian Vaughn runs **Off the Hook Charters** (68 Helmsman Way,

843/298-4376, www.offthehookcharters.com), which offers fully licensed half-day trips ($400). **Miss Carolina Sportfishing** (168 Palmetto Bay Rd., 843/298-2628, www.misscarolinafishing. com) offers deep-sea action at a little over $100 per hour. Captain Dave Fleming of **Mighty Mako Sport Fishing Charters** (164 Palmetto Bay Rd., 843/785-6028, www.mightymako. com) can take you saltwater fishing, both backwater and near-shore, on the 25-foot *Mighty Mako* for about $400 for a half-day. If you're at the South Beach Marina area of Sea Pines Plantation, head into **Blue Water Bait and Tackle** (843/671-3060) and see if they can hook you up with a trip.

Public landings in the Hilton Head area include the Marshland Road Boat Landing and the Broad Creek Boat Ramp under the Charles Fraser Bridge, and the Haigh Landing on Mackay Creek.

Hiking and Biking

Although the very flat terrain is not challenging, Hilton Head provides some scenic and relaxing cycling opportunities. Thanks to wise planning and foresight, the island has an extensive award-winning 50-mile network of biking trails that does a great job of keeping cyclists out of traffic. A big plus is the long bike path paralleling the William Hilton Parkway, enabling cyclists to use that key artery without braving its traffic. There is even an underground bike path beneath the Parkway to facilitate crossing that busy road. In addition, there are also routes along Pope Avenue as well as North and South Forest Beach Drive. Go to www.hiltonheadisland.org/biking to download a map of the entire island bike path network.

For biking purposes, be aware that on some private resort developments, access technically is limited to residents, and you may be challenged and asked where you're residing. Also, pay attention to the miniature stop signs on the bike paths, ignorance of which can lead to some nasty scrapes or worse.

Palmetto Dunes Oceanfront Resort (4 Queens Folly Rd., 800/827-3006, www.palmettodunes.com) has a particularly nice 25-mile network of bike paths that all link up to the island's larger framework. Within the resort is **Palmetto Dunes Outfitters** (843/785-2449, www.pdoutfitters.com, daily 9 A.M.-5 P.M.), which will rent you any type of bike you might need. Sea Pines Plantation also has an extensive 17-mile network of bike trails; you can pick up a map at most information kiosks within the plantation.

But the best bike path on Hilton Head is the simplest of all, where no one will ask you where you're staying that night: the beach. For a few hours before and after low tide, the beach effectively becomes a 12-mile bike path around most of the island, and a pleasant morning or afternoon ride may well prove to be the highlight of your trip.

There's a plethora of bike rental facilities on Hilton Head with competitive rates. Be sure to ask if they offer free pickup and delivery. Try **Hilton Head Bicycle Company** (112 Arrow Rd., 843/686-6888, Mon.-Sat. 9 A.M.-5 P.M., Sun. noon-5 P.M.).

Hikers will particularly enjoy Pinckney Island National Wildlife Refuge, which takes you through several key Lowcountry ecosystems, from maritime forest to salt marsh. Other peaceful, if nonchallenging, trails are at the Audubon-Newhall Preserve.

Horseback Riding

Within the Sea Pines Forest Preserve is **Lawton Stables** (190 Greenwood Dr., 843/671-2586, www.lawtonstableshhi.com), which features pony rides, a small animal farm, and guided horseback rides through the preserve. You don't need any riding experience, but you do need reservations.

Bird-Watching

The premier birding locale in the area is the **Pinckney Island National Wildlife Refuge** (U.S. 278 east, just before Hilton Head,

912/652-4415, www.fws.gov, free). You can see bald eagles, ibis, wood storks, painted buntings, and many more species. Birding is best in spring and fall. The refuge has several freshwater ponds that serve as wading bird rookeries. During migratory season, so many beautiful birds make such a ruckus that you'll think you've wandered onto an Animal Planet shoot.

Another good bird-watching locale is **Victoria Bluff Heritage Preserve** (803/734-3886, daily dawn-dusk, free), a 1,100-acre pine-and-palmetto habitat. Get here from Hilton Head by taking U.S. 278 off the island. Take a right onto Sawmill Creek Road heading north. The parking area is shortly ahead on the right. Note that there are no facilities here.

Golf

Hilton Head is one of the world's great golf centers, with no less than 23 courses, and one could easily write a book about nothing but that. This, however, is not that book. Perhaps contrary to what you might expect, most courses on the island are public, and some are downright affordable. All courses are 18 holes unless otherwise described; green fees are averages and vary with season and tee time.

The best-regarded course, with prices to match, is **Harbour Town Golf Links** (Sea Pines Plantation, 843/363-4485, www.seapines.com, $239). It's on the island's south end at Sea Pines and is the home of the annual RBC Heritage Classic, far and away the island's number-one tourist draw.

There are two Arthur Hills-designed courses on the island, **Arthur Hills at Palmetto Dunes Resort** (843/785-1140, www.palmettodunes.com, $125) and **Arthur Hills at Palmetto Hall** (Palmetto Hall Plantation, 843/689-4100, www.palmettohallgolf.com, $130), both of which now offer the use of Segway vehicles on the fairways. The reasonably priced **Barony Course** at Port Royal Plantation (843/686-8801, www.portroyalgolfclub.com, $98) also boasts some of the toughest greens on the island. Another

challenging and affordable course is the **George Fazio** at Palmetto Dunes Resort (843/785-1130, www.palmettodunes.com, $105).

Hilton Head National Golf Club (60 Hilton Head National Dr., 843/842-5900, www.golf-hiltonheadnational.com), which is actually on the mainland just before you cross the bridge to Hilton Head, not only boasts a total of 27 challenging holes but is consistently rated among the best golf locales in the world for both condition and service. *Golf Week* has named it one of the country's best golf courses. All three courses are public and green fees at each are below $100.

It's a good idea to book tee times through the **Golf Island Call Center** (888/465-3475, www.golfisland.com), which can also hook you up with good packages.

Tennis

One of the top tennis destinations in the country, Hilton Head has over 20 tennis clubs, some of which offer court time to the public (walk-on rates vary; call for information). They are: **Palmetto Dunes Tennis Center** (Palmetto Dunes Resort, 843/785-1152, www.palmettodunes.com, $30 per hour), **Port Royal Racquet Club** (Port Royal Plantation, 843/686-8803, www.portroyalgolf-club.com, $25 per hour), **Sea Pines Racquet Club** (Sea Pines Plantation, 843/363-4495, www.seapines.com, $25 per hour), **South Beach Racquet Club** (Sea Pines Plantation, 843/671-2215, www.seapines.com, $25 per hour), and **Shipyard Racquet Club** (Shipyard Plantation, 843/686-8804, $25 per hour).

Free, first-come-first-served play is available at the following public courts, maintained by the Island Recreation Association (www.islandreccenter.org): **Chaplin Community Park** (Singleton Beach Rd., four courts, lighted), **Cordillo Courts** (Cordillo Pkwy., four courts, lighted), **Fairfield Square** (Adrianna Lane, two courts), **Hilton Head High School** (School Rd., six courts), and **Hilton Head Middle School** (Wilborn Rd., four courts).

BEAUFORT

ACCOMMODATIONS

Generally speaking, accommodations on Hilton Head are often surprisingly affordable given their overall high quality and the breadth of their amenities.

Under $150

You can't beat the price at **Park Lane Hotel and Suites** (12 Park Lane, 843/686-5700, www.hiltonheadparklanehotel.com, $130). This is your basic suite-type hotel (formerly a Residence Inn) with kitchens, laundry, a pool, and a tennis court. The allure here is the price, hard to find anywhere these days at a resort location. For a nonrefundable fee, you can bring your pet. The one drawback is that the beach is a good distance away. The hotel does offer a free shuttle, however, so it would be wise to take advantage of that and avoid the usual beach parking hassles. As you'd expect given the price, rooms here tend to go quickly; reserve early.

$150-300

By Hilton Head standards, the 【**Main Street Inn & Spa** (2200 Main St., 800/471-3001, www.mainstreetinn.com, $160-210) can be considered a bargain stay, and with high quality to boot. With its Old World touches, sumptuous appointments, charming atmosphere, and attentive service, this 33-room inn and attached spa on the grounds of Hilton Head Plantation seem like they would be more at home in Charleston than Hilton Head. The inn serves a great full breakfast—not continental—daily 7:30-10:30 A.M. As a bonus, most of the less-expensive guest rooms have a great view of the formal garden, another part of that old Lowcountry appeal that's hard to come by on the island. If you want to upgrade, there are larger guest rooms with a fireplace and a smallish private courtyard for not much more. Overall, it's one of Hilton Head's best values.

Another good place for the price is the **South Beach Marina Inn** (232 S. Sea Pines Dr.,

843/671-6498, www.sbinn.com, $186) in Sea Pines. Located near the famous Salty Dog Cafe and outfitted in a similar nautical theme, the inn not only has some pretty large guest rooms for the price, it offers a great view of the marina and has a very friendly feel, great for families with kids and romantic couples alike (especially with a beach on calm Calibogue Sound only a few minutes' walk away). As with all Sea Pines accommodations, staying on the plantation means you don't have to wait in line with other visitors to pay the $5-per-day "road fee." Sea Pines also offers a free trolley to get around the plantation.

One of Hilton Head's favorite hotels for beach lovers is the **Holiday Inn Oceanfront** (1 South Forest Beach Dr., 843/785-5126, www.hihiltonhead.com, $200), home of the famed Tiki Hut bar on the beach. Staff turnover is less frequent here than at other local accommodations, and while it's no Ritz-Carlton and occasionally shows signs of wear, it's a good value on a bustling area of the island. Parking has always been a problem here, but at least there's free valet service.

One of the better resort-type places for those who prefer the putter and the racquet to the Frisbee and the surfboard is the **Inn at Harbour Town** (7 Lighthouse Lane, 843/363-8100, www.seapines.com, $199) in Sea Pines. The big draw here is the impeccable service, delivered by a staff of "butlers" in kilts, mostly Europeans who take the venerable trade quite seriously. While it's not on the beach, you can take advantage of the free Sea Pines Trolley every 20 minutes.

Recently rated the number-one family resort in the U.S. by *Travel + Leisure,* the well-run 【 **Palmetto Dunes Oceanfront Resort** (4 Queens Folly Rd., 800/827-3006, www.palmettodunes.com, $150-300) offers something for everybody in terms of lodging. There are small, cozy condos by the beach or larger villas overlooking the golf course and pretty much everything in between. The prices are perhaps

The Crowne Plaza has expansive, relaxing grounds.

disarmingly affordable considering the relative luxury and copious recreational amenities, which include 25 miles of very well-done bike trails, 11 miles of kayak and canoe trails, and, of course, three signature links. As with most developments of this type on Hilton Head, most of the condos are privately owned, and therefore each has its particular set of guidelines and cleaning schedules.

A little farther down the island you'll find the **Crowne Plaza Hilton Head Island** (130 Shipyard Dr., 877/620-1682, www.cphiltonhead.com, $160-200), which styles itself as Hilton Head's only green-certified accommodations. The guest rooms are indeed state-of-the-art, and the expansive shaded grounds near the beach are great for relaxation. No on-site golf here, but immediately adjacent is a well-regarded tennis facility with 20 courts.

Another good resort-style experience heavy on the golf is on the grounds of the Port Royal Plantation on the island's north side, **The Westin Resort Hilton Head Island** (2 Grasslawn Ave., 843/681-4000, www.westin.com/hiltonhead, from $200), which hosts three PGA-caliber links. The beach is also but a short walk away. This AAA four diamond-winning Westin offers a mix of suites and larger villas.

Vacation Rentals

Many visitors to Hilton Head choose to rent a home or villa for an extended stay, and there is no scarcity of availability. Try **Resort Rentals of Hilton Head** (www.hhivacations.com) or **Destination Vacation** (www.destinationvacationhhi.com).

FOOD

You'll have no problem finding good restaurants in and around Hilton Head, with a great combination of taste and a comparatively casual atmosphere. Because of the cosmopolitan nature of the population, with so many transplants from the northeastern United States and Europe, there is uniformly high quality.

Because of another demographic quirk of the area, its large percentage of senior citizens, you can also find some great deals by looking for some of the common "early bird" dinner specials, usually starting around 5 P.M.

Breakfast and Brunch

There are a couple of great diner-style places on the island. Though known more for its hamburgers and Philly cheesesteaks, **◖ Harold's Diner** (641 William Hilton Pkwy., 843/842-9292, Mon.-Sat. 7 A.M.-3 P.M., $4-6) has great pancakes as well as its trademark brand of sarcastic service. Unpretentious and authentic in a place where those two adjectives are rarely used, it has been said of Harold's that "the lack of atmosphere *is* the atmosphere." Be aware that the place is small, popular, and reservations are not taken.

If you need a bite in the Coligny Plaza area, go to **Skillets** (1 N. Forest Beach Dr., 843/785-3131, www.skilletscafe.com, breakfast daily 7 A.M.-5 P.M., dinner daily 5-9 P.M., $5-23) in Coligny Plaza. Their eponymous stock-in-trade is a layered breakfast dish of sautéed ingredients served in a porcelain skillet, like the "Kitchen Sink" (pancakes ringed with potatoes, sausage, and bacon, topped with two poached eggs).

A great all-day breakfast place with a twist is **◖ Signe's Heaven Bound Bakery & Café** (93 Arrow Rd., 843/785-9118, www.signesbakery.com, Mon.-Fri. 8 A.M.-4 P.M., Sat. 9 A.M.-2 P.M., $5-10). Breakfast is tasty dishes like frittatas and breakfast polenta, while the twist is the extensive artisanal bakery, with delicious specialties like the signature key lime pound cake. You'll be surprised at the quality of the food for the low prices. Expect a wait in line at the counter during peak periods.

A fairly well-kept local secret is the **French Bakery and Courtyard Cafe** (430 William Hilton Pkwy./U.S. 278, 843/342-5420, www.frenchbakeryhiltonhead.com, Mon.-Sat. 8:30 A.M.-4 P.M., $5). Set inside the Pineland Station shopping center and with nice open-air seating, French Bakery offers a full range of fresh-baked goods like quiches, croissants, paninis, artisanal breads, cakes, and gourmet pastries.

German

I'm pretty sure you didn't come all the way to South Carolina to eat traditional German food, but while you're here...check out **◖ Alfred's** (807 William Hilton Pkwy./Hwy. 278, 843/341-3117, wwww.alfredsofhiltonhead.com, $20-30), one of the more unique spots on Hilton Head and a big favorite with the locals. Expect a wait. Bratwurst, veal cordon bleu, and of course wiener schnitzel are all standouts. I recommend the German Mix Platter ($25), which features a brat, some sauerbraten, and a schnitzel. That said, owner-chef Alfred Kettering actually offers a lot more than just German food, with a killer veal scaloppine and great grilled salmon, among others. Interestingly, the extensive wine list is overwhelmingly Californian, with only a single German entry, a riesling.

Mediterranean

For upscale Italian, try **Bistro Mezzaluna** (55 New Orleans Rd., 843/842-5011, daily 5-9:30 P.M.). Known far and wide for its osso buco as well as its impeccable service, there's also a great little bar for cocktails before or after dinner.

Mexican

There are a couple of excellent and authentic Mexican restaurants on the island. Just off the William Hilton Parkway near the island's entrance is **◖ Mi Tierra** (160 Fairfield Square, 843/342-3409, lunch daily 11 A.M.-4 P.M., dinner Mon.-Fri. 4-9 P.M., Sat.-Sun. 4-10 P.M., $3-15). You'll find lots of traditional seafood dishes, like seviche, octopus, shrimp, and oysters. On Mondays there is often a real mariachi band.

Another great Mexican place—also with a Bluffton location—is **Amigo's Café Y Cantina** (70 Pope Ave., 843/785-8226, Mon.-Sat.

11 A.M.-9 P.M., $8). While its strip-mall locale is not great, the food is fresh, simple, excellent, fast, and inexpensive.

Middle Eastern

Hard to describe but well worth the visit, **((** **Daniel's Restaurant and Lounge** (2 N. Forest Beach Dr., 843/341-9379, http://danielshhi.com, daily 4 P.M.-2 A.M., tapas $10-12) combines elements of a traditional Middle Eastern eatery, an upscale tapas place, a beach spot, and a swank bar scene to create one of the more memorable food-and-beverage experiences on the island. Add in the fact that the prices are actually quite accessible and you've got a must-visit. Their "big small plates," meaning larger-portion tapas, run about $10-12 per plate. While they market their Middle Eastern flavor with plates like the cinnamon lamb kebab, their tapas have a cosmopolitan feel and range from a Caribbean salmon steak to chicken pesto sliders.

New Southern

A fairly new addition to the island's foodie scene, **Robert Irvine's Eat!** (1000 William Hilton Pkwy./Hwy. 278, 843/785-4850, www.eathhi.com, dinner Mon.-Sat. from 5 P.M., $15-30), in the Village at Wexford shopping center, is of course a creation of the eponymous Food Channel celebrity chef, who is often seen in the restaurant. The menu tends toward Charleston-esque upgrades of traditional classics, such as the fennel-brined pork chop, blackened snapper and grits, and an extensive tapas menu that includes a she-crab bisque and, yes, fried green tomatoes. Reservations are strongly recommended.

For a casual but tasty sandwich in Coligny Plaza, go straight to **((** **Bombora's Grille and Chill Bar** (101 Pope Ave., 843/689-2662, www.bomborasgrille.com, Mon.-Tues. 1 P.M.-midnight, Wed.-Fri. 11 A.M.-midnight, Sat.-Sun. noon-midnight, $10-15) and order the pulled pork sandwich. Though technically the lack of sauce means it's not barbecue—hence the name—this is an excellent and hearty dish that can stand alongside the 'cue at more "authentic" places. Even the fries are delicious. Wash it all down with a selection from their wide range of handcrafted beers in regular or large growler size.

Seafood

Not to be confused with Charley's Crab House next door to Hudson's, seafood lovers will enjoy the experience down near Sea Pines at **((** **Charlie's L'Etoile Verte** (8 New Orleans Rd., 843/785-9277, http://charliesgreenstar.com, lunch Tues.-Sat. 11:30 A.M.-2 P.M., dinner Mon.-Sat. 5:30-10 P.M., $25-40), which is considered by many connoisseurs to be Hilton Head's single best restaurant. The emphasis here is on "French country kitchen" cuisine—think Provence, not Paris. In keeping, each day's menu is concocted from scratch and handwritten. Listen to these recent entrées and feel your mouth water: flounder sauté meunière, grilled wild coho salmon with basil pesto, and breast of duck in a raspberry demi-glace. Get the picture? Of course, you'll want to start with the escargot and leeks vol-au-vent, the house pâté, or even some pan-roasted Bluffton oysters. As you'd expect, the wine selection is celestial. Reservations are essential.

A longtime Hilton Head favorite is **((** **Red Fish** (8 Archer Rd., 843/686-3388, www.redfishofhiltonhead.com, lunch Mon.-Sat. 11:30 A.M.-2 P.M., dinner daily beginning with early-bird specials at 5 P.M., $20-37). Strongly Caribbean in decor as well as the menu, with romanticism and panache to match, this is a great place for couples. The creative but accessible menu by executive chef Sean Walsh incorporates unique spices, fruits, and vegetables for a fresh, zesty palette. The recommended course of action is to pick your own wine from the vast, 1,000-plus-bottle award-winning selection in the attached wine shop and cellar to go

BEAUFORT

with your dinner. Recent highlights from the rotating seasonal menu include the grilled sea bass, the Latin ribs, and yes, the vegetable strudel. Reservations are essential.

Fresh seafood lovers will enjoy one of Hilton Head's staples, the huge **Hudson's on the Docks** (1 Hudson Rd., 843/681-2772, www.hudsonsonthedocks.com, lunch daily 11 A.M.-4 P.M., dinner daily from 5 P.M., $14-23) on Skull Creek just off Squire Pope Road on the less-developed north side. Much of the catch—though not all of it, by any means—comes directly off the boats you'll see dockside. Built on the old family oyster factory, Hudson's is now owned by transplants from, of all places, Long Island, New York. Try the stuffed shrimp filled with crabmeat, or just go for a combination platter. Leave room for one of the homemade desserts crafted by Ms. Bessie, a 30-year veteran employee of Hudson's.

INFORMATION AND SERVICES

The best place to get information on Hilton Head, book a room, or secure a tee time is just as you come onto the island at the **Hilton Head Island Chamber of Commerce Welcome Center** (100 William Hilton Pkwy., 843/785-3673, www.hiltonheadisland.org, daily 9 A.M.-6 P.M.).

Hilton Head's newspaper of record is the *Island Packet* (www.islandpacket.com).

Hilton Head's main **post office** (213 William Hilton Pkwy., 843/893-3490) is in an easy-to-find location.

GETTING THERE AND AROUND

A few years back, the **Savannah International Airport** (SAV, 400 Airways Ave., Savannah, 912/964-0514, www.savannahairport.com) added Hilton Head to its name specifically to identify itself with that lucrative market. It has been a success, and this facility remains the closest large airport to Hilton Head Island and Bluffton. From the airport, go north on I-95 into South Carolina, and take exit 8 onto U.S. 278 east. There is a local regional airport as well, the **Hilton Head Island Airport** (HXD, 120 Beach City Rd., 843/689-5400, www.bcgov.net). While very attractive and convenient, keep in mind that it only hosts propeller-driven commuter planes because of the runway length and concerns about noise.

If you're entering the area by car, the best route is exit 8 off I-95 onto U.S. 278, which takes you by Bluffton and right into Hilton Head. Near Bluffton, U.S. 278 is called Fording Island Road, and on Hilton Head proper it becomes the William Hilton Parkway business route. Technically, U.S. 278 turns into the new Cross Island Parkway, but when most locals say "278" they're almost always referring to the William Hilton Parkway.

Other than taxi services, there is no public transportation to speak of in the Lowcountry, unless you want to count the free shuttle around Sea Pines Plantation. Taxi services include **Yellow Cab** (843/686-6666), **Island Taxi** (843/683-6363), and **Ferguson Transportation** (843/842-8088).

Bluffton and Daufuskie Island

Just outside Hilton Head are two of the Lowcountry's true gems, Bluffton and Daufuskie Island. While Bluffton's outskirts have been taken over by the same gated community and upscale strip-mall sprawl spreading throughout the coast, at its core is a delightfully charming little community on the quiet May River, now called Old Bluffton, where you'd swear you just entered a time warp.

Daufuskie Island still maintains much of its age-old isolated, timeless personality, and the island—still accessible only by boat—is still one of the spiritual centers of the Gullah culture and lifestyle.

◖ OLD BLUFFTON

Similar to Beaufort, but even quieter and smaller, historic Bluffton is an idyllic village on the banks of the hypnotically serene and well-preserved May River. Bluffton was the original hotbed of secession, with Charleston diarist Mary Chesnut famously referring to the town as "the center spot of the fire eaters." While its outskirts (so-called "Greater Bluffton") are now a haven for planned communities hoping to mimic some aspect of Bluffton's historic patina, the town center itself remains an authentic look at old South Carolina. Retro cuts both ways, however, and Bluffton has been a notorious speed trap for generations. Always obey the speed limit. During their Civil War occupation, Union troops repaid the favor of those original Bluffton secessionists, which is why only nine homes in Bluffton are of antebellum vintage; the rest were torched in a search for Confederate guerrillas.

The center of tourist activity focuses on the **Old Bluffton Historic District,** several blocks of 1800s-vintage buildings clustered between the parallel Boundary and Calhoun Streets (old-timers sometimes call this "the original square mile"). Many of the buildings are private residences, but most have been converted into art studios and antiques stores. The wares feature a whimsical folk-art quality very much in tune with Bluffton's whole Southern Shangri-la feel. While the artists and shopkeepers are serious about their work, they make it a point to warmly invite everyone in, even when they're busy at work on the latest project.

Heyward House Historic Center

The Heyward House Historic Center (70 Boundary St., 843/757-6293, www.heywardhouse. org, Mon.-Fri. 10 A.M.-4 P.M., Sat. 11 A.M.-2 P.M., tours $5 adults, $2 students) is not only open to tours but serves as Bluffton's visitors center. Built in 1840 as a summer home for the owner of Moreland Plantation, John Cole, the house was later owned by George Cuthbert Heyward, grandson of Declaration of Independence signer Thomas Heyward. (Remarkably, it stayed in the family until the 1990s.) Of note are the intact slave quarters on the grounds.

The Heyward House also sponsors walking tours of the historic district (843/757-6293, $15, by appointment only). Download your own walking-tour map at www.heywardhouse.org.

Church of the Cross

Don't fail to go all the way to the end of Calhoun Street, as it dead-ends on a high bluff on the May River at the Bluffton Public Dock. Overlooking this peaceful marsh-front vista is the sublimely photogenic Church of the Cross (110 Calhoun St., 843/757-2661, www.thechurchofthecross.net, free tours Mon.-Sat. 10 A.M.-2 P.M.). The current sanctuary was built in 1854 and is one of only two local churches not burned in the Civil War, but the parish itself began in 1767, with the first services on this spot held in the late 1830s. Standing here on the bluff, with the steady south breeze blowing the bugs away and relieving you of the Lowcountry heat, you can see why affluent South Carolinians began building summer homes here in the 1800s. While the church looks as if it were made of cypress, interestingly it's actually constructed of heart pine.

Bluffton Oyster Company

You might want to get a gander at the state's last remaining working oyster house, the Bluffton Oyster Company (63 Wharf St., 843/757-4010, Mon.-Sat. 9 A.M.-5:30 P.M.), and possibly purchase some of their maritime bounty. The adjoining five acres were recently purchased by the Beaufort County Open Land Trust with the intention of evolving the area into a community green space celebrating a key aspect of local heritage, the celebrated May River oyster. Meanwhile, Larry and Tina Toomer continue to oversee the oyster harvesting-and-shucking

family enterprise, which has roots going back to the early 1900s.

Waddell Mariculture Center

While the oysters are growing scarce on the May River, get a close-up look at an interesting state-funded seafood farm on the Colleton River estuary, the Waddell Mariculture Center (Sawmill Creek Rd., 843/837-3795). Free tours are available Monday-Wednesday and Friday mornings. Shrimp, fish, and shellfish are some of the "product" raised and harvested here. Get to Waddell by taking U.S. 278 east from Bluffton and then taking a left on Sawmill Creek Road.

SHOPPING

Bluffton's eccentric little art studios, most clustered in a two-block stretch on Calhoun Street, are by far its main shopping draw. Named for the Lowcountry phenomenon you find in the marsh at low tide among the fiddler crabs,

Bluffton's Calhoun Street hosts many offbeat galleries.

© JIM MOREKIS

Bluffton's **Pluff Mudd Art** (27 Calhoun St., 843/757-5551, Mon.-Sat. 10 A.M.-5:30 P.M.) is a cooperative of 16 great young painters and photographers from throughout the area. The **Guild of Bluffton Artists** (20 Calhoun St., 843/757-5590, Mon.-Sat. 10 A.M.-4:30 P.M.) features works from many local artists, as does the outstanding **Society of Bluffton Artists** (48 Boundary St., 843/757-6586). For cool, custom handcrafted pottery, try **Preston Pottery and Gallery** (10 Church St., 843/757-3084). Another great Bluffton place is the hard-to-define **Eggs'n'tricities** (71 Calhoun St., 843/757-3446). The name pretty much says it all for this fun and eclectic vintage, junk, jewelry, and folk art store.

If you want to score some fresh local seafood for your own culinary adventure, the no-brainer choice is the **Bluffton Oyster Company** (63 Wharf St., 843/757-4010, Mon.-Sat. 9 A.M.-5:30 P.M.), the state's only active oyster facility. They also have shrimp, crab, clams, and fish, nearly all of it from the nearly pristine May River on whose banks it sits.

For a much more commercially intense experience, head just outside of town on U.S. 278 on the way to Hilton Head to find the dual **Tanger Outlet Centers** (1414 Fording Island Rd., 843/837-4339, Mon.-Sat. 10 A.M.-9 P.M., Sun. 11 A.M.-6 P.M.), an outlet-shopper's paradise with virtually every major brand represented, including Nine West, Ralph Lauren, Abercrombie & Fitch, and dozens more, along with new additions Skechers and the Limited Too. A serious shopper can easily spend most of a day here between its two sprawling malls, Tanger I and Tanger II, so be forewarned.

SPORTS AND RECREATION

A key kayaking outfitter in Bluffton is **Native Guide Kayak Tours** (8 2nd St., 843/757-5411, www.nativeguidetours.com), which features tours of the May and New Rivers led by native Ben Turner. Another good outfit is **Swamp Girls Kayak Tours** (843/784-2249, www.swampgirls.com), the labor of love of Sue Chapman and Linda Etchells.

To put in your own kayak or canoe on the scenic, well-preserved May River, go to the **Alljoy Landing** at the eastern terminus of Alljoy Road along the river. Or try the dock at the end of Calhoun Street near the Church of the Holy Cross. There's also a rough put-in area at the Bluffton Oyster Company (63 Wharf St.), which has a public park adjacent to it. For fishing, public landings include the dock on Calhoun Street, Alljoy Landing, and Bluffton Oyster Company.

For a much more wild hiking and bird-watching experience, go north of Bluffton to **Victoria Bluff Heritage Preserve** (803/734-3886, daily dawn-dusk, free), a 1,100-acre flat-woods habitat notable for featuring all four native species of palmetto tree. There are no facilities, and a lot of hunting goes on in November-December. Get here from Bluffton by taking Burnt Church Road to U.S. 278. Take a right onto U.S. 278 and then a left onto Sawmill Creek Road heading north. The parking area is shortly ahead on the right.

The closest public golf courses to Bluffton are the Arnold Palmer-designed **Crescent Pointe Golf Club** (1 Crescent Pointe Dr., 888/292-7778, www.crescentpointegolf.com, $90) and the nine-hole **Old Carolina Golf Club** (89 Old Carolina Rd., 888/785-7274, www.oldcarolinagolf.com, $26), certainly one of the best golf deals in the region.

ACCOMMODATIONS
Under $150

A quality bargain stay right between Bluffton and Hilton Head is the **Holiday Inn Express Bluffton** (35 Bluffton Rd., 843/757-2002, www.ichotelsgroup.com, $120), on U.S. 278 as you make the run onto Hilton Head proper. It's not close to the beach or to Old Town Bluffton, so you'll definitely be using your car, but its central location will appeal to those who want to keep their options open.

BEAUFORT

Over $300

For an ultra-upscale spa and golf resort environment near Bluffton, the clear pick is the **Inn at Palmetto Bluff** (476 Mt. Pelia Rd., 843/706-6500, www.palmettobluffresort.com, $650-900) just across the May River. This Auberge property was picked recently as the number-two U.S. resort by *Condé Nast Traveler* magazine. Despite its glitzy pedigree and extremely upper-end prices, it's more Tara than Trump Tower. The main building is modeled after a Lowcountry plantation home, and the idyllic views of the May River are blissful. Lodging is dispersed among a series of cottages and "village home" rentals. Needless to say, virtually your every need is provided for here, though the nearest off-site restaurant of any quality is quite a drive away. That will likely make little difference to you, however, since there are three top-flight dining options on the grounds: the fine dining **River House Restaurant** (843/706-6542, breakfast daily 7-11 A.M., lunch or "porch" menu daily 11 A.M.-10 P.M., dinner daily 6-10 P.M., $30-40); the **May River Grill** (Tues.-Sat. 11 A.M.-4 P.M., $9-13) at the golf clubhouse; and the casual **Buffalo's** (843/706-6630, Sun.-Tues. 11:30 A.M.-5 P.M., Wed.-Sat. 11:30 A.M.-9 P.M., $10-15).

FOOD
Breakfast and Brunch

No discussion of Bluffton cuisine is complete without the famous **Squat 'n' Gobble** (1231 May River Rd., 843/757-4242, daily 24 hours), a wholly local phenomenon not to be confused with a similarly named chain of eateries in California. Long a site of gossiping and politicking as well as, um, squatting and gobbling, this humble diner on the May River Road in town is an indelible part of the local consciousness. Believe it or not, despite the totally unpretentious greasy-spoon ambience—or because of it—the food's actually quite good.

They specialize in the usual "American" menu of eggs, bacon, hamburgers, hot dogs, and fries. There's a tie for best thing on the menu—I can't decide whether the Greek pizza or the barbecue is better, so I'll go with both.

Classic Southern

Another beloved Bluffton institution (and Blufftonians love their institutions) is **Pepper's Porch** (1255 May River Rd., 843/757-2295, Tues.-Sun. 11:30 A.M.-9 P.M., $12-20). Housed in an old barn for drying a local herb called deer tongue, this is the kind of distinctly Southern place where they bring out a basket of little corn muffins instead of bread. Entrées include a great stuffed grouper and delicious, fresh-fried shrimp. Don't miss the fried strawberry dessert, which tastes a million times better than it sounds. Weekends see live music and karaoke in the aptly named Back Bar, a favorite local hangout.

Prime rib is the house specialty at **Myrtle's Bar & Grill** (32 Bruin Rd., 843/757-6300, lunch Tues.-Fri. 11:30 A.M.-2:30 P.M., dinner Tues.-Sat. 5-9:30 P.M., brunch Sun. 10 A.M.-2 P.M.), generally served on Tuesday nights. They also do a mean flounder. Housed in the old post office, Myrtle's is a favorite local hangout and has recently begun hosting an interactive murder-mystery dinner theater show.

French

Most dining in Bluffton is pretty casual, but you'll get the white tablecloth treatment at **Claude & Uli's Signature Bistro** (1533 Fording Island Rd., 843/837-3336, lunch Mon.-Fri. 11:30 A.M.-2:30 P.M., dinner Mon.-Sat. from 5 P.M., $18-25) just outside of town in Moss Village. Chef Claude has brought his extensive European training and background (which includes Maxim's in Paris) to this romantic little spot. Claude does a great veal cordon bleu as well as a number of fine seafood entrées, such as an almond-crusted tilapia and an excellent seafood pasta. Don't miss

WHO ARE THE GULLAH?

A language, a culture, and a people with a shared history, Gullah is more than that—it's also a state of mind. Simply put, the Gullah are African Americans of the Sea Islands of South Carolina and Georgia. (In Georgia, the term *Geechee*, from the nearby Ogeechee River, is more or less interchangeable.) Protected from outside influence by the isolation of this coastal region after the Civil War, Gullah culture is the closest living cousin to the West African traditions of their ancestors imported as slaves.

While you might hear that *Gullah* is a corruption of "Angola," some linguists think it simply means "people" in a West African language. In any case, the Gullah speak what is known as a creole language, meaning one derived from several sources. Gullah combines elements of Elizabethan English, Jamaican patois, and several West African dialects; for example "goober" (peanut) comes from the Congo *n'guba*. Another creole element is a word with multiple uses, for example Gullah's *shum* could mean "see them," "see him," "see her," or "see it" in either past or present tense, depending on context. Several white writers in the 1900s published collections of Gullah folk tales, but for the most part the Gullah tongue was simply considered broken English. That changed with the publication of Lorenzo Dow Turner's groundbreaking *Africanisms in the Gullah Dialect* in 1949. Turner traced elements of the language to Sierra Leone in West Africa and more than 300 Gullah words directly to Africa.

Gullah is typically spoken very rapidly, which of course only adds to its impenetrability to the outsider. Gullah also relies on colorful turns of phrase. *"E tru mout"* ("He true mouth")

means the speaker is referring to someone who doesn't lie. *"Ie een crack muh teet"* ("I didn't even crack my teeth") means "I kept quiet." A forgetful Gullah speaker might say, *"Mah head leab me"* ("My head left me").

Gullah music, as practiced by the world-famous Hallelujah Singers of St. Helena Island, also uses many distinctly African techniques, such as call and response (the folk hymn "Michael Row the Boat Ashore" is a good example). The most famous Americans with Gullah roots are boxer Joe Frazier (Beaufort), hip-hop star Jazzy Jay (Beaufort), NFL great Jim Brown (St. Simons Island, Georgia), and Supreme Court Justice Clarence Thomas (Pin Point, Georgia, near Savannah).

Upscale development continues to claim more and more traditional Gullah areas, generally by pricing them out through rapidly increasing property values. Today, the major pockets of living Gullah culture in South Carolina are in Beaufort, St. Helena Island, Daufuskie Island, Edisto Island, and a northern section of Hilton Head Island.

The old ways are not as prevalent as they were, but several key institutions are keeping alive the spirit of Gullah: the **Penn Center** (16 Martin Luther King Dr., St. Helena, 843/838-2474, www.penncenter.com, Mon.-Sat. 11 A.M.-4 P.M., $4 adults, $2 seniors and children) on St. Helena Island near Beaufort; the **Avery Research Center** (66 George St., Charleston, 843/953-7609, www.cofc.edu/avery, Mon.-Fri. 10 A.M.-5 P.M., Sat. noon-5 P.M.) at the College of Charleston; and **Geechee Kunda** (622 Ways Temple Rd., Riceboro, Georgia, 912/884-4440, www.geecheekunda.net) near Midway off U.S. 17.

their specialty soufflé for dessert, which you should order with dinner as it takes almost half an hour to bake.

Mexican

My favorite restaurant in Bluffton by far is a near-copy of an equally fine Mexican restaurant in Hilton Head, ◖ **Mi Tierra** (101 Mellichamp Center, 843/757-7200, lunch daily 11 A.M.-4 P.M., dinner Mon.-Fri. 4-9 P.M., Sat.-Sun. 4-10 P.M., $3-15). They have very high-quality Tex-Mex-style food in a fun atmosphere at great prices. Another highly regarded Mexican place in Bluffton is **Amigo's Café Y Cantina** (133 Towne Dr., 843/815-8226, Mon.-Sat. 11 A.M.-9 P.M., $8).

INFORMATION AND SERVICES

You'll find Bluffton's visitors center in the **Heyward House Historic Center** (70 Boundary St., 843/757-6293, www.heyward-house.org).

A good Bluffton publication is *Bluffton Today* (www.blufftontoday.com).

If you need postal services, Bluffton also has its own **post office** (32 Bruin Rd., 843/757-3588).

DAUFUSKIE ISLAND

Sitting between Savannah and Hilton Head Island and accessible only by water, Daufuskie Island has about 500 full-time residents, most of whom ride around on golf carts or bikes (there's only one paved road, Haig Point Road, and cars are a rare sight). Once the home of rice and indigo plantations and rich oyster beds—the latter destroyed by pollution and overharvesting—the two upscale residential resort communities on the island, begun in the 1980s, give a clue as to where the future lies, although the recent global economic downturn slowed development to a standstill.

The area of prime interest to visitors is the unincorporated western portion, or **Historic District,** the old stomping grounds of Pat Conroy during his stint as a teacher of resident African American children. His old two-room schoolhouse of *The Water is Wide* fame, the **Mary Field School,** is still here, as is the adjacent 140-year-old **Union Baptist Church,** but Daufuskie students now have a surprisingly modern new facility (middle school students are still ferried to mainland schools every day). Farther north on Haig Point Road is the new **Billie Burn Museum,** housed in the old Mt. Carmel Church and named after the island's resident historian. On the southern end you'll find the **Bloody Point Lighthouse,** named for the vicious battle fought nearby during the Yamasee War of 1815 (the light was actually moved a 0.5 miles inland in the early 1900s). Other areas of interest throughout the island include Native American sites, tabby ruins, the old Baptist Church, and a couple of cemeteries. Otherwise there's really not much to do on Daufuskie. It's a place where you go to see a slice of Sea Island and Gullah history and relax, relax, relax. While at one time there was an operating resort and spa on the island, as of this writing it was bankrupt and closed, with no clear plans to reopen.

For overnight stays, you can rent a humble cabin at **Freeport Marina** (843/785-8242, rates vary). For the freshest island seafood, check out the **Old Daufuskie Crab Company** (Freeport Marina, 843/785-6652, daily 11:30 A.M.-9 P.M., $7-22).

A public ferry between Daufuskie and Hilton Head is **Calibogue Cruises** (843/342-8687). It brings you in on the landward side of the island, and from there you can take shuttles or rent golf carts or bikes.

Points Inland

It's very likely that at some point you'll find yourself traveling inland from Beaufort, given that area's proximity to I-95. While generally more known for offering interstate drivers a bite to eat and a place to rest their heads, there are several spots worth checking out in their own right, especially Walterboro and the Savannah National Wildlife Refuge.

WALTERBORO

The very picture of the slow, moss-drenched Lowcountry town—indeed, the municipal logo is the silhouette of a live oak tree—Walterboro is a delightful, artsy oasis. Right off I-95, Walterboro serves as a gateway of sorts to the Lowcountry, and the cheap commercial sprawl on the interstate shows it. But don't be put off by this ugliness—once you get into town it's as charming as they come, with roots dating back to 1783 and offering the added bonus of being one of the best antiquing locales in South Carolina. Convenient and eminently walkable, the two-block Arts and Antiques District on Washington Street centers on over a dozen antiques and collectible stores on the town's main drag, interspersed with gift shops and eateries.

Sights

◖ SOUTH CAROLINA ARTISANS CENTER

If you're in town, don't miss the South Carolina Artisans Center (334 Wichman St., 843/549-0011, www.scartisanscenter.com, Mon.-Sat. 10 A.M.-6 P.M., Sun. 1-6 P.M., free), an expansive and vibrant collection of the best work of local and regional painters, sculptors, jewelers, and other craftspeople, for sale and for enjoyment.

© JIM MOREKIS

the South Carolina Artisans Center in Walterboro

BEAUFORT

Imagine a big-city folk art gallery, except without the pretension, and you get the idea. It's not on the main drag, but it's only about a block around the corner, so there's no excuse not to drop in. You can find most any genre represented here, including jewelry, watercolors, shawls, photography, and sweetgrass baskets. The Artisans Center hosts numerous receptions, and every third Saturday of the month they hold live artist demonstrations 11 A.M.-3 P.M.

MUSEUMS

Walterboro boasts three museums. The newly relocated and upgraded **Colleton Museum** (506 E. Washington St., 843/549-2303, www.colletonmuseum.com, Tues. noon-6 P.M., Wed.-Fri. 10 A.M.-5 P.M., Sat. 10 A.M.-noon, free) is one of the best examples of a small town museum you're likely to find anywhere. In aesthetically pleasing fashion, it houses some perhaps surprisingly lively exhibits exploring area history and culture from prehistory to the present day, all packed with charmingly unique and interesting artifacts of everyday life in this historic community.

The **Bedon-Lucas House Museum** (205 Church St., 843/549-9633, Thurs.-Sat. 1-4 P.M., $3 adults, free under age 8) was built by a local planter in 1820. An example of the local style of "high house," built off the ground to escape mosquitoes and catch the breeze, the house today is a nice mix of period furnishings and unadorned simplicity.

The **Slave Relic Museum** (208 Carn St., 843/549-9130, www.slaverelics.org, Mon.-Thurs. 9:30 A.M.-5 P.M., Sat. 10 A.M.-3 P.M., $6 adults, $5 children) houses the area Center for Research and Preservation of the African American Culture. It features artifacts, photos, and documents detailing the Atlantic passage, slave life, and the Underground Railroad.

TUSKEGEE AIRMEN MEMORIAL

Yes, the Tuskegee Airmen of World War II fame were from Alabama, not South Carolina. But a contingent trained in Walterboro, at the site of the present-day Lowcountry Regional Airport (537 Aviation Way, 843/549-2549) a short ways south of downtown on U.S. 17. Today, on a publicly accessible, low-security area of the airport stands the Tuskegee Airmen Memorial, an outdoor monument to these brave flyers. There's a bronze statue and several interpretive exhibits.

GREAT SWAMP SANCTUARY

A short ways out of town in the other direction is the Great Swamp Sanctuary (www.thegreatswamp.org, daily dawn-dusk, free), a still-developing ecotourism project focusing on the Lowcountry environment. Located in one of the few braided-creek habitats accessible to the public, the 842-acre Sanctuary has three miles of walking and biking trails, some along the path of the old Charleston-Savannah stagecoach route. Kayakers and canoeists can paddle along over two miles of winding creeks. A 10,000-square-foot interpretive center is in the works. There are three entry points to the Great Swamp Sanctuary, all off Jefferies Boulevard. In west-to-east order from I-95: north onto Beach Road, north onto Detreville Street (this is considered the main entrance), and west onto Washington Street.

Festivals and Events

In keeping with South Carolina's tradition of towns hosting annual events to celebrate signature crops and products, Walterboro's **Colleton County Rice Festival** (http://thericefestival.org, free) happens every April. There's a parade, live music, a 5K run, the crowning of the year's "Rice Queen," and you just might find yourself learning something about the unique coastal lifestyle built around this ultimate cash crop of the early South.

Accommodations and Food

If you're looking for big-box lodging, the section of Walterboro close to I-95 is chockablock

TUSKEGEE AIRMEN IN WALTERBORO

In a state where all too often African American history is studied in the context of slavery, a refreshing change is the tale of the Tuskegee Airmen, one of the most-lauded American military units of World War II. Though named for their origins at Alabama's Tuskegee Institute, the pilots of the famed 332nd Fighter Group actually completed final training in South Carolina at Walterboro Army Airfield, where the regional airport now sits.

The U.S. military was segregated during World War II, with African Americans mostly relegated to support roles. An interesting exception was the case of the 332nd, formed in 1941 as the 99th Pursuit Squadron by an act of Congress and the only all-black flying unit in the American military at the time. For the most part flying P-47 Thunderbolts and P-51 Mustangs, the pilots of the 332nd had one of the toughest missions of the war: escorting bombers over the skies of Germany and protecting them from Luftwaffe fighters. Though initially viewed with skepticism, the Tuskegee Airmen wasted no time in proving their mettle.

In fact, it wasn't long before U.S. bomber crews—who were, needless to say, all white—specifically requested that they be escorted by the airmen, who were given the nickname "Red-tail Angels" because of the distinctive markings of their aircraft. While legend has it that the 332nd never lost a bomber, this claim has been debunked. But as Tuskegee Airman Bill Holloman said, "The Tuskegee story is about pilots who rose above adversity and discrimination and opened a door once closed to black America, not about whether their record is perfect." The 332nd's reputation for aggressiveness in air combat was so widely known that the Germans also had a nickname for them—*Schwartze Vogelmenschen*, or "Black Birdmen."

Today Walterboro honors the Airmen with a monument on the grounds of the Lowcountry Regional Airport, on U.S. 17 just northeast of town. In an easily accessible part of the airport grounds, the monument features a bronze statue and several interpretive exhibits. Another place to catch up on Tuskegee Airmen history is at the **Colleton Museum** (506 E. Washington St., 843/549-2303, www.colletonmuseum.com, Tues. noon-6 P.M., Wed.-Fri. 10 A.M.-5 P.M., Sat. 10 A.M.-noon, free), which has a permanent exhibit on the pilots and their history in the Walterboro area.

Walterboro Army Airfield's contribution to the war effort was not limited to the Tuskegee Airmen. Seven of the famed Doolittle Raiders were trained here, there was a compound for holding German prisoners of war, and it was also the site of the U.S. military's largest camouflage school.

with it. The quality is surprisingly good, perhaps because they tend to cater to Northerners on their way to and from Florida. A good choice is **Holiday Inn Express & Suites** (1834 Sniders Hwy., 843/538-2700, www.hiexpress. com, $85), or try the **Comfort Inn & Suites** (97 Downs Lane, 843/538-5911, www.choice-hotels.com, $95).

If you'd like something with a bit more character, there are two B&Bs on Hampton Street downtown. **Old Academy Bed & Breakfast** (904 Hampton St., 843/549-3232, www.old-academybandb.com, $80-115) has four guest rooms housed in Walterboro's first school building. They offer a full continental breakfast. Note that credit cards are not accepted. Although built recently, by local standards, the 1912 **Hampton House Bed and Breakfast** (500 Hampton St., 843/542-9498, www.hampton-housebandb.com, $125-145) has three well-appointed guest rooms and offers a full country breakfast. By appointment only, you can see the Forde Doll and Dollhouse Collection, with over 50 dollhouses and oodles of antique dolls.

The story of food in Walterboro revolves around ◖ **Duke's Barbecue** (949 Robertson Blvd., 843/549-1446, $7), one of the best-regarded barbecue spots in the Lowcountry and one of the top two joints named "Duke's" in the state (the other, by common consensus, is in Orangeburg). The pulled pork is delectable, cooked with the indigenous South Carolina mustard-based sauce. Unlike most area barbecue restaurants, some attention is devoted to the veggies, such as collard greens, green beans, and black-eyed peas with rice.

HARDEEVILLE

For most travelers, Hardeeville is known for its plethora of low-budget lodging and garish fireworks stores at the intersection of I-95 and U.S. 17. Truth be told, that's about all that's here. However, train buffs will enjoy getting a gander at the rare and excellently restored **Narrow Gauge Locomotive** near the intersection of U.S. 17 and Highway 46. Donated by the Argent Lumber Company in 1960, Engine No. 7 memorializes the role of the timber industry in the area.

If you're hungry in Hardeeville, go straight to **Mi Tierrita** (U.S. 17 and I-95, 843/784-5011, $5), an excellent, authentic Mexican restaurant near the I-95-U.S. 17 confluence. It's pretty beat-up on the inside, but the food is delicious and many steps above the typical watered-down Tex-Mex you find in the Southeast. If barbecue is your thing, go on Highway 170A on the "backside" of Hardeeville in the hamlet of Levy to **The Pink Pig** (3508 S. Okatie Hwy., 843/784-3635, www.the-pink-pig.com, Tues.-Wed. and Sat. 11 A.M.-3 P.M., Thurs.-Fri. 11 A.M.-3 P.M. and 5-7 P.M., $5-15). They offer three sauces: honey mustard, spicy, and "Gullah." The place is surprisingly hip, with good music piped in and a suitably cutesy, kid-friendly decor with plenty of the eponymous rosy porcine figures.

SAVANNAH NATIONAL WILDLIFE REFUGE

Roughly equally divided between Georgia and South Carolina, the sprawling, 30,000-acre Savannah National Wildlife Refuge (912/652-4415, www.fws.gov/savannah, daily dawn-dusk, free) is a premier bird-watching and nature-observing locale in the Southeast. As with many refuges in the coastal Southeast, it's located on former plantations. The system of dikes and paddy fields once used to grow rice now helps make this an attractive stopover for migrating birds. Bird-watching is best October-April, with the winter months best for viewing migratory waterfowl. While you can kayak on your own on miles of creeks, you can also call **Swamp Girls Kayak Tours** (843/784-2249, www.swampgirls.com), who work out of nearby Hardeeville, for a guided tour. To get here, take exit 5 off I-95 onto U.S. 17. Go south to U.S. 170 and look for the Laurel Hill Wildlife Drive. Be sure to stop by the brand-new visitors center.

COLUMBIA AND THE MIDLANDS

The "real" South Carolina, this large area stretching across the wide waist of the state, tends to be left out of many discussions of Palmetto State tourism. Between the living movie set that is the Lowcountry and the more dramatic landscape of the Upstate, the Midlands—flat and crisscrossed with interstate highways—sometimes seem plain by comparison.

But the Midlands have long been something of an honest broker between the Lowcountry and the Upcountry, from Columbia's original role as compromise state capital to the region's default mode as a cultural buffer zone between the insouciant coast and the staunch mountains.

It's quite a menu, actually: There are the considerable cultural offerings of Columbia and any number of picturesque smaller cities, such as horse-centric Camden. There are the old tobacco towns of the Pee Dee, such as Hartsville and Cheraw. And once you've tasted it, you can't forget that distinctive Midlands-style barbecue, in an unusual but oddly addictive mustard-based sauce, courtesy of the region's original contingent of German settlers.

Anglers in particular will enjoy the Midlands, home to several excellently stocked freshwater lakes, among them Lake Murray near Columbia. In Santee Cooper, the huge Lake Marion and its slightly smaller sibling,

© JIM MOREKIS

COLUMBIA

HIGHLIGHTS

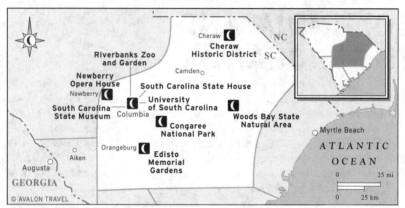

LOOK FOR ◖ TO FIND RECOMMENDED SIGHTS, ACTIVITIES, DINING, AND LODGING.

◖ **South Carolina State House:** The resilient and grand state capitol features gorgeous grounds and interesting monuments (page 255).

◖ **South Carolina State Museum:** Learn all about the Palmetto State in an excellently restored warehouse in the Congaree Vista (page 259).

◖ **University of South Carolina:** The quietly elegant Horseshoe area is a slice of history at one of the South's oldest universities (page 260).

◖ **Riverbanks Zoo and Garden:** One of the country's best all-around zoos has a dynamic educational and conservation component as well as a beautiful botanical garden (page 263).

◖ **Congaree National Park:** This park features an ancient cypress swamp with what may

be the tallest old-growth canopy remaining on earth (page 280).

◖ **Newberry Opera House:** A lovingly restored building that still hosts regular performances in historic Newberry (page 285).

◖ **Cheraw Historic District:** The birthplace of Dizzy Gillespie also boasts one of the cutest downtown areas in the state (page 289).

◖ **Woods Bay State Natural Area:** A very well-preserved Carolina bay that features a canoe trail and scenic boardwalk (page 294).

◖ **Edisto Memorial Gardens:** The pride of Orangeburg showcases thousands of varieties of roses (page 301).

Lake Moultrie, host a cottage industry catering to serious professionals and casual anglers. In addition to fishing, throughout the region there's an abundance of outdoor activity, including some of the best white-water rafting in the South near Columbia and the altogether unique Congaree National Park, home to some of the most ancient old-growth forest on the planet.

PLANNING YOUR TIME

Columbia is an easy city to get around in and enjoy. Reserve half a day for the Riverbanks Zoo and a minimum of another half day for the other major sights. The best way to enjoy the city, however, is to have a couple of days. This will allow you to see more of the city, including a night out in the Vista and an evening in Five Points.

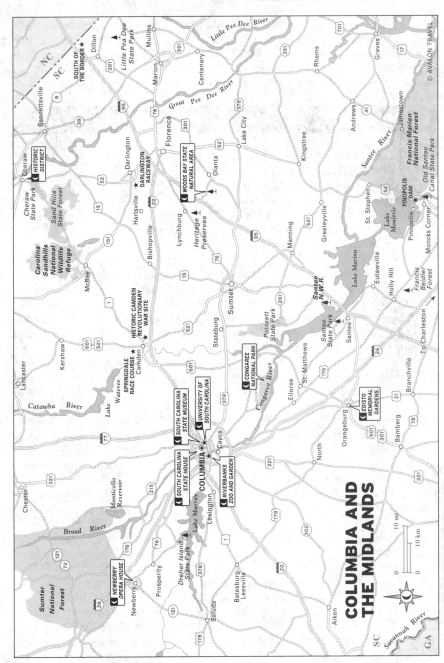

COLUMBIA AND
THE MIDLANDS

COLUMBIA

Because of the physical breadth of the Midlands, one day is not nearly enough to enjoy the rest of the region outside Columbia. You should reserve half a day alone for Congaree National Park, for example. If you only have a day or a day and a half, choose between two areas: either the Pee Dee, with stops in Camden, Cheraw, and Hartsville, or Santee Cooper, with stops in Orangeburg and Moncks Corner.

Columbia

I find Columbia to be a nice break from the typical South Carolina template. There's a ton of history, but you don't get the often stultifying nostalgia present in some of the state's older cities. This freshness, it must be said, is largely because most of Columbia's history was burned down in the Civil War.

Columbia's broad, inviting avenues—a necessity of the rebuilding after Sherman's torching, now considered a civic signature—are a welcome break from the winding, often-cramped streets of Charleston and the predictable Main Streets of dozens of South Carolina hamlets. Because of its relatively modern layout, not to mention its function as the seat of state government, Columbia has a forward-looking spirit that still manages to retain much of the genteel nature of South Carolina society.

And while it seems that almost every little burg you drive through in this state has its own little private college—certainly not an unattractive trait—Columbia has the big enchilada, the University of South Carolina, which brings with it that comparatively rare thing in the Palmetto State: a genuine, honest-to-goodness college-town vibe, as opposed to just a town with a college.

Columbia's main attractions are threefold: the excellent Riverbanks Zoo and Garden; the Five Points area, good for shopping and nightlife; and the Congaree Vista (more commonly called just "the Vista"), a restored warehouse district that now hosts the city's hippest restaurants and shops.

HISTORY

> They spoiled a damn fine plantation to make a damn poor town.
>
> Thomas Taylor,
> on whose land Columbia was built

The first planned capital in the United States and only the second planned city in the nation (after Savannah, Georgia), Columbia was born in compromise, bred in governance, and tempered by war. Shortly after the Revolution and statehood, South Carolina was in need of a state capital. However, generations of resentment by Upcountry farmers toward their much wealthier agricultural counterparts in the Lowcountry meant that the capital would likely be nowhere near the slave-tended rice fiefdoms of Charleston and surrounding area. Therefore, in the democratic spirit of the new nation, it was decided to locate the new capital as close as possible to the geographic center of the Palmetto State. In 1786 the compromise site was narrowed down to the area around the Congaree River. Because of its location on the fall line and its navigable waterways, there was already a thriving trading post here. But the site finally agreed on would be on The Plains, the family plantation of Thomas Taylor, whose dissatisfaction with the final product is noted above.

The name of the new city would reflect the symbol of the new nation, a feminine figure who was the Uncle Sam of her day. The name Columbia won the vote in the state Senate 11 to

7, beating out—you guessed it—Washington. The state legislature met in Columbia for the first time in 1790 in the still unfinished first State House, now long gone. The following year, George Washington came to town while on his national tour, describing Columbia as "an uncleared wood with very few houses in it."

But by 1800, serious commerce had sprung up in politics' wake, including riverboats from Charleston, slave labor, and the core of the city's nascent textile industry. What would become the University of South Carolina was founded in 1801. In December 1860, Columbia's First Baptist Church, still standing, hosted the state Secession Convention, which voted formally to remove South Carolina from the union. During the Civil War, Columbia became something of a safe haven for refugees from all over the South. Its population swelled—women and children, mostly—and wealth was moved from more vulnerable areas in the Lowcountry, then under heavy Union pressure from sea and from land.

For reasons still unknown to history, though long debated, General William Sherman took a big left turn into South Carolina upon ending his March to the Sea at Savannah. Was Charleston, which fired the first shots of the war, spared the torch because of Sherman's fond memories of when he was stationed there? Or, more likely, was it just too difficult to get his massive army through the marshes of the Lowcountry? In any case, the wrath that could have been Charleston's was visited on Columbia in February 1865. The circumstances are hazy to this day. We do know that Union shelling from across the Congaree River came on February 16, and shortly thereafter Mayor Goodwyn surrendered the city to Sherman, meeting the general's representatives at 5th Street and River Drive.

What happened next is more murky. Sherman promptly set up his occupation headquarters at 1615 Gervais Street, promising that order would prevail. However, the very next night a third of the city went up in flames, with over 300 acres and nearly 1,400 buildings destroyed. On Columbia's key thoroughfare, Main Street, only the unfinished new State House and the French consulate remained standing. Sherman would later essentially blame the townspeople themselves, saying the fire was caused by the combustion of carelessly stacked cotton bales. But many eyewitness reports blame a series of fires set by vengeful (and drunk) Union troops.

The war's aftermath was particularly difficult in Columbia, with an ethically challenged Reconstruction government wasting already slim state funds and the Ku Klux Klan terrorizing local African Americans. A semblance of order was essentially forced on the city by the "Red Shirts" of Governor Wade Hampton III, former Confederate general elected to the governor's office in 1876. His paramilitary organization moderated among extremist militias on both sides of the racial divide, and an uneasy truce came to Columbia.

Important though Columbia was, it wouldn't have its first paved street until 1908. A construction boom soon followed, with banking in particular being a main economic engine. As with many areas of the South, the World War II era provided an enormous economic lift. The sprawling Fort Jackson opened on the city's east side in 1940. After the war's beginning, General Jimmy Doolittle's famous Tokyo raiders trained at what is now Columbia International Airport, using an island in the middle of Lake Murray for bombing practice.

The Civil Rights era was relatively tame in Columbia, which saw its first lunch-counter strike in August 1962. The University of South Carolina admitted its first black students since Reconstruction in 1963, and around the same time most of the old Jim Crow laws began going by the wayside. Indeed, Columbia was so progressive compared to most of the South at the time that in 1965 *Newsweek* magazine wrote that the city had "liberated itself from the plague of doctrinal apartheid."

Like Charleston and Savannah, a wave of grassroots activism in the 1960s conserved many older buildings from the wrecking ball and made possible the ensuing tourism and recreation boom of the 1970s and 1980s. In the 1990s the city renovated the once-seedy Congaree Vista warehouse area, now a thriving center of shopping, dining, and nightlife near the State House.

ORIENTATION

Columbia lies at the confluence of the Broad and Saluda Rivers, which form the Congaree River immediately below the city. As its history indicates, it is almost exactly in the center of the state, served by a convenient network of interstate highways: I-20, I-26, and I-77, with a perimeter highway, I-126. Consequently, Columbia is a very easy town both to get to and to get around.

Routes into downtown are many; among them: I-126 to Huger Street; Charleston Highway (U.S. 321) to Knox Abbott Drive, which turns into Blossom Street over the river into downtown; I-26 to U.S. 1, which turns into Meeting Street in West Columbia and then Gervais Street into downtown; and from the northwest, I-20 to U.S. 1 (Two Notch Rd.), which turns into Gervais Street on the east side of town.

As far as downtown goes, Main Street stretches north and south from the capitol, with Assembly Street the other main north-south artery. Gervais Street cuts through downtown and includes the restored Congaree Vista area near the river. The University of South Carolina takes up the southern portion of downtown, with Five Points—the intersection of Devine, Harden, and Santee Streets—at one corner.

The main suburbs are both on the west bank of the Congaree River: West Columbia, which includes the Riverbanks Zoo and Garden; and Cayce, immediately to the south, a major residential area.

SIGHTS

Columbia keeps a nice balance of the old and the new. Among the historic house museums are some of the precious few homes to survive the Union burning of the city, and South Carolina's capital also has some more wide-ranging and contemporary offerings. While the "must-see" picks are limited here to specific attractions, any local will tell you that no trip to Columbia is complete without stops at Five Points and the Congaree Vista (more often "the Vista"), both downtown.

Robert Mills House

Not the oldest but certainly the most architecturally significant of the three antebellum homes to survive Sherman's torching, the Robert Mills House (1616 Blanding St., 803/252-7742, www.historiccolumbia.org, Tues.-Sat. 10 A.M.-4 P.M., Sun. 1-5 P.M., $6 adults, $3 children, free under age 6) is named for its designer, whose impressive oeuvre includes the Washington Monument. Built in 1823 for local merchant Ainsley Hall, this brick Classical Revival building soon metamorphosed into something else entirely.

With Hall's untimely death and the dispersal of his estate before the house was finished, it was soon purchased by the local Presbyterian synod. A seminary began holding classes here in 1831, and Woodrow Wilson's father and uncle, both Presbyterian ministers, were on the faculty.

When the seminary moved in 1927, the old mansion fell into disrepair and was slated for demolition after World War II. But as with Charleston and Savannah, a grassroots conservation effort saved the house in the mid-1960s, and it's now administered by the Historic Columbia Foundation. The interior hosts a range of furniture and decorative arts, including examples of American Federal, English Regency, and French Empire styles.

Don't forget that you can get a combo ticket (803/252-7742, $15 adults, $8 children, free

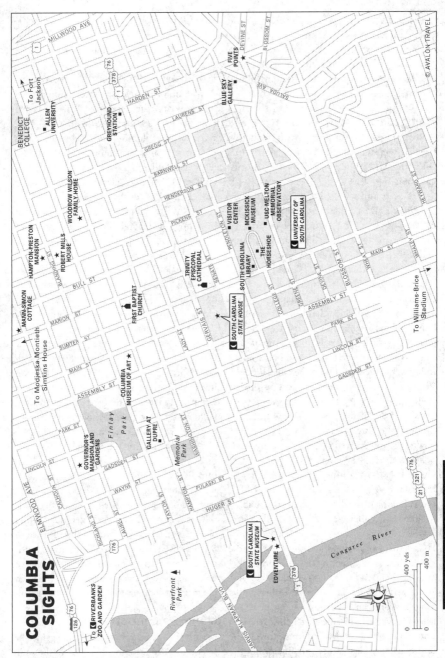

COLUMBIA SIGHTS

© AVALON TRAVEL

MILLWOOD AVE
To Fort Jackson
BENEDICT COLLEGE
★ ALLEN UNIVERSITY
GREYHOUND STATION
HARDEN ST
LAURENS ST
GREGG ST
BARNWELL ST
HENDERSON ST
PICKENS ST
WOODROW WILSON FAMILY HOME
HAMPTON-PRESTON MANSION
★ ROBERT MILLS HOUSE
BLANDING ST
BULL ST
★ MANN-SIMON COTTAGE
To Modjeska Monteith Simkins House
MARION ST
SUMTER ST
MAIN ST
ASSEMBLY ST
FIRST BAPTIST CHURCH
★ COLUMBIA MUSEUM OF ART
GERVAIS ST
LADY ST
SENATE ST
PENDLETON ST
TRINITY EPISCOPAL CATHEDRAL
VISITOR CENTER
MCKISSICK MUSEUM
USC MELTON MEMORIAL OBSERVATORY
THE HORSESHOE
SOUTH CAROLINA LIBRARY
★ UNIVERSITY OF SOUTH CAROLINA
BLUE SKY GALLERY
FIVE POINTS ★
DEVINE ST
BLOSSOM ST
SALUDA AVE
HEYWARD ST
WHALEY ST
S. MAIN ST
DEVINE ST
GREENE ST
COLLEGE ST
BLOSSOM ST
ASSEMBLY ST
PARK ST
LINCOLN ST
GADSDEN ST
★ SOUTH CAROLINA STATE HOUSE
To Williams-Brice Stadium
GOVERNOR'S MANSION AND GARDENS
Finlay Park
GALLERY AT DUPRE
Memorial Park
WASHINGTON ST
PARK ST
LINCOLN ST
RICHLAND ST
LINCOLN ST
CALHOUN ST
ELMWOOD AVE
GADSDEN ST
WAYNE ST
LAUREL ST
TAYLOR ST
HAMPTON ST
PULASKI ST
HUGER ST
To RIVERBANKS ZOO AND GARDEN
Riverfront Park
SOUTH CAROLINA STATE MUSEUM
EDVENTURE ★
Congaree River
Congaree River
0   400 yds
0   400 m

COLUMBIA

under age 6) at the Mills House for all the Foundation's house museums, including the Hampton-Preston Mansion and the Mann-Simon Cottage. The last tour at each house begins Tuesday-Saturday at 3 P.M. and Sunday at 4 P.M.

Hampton-Preston Mansion

Across the street from the Mills House is the 1818 Hampton-Preston Mansion (1615 Blanding St., 803/252-7742, www.historic-columbia.org, Tues.-Sat. 10 A.M.-4 P.M., Sun. 1-5 P.M., $6 adults, $3 children, free under age 6). This classic example of an elite planter's domicile was built for cotton merchant Ainsley Hall, who also had the Mills House built several years later, but soon ended up in the hands of an even wealthier planter, Wade Hampton, who at his death in 1835 was widely held to be the richest man in the United States.

Hampton's daughter Caroline and her husband, John Preston, moved in after the patriarch's passing, and it is during this period that many of the fine furnishings in the house today were acquired. Quite the collectors, the Prestons purchased many fine pieces during their many tours of Europe. The size of the house was doubled in 1845-1850 with the addition of the north facade.

The mansion served as a Union Army headquarters during the Civil War occupation of Columbia. In an all-too-familiar story for so many of these grand old Southern houses, after the war the owners had to sell it, and the building fell into neglect after a succession of small colleges also left the premises. The Historic Columbia Foundation, which continues to administer the property, saved it, acquiring the building in 1969 and opening it to the public a year later.

Tickets are purchased at the Robert Mills House. You can also buy a combo ticket (803/252-7742, $15 adults, $8 children, free under age 6) at the Mills House for all the Foundation's house museums, including the

Robert Mills House and Mann-Simon Cottage. The last tour at each house begins Tuesday-Saturday at 3 P.M. and Sunday at 4 P.M.

Woodrow Wilson Family Home

Perhaps unfortunately for visitors but fortunately for posterity, the Woodrow Wilson Family Home (1705 Hampton St., 803/252-7742, www.historiccolumbia.org) is closed for massive restoration at least through 2012 and possibly longer. Still, this attractive Victorian cottage, built in 1872, is a vital piece of Columbia history that's easily viewed from the street.

The Wilson family arrived in Columbia from Augusta, Georgia, during Reconstruction, when the future president's father, Joseph Ruggles Wilson, took a job at the Presbyterian Theological Seminary, housed in what's now the Mills House. Woodrow Wilson, who went by the name Tommy at the time, was 14 years old. Woodrow's mother, Jessie, held sway over the extensive gardens and planted the magnolias in the front yard, which can be seen from Hampton Street. The Wilsons only stayed in the house for a couple of years. Dr. Wilson became involved in an internal political squabble at the seminary and in 1874 resigned for a job in North Carolina. However, the Wilsons remained close to many people in Columbia and returned often.

By Southern standards, the grassroots movement that saved the Woodrow Wilson home came very early, in 1928, with the house opening to the public in 1932. Clearly the move to save the house was spurred in no small part by the president's 1924 death. When the home reopens, its collections will reflect the era when the Wilsons lived here; however, few will be former possessions of the family. Historically, the key object in the collection is the bed in which the president was born in 1856 in Staunton, Virginia.

Mann-Simon Cottage

No one is quite sure how Celia Mann gained her freedom. Born into slavery near Charleston in

1799, she somehow escaped servitude and made her way to Columbia to serve as a midwife; legend says she walked the entire way. By 1844 she was living in the Mann-Simon Cottage (1403 Richland St., 803/252-7742, www.historiccolumbia.org, Tues.-Sat. 10 A.M.-4 P.M., Sun. 1-5 P.M., $6 adults, $3 children, free under age 6), one of a precious handful of antebellum homes in South Carolina owned by free blacks.

Intriguingly, the house was actually acquired by Celia's husband, Ben DeLane, also a free African American from Charleston. He either bought or constructed the house sometime before her arrival in town. Perhaps even more intriguingly, the 1850 census describes Celia as a "mulatto" who owned a 77-year-old slave herself. While the phenomenon of free blacks owning slaves did occur in the South, it's likely that the elderly woman in the census was a relative of Celia's—perhaps even her mother.

Celia—described in a chronicle of the time as a "respected colored nurse"—helped found what would become the First Calvary Baptist Church of Columbia, which began meeting in the basement of the cottage after splitting off from the First Baptist Church when that edifice hosted the first Confederate Secession Convention in 1860. Contrary to popular belief, before the Civil War the races often worshiped together in the South, albeit in separate seating sections. It was only after the war that the strict physical segregation of the Jim Crow era became commonplace.

At the cottage, take note of how subsequent generations of the Mann and Simons families, all Celia's descendants, added onto the house. Much more than a museum, this is a living chronicle of one remarkable family's history. The cottage stayed in the Mann family all the way into the 1960s, and a grassroots conservation effort in 1970 saved the historic structure from demolition. Inside you'll find an exhibit on Celia and her descendants as well as one on the archaeology of the site. The collections within represent the typical pursuits of freed people of color at the time: bakers, tailors, musicians, and (after Reconstruction) educators.

Admission tickets are purchased at the Robert Mills House. You can also buy a combo ticket (803/252-7742, $15 adults, $8 children, free under age 6) at the Mills House for all the Foundation's house museums, including the Hampton-Preston Mansion and the Robert Mills House. The last tour at each house begins Tuesday-Saturday at 3 P.M. and Sunday at 4 P.M.

South Carolina State House

South Carolina is a pretty small state, both in area and in population. But the South Carolina State House (1101 Gervais St., 803/734-2430, www.discoversouthcarolina.com, www.scstatehouse.gov, grounds daily dawn-dusk, free), whose grounds cover nearly 20 acres, is one of the grandest state capitols in the nation, steeped not only in history but also in natural and architectural beauty. Free guided tours of the entire capitol are available Monday-Saturday and the first Sunday of the month.

HISTORY

The history of the State House is remarkable; its construction alone spanned generations. The current structure is not the first capitol built on the old Taylor tract, chosen in 1786. The first edifice, poorly made of wood, was built in 1794 and almost immediately proved inadequate. In 1853 Governor John Manning, a wealthy planter in his own right, pushed for the funding and construction of a much more ambitious building. After an abortive start—the state lost nearly $75,000 when it had to fire the first architect and start over from scratch—the State House took shape under Baltimore architect John R. Niernsee, whose portfolio included work on the Smithsonian. At the outbreak of the Civil War in 1861, the State House—made of native granite quarried a few miles away—was just about ready for a roof. Niernsee

COLUMBIA

© JIM MOREKIS

statue of George Washington on the State House steps

promptly joined the Confederate Army, and work on the building slowed to a crawl.

Fast forward to 1865: General William Sherman and his army assailed the city, and the still incomplete State House took several cannonballs (you can still see the spots where the shells hit). Once in Columbia, the Yankees promptly burned the old State House to the ground along with just about everything else in town. While legend has it that Sherman spared the new building because it wasn't actually where the legislature approved secession, this isn't quite right. The truth is that the Union troops did set fire to the interior of the new State House, and a good bit of damage was sustained. Still, those granite walls stood firm. A temporary roof was added after the war, but otherwise the State House was to sit idle and unfinished for years.

The election of former Confederate general Wade Hampton as governor in 1876 signaled the end of Reconstruction in South Carolina and the resurgence of the Democratic old guard to power. The State House was in focus once again, and funding began to flow its way. Niernsee was brought back to oversee its completion in 1883, but he died before he could really do much. His son Francis was appointed chief architect in 1888, but it was left to yet another designer, the much-maligned Frank Pierce Milburn, to finish the State House. Hired in 1900, Milburn completed the building three years later, but due to graft, shoddy workmanship, and undoubtedly too many cooks spoiling the broth, his work came under fire as inadequate.

It was only in 1907—more than half a century after the first steps were taken—that the State House was considered truly finished, after a series of structural repairs overseen by noted architect Charles Coker Wilson. Along the way, a host of monuments and gardens, a veritable cornucopia of South Carolina history, were erected and planted on the surrounding grounds. And a series of major renovations in the late 1990s brought the building up to speed for a new century of governance.

A WALKING TOUR OF THE
STATE HOUSE GROUNDS

One of the most satisfying things to do on a nice day in Columbia is stroll the expansive grounds of the State House. It's pleasant and relaxing, and interesting as well—the various tributes and monuments, many of them somewhat politically incorrect, are a lively and evolving chronicle of the state's history and quirky politics. Below is a walking tour of the highlights. As you take it all in, note the abundance of plant and tree life, all lovingly landscaped.

Start at the entrance on Gervais Street, at the **Confederate Monument.** At one time, the rebel Stars and Bars flew over the State House. However, after negative media attention in the 1990s and a threatened national boycott, the Confederate battle flag was moved to fly alongside this 1879 monument instead. To the immediate left is the 1941 **Spanish-American War Monument.** In the same vein, continue east to find the **Gun from the USS *Maine*,** an artifact from the ship whose destruction started the conflict with Spain.

Continue on the curved walkway until it parallels Sumter Street. Here you'll find the **Revolutionary War Generals Monument,** commemorating that menagerie of guerrilla freedom fighters: Francis "Swamp Fox" Marion, Thomas "Gamecock" Sumter, and Andrew "Wizard Owl" Pickens. A short distance south is a time capsule set to be opened on the 250th anniversary of the founding of Columbia.

Now walk along the pathway directly toward the State House to the **African American History Monument,** a comparatively late addition to the grounds and the first of its kind on any American capitol grounds. The dozen vignettes on the monument depict various chapters in the struggle for civil rights from slavery through today. At the base of the monument are four rubbing stones, each representing a different region of Africa from which slaves were imported.

Walk south to the big equestrian statue. This is **Wade Hampton III,** a general turned progressive governor, who despite his impeccable Confederate pedigree did a remarkable amount for African Americans after Reconstruction. The statue was erected in 1906, a scant four years after the influential war hero and statesman's death.

Continue west to the **Strom Thurmond Monument,** one of the more controversial memorials on the State House grounds. Though the statue depicts the longtime senator and conservative icon at the ripe young age of 60, Thurmond himself attended the unveiling of it in 1999, when he was 97. He would eventually retire from the Senate at age 100 as the nation's longest-serving senator, and he died in 2003. Most interestingly—and ironically, given Thurmond's long support of segregation and opposition to civil rights—the list of his children was amended to include a mixed-race daughter he had out of wedlock, Essie Mae Washington-Williams, now 87. Her mother, Carrie Butler, had an affair with Thurmond when she was 15 while serving as the family maid, and her daughter kept the secret until after his death. Ms. Washington-Williams now lives in Los Angeles and wrote an account of her life and relationship with Thurmond, *Dear Senator*, in 2005.

Now walk on the west side of the State House and look at its walls. Here you will see brass stars marking six **Union cannonball hits** on the State House during the bombardment before Sherman took the city. The large memorial nearby is the **Palmetto Regiment Memorial,** oldest monument on the grounds and commemorating the service and sacrifice of this regiment during the Mexican-American War.

Now head east to Assembly Street and find the **grave of Captain Swanson Lunsford.** This is the only tomb on the grounds, the final resting place of this Revolutionary War hero, whose family once owned the land where he is buried. Continue north a short distance parallel to Assembly Street and find the **Veterans Monument,** newest addition to the grounds and a memorial to all South Carolina veterans, in peacetime and in war.

Walk to the extreme northwest corner of the State House grounds at Assembly and Gervais Streets to find one of its most interesting markers, the **Dr. J. Marion Sims Monument.** The good doctor is widely considered the father of modern gynecology. The South Carolina native is not without controversy, however; some historians have concluded that he performed much of his research on female slaves against their will—and in some cases, apparently, without anesthetic.

Walk east again parallel to Gervais Street. Just before the Confederate Monument, where you began your walking tour, are two important spots. The first is the statue of Benjamin "Pitchfork Ben" Tillman, populist governor

of South Carolina in the 1890s and prime author of the supremacy of the Baptist Upstate over the Episcopalian Lowcountry. Yet another of the State House's controversial politically incorrect memorials, this statue in effect honors an avowed white supremacist who introduced the segregationist Jim Crow laws to the Palmetto State. Nearby is a much more wholesome monument, the **Washington Elm.** This beautiful tree is a granddaughter of the elm tree in Cambridge, Massachusetts, under which George Washington took command of the Continental Army in 1775. It was awarded to the South Carolina Daughters of the American Revolution in 1947.

Speaking of our first president, we've saved the best for last: the imposing and impressive **George Washington Statue** at the capitol's front steps. Sculpted of bronze on a granite base, the statue is Washington's exact height (as closely as historians can figure): six feet, two inches tall. If you're here after hours, you may notice joggers running up and down the front steps, Rocky-style.

Trinity Episcopal Cathedral

The beautiful buffed-brick Trinity Episcopal Cathedral (1100 Sumter St., 803/771-7300, www.trinitysc.org), near the State House, is a fine example of Gothic Revival church architecture, and a recent renovation has made it even more attractive. Its congregation has roots back to the very first backcountry Episcopalian church in the state, around 1812.

Designed by Edward Brickell in 1840, the current sanctuary boasts stained-glass windows from Munich, a gorgeous baptismal font, and a host of deceased luminaries in the attached cemetery, including five governors of South Carolina and three Confederate generals (and one who was both: Wade Hampton III). Good construction and benevolent wind patterns (and divine intervention?) saved the church from Yankee fires in 1865.

© JIM MOREKIS

COLUMBIA

Trinity Episcopal Cathedral

the South Carolina Relic Room, next to the State Museum

⬛ South Carolina State Museum

The mother lode of all history of the Palmetto State, the South Carolina State Museum (301 Gervais St., 803/898-4921, www. southcarolinastatemuseum.org, Labor Day-Memorial Day Tues. 10 A.M.-8 P.M., Wed.-Fri. 10 A.M.-5 P.M., Sat. 10 A.M.-6 P.M., Sun. 1-5 P.M., Memorial Day-Labor Day Mon. and Wed.-Fri. 10 A.M.-5 P.M., Tues. 10 A.M.-8 P.M., Sat. 10 A.M.-6 P.M., Sun. 1-5 P.M., $7 adults, $5 children, free under age 3) occupies the 1893 Columbia Mill textile building, the first electrically powered one in the country, in the restored Vista district downtown, next to the historic Gervais Street Bridge over the Congaree River.

Open since 1988, there are over 70,000 artifacts in its growing collection. There's a constant menu of rotating exhibits as well as a standing collection of art, archaeology, and natural history. Kids love the giant shark display, a 43-foot-long replica of a prehistoric shark skeleton typical of the species that once roamed this area back when water levels were significantly higher than today.

But the real highlights are the detailed and vibrant exhibits on particular segments of the human history of South Carolina. As you'd expect, the Civil War exhibit is particularly vivid, but that is by no means the only high point. There's excellent interpretation of the state's colonial history, including the lives of Native Americans and Africans both enslaved and free.

A nice plus for those interested in digging deeper, so to speak, into South Carolina history are the exhibits on various industries that have meant so much to the state, such as mining, forestry, agriculture, and shrimping. A life-size replica of the *Best Friend of Charleston* train—the first locomotive built in the United States—is great fun for kids.

Housed within the State Museum complex is the small but well-tended **South Carolina Relic Room & Military Museum** (301 Gervais St., 803/737-8095, www.crr.sc.gov, Tues.-Sat. 10 A.M.-5 P.M., 1st Sun. of the month 1-5 P.M., $5 adults, $2 youth, free under age 12, $1 1st Sun. of the month), which has occupied

COLUMBIA

© JIM MOREKIS

Columbia Museum of Art

several locations over the years but still maintains an interesting collection of artifacts and memorabilia highlighting the state's significant contributions to American military history, with a strong focus on the Civil War era. Since it is well worth visiting, and the entrance is a stone's throw away from the entrance to the State Museum proper, I suggest getting a combo ticket ($9), which provides admission to both the State Museum and the Relic Room & Military Museum.

EdVenture

The new-fangled children's museum EdVenture (211 Gervais St., 803/779-3100, www.edventure.org, Tues.-Sat. 9 A.M.-5 P.M., Sun. noon-5 P.M., $9.50), within the State Museum complex but in a separate building, was built specifically for those ages 12 and under. In it are over 350 hands-on exhibits, mostly concentrating on science and nature. A highlight is "Eddie," a 40-foot-tall schoolboy

within whose simulated innards kids can climb and slide on.

Columbia Museum of Art

The small but well-done Columbia Museum of Art (Main St. and Hampton St., 803/799-2810, www.columbiamuseum.org, Tues.-Fri. 11 A.M.-5 P.M., Sat. 10 A.M.-5 P.M., Sun. noon-5 P.M., $10 adults, $5 children, free under age 5) is in a suitably modern-looking building, erected in 1998. The highlight of its permanent collection is the Samuel H. Kress Collection on the upper floor, including some wonderful Renaissance and baroque pieces. The most notable single works here are Botticelli's matchless *Nativity* and Claude Monet's *The Seine at Giverny.* Occasionally hours and prices are different during special exhibits; check the website for details.

Also of interest is the museum's growing Asian collection, and don't forget to check out the Tiffany glass. And, of course, there's a nice museum gift shop as well—good luck tearing the kids out of that one.

◖ University of South Carolina

Columbia isn't just the state capital; it's a college town as well. The University of South Carolina (USC, 803/777-0169, www.sc.edu) hosts nearly 30,000 students at its main campus in Columbia, although apparently only a few attend during summer, which is dead compared to the busy fall and spring.

While the institution has seven other campuses around the state, this is the flagship, dating from its establishment in 1801 as part of a flurry of Southern public universities set up after the Revolution (Georgia, North Carolina, and Virginia also established public universities during this time). Significantly, USC was the only one to grant degrees to African Americans during Reconstruction—though admittedly this was under duress from the federal government and resulted in the temporary closure of the university in 1877 when the old guard returned to power.

Riding the changing tides of state and national history, USC—it's still called that here despite a recent court decision giving the University of Southern California marketing rights to the acronym—went through various incarnations from its founding, from college to university to agricultural school. In 1906, however, it acquired its current and hopefully final designation. Other key dates in USC history are 1893, when it became coed, and 1963, when the school integrated for the first time since Reconstruction.

On Sumter Street at College Street you'll find the wrought iron gates opening onto **The Horseshoe,** the oldest and most beautiful part of campus. The first building here, Rutledge College, was built in 1805, and hosted nine students and two professors. It was followed in short order by the original President's House, DeSaussure College (designed as the mirror image to Rutledge), and the remaining eight buildings of the originally planned 11. The buildings survived the Union burning of the city because they were used to house wounded soldiers of both armies.

A smaller, lusher version of Harvard Yard, the Horseshoe today remains the iconic image of the University of South Carolina, a tree-lined quad intersected by narrow walkways. Some of the bricks you will walk on come from the old Booker T. Washington High School building, the first black high school in Columbia, purchased and torn down by USC. Despite the enormous physical expansion of USC throughout the city—sometimes in Columbia it seems like you're never more than 20 feet away from a government office or a university facility, or both—the Horseshoe remains the spiritual center of campus and a fond memory for all alumni.

In 1939 the grand **McKissick Museum** (816 Bull St., 803/777-7251, www.cas.sc.edu, Mon.-Fri. 8:30 A.M.-5 P.M., Sat. 11 A.M.-3 P.M., free), a New Deal-era public works project, replaced the President's House, which would eventually

be relocated to the Horseshoe in 1952. Since the 1970s the McKissick has housed USC's many collections and has diverse exhibits on public life and history in the state. There are two galleries on the second floor, a natural history component on the third floor, and a small collection of Baruch silver within the Visitors Center on the first floor.

The key building to note during your walking tour of the Horseshoe is one near the Sumter Street entrance, the **South Caroliniana Library** (910 Sumter St., 803/777-3131, www.sc.edu, Mon.-Fri. 8:30 A.M.-5 P.M., Sat. 9 A.M.-1 P.M., free). Designed by renowned American architect Robert Mills, who also designed Columbia's premier house museum, the Caroliniana is the first freestanding college library in the country (two fireproof wings were added in 1927). Adding to the slight air of eccentricity is the tomb in front of the library, that of longtime USC President J. Rion McKissick. The library has one of the most significant collections on Southern history anywhere, with a particularly distinguished reading room full of stately busts and Harry Potter-esque alcoves. It's open to the public; all you need is a photo ID. Keep in mind that it's open only when classes are in session.

In the autumn, the center of campus is **Williams-Brice Stadium** (803/777-4274, www.gamecocksonline.com), the 85,000-seat venue where the South Carolina Gamecocks play football. Interestingly, the bones of the stadium date back to the New Deal, when the Works Progress Administration built Carolina Stadium in 1934. The team plays in the always-tough Southeastern Conference, generally finishing in the middle of the pack or worse. Despite this, the Gamecocks have some of the most passionate fans in the country.

Not all here is athletics, however. The **USC Melton Memorial Observatory** (803/777-4180, www.physics.sc.edu, free), on campus right off Greene Street, hosts public viewing sessions of

WALTER EDGAR'S JOURNAL

He's originally from Alabama, but you could call University of South Carolina professor Walter Edgar the modern voice of the Palmetto State. From the rich diversity of barbecue to the inner workings of the poultry business and the charms of beach music, Edgar covers the gamut of South Carolina culture and experience on his popular weekly radio show *Walter Edgar's Journal*, airing on South Carolina public radio stations throughout the state.

Currently director of the USC Institute of Southern Studies, the Vietnam vet and certified barbecue contest judge explains the show like this: "On the *Journal* we look at current events in a broader perspective, trying to provide context that is often missing in the mainstream media." More specifically, Edgar devotes each one-hour show to a single guest, usually a South Carolinian—by birth or by choice—with a unique perspective on some aspect of state culture, business, arts, or folkways. By the time the interview ends, you not only have a much deeper understanding of the topic of the show but of the interviewee as well. And because of Edgar's unique way of tying strands of his own vast knowledge and experience into every interview, he'll also leave you with a deeper understanding of South Carolina itself.

In these days of media saturation, a public radio show might sound like a rather insignificant perch from which to influence an entire state. But remember that South Carolina is a small, close-knit place, a state of Main Street towns rather than impersonal metro areas. During any given show, many listeners in Edgar's audience will know his guests on a personal basis. And by the end of the show, the rest of the listeners will feel as if they did.

Listen to *Walter Edgar's Journal* Friday at noon on South Carolina public radio, with a repeat Sunday at 8 P.M. Hear podcasts of previous editions at www.scetv.org.

the night sky (Apr.-Sept. Mon. 9:30-11:30 P.M., Oct.-Mar. Mon. 8-10 P.M.) on clear evenings.

To learn more about USC and campus life, visit its excellent **Visitors Center** (1500 Pendleton St., 803/777-0169, www.sc.edu/visitorcenter, Mon.-Fri. 8:30 A.M.-5 P.M., Sat. 11 A.M.-3 P.M.) within the McKissick Museum building. Public parking is adjacent to the building. They hold regular free walking tours of the campus, led by specially trained University Ambassadors. The tours last over two hours, so wear your walking shoes.

Notable alumni include former *Entertainment Weekly* host Leeza Gibbons, all members of Hootie and the Blowfish, world-renowned painter Jasper Johns, former New York Mets great Mookie Wilson, Heisman Trophy winner George Rogers, and a host of assorted South Carolina governors, senators, and representatives. Perhaps the most famous faculty member was poet and *Deliverance* author James Dickey.

First Baptist Church

There are a lot of places in South Carolina that can lay claim to being the cradle of secession. The first Ordinance of Secession was drawn up in Beaufort, while the first shots of the war were fired in Charleston. But it was at the First Baptist Church (1306 Hampton St., 803/256-4251, www.fbccola.com) in Columbia where a state convention in December 1860 voted unanimously for South Carolina to leave the union. The 1856 Greek Revival structure was the only building in town large enough to hold the delegation at the time.

Confusingly even today, the *first* First Baptist Church was built in 1811 on Sumter Street. When the Yankees came to town looking for revenge, local lore has it that a quick-thinking African American deacon sent them down the street. So they mistakenly burned down the original edifice, leaving the actual site of the convention untouched.

Don't look for any of this possibly embarrassing history on the church website; they're too busy ministering and televising their very popular 10:30 A.M. Sunday service.

COLUMBIA

Modjeska Monteith Simkins House

Named for its groundbreaking resident, the Modjeska Monteith Simkins House (2025 Marion St., 803/252-7742) is an interesting bit of little-known Columbia history. Modjeska Monteith Simkins became the state's first full-time African American public health worker in the 1930s, doing important work to stem the epidemic spread of tuberculosis and pellagra among the area's black population. By extension, her work brought her into the field of social justice, and in her regular meetings at this house she was soon hosting figures such as future Supreme Court justice Thurgood Marshall, who was barred from staying at Columbia hotels because of his race. Simkins went on to be a leading civil rights figure, instrumental in the desegregation of the local school system. She died in 1992.

the botanical garden at Riverbanks Zoo

© SOPHIA MOREKIS

Governor's Mansion and Gardens

Not to be confused with the home of the Palmetto State's legislative branch, the State House, the executive branch is headquartered at the Governor's Mansion and Gardens (800 Richland St., 803/737-1710, www.scgovernorsmansion.org, gardens Mon.-Fri. 9 A.M.-5 P.M., free), a complex of structures on an attractively landscaped nine-acre parcel on the high ground of Arsenal Hill. Built in 1855 as the Arsenal Military Academy, the building, which now houses the governor and family, survived the burning of the city in 1865 and hosted its first chief executive in 1869.

The guest quarters next door, the 1855 Lace House, was purchased in 1968. The 1830 Caldwell-Boylston House, also on the grounds, was bought by the state in 1978 and now houses staff offices and a nice gift shop for visitors to the mansion and grounds. The six rooms of the Mansion open to the public contain an impressive collection of furnishings and artwork from various eras. Call to set up a free tour.

◀ Riverbanks Zoo and Garden

One of the nation's best, if underrated, zoos and South Carolina's most popular single attraction, Riverbanks Zoo and Garden (500 Wildlife Pkwy., 803/779-8717, www.riverbanks.org, fall-winter daily 9 A.M.-5 P.M., spring-summer Mon.-Fri. 9 A.M.-5 P.M., Sat.-Sun. 9 A.M.-6 P.M., $11.75 adults, $9.25 children, free under age 2) is a fairly unique combo site. Not only do you get a crackerjack zoo, with nearly 400 species represented and an extensive environmental and educational component, but there's a beautiful and well-done botanical garden as well.

The seriousness of Riverbanks's mission is underscored by the fact that their two best exhibits might be something of a surprise. The 20,000-square-foot **Aquarium Reptile Complex** is a stunning and vibrantly colorful collection of reptiles, fish, amphibians, and invertebrates. It may not sound like much fun just reading about it, but this will be one of the highlights of your trip.

Another particularly outstanding collection is the **Birdhouse,** which actually comprises three separate avian habitats: Penguin Coast, featuring several different species of the always popular swim-happy birds; Asian Trek, featuring many exotic species from the Far East; and Savanna Camp, with birds from Africa and South America. You'll also get plenty of meat-and-potatoes zoo action as well, with a focus on a typical range of African mammals, including elephants, zebras, giraffes, and a particularly good gorilla exhibit.

When my daughter and I visited in summer 2008, a gorgeous litter of the cutest lion cubs you've ever seen was on display, spending most of their time sleeping and drinking milk from a bottle. They're not cubs anymore, and those lions now have their own dedicated habitat. And speaking of lions—sea lions, that is—Riverbanks has a large sea lion habitat with regular shows and feedings (daily 10:30 A.M. and 3 P.M.).

The zoo is only part of the picture, however. Take a free regular tram from the zoo grounds to the 70-acre **botanical garden,** one of the most extensive in the South. The tram drops you at a nice little visitors center run by Clemson University. The highlight of the site is the 34,000-square-foot Walled Garden, intricate with mazes and lush with colorful flowers. There's also a Bog Garden, for water-loving plants; a peaceful Shade Garden; an exquisite Rose Garden, with a nice selection of Noisette roses, a popular native flower; and the eccentric Dry Garden out front in the parking lot, featuring drought-resistant species.

The river in Riverbanks is the Saluda River, across which the tram travels between the two attractions. A River Trail in the botanical garden takes you from the Saluda River Bridge down along a path to the ruins of the old **Saluda River Factory.** Dating from 1830, the Factory is one of the state's oldest textile mills,

and at one time the largest in the South. This is actually a separate historic district in its own right, since at one time it was home to a general store, a tavern, and several boarding houses.

If zoos aren't your thing, or if you object to them on ethical grounds, you can simply visit the botanical garden by itself; it has its own separate entrance (Mohawk Dr. and Botanical Pkwy.) on the West Columbia side. Admission is the same whether you go to the zoo or not, however.

Some tips on enjoying Riverbanks: It gets hot in Columbia. Go early or late in the day to see the animals at their best. Regardless of the heat, Riverbanks begins attracting heavy crowds just before lunchtime. If crowds bother you, get there right as it opens. When you enter, take stock of the rotating schedule of exhibits, programs, showtimes, and feeding times *before* you set off on your trek through the zoo.

Riverbanks couldn't be easier to get to. It's just off I-26 at the Greystone Boulevard exit.

Fort Jackson

One of the U.S. Army's largest training areas, Fort Jackson is the focal point of enormous economic, professional, and social activity in Columbia, although it's of little interest or even noticeable to the civilian visitor. There is, however, the **Fort Jackson Museum** (4442 Jackson Blvd., 803/751-7419, Mon.-Fri. 9 A.M.-4 P.M., free), across from post headquarters, which contains thousands of artifacts of Army history dating from roughly World War I to the present. Get a visitors pass at the front gate. As with any U.S. military facility, make sure you have your auto registration or rental car contract in hand along with proof of insurance, and always obey the speed limit.

Fort Jackson also hosts several smaller, more focused museums that might be of great interest to the hard-core military buff. The **U.S. Army Adjutant General's Corps Museum** (Bldg. 4392, Strom Thurmond Blvd., 803/751-1747, www.jackson.army.mil/!2009_pages/museum/index.html, Tues.-Fri. noon-4 P.M., free) details the history of the Army's "human resource" component, including bands, postal service, and morale. The **U.S. Army Chaplain Museum** (10100 Lee Rd., 803/751-8079, Mon.-Fri. 9 A.M.-4 P.M., free) chronicles the history of Army chaplains of all faiths from the Revolution to the present day. And the **U.S. Army Finance Corps Museum** (803/751-3771, Mon.-Fri. 9 A.M.-4 P.M., free), honors the unit of the Army responsible for meeting its huge payroll.

ENTERTAINMENT AND EVENTS

Columbia is a fun town with plenty of nightlife, especially when USC is in session. In addition to its cultural offerings, there are two main areas to remember for entertainment, dining, and shopping: Five Points, the intersection of Harden and Greene Streets, and Saluda Avenue; and the Vista (sometimes called the Congaree Vista), a more recently restored area closer to downtown amid the old mill buildings.

Nightlife

As you'd expect, nightlife here is plentiful, boisterous, and centers around the college scene, especially in Five Points. The Vista appeals to visitors as well as trendy and well-heeled locals. There's no smoking in all bars, restaurants, and public places in Columbia.

Any discussion of nightlife in Columbia, and specifically in Five Points, should begin with **Jake's Bar & Grill** (2112 Devine St., 803/252-5253, Mon.-Thurs. 4 P.M.-2 A.M., Fri. 3 P.M.-2 A.M., Sat.-Sun. noon-2 A.M.). Formerly called Rockafella's, it often hosted Hootie and the Blowfish when they were getting their start, and it remains the quintessential Five Points neighborhood joint despite its new name. The beer list is long, and the outdoor deck is a great place to chill on a nice night. Speaking of

© JIM MOREKIS

Five Points is the birthplace of Hootie and the Blowfish.

Hootie and the Blowfish, the space where they first played in Five Points is at **Pub on Santee** (733 Santee St., 803/256-4292), back when it was called Monterrey Jack's.

Not to be outdone is **Five Points Pub** (2020 Devine St., 803/253-7888, Mon. and Sat. 8 P.M.-2 A.M., Tues.-Fri. 5 P.M.-2 A.M.). With one entrance on Devine Street and another on Santee Avenue, this cavernous space might confuse you into thinking it is two establishments. This is the place to go for live music, good company, and passable bar food.

Probably the most happening college-town bar experience in Five Points these days is at **Group Therapy** (2107 Greene St., 803/256-1203, www.grouptherapybar.com, Mon.-Fri. 4:30 P.M.-2 A.M., Sat.-Sun. 7 P.M.-2 A.M.), pretty much guaranteed to be jam-packed on weekend nights whenever the university is in session.

For a more laid-back, Deadhead vibe and a late, late-night scene, go to **Tavern on Greene** (2002-C Greene St., 803/252-7265, Mon.-Fri. 4 P.M.-4 A.M., Sat.-Sun. 6 P.M.-2 A.M.), commonly known as Five Points's "hippie bar."

One night when I was in **Goatfeather's** (2017 Devine St., 803/256-3325, daily 4 P.M.-2 A.M., kitchen until 9 P.M. Sun.-Wed., until 10 P.M. Thurs.-Sat.) in Five Points, they had a massive "Obama" banner hanging over the bar. While Goatfeather's is probably not much fun if you're a conservative, its hipster appeal, swank furnishings, and dimly lit retro vibe definitely make for a fun bar scene, and the kitchen fare is outstanding.

Another popular Five Points locale is **Delaney's Music Pub** (741 Saluda Ave., 803/779-2345, daily 11 A.M.-2 A.M.), which, as the name possibly implies, is modeled on a traditional Irish pub. For what's widely considered the best beer in town, try the **Hunter Gatherer Brewery** (900 Main St., 803/748-0540, Tues.-Sat. 4 P.M.-midnight), which, though considerably more artsy than your typical brewpub, offers some delectable artisanal beers on tap. Serious

beer connoisseurs should also consider the **Flying Saucer** (931 Senate St., 803/933-9997, www.beerknurd.com, Mon.-Wed. 11 A.M.-1 A.M., Thurs.-Sat. 11 A.M.-2 A.M., Sun. noon-midnight), which offers—wait for it—over *80 beers on tap,* in addition to nearly 150 bottled brands.

The closest thing to a Five Points-style dive in the Vista is **The Whig** (1200 Main St., 803/931-8852, daily 4 P.M.-2 A.M., kitchen until 10 P.M.), a bohemian-slacker joint with what's generally considered the best jukebox in town. If you're a pool shark, head down to **Jillian's** (800 Gervais St., 803/779-7789, Mon.-Wed. 11:30 A.M.-midnight, Thurs. and Sun. 11:30 A.M.-1 A.M., Fri. 11:30 A.M.-3 A.M., Sat. 11:30 A.M.-2 A.M.), a pool hall-sports bar in the Vista. If you can't hustle a game at a table, you can certainly watch a game on any one of nearly 30 big-screens. The only rooftop bar in town is in the **Carolina Ale House** (798 Lady St., 803/227-7150, www.carolinaalehouse.com, daily 11 A.M.-2 A.M.) in the Vista, also known for its hearty grill items and its late kitchen hours.

But taking the cake for interesting and eclectic Columbia nightlife experiences is **The Art Bar** (1211 Park St., 803/929-0198, Sat.-Wed. 8 P.M.-2 A.M., Thurs. 8 P.M.-3 A.M., Fri. 8 P.M.-4 A.M.), down by the Vista. Impossible to pigeonhole, The Art Bar is a college dive, a hipster hangout, a Goth gathering place, a live music mecca, a crazy karaoke scene, and a gay bar, all in one intriguing package. Just come with an open mind, and you'll find a way to fit right in. The main gay and lesbian bar in town is **PTs 1109** (1101 Harden St., 803/758-6090, www.pts1109.com, Mon.-Sat. 8 P.M.-close). They have various drag and cabaret shows with varying cover charges.

Performing Arts

The nearly half-century-old **South Carolina Philharmonic** (721 Lady St., 803/771-7937, www.scphilharmonic.com) plays most of its classical music concerts at the **Koger Center** for the Arts (1051 Greene St., 803/777-7500, www.koger.sc.edu) under the baton of Morihiko Nakahara.

Columbia City Ballet (www.columbiacityballet.com), a professional troupe, generally dances at the Koger Center for the Arts. They offer one of the more eclectic seasons you'll find outside New York, with a ballet about Dracula every Halloween, and even a ballet chronicling the history of Hootie and the Blowfish. Of course, there's an annual holiday *Nutcracker* as well. Another local troupe, Columbia Classical Ballet (803/252-9112, www.columbiaclassicalballet.org), also dances at the Koger Center.

The South Carolina Shakespeare Company (803/787-2273, www.shakespearesc.org, $12 adults, free under age 12) holds vibrant outdoor performances of the Bard's work each fall at the amphitheater in Finlay Park downtown. Boasting one of the oldest community theater histories in the country is Town Theatre (1012 Sumter St., 803/799-2510, www.towntheatre.com, $10-15), a project of the Columbia Stage Society. Housed in the 1924 venue of the same name, Town Theatre concentrates on popular chestnuts like *West Side Story* and *Little Shop of Horrors*.

The University of South Carolina sponsors Theatre South Carolina (803/777-5208, www.cla.sc.edu/thea), which holds most of its performances at Drayton Hall (1214 College St.) and Longstreet Theatre (1300 Greene St.), with more experimental shows at the Lab Theatre (1400 Wheat St.). Though not affiliated with the university, Trustus Theatre (520 Lady St., 803/254-9732, www.trustus.org, $20-25) relies on a core of performers trained in the USC performing arts program to deliver a season mixing standbys (*Evita*) with more daring productions (*Doubt: A Parable*).

Probably the most offbeat bunch in town is Workshop Theatre of South Carolina (1136 Bull St., 803/799-4876, www.workshoptheatre.com, $10-20), which brings an interesting and eclectic season to its stage, from *High School Musical* to *Les Liaisons Dangereuses*.

Cinema

The place to see indie film in Columbia is at The Nickelodeon (937 Main St., 803/254-3433 www.nickelodeon.org, $7.50) downtown next to the USC campus. Run by the nonprofit Columbia Film Society, a year's membership costs $35 and gets you discounted admission. They hold various tiny film festivals throughout the year, including the "Indie Grits" festival (Apr.), a Native American festival (Nov.), a Latin festival (Sept.-Oct.), an African American festival (Jan.-Feb.), and a Jewish festival (Mar.-Apr.).

Otherwise, you'll have to go to the suburban multiplexes for movie action, including Regal Sandhill Stadium 16 (450 Town Center Place, 803/736-1811) and Regal Columbiana Grande Stadium 14 (1250 Bower Pkwy., 803/407-9898) out at the Columbiana Mall, off I-26 a little way north of town.

Festivals and Events

The South Carolina Book Festival (www.scbookfestival.org, free) happens each February, bringing dozens of nationally acclaimed authors to the Columbia Metropolitan Convention Center (1101 Lincoln St.).

The main public event on the calendar for downtown Columbia is March's annual St. Patrick's Day Festival (www.stpats5points.com, $15) in Five Points. It doesn't hold a handle to Savannah's yearly event, but the conglomeration of bars and the cozy streets make for a vivacious Celtic celebration. There are five stages of live music, various kids' activities, and, of course, a big parade.

In April comes the Columbia International Festival (803/799-3452, www.cifonline.org, $5 adults, $1 children), an eclectic celebration of the various cultures, both homegrown and from abroad, in South Carolina. Held at the state fairgrounds near Williams-Brice Stadium, this event offers entertainment, exhibits, and, of course, lots and lots of international food. Also in April is the unique **Indie Grits Film Festival** (803/254-8234, www.indiegrits.com), a fun and quirky little film fest hosted by **The Nickelodeon** (937 Main St., 803/254-3433, www.nickelodeon.org), the city's art house theater.

In September, the congregation of the Holy Trinity Greek Orthodox Church hosts the **Columbia Greek Festival** (803/461-0248, www.columbiasgreekfestival.com) at the corner of Calhoun and Sumter Streets downtown. There's food, dance, music, and Greek goodies for sale.

Each October, Five Points hosts the **Columbia Blues Festival** (803/733-8452, www.wordofmouthproductions.org), a celebration of that indigenous American art form, mostly relying on regional talent. Also in October comes the biggest single local event, the **South Carolina State Fair** (1200 Rosewood Dr., 803/799-3387, www.scstatefair.org, $8 adults, $2 children) at the sprawling state fairgrounds near Williams-Brice Stadium. With roots going back to the 1830s, this is one of the largest such events in the Southeast, with over 500,000 attendees each year. Rides, food, livestock, and agriculture shows keep the huge crowd entertained, with the highlight being the colorful competitive exhibits. A series of concerts (about $15 pp) livens up the evenings.

Perhaps the quirkiest event in Columbia is the **Five Points Festivus** (www.fivepointscolumbia.com) in December. Taking its name from a famous *Seinfeld* episode, this merchant-driven affair features a strange parade, music, a tree lighting, and an "Airing of Grievances" pub crawl.

SHOPPING

Other than malls, the main shopping area in Columbia is at Five Points. The Vista also has a growing range of good stores.

Antiques

As with much of South Carolina, the capital has some good antiques action. The largest antiques malls near Columbia proper are in the Vista: **City Market Antiques Mall** (707 Gervais St., 803/799-7722, Tues.-Sat. 10 A.M.-5 P.M., Sun. 2-5 P.M.), with over 65 dealers; and the massive **Columbia Antique Mall** (602 Huger St., 803/765-1584, Mon.-Sat. 10:30 A.M.-5:30 P.M., Sun. 1:30-5:30 P.M.).

Over the river, West Columbia has a sort of antiques colony of its own, at **763 Meeting Street Antique Mall** (763 Meeting St., 803/796-1516, Mon.-Sat. 10 A.M.-5:30 P.M., Sun. 1:30-5:30 P.M.), **Antiques on Meeting** (614 Meeting St., 803/791-0008, Mon.-Sat. 10:30 A.M.-5:30 P.M.), and **Marketplace on Meeting** (550 Meeting St., 803/794-1000, Mon.-Fri. 10 A.M.-3 P.M.).

Art Galleries

The acclaimed **Blue Sky Gallery** (733 Saluda Ave., 803/779-4242, www.blueskyart.com, by appointment) in Five Points is the place where you'll find original work from none other than Blue Sky himself, a.k.a. Warren Edward Johnson, a nationally renowned local artist who specializes in murals and folk art. Call for an appointment, because he doesn't keep regular hours at the gallery anymore.

The Vista hosts a number of great galleries in the restored old warehouse spaces, including the modern-tinged **if** (1223 Lincoln St., 803/238-2351, Mon.-Fri. 11 A.M.-7 P.M., Sat. 11 A.M.-5 P.M.) and the eclectic **Gallery at DuPre** (807 Gervais St., 803/546-1143).

Books

Over the river in West Columbia is **Ed's Editions** (406 Meeting St., 803/791-8002, www.edseditions.com, Mon.-Sat. 10 A.M.-6 P.M., Sun. 1-5 P.M.), generally considered the city's best used bookstore. Serious bibliophiles shouldn't miss the Rare Book Room.

Though a good bit off-campus, the main USC-related bookshop is **Addam's University Bookstore** (152 Assembly St., 803/256-6666, daily 8:30 A.M.-6 P.M.), which in addition to

COLUMBIA

providing any book a student would need also has a huge stock of Gamecock gear.

If you like a jolt of java along with your metaphysical reading, try **Higher Grounds Books & Beans** (1306 Hampton St., 803/217-3247, Mon.-Tues. and Thurs.-Fri. 8 A.M.-3 P.M., Wed. 8 A.M.-7 P.M., Sun. 9 A.M.-noon) at the corner of Hampton and Sumter, which specializes in Christian reading material and coffee.

Clothes

Sid Nancy (733 Saluda Ave., 803/779-6454, Mon.-Fri. noon-8 P.M., Sat. 11 A.M.-7 P.M., Sun. 1-3 P.M.) in Five Points, as the name might indicate, is an awesome vintage and thrift store with a definite cutting-edge postpunk appeal.

Adjacent is the excellent consignment shop **Revente** (737 Saluda Ave., 803/256-3076), which tends to cater to the upper end of the scale, though with some great bargains if your timing is right.

Papa Jazz, a great music store in Five Points

© JIM MOREKIS

A couple of streets over, **Natural Vibrations** (719 Harden St., 803/771-4144, Mon.-Sat. 11 A.M.-6 P.M., Sun. 1-6 P.M.) deals on the Rasta end of the scale, with hemp products, T-shirts, and various reggae-related merch.

For various University of South Carolina burgundy-and-white gear, try the **Gamecock Stop** (1928 Rosewood Dr., 803/748-0487, Mon.-Sat. 9 A.M.-6 P.M.), although the selection at **Addam's University Bookstore** (152 Assembly St., 803/256-6666) is great.

Specialty Shops

Three Dog Bakery (625 Harden St., 803/312-9988, Mon.-Sat. 10 A.M.-6 P.M.) has some delicious-looking confections that you'll be tempted to sample, but don't—they're just for Rover.

Seminal Columbia institution **Cromer's P-Nuts** (1700 Huger St., 803/779-2290, www.cromers.com, Mon.-Fri. 9 A.M.-6 P.M., Sat. 9 A.M.-5 P.M.) in the Vista has a strange twist on truth in advertising: Their slogan is "Guaranteed Worst in Town." The story goes that during the Great Depression, Julian Cromer found he had some competition for his once-dominant one-man roasted peanut stand downtown. Since the competition was making some headway claiming not only that they had the best peanuts in town but that Mr. Cromer's were demonstrably the worst, Mr. Cromer had an idea. He put up a sign bearing his now-famous credo, and shortly he was back on top of Columbia's cutthroat roadside roasted peanut business. Today, the store remains in family hands, and you can buy a range of snacks, party supplies, and, of course, peanuts.

Music

Serious vinyl junkies should head straight to Five Points to check out **Papa Jazz** (2014 Greene St., 803/256-0096, www.papajazz.com, Mon.-Sat. 10 A.M.-7 P.M., Sun. 1-6 P.M.). Besides the eponymous genre, they deal in used vinyl of all types, including rare funk records

COLUMBIA

and the occasional punk gem. It's a tiny store packed to the gills with music, but it has been a Columbia tradition for over 25 years.

Malls

The city's premier mall is **Columbiana Centre** (100 Columbiana Circle, 803/732-6255, www.columbianacentre.com, Mon.-Thurs. 10 A.M.-9 P.M., Fri.-Sat. 10 A.M.-10 P.M., Sun. 1:30-7 P.M.) off I-26 a little northwest of town. Its anchor stores are Dillard's, Sears, J. C. Penney, and Belk. **Columbia Place** (7201 Two Notch Rd., 803/788-4676, Mon.-Sat. 10 A.M.-9 P.M., Sun. noon-6 P.M.) offers anchor stores such as Old Navy, Macy's, Sears, and Burlington Coat Factory.

Farmers Markets

The granddaddy of them all is **Columbia State Farmers Market** (1001 Bluff Rd., 803/737-4664, Mon.-Sat. 6 A.M.-9 P.M., Sun. 1-6 P.M.), in operation at this same 50-acre site, with a 100,000-square-foot drive-through building. This state-operated facility, one of three in South Carolina, has 500 stalls, 100 wholesale outlets, about 40 retail outlets, and even its own U.S. Post Office location.

Downtown, the **Trinity Episcopal Church Farmers Market** (1100 Sumter St., 803/771-7300, Sun. 8:30 A.M.-noon) sells local produce each Sunday in the warm seasons.

In the Vista you'll find the **All-Local Farmers Market** (www.stateplate.org), held every second Saturday of the month 8 A.M.-noon on the patio of the popular local restaurant Gervais & Vine (620A Gervais St.) and every fourth Saturday at Rosewood Market (2803 Rosewood Dr.).

SPORTS AND RECREATION
Kayaking, Canoeing, and Rafting

Because of its position at the confluence of the Saluda, Broad, and Congaree Rivers and the presence of Lake Murray nearby, Columbia is a haven for water-based pastimes. These rivers are undeveloped or less-developed along much of their length through and around the city, and they provide a peaceful paddle with a minimum of fuss.

Generally speaking, most put-in spots are in West Columbia, using the large Gervais Street Bridge from downtown as a major landmark. The **Three Rivers Greenway** (www.riveralliance.org, daily dawn-dusk, free) joins several different hiking and biking paths as well as provides numerous river access points.

A deceptively easy put-in that will eventually lead to some fun Class II-III white water is from the ramp on the Saluda at the Riverbanks Zoo and Garden parking lot. From there, you can take out at the Gervais Street Bridge at the West Columbia Riverwalk. Besides the rapids, there's a lot of good nature viewing on this stretch as well.

A great place to put in on the Saluda River is **Saluda Shoals Park** (5605 Bush River Rd., 803/731-5208, www.icrc.net, daily dawn-dusk, $4 per vehicle), a 350-acre park on the Saluda River outside of town with a good launch ramp. They offer periodic guided kayak trips; call for details. To get here, take I-26 west, exit at Piney Grove Road, and turn left. Go about 1.5 miles to St. Andrews Road and turn right, then left at the first traffic light. Saluda Shoals Park is nearly two miles farther up on the left.

The Broad River is more peaceful. There's a dam at Broad River Road you can use as a launching spot, and from there you can paddle to the West Columbia Amphitheater at the Gervais Street Bridge. The Congaree River is also mellow, with a good put-in spot at the West Columbia Riverwalk at the Gervais Street Bridge, with a takeout at the Rosewood Drive landing. On this run you can paddle through the old canal locks.

There are several good outfitters in town for rental, purchase, or guided tours. **Adventure Carolina** (1107 State St., 803/796-4505, www.adventurecarolina.com) runs several trips on all area rivers, including a quick and easy selection of three-hour, three-mile paddles (about $50 pp). They also rent anything you might need. **River Runner Outdoor Center** (905 Gervais St., 803/771-0353, www.riverrunner.us, Mon.-Sat. 10 A.M.-6 P.M.) is the designated outfitter for Saluda Shoals Park but will rent for any trip at about $40 per day. River Runner has an impressive inventory of regionally made kayaks and canoes for purchase. They run periodic paddles throughout the year; check the website or call for details.

Fishing and Boating

Columbia is fishing crazy, and fishing around here mostly means **Lake Murray** (www.scjewel.com). This 50,000-acre lake boasts 650 miles of shoreline. Because of its artificial origin as a hydroelectric resource managed by South Carolina Electric and Gas (SCE&G), you can encounter some unseasonably cold water when you're fly-fishing due to the deep, frigid currents swirling from the bottom of the dam. But, as they say, that makes the fish all the happier.

Lake Murray was used for bombing practice by General Jimmy Doolittle's raiders in World War II; in fact, the island in the middle now called Lunch Island is still known to generations of Columbians as "Bomb Island." Whatever you call it, it's still home to thousands of purple martins who stop over each year.

To rent boats on Lake Murray, go to www.lakemurraycountry.com. The easiest access point for the lake is from **Dreher Island State Recreation Area** (3677 State Park Rd., 803/364-4152, www.southcarolinaparks.com, daily dawn-dusk, $2, free under age 16).

If lake fishing isn't for you, you can always fish the rivers from the **Three Rivers Greenway** (803/765-2200, www.riveralliance.org, daily dawn-dusk, free), along the banks of the Congaree and Broad Rivers.

Hiking and Biking

South Carolina's capital city is on the cutting edge of creative and user-friendly urban green-space design. Combine that with the generally excellent weather and friendly people, and you have a recreation home run.

The premier walking and biking site in Columbia is the excellent **Three Rivers Greenway** (803/765-2200, www.riveralliance.org, daily dawn-dusk, free), actually an umbrella project comprising three separate river walks on the banks of the Congaree and Broad Rivers, most directly connected. There are lighted and paved trails, boardwalks, and overlooks all along the nearly nine-mile collective Greenway, and future extensions are underway. All paths are accessible to people with disabilities; you can even take baby strollers along with no problem. Plenty of designated public parking is available at all entrances to the Three Rivers Greenway.

The key segments on the east side of the rivers, closest to downtown, are **Granby Park** (accessible via Huger St. past Blossom St. and onto Catawba St.) and **Riverfront Park** (accessible via Huger St. to Laurel St.). While at Riverfront Park, you can see the cool remains of the city's 1906 waterworks, integrated into the park design.

On the other side of the rivers in West Columbia and the suburb of Cayce are the **West Columbia Riverwalk** (from town, cross over the Gervais St. Bridge, take a left on Alexander Rd., and you'll see the amphitheater and parking lot on the left) and the **Cayce Riverwalk** (take Blossom St. over the river, a left onto Axtell Dr./Jessamine St., and the entrance is on the left).

Harbison State Forest (5500 Broad River Rd., 803/896-8890, www.state.sc.us/forest/refharb.htm, free) features over 12 miles of trails through the hardwood forest down to the Broad River.

A 14-mile segment of the ambitious, statewide **Palmetto Trail** (www.palmettoconservation.org) cuts through Fort Jackson on the east side of town. Access it through Gate 1, where you can park your car at the trailhead.

Sesquicentennial State Park

The Civilian Conservation Corps-era Sesquicentennial State Park (9564 Two Notch Rd., 803/788-2706, www.southcarolinaparks. com, daily dawn-dusk, $2, free under age 16), close to Columbia, has a nice 30-acre lake surrounded by a two-mile trail. Check for occasional interpretive nature programs.

Dreher Island State Recreation Area

Located on Lake Murray about 30 minutes north of town, Dreher Island State Recreation Area (3677 State Park Rd., 803/364-4152, www. southcarolinaparks.com, daily dawn-dusk, $2, free under age 16) actually comprises three islands linked to the mainland. In addition to the great fishing, there's camping and a nature trail.

Bird-Watching

Each July and August, on little Lunch Island in the middle of Lake Murray (old-timers call it "Bomb Island" for its role as target practice for Doolittle's raiders), nearly one million purple martins gather to rest on their way south for the winter. Each day that they're here, before dawn and after dusk, they fill the skies to chow down on mosquitoes and gnats. It's quite a beautiful, almost stunning display, and it's the largest natural roosting sanctuary in North America. Note that September is too late to see them.

The 65-foot **Southern Patriot** (803/749-8594, www.lakemurraytours.com, $27) offers three-hour evening tours specifically to observe the purple martins during summer.

Golf

Columbia doesn't have South Carolina's best golf, but there are 17 courses in the area. Probably the best public links—and a great value to boot—is **Oak Hills Golf Club** (7629 Fairfield Rd., 800/263-5218, www.oakhillsgolf.

com, $30), a combined effort of Steve Melnyk and Davis Love III.

Spectator Sports

Spectator sports in Columbia essentially begin and end with **University of South Carolina athletics** (www.gamecocksonline.cstv.com). As part of the Southeastern Conference, the Gamecocks play football at **Williams-Brice Stadium** (1127 George Rogers Blvd., 803/254-2950), basketball at the **Colonial Center** (801 Lincoln St., 803/576-9200), and baseball at a new field on Williams Street. Good luck getting tickets, especially for home football games. Regardless of how the 'Cocks are doing on the gridiron, their games are always attended by fiercely passionate, sold-out crowds.

There is serviceable professional minor-league ball courtesy of the **Columbia Blowfish** (301 Assembly St., 803/254-3474, www.blow-fishbaseball.com), a New York Mets affiliate that plays home games in the circa-1940s Capital City Stadium ("The Cap") as part of the Coastal Plain League. A team called the Bombers, in tribute to General Doolittle and his World War II raiders, played here until leaving town for Greenville in 2005 (they're now called The Drive). In their inaugural season in 2006, the new Blowfish led the league in attendance.

ACCOMMODATIONS

Columbia has plenty of lodging but is somewhat underserved in terms of quality accommodations for travelers and businesspeople. This is slowly changing, however. These are the best picks close to major attractions.

Under $150

Perhaps the most beloved stay in Columbia is the ◖ **Inn at USC** (1619 Pendleton St., 866/455-4753, www.innatusc.com, $145), a real hidden gem right on campus. While intended primarily as a stop for alumni and those on Gamecock business, the general public has taken to this popular boutique property, which is managed by the Hampton chain. A particular emphasis is placed on a certain clubby collegiality, down to the rotating (and quite good) art exhibits gracing the walls. Another big plus is the complimentary cooked-to-order breakfast in the Palmetto Room.

A newer property downtown is the **Sheraton Columbia Downtown** (1400 Main St., 803/988-1400, www.starwoodhotels.com, $145), housed in a particularly well-restored former bank building; you'll actually find a hip little bar in the old bank vault. The guest rooms are similarly well appointed, with a real attempt made at something close to period furnishing.

The **Courtyard by Marriott Downtown at USC** (630 Assembly St., 803/799-7800, www.marriott.com, $120-125) was actually a Holiday Inn not long ago. An extensive makeover has put the facility more in line with the Marriott chain's self-consciously minimalist design. The location puts you a short walk from several performing arts facilities, the State House, and the Vista. Parking is extra, but on the weekend you should have no problem finding street parking. The key downside is that the rooftop swimming pool is pretty small and windy.

It's not in downtown proper, but the **Embassy Suites** (200 Stoneridge Dr., 803/252-8700, www.embassysuitescolumbia.com, $130) right next to the Riverbanks Zoo and Garden is a handy, well-run place to stay near Columbia's main attraction, just off I-126 and minutes away from downtown. The complimentary breakfast is particularly good and extensive, and as suburban hotel bars go, it's rockin'.

There aren't many bed-and-breakfasts in Columbia—thanks to General Sherman, the stock of nostalgic old homes is low—but one well-regarded B&B is the **1425 Inn** (1425 Richland St., 803/252-7225, www.the1425inn.com, $130-150). Formerly the Richland Inn, this property has had a slight but still tasteful makeover since a management change. However, its tradition of Southern hospitality has stayed intact, with its five guest rooms sumptuously appointed and the breakfasts hot and delicious.

$150-300

It's hard to beat the ◖**Hampton Inn Downtown** (822 Gervais St., 803/231-2000, www.hamptoninncolumbia.com, $159) for its combination of location and service. Right in the Vista and close by the State House, this property has the usual high standards associated with the Hampton brand, along with the usual price premium. The only problematic thing about this property is its continuing tight parking issue.

Housed in a former bakery building, the **Inn at Claussen's** (2003 Greene St., 803/765-0440, www.theinnatclaussens.com, $150-200) is the premier lodging in Five Points proper. It's not as chichi as some of the plusher new places nearer the Vista, but the guest rooms are particularly large and comfortable. And, of course, being steps away from the nightlife and shopping at Five Points is a big plus.

FOOD

Columbia may not be challenging Charleston on the food front anytime soon, but a growing number of very tasty establishments have sprung up in the Five Points and Vista districts to go along with other longtime favorites in town. And if you're a barbecue fan, you're definitely in luck.

American

The issue of where to find the best burger in town is an ongoing spirited debate in Columbia. There are certainly plenty of great places to choose from, making it an enjoyable discussion. It's an acquired taste, but many Columbians swear by the pimento cheeseburgers and the pimento cheese fries at **Rockaway's** (2719 Rosewood Dr., 803/256-1075, daily 11 A.M.-11 P.M., $8), an under-the-radar locals-only type place in a nondescript building on the south side of the USC campus.

COLUMBIA
ACCOMMODATIONS
AND FOOD

© AVALON TRAVEL

For a brewpub, **Hunter Gatherer Brewery** (900 Main St., 803/748-0540, Tues.-Sat. 4 P.M.-midnight, $10) has an excellent kitchen, and many locals insist the best burger in town is actually here.

As for good old hot dogs, another Columbia staple near the north side of the USC campus is **Sandy's Famous Hot Dogs** (825 S. Main St., 803/254-6914, Mon.-Thurs. 11 A.M.-9 P.M., Fri.-Sat. 11 A.M.-10 P.M., Sun. noon-9 P.M., $2-5). It specializes in the unusual but oddly endearing slaw dog, topped with ground beef, coleslaw, mustard, and diced onions. It's a mess, but one of the tastier messes you'll ever have.

Asian

For a ridiculously hip night out with some ridiculously tasty Pacific Rim cuisine, go straight to **C SakiTumi** (831 Gervais St., 803/931-0700, www.sakitumigrill.com, Mon.-Wed. 4:30-10 P.M., Thurs.-Sat. 4:30 P.M.-midnight,

© SOPHIA MOREKIS

SakiTumi in the Vista

$12-18) in the Vista, with its somewhat hard-to-find entrance off Gervais Street. It's loud, it's dark, and the bar scene is as intriguing as its sushi rolls. Any tuna sushi or sashimi is the way to go; they bring in whole tuna loins, cut to order on the spot. And do I have to tell you there's a huge variety of hot and cold sake? Note that reservations are not accepted.

Nearby you'll find **Tsunami** (700C Gervais St., 803/312-9911, www.tsunamicompany. com, daily 4:30 P.M.-midnight, $15-20), part of a South Carolina chain that specializes in both sushi and tasty hibachi entrées like scallops and filet mignon. Like SakiTumi, this is a dark hip haven for Columbia's beautiful people.

Barbecue and Ribs

While his politics are an acquired taste, **Maurice's Gourmet Barbecue** (1600 Charleston Hwy., 803/796-0220, www.mauricesbbq.com, Sun.-Thurs. 10 A.M.-10 P.M., Fri.-Sat. 10 A.M.-11 P.M., $7-12) in West Columbia is the real thing: mustard-based Carolina pulled pork, and lots of it. In the 1950s, Maurice Bessinger inherited the family barbecue joint from his daddy, Big Joe (Maurice, interestingly, was called Little Joe), but he had a much bigger vision. In a few years, his "Piggie Park" drive-ins were the toast (and the onion rings, and the hushpuppies) of the Palmetto State, specializing in big servings of serious barbecue, burgers, and brisket and gallons of sweet tea. The Charleston Highway location across the river from downtown is the original, but there are five more locations in Columbia alone, and 17 total in the state; see the website for an interactive map. A quick way to get here is by exit 113 off I-26. Two caveats: First, Maurice's barbecue is the traditional Midlands variety, in a yellow mustard sauce. It's not for everybody, but you can't argue with success—Maurice claims to have delivered over 30 million servings at his chain of restaurants around the state. If you fall in love with it, you can leave with armloads of the stuff from the gift shop. Second, Maurice wears his right-wing neo-Confederate politics on his sleeve. While he claims to have had a religious conversion that cured him of his once outspoken segregationist leanings—he tried to keep African Americans from eating at his restaurants as late as 1968—cynics say his epiphany had more to do with keeping his business intact in a changing world than with any real change in his worldview. If you can deal with the atmosphere—rebel flags, revisionist history pamphlets, and the like—then you will enjoy Maurice's. If not, consider yourself forewarned.

While Maurice gets way more press, many locals insist the totally nonpartisan **◖ Little Pigs** (4927 Alpine Rd., 803/788-8238, www.littlepigs.biz, Wed. 11 A.M.-2 P.M., Thurs.-Sat. 11 A.M.-9 P.M., $8) outside of downtown near Fort Jackson has much better 'cue, despite not cooking with wood (a sticky issue with connoisseurs). This is all-you-can-eat buffet-style dining in a simple setting, with the focus purely on the pig itself—literally, since you can see it all right there in the buffet line.

If you don't want to drive that far, **Palmetto Pig** (530 Devine St., 803/733-2556, $5-10) is right near the USC campus. They offer a particularly tasty nonmustard sauce based on some old Orangeburg recipes.

Hudson's Smokehouse (4952 Sunset Blvd., 803/356-1070, www.hudsonssmokehouse.com, Mon.-Sat. 10:30 A.M.-9 P.M., Sun. 3-9 P.M., $8-14) is a newer joint, which in the world of barbecue is a strike against them, but they're building a big clientele with the quality of their pulled pork, offered in either South Carolina mustard-based sauce, traditional Southern vinegar-based sauce, or tomato-based sauce.

The best ribs in the Vista are at **Carolina Wings & Rib House** (600 Gervais St., 803/256-8844, www.carolinawings.com, Sun.-Thurs. 11 A.M.-10 P.M., Fri.-Sat. 11 A.M.-11 P.M., $5-20). Along with killer ribs, they offer Carolina-style pork and chicken entrées. A big plus is the extensive beer list.

Classic Southern

Not Columbia's best restaurant, but certainly its best-known, **◖ Yesterday's** (2030 Devine St., 803/799-0196, www.yesterdayssc.com, Sun.-Thurs. 11:30 A.M.-midnight, Fri.-Sat. 11:30 A.M.-1 A.M., $6-12), in the heart of Five Points, is as close to a Southern institution as the city offers. Founded in 1976, Yesterday's occupies the distinctive Flatiron Building-shaped structure at the corner of Devine and Harden Streets and was singularly instrumental in the revival of the Five Points area. This simple, always-crowded diner has a menu perfect for a Southern game-day meal for the whole family: "Confederate fried" steak, special-recipe fried chicken, fried catfish, and, of course, the signature meatloaf. Yes, meatloaf. They also have all kinds of sandwiches, including wraps, burgers, clubs, and southwestern chicken.

What the heck is a **Lizard's Thicket** (818 Elmwood Ave., 803/779-6407, www.lizardsthicket.com, daily 6-10 A.M., $7-15)? It's a very popular local chain featuring Southern meat-and-three home cooking in a relaxed atmosphere. The key location is probably the one downtown near the USC campus, although there are 10 other locations around the Columbia metro area. This is the kind of place where the Sunday special is a pot roast and nearly all the vegetable dishes are seasoned with real pork.

Coffee, Tea, and Sweets

Probably the best cuppa joe in Columbia is at the relatively new **Drip** (729 Saluda Ave., 803/661-9545, www.dripcoffeecolumbia.com, Mon.-Sat. 7 A.M.-6 P.M., Sun. 8 A.M.-6 P.M.) in the heart of Five Points, which, as the name implies, specializes in the hot newish trend of pour-over drip coffee; each individual cup is made in this way. There is also wine and beer, a nice plus.

The popular **Immaculate Consumption** (933 Main St., 803/799-9053, Mon.-Fri. 8 A.M.-7 P.M.) near the State House isn't a peaceful oasis but more of a community

© JIM MOREKIS

Drip, in the heart of Five Points, offers some of the best coffee in town.

gathering place. The bakery items should be tasted to be believed, and their lunch items are worth checking out for taste as well as for convenience. And in a town better known for sweet tea, the coffee selection is excellent. The only drawback is the short hours.

More like the classic college coffeehouse with long hours to match, **Cool Beans Coffee** (1217 College St., 803/779-4277, Mon.-Fri. 7 A.M.-midnight, Sat.-Sun. 9 A.M.-midnight) hosts an eclectic crowd, all chilling to indie tunes.

A favorite, if quirky, spot in the Vista is **Nonnah's** (930 Gervais St., 803/779-9599, Mon.-Fri. 11:30 A.M.-2 P.M. and 5-10 P.M., Sat. 6 P.M.-midnight), an eatery better known for its bar scene and for its great desserts.

Mediterranean and Middle Eastern

Generally considered one of the best restaurants in Columbia and certainly the most romantic, ◖ **Gervais & Vine** (620A Gervais St., 803/799-8463, www.gervine.com, Mon.-Sat.

4:30 P.M.-close, $8-10) specializes in Spanish-style tapas. An extensive vibrant menu of both hot and cold tapas awaits, including seared pork tenderloin with cucumber-melon salsa and lavender honey, and marinated manchego cheese with thyme and garlic. The hot tapas tend to cluster around $8, and the cold tapas are about $5 each. Don't overlook the stone-oven pizza, each under $10, offered in several tasty varieties from the *margherita* to the Greek, or you can design your own. Keep in mind that reservations are not accepted. The wine list, as you'd expect, is quite impressive, with over 40 varieties offered by the glass. Each year on the third Thursday in November, Gervais & Vine celebrates the release of the newest Beaujolais with a huge party.

Columbia's premier Italian restaurant is **Ristorante Divino** (803 Gervais St., 803/799-4550, www.ristorantedivino.com, Mon.-Sat. 6-10 P.M., $20-30), which concentrates on northern Italian cuisine and specializes in an extensive wine list. While it doesn't stack up to even a middle-of-the-road Italian place in New York or Boston, Ristorante Divino will do just fine for the Deep South.

If you're in Five Points and have a hankering for a pizza and a pitcher, go no farther than the **Village Idiot** (2009 Devine St., 803/252-8646, www.villageidiotpizza.com, Mon. 4 P.M.-midnight, Tues.-Fri. 4 P.M.-2 A.M., Sat. 11:30 A.M.-2 A.M., Sun. 11:30 A.M.-midnight, $10-15). They have an awe-inspiring menu of specialty pizzas, available half-and-half, including the Rucker (ranch sauce topped with chicken and bacon) in honor of Hootie & the Blowfish lead singer Darius Rucker. Or you can just build your own pie or slice.

Mexican

For a quick, fun, and tasty south-of-the-border bite in the Vista, try **Monterrey Restaurante** (931 Senate St., 803/765-1465, Mon.-Thurs. 11 A.M.-10 P.M., Fri. 11 A.M.-11 P.M., Sat.-Sun. 11:30 A.M.-10 P.M., $8-14), the best Mexican place in Columbia. It's the usual salsa-and-cerveza vibe, but the entrées are lighter and tastier than most Mexican joints.

New Southern

A longtime favorite with locals, visitors, and the college crowd alike, the **Blue Marlin** (1200 Lincoln St., 803/799-3838, www.bluemarlin-columbia.com, lunch Mon.-Fri. 11:30 A.M.-2:30 P.M., dinner Mon.-Thurs. 5-10 P.M., Fri. 5-11 P.M., Sat. 4-11 P.M., Sun. 11:30 A.M.-9 P.M., $16-25) in the Vista is known for its mix of Lowcountry and New Orleans-style entrées, like the oyster and shrimp Bienville, seafood gumbo, and shrimp and grits. You might also want to go for any of their delectable fried takes, such as the Blue Marlin sampler of crispy flounder, crab cakes, and shrimp. In a unique and delicious touch, each table gets a community-style bowl of collard greens.

My favorite restaurant in Five Points is

Goatfeathers (2107 Devine St., 803/256-3325, Mon.-Sat. 5:30-10 P.M., $10-22). This dark, stylish place has acquired a reputation as something of a hipster hangout, but the food is incredible. Look to the specials board, where you will find treats like delectable bacon and scallops or a unique take on salmon. Even the Goatfeathers burger, one of the best I've had anywhere, will do fine in a pinch. Don't forget to save room for one of the signature desserts, themselves a famous local draw. Another big plus is the good wine list and the altogether excellent beer list. The bar stays open until 2 A.M. on weekends.

Possibly the most unique fine-dining spot in Columbia—as well as the oldest in the Vista—is **Motor Supply Company Bistro** (920 Gervais St., 803/256-6687, lunch Tues.-Sat. 11:30 A.M.-2:30 P.M., Sun. 11:30 A.M.-3 P.M., dinner Tues.-Thurs. 6-10 P.M., Fri.-Sat. 6-11 P.M., Sun. 6-9 P.M., $17-27). Because the menu changes as often as twice daily, it's hard to pin down specifics. You might get a succulent pork-chop dish, a pan-roasted tenderloin, or an adventurous truffle-scented egg pasta tossed with mushrooms and garlic. The wine list is commonly considered the best in town.

Vegetarian

The premier vegan and vegetarian spot in Columbia is **Blue Cactus Café** (2002 Greene St., 803/929-0782, Tues.-Fri. 11 A.M.-3 P.M. and 5-9 P.M., Sat. noon-9 P.M., $7-10). While the veggie burrito is to die for, carnivores will be pleased at the various spicy meat dishes offered, especially in Southwestern and Korean—yes, Korean—cuisine. This is the kind of place where the service is as slow as it is friendly, so consider it a lifestyle decision rather than a quick stop.

INFORMATION AND SERVICES
Visitors Centers

The main visitors center in the area is the **Columbia Regional Visitors Center** (1101 Lincoln St., 803/545-0000, Mon.-Fri.

8 A.M.-6 P.M., Sat. 10 A.M.-4 P.M., Sun. 1-5 P.M., www.columbiacvb.com) on the upper floor of the Convention Center in the Vista. The Lake Murray area has its own, the **Capital City/Lake Murray Country Visitors Center** (2184 North Lake Dr., Irmo, 800/725-3935, www.scjewel.com, Mon.-Fri. 9 A.M.-5 P.M., Sat. 10 A.M.-4 P.M., Sun. 1-5 P.M.), northwest of town near the lake. The university runs an excellent visitors center as well, the **University of South Carolina Visitors Center** (816 Bull St., 803/777-0169, www.sc.edu/visitor, Mon.-Fri. 8:30 A.M.-5 P.M., Sat. 11 A.M.-3 P.M.) in the historic McKissick Museum at the USC Horseshoe. Visitor parking is available at the corner of Pendleton and Bull Streets.

Hospitals and Police
The main hospital is **Palmetto Health Baptist Columbia** (Taylor St. and Marion St., 803/296-5010, www.palmettohealth.org), one of the best in the Southeast. The Columbia metro area is served by the **Columbia Police Department** (803/545-3500, www.columbiapd.com).

Media
The newspaper of record in Columbia is also South Carolina's main paper, *The State* (www.thestate.com). The free independent weekly, a great source of music and entertainment news, is the *Columbia Free Times* (www.free-times.com), which comes out on Wednesday.

Services
The main **U.S. Post Office** (1601 Assembly St. 800/275-8777, Mon.-Fri. 7:30 A.M.-6 P.M.) is downtown. There's also a Five Points location (2108 Greene St., 800/275-8777, Mon.-Fri. 8:30 A.M.-5 P.M.).

The main branch of the **Richland County Public Library** (1431 Assembly St., 803/799-9084, www.richland.lib.sc.us, Mon.-Thurs. 9 A.M.-9 P.M., Fri.-Sat. 9 A.M.-6 P.M., Sun. 2-6 P.M.) is at the corner of Assembly and Hampton Streets downtown. The **South Caroliniana Library** (910 Sumter St., 803/777-3131, www.sc.edu, Mon.-Fri. 8:30 A.M.-5 P.M., Sat. 9 A.M.-1 P.M., free) in the USC Horseshoe is oldest freestanding college library in the United States, boasting a large collection of local and regional documents, archives, and books. The main USC library is the **Thomas Cooper Library** (Blossom St. and Sumter St., 803/777-3142, www.sc.edu/library, Mon.-Thurs. 7:30 A.M.-11 P.M., Fri. 7:30 A.M.-7 P.M., Sat. 10 A.M.-7 P.M., Sun. 10 A.M.-11 P.M.), where visitors are welcome.

GETTING THERE
Columbia is served by **Columbia Metropolitan Airport** (CAE, 3000 Aviation Way, www.columbiaairport.com), southwest of town, which hosts American, Delta, United, and US Airways.

If you're driving, three interstate highways—I-20, I-26, and I-77—intersect with each other near the city. Signage is plentiful and accurate from all three.

Amtrak (850 Pulaski St., 803/252-8246 or 800/872-7245, www.amtrak.com) has a station downtown with daily New York-Miami *Silver Star* trains. There's a **Greyhound** bus station (2015 Gervais St., 803/256-6465, www.greyhound.com, daily 24 hours) downtown as well.

GETTING AROUND
The airport has numerous **rental car** kiosks, including Alamo, Avis, Budget, Hertz, and Thrifty. In town you'll find an abundance of Enterprise (www.enterprise.com) locations; several Hertz locations, including one downtown (508 Gervais St., 803/252-2561, www.hertz.com); and a Budget location downtown (408 Blossom St., 803/779-3707, www.budget.com).

The **Central Midlands Regional Transit Authority** (803/255-7100, www.gocmrta.com) is the city's public transportation system. Buses run throughout the area, including a full schedule of downtown routes. Single trips are $1.50, or you can purchase a 10-ride pass for $10.

COLUMBIA

There are plenty of taxi services in Columbia, with **Checker Yellow Cab** (1715 12th St., 803/799-3311) and **Carlton's Discount Taxi Service** (803/381-6222) two good bets.

While Columbia is easy to navigate, parking remains an issue most times of year, with summer a notable exception. Metered parking is available, of course, but it's competitive. A welcome addition is the 675-car **Lincoln Street Parking Garage** (Washington St. and Lincoln St.) in the Vista. Other downtown garages that offer hourly rates include **Lady Street Garage** (1100 Lady St.), **Park Street Garage** (1007 Park St.), and the **Sumter Street Garage** (1400 Sumter St.). All offer rates of about $1 per hour, $10 per full day.

Outside Columbia

◀ CONGAREE NATIONAL PARK

There's literally nothing like it on the planet. Set on a pristine tract of land close to Columbia's sprawl but seemingly a galaxy away, Congaree National Park (100 National Park Rd., 803/776-4396, www.nps.gov/cosw, daily dawn-dusk, free) contains the most ancient stands of old-growth cypress left in the world. It is, quite simply, one of my favorite places. And like many truly great experiences, it's free.

Adjacent to the **Harry Hampton Visitor Center** (daily 8:30 A.M.-5 P.M.), which has a great gift shop in addition to good educational exhibits, you'll embark on a system of elevated boardwalks and trails, 20 miles in total, that takes you into and through a good portion of Congaree's 22,000 acres. A well-done self-guided tour brochure explains the fascinating aspects of this unique environment, almost unknown today.

You'll see cypresses towering over 130 feet into the air (Congaree is said to have the tallest forest canopy on earth, taller than the boreal forests of Canada and the Himalayas). At ground level you'll see hundreds of cypress "knees," parts of their root system that jut above ground. You'll see unbelievably massive loblolly pines—a larger, immeasurably grander species than the sad slash pine tree farms that took over much of the South's available acreage with the arrival of the big paper plants in the 1930s.

You'll have the rare experience of seeing what an old-growth forest actually looks like and why it's so peaceful: Because the canopy shuts off so much light, there is almost no understory. You can walk among the great trees as if you were in a scene from *Lord of the Rings*. You'll view gorgeous Weston Lake, actually an oxbow lake that was once part of the Congaree River, isolated as the river changed course over time. You'll see—and much more often, hear—a wide range of wildlife, including owls, waterfowl, and several species of woodpecker, including the rare red-cockaded woodpecker.

You can kayak the Cedar Creek, or take one of the free guided canoe tours every Saturday and Sunday, with canoes provided. And serious hikers will enjoy the expansive series of trails that go even deeper into the wilderness than the standard boardwalk loop (sorry, pedal-pushers—no bikes are allowed on the trails or boardwalks). As you experience the park—its name was recently changed from Congaree National Swamp—take in some deep breaths. Notice the crisp, clean smell—really more a *lack* of smell. You definitely get the sense of stepping back in time, and you might find yourself expecting to see a pterodactyl circling overhead.

As awesome as Congaree National Park is, I don't recommend a visit in the depth of the Carolina summer. Fall is my favorite time to visit—the air is crisp, and the foliage is stunning. While the park generally closes at 5 P.M., occasionally it stays open later for various special ranger programs; call or consult the website for more info. If you're really into it, you can even primitive camp here for free; get a permit from the Visitor Center.

CAMDEN

Founded in 1733 and South Carolina's oldest inland city, Camden is considered by marketing types to be a part of the state's so-called Old English District of the Upstate. The truth is that it's physically much closer to Columbia, about 30 minutes' drive, and more in tune with the Columbia area both in economy and in spirit.

Camden's attractive and practical geographic location on the Wateree River also got the notice of Native Americans. The town's main drag, Broad Street, is actually on the route of the old Catawba trading path. Archaeologists now think the great and influential Creek town of Cofitachequi, which gained fame for its contact with Spanish explorer Hernando De Soto, was headquartered nearby.

Two key redcoat-versus-Tory engagements happened nearby as well, both defeats: the battles of Camden and Hobkirk's Hill. The Civil War saw little action here, other than as a hospital area for wounded troops. Most notably, it was the home of Mary Boykin Chesnut, famed Civil War diarist.

Camden's resurgence came in the late 1800s, when it became home to a series of wealthy Northerners who brought their wealth and their love of horses to town. To this day Camden is a major equestrian center, nicknamed the "Steeplechase Capital of the World."

Camden's most famous native son is Bernard Baruch, wealthy investment banker of the 1920s and adviser to presidents Woodrow Wilson and Franklin Roosevelt. His boyhood home is long gone, but a marker on Broad Street records its location.

Historic Camden Revolutionary War Site

Unlike most historic battlefields in the state, the Historic Camden Revolutionary War Site (803/432-9841, www.historic-camden.net, Tues.-Sat. 10 A.M.-5 P.M., Sun. 2-5 P.M., free) commemorates a British victory. In this "Empire Strikes Back" scenario, American general Horatio Gates, hero of the Battle of Saratoga, and his combined force of Continental troops and untrained militia met a large British force from Charleston under the command of Lord Cornwallis, better known to history for surrendering to George Washington at Yorktown several years later.

Cornwallis had the last laugh this August day in 1780, however. When the overconfident American troops attacked at daybreak, his redcoat veterans counterattacked with a bayonet charge. Gates's militia panicked and fled the field of battle, some without firing a shot. Gates accompanied his men on their ignominious flight, during which at least 1,000 were killed. Because of the scale and circumstances of the rout, Camden was the worst American defeat of the Revolutionary War.

Despite the unhappy ending for the home team, there is a lot to see, although much of it fairly low-key. The 107-acre "outdoor museum" includes the town site of Camden, the oldest inland city in South Carolina. Sprinkled around the grounds are a variety of restored historic buildings, such as the 1785 John Craven House, the 1830 Cunningham House, and the grand Joseph Kershaw mansion, which served as Lord Cornwallis's headquarters. There's also a 0.5-mile nature trail.

One caveat: This is not the actual battle site, which is several miles away and largely uninterpreted. This site is meant to provide background and flavor rather than an up-close look at the fighting. To get to the actual battlefield, go north from Historic Camden about seven miles on U.S. 521, then take a left onto Flat Rock Road. The marker commemorating the battle is about two miles up on the right.

You can choose self-guided tours or an

assortment of guided tours, such as the full guided tour (Tues.-Fri. 10:30 A.M. and 3 P.M., Sat. 10:30 A.M. and 1:30 P.M., Sun. 2:30-4 P.M., $5 adults, $3 ages 6-17, free under age 6), including a tour of the Kershaw-Cornwallis headquarters mansion, the main historic building at the site.

Although the battle was fought in the heat of a Carolina summer, the first weekend in November (Sat.-Sun. 10 A.M.-5 P.M.) you can experience a full-on black-powder reenactment of the battle near the Kershaw-Cornwallis House in more pleasant temperatures.

Camden Historic District

A short drive north from the Revolutionary War site, the small and tidy downtown area hosts over 60 antebellum structures. It has seen more vibrant days, but there are a number of key historic buildings. Your first stop should be the **Robert Mills Courthouse** (Mon.-Fri. 9 A.M.-5 P.M., Sat. 11 A.M.-4 P.M., Sun. 1:30-5 P.M., free), fully restored to its original 1845 state as designed by the great Robert Mills, and now the home of the **Kershaw County Chamber of Commerce and Visitors Center** (800/968-4037, www.camden-sc.org). Get a brochure for a self-guided walking tour of downtown, and enjoy the handiwork of Mills, architect of the Washington Monument and protégé of Thomas Jefferson.

The stately **Camden Archives and Museum** (1314 Broad St., 803/425-6050, Mon.-Fri. 8 A.M.-5 P.M., Sat. 10 A.M.-4 P.M., first Sun. of the month 1-5 P.M., free), housed in a former Carnegie Library built in 1915, is a great way to soak in the details of local history. One of the coolest artifacts is the De Saussure Weather Book, containing some of the oldest known meteorological records in the state. The South Carolina Daughters of the American Revolution are based in the building, and the South Carolina Society of Colonial Dames has its genealogical libraries here.

Another notable building is the restored

Bonds Conway House (811 Fair St.), an 1812 structure that was once the home of the eponymous Mr. Conway and family, the first African Americans in town to purchase their freedom. This well-restored vernacular cottage, with extensive heart-pine interiors, now houses the **Kershaw County Historical Society** (803/425-1123, Thurs. 1-5 P.M., free).

The very symbol of Camden is on top of the circa-1886 **Opera House Tower** (Broad St. and Rutledge St.). Now a private storefront, the Opera House is topped by a large weathervane depicting King Haiglar, a local Catawba chief who befriended early settlers to the area.

Still in use today, the **Quaker Cemetery** (700 Meeting St., 803/432-4356, daily 8 A.M.-6 P.M.) only contains a few actual Quaker graves, with no headstones and recognized only by the distinctive brick arch (Quakers frown on monuments). Here you'll find the final resting place of several historical figures, most notably Abraham Lincoln's brother-in-law, George Rogers Clark Todd. Find the Neil Smith monument and note the scars; these are bullet marks made by Henry Nixon as he prepared for a duel with Thomas Hopkins (Nixon lost, and he's actually buried nearby). But the most poignant graves here are much younger—the triple plots of the Roberts brothers, all killed in the line of duty in World War II.

Adjoining the Quaker Cemetery are two other small burial grounds, the Beth El and Old Presbyterian cemeteries.

Springdale Race Course

Northwest of town is the nearly 100-year-old Springdale Race Course (200 Knights Hills Rd., 803/432-6513), which also hosts the town's two biggest steeplechase events. At the entrance to the track you'll find the **National Steeplechase Museum** (803/432-6513, www.nationalsteeplechasemuseum.org, Sept.-May Wed.-Sat. 10 A.M.-4 P.M., other times by appointment, free), containing a well-managed

Camden's National Steeplechase Museum

© JIM MOREKIS

and exhaustive collection of vintage photos, artifacts, trophies, racing colors, and archival records detailing the rich history of steeplechase in the United States, with a focus on South Carolina's key role in that equestrian genre.

Get to Springdale Race Course by taking U.S. 521 (Broad St.) north through Camden, and then turn left onto Knights Hill Road. The track is a little way up on the right.

EVENTS

The key events in Camden are three important equestrian events at the Springdale Race Course. The **Carolina Cup** (www.carolina-cup.org, $30-45) steeplechase happens on a Saturday in late March and brings almost 70,000 attendees to the events. The smaller **Colonial Cup** (www.carolina-cup.org, $20-25) steeplechase takes place on a Sunday in mid-November. The events are a lot of fun, with tailgating and beautiful spring and fall fashions, not to mention the great equestrian action

on the track. (Gambling on any horse sport is illegal in South Carolina.) While prime parking spots at Springdale go for $200 and up, there is $10 general admission parking available.

The third major equestrian event involves polo, specifically the **Camden Polo Cup** (803/425-7676, adults $10, children $5) the first weekend in May, which raises funds for the Fine Arts Center downtown. As home of the second-oldest polo track in the country, Camden takes its polo seriously. But this Sunday event is a hoot, and if you can't make it to the polo matches over in Aiken, this is a great substitute.

Shopping

Camden is known far and wide as one of South Carolina's premier antiques towns. Head straight to the **Camden Antique and Arts District** (803/432-2525) downtown to find about two dozen shops, all in close proximity and all with a very keen and serious eye. Keep in mind many shops are closed on Sunday. Key purveyors are **Andries Van Dam Investment Art and Antiques** (914 Market St., 803/432-0850, Thurs.-Sat. 10 A.M.-5:30 P.M.), **Camden Antiques Market** (830 S. Broad St., 803/432-0818, daily 10 A.M.-6 P.M.), **Heritage Antique Mall** (113 E. DeKalb St., 803/425-4191, Tues.-Sat. 10 A.M.-6 P.M., Sun. 1-6 P.M.), and **Springdale Antiques** (951 Broad St., 803/432-0312).

Some artist and artisan galleries within the downtown area worth checking out are the **Fine Arts Center of Kershaw County** (810 Lyttleton St., 803/425-7676, Mon.-Fri. 10 A.M.-5 P.M.), a three-building complex featuring exhibits and performance space; **Philip's Woodworks** (621 Rutledge St., 803/432-5454); **The Potter's Hand** (938 Broad St., 803/424-1120); and **Olde Gin Woodworks** (909 Market St., 803/432-5678).

Sports and Recreation

Paddlers in particular will enjoy **Goodale**

COLUMBIA

State Park (650 Park Rd., 803/432-2772, www.southcarolinaparks.com, Fri.-Sun. 9 A.M.-6 P.M., free) a little way northeast of Camden. The only drawback is the curtailed days of operation. A Civil War-era millpond combines with a nice cypress ecosystem. There's a marked three-mile canoe-kayak trail through the cypress swamp, which includes a pass by a great heron rookery. You can rent a canoe ($12 per day).

Accommodations and Food

If all you're looking for is a clean and well-run chain hotel, take exit 98 off I-20 and look for the **Comfort Inn and Suites** (220 Wall St., 803/425-1010, www.comfortinn.com, $95) or the **Holiday Inn Express** (419 Sumter Hwy., 803/424-5000, www.hiexpress.com, $105) next door.

There are several great B&Bs in town, chief among them the outstanding **Bloomsbury Inn** (1707 Lyttleton St., 803/432-5858, www.bloomsburyinn.com, $150-180), widely rated one of the best in the United States. The owners, Bruce and Katherine Brown, were voted Innkeepers of the Year in 2008. Both retired Air Force colonels, they run the Bloomsbury with a mixture of genuine Southern hospitality and military-style attention to detail. The 1849 property itself is of great historical importance as the onetime home of James and Mary Chesnut, he a Confederate general and she a famous wartime diarist. While the interior furnishings in the public areas and in the four guest rooms are all you'd expect and then some, the two-acre grounds are gorgeous as well, with a full range of evocative Southern flora.

Another great stay is the **Camden House** (1502 Broad St., 803/713-1013, www.camden-house.us, $110-150) with four spacious guest rooms. As you'd expect from a horsey, antiquey town like Camden, the furnishings are sumptuous and immaculately tasteful within this fairly rare example of an "in-town" plantation house.

The best-regarded eating spot in the Camden area is actually a short drive outside Camden in Boykin, a historic little hamlet just south of town on U.S. 521, past I-20. **The Mill Pond Steakhouse** (84 Boykin Mill Rd., 803/424-0261, www.themillpondsteakhouse.com, Tues.-Sat. 5-10 P.M., $20-40) serves awesome high-end connoisseur-style steaks and Southern classics like crab cakes and shrimp and grits. The restaurant offers a scenic view of Mill Pond, an impounded body of water that saw intensive action during the Civil War. In fact, seated in the dining room, you're roughly in the center of the Confederate line, which failed in its bid to hold back Union troops that included members of the famous 54th Massachusetts Volunteers, the African American unit chronicled in the movie *Glory*.

NEWBERRY

In some ways the very model of the picturesque South Carolina "Main Street" town, Newberry has prospered while many similar towns in the state have not. This is mostly due to its well-preserved, vibrant downtown, its location right between two fast-growing metro areas (Columbia and Greenville-Spartanburg), and proximity (but not *too* close) to I-26.

Its original settlers were the typical Midlands mix of Scots-Irish and German settlers who came in the late 1700s. By the mid-1800s Newberry had become a major rail center for the shipment of cotton. Historic Newberry College was built in 1856 and served as a hospital for Union and Confederate troops during the Civil War. Reconstruction brought a particularly unsettled vibe to the city, at the time a hotbed of Ku Klux Klan activity—though you'd certainly never know it today, other than perhaps the frieze on the courthouse, showing a mean-looking American eagle uprooting a South Carolina palmetto tree.

Consistently voted one of the best small towns in the United States to live in, Newberry is the kind of place where nice, quiet B&Bs

are a short walk from downtown, most everyone is polite and helpful, and the pace is slow but standards are still high. A good first stop is the **Newberry Visitors Center** (1109 Main St., 803/276-4274, www.newberrycounty.org, Mon.-Fri. 9 A.M.-5 P.M., Sat. 10 A.M.-2 P.M.), located in the historic Public Lounge where women and children would gather in the early 1900s while the menfolk did their important man-type business on Main Street.

While in downtown Newberry, architectural enthusiasts will want to closely examine some of the buildings. Cornices, windows, and doors often boast nice examples of corbeled brick. A particularly unusual feature is the prevalence of pressed tin decorations on facades, and in some cases in the interiors.

◀ Newberry Opera House

The best-known sight in town, bordering on the iconic, is the Newberry Opera House (1201 McKibben St., 803/276-6264, www.newberryoperahouse.com). Built at the height of the Victorian era in 1882 for $30,000, this impressive French Gothic structure underwent an extensive multimillion-dollar renovation in the mid-1990s.

During its heyday, the stage was lit by extensive gaslights and hosted the country's best singers and actors in traveling road shows. In the early years of the 20th century it began hosting silent-film screenings. A showing of a Thomas Edison "talkie" turned out to be a precursor of sorts, and by the 1920s the Opera House was remodeled as a full-on movie theater.

But as with so many things, the postwar era brought change. The Opera House hosted its last movie, *The Outlaw,* in 1952. In a story from the 1950s and 1960s so familiar to so many older Southern cities, the Opera House was saved from imminent demolition by a grassroots conservation effort. Now owned and operated by the city of Newberry, this 426-seat venue is fully restored and equipped for a more modern entertainment age.

So is opera actually performed in the Opera House? Yes, courtesy of the South Carolina Opera Company, the Asheville Lyric Opera, and various traveling companies. They combine to put on a short annual season of classics (about $40 per performance), featuring light opera chestnuts such as *The Pirates of Penzance* and heavy-duty productions like *La Bohème*. That's not all—the Opera House hosts a very full, almost hectic schedule of performances and concerts throughout the year. Locals come, to be sure, but the Opera House is a draw all over the Midlands.

Newberry College

Just north of downtown you'll find the scenic 90-acre campus of Newberry College (2100 College St., 803/276-5010, www.newberry.edu). Founded in 1828, today this Lutheran-affiliated college hosts about 900 students on its calming grounds, which center on the abundantly landscaped quadrangle, a legacy of the school's founder, the Reverend John Bachman, amateur naturalist and close friend of the great John James Audubon.

There's an ornate copy of the Book of Kells in the special collections room of the **Wessels Library** just off the quad. A short walk to the other side of the quad is the **Wiles Chapel,** with its beautiful stained-glass windows.

A sore topic in Newberry involves the college, specifically the forced retirement in 2008 of its sports teams' moniker, "Indians." Under pressure from a new policy of the National Collegiate Athletic Association (NCAA), Newberry appealed, saying that its team name did not flout the directive against "hostile and abusive" imagery. While the NCAA allowed larger and wealthier schools such as Florida State University (the Seminoles) and the University of Illinois (the Fighting Illini) to keep their Native American-inspired names, it denied Newberry's appeal and threatened sanctions if it did not comply. In true South

Carolina tradition, the school originally intended to defy the NCAA ruling and continue calling its teams "Indians." However, they've since relented, and even the local Indian Club of boosters is now simply the Athletic Club, while the erstwhile mascot of the sports teams, for the time being, is simply a large N.

While there are surely two sides to every story, the stigma of racial insensitivity is ironic considering that Newberry College's founder, the Reverend Bachman, was one of the first Southern pastors to argue against slavery. Each spring the college hosts the **John Bachman Symposium** (www.johnbachman.org, free) to celebrate his life and writings.

Other Sights

South Carolina is an orchid-crazy state, with growers and connoisseurs sprinkled throughout. Perhaps the leading purveyor is **Carter & Holmes Orchids** (629 Mendenhall Rd., 803/276-0579, www.carterandholmes.com, Mon.-Sat. 9 A.M.-5 P.M.) a few miles south of Newberry, which began as a corsage dealer after World War II. Today, you can tour the 18 greenhouses and admire the many orchids. And yes, they'll ship directly to you.

If wine is more your thing, head about four miles outside town just off Highway 34 and visit the **Enoree River Vineyard** (1650 Dusty Rd., 803/276-2855, www.enoreeriverwinery.com, Tues.-Sat. 10 A.M.-6 P.M.), opened in 2006 by Richard and Laura LaBarre. You can tour the grounds, purchase gourmet goods and wine made from their homegrown muscadine grapes, and of course, sample the wares.

To learn more about area history, visit the **Newberry County Historical Museum** (1503 Nance St., www.newberrycountyhistory.com, 1st and 3rd Sat. of the month 1-4 P.M., donation) within the circa 1820 E.S. Coppock House.

Shopping

Like Camden, Newberry is big on antiques.

The main drag for antiquing in Newberry is, fittingly, Main Street, where you'll find the densely appointed **Newberry Antiques Mall** (1530 Main St., 803/321-5800) and the excellent **As Time Goes By** (1300 Main St., 803/276-4715). You'll also find **Eurolux Antiques** (1409 Main St., 803/276-4001), which focuses on continental pieces, **Shop Around the Corner** (1510 Main St., 803/321-0596), which also has thrift items, and **Nichols Studio** (1311 Main St., 803/321-0080), which deals in vintage photos.

Sports and Recreation

The 276-acre **Lynch's Woods Park** (803/276-0032, daily dawn-dusk, free), just on the outskirts of town, has plenty of wooded trails for hiking, bicycling, and horseback riding. Part of the statewide **Palmetto Trail** (www.palmettotrail.org) goes through here. Get to the park from downtown Newberry by taking Main Street east to U.S. 76 (Wilson Rd.). Look for the sign on your left. From I-26, take exit 74 and head west on Highway 34 for two miles. Take a left onto U.S. 76 and look for the sign.

Accommodations and Food

Sadly, Newberry's once impressive collection of B&Bs has pretty much all closed. But for good chain accommodations in an unbeatable location, try the **Hampton Inn Newberry-Opera House** (1201 Nance St., 803/276-6666, $110) right across the street from, yes, the Opera House.

The best-regarded restaurant downtown is **Delamater's** (1117 Boyce St., 803/276-3555, www.delamaters.com, Mon.-Sat. 11:30 A.M.-2 P.M. and 5-10 P.M., $10-20), a short jaunt from the Opera House. It offers a tasty line of gourmet "dinner sandwiches" as well as classics like shrimp and grits.

Just around the corner, the most hopping nightspot downtown is **The Storm Cellar** (1215 Boyce St., 803/405-0000, www.thecabanainc.com), a wine and cigar bar downstairs from the **Cabana Restaurant** (www.thecabanainc.com, lunch Tues.-Fri. 11 A.M.-3:30 P.M., dinner Tues.-Sat. 5-11 P.M., $10-25).

SUMTER

While only incorporated in 1845, the Sumter area was settled and farmed as far back as the 1740s. It is named for General Thomas Sumter, a.k.a. "The Fighting Gamecock," one of several guerrilla leaders that fought the British during the American Revolution. Born in Virginia, Sumter founded the nearby town of Statesburg in the 1760s. Legend has it that he became an implacable foe of the British when a party of redcoats plundered his home and forced his invalid wife to watch it burn to the ground.

For a long time largely dependent on nearby Shaw Air Force Base, Sumter is a quiet and growing city about 45 miles east of Columbia that's gradually turning to retirees and tourism to diversify its economy. Public policy geeks might be interested to know that in 1912, Sumter was the first city in the United States to adopt the council-manager form of government in which an appointed professional city manager runs day-to-day operations.

Sights

For such a relatively large city—the eighth largest in the state—there are comparatively few sights. The main attraction in Sumter by far is **Swan Lake Iris Gardens** (822 W. Liberty St., 803/436-2640, www.sumter-sc.com, daily 7:30 A.M.-dusk, free), begun in 1927 as the labor of love of regional business titan and amateur botanist Hamilton Carr Bland. Legend has it that Bland's initial iris planting failed so badly that, out of frustration, he told his gardener to dump the bulbs in the nearby blackwater lake. The irises then bloomed on their own with no trouble, resulting in the first inkling of the magnificent displays you see today. A trail runs around the lake, while a boardwalk leads 1,000 feet into the surrounding swamp. The

best time to come is May-June, when the irises are in bloom. Around the last weekend in May is the **Iris Festival,** a four-day event. December 1 marks the month-long "Fantasy of Lights," in which the grounds are lit with—no joke—about one million Christmas lights.

The 150-acre grounds also host eight species of swans, the only public site in the country to host every indigenous species (for the record, they are: royal white mutes, black-necked swans, Coscorobas, whoopers, trumpeters, black Australians, whistlers, and Bewick's swans). You can feed them bread and crackers, but I recommend keeping your distance during mating season (early spring). If you want to feed yourself, go to the **Iris Market** (Thurs.-Fri. 11 A.M.-2 P.M., Sat. noon-5 P.M., Sun. 1-5 P.M.) on-site.

The center of civic and cultural life in town is the **Sumter Opera House** (21 N. Main St., 803/436-2640), which in addition to hosting multiple performances also hosts city hall. There's a regular schedule of Friday night events at the Opera House throughout the month, including films and live performances, all reasonably priced.

Accommodations and Food

For its not inconsiderable size, Sumter has a dearth of quality accommodations and food. Try the **Hampton Inn Sumter** (1370 Broad St., 803/469-2222, www.hamptoninn.com, $99). To cool off with a cone or other treat, try the favorite downtown institution **Dairy Cream** (267 Broad St., 803/775-1908, Mon.-Thurs. 10:30 A.M.-10 P.M., Fri.-Sat. 10:30 A.M.-10:30 P.M., Sun. noon-10:30 P.M.). Another longtime favorite is the nostalgia-tinged **Pizza Lane** (460 Broad St., 803/773-4351, www.pizzalane.com, Mon.-Thurs. 11 A.M.-9 P.M., Fri.-Sun. 11 A.M.-10 P.M., $10), known for its pizza buffet.

POINSETT STATE PARK

One of the more expansive Civilian Conservation Corps-built state parks, Poinsett

State Park (6660 Poinsett Park Rd., 803/494-8177, www.southcarolinaparks.com, daily 9 A.M.-9 P.M., free) is known for its particular appeal to hikers. The extensive system of in-park foot, bike, and horse trails link up with the Palmetto Trail (www.palmettoconservation.org), which goes on into the adjacent Manchester State Forest.

Because of its key location where the Midlands sand hills meet the coastal plain, the topography is unusually interesting for this usually flat area. Wildflower displays in May are particularly nice. The 10-acre lake has a coquina bathhouse from the 1930s, and you can rent a boat to do some angling.

There are 24 campsites with water and electricity ($12), and 26 designated tent sites with just water ($9). For a decidedly plusher stay, there are five fully furnished cabins ($45-100) complete with fireplaces.

INFORMATION AND SERVICES
Visitors Centers

Congaree National Park has the excellent **Harry Hampton Visitor Center** (daily 8:30 A.M.-5 P.M.), which has extensive educational exhibits. In Camden, the old courthouse downtown hosts the **Kershaw County Chamber of Commerce and Visitors Center** (607 S. Broad St., 800/968-4037, www.camden-sc.org, Mon.-Fri. 9 A.M.-5 P.M., Sat. 11 A.M.-4 P.M., Sun. 1:30-5 P.M.), where you can get brochures and information on self-guided walking tours. In Newberry, check out the **Newberry Visitors Center** (1109 Main St., 803/276-4274, www.newberrycounty.org, Mon.-Fri. 9 A.M.-5 P.M., Sat. 10 A.M.-2 P.M.) downtown. In Sumter, visit the **Sumter Convention and Visitors Bureau** (822 W. Liberty St., 803/436-2640, www.sumtertourism.com, Mon.-Fri. 8:30 A.M.-5 P.M.).

Hospitals

While the bigger hospitals are in the larger cities of Columbia and Florence, in Camden you'll find the main branch of the **Kershaw County Medical Center** (1315 Roberts St., 803/432-4311, www.kcmc.org). If you need medical attention in Newberry, there's the **Newberry County Memorial Hospital** (2669 Kinard St., 803/924-8126, www.newberryhospital.org). In Sumter, try the **Tuomey Regional Medical Center** (129 N. Washington St., 803/774-9000, www.tuomey.com).

The Pee Dee

Named for the Pee Dee River running through it, this region in the extreme northeast of the state—always called "the Pee Dee," not just "Pee Dee"—is largely off the tourism radar. That's a shame, because it offers a particularly relaxing, rolling landscape and a plethora of charming small towns. The nice homes dotted throughout those towns testify to the Pee Dee's former status as a key cotton and tobacco-growing area, activities aided immensely by the river's ability to conveniently transport goods to market. Although today the Pee Dee is one of the most economically depressed areas of the state, it does have pockets of rapid growth, and cotton fields still line the highways throughout. And, of course, stock car fans can make the pilgrimage to the grandfather of all tracks, Darlington International Raceway.

The region's location near the junction of I-95 and I-20 is both a blessing and a curse for the Pee Dee. The increased traffic has brought development along those routes, but often to the detriment of the pleasant small towns in the surrounding area. I encourage you to use local roads, such as Highway 9 and U.S. 52, whenever possible to get a real feel of the place.

Though Florence is by far the major city in the region—largely due to its location straddling the aforementioned interstates—it has comparatively little to offer. Where possible, stay off the beaten path to explore the region further.

CHERAW AND VICINITY

This beguiling little town on the river is my favorite place in the Pee Dee and one of the Palmetto State's great, but underrated, gems. How gemlike? To tour some of its historic buildings, you simply sign out the keys at the little visitors center. Only in South Carolina, folks.

Primarily known today as the birthplace of jazz great Dizzy Gillespie, it's actually one of the first settlements in the state, dating from the 1730s. Its heyday came in the early 1800s as a central brokerage point for cotton. Because Cheraw—pronounced "chuh-RAW"—sits where the Pee Dee River first becomes navigable, cotton farmers sent their crop here for barge transport down the river to the seaport of Georgetown.

Cheraw played a role in both the American Revolution and the Civil War. The Revolutionary War saw General Nathanael Greene's army encamp nearby, and General Sherman brought a large number of troops here during the Civil War—thankfully with little destruction. Sherman's dirty work was largely done for him by the time he came; an 1835 fire destroyed many buildings in Cheraw, and a wartime powder explosion wrecked the Village Green area.

◖ Cheraw Historic District

To fully enjoy the 213-acre Cheraw Historic District (843/537-8425, www.cheraw.com), remember that there are three basic components: Market Street, the main drag, which includes the Village Green and is mostly Victorian; perpendicular 3rd Street, where the grandest antebellum homes are located; and the Riverside, which includes a historic church and a river walk on the Pee Dee itself.

The **Cheraw Visitors Bureau** (221 Market

St., 843/537-8425, Mon.-Fri. 9 A.M.-5 P.M., www.cheraw.com) inside the Chamber of Commerce building puts out an excellent walking-tour map. Call or go by to get one. You can even make appointments to tour sites on the weekend, but make sure to call ahead.

A natural first stop is the place where Cheraw's favorite son grew up, the **Dizzy Gillespie Home Site Park** (300 block of Huger St., dawn-dusk, free). Get here by taking Huger Street a couple of blocks north of Market Street as you come into town. No building stands here today, just some benches, attractive flowers, and a number of striking modernist sculptures invoking the spirit of jazz. A particularly cool aspect of the park is the chrome fence along Huger Street, illustrating several bars from Gillespie's biggest hit, "Salt Peanuts." (No statue of Dizzy? No worries. There's a nice one a few blocks farther into town.)

Scoot a block north and ease onto McIver Street to see the grand **Powe House** (143 McIver St.), used by General Sherman as headquarters during his occupation. A few doors down is the **Enfield House** (135 McIver St.), headquarters of Union general Oliver Howard.

MARKET STREET

On Market Street you'll find several key structures along the **Village Green.** First is the **Merchant's Bank Building** (232 Market St.), which before the Civil War housed the largest bank in South Carolina outside Charleston; it was the last known bank to honor Confederate money. Next door is the tiny circa-1820 **Lyceum Museum** (843/537-8425, Mon.-Fri. 9 A.M.-5 P.M., free), first a chancery court, then a library, then a telegraph office, and now containing artifacts of local history. Get the keys from the Visitors Bureau (221 Market St.). The building next to the Lyceum is the circa-1858 **Town Hall,** still used as municipal offices.

Directly across the street is the also tiny 1820 **Inglis-McIver Law Office.** This building

COLUMBIA

© JIM MOREKIS

Dizzy Gillespie Home Site Park, in Cheraw

was actually moved here from Front Street in 1948. It once housed the office of John A. Inglis, chairman of the committee that drew up the original South Carolina Ordinance of Secession. Next door is the **Market Hall,** dating from 1837. Once a public market, it's now used for civic functions.

A few yards away in the 200 block of Market Street is a small park with a wonderful Ed Dwight-designed statue of Dizzy Gillespie, complete with trademark upward-bent horn and puffed-out cheeks. If you're really into your Dizzy history, go see the **Wesley United Methodist Church** (307 Greene St.), where he attended services as a child.

3RD STREET

Drive or walk up and down 3rd Street, admiring the stately old homes (all privately owned; don't trespass). Of particular interest is the 1823 **Lafayette House** (235 3rd St.), a two-story affair that hosted the Marquis de Lafayette during his 1825 American tour. Another beauty is **The Teacherage** (230 3rd St.), considered the oldest extant building in Cheraw, built before 1785, with a wing added in the 1840s, and named for its 20th-century role as a teachers' boarding house. The Malloy family entertained Woodrow Wilson's father here in the 1800s.

THE RIVERSIDE

Old St. David's Church (Church St., Mon.-Fri. 9 A.M.-5 P.M., free) is a wonderfully well-preserved example of an elegantly simple Upcountry Episcopal sanctuary. Why "old"? There are no services held here now—the congregation worships at "new" St. David's on Market Street, which is actually still pretty old, considering it was built in 1916. To get to the old church, go east on Market Street until it dead-ends on Front Street; then take a right and then another right onto Church Street. The church was used as a hospital by British and colonial troops during the Revolution. To tour the interior, go by the Visitors Bureau (221 Market St., 843/537-8425) and pick up the keys; it's a good idea to call ahead.

The adjacent graveyard is worth a walk and contains several notable burial sites including that of Moses Rogers, captain of the SS *Savannah,* the first steamship to cross the Atlantic. Also nearby is the **Confederate Monument,** which is distinguished from countless others like it in small towns throughout the South by the fact that it was the very first in existence—so early, in fact, that the original inscription made no mention of Confederate forces so as not to offend the Union troops still occupying Cheraw.

East of the church is the little **Riverside Park** (843/537-8425, daily dawn-dusk, free), where a viewing platform and a short nature trail provide nice views of the peaceful, dark Pee Dee River. This, the first navigable point on the waterway, was once the site of the old Kershaw Ferry and steamboat landing.

Cheraw State Park

The excellent Cheraw State Park (100 State Park Rd., 843/537-9656, www.southcarolinaparks.com, daily 7 A.M.-9 P.M., free), just outside town on U.S. 52, is actually the first state park in South Carolina, established in 1934 by the Works Progress Administration. There's plenty to do: fishing on Lake Juniper, nature walks, camping, and a quite well-regarded 18-hole golf course (843/537-2215) designed by Tom Jackson. You can rent fishing boats ($12 per day) and canoes or kayaks ($15 per day).

Cheraw Fish Hatchery

Farther out of town is the Cheraw Fish Hatchery (U.S. 1, 843/537-7628, Mon.-Fri. 8 A.M.-4 P.M., free), which stocks lakes throughout the region with about two million fish each year. Tour the hatchery itself and stay for a picnic.

Sand Hills State Forest

The vast and unusual Sand Hills State Forest (16218 U.S. 1, 843/498-6478, www.state.sc.us, office daily 8 A.M.-4:30 P.M., free), between the towns of McBee and Patrick, comprises 46,000 acres of recreational opportunities, including hunting, fishing, biking, horseback riding, and bird-watching. The rare red-cockaded woodpecker calls the forest home, and there are a copious variety of fish in the forest's 13 ponds. The eponymous sand hills are vestiges of sand deposits made millions of years ago. They're lovely to look at, but they are infertile, which led the feds to buy the land from hardscrabble farmers in the 1930s.

Most activity here centers on Sugar Loaf Mountain—actually a 100-foot natural sand pile—around which wind numerous hiking trails. Horseback riding on the trails is encouraged, but you need a permit in advance ($5 per day). There are also several campsites ($10-15).

Carolina Sandhills National Wildlife Refuge

Established in 1939, Carolina Sandhills NWR (23734 U.S. 1, 843/335-8401, www.fws.gov/carolinasandhills, daily dawn-dusk, free) is one of the last, best places to find the once-ubiquitous longleaf pine and wiregrass habitat, home of the endangered red-cockaded woodpecker. In eons long past, bison and Florida panthers roamed here as well.

Several well-maintained hiking trails allow you to fully explore and observe this rare ecosystem, and a handful of lakes are available for fishing (state license required). One lake, Lake Bee, bisects the refuge. Two observation towers are available for bird and nature watching, and there's even a dedicated photographer's blind on Martins Lake.

A great way to enjoy the refuge is on bicycle, since there are plenty of bike trails, but keep in mind that bikes are not allowed on the foot trails. Don't be surprised to come across a wild turkey or two, and note that hunting is allowed on the refuge in season.

COLUMBIA

Events

The premier event in Cheraw, as you'd expect, given its favorite son, is the **South Carolina Jazz Festival** (various venues, 843/537-8420, www.scjazzfestival.com, $20 per day). For such a small town, this event attracts a good number of quality performers over its two-day span each autumn. Highlights include a combined jazz and art event on the Town Green and, of course, a concert at the Dizzy Gillespie Home Site Park.

Accommodations and Food

The best place to stay in Cheraw is the **C Spears Guest House** (228 Huger St., 843/537-1097, www.spearsguesthouse.com, $75) off the main drag of Market Street. Kay and Larry Spears are delightful hosts, and their restored B&B, with four small but charming guest rooms, is great for relaxation. The breakfast is self-serve continental from the house's well-equipped kitchen. Interestingly, Larry says they're busiest during the week, which is when business travelers are likely to be passing through Cheraw. This means more room at the inn for the weekend visitor, however, so you may as well take advantage.

If camping's your bag, go straight to the Works Progress Administration-era **Cheraw State Park** (100 State Park Rd., 843/537-9656, www.southcarolinaparks.com, daily 7 A.M.-9 P.M., free) outside town on U.S. 52. There are eight well-equipped one-bedroom rental cabins ($65-82), 17 electric-and-water camping sites ($17), and boat-in backcountry camping ($5) at the landing on Lake Juniper.

For a tasty bite in Cheraw, there's a great Mexican place, **Fiesta Tapatia** (807 Market St., 843/921-0200, daily 11 A.M.-10 P.M., $10). For more typical Southern home cooking—smothered or fried everything—go to **River's Edge** (162 2nd St., 843/537-1109, lunch Mon.-Wed. 11 A.M.-2:30 P.M., Thurs.-Sat. 11 A.M.-2:30 P.M., dinner Thurs.-Sat. 5:30-9:30 P.M., $8-12). Hungry for pizza? Check out **El**

Sherif's (217 2nd St., 843/921-0066, lunch Mon.-Sat. 11 A.M.-2:30 P.M., dinner Mon.-Sat. 5-10 P.M., $6-10), which also has killer subs and a good selection of Greek cuisine.

DARLINGTON

Although little Darlington has been largely subsumed within Florence's sprawl, it still stubbornly retains its own quirky personality. The Darlington Guards infantry were among the first soldiers to volunteer for service in the Civil War and for the Spanish-American War 40 years later.

Legend has it that Darlington was spared Sherman's torch because the officer sent to carry out the deed was an architect in civilian life. Seeing a house he'd designed, he allegedly called the whole thing off.

Though Darlington's cash crop was tobacco for most of the 20th century, cotton has always been part of the local DNA. Plenty of cotton fields still abound in the surrounding area. Its biggest event, though, is the **Sweet Potato Festival** (Public Square downtown, www.visitdarlingtoncounty.org, free) each October.

Darlington Raceway

Celebrating over 60 years of racing, Darlington Raceway (1301 Harry Byrd Hwy./U.S. 52, 843/395-8499, www.darlingtonraceway.com, dates vary, $35-150) is the granddad of all NASCAR tracks, the first ever to host a major race. While it's not as plush as the newer, ritzier raceways built to accommodate the sport's push to gentrify its ranks, this is still an impressive sight right on U.S. 52 and a bit of living history.

Darlington has thus far resisted attempts to marginalize it by the PR-conscious NASCAR, which increasingly prefers that its sport be seen as the province of Northeasterners near major metro areas for whom racing is a mere diversion, rather than a haven for Southerners with racing in their blood but perhaps thinner wallets.

Indeed, racing fans can celebrate the "return"

THE TRACK TOO TOUGH TO TAME

Darlington Raceway, the "track too tough to tame," began as a labor of love by Harold Brasington in 1949, when he bought some peanut and cotton fields and began turning them into a racing oval. Well, almost an oval—a neighbor didn't want his minnow pond disturbed, so what would become Turns 3 and 4 were narrowed, resulting in Darlington's unique egg shape, pinched at one end.

Now coming in at precisely 1.366 miles, "Harold's Folly," as disbelieving locals first called it, is the grandfather track of stock car racing. The first race was on Labor Day 1950, and when an expected crowd of 10,000 turned out instead to number over 25,000, nobody called it a folly anymore. Now seating upward of 65,000, Darlington is a delight for fans and a challenge for drivers, who routinely hit the wall while trying to negotiate its weird geometry at over 200 mph.

Darlington Raceway has faced a threat in the face of NASCAR's continuing attempts to Disney-fy the sport. By holding races in more heavily populated areas near major metro areas, NASCAR has signaled its desire to draw a new generation of more moneyed, more casual fans to the sport—to the detriment of historic tracks like Darlington, set in an economically depressed area of the Deep South far away from any large population center. An extensive series of renovations in 2007 seems to have lifted its stock, however, and while the marquee Southern 500 race is no longer a staple of Labor Day (it's on Mother's Day weekend instead), the granddaddy of them all seems to be alive and kicking.

---

of the NASCAR Sprint Cup Series Southern 500, a beloved Labor Day race that was briefly removed from the Series in 2005-2008. Now held the Saturday before Mother's Day, the huge raceway is filled to the brim, RVs packing the infield, for the Southern 500 and its lead-in race the Friday before, the Diamond Hill Plywood 200. If you're not in town that weekend, you can call ahead for tours (Mon.-Fri., $5 pp). Or for a quick peek, just stop at the security guard's hut at the museum and sign in.

Sharing a parking area with the security guard is the **Darlington Raceway Stock Car Museum** (1301 Harry Byrd Hwy./U.S. 52, 843/395-8862, www.darlingtonraceway.com, Mon.-Fri. 10 A.M.-5 P.M., Sat. 10 A.M.-4 P.M., Sun. 11 A.M.-4 P.M., $5 adults, free under age 13). It has a small but interesting historical collection and, of course, a gift shop.

Pim's Maze

You've heard of crop circles? Pim's Maze (464 Dovesville Hwy., 888/277-7815, www.cornfieldmaze.com, Sept.-Nov. Sat. 10 A.M.-9 P.M., Sun. 2-9 P.M., Wed. 6-8 P.M., $7 adults, $6 children, free under age 4) is an elaborate version made by humans, not aliens. This labyrinth in a local cornfield is a beguiling way to spend an hour or two and let the kids blow off some steam in a natural setting. It's between Darlington and Hartsville on Dovesville Highway, a short stretch joining U.S. 15 and U.S. 52.

FLORENCE AND VICINITY

It's sad that a city with such a pretty name—it honors the daughter of city founder William Harlee—is so hard to look at sometimes. Downtown Florence is depressing, seemingly a place where zoning took a permanent vacation, not to be seen or heard from since. That said, this is the Pee Dee's largest city, helped greatly by its position at the junction of I-95 and I-20.

While a wag would say that the area's impressive influx of hospitals and health care firms has more to do with the citizenry's unhealthy diet than any fiduciary foresight, there's no question that Florence has made a name for itself as a regional medical hub.

Easy transportation has always been key

to Florence's history. Though technically it began as a township in the early 1700s, for practical purposes its history began in the mid-1800s when it became a major rail center. After Sherman's victory at Atlanta, the Confederates moved many Union POWs from Andersonville, Georgia, to Florence. The Florence Prison Stockade, a rank, brutal place, just as Andersonville was, operated for a comparatively short time, only five months. But during that time, about 3,000 of the 18,000 prisoners died, and many were buried as unknowns in Florence National Cemetery.

So, assuming you don't get sick while you're here, is there much to do? Yes, there are a few things worth seeing in Florence; they even have a symphony orchestra, no small feat for any midsize city in the country in these financially strapped times. And as with all of South Carolina, the people are delightful.

Museums

For a look into the history of the area as well as a rotating art gallery, check out the **Florence Museum of Art, Science, and History** (558 Spruce St., 843/662-3351, www.florence-museum.org, Tues.-Sat. 10 A.M.-5 P.M., Sun. 2-5 P.M., $1). Standing exhibits include an Asian and African collection, Mediterranean artifacts, Pueblo pottery, and artifacts from the infamous Mars Bluff incident of the Cold War era in which an atomic bomb was accidentally dropped in the area, the nonnuclear portion exploding.

Housed in a renovated boxcar and caboose, the **Florence Railroad Museum** (Irby St. and Baroody St., 843/662-3351, Jun.-Aug. Sat.-Sun. 2-5 P.M.) pays homage to the city's roots as a key railroad center in the 1800s. Check in the Florence Museum for entrance info.

As you'd expect from its name, the **War Between the States Museum** (107 S. Guerry St., 843/669-1266, Wed. and Sat. 10 A.M.-5 P.M., $2 adults, $1 children) focuses on local life during the Civil War, including a scale model of the Florence Stockade. Note the unusual days of operation.

Florence National Cemetery

Located 0.25 miles north of the old Florence Stockade—which sadly provided many of the bodies for this site—Florence National Cemetery (803 E. National Cemetery Rd., 843/669-8783, daily dawn-dusk, free) was established as a national cemetery at the end of the Civil War. It contains the remains of not only many of the Union POWs who perished a short distance away but Confederate soldiers who gave their lives for the lost cause.

A large portion comprises graves of unknowns, but one exception is the final resting place of Florena Budwin, the first female interred at a national cemetery. Legend has it that Florena disguised herself as a man in order to follow her husband, a captain serving in a Pennsylvania regiment. Her identity was discovered while she was imprisoned at the stockade, where she cared for injured Union soldiers until she fell ill and died shortly before war's end. She has the only marked grave in Row 13.

◖ Woods Bay State Natural Area

The best site associated with Florence is actually south of town in the country, near tiny Olanta but still conveniently close to I-95. Woods Bay State Natural Area (11020 Woods Bay Rd., 843/659-4445, www.south-carolinaparks.com, daily 9 A.M.-6 P.M., free) is one of the largest remaining Carolina bays, a unique and somewhat mysterious geological phenomenon. These elliptical depressions, scattered throughout the Carolinas and all oriented in a northwest-southeast direction, are typified by a cypress-tupelo bog environment. There's also a rich variety of flora and fauna, including the rare Cooper's hawk and southern twayblade orchid.

Woods Bay's 1,600 acres are a particularly nice example, with a meandering 500-foot

© JIM MOREKIS

Woods Bay State Natural Area features a preserved Carolina bay.

boardwalk that takes you right out into the middle of the swamp, which usually has at least three feet of water. A nature trail goes around the circumference of the bay. Fishing is permitted in its waters with a valid state fishing license (www.dnr.sc.gov). An adjacent heritage preserve protects the bay's sand rim, a distinctive feature of Carolina bays. Bicycles are not allowed anywhere on the site.

Although the signage is good, it can still be a little tricky getting here. The quickest route is I-95 exit 146, but if you're coming from Florence, take U.S. 52 (Irby St.) through the city and take a right on U.S. 301 south of town. When you get to Olanta, start looking for the brown signs for Woods Bay. To get back on I-95, take a left onto Woods Bay Road and continue on to little Shiloh. I-95 is a short distance away.

Heritage Preserves

Just on the other side of I-95 from Woods Bay State Natural Area, near the town of Lynchburg, are two adjacent heritage preserves devoted to a unique and rapidly diminishing ecosystem.

The **Longleaf Pine Heritage Preserve** (803/734-3886, www.dnr.sc.gov, daily dawn-dusk, free) is an echo of what was once the dominant habitat throughout the Southeast, featuring a very different and more aesthetically pleasing species of pine than the typical slash pine monoculture that replaced it to feed the pulp and paper industry. Longleaf pine is a fire-dependent ecosystem, so this preserve is managed through prescribed burns by the state's Department of Natural Resources. Bird-watchers can find the endangered red-cockaded woodpecker here, and botanists will enjoy the wildflower displays as well as the presence of the rare Canby's dropwort. Get to the Longleaf Pine Heritage Preserve from I-95 exit 141. Take Highway 53 south to Three Mile Branch Road, and take a right. Continue to Road S-31-101. Take a right, and the preserve entrance is close by, a couple of miles ahead.

The **Lynchburg Savanna Heritage Preserve** (803/734-3886, www.dnr.sc.gov, daily dawn-dusk, free) also features the longleaf pine habitat, some pond-cypress savanna, the unusual pocosin bog habitat, and some distinctive "fern fields." The whole mix brings a nice variety of flora and fauna to the area, and botanists in particular will love this preserve and its whopping 10 species of rare carnivorous plants. In winter, bird-watchers can find four species of sparrows rarely seen in one place: Bachman's, song, Lincoln's, and field sparrows. To get to Lynchburg Savannah Heritage Preserve from Longleaf Pine Heritage Preserve, continue east on County Road 101 and take a left on Highway 53. Continue past Atkins and take a left onto Road S-31-327. The preserve is about five miles ahead on the right.

Keep in mind there are no facilities at either location, and hunting is sometimes permitted.

Accommodations and Food

There's always room at the inn in Florence. The

COLUMBIA

plethora of chain hotels off I-95 is largely due to the city's status as roughly the halfway point between New York City and Miami. However, the quality is often below par. Probably the best box hotel is **Holiday Inn Express Hotel & Suites** (3440 W. Radio Dr., 843/432-1500, www.ichotelsgroup.com, $99), conveniently near the junction of I-95 and I-20. There are a couple of good Marriott properties, with the usual price premium of that chain. Near the junction of I-95 and I-20 is the well-regarded **Courtyard Florence** (2680 Hospitality Blvd., 843/662-7066, www.marriott.com, $100). There's also the **Fairfield Inn Florence** (140 Dunbarton Dr., 843/669-1666, www.marriott.com, $100).

There is one B&B of note in town, **Ambrias Garden Manor** (111 Kuker St., 843/661-6060, http://ambriasgardenmanor.com, $135), set in a 1920s mansion downtown and boasting a lovely camellia garden.

If you like fast food, you'll love Florence. If you don't, the best of Florence's handful of good restaurants is **◖Redbone Alley** (1903 W. Palmetto St., 843/673-0035, www.redbonealley.com, Mon.-Thurs. 11:30 A.M.-10 P.M., Fri.-Sat. 11:30 A.M.-11 P.M., Sun. 11:30 A.M.-9 P.M., $15-20), which offers a good shrimp-and-grits entrée as well as some tasty Southern takes on chicken and pork. Another favorite for locals is **Percy & Willie's Food and Spirit** (2401 David H. McLeod Blvd., 843/669-1620, Sun.-Thurs. 11 A.M.-10 P.M., Fri.-Sat. 11 A.M.-11 P.M., $15-20), always good for a juicy steak and a good time. For a taste of world cuisine, head straight to **Ann's Kitchen & Taste of Thai** (914 S. Cashua Dr., 843/679-9678, lunch Tues.-Fri. 11 A.M.-2 P.M., dinner Tues.-Sat. 5-9 P.M., $10-15). The name says it all.

HARTSVILLE

Unlike many towns in the hardscrabble Pee Dee, tidy and picturesque Hartsville is quite affluent. This is largely due to its diversified economy, which includes not only a well-regarded

liberal arts institution with a fat endowment and a scenic campus, **Coker College** (300 E. College Ave., 843/383-8000, www.coker.edu), but a big paper plant and a nuclear power facility. The downtown historic district, centering on Centennial Park and its well-landscaped fountain, is a fun place to stroll, dine, and shop.

Kalmia Gardens

A project of Coker College—but on the other end of Hartsville from the campus—is scenic Kalmia Gardens (1624 W. Carolina Ave., 843/383-8145, www.coker.edu/kalmia, daily dawn-dusk, free). This small but colorful garden, first planted in 1935, has several components: the 1820 Hart House, former home of the town's founder, Thomas Hart; a formal garden near the parking lot; a steep boardwalk down a 60-foot bluff—the gardens straddle the fall line—populated by the distinctive species of mountain laurel (*Kalmia latifolia*) for which the gardens are named; a small bridge over the Black Creek; and the contiguous and somewhat dense Segars-McKinnon Heritage Preserve, just over the bridge.

The mountain laurel generally blooms in May; other notable floral displays are azaleas, camellias, day lilies, tea olive, and wisteria. Get here by taking West Carolina Avenue south of downtown and look for the entrance on the right.

Museums and Historic Homes

The **Hartsville Museum** (222 N. 5th St., 843/383-3005, www.hartsvillemuseum.org, Mon.-Thurs. 10 A.M.-5 P.M., Fri. 10 A.M.-noon and 1-5 P.M., Sat. 10 A.M.-2 P.M., free) contains a range of exhibits on the town's history, set inside a former 1930s post office. Outdoors is a fun Sculpture Courtyard.

The oldest building downtown is the **John Lide Hart Cottage** (116 E. Home Ave., 843/332-8017, Feb.-Dec. 1st Sun. of the month 3-5 P.M.), the last remaining structure from the original Hart Plantation, on which the town was later built. They hold an annual holiday tour with costumed docents the first Sunday in December 3-5 P.M.

Three miles west of town is the **Jacob Kelley House Museum** (578 Kelleytown Rd., 843/427-8720, Feb.-Dec. 1st Sun. of the month 3-5 P.M.), built in 1820 and occupied by Union troops at the end of the Civil War. Annual events include a Confederate Memorial Service the first Sunday in May and a holiday tour the first Sunday in December.

Accommodations and Food

The **Oak Manor Inn** (314 E. Home Ave., 843/383-9553, $85) is the town's main B&B. They cater mostly to business travelers, but it's still a quality stay for casual visitors. The **Fairfield Inn Hartsville** (200 S. 4th St., 843/332-9898, www.marriott.com, $99-109) is a well-run chain hotel right downtown.

The main hangout in Hartsville is the eclectic **Midnight Rooster** (136 E. Carolina Ave., 843/383-0800, http:/midnightrooster.com), a combined coffeehouse, eatery, sushi bar, and live-music spot. The hours are pretty odd and somewhat confusing, so I'd suggest going straight to the website to see which portion is open when. It's definitely worth the visit.

A good place for barbecue is **Shug's Smokehouse** (2404 Kelleytown Rd., 843/383-3747, www.shugssmokehouse.com, Mon. 4-9 P.M., Tues.-Thurs. 11 A.M.-9 P.M., Fri.-Sat. 11 A.M.-10 P.M., $10-20).

BISHOPVILLE

The beginning of the state's South Carolina Cotton Trail tourism route (www.sccottontrail.com), Bishopville began at the intersection of two old Indian trails, known to early colonists as Singleton's Crossroads. It got its current name in 1888 when it was named after leading citizen Dr. Jacques Bishop. Its most famous native is "Doc" Blanchard, star running back for the dominant Army football teams of the 1940s.

Pearl Fryar's Topiary Garden

A combination of classic South Carolina kitsch and sincere artistic achievement, Pearl Fryar's Topiary Garden (145 Broad Acres Dr., www.fryarstopiaries.com, Tues.-Sat. 10 A.M.-4 P.M., donation) is one of the most unique stops in the state. Pearl—an elderly man, not a woman—began this labor of love in 1984, supposedly as an attempt to win "Yard of the Month." Safe to say, mission accomplished.

Now having contributed his work to Spoleto in Charleston and the State Museum in Columbia, the amiable Pearl has become one of South Carolina's most popular folk artists. His delicately carved living garden sculptures take up about three acres, using plants as diverse as boxwood, cherry laurel, and eight types of holly.

You can enjoy them alone, but it's worth a call to see if Pearl can give you a personalized tour. It's all free of charge, but leave a donation so that Pearl and his associated nonprofit, the Friends of Pearl, can keep the garden growing.

Bishopville Opera House

The old Opera House (109 N. Main St., 803/484-5090, www.peedeetourism.com, Mon.-Fri. 1-5:30 P.M., free), which has never actually hosted an opera performance, was built in the 1890s as a temporary courthouse. Renovated in 1993, it now hosts local artist and artisan exhibits and community events.

South Carolina Cotton Museum

As you'd expect, the South Carolina Cotton Museum (121 W. Cedar Lane, 803/484-4497, www.sccotton.org, Mon.-Sat. 10 A.M.-4 P.M., $6 adults, $3 students) covers all aspects and effects that the staple crop had on the Pee Dee. There's farm equipment and a life-size farmhouse replica meant to simulate the "shotgun house" of a sharecropper (so named because a shotgun blast could shoot through every room due to its narrow frontage). The gift shop offers a cool range of cotton-oriented items,

COLUMBIA

and there's a tribute to native son Felix "Doc" Blanchard, star Army football player.

Button King Museum

Another kitschy but folksy side of the Pee Dee, the Button King Museum (55 Joe Dority Rd., no phone, www.scbuttonking.com, donation) honors the life and art of the eponymous folk artist, whose real name is Dalton Stevens. His stock-in-trade is his passion—one might even say obsession—for attaching colorful shiny buttons all over everything he owns, including his car and his piano.

Stevens says his hobby began as a response to insomnia, and it has continued on as a life's mission, documented in a number of media appearances that he has thoughtfully compiled onto DVDs available for sale, along with musical recordings of him playing his guitar and banjo (yup, both also covered with buttons). Admission is free but donations are welcome and appreciated.

Getting here is a little tricky. When near town, take Highway 34 west and then take a left onto Johnson's Pond Road, watching for signage. After about one mile, take the fork to the right and turn onto Joe Dority Road. Look for the sign.

Lynches River

A 54-mile stretch of Lynches River (www.dnr.sc.gov) was named an official state Scenic River in 1994. This heavily forested, virtually pristine section of the blackwater river, which was named for Declaration of Independence signer Thomas Lynch, looks like something out of a movie and has stories to match. It was once a hiding ground for escaped slaves, and the state's last duel took place on its banks. While 1989's Hurricane Hugo felled many trees, making navigation difficult, they are gradually being cleared.

There are two great ways to enjoy the Lynches River: **Lee State Natural Area** (487 Loop Rd., 803/428-5307, www.southcarolinaparks.com, daily 9 A.M.-9 P.M., free), a Civilian Conservation Corps-era state park conveniently right off I-20 at exit 123, and **Lynches River County Park** (1110 Ben Gause Rd., 843/389-2785, www.florenceco.org, daily dawn-dusk, free), farther downstream near Florence.

You can put in a canoe or kayak at either site, or go even farther upstream at the public landing off U.S. 15, which marks the beginning of the Scenic River designation. Canoe and kayak rental is available at Lynches River County Park (843/667-0920, about $30 per day); call for rental information. In addition, both sites offer hiking trails. You can camp at Lee State Natural Area, which has 25 sites ($12-13) with electricity and water.

Lots of folks fish for sunfish, catfish, and bass on the Lynches, but you do need a valid state fishing license (www.dnr.sc.gov). Lee State Natural Area has an artesian spring-fed lake stocked with catfish.

MULLINS

Primarily known to history as the birthplace of boxing champion Sugar Ray Leonard, Mullins made its bones as a key tobacco market, and you can learn all about it at the **South Carolina Tobacco Museum** (Front St. and Main St., 843/464-8194, www.mullinssc.us, Mon.-Fri. 9 A.M.-5 P.M., $2 adults, $1 children), located in the old train depot. It recreates the life cycle of the plant from field to harvest, and there's even a growing-research library. Mullins also celebrates its nicotine heritage in the **Golden Leaf Festival** (843/464-5200, www.mullinssc.us, free), held each September in the cute downtown area.

A good B&B in Mullins is **O'Hara's Century House Inn** (123 E. Wine St., 843/464-7287, $50), which in true Pee Dee fashion also hosts a public buffet on weekdays and dinners on weekends. The best place to get a bite in Mullins is at **Webster Manor** (115 E. James St., 843/464-9632, Mon.-Fri. 10:30 A.M.-2 P.M., $10-15). While also a B&B, Webster's main claim to fame is its outstanding lunchtime buffet, for which people drive from miles around.

LITTLE PEE DEE STATE PARK

Scenic and convenient to I-95, Little Pee Dee State Park (1298 State Park Rd., 843/774-8872, www.southcarolinaparks.com, daily 9 A.M.-9 P.M., free) near Dillon is one of South Carolina's most well-rounded and enjoyable state parks, although it is pretty much isolated from the rest of the state. Anglers and naturalists can enjoy not only the blackwater Little Pee Dee River but also a largely intact 54-acre Carolina bay. Rent a boat with a trolling motor ($25 per day) or a canoe or kayak ($12 per day). A fun hike is the short trail to Beaver Pond, where you might see—you guessed it—some beavers. There are 32 campsites with electricity and water ($13) and 18 designated tent sites ($10).

SOUTH OF THE BORDER

For generations, travelers along I-95 were treated to billboards for hundreds of miles with a stereotyped Mexican named Pedro with a penchant for puns ("chile today, hot tamale") lazily exhorting people to visit South of the Border (I-95 and U.S. 301/501, 843/774-2411, www.thesouthoftheborder.com, daily 24 hours, free). Begun in 1950 by Al Schafer as a beer stand servicing a dry North Carolina county just across the state line—"south of the border," get it?—the entertainment empire near Dillon gradually grew to encompass motels, restaurants (Mexican and otherwise), gas stations, RV campgrounds, fireworks stands, sprawling gift shops, and even an adult entertainment store, the Dirty Old Man's Shop. At one point, South of the Border, which covers nearly 150 acres, had its own police and fire departments.

A changing world and vastly increased entertainment options mean that South of the Border is but a shadow of its former self. Schafer gradually became South Carolina's reclusive, eccentric version of Howard Hughes, dying in 2001 at age 87. Employees no longer wear "Pedro" nametags. The borderline racist content of the billboards was watered down for a more evolved world in 1997 ("These baby boomers do not have a sense of humor," Schafer said at the time).

The main landmark is the 75-foot sombrero-clad Pedro himself, between whose massive legs you can drive your car. He sports a new neon paint scheme to fit the new times. While a mere $0.50 gets you a trip to the top to view the surrounding countryside, unfortunately the elevator breaks down a lot, and you won't be allowed up at all on a windy day.

While its best days are clearly behind it, South of the Border retains its off-the-chart kitsch quotient and is still a welcome respite from that particular stretch of mind- and body-numbing boredom along I-95. There are over 300 guest rooms at the **South of the Border Motor Inn** ($55-75), which might surprise you with the comparatively high quality of the rooms given the bargain rates.

Strange-but-true fact: Federal Reserve Chairman Ben Bernanke once worked here when he was a teenager.

INFORMATION

When in Cheraw, get your info at the **Cheraw Visitors Bureau** (221 Market St., 843/537-8425, www.cheraw.com, Mon.-Fri. 9 A.M.-5 P.M.) downtown. The main clearinghouse for all Darlington County information is in Hartsville at the **Darlington County Tourism Office** (214 N. 5th St., 843/339-9511, www.darlingtoncounty.org). For tourism info in Florence, go to the **Florence Convention & Visitors Bureau** (3290 W. Radio Dr., 843/664-0330, www.florencesccvb.com).

The main newspaper in the region is the **Florence Morning News** (www.scnow.com). Cheraw boasts the **Cheraw Chronicle** (www.thecherawchronicle.com), and Hartsville has **The Messenger** (www.scnow.com).

SERVICES

Florence has an assortment of quality health care facilities, chiefly the **McLeod Regional Medical**

CAROLINA KITSCH

Every state in the country has a certain amount of weird but harmless Americana. South Carolina, however, seems to have more than its share; a cynic might even say the whole place is one big ball of kitsch. The state's eccentric throwback personality is reflected in its plethora of unselfconscious quirky attractions.

While a separate volume could be devoted to the state's entire roster, here's a list of the oddball attractions mentioned in this book, beginning with the King Daddy of them all, South of the Border in the Midlands.

- South of the Border, Dillon (page 299)
- Pearl Fryar's Topiary Garden, Bishopville (page 297)

- Button King Museum, Bishopville (page 298)
- Pim's Maze, Darlington (page 293)
- Coburg Cow, Charleston (page 64)
- Littlest Church in South Carolina, Conway (page 166)
- Oyotunji Village, Sheldon (page 205)
- Fireworks stores, Hardeeville (page 246)
- God's Acre Healing Springs, Blackville (page 335)
- Monetta Drive-In, Monetta (page 331)
- The Peachoid, a.k.a. the "Big Butt," Gaffney (page 369)
- Stumphouse Tunnel, Walhalla (page 382)

Center (555 E. Cheves St., 843/777-2200, www.mcleodhealth.org). Cheraw has the much smaller **Chesterfield General Hospital** (711 Chesterfield Hwy., 843/537-7881, www.chesterfieldgeneral.com). In Hartsville you'll find **Carolina Pines Regional Medical Center** (1304 W. Bobo Newsom Hwy., 843/339-2100, www.cprmc.com).

GETTING THERE AND AROUND
By Air
The airport serving the Pee Dee is **Florence Regional Airport** (FLO, 2100 Terminal Dr., 843/669-5001, www.florencescairport.com), which hosts Delta and U.S Airways. However, most travelers drive to the Pee Dee or arrive at larger airports in the region, such as Greenville, Charleston, or Charlotte.

By Car
Interstate highways I-95 and I-20 intersect in the Pee Dee, and they are by far the dominant arteries. Other major highways include U.S.

1 from Camden to Cheraw; U.S. 301, which largely parallels I-95 to the east; and U.S. 52 from Cheraw through Darlington to Florence.

Florence Regional Airport has several **car rental** kiosks, including Hertz, Budget, and Avis. There's an Enterprise location (213 S. Coit St., 843/317-6857) downtown. Hartsville has a couple of locations, including Hertz (1 N. 2nd St., 843/662-7930) and Enterprise (826 N. 5th St., 843/857-9088).

By Train
Two cities in the Pee Dee have **Amtrak** (www.amtrak.com) passenger train stations with daily New York City-Miami *Silver Meteor* trains: Florence (807 E. Day St.) and Dillon (100 N. Railroad Ave.), near the North Carolina border.

By Bus
Greyhound (www.greyhound.com) has bus stations in Florence (611 S. Irby St., 843/662-8407) and in Sumter (129 S. Harvin St., 803/775-3849).

COLUMBIA

The Santee Cooper Region

During family drives up and down boring old I-95 as a kid, I always perked up when we hit the long, low bridge over Lake Marion. That such a vast, deep blue body of water, brimming with whitecaps on a windy day, would seemingly pop up out of nowhere in this flat, nondescript country was impressive enough; add in hundreds of partially submerged cypress trees poking out of the water and the mystique of the Swamp Fox, for whom the lake is named, and it became a lifelong fascination.

As primordial as Lakes Marion and Moultrie seem to be, they're actually artificial. Both are byproducts of a New Deal-era hydroelectric project under the auspices of the Santee Cooper Authority, named after the two rivers impounded to form the lakes. In the name of rural electrification, vast tracts of land were acquired by the government in the 1930s, with over 900 families—most African American and poor—forcibly bought out.

Beginning in 1939, the virgin hardwood forests around the Santee and Cooper Rivers were carved out and flooded. World War II interrupted the completion of the clearing of Lake Marion— hence all those gnarled cypress trees still poking above the waves to this day. Somewhere under its waters, in fact, is Pond Bluff, the old homestead of the Swamp Fox himself.

One of the largest public works projects in history, the Santee Cooper project was so expansive that eventually the entire region would be known by the same name; the area's chief utility company also goes by that moniker. While today Santee Cooper is a sports enthusiast's paradise, if all you want is a taste of life here, it's an easy enough visit, since I-95 makes transportation a breeze.

Key stops include Orangeburg, home of the popular annual Festival of the Roses; Moncks Corner, the gateway to Charleston; a great

wildlife refuge on Lake Marion; and a neat canal and museum on Lake Moultrie.

Oh, and one other thing: The best barbecue in South Carolina is in Santee Cooper.

ORANGEBURG

Considered unusual even within South Carolina, Orangeburg is hard to figure out. In this Anglophilic state, it's named for a Dutchman, William Prince of Orange, and was originally settled by Swiss and German immigrants. The people are friendly, although this remains one of the most racially segregated towns in the United States. The downtown area around Russell Street has great potential and has been improved but just can't seem to get anything going. They have a couple of great barbecue places, but almost no other noteworthy restaurants. Topping it off, the locals even have their own dialect, a nice blend of the Upcountry's twang and the Lowcountry's drawl.

Probably the best-known Orangeburg native is Pulitzer Prize-winning *Washington Post* columnist and TV analyst Eugene Robinson.

◖ Edisto Memorial Gardens

By far the main attraction in Orangeburg is Edisto Memorial Gardens (200 Riverside Dr., 800/545-6153, www.orangeburg.sc.us/gardens, daily dawn-dusk, free). The "memorial" aspect is because they're dedicated to the memory of local veterans who died in both world wars. But other than the nice sculpture at the entrance, there is little else remotely military about this wonderful free venue right next to Orangeburg's downtown.

As a nod to the city's annual popular Festival of Roses, the keynotes are the vast fields of heirloom roses in a dazzling variety of colors, which you'll be able to see approximately April-November, with May being the best month.

COLUMBIA

© JIM MOREKIS

outdoor sculpture at Edisto Memorial Gardens

You can't pick the roses, but you can just about get lost wandering among the rows. A scenic duck pond provides a relaxing backdrop.

My favorite part of the Gardens is a relaxing walk on the elevated boardwalk along the banks of the north fork of the Edisto River, which meanders through the site. This blackwater river originates not far from town, and looking at it takes you right back into the old South—down to the old water-powered mill, still churning away at one bend.

Edisto Memorial Gardens is owned and operated by the city of Orangeburg, and while it's free of charge, some maintenance is occasionally overdue. Just pay attention—any unsafe sections are clearly marked. The site takes on added brilliance—literally—in November and December, as Christmas-themed light displays occupy seemingly every corner of the gardens.

Other Sights

Orangeburg hosts the historically black **South Carolina State University** (300 College St., 803/536-7000, www.scsu.edu), founded in 1896. On campus you'll find the **I.P. Stanback Museum and Planetarium** (803/536-7174, www.scsucrash.blogspot.com, free), a 16,000-square-foot complex with a good regional art gallery, a steady schedule of events, and a 40-foot dome in the planetarium. Call ahead for hours.

An even older historically black college, the first in the state, is **Claflin College** (400 Magnolia St., 803/535-5000, www.claflin.edu), just southeast of downtown. Founded in 1869 at the height of Reconstruction, Claflin has its own historic district on campus, including the 1898 **Arthur Rose Museum** (Mon.-Fri. 9 A.M.-5 P.M., free), formerly the Lee Library, a nice Victorian built of bricks fired on campus. It now has a college-related art collection. **Tingley Memorial Hall,** with its distinctive cupola, was built in 1908 and is on the National Register of Historic Places.

From Edisto Gardens, travel a few blocks north on Russell Street. The stretch of Russell Street between Broughton and Church Streets is the main business district, with several well-preserved commercial buildings, such as the turreted 1904 **Louis Building** (1198 Russell St.) and the 1941 **Bluebird Theatre** (1141 Russell

THE ORANGEBURG MASSACRE

Orangeburg was the scene of a terrible incident in 1968 that tends to get swept under the rug given all the other key events in that turbulent year. In a ham-handed effort to comply with new integration laws, Harry Floyd, owner of the All Star Triangle bowling alley (1543 Russell St.), took down his "Whites Only" sign and replaced it with one saying "Privately Owned." Floyd turned down the fairly modest request of some local African Americans to bowl there one night a week.

On February 5 a group of black students tried to gain entrance to the bowling alley, only to be turned away. In the ensuing often-violent demonstrations that followed, one thing led to another, and local police officers mistakenly thought that one of their own had been shot in the head (in reality he'd been knocked out by a thrown object). Police opened fire on the crowd with shotguns, killing three men and wounding nearly 30 more.

In a denouement that could only happen in South Carolina, the All Star Triangle Bowl finally opened its doors to black patrons, Harry Floyd went unpunished, and the bowling alley remained open and quite popular with both white and black patrons until 2007, when it closed due to financial difficulties. However, the building remains on the National Register of Historic Places.

To learn more about what became known as the Orangeburg Massacre, visit www.orangeburgmassacre1968.com.

St.), now home of the **Orangeburg Part-Time Players** (www.optp.org).

A short way off Russell you'll find the **Briggman House** (1156 Amelia St.), a.k.a. "Briggman's Folly," built in 1850 by Orangeburg's first mayor, a German immigrant named Frederick Briggman, and held together with wooden pegs.

Events

The key event of the year is the **Festival of Roses** (803/534-6821, www.festivalofroses.com, free), held, fittingly, the weekend before Mother's Day. About 30,000 people attend this weekend-long event, which culminates in a Parade of Roses downtown, with a special float carrying the Queen of Roses.

The nearly 50-year-old **Grand American Hunt** (803/534-6821) brings tens of thousands of hunters and their canines to the area each January for a massive raccoon hunting expedition—although the cute masked critters are not actually harmed, just tracked by specially trained dogs.

Accommodations and Food

There are plenty of chain accommodations in and around Orangeburg, but little of note. Try the **Hampton Inn** (3583 St. Matthews Rd., 803/531-6400, www.hamptoninn.com, $84-104) off I-26.

Food in Orangeburg largely begins and ends with **◖ Duke's Barbecue,** the legacy of the legendary Earl Duke. There are two locations, one uptown (789 Chestnut St., 803/534-9418, call for hours, $8) and one downtown (1298 Whitman St., 803/534-2916, call for hours, $8). Connoisseurs of 'cue clearly prefer the original, more Spartan spot on Whitman Street downtown, commonly referred to around town as "the one by the Pepsi plant." In both cases, you get freshly cooked pulled pork served all-you-can-eat buffet-style with a local version of the indigenous mustard-based sauce, plenty of sweet tea, and loaves of Sunbeam white bread on the tables. Both locations serve what could be the finest examples of the traditional South Carolina side called hash, a pork-based stew. I strongly urge you to call ahead for hours.

In the South Carolina equivalent of the intrigues of the Italian Renaissance, an "upstart" 'cue spot, **Antley's** (1370 Sims St.,

COLUMBIA

803/531-0444, call for hours, $8), has split off from the Duke barbecue dynasty, taking some longtime Duke's customers with them.

LAKES MARION AND MOULTRIE

The primary purpose of these lakes was to provide hydroelectric power to the Midlands and Lowcountry. Their secondary purpose was to provide a navigable channel from Columbia down to Charleston. That said, most folks value Lakes Marion and Moultrie because together they are one of the best freshwater fishing locales in the country, chalking up many world record-holding catches. And because of their location in the Deep South, they never freeze over and thus are fishable all year.

Wild-looking Lake Marion on the Santee River, known for its plethora of striped bass, is the largest and northernmost of the two, covering over 100,000 acres. More manicured Lake Moultrie on the Cooper River covers about 60,000 acres and is known for its massive catfish; blue cats over 40 pounds are not uncommon, and some over 50 pounds have been caught.

Since its inception in 1934, the Santee Cooper project's credo has been "For the benefit of all." Because of this, you'll find no elitism, no exclusivity, nor any serious attempt to limit access to the lakes. There are numerous marinas, public landings, and fish camps all around the circumference of both lakes.

Santee National Wildlife Refuge

Located an easy jaunt off I-95, the user-friendly Santee NWR (2125 Fort Watson Rd., 803/478-2217, www.fws.gov/santee, daily dawn-dusk, free) actually comprises several federally run locations on the eastern shore of Lake Marion. It combines hiking and biking trails, history, some of the best inland bird-watching in the state, and even a beach of sorts. The well-done **visitors center** (Tues.-Fri. 8 A.M.-4 P.M., 1st, 2nd, and 3rd Sat. of the

month 8 A.M.-4 P.M.) is at the main Bluff Unit of the refuge, with a nice overlook of the lake and an easy walk down to the sandy shore.

A very short drive away is the site of Fort Watson, built by the British on a 3,000-year-old Indian mound, which was then on the shores of the Santee River. Francis Marion caused the British surrender of Fort Watson in 1781 by building a log tower from which to lay down artillery fire. Each October sees a Revolutionary War encampment on-site in honor of the victory.

The Indian mound, the largest known example on the American coastal plain, still remains today, overgrown with vegetation and complete with wooden stairs to the top. Don't bother looking for artifacts; there really aren't any left, and besides, it's illegal to take any out of the park.

On the south side of I-95 is the Dingle Unit, home to a Carolina bay and an extensive walking trail. Farther to the east is the Pine Island Unit, which you have to drive and hike to. It has a boat ramp and is thus accessible by water. Just to the east of Pine Island is the Cuddo Island Unit, which features nearly eight miles of driving and three miles of hiking and biking trails through its rich habitat.

Bird-watchers throughout Santee NWR will particularly enjoy the rich variety of migratory ducks, geese, and swans that make their way here November-February. A variety of raptors, warblers, and other birds fill the refuge as well. Keep in mind that during particularly sensitive times of the year, certain parts of the refuge are closed to protect the wildlife; call ahead.

Elloree

One of the better downtown renovations in the area is in tiny Elloree. Unlike most towns in these parts with an Indian name, Elloree's is not an old usage. In 1886 city fathers adopted the moniker, which ostensibly means "The home I love" in a Native American language.

Elloree made a name for itself as an

antiquing town, but in recent years the economic downturn hit the town hard, and nearby Walterboro has taken over as the region's primary antiques hub. But there's still good antiquing here, mostly up and down the main drag of Cleveland Street.

For a closer look at area history, drop by the **Elloree Heritage Museum and Cultural Center** (2714 Cleveland St., 803/897-2225, www.elloreemuseum.org, Wed.-Sat. 10 A.M.-5 P.M., $5 adults, $3 children), which has recently added a wing on rural farm life in the region. By far the biggest thing happening in town is the **Elloree Trials** (803/897-2616, $15, free under age 12), a thoroughbred and quarter horse event over Easter weekend featuring about a dozen races and with nearly 10,000 people in attendance—not bad for a town with less than 1,000 residents.

Pinopolis Dam

The tallest single-step lock in North America and the second tallest in the world, the Pinopolis Dam at the south end of Lake Moultrie separates the impounded lake from the Cooper River. If you're in a boat or kayak, it's a whopping 75-foot, half-hour drop from the lake to the 1940s-era Tailrace Canal, a short trip on which takes you to the river.

Generally, unpowered craft are not allowed in the lock. But for a guided kayak tour that includes a jaunt through the lock, contact **Blackwater Adventures** (843/761-1850, www.blackwateradventure.com, about $50). The trip includes a two-mile leg down the Cooper River.

Francis Beidler Forest

The Francis Beidler Forest (336 Sanctuary Rd., Harleyville, 843/462-2150, www.sc.audubon.org, Tues.-Sun. 9 A.M.-5 P.M., $8 adults, $4 ages 6-18, free under age 6) is jointly owned by the Nature Conservancy and the Audubon Society to conserve this rare and special 15,000-acre habitat in the blackwater Four Holes Swamp. A 1,800-acre section of the forest contains some of the largest and most ancient old-growth stands of bald cypress and tupelo trees in the world, with some trees well over 1,000 years old. Explore this section on a two-mile boardwalk.

To get here from Charleston, take I-26 west out of town to exit 187. Make a left onto Highway 27 south to U.S. 78, where you turn right. Veer right on U.S. 178, and then take a right on Francis Beidler Forest Road. To get to the visitors center, veer right onto Mims Road after a few miles.

Branchville

Although technically one of the oldest settlements in South Carolina—founded by a Prussian immigrant in 1734—little remains of Branchville's distant past. Today the burg is best known for being the first railroad junction in history. Originally on the Charleston-Hamburg line—itself the first scheduled train in the U.S.—Branchville became a junction in 1838 when a line from Columbia was completed. Its heyday was brief, however, as General Sherman's men tore up the rail lines at war's end.

The original historic depot was heavily damaged by fire in the 1990s, but an extensive renovation has been done. The depot currently houses the cute and very attractively done **Branchville Railroad Museum and Shrine** (7204 Freedom Rd., 803/274-8820, Fri.-Sat. 10 A.M.-2 P.M., Sun. 2-5 P.M., free), which contains many original artifacts from the town's glory days, including a replica of *The Best Friend of Charleston* steam locomotive.

Every September brings the very popular **Raylrode Daze** festival, honoring the area's contribution to railroad lore, complete with mock gunfights, cancan girls, a pet show, a street dance, and even a Kangaroo Court for attendees not deemed to be in enough train-spotting spirit.

Sports and Recreation

ON THE WATER

A good way for the casual traveler to enjoy the lakes is at **Santee State Park** (251 State Park Rd., 803/854-2408, www.southcarolinaparks. com, Mon.-Sun. 6 A.M.-10 P.M., $2 adults, free under age 16) on Lake Marion near the town of Santee. This very popular park is focused exclusively on lakefront living and recreation, with cabins galore. A nature-based boat tour of the lake (Wed. and Fri.-Sun., call for times) run by Fish Eagle Tours (803/854-4005) departs from the Tackle Shop. The park also has two boat ramps on-site.

An easy way to fish is on the old bridge over Lake Marion, parallel to I-95 and now used as a fishing pier. Serious anglers, however, gravitate toward the many fish camps and marinas all around the huge circumference of the lakes. Some are quite plush by semirural standards, featuring cabins, lighted fishing piers, and attached restaurants. Notable examples are **Randolph's Landing** (122 Randolph's Landing Way, 803/478-2152, www.randolphs-landing. com), up at the Santee Dam; **Cooper's Landing** (1526 Gordon Rd., 803/478-2549), just off I-95; and **Harry's Heart of the Lakes** (320 Harry's Camp Circle, 843/351-4561, www.harrysfish-camp.net), at the southern tip of Lake Marion.

A fishing guide always comes in handy, especially on a body of water like Lake Marion, which has many stumps lurking beneath the surface. While most fishing camps offer guides, some key independent operators are bass specialist **Inky Davis** (803/478-7289, www.inky-davis.com) out of Manning, redfish and bass man **Captain Jimmie** (843/553-1139, www. jimmiehair.com) out of Eutaw Springs, catfish hunter **Joe Drose** (843/351-2860, www.san-teecoopercats.com) out of Pineville, and catfish veteran **Captain Casey** (843/761-3092) out of Moncks Corner at the southern tip of Lake Moultrie. Generally speaking, a full day out on the water will run about $300 for 1-2 people.

All fishing on the lakes for those over age 16 requires a valid South Carolina fishing license, available at any tackle shop, online (www.dnr. sc.gov), or by phone (888/434-7472). A seven-day nonresident license is $11. A total of 40 game fish can be kept any one day, with no more than 10 black bass, 5 striped bass, and only 1 catfish over 36 inches long.

Kayakers can put in at many spots on the lakes, including Santee State Park. Of particular interest is the **Berkeley County Blueways** (843/719-4146, www.berkeleyblueways.com), 175 miles of paddling trails from lower Lake Marion all the way southeast to Francis Marion National Forest. **Blackwater Adventures** (843/761-1850, www.blackwateradventure. com) and **Nature Adventures** (843/928-3316, www.natureadventuresoutfitters.com) offer various kayak and canoe tours along with rentals.

There's even a beach of sorts on Lake Moultrie called **Overton Park** (843/761-8039, Memorial Day-Labor Day daily 10 A.M.-6 P.M., $2). It's at the southern tip of the lake at the Pinopolis Dam; get here by taking U.S. 52.

An outstanding recreation guide is available at www.santeecoopercountry.org.

ON LAND

Generations of golfers, most from the Northeast and Midwest, have taken advantage of Santee Cooper's location near I-95. While these duffers are more downscale than their counterparts in Hilton Head or Charleston, they seem to have more fun and pay a good bit less for the privilege.

There are three courses of note on Lake Marion around the town of Santee: **Santee Cooper Country Club** (630 Santee Dr., 803/854-2467, www.santeecoopergolf.com, $30-60), the area's first; **Lake Marion Golf Course** (9069 Old Hwy. 6, 803/854-2554, www.santeecoopergolf.com, $27-51), built in 1979; and **Santee National Golf Club** (8638 Old Hwy. 6, 803/854-3531, www.santeen-ational.com, $40-60). But the best course might well be **Wyboo Golf Club** (1 Warrens Way, 803/478-7899, www.wyboogolfclub.com, $40-50), a Tom Jackson design near Manning (take I-95 exit 119), which is the best course in Clarendon County and consistently rated one of the top 10 public courses in South Carolina. There are tons of golf packages available in the area; call the Santee Cooper Country commission (800/227-8510) for more info.

Hikers can traverse a segment of the **Palmetto Trail** (www.palmettoconservation. org) on Lake Moultrie. The trailhead is at the U.S. Forest Service Canal Recreation Area on the west side of U.S. 52.

Accommodations

There's a plethora of fishing-related lodging and RV-style camping all around the lakes—about two dozen places in all, the vast majority on Lake Marion. For a comprehensive look, go to www.santeecoopercountry.org. A lot of folks opt for vacation rentals on the lakes; go to www.lakemarionvacation.com for more information.

A fun place to stay near the lakes is **Santee State Park** (251 State Park Rd., 803/854-2408, www.southcarolinaparks.com). Ten well-furnished cabins are situated on a long pier over Lake Marion, with another 20 cabins on the lake itself. While all are two-bedroom, sleeping a maximum of six, they run $80-120, depending on size. Call or go to the website well in advance to reserve a cabin. There are also 158 lakeside campsites ($16-18).

There are several primitive campgrounds along the **Lake Moultrie Passage** of the Palmetto Trail (www.palmettoconservation.org). Remember that August-December is hunting season.

Elloree has had quite a bit of national press for its picturesque qualities. While the exterior of the 1906 **Elloree Bed and Breakfast** (660 W. Hampton St., 803/897-2225, www.elloreebandb.com) doesn't provide the best architectural example in town, its guest rooms are particularly well-appointed. Owners Jack and Cindy Lane offer two guest rooms: The Old Carolina Room ($100) is actually a suite, with a large and lovely sitting room, while the Angel Room ($80) is a bit smaller, though just as tastefully appointed.

Food

Any discussion of great food in Santee Cooper—and by some gourmands' estimation, in all of South Carolina—must begin with **(Sweatman's Bar-b-que** (1313 Gemini Dr., 803/492-7543, Fri.-Sat. 11:30 A.M.-9:30 P.M., $8-15, cash only). Located outside the small town of Holly Hill on the western side of the lakes, there's nothing else of note near the restaurant. But that's OK, since Sweatman's alone is worth the trip. Indeed, I've heard of people driving 2-3 hours, literally from the other side of the state, just to eat here on a weekend. While a certain amount of this popularity is driven by the media's trendy fondness for "authentic" Americana—Sweatman's proudly displays signed items by TV gourmand Anthony Bourdain—there's no doubt that this is a special kind of place, if a humble one.

Sometime in the 1970s this old farmhouse in the country off Highway 453 morphed into a roadhouse. They cook their pork the old-fashioned way: the proverbial whole hog, slow-cooked over wood in a blockhouse out back. The result is served buffet-style, in two types: the dry white portion, the "inside meat," and the glazed outer portion, "the outside meat." Don't miss the "cracklin's," delicious crunchy portions of fried pigskin. You get your choice of sauces, either the indigenous mustard sauce or vinegar-based. You also get the requisite serving of the staple South Carolina hash, some coleslaw and rice, and, of course, sweet tea.

Sweatman's closes for most of August—it's too hot to tend the pit then—so if you're vacationing during that time, you're out of luck. And remember, they only take cash. To get here, take I-95 exit 90 and then head east

Sweatman's Bar-b-que, near Holly Hill

© JIM MOREKIS

on U.S. 176, which becomes Main Street in Holly Hill. Turn left onto Highway 453 and head north for a few miles, and Sweatman's is on the right. When in Holly Hill looking for the turn, keep in mind that Highway 453 is not contiguous through town. You're looking for the spur of Highway 453 that begins on the west side of the railroad tracks.

In terms of culinary 'cue, Sweatman's has only one serious competitor in the area, and that's **☾ McCabe's Bar-B-Que** (480 N. Brooks St., 803/435-2833, Thurs.-Sat. 5:30-9 p.m., $10) on the eastern side of Lake Marion in the town of Manning. (While technically part of the Pee Dee, I include McCabe's here because, for all intents and purposes, Manning is part of the lake country and markets itself as such.) The pork is finely pulled, and the sauce is the tangy, kicky Pee Dee-style pepper-and-vinegar variety. Served with that distinctive hash side dish and sliced tomatoes, this plate is often considered the

equal of Sweatman's—although because I don't wish to start another civil war, I leave that call up to you.

If you're in Santee and need a meal, hit **Clark's Family Restaurant** (8920 Old Hwy. 6, 803/854-2101, Sun.-Thurs. 6 a.m.-9 p.m., Fri.-Sat. 6 a.m.-10 p.m., $10), an old mom-and-pop establishment known to generations of locals as well as travelers on I-95 (take exit 98). As you'd expect given its lakeside location, the fried catfish is primo, but I'd refrain from describing it that way out loud.

Although not the best barbecue in the region, **Lone Star Barbecue & Mercantile** (2212 State Park Rd., 803/854-2000, Thurs.-Sat. 11 a.m.-9 p.m., Sun. 11 a.m.-4 p.m., $10) in Santee is certainly well respected, with the all-you-can-eat buffet typical of the area.

MONCKS CORNER

The town of Moncks Corner, seat of Berkeley County, is at the southern tip of Lake Moultrie

COLUMBIA

at the headwaters of the Cooper River; it is a gateway of sorts to the greater Charleston area.

Mepkin Abbey

The burg of Moncks Corner is actually named for a person, not a vocation, but nonetheless that's where you'll find a fully active, practicing Trappist monastery, Mepkin Abbey (1098 Mepkin Abbey Rd., 843/761-8509, www.mepkinabbey.org, Tues.-Fri. 9 A.M.-4:30 P.M., Sat. 9 A.M.-4 P.M., Sun. 1-4 P.M., free), notable for the fact that it's not only open to visitors but welcomes them.

The beautiful abbey and grounds on the Cooper River is on what was once the plantation of great Carolina statesman Henry Laurens, whose ashes are buried here, and later the home of the famous publisher Henry Luce and his wife, Clare Boothe Luce. The focal point of natural beauty is the Luce-commissioned **Mepkin Abbey Botanical Garden** (Tues.-Sun.), a 3,200-acre tract with a camellia garden designed by noted landscape architect Loutrel Briggs, a native New Yorker who made Charleston his adopted home.

When they're not in prayer, the monks generally observe silence. In accordance with the emphasis the order puts on the spiritual value of manual labor, farming is the main physical occupation, with the monks' efforts producing eggs, honey, preserves, soap, and even compost from the gardens, all of which you can purchase in the abbey gift shop in the reception center, which will always be your first stop. Tours of the abbey itself are usually given Tuesday-Sunday 11:30 A.M. and 3 P.M.

The majority of visitors to the abbey are day visitors here to enjoy the quiet, the breeze, and the humming of the honeybees. But for those who want a contemplative, quiet retreat of a distinctly Christian nature, the abbey lets you stay up to six nights in one of their guesthouses (married couples can also take advantage of this).

As you'd imagine, the accommodations are Spartan—a bed, a desk, a reading chair, and a private bathroom. Linens, towels, and soap are provided, but other than access to the library, there's no other modern stimulation.

Retreatants eat with the monks, enjoying the same strict vegetarian diet and the same strict mealtime silence (although at lunch, a single monk reads aloud from a book). Monks will assist retreat guests in the protocols of the abbey's prayer schedule.

Cypress Gardens

Nature lovers can also enjoy Cypress Gardens (3030 Cypress Gardens Rd., 843/553-0515, www.cypressgardens.info, daily 9 A.M.-5 P.M., last admission 4 P.M., $10 adults, $5 ages 6-12), which carries with it a lot of the same quiet, meditative nature of the abbey, although it's entirely secular.

One of the first nature preserves in the Lowcountry, Cypress Gardens is the life's work of Benjamin R. Kittredge and his son Benjamin Jr. Together they brought back the former glory of the old Dean Hall plantation, which the elder Kittredge, a New Yorker who married into a wealthy Charleston family, had bought in 1909. Instead of rice, the main crop was to be flowers—millions of flowers, including azaleas, daffodils, camellias, wisteria, dogwoods, roses, lotuses, and more. The old paddy system was made navigable for small boats—today they're glass-bottomed—to meander among the tall cypress trees. The city of Charleston acquired the tract from the family, and later Berkeley County would come into possession of it.

The current 170-acre park was heavily damaged during Hurricane Hugo in 1989, but it has made quite a comeback, and its inspiring and calming natural beauty remains true to the vision of the Kittredges. The founders would certainly approve of a particularly modern addition, the Butterfly House, a 2,500-square-foot building packed full of butterflies, caterpillars,

COLUMBIA

THE MONKS OF MONCKS CORNER

COURTESY OF CHARLESTONCVB.COM

Cistercians of the Strict Observance, more commonly known simply as Trappists. With the credo "pray and work," the Trappists believe manual labor provides worshippers with the best opportunity to share and experience creation and restoration. They also view manual labor as following in the footsteps of the "Poor Christ"—since their work enriches and provides for the surrounding community, especially the disadvantaged.

Much of the monks' labor centers on various farm activities. Until recently, the harvesting of chicken eggs—almost 10 million annually—was the main source of revenue to maintain the abbey. In the wake of a controversy surrounding those eggs—which began when a member of the animal rights group PETA came as a retreat guest and secretly filmed the abbey's chicken coops—the abbey has decided to phase out egg production and sale and turn to other products to raise money.

As part of their vows, Mepkin Abbey's monks remain silent during the early and late parts of the day. Their daily schedule is very strict, as follows:

- 3 A.M.: Rise

- 3:20 A.M.: Vigils, followed by half an hour of meditation, then a reading or private prayer

- 5:30 A.M.: Lauds, followed by breakfast

- 7:30 A.M.: Eucharist, followed by 15 minutes thanksgiving and Terce

- 8:30-11:30 A.M.: Silence ends and morning work period begins

- Noon: Midday prayer followed by lunch

- 1-1:40 P.M.: Siesta (optional)

- 1:45-3:30 P.M.: Afternoon work period

- 5 P.M.: Supper

- 6 P.M.: Vespers

- 7:35 P.M.: Compline

- Silence begins as monks retire for the day.

Near Moncks Corner, South Carolina, the old Mepkin Plantation is now the home of the monks of Mepkin Abbey. How and why a monastery came to be in this semirural corner of the Deep South is worth a closer look.

Originally the plantation of the great South Carolina statesman and Revolutionary War hero Henry Laurens, by 1936 the grounds had come into the hands of famed *Time* magazine publisher Henry Luce. In 1949, Henry and his wife, Clare Boothe Luce, a renowned congresswoman and playwright, donated a large portion of Mepkin to the Roman Catholic Church to be used as a monastery. In response, 29 monks from the Abbey of Gethsemane in Kentucky answered the call and moved to the Lowcountry to begin Mepkin Abbey. Although it does contain actual monks, the little town of Moncks Corner north of Charleston was actually named for Thomas Monck, a merchant in the area.

Mepkin Abbey's monks are of the Order of

COLUMBIA

turtles, and birds. Just go in quietly, remain as quiet as you can, and the butterflies will find you, an unforgettable experience for children and adults alike.

You can also walk two nature trails and enjoy the flora and fauna of this area, untouched by modern development. There's a new Crocodile Isle exhibit with several rare species of the reptile. A freshwater aquarium has 30 species of fish and about 20 species of reptiles and amphibians. Out on the water, you can enjoy one of those glass-bottomed boat rides on the blackwater, or—and this is what I recommend—paddle yourself in a canoe (included in the admission price) among the gorgeous cypress trees.

Old Santee Canal Park

Back in the 1700s, rice and other crops from the upcountry made their way to market by way of the Santee River and then to the Atlantic for a coast-hugging journey to Charleston for export. By 1770, Charleston city fathers had decided that linking the Santee directly with Charleston's wharves on the Cooper River was the way to go. While the Revolutionary War held up the works for a while, by 1793 nearly 1,000 workers dug for seven years to complete the project. By 1800 the 22-mile, 10-lock Santee Canal was in operation, the first true canal in the United States.

George Washington was so impressed that he remarked, "It gives me great pleasure to find a spirit of inland navigation prevailing so generously. No country is more capable of improvements in this way than our own." His words proved prophetic when an even greater engineering feat—the railroad—signaled the end of the canal's viability in the mid-1800s.

Today, most of the canal is under the waters of another immense engineering project, Lake Moultrie. However, Old Santee Canal Park (900 Stony Landing Rd., 843/899-5200, www.oldsanteecanalpark.org, daily 9 A.M.-5 P.M., $3) is located at a point where you can see part of

the canal enter Biggin Creek, the headwaters of the Cooper River.

On the Stony Landing bluff stands an 1843 plantation house built by Charleston merchant John Dawson. You can tour the restored house, view exhibits in the excellent 11,000-square-foot Interpretive Center, and view the 1940s-era Tailrace Canal, which connects Lake Moultrie to the Cooper River.

Lots of school groups tour the site throughout the year, and a highlight for them are the various snake exhibits on-site, this swampy area being particularly suitable for the legless reptiles. Naturalists will note the unusual plant life typical of an area, with limestone-heavy underlying soil, or marl.

Sharing the 195-acre grounds with the Old Santee Canal Park—and included in the cost of admission—is the **Berkeley Museum** (950 Stony Landing Rd., 843/899-5101, www.gobcweb.com, Mon.-Sat. 9 A.M.-5 P.M., Sun. 1-5 P.M.), which traces area history from prehistoric times to the present, including, naturally, a good section on Berkeley County's most famous native son, Francis Marion, the legendary Swamp Fox of Revolutionary War fame. The museum also boasts a replica of the Confederate torpedo boat CSS *David,* built here at Stony Landing. In October 1863 the *David* attacked the USS *New Ironsides,* seriously damaging the Union ironclad. The *David* survived to fight another day, although its next attack, on the USS *Wabash,* was unsuccessful. No one really knows what happened to the *David* next, but its spirit lives on at the Berkeley Museum.

Francis Marion Gravesite

Francis Marion's main homestead, Pond Bluff near Eutawville, now lies submerged under the waters of Lake Marion. But you can pay your respects to the Swamp Fox without scuba gear. The final resting place of Marion and his wife is on the old Belle Isle Plantation Cemetery (daily dawn-dusk), on Highway 45 between Highway 6 and

COLUMBIA

Eadytown. Be aware that this is only a cemetery with a historic marker, and there are no facilities.

Marion's tombstone reads in part: "History will record his worth, and rising generations embalm his memory, as one of the most distinguished Patriots and Heroes of the American Revolution: which elevated his native Country to honor and independence and secured to her the blessings of liberty and peace."

Accommodations and Food

Moncks Corner isn't awash in world-class lodging, but you might try the **Holiday Inn Express** (505 Rembert C. Dennis Blvd., 843/761-7509, $100-140). If you get hungry while you're here, your best bet is to go for seafood at **Gilligan's at the Dock** (582 Dock Rd., 843/761-2244, Sun.-Thurs. 11 A.M.-9 P.M., Fri.-Sat. 11 A.M.-10 P.M., $12-20). They have awesome fried catfish and a nice view of the Cooper River.

INFORMATION AND SERVICES

The centrally located visitors center for Santee Cooper is the **Santee Cooper Country Visitor Information Center** (9302 Old Hwy. 6, 803/854-2131, www.santeecoopercountry.org) in the town of Santee right off I-95.

Key newspapers in the area are the Orangeburg **Times and Democrat** (www.thetandd.com) and the Moncks Corner **Berkeley Independent** (www.berkeleyind.com).

There are two main hospitals in the area: **The Regional Medical Center** (3000 St. Matthews Rd., 803/533-2200) in Orangeburg, and **Roper Berkeley Center** (703 Stony Landing Rd., 843/899-7700) in Moncks Corner.

GETTING THERE AND AROUND

I-95 goes directly through Santee Cooper, making it one of the more accessible parts of South Carolina. U.S. 301 is another key route, cutting through the region and serving Orangeburg before briefly joining I-95 and crossing Lake Marion to Manning. U.S. 17 is the main road to Moncks Corner.

A car is a must in Santee Cooper, unless you're planning on simply boating to the lakes from the Intracoastal Waterway, although this is theoretically possible. Rental cars are available in Orangeburg from **Enterprise** (1624 Saint Matthews Rd., 803/534-0143, www.enterprise.com) and **Hertz** (907 Chestnut St., 803/534-0447, www.hertz.com).

AIKEN AND HORSE COUNTRY

Contrary to media stereotypes of the South, we're not talkin' rodeo here, folks. Horse action in South Carolina's thoroughbred country is of the serious upper-crust variety. As a result, towns hereabouts have avoided the economic malaise often found in small towns throughout the state. Money may not buy happiness, but it can get you a pretty good facsimile.

That said, there's more going on than just horses and the affluence that inevitably accompanies them. You'll find some of the state's nicest people—which is saying a lot—and a delightful rolling countryside that, with or without horses, will bring peace to your soul.

One key part of local life that you won't see much of is the massive and environmentally troublesome Savannah River Site (SRS), a "nuclear materials processing center" (seemingly a euphemism for "former bomb plant that desperately needs cleaning up"), owned by the federal Department of Energy and located about 10 miles south of Aiken. SRS's huge job presence in the region means that the locals don't care to hear lectures about possible radioactive contamination of the groundwater or of the morals involved in making nuclear weapons in the first place. Rather, most locals take the sincere view that it's an honor to host a facility with such a vital role in defending the American way of life. This sense of civic duty and sacrifice—often bordering

HIGHLIGHTS

SOUTH CAROLINA

Winter Colony
Hitchcock Woods
Hopelands Gardens
Aiken
Carolina Bay Nature Preserve
Augusta
God's Acre Healing Springs
Redcliffe Plantation State Historic Site
Blackville
Barnwell
Church of the Holy Apostles

0   10 mi
0   10 km

GEORGIA

NC
GA

© AVALON TRAVEL

LOOK FOR ☾ TO FIND RECOMMENDED SIGHTS, ACTIVITIES, DINING, AND LODGING.

☾ **Aiken Winter Colony:** Cozy, historic cottages of the wealthy Northerners who put Aiken on the map (page 317).

☾ **Hopelands Gardens:** This relaxing formal garden hosts the Thoroughbred Racing Hall of Fame (page 319).

☾ **Carolina Bay Nature Preserve:** A scenic and accessible Carolina bay that features a good walking trail all around its circumference (page 320).

☾ **Hitchcock Woods:** The country's largest urban forest is a great place to exercise or get away (page 320).

☾ **Church of the Holy Apostles:** You'll marvel at the beauty of this historic sanctuary hewn of gorgeous cypress (page 334).

☾ **God's Acre Healing Springs:** The clear waters of this creek outside Blackville have been revered for centuries (page 335).

☾ **Redcliffe Plantation State Historic Site:** This grand Greek Revival mansion sits amid 150-year-old magnolias (page 338).

on naïveté—is common in the South, and particularly common here (in nearby North Augusta, there's even an "Atomic Road"). You're free to agree or disagree, of course, but you're unlikely to change many minds in voicing your principled opposition. My advice? Stick to bottled water, enjoy the scenery, relax, and have a good time.

PLANNING YOUR TIME

Aiken is a small town and is easily enjoyable in a single day, or even a busy half-day. An additional drive out to other sections of horse country, for example to Edgefield and to Blackville, will take the better part of a day. If you want to enjoy equestrian sports, remember that during polo season, games are on Sunday afternoons. Autumn sees the beginning of fox hunting season.

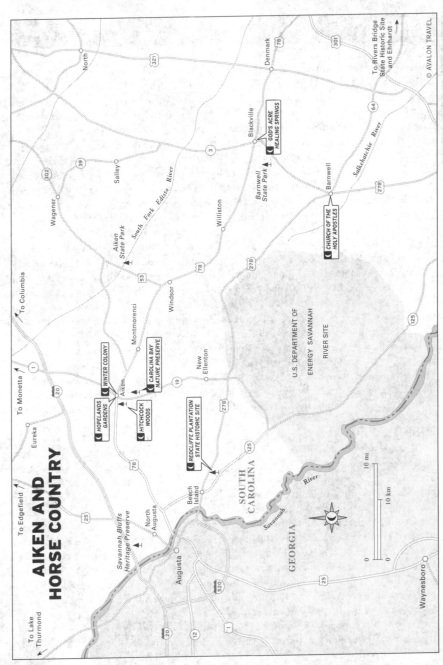

© AVALON TRAVEL

AIKEN AND HORSE COUNTRY

To Edgefield

To Lake Thurmond

To Columbia

To Monetta

North

321

302

39

Salley

Wagener

1

Eureka

20

25

North Augusta

Savannah Bluffs Heritage Preserve

78

Montmorenci

53

Aiken State Park

South Fork Edisto River

Williston

78

Windsor

Denmark

78

301

To Rivers Bridge State Historic Site and Ehrhardt

Blackville

3

GOD'S ACRE HEALING SPRINGS

64

Barnwell State Park

Barnwell

278

Salkehatchie River

CHURCH OF THE HOLY APOSTLES

278

WINTER COLONY

CAROLINA BAY NATURE PRESERVE

HOPELANDS GARDENS

HITCHCOCK WOODS

Aiken

19

New Ellenton

278

125

U.S. DEPARTMENT OF ENERGY SAVANNAH RIVER SITE

125

REDCLIFFE PLANTATION STATE HISTORIC SITE

Beech Island

SOUTH CAROLINA

GEORGIA

Savannah River

Augusta

520

20

12

1

25

Waynesboro

10 mi

10 km

0

0

Aiken

There are towns with horses, and then there are horse towns. Aiken is the latter. How can you tell the difference? Let's put it this way: Horses have the right of way over cars within Aiken city limits. Another way to tell is the little image of a horse's head on each street sign, many of which bear the names of famous horses, stables, and races, such as Kelso Drive, Ruffian Road, Calumet Court, and Derby Lane. Indeed, roads in Aiken's Horse District are intentionally kept unpaved so as not to cause stress to tender equine hooves.

Several Kentucky Derby winners have Aiken roots, including Pleasant Colony (1981), Swale (1984), and Sea Hero (1993). Thoroughbred racing, polo, steeplechase, fox hunting—virtually the entire history of equestrian activity in the country—is here in one form or another. That said, the amount of nonhorsey things to do here might surprise you. Visitors can enjoy the clean retro-tinged downtown area, with its wide attractive streets and its very good selection of cafés, restaurants, and stores, a clear cut above most South Carolina towns its size.

HISTORY

For hundreds of years, Native Americans made their homes on and near the banks of the great Savannah River. Everything changed in 1540, however, when the dangerous and daring Hernando de Soto met emissaries of the great chiefdom of Cofitachequi along the shores of the river. While the Spanish never established a major presence in this part of the South, English settlers did. With the establishment of several nearby trading posts in the early 1700s, including Augusta, Georgia, and Beech Island, South Carolina, the area became a key stop in the thriving deerskin trade that drove much of the backcountry economy in the earliest days of American settlement.

The modern history of Aiken begins a good bit later, in the early 1800s. William Aiken, president of the South Carolina Canal and Railroad Company, commissioned the construction of a railroad from Charleston on the coast to Hamburg on the Savannah River. Work began on the railroad in 1830, with the town of Aiken, named after the company president, laid out in 1834. In a familiar pattern in South Carolina history, the area quickly became a summer retreat for wealthy Charlestonians looking to get away from the humid marshes of the Lowcountry. Aiken hosted something of a rarity in 1865, near the war's end: General Joseph Wheeler stopped an advancing Union force in the Battle of Aiken, one of a handful of times a Confederate force ever got the upper hand over General William Sherman.

Unlike many South Carolina towns, stuck in the recrimination and miasma of Reconstruction, Aiken recovered quickly, again through the desire of the wealthy to get away from it all. But in this case it was wealthy Northerners, escaping not malarial summers but frigid New York winters. Thus was established Aiken's famous Winter Colony, a time of cottages, artistic pursuits, and, of course, anything having to do with horses. One of those wealthy New Yorkers, Thomas Hitchcock, was a crackerjack polo player, and it's largely due to him that Aiken is to this day a national polo center. One of Aiken's key attractions, Hitchcock Woods, is the site of his former polo and hunting grounds. Other notable names from this golden time in Aiken in the late 1800s and early 1900s included Winston Churchill, the Vanderbilts, and the Mellons.

ORIENTATION

The main drag in Aiken is U.S. 78/U.S. 1, known as Richland Avenue for most of its

© JIM MOREKIS

equine statue in downtown Aiken

east-west length through town. Other than a couple of fun downtown blocks to the north of Richland Avenue, most things of note in Aiken are south of this demarcation line. The main north-south avenue, along which you almost surely will travel at some point during your visit, is Whiskey Road (called Chesterfield Street downtown).

Like most South Carolina towns, Aiken has a clearly defined center. Find it at the intersection of Richland Avenue and Laurens Street, marked by a cute little fountain smack-dab in the middle of the intersection. One of many distinctive "parkways" (squares) in downtown Aiken, the fountain is a great landmark if you need to get someone in your party to meet you after going your separate ways for a while.

SIGHTS

Aiken manages a good mix of horse-related attractions and those having nothing to do with our fast four-legged friends. The majority of attractions in town, whether horsey or not, make the most of Aiken's scenic easygoing natural beauty and optimistic all-American atmosphere.

◖ Winter Colony

The old homes of the wealthy Northerners who really put Aiken on the map are almost all privately owned. But a drive or a walk through the Winter Colony Historic Districts (www.nationalregister.sc.gov), which are three nationally recognized areas, will give you a good idea not only of their wealth but of their taste as well.

Major sectors include the area just west of the intersection of Richland Avenue and Laurens Street; Highland Park Drive near the railroad tracks; the Hitchcock Woods-Hopelands-Rye Patch area off Whiskey Road, south of downtown; and the matchless oak-lined canopy along Boundary Street. Key estates—all private—in the Winter Colony include **Let's Pretend, Joye Cottage,** and

AIKEN

Sandhurst. The best way to tour the historic areas of Aiken, including the Winter Colony, is to join the city's tour (803/642-7631, www.cityofaikensc.gov, Sat. 10 A.M., $15) leaving from the new Visitors Center and Train Museum downtown.

You'll often hear the phrase **Horse District** in Aiken. This is actually an informal name for the residential area within the Winter Colony near two vintage racetracks, the Aiken Mile Track (Banks Mill Rd.) and the Aiken Training Track (538 Two Notch Rd.), both on the National Register of Historical Places. Found mostly east of Whiskey Road south of downtown, the Horse District features mostly unpaved roads, the better to keep those expensive horse's tootsies healthy. But you can drive on 'em just the same (the speed limit is a strict 15 mph), admiring the meadows, fine homes, and occasional glimpse of a horse.

Keep in mind that during the warmer months there are precious few horses to

© AVALON TRAVEL

see—most will be racing or training up North (this is, after all, a winter colony).

Aiken Railroad Depot

The newest attraction in town is the Aiken Railroad Depot, also called the **Visitors Center and Train Museum** (406 Park Ave., 803/293-7846, www.aikenrailroaddepot.com, Wed.-Fri. 10 A.M.-5 P.M., Sat. 9 A.M.-2 P.M., free). Based in the old 1899 Southern Railway Depot, this beautifully restored facility now centers around nine HO-gauge model train dioramas depicting stops in the historic railroad, from Charleston on the coast on up to Aiken. There's also a 3.25-inch-gauge model of the old New York-Aiken train that brought all those rich folks down here to play back in the day.

Aiken County Historical Museum

For a good look at area history, housed within a beautiful historic building, check out the Aiken County Historical Museum (433 Newberry St., 803/642-2015, http://aiken-county.net, Tues.-Sat. 10 A.M.-5 P.M., Sun. 2-5 P.M., free). While the exhibits are OK, you might honestly be more impressed by the 32-room great house itself, called Banksia (after a variety of rose).

During the Great Depression, onetime International Harvester president Richard Howe of New York acquired the older section, which was built in 1860, and promptly added a larger brick section in 1931. Easily the most compelling—downright heartbreaking, really—exhibit within the museum is the display about Ellenton, a nearby town that was literally destroyed and all its inhabitants forcibly removed to make way for the Savannah River Site in the 1950s.

❮ Hopelands Gardens

The gently meandering, exquisitely done outdoor arboretum called Hopelands Gardens

(1700 Whiskey Rd., 803/642-7631, daily 10 A.M.-dusk, free) is, like many sights in Aiken, a legacy of transplanted Northern wealth. Hope Iselin, widow of a wealthy industrialist, gave this 14-acre estate to the city as a public garden in the 1960s on her death at age 102. It's believed that she herself planted some of the cedars and live oaks.

Walking the grounds is a peaceful, lush experience for both the dedicated botanist and the casual visitor alike. Monday nights in May-August bring free outdoor evening concerts to the Roland H. Windham Performing Arts Stage at the rear of the gardens. Bring a blanket and a picnic and enjoy the music.

Also on the grounds is the Dollhouse, once a playhouse and erstwhile schoolroom of the Iselin kids. Actually an old Sears & Roebuck catalog house, today the Dollhouse hosts the Aiken Garden Club Council. It's open to the public every Sunday 2-5 P.M., and during the Christmas season it is decorated in fine holiday fashion.

To get here from downtown, just head south on Chesterfield Street, which shortly turns into Whiskey Road.

Thoroughbred Racing Hall of Fame and Museum

Set in the restored old Iselin carriage house (natch) in a corner of Hopelands Gardens is the Thoroughbred Racing Hall of Fame and Museum (803/642-7631, aikenracinghall-offame.com, Sept.-May Tues.-Fri. and Sun. 2-5 P.M., Sat. 10 A.M.-5 P.M., June-Aug. Sat. 10 A.M.-5 P.M., Sun. 2-5 P.M., free). Hope Iselin, who bequeathed Hopelands to the city, was quite a horse maven in addition to an amateur horticulturalist, and this is another component of her legacy to Aiken. Staffed by volunteers, this is the kind of humble, underfunded, but achingly sincere museum that makes up in spirit what it lacks in the wow factor.

Downstairs is the actual Hall of Fame, a

suitably clubby-looking collection of actual racing silks from famous horses that have trod local tracks, along with all kinds of historical and pedigree information on them. Upstairs is a rambling series of rooms devoted to Aiken's long and distinguished polo and steeplechase history, with trophies and mallets galore. If the kids get bored with the sports aspect of it all—such as the reading rooms stocked with a collection of historic racing magazines—there's a little children's area with horse-themed activities.

Rye Patch

The 10-acre Rye Patch (803/642-7631, daily 10 A.M.-dusk, free) adjacent to Hopelands Gardens, was bequeathed to the city in 1984 by yet more transplanted wealthy Northerners, the Rogers family. It's certainly less impressive than Hopelands, but there is a nice rose garden on-site. May is the best time to see the roses in full bloom.

Also at Rye Patch is the **Carriage Museum** (803/642-7631, free), housed in the former Rogers carriage house and which is home to a variety of historic carriages, buggies, and surreys. Call ahead if you want to see inside, however, as the hours are a little "buggy" themselves.

◖ Carolina Bay Nature Preserve

Easily Aiken's most underrated attraction, the Carolina Bay Nature Preserve (Whiskey Rd. and Price Ave., daily dawn-dusk, free) is one of the few sights in town not associated with rich people, horses, or both. Owned by the city and protected by the Aiken County Open Land Trust, this lush wetland just across the street from a municipal recreation facility is one of thousands of Carolina bays—elliptical depressions whose origins are shrouded in mystery—found throughout the mid-Atlantic and Southeastern United States.

Like most Carolina bays, Aiken's is far from pristine, having been farmed for many years. But this particular specimen is a great example

of a restored Carolina bay, with some indigenous flora reintroduced, including a wildflower meadow. A discreet system of pumps keeps it full of water and conversely keeps it from overflowing and flooding the surrounding development. More and more birds have begun visiting the bay as the years go by. A trail takes you all around the circumference of the bay, and the scenery is beautiful at each point; you can even fish.

To get here, take Whiskey Road well south of Hopeland Gardens until you get to Price Avenue, where you turn east; the preserve parking area is shortly ahead on the left.

◖ Hitchcock Woods

Once the fox hunting grounds of Thomas Hitchcock, New Yorker and avid sportsman, Hitchcock Woods (South Boundary Rd. and Whiskey Rd., 803/642-0528, www.hitchcockwoods.org, daily dawn-dusk, free) is now considered the largest urban forest preserve in the country at a whopping 2,000 acres. It's a great place to hike and stroll, though oddly—given that any number of horse-related activities is allowed—no bicycling is allowed.

There are several interesting aspects of Hitchcock Woods from a naturalist's perspective. First is the vestigial "river" of white sand, related to the sand-hill ecosystem found throughout this area and the Midlands. There are also some low cliffs of kaolin, a natural clay. Bird-watching is pretty good here too.

There are seven main entrances, each with a kiosk that has maps to the woods; or go to the website for a printable, delightfully *Lord of the Rings*-like map. The closest entrance to downtown is on South Boundary Road west of Laurens Street. Another is on Coker Spring Road just west of the spring.

At various times of year, fox hunts of a sort are still conducted in Hitchcock Woods, with the hounds chasing a dragged scent rather than cute little foxes, thank goodness.

Carolina Bay Nature Preserve

Dupont Planetarium

On the campus of the University of South Carolina Aiken, within the Ruth Patrick Science Education Center, you'll find the Dupont Planetarium (471 University Pkwy., 803/641-3654, http://rpsec.usca.edu/planetarium), which holds public shows every Saturday ($4-6 pp, depending on the program and time of day). The attached observatory is open to the public after the evening planetarium shows. Within the Science Center you'll also find a gift shop called the **Science Store** (Mon.-Fri. 9 A.M.-5 P.M. and during public planetarium shows).

St. Thaddeus Episcopal Church

Built in 1842, the handsome St. Thaddeus Episcopal Church (125 Pendleton St., 803/648-5497, www.stthaddeus.org) is the oldest church in Aiken. Key figures buried in the attached cemetery include renowned botanist Henry William Ravenel and poet

James Matthews Legaré. Some Confederate soldiers killed in the Battle of Aiken are buried here as well; Union casualties are interred in the First Baptist Church cemetery (120 Chesterfield St.).

Coker Spring

The ruins of Coker Spring (Coker Spring Rd., www.aiken.net, daily dawn-dusk, free) belie the archaeological evidence that this natural spring provided fresh clean drinking water as far back as prehistoric times. The first recorded owner was Ephraim Franklin, who obtained it as part of a larger land grant in 1787. At one point the mouth of the spring was sheltered by a springhouse of brick and stucco, since restored, with an ornate pedimented entrance.

Before the railroad signaled the founding of Aiken, the spring was a key watering stop on the stagecoach route from Charleston to Abbeville. Local lore has it that any visitor

KUDZU'S CREEP

The fast-growing leafy kudzu vine (*Pueraria lobata*) is a ubiquitous sight as you enter the foothills around the Appalachians. Along with pickup trucks and roadside fruit stands, it has become an iconic image of the rural South, as evidenced by the classic cover for R.E.M.'s *Murmur* album and the poem titled "Kudzu" by Georgia poet James Dickey.

Beginning around the fall line across the middle of the state, South Carolina has more than its share of the stuff, scornful of artificial boundaries as kudzu always is. However, while kudzu's voracious tendency to engulf entire forests is no doubt dramatically picturesque, the vine is neither benign nor indigenous to the South. Originally native to Japan, kudzu was deliberately imported as an ornamental into the United States in 1876 at the Philadelphia Centennial Exposition. The real problem began in the 1930s, when the federal government encouraged Southern farmers to plant kudzu everywhere they could as a way to reduce soil erosion. Its prime exponent during that time was FDR's Civilian Conservation Corps, also responsible for many of the fine state parks in South Carolina today. By the end of World War II, 500,000 acres of kudzu had been planted in the Southeast.

Farmers soon discovered to their chagrin that the hardy plant was also incredibly fast-growing—up to a foot a day, or an incredible 90 feet per growing season. By the 1950s the feds—a day late and a dollar short, as we say in the South—decided kudzu was no longer a beneficial plant but a pest weed. A 1993 Congressional estimate concluded that kudzu cost the region at least $50 million each year in lost cropland and the cost of trying to control its further spread.

The bright side is that natural forests are much more resistant to kudzu than domesticated crops or tree farms. And in South Carolina in particular, kudzu doesn't propagate as easily as in other climes. Further, kudzu has its uses, as Asians have known for centuries. High in vitamins A and C, the leaves are edible, either as salad or as a cooked vegetable. The long purple flowers can by battered and fried, or rendered into a sweet jelly. And the roots can be prepared as you would a beet.

Its main value, however, is psychological. Since you can't beat kudzu, Southerners have learned to cope with it, even admire it for its stubborn resilience—so like the Southern spirit itself.

who sips from the spring is fated to return to Aiken. To take your chances on the old legend, take Whiskey Road south of downtown. Just after the intersection of Whiskey Road and Easy Street, veer right onto the short Coker Springs Road.

Tours

The key tour in Aiken is provided by the city (803/642-7631, www.cityofaikensc.gov, Sat. 10 A.M., $15) leaving from the new Visitors Center and Train Museum downtown. Lasting about two hours, it takes you by trolley to all significant areas of town, including through the Winter Colony, with a stop for a walk through Hopelands Gardens. Call for reservations or information.

ENTERTAINMENT AND EVENTS
Equestrian Events

As you've figured out by now, life in Aiken revolves around horses. Polo, in particular, is a local favorite, with Aiken the acknowledged center of the sport on the East Coast—nine polo fields are within city limits, and nearly fifty pro players live here. Polo has a long history here, going back to 1882, and it has seen quite a resurgence of late, which is ironic considering the general decline in some other equestrian sports.

You don't have to play polo or even know how to ride a horse to enjoy it. It's a spectator sport that, like any other, can be a lot of fun when you get in the mood and soak in the vibe. And like any spectator sport, it has a season, or rather

Aiken is a major equestrian center.

a couple of them: September-November and March-May.

The center of the polo universe in Aiken is **Whitney Field** (Mead Ave.), a historic site that has the distinction of being the oldest polo field in continuous service in the United States. Regular games of the Aiken Polo Club (www.aikenpoloclub.org, Sun. 3 P.M., $5) happen each Sunday during the season. Tournaments occur throughout the two playing seasons; go to the website for dates and times.

By far the main equestrian event in Aiken happens each March with the **Aiken Triple Crown,** which actually comprises three weeks of activity. The Aiken Trials (www.aikentrainingtrack.com, $10), a race, happens at the Aiken Training Track the first week. The Aiken Steeplechase (www.aikensteeplechase.com, $15) happens during the second week at Ford Conger Field. Polo (www.aikenpoloclub.org, $10) finishes the event in the third week at Whitney Field.

Another key event, with even more aristocratic overtones, happens just after the Triple Crown, when Hitchcock Woods hosts the **Aiken Horse Show** (www.aikenhorseshow.org, $10 per vehicle), a weekend event in which entrants show off their jumping and "under saddle" (walking, trotting, and cantering) skills. All proceeds go to the Hitchcock Woods Foundation. Interestingly, this is the only time when cars are allowed in the Woods.

Fox hunting is an established tradition in Aiken, though these days the hounds chase dragged scents rather than actual foxes. October-March is fox-hunting season, and Hitchcock Woods is the usual site of the hunts, or "drags," sponsored by the largest club in town, **Aiken Hounds** (803/643-3724, www.aikenhounds.com). The public is invited to watch their regular hunts (Tues. 2 P.M., Sat. 9 A.M.), all leaving from the Memorial Gate within Hitchcock Woods. The season opens Thanksgiving Day at 11 A.M. with a hunt, before which the hounds are blessed by an Episcopal priest. **Whiskey Road Fox Hounds** (803/649-0638, www.whiskeyroadfoxhounds.com) runs drags October-March Thursday and Sunday mornings.

Other key equestrian events include the **Fall Steeplechase** (www.aikensteeplechase.com, $15) in October at Ford Conger Field; progressive show jumping (www.psjshows.com) at Highfields Event Center (198 Gaston Rd., 803/649-3505); and about nine tournaments sponsored by the Aiken Polo Club (www.aikenpolo.net).

GETTING TO THE FIELDS

To get to **Whitney Field** from downtown, turn south on Chesterfield Street, which becomes Whiskey Road. Go one mile and turn left onto Mead Avenue. The entrance to Whitney Field is shortly ahead on your right. To get to the **Aiken Training Track** from downtown, turn south on Chesterfield Street, which becomes Whiskey Road. Take a left onto Grace Avenue and then a right on Two Notch Road; the track is shortly ahead on the left. **Ford Conger Field** is at the intersection of Audubon Drive and Powderhouse Road, south of downtown.

Other Events

To see, feel, and hear what one of the last engagements of the Civil War—and one of the last Confederate victories—was like, check out the **Battle of Aiken Reenactment** (1210 Powell Pond Rd., www.battleofaiken.org, Sat.-Sun. 9 A.M.-5 P.M.), which happens the last weekend in February. This is quite a production, attracting over 10,000 visitors, and those new to the field of historic reenactment will be amazed at the scale. The battle is reenacted with exhaustive attention to detail on each of the two days at 2 P.M. Bring a blanket or lawn chair. The rest of the time you can enjoy other, more peaceful reenactments, along with food, crafts, and entertainment, all historically correct. There's even a period church service

Sunday at 11 A.M. Kids are encouraged to ask any of the "soldiers" questions all weekend long—except, of course, when they're firing blanks at each other with their black-powder muskets. To get to the site, take Highway 19 north out of Aiken and turn right on Powell Pond Road.

What's the first thing that comes to mind when you think of a small, landlocked Southern town? Why, Maine lobsters, of course. Those are the participants in the **Lobster Race** (1st Fri. in May, 5:30-11:30 P.M., $5), a very popular charity benefit held downtown in two locations: The Alley just off Laurens Street south of Richland Avenue; and Newberry Street between Park and Richland Avenues. In addition to the eponymous crustacean speed event, there's food, music, and rides.

A unique juried arts and crafts show downtown is **Aiken's Makin'** (803/641-1111, www.aikensmakin.net, free), which happens on a weekend in September. Over 70 artisans and two dozen food vendors combine for a family event celebrating the work of the many creative artists in the area. You can browse or shop. The only condition: the wares have to be made by the seller.

Christmas is a great time to visit **Hopelands Gardens** (803/642-7631, daily 10 A.M.-dusk, free), which is decorated for the season and throws the doors of its buildings open for tours, complete with hot chocolate and cider.

Nightlife

Aiken is not much of a party town, but you'll usually find a party at the Hotel Aiken's **Polo Tavern** (235 Richland Ave., 803/648-4265, www.hotelaiken.com, Mon.-Sat. 3 P.M.-2 A.M., Sun. 4 P.M.-2 A.M.). Also within the historic structure is a trendy wine-and-tapas bar, **One Hundred Laurens** (235 Richland Ave., 803/648-4265, Thurs.-Sat. 4 P.M.-2 A.M.).

The **Aiken Brewing Company** (140 Laurens St., 803/502-0707, www.aikenbrewing-company.com, Mon.-Sat. 11 A.M.-2 A.M.)

has a wide and tasty selection of artisanal home-brewed beers, including its signature Thoroughbred Red and a Steeplechase Oatmeal Stout.

Performing Arts

Most arts activity in Aiken centers around the **Aiken Center for the Arts** (122 Laurens St., 803/641-9094, www.aikencenterforthearts. org, gallery Mon.-Sat. 10 A.M.-4 P.M.). This multiuse facility hosts frequent concerts and performances throughout the year but is better known for its visual arts component, including various rotating art exhibits and a steady slate of workshops and classes. The **Aiken Civic Ballet** (803/648-5771, www.aikencivicballet. com), the state's longest continuously operating dance company, performs several times a year at the Aiken Center for the Arts.

Aiken does not have a symphony orchestra per se, but it has a fruitful relationship with the **Augusta Symphony Orchestra** (www.augustasymphony.org), headquartered across the Savannah River in Augusta, Georgia. They perform at various times throughout the year at the **Etherredge Center** (471 University Pkwy., 803/648-6851, www.usca.edu) on the Aiken campus of the University of South Carolina.

The **Aiken Community Playhouse** (www. aikencommunityplayhouse.com) performs downtown in the **Washington Center for the Performing Arts** (126 Newberry St., 803/648-1438).

SHOPPING

Due largely to its affluence and ease of navigation, Aiken is a fun and enticing place to shop. There are a variety of midrange and upscale shops in the central downtown area as well as some very good antiquing.

Antiques

There are at least half a dozen antiques shops downtown, many with Sunday hours—a nice change from a lot of sleepy South Carolina towns. The most notable examples are **Aiken Antique Mall** (112 Laurens St., 803/648-6700, Mon.-Sat. 10 A.M.-6 P.M., Sun. 1:30-6 P.M.), **Aiken Antiques and Auction** (1060A Park Ave., 803/642-0107, Mon.-Sat. 9 A.M.-6 P.M., Sun. 1:30-6 P.M.), and **Swan Antique Mall** (321 Richland Ave., 803/643-9922, Mon.-Sat. 10 A.M.-5:30 P.M., Sun. 1-5 P.M.). **The Iron Pony** (210 York St., 803/642-5004, Wed.-Sat. 11 A.M.-5 P.M.) is set in an antebellum home.

Arts and Crafts Galleries

If you like paintings of horses, boy, are you in luck. **Equine Divine** (135 Laurens St., 803/642-9772, www.equinedivineonline.com, Mon.-Sat. 10 A.M.-5 P.M.) deals in plenty of equestrian-related artwork and doodads, and it even stays open an hour later during polo season.

Jackson Gallery (300 Park Ave., 803/648-7397, by appointment) features high-end horse sculpture. **Artist's Parlor** (126 Laurens St., 803/648-4639, Mon.-Fri. 9:30 A.M.-6 P.M., Sat. 9:30 A.M.-5:30 P.M.) features jewelry and pottery. **Beads and Baubles** (226 Park Ave., 803/648-6858, Tues.-Wed. and Fri. 11 A.M.-5 P.M., Thurs. 11 A.M.-7:30 P.M., Sat. 11 A.M.-4 P.M., Sun. 1-5 P.M.), as the name indicates, focuses on the beading arts.

Cobalt Cat Glass Designs (116F Laurens St., 803/599-0183, call for hours) features stained glass, paintings, ceramics, pottery, and furniture. **Southern Moon Pottery** (310 Richland Ave., 803/641-2309, Mon.-Fri. 10 A.M.-5 P.M.) features the work of local and regional potters.

Specialty Shops

If you're a dog lover in this horse town, check out **Bone-I-Fide Bakery** (127 Laurens St., 803/644-7278, www.theboneifidebakery.com, Mon.-Sat. 10 A.M.-5 P.M.), which features delicious (and not cheap!) baked treats for your pup. **Birds and Butterflies** (117 Laurens St.,

803/649-7999, Mon.-Fri. 9:30 A.M.-6 P.M., Sat. 9:30 A.M.-5 P.M.) has some delightful items for the garden. One of the best kitchen shops I've ever seen is in Aiken: **Plum Pudding** (101 Laurens St., 803/644-4600, www.plumpuddingkitchen.com, Mon.-Sat. 10 A.M.-6 P.M.), which features all kinds of useful and cool kitchen gear in addition to gourmet goods.

Malls and Markets

If you insist on going to a mall, there's the **Aiken Mall** (2441 Whiskey Rd., 803/649-0897, Mon.-Sat. 10 A.M.-9 P.M., Sun. 1:30-6 P.M.), with Dillard's, The Gap, and other national stores.

At the corner of Richland Avenue and Williamsburg Street downtown you'll find the venerable, over half-century-old **Aiken County Farmers Market** (Apr.-Nov. Mon.-Sat. 7:30 A.M.-4:30 P.M.), which offers an impressive and extensive variety of regionally grown fruit and produce.

SPORTS AND RECREATION
Natural Areas

The 1,000-acre **Aiken State Natural Area** (1145 State Park Rd., 803/649-2857, www.southcarolinaparks.com, daily 9 A.M.-dusk, $2 adults, free under age 16) is right on the blackwater South Edisto River about 15 miles east of town. You can canoe or kayak (rentals $15 per day), fish on any of four spring-fed lakes (state fishing license required), enjoy some great birdwatching, and hike on the Jungle Nature trail, a two-mile loop through various habitats. RV and tent camping is available ($12-13).

Aiken State Natural Area has a unique story even among South Carolina's many fine parks built by the Civilian Conservation Corps (CCC) during the Great Depression; it was built by an African American detachment of the CCC. Interpretive signs tell their story throughout the park. To get to Aiken State Natural Area, take Whiskey Road south of Aiken and make a right onto Silver Bluff Road (Hwy. 302), which turns into State Park Road.

A wholly unique natural site south of town is the **Aiken Gopher Tortoise Heritage Preserve** (www.dnr.sc.gov, daily dawn-dusk, free), 1,500 acres devoted to the northernmost habitat of the endangered gopher tortoise. The cute, but surprisingly large, critters are key to the Southern wiregrass habitat because their 10-foot-deep burrows are often used by other animals as well. Aiken County has some of the largest remaining stands of wiregrass and longleaf pine habitat, once the norm throughout huge swaths of the Southeast. Over 16 miles of trails take you through the heart of the preserve, but bicycles are not allowed, and there are no facilities. To get here, drive south from Aiken on U.S. 78 for 12 miles to Windsor. Take a left onto Spring Branch Road, which turns into unpaved Windsor Road after 1.5 miles.

Kayaking and Canoeing

At **Aiken State Natural Area** (1145 State Park Rd., 803/649-2857, www.southcarolinaparks.com, daily 9 A.M.-dusk, $2 adults, free under age 16), popular canoeing programs include a basic skills workshop in July-August and "Canoeing with a Ranger" down the South Edisto River June-mid-August every Thursday evening. You can rent canoes (about $15 per day).

There are plenty of public landings all along the banks of the South Edisto River, including Keadle's Bridge Landing at Windsor Road and Highway 4, and Edisto River Landing on U.S. 21.

Equestrian

As you'd expect, there are plenty of riding facilities in Aiken, ranging from spectacularly well-equipped to merely very well-equipped. Most are open by appointment only. One of the largest is **Black Forest Equestrian Center** (4343 Banks Mill Rd., 803/644-6644, www.blackforestfarm.com), which has four arenas and 12 miles of trails. Another is **Jumping Branch Farm** (179 Fox Pond Rd., 803/642-3484, www.

jbfarm.com). For trail riding, try **Fox Hollow Stable** (803/640-6202).

Golf

There are several good public courses in the Aiken area, chief among them the Donald Ross-designed **Aiken Golf Club** (555 Highland Park Dr., 803/649-6029, www.aikengolfclub. com, $32-37), which, in a nice (and dwindling) touch, allows you to walk the course if you'd like. Reservations are required. Another is **Cedar Creek** (2475 Club Dr., 803/648-4206, www.cedarcreek.net, $36-52), which is within a gated community but welcomes the public.

ACCOMMODATIONS

The most important thing to remember about staying in Aiken is that all lodging is at a premium during the week of the Masters golf tournament, held each year in early April in nearby Augusta, Georgia. Rates are massively higher, and rooms generally fill up very far in advance.

Under $150

For an interesting and remarkably inexpensive stay right downtown, try the **Hotel Aiken** (235 Richland Ave., 803/648-4265, www.hotelaiken.com, $65-100), a historic property built in 1898 at the height of the Winter Colony's glory. Renovated in 2001, it still retains a certain well-worn patina. However, this isn't where to go for peace and quiet: The hotel's two attached bars, the clubby **Polo Tavern** and the ritzy **One Hundred Laurens** are centers of downtown nightlife. In fact, things get so noisy that the guest rooms directly over the bar area are discounted.

The circa-1872 **Carriage House Inn** (139 Laurens St., 803/644-5888, www.aikencarriagehouse.com, $110-145) offers 16 guest rooms in a gorgeous historic house downtown. The appointments are simpler than at some B&Bs but are elegant in their simplicity.

$150-300

For a truly grand historic hotel experience downtown, try **⚑ The Willcox** (100 Colleton Ave., 877/648-2200, www.thewillcox.com, $185-425), which once hosted Franklin D. Roosevelt as well as a host of well-heeled visitors during Aiken's Winter Colony glory days. Kind of a cross between a boutique hotel and a B&B, The Willcox features 15 quite luxurious guest rooms, an on-site spa, and a delicious full Southern breakfast each morning. Bring your "well-trained" pet for a one-time $50 charge.

Camping

Aiken State Natural Area (1145 State Park Rd., 803/649-2857, www.southcarolinaparks. com) offers 25 RV and tent sites ($12-13).

FOOD

Good dining options are scattered throughout the central downtown area, with several in "The Alley," a short lane off Laurens Street between Park and Richland Avenues.

American

The **Aiken Brewing Company** (140 Laurens St., 803/502-0707, www.aikenbrewingcompany. com, Mon.-Sat. 11 A.M.-2 A.M., $10) is a popular restaurant and microbrewery at the entrance to the Alley. While it is best known for its surprisingly wide selection of handcrafted brews, it also offers above-average bar food, such as quesadillas and beer-battered (of course) chicken tenders and wings.

One of the older places in town, also in the Alley, is the **West Side Bowery** (151 Bee Lane, 803/648-2900, www.westsidebowery.com, Mon.-Sat. 11:30 A.M.-10 P.M., $8-15), which serves a nice selection of basic American-style restaurant food in a relaxed setting.

Classic Southern

In addition to being one of the South's great stays, **The Willcox** (100 Colleton Ave.,

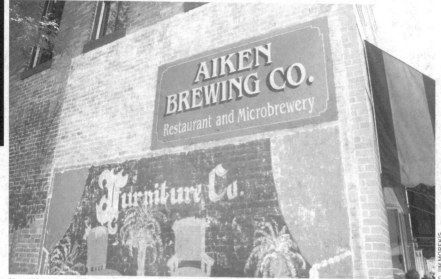

© JIM MOREKIS

the Aiken Brewing Company, downtown

877/648-2200, www.thewillcox.com, Mon.-Sat. 11:30 A.M.-9 P.M., Sun. 9 A.M.-9 P.M., $12-36) also sports a gourmet restaurant open to the public, specializing in Southern high tea-style beverages and sandwiches.

Coffee and Treats
For a cup of joe, some hipster attitude, and a light wrap, sandwich, or sweet treat, go to **K New Moon Cafe** (116 Laurens St., 803/643-7088, http://newmoondowntown.com, Mon.-Fri. 8 A.M.-5 P.M., Sat.-Sun. 9 A.M.-2 P.M., $5), certainly the closest thing to an alternative place in this preppy town, although note the weird hours.

Cuban
K Cafe Rio Blanco (148 Laurens St., 803/643-7075, Mon.-Wed. 11:30 A.M.-6:30 P.M., Thurs.-Sat. 11:30 A.M.-7:30 P.M., $7-10) offers a full and fresh Cuban buffet, daily specials, tasty Cuban sandwiches, and, of course, delectable (and sweet!) Cuban coffee with flan for dessert.

When he's in the mood, the chef riffs Latin jazz on his sax in the kitchen.

Pizza
For straight-up pizza, go straight to **Acropolis Pizza** (1647 Richland Ave., 803/649-7601, $8), which specializes in Northeastern-style pie along with some tasty Greek items.

INFORMATION AND SERVICES
The main **Aiken Visitor Center** (113 Laurens St., 803/642-7557, www.aikenis.com) has moved and is now inside the historic Holley Building. The **Visitors Center and Train Museum** (406 Park Ave., 803/293-7846, www.aikenrailroad-depot.com) also features good visitor info.

The newspaper of record in Aiken is the *Aiken Standard* (www.aikenstandard.com), while the equestrian community is well served by *The Aiken Horse* (www.theaikenhorse.net), available for free all over town.

The main medical facility in town is **Aiken Regional Medical Center** (302 University Pkwy.,

803/641-5000, www.aikenregional.com) on the north side of town near the USC Aiken campus. The main station of the **Aiken Police Department** (251 Laurens St., 803/642-7620) is downtown.

If you need to mail a letter or get some stamps, go to Aiken's **post office** (307 Laurens St., 800/275-8777, www.usps.com, Mon.-Fri. 8:30 A.M.-5 P.M., Sat. 9 A.M.-noon).

GETTING THERE

Aiken is very accessible either from I-20 just to the north or directly from Augusta, Georgia, via U.S 78, which is called Jefferson Davis Highway in Augusta and becomes Richland Avenue in downtown Aiken.

The closest airport to Aiken is the small **Augusta Regional Airport** (AGS, 1501 Aviation Way, 706/798-3236, http://ags.sky-harbors.com) in Georgia, hosting carriers Delta Connection and U.S. Airways Express. Indeed, when in Aiken it's important to remember that the much larger Augusta is a short drive away and is for all intents and purposes considered a part of the local economy.

In Aiken, there's a **Greyhound bus station** (153 Pendleton St., 803/648-6894, www.greyhound.com).

GETTING AROUND

Aiken is remarkably easy to navigate and get around, with the possible exception of its many "parkways" (decorated traffic circles). While pretty, they're difficult to navigate. Here are the rules:

- If facing a red stop signal, stop completely.
- If traffic allows, turn into traffic and join the flow.
- You can turn left on red in a parkway to join the flow—the only place in the state where that's legal.
- Don't cross the intersection until the light turns green.
- If it's a "round" intersection, you can exit the intersection whenever it's clear.

While a car is required for maximum access, the county-run **Best Friend Express** (www.bestfriendexpress.com, Mon.-Sat., $2) provides a cheap and efficient mode of transportation between Aiken and North Augusta using small biodiesel buses, which make a full circuit of the area every two hours. The Aiken Metro route and the Aiken North-South routes are the ones you will likely use. A nice plus is that they will usually pick you up when you flag them, as opposed to being limited to designated stops. They don't run on Sunday, though.

In terms of auto travel within horse country, the main roads are U.S. 25, which takes you from Edgefield down to Trenton and on into North Augusta; and U.S. 78, east of Aiken, which more or less parallels the old railroad track and takes you to those first stops on the Charleston-Hamburg line: Blackville, Denmark, Bamberg, and Branchville.

Keep in mind that speed limits are strictly enforced on highways and in towns in this part of South Carolina.

Outside Aiken

While Aiken is the main tourism draw in the South Carolina horse country, take some time to check out some of the beguiling towns dotting the countryside around it, Edgefield and Blackville in particular. All of them have their own distinct personality, but all share the innate grace prevalent in this historic region in the watershed of the mighty Savannah River.

As in most small towns in the state, stay strictly within the speed limit. There's not much crime around here, so the police have a lot of extra time on their hands.

NORTH OF AIKEN
Edgefield

On U.S. 25 between Greenwood and Aiken is proud little Edgefield, which for some reason was the home town of no fewer than 10 governors of South Carolina. The most famous is Strom Thurmond, later a U.S. senator, a well-done modernist statue of whom dominates the charming and attractive town square. The other thing Edgefield is known for is being the epicenter of the beautiful, unique, and utilitarian art form called Edgefield pottery.

OLD EDGEFIELD POTTERY

The main purveyor of the most famous indigenous art form is Old Edgefield Pottery (230 Simkins St., 803/637-2060, Tues.-Sat. 10 A.M.-6 P.M., donation) in a small freestanding building right off the main square down Potter's Alley. This is not a retail store per se but the real workshop of master potter Stephen Ferrell, with some truly amazing specimens of pottery in various states of completion.

© JIM MOREKIS

Edgefield was home to 10 South Carolina governors.

TOMPKINS LIBRARY

The main attraction on the town square is the Tompkins Library and Welcome Center (104 Courthouse Square, 803/637-4010, Mon.-Fri. 9 A.M.-4 P.M.), where you can find visitor information and extensive genealogical research resources, including a "Trailing Your Ancestors" exhibit. While on this side of the square, note the ornamental mosaic entranceways to several of the buildings.

FRESHWATER COAST DISCOVERY CENTER

On the state's "Discovery Corridor," the Joanne T. Rainsford Region 2 Discovery Center (405 Main St., 803/734-0767, www.sc-heritagecorridor.org, Tues.-Sat. 10 A.M.-5 P.M., free), sometimes called the Freshwater Coast Discovery Center, features exhibits about the history of Edgefield and the surrounding area. This is also a good place to get brochures and tips about refining your visit.

OAKLEY PARK MUSEUM

A few blocks south of the square, behind a gated drive, is the Oakley Park Museum (300 Columbia Rd., 803/637-4027, Wed.-Fri. 10 A.M.-4 P.M. or by appointment, nominal fee), home of Confederate general Martin W. Gary. The stately mansion is now operated by the local Daughters of the Confederacy as a museum and self-professed "shrine" to the Red Shirts, a vaguely threatening paramilitary group of the Reconstruction era who ensured the return of the old guard in the 1876 elections. There's even an actual historical Red Shirt on display. It's a fascinating glimpse into a drastically underreported—and darkly fascinating—portion of American history.

TEN GOVERNORS RAILS TO TRAILS

Continue south to find a much more innocent pleasure, the Ten Governors Rails to Trails (803/637-4014, daily dawn-dusk, free), a one-mile passage that incorporates an old train trestle over U.S. 25. It's a relaxing and scenic way to get some exercise or let the kids (and dogs) blow off some steam. Park in the lot south of the intersection of Main and Mims Streets.

NATIONAL WILD TURKEY FEDERATION

Just outside Edgefield on U.S. 25 is the National Wild Turkey Federation Visitor Center and Museum (770 Augusta Rd., 803/637-3106, www.nwtf.org, Mon.-Fri. 8:30 A.M.-5 P.M., free). No, it's not dedicated to the beloved Kentucky bourbon; it's the national headquarters of the society dedicated to the study and conservation of one of South Carolina's great game birds and Benjamin Franklin's unsuccessful choice for our national symbol. The campus includes the 60,000-square-foot Wild Turkey Center, a wild turkey museum (including the world's largest box call, a gift shop called the Turkey Shoppe, natch), and a 125-acre outdoor education center. In front of the complex you'll find a huge bronze turkey, sculpted by Cody Houston.

TRENTON PECAN GROVE

An unusual and beautiful roadside sight is near the village of Trenton just south of Edgefield. U.S. 25 passes between two rows of fine old pecan trees, planted with care many years ago along the road.

Monetta

About 30 minutes north of Aiken en route to Columbia on U.S. 1 is tiny Monetta, chiefly known for hosting one of only two working drive-in theaters remaining in South Carolina (the other is near Beaufort). A real blast from the past, the **Monetta Drive-In** (5822 Columbia Hwy., 803/685-7949, www.thebigmo.com, Mar.-Nov., $7 adults, $4 children, free under age 4), a.k.a. "The Big Mo," shows current releases, with audio tracks broadcast over two FM frequencies. While they do have tasty concessions, you can bring your own eats in—but no grilling, please. You can sit outside in a lawn chair or on a blanket, but they do ask that you

EDGEFIELD POTTERY

© JIM MOREKIS

Edgefield pottery has become a hot commodity.

Currently one of the hottest-selling categories of folk art in the world, Edgefield pottery embodies the ideal of elegant simplicity and the effortless grace of functional art. Named for the old Edgefield District along the banks of the mighty Savannah River (now split into Aiken and Edgefield Counties), Edgefield pottery began around 1810 on the plantation of Dr. Abner Landrum. He had his African American slave potters take the excellent clay from this area along the mighty Savannah River, throw it on the wheel, fire it in a kiln, and glaze the resulting stoneware with versatile and attractive alkaline glazes. It sounds simple to us, but it was groundbreaking at the time, a period when toxic lead-based glazes were commonplace. The only other known use of alkaline pottery glaze was in China about 2,000 years ago.

Generally speaking, Edgefield pottery dates from the early 1800s through the early 20th century. While both white and African American potters made it, the bulk of it was made by African American potters on plantations. Some key potters made many thousands of pieces during their lifetimes, but not to sell: This pottery was always intended for heavy use. While the identity of most of the potters is lost to history, we know some by name, including "Dave the Slave," subject of the best-selling book *Carolina Clay.* As you'd expect, signed pieces of Edgefield pottery fetch the highest prices, as do examples bearing decorations—typically swirly designs with rough human figures.

Unlike much vintage pottery, Edgefield pottery can still be used in your kitchen with no harmful side effects because of its safe alkaline glaze. A great place to pick up some amazing examples—from as low as $35 up to several thousand dollars—is **Past Times** (165 S. Mechanic St., 864/654-5985, Tues.-Sat. 11 A.M.-5 P.M.) in Pendleton, near Clemson. In Edgefield, visit **Old Edgefield Pottery** (230 Simkins St., 803/637-2060, Tues.-Sat. 10 A.M.-6 P.M., donation) just off the town square. Artist-in-residence Stephen Ferrell is nationally known for the beautiful and historically authentic work he does in this rough-hewn little studio.

NEW ELLENTON, ATOMIC CITY

If you take Whiskey Road out of Aiken, you'll come directly to New Ellenton, "South Carolina's Atomic City." It's a sad little town with a sad tale to tell.

In the early 1950s, the now-extinct town of Ellenton was depopulated by the U.S. government to build the massive Savannah River Site nuclear facility, used during the Cold War to build hydrogen bombs. The entire population of 6,000 people—mostly poor, mostly black—was bought out of their homes and moved 14 miles north to a place that would become known as New Ellenton. Often, entire homes and churches were put on flatbed trucks and driven to the new site. When possible, bodies in cemeteries were exhumed and moved as well.

There has even been an opera of sorts written about the episode: *I Don't Live There Anymore: The Ellenton Story* (www.idlta.com). It was performed at Charleston's Spoleto Festival in 1993. Each October the town holds the **Atomic Festival** (www.newellentonsc.com), a festive outdoor event with music and food, to honor the former town of Ellenton. New Ellenton's chief claim to fame these days—other than having one of the best barbecue joints in the South—is its reputation as a speed trap; always obey the speed limit.

not sit on your car. Gates open at 6:30 P.M., with the flicks starting about 7:30 P.M. It's cash only for admission, but plastic is accepted for concessions. Get to The Big Mo by taking U.S. 1 about a mile north of Monetta.

About two miles south of Monetta is the 30-acre **Janet Harrison High Pond Heritage Preserve** (803/734-3886, www.dnr.sc.gov, daily dawn-dusk, free), named for the regional colloquialism for the well-preserved Carolina bay within its confines—"high pond." You might hear the place referred to as the "windmill high pond" because of the landmark old windmill

near one of the trails. Note that no facilities are available. To get to the preserve, take Highway 39 southeast of its intersection with U.S. 1.

EAST AND SOUTH OF AIKEN
Montmorenci

Take U.S. 78 a few miles east of Aiken to find tiny Montmorenci, a charming town known for two things: a cute vineyard and an awesome B&B.

Unlike the operation in Aiken calling itself a winery, **Montmorenci Vineyards** (2989 Charleston Hwy., 803/649-4870, Wed.-Sat. 10 A.M.-6 P.M.) actually makes wine from its own grapes. There's a tasting room and, of course, a gift shop.

One of the great Southern B&Bs, the 11-room **☾ Annie's Inn** (3083 Charleston Hwy., 803/649-6836, http://anniesinnbnb.com, $110-135) is the labor of love of Dallas and Scottie Ruark. They have tastefully restored this antebellum gem, adding several guest cottages to the grounds, which were once one of the area's biggest cotton plantations. Breakfast is served in a rustic-style country kitchen atmosphere. For those into such things, there's a legend that the ghost of a little girl wanders the halls, calling for her mother.

Salley

South Carolina is chock-full of small-town agricultural festivals, and perhaps the quirkiest is in the tiny town of Salley, population 398. That number balloons to about 30,000 every year on the Saturday after Thanksgiving for the annual **Chitlin' Strut** (www.chitlinstrut.com, free), celebrating that vernacular Southern delicacy made of, yes, fried pig intestines.

Enjoy a parade, a beauty pageant, rides, a tractor show, a "Chitlin' Strut Idol" contest, and, of course, hog calling.

Barnwell

Chiefly known to the world as the birthplace of music legend James Brown, Barnwell was once a powerhouse in state politics, and it still serves as the government seat of Barnwell County. The town's signature landmark is the altogether unique **Barnwell Sundial** (141 Main St., www.barnwellcounty.sc.gov), billed as the world's only freestanding vertical sundial. You can't miss it; it sits next to the traffic circle in front of the imposing county courthouse. A wealthy resident and state senator, Joseph D. Allen, had the sundial made in Charleston in 1858 and brought here. Although it was erected two years prior to the establishment of standard time, they say it keeps within two minutes of it.

CHURCH OF THE HOLY APOSTLES

A few blocks away is the hauntingly beautiful Church of the Holy Apostles (228 Hagood Ave., 803/259-3477, www.holyapostlesbarnwell.org), built in the 1850s of cypress from local swamps, with heart-pine pews. General Sherman wanted Barnwell burned to the

ground because it was named for a leading secessionist. While most of the town was indeed burned, about a dozen antebellum homes and all churches survived more or less intact. However, in what became a fairly routine act of sacrilege at war's end, Union cavalrymen used this church as a stable and watered their horses from the baptismal font, which supposedly dates from medieval times. Hoof prints are still visible on the floors.

But in an act of good karma, a deserter from Sherman's army, James Bolen, ordered a bell made for the church when he noticed it didn't have one. Today it is rung once for each apostle except Judas. The first time it rang, in fact, was for Bolen's funeral; he is buried in the adjoining churchyard. A former governor of the state, Johnson Hagood, is buried here also.

OTHER SIGHTS

There are several other historic churches in Barnwell—though none as magnificent as Holy Apostles—including **St. Andrew's Catholic Church** (168 Madison St., 803/259-7593), the oldest Roman Catholic sanctuary in South Carolina.

The **Circle Theater** (325 Academy St., 803/259-7046, http://barnwellcircletheatre.com), which presents several performances each year, is housed within the former Barnwell Presbyterian Church, built in 1848 and serving as courthouse during the Union occupation (the Yankees burned down the actual courthouse).

Bethlehem Baptist Church (177 Wall St., 803/259-7306), an 1889 structure using some materials from the original 1829 church, is one of the first African American churches organized before the Civil War.

Blackville

There's not much going on in little Blackville, a tidy, law-abiding (the speed limit is a strict 35 mph) hamlet that began as a stop on the old Charleston-Hamburg rail line. Now it's known chiefly for its Mennonite presence—a

© JIM MOREKIS

Church of the Holy Apostles, in Barnwell

© JIM MOREKIS

Locals enjoy loading up on water from God's Acre Healing Springs.

fairly recent addition from the 1970s—and its legendary springs.

◖ GOD'S ACRE HEALING SPRINGS

Yes, the man upstairs himself is listed on county records as property owner of God's Acre Healing Springs (Healing Springs Rd., daily dawn-dusk, free), since its last mortal owner, L. P. Boylston, bequeathed it to Him in 1944. Low, burbling, and tree-lined, with several open spigots installed on its banks, the Healing Springs—actually more of a creek—attracts locals who bring their own jugs to fill up with water and take home for kitchen and bathing use.

Though primarily seen today as an inspiring Christian phenomenon—don't be surprised to see people fervently praying over the water—the spring's legend goes back to the Native Americans, who were frequently in and around the area because of two key transport routes, the Cherokee Trail and the Edisto River. Lore has it that some Native Americans, fighting with the

British during the Revolution, brought some wounded redcoats here after a firefight with some colonists. After word spread of their apparently miraculous recovery, local Christians adopted the Native Americans' reverence of this unique and quietly inspiring natural highlight.

The Healing Springs are just north of Blackville on Highway 3 (adhere to the speed limit religiously—no pun intended). Follow the signs for the Healing Springs Baptist Church and take a right onto Healing Springs Road. In the church parking lot you'll see signs to lead you about 100 yards to the springs, where you can drive up and park.

OTHER SIGHTS

Part of the state's "Discovery Corridor," the **Rivers, Rails, and Crossroads Discovery Center** (U.S. 278, 803/284-3976, www.sc-heritagecorridor.org, Tues.-Sat. 10 A.M.-5 P.M., free) about three miles west of Blackville, memorializes the role of this area of South Carolina in

HIGH COTTON AND HOT STEAM

The big cotton boom of the early 1800s in South Carolina created a demand for a quick way to get the cash crop to market in Charleston, then hotly competing with Savannah, Georgia, for the title of nation's leading cotton export center. That's how South Carolina became home to the first steam rail system in the world, an incredibly little-known fact today.

In 1827, the South Carolina Canal and Rail Road Company was chartered to build a line that would expedite trade from the Upcountry. The resulting 137-mile Charleston-Hamburg line, begun in 1833, was at the time the longest railroad in the world. By 1858 the line was joined with tracks going all the way to Memphis, Tennessee.

However, competing railroads—such as subsequent tracks to Greenville and Augusta—kept profit margins on the Charleston-Hamburg line so low that further expansion was not feasible. With the rise of Augusta and then Atlanta as major rail centers, the line gradually became a backwater run. While the original line stayed in some form of service until the 1980s, its glory days were far in the past.

Today, U.S. 78 roughly follows the old rail bed through towns like Aiken, Blackville, Williston, and, of course, tiny Branchville, which became the world's first rail junction when a spur to Columbia was built off the Charleston-Hamburg line.

the burgeoning rail industry of the early 1800s, when the Charleston-Hamburg line was the longest in the world and hosted the first-ever scheduled train service.

Another interesting sight in town is the **Blackville Public Library** (19420 Solomon Blatt Ave., 803/284-2295, Mon.-Tues. and Thurs. 10 A.M.-1 P.M. and 2-6 P.M., Wed. 2-6 P.M.), inside the restored train depot.

Denmark

Founded in the 1830s, one of the first stops on the Charleston-Hamburg line—called Graham's Turnout until 1893—Denmark is mostly known today for the **Jim Harrison Gallery** (4716 Carolina Hwy., 803/793-5796, www.jimharrison.com, Tues. and Thurs.-Fri. 11 A.M.-5 P.M., Wed. and Sat. 11 A.M.-3 P.M., Sun. 1-4 P.M.), home base of the well-regarded regional artist of the same name, famous for his rural imagery and liberal use of the Coca-Cola logo. Set in the sprawling former Denmark Tea Room, once a thriving restaurant catering to rail travelers, the gallery now houses many examples of Jim's work as well as studio space.

Just down the road the restored historic **Denmark Depot** is still an active Amtrak station.

From the Harrison Gallery, look across the intersection to see the historic AT&T building, site of the first transatlantic phone call in 1915. Within the AT&T building you'll find the **Caroline Collection** (4659 Carolina Hwy., 803/793-4739, Mon.-Sat. 10 A.M.-6 P.M.), which has an extensive collection of American, English, and Continental antiques from the 1700s through the 20th century, spanning three stories.

Rivers Bridge State Historic Site

As synonymous as South Carolina is with the Civil War, it might shock you to know that there is only one preserved battlefield in the entire state from that conflict. It is at the Rivers Bridge State Historic Site (325 State Park Rd., 803/267-3675, www.southcarolinaparks.com, Thurs.-Mon. 9 A.M.-6 P.M., free), a small but well-managed facility just south of the little town of Ehrhardt. In February 1865 a ragtag group of Confederates held out for two days against a larger contingent of General Sherman's mighty army. Rebel earthworks still remain on-site, and there is a 0.75-mile interpretive trail with occasional ranger-led tours.

Food

In Blackville, by all means stop at **☕ Miller's**

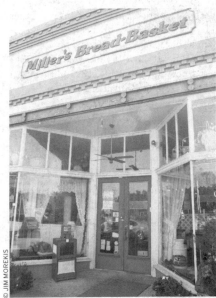

© JIM MOREKIS

the Mennonite-run Miller's Bread Basket, in Blackville

$7.50). Within its suitably Spartan locale you'll find a delectable buffet of smoked pulled pork with two sauces available as well as the requisite sides of hash, cracklin's, and hush puppies.

WEST OF AIKEN
Beech Island

Just below North Augusta on the Savannah River is the historic township of Beech Island, founded in 1685 and one of the earliest inland trading posts in the country. The location was essentially the intersection of several major Indian trails, some of which went all the way to the Mississippi River. Soon after you arrive you'll note that Beech Island is no island at all—the modern name is likely a corruption of "Beech Highland," a reference to the river bluffs and the species of water-loving tree, which presumably grew all around.

To learn more about the fascinating discoveries still being made along the ancient Savannah River, visit **Silver Bluff Audubon Center and Sanctuary** (4542 Silver Bluff Rd., 803/471-0291, www.scaudubon.org, Mon.-Sat. 9 A.M.-5 P.M., free), a wildlife sanctuary and environmental education center occupying two square miles of the former Kathwood Plantation along the river. At least 200 birds live in or visit the area throughout the year. Don't miss the feeding ponds for the endangered wood storks.

The Silver Bluff site has seen some amazing events in history, including extensive Native American habitation, the arrival of Hernando de Soto, a visit by naturalist William Bartram, and a Revolutionary War skirmish. Ongoing archaeological work at the site is done under the auspices of the **Savannah River Archaeological Research Program** (www.srarp.org), which performs the work at the behest of the Department of Energy, which owns much of the land along the river. To get to Silver Bluff, take U.S. 278 south and make a right onto Silver Bluff Road. Continue toward

Bread Basket (438 Main St., 803/284-3117, Tues. and Thurs.-Fri. 11 A.M.-5 P.M., Wed. and Sat. 11 A.M.-3 P.M., $5-10) on the town's main drag. The women who cook and serve the food wear the traditional simple dresses particular to this strand of the church known as Beachy Mennonites (think less-strict Amish). Load up on the simple but tasty Dutch-influenced Southern buffet, but don't neglect to buy a loaf or two of their famous fresh-baked Mennonite bread.

Just down the road you'll find **Dukes Bar-B-Q** (19355 Solomon Blatt Ave., 803/284-3546, Thurs.-Sat. 11 A.M.-9 P.M., $5-10), a fine and typically Spartan example of these widespread but largely unaffiliated barbecue joints in South Carolina sharing the same name.

South of Aiken, the town of New Ellenton, known as "South Carolina's Atomic City," hosts one of the best barbecue joints in the South: ◖ **Carolina Bar-B-Que** (109 Main St., 803/652-2919, Thurs.-Sat. 11 A.M.-8 P.M.,

the river, crossing Old Jackson Highway and the railroad tracks.

Nearby, **Silver Bluff Missionary Baptist Church** (360 Old Jackson Hwy., 803/827-0706) is one of the oldest (they claim to be *the* oldest) black Baptist church in the United States. While the present building is a young whippersnapper built in 1948, the congregation traces its roots to 1750, when founding citizen, trader, and planter George Galphin encouraged his slaves to help spread the gospel—quite a daring move for the time.

◖ Redcliffe Plantation State Historic Site

Beech Island's most famous citizen was South Carolina Governor and U.S. Senator James Hammond, who in 1857 began the construction of his grand Greek Revival home, now part of Redcliffe Plantation State Historic Site (181 Redcliffe Rd., 803/827-1473, www.south-carolinaparks.com, Thurs.-Mon. 9 A.M.-5 P.M., free). Once a plantation with nearly 1,000 African American slaves working here—Hammond, after all, was the man who famously declared "Cotton is king" on the floor of the Senate—Redcliffe was donated to the state in 1973 by a descendant, *Time* magazine editor John Shaw Billings.

Legend has it that Hammond was particularly proud of the fact that he could see the church steeples in Augusta, Georgia, from his upper floor. You can tour the extensively restored and appointed house (Thurs.-Mon. 1 P.M., 2 P.M., 3 P.M., $4 pp). In addition, there is a 1.5-mile nature trail with great bird-watching through Redcliffe's hardwood forest, a historic cemetery with Hammond's grave, and some particularly well-preserved slave quarters. The site hosts a number of special events throughout the year, including the African American Experience in February, Children's Day in April, Archaeology Day in September, and Christmas in the Quarters in December, which examines

the holiday customs of the African Americans who worked and lived at Redcliffe. Consult the website or call for more information.

Redcliffe is about 14 miles from I-20. Take exit 1 onto Martintown Road, and then turn left onto Atomic Road after about four miles. Turn right onto Beech Island Avenue and then left onto U.S. 278. After two miles, take a right onto Hammond Road, then a right onto Redcliffe Road. Note the site is closed Tuesday-Wednesday.

Near the entrance to Redcliffe on U.S. 278 is historic **All Saints Episcopal Church** (1595 Williston Rd., 803/302-9900), built in 1831 and site of the baptism of Woodrow Wilson's wife, Ellen Axson. The future president met her here.

North Augusta

Right on the Savannah River just above Beech Island is the growing town of North Augusta, not to be confused with the larger and older city of Augusta, Georgia, across the river in the Peach State. While it has its roots as one of a cluster of deerskin trading posts in the earliest colonial days, North Augusta was not a town until 1906, when it was founded by James U. Jackson as a resort stop on the old Aiken-Augusta trolley line.

Nowadays, North Augusta is a placid but pleasant community with a particularly well-done trail along the scenic Savannah River, the **North Augusta Greeneway** (803/441-4310, daily dawn-dusk, free), an eight-mile jaunt along the waterfront on a converted railroad right-of-way. Benches and water fountains are available in the more urban portions, and a surprisingly large amount of wildlife can be seen at points. As you're coming into town, look for the "Riverview Park" signs. (One of the routes seems a little odd in that you have to drive through a brand-new mixed-use subdivision, Hammonds Ferry. It seems like a private community, but there's no gate and you just drive through to the Greeneway.)

Nearby is the **Living History Park** (299 W. Spring Grove Ave.), a natural amphitheater that hosts the popular **Colonial Days** (803/279-7560, www.colonialtimes.us, free) event the third weekend in October. The event features reenactments, demonstrations, and voluntary (and very temporary!) enlistment in the local "militia."

The chief equestrian facility in town is the massive **Hippodrome** (5540 Jefferson Davis Hwy., 803/278-4785, www.northaugustahippodrome.com), with a 45,000-square-foot indoor arena and a 52,000-square-foot outdoor arena that together host at least 30 major equestrian events each year at various prices.

A couple of good antiques shops in town are **Riverfront Antique Mall** (5979 Jefferson Davis Hwy., 803/279-0900, Tues.-Sun. 10 A.M.-7 P.M.) and **Singing Hills Antiques** (415 West Ave., 803/441-8805, Tues.-Sat. 10 A.M.-5 P.M.).

ACCOMMODATIONS AND FOOD

The best place to stay in North Augusta is **Rosemary Hall** (804 Carolina Ave., 803/278-6222, http://rosemaryinnbb.com, $129-179), built by town founder James U. Jackson. You can be a guest in one of the homes' six guest rooms and enjoy the beautiful furnishings, excellent breakfast, afternoon tea, and great views. Right across the street is Lookaway Hall, built in 1895 after a bet between James Jackson and his brother Walter. They cut a deck of cards (or in some versions of the tale, flipped a coin) to see who would get to build on this lot, which has a great view overlooking Calhoun Park; Walter won.

For an interesting camping experience right on the river, go to the landing at **Riverview Park** (Hammond Ferry Rd., 803/441-4310), which has several primitive campsites that must be reserved in advance.

For good eats in North Augusta, don't miss the old-fashioned charms of the **SNO-CAP Drive-in** (618 West Ave., www.snocapdrivein.

com), which has dispensed root beer floats, milk shakes, cherry Cokes, ice cream cones, burgers, and onion rings for nearly 50 years. Some weekends you'll find a vintage car show going on in the parking lot. SNO-CAP is close to the Living History Park downtown, a short way off Georgia Avenue, the main drag.

Savannah Bluffs Heritage Preserve

Just north of North Augusta is Savannah Bluffs Heritage Preserve (803/734-3886, www.dnr.sc.gov, daily dawn-dusk, free), a small (less than 100 acres), rustic, but pretty sanctuary along the Savannah River featuring a great and somewhat unusual mix of coastal plain and piedmont habitats. This site is not particularly user-friendly, but it is a paradise of sorts for botany buffs as one of the only habitats of the rocky shoals spider lily, found on the river shoals that are part of the preserve. They bloom spectacularly in June. There are even rarer specimens, such as relict trillium, a perennial herb that flowers in the spring. The rock formations may be remnants of Native American fishing weirs.

The preserve is tricky to get to but worth it for nature lovers. From I-20 exit 1, take Highway 230 southeast about five miles. Turn on the first road on the right, and after about 0.25 miles, turn right again. After about 0.3 miles you'll pass through an aluminum gate. The parking lot is shortly ahead on the left. Beyond the parking lot, follow the power line right-of-way to the trail itself. No facilities are available here.

LAKE THURMOND

South Carolina markets its artificial reservoirs on the Savannah River as the state's "freshwater coast," and they are particularly conducive to recreation. The largest and southernmost location on the freshwater coast is 70,000-acre Lake Strom Thurmond (www.sas.usace.army.mil/lakes/thurmond), still known to old-timers as "Clark's Hill," the reservoir's former name. Along its 70,000 acres are no less than three

THE IRISH TRAVELERS

We know that the clan of nomads called the Irish Travelers arrived in South Carolina sometime in the mid-1800s. But before that, their past is murkier. Some scholars say the Travelers were refugees from Cromwell's pillage of Ireland in the 1600s. Others say they fled the Irish Potato Famine in the 1800s. The Travelers themselves claim to descend from wandering tinkers, or tin sellers, of medieval times. But the locals around North Augusta simply call them "Gypsies."

Whatever their origin, the Irish Travelers are one of the most interesting sociological phenomena in South Carolina. Numbering about 3,000, the community supports itself mostly by spending much of the year traveling around the Southeast doing odd jobs and day labor. When among non-Travelers—whom they call "country people"—they've been known to speak a quirky dialect, vaguely related to Gaelic, called "the Cant" or "Shelta." As with carnie lingo, the Cant isn't taught to anyone outside the Traveler family. So what are the Travelers hiding? Law-enforcement officials around the country say that in many cases, the "odd jobs" the Travelers do for unsuspecting clients—roofing and driveway painting, for example—are elaborate scams.

The Traveler lifestyle is a fascinating, often disturbing glimpse into an age gone by. Children are sometimes taken out of school after eighth grade—the legal limit—in order to take them on the road and teach them the trade. To maintain privacy, many Travelers marry only other Travelers, often in arranged marriages at ages as young as 12 (although that practice seems to be dying out). Years of intermarriage

mean there are only a handful of Traveler surnames, chief among them Carroll, Gorman, Riley, and Sherlock.

South Carolina hosts the bulk of Travelers in the United States, with North Augusta hosting the largest single group in the country. In fact, they have their own subdivision, called Murphy Village after the priest who made the community possible in the 1960s. Contrary to any mental images you may have, many Travelers drive new upscale cars and big shiny pickup trucks. Murphy Village is chockablock with spacious new McMansions, many of which boast large Madonna statues in the front yard.

You literally can't miss Murphy Village. It's on both sides of U.S. 25 on the border of Edgefield County and Aiken County. Just look for the statuary and the big nice houses. Many of the McMansions have their windows covered with butcher paper and sit side-by-side with well-maintained double-wide trailers. Local lore has it that the big houses are part of the dowry of Traveler daughters, intended for the long-engaged couple to move into when they come of age. Another version has it that the paper is to keep *haints* (evil spirits) out of the houses while they're unoccupied.

While the Travelers are not particularly welcoming of curiosity-seekers driving through their community, they'll cause you no harm. In fact, unless you're here in the winter, it's rare to come into contact with the Travelers at all. In the warmer months many are out on the road, doing their thing.

state parks in addition to many private facilities. Fishing highlights include bass, crappie, catfish, bream, and striper (valid state fishing license required; go to www.dnr.sc.gov).

For more information, or to sign up for a tour of the huge dam and power plant on the lake, go to the **Thurmond Lake Office & Visitor Center** (510 Clarks Hill Hwy., 864/333-1147, www.sas.usace.army.mil/lakes/thurmond, daily 8 A.M.-4:30 P.M.).

Hickory Knob State Resort Park

Why is the "r" word in the name of Hickory Knob State Resort Park (1591 Resort Dr., 864/391-2450, www.southcarolinaparks. com, daily 24 hours, free)? The 18-hole Tom Jackson-designed golf course gives you a hint, as does the 78-room lodge, the tennis courts, the swimming pool, the free wireless Internet, and the archery and skeet ranges. In short, as plush as many South Carolina state parks tend

North Augusta's SNO-CAP Drive-in

to be, 1,000-acre Hickory Knob is first among equals in the luxury department.

Lodging is copious and relatively inexpensive. There are 18 fully equipped one-bedroom cabins ($68-105) and a restored historic two-bedroom villa, the Guillebeau House ($87-135). The motel rooms ($48-82) are the standard 2-4-person spaces with TVs, phones, and coffeemakers, and there is a large buffet-style restaurant on the grounds.

Campers will find 44 sites, 21 of them lakefront, with electricity and water ($15-17). Unfortunately there is no designated tent camping area, and the park tends to be dominated by RVs; tent campers might want to check out nearby Bakers Creek State Park.

There is a boat ramp in the park, available for day use for a small fee. You can rent kayaks ($12 per day) to put in on Lake Thurmond. There is a swimming pool, but it's only open for cabin and lodge guests. Nonaquatic recreation includes free tennis courts, 12 miles of

bike trails, a skeet range (reservation required, $11-16 per round), and an archery range (reservation required, $2-10). The on-site golf course is fully tricked out, with a driving range, a practice green, and a clubhouse. Green fees max out at $20, with cart fees around $15.

Bakers Creek State Park

A few minutes upstream from Hickory Knob is the much smaller, seasonal Bakers Creek State Park (863 Baker Creek Rd., 864/443-2457, www.southcarolinaparks.com, Mar.-Dec. daily 6 A.M.-9 P.M., $2 adults, free under age 16). There are no boat rentals, but there are two boat ramps on Lake Thurmond. There's a one-mile hiking trail and a nice 10-mile bike trail. There are two campgrounds at Bakers Creek; Campground One is best for tent campers, featuring 50 sites with water and no electricity ($10-14). Campground Two has 50 sites with electricity and water ($15-18).

Hamilton Branch State Recreation Area

While it has no designated tent sites, overall the most rustic and nature-oriented facility on Lake Thurmond is Hamilton Branch State Recreation Area (111 Campground Rd., 864/333-2223, www.southcarolinaparks.com, daily 6 A.M.-9 P.M., $2 adults, free under age 16). Located on a spit of land jutting into the lake, it offers scenic views, nice fishing spots, and richly wooded terrain—a big plus in hot weather. There are two boat ramps on the lake. There are no cabins or villas, just 140 campsites with electricity and water ($15-17). Almost every site is right on the lake.

Army Corps of Engineers Recreational Areas

The U.S. Army Corps of Engineers manages over 500 campsites on both sides of Lake Thurmond. Four of its campgrounds are on the South Carolina side. Find full campground maps at www.sas.usace.army.mil/lakes/thurmond. They also run several day-use areas on the South Carolina side.

Hawe Creek Campground (877/444-6777, www.recreation.gov, daily 7 A.M.-10 P.M.) has 28 campsites, all lakefront, with water and electricity ($22-24).

For a genuinely rustic experience, try one of the 10 primitive campsites ($6) at **Leroys Ferry Campground** (877/444-6777, www.recreation.

gov, daily 7 A.M.-10 P.M.). The campground has water, a boat ramp, and primitive toilets.

Another good natural experience is at **Mount Carmel** (877/444-6777, www.recreation.gov, daily 7 A.M.-10 P.M.), or "Hesters Bottom," which has 39 sites near the lake plus five tent sites ($18-24).

The **Modoc Campground** (877/444-6777, www.recreation.gov, daily 7 A.M.-10 P.M.) is the most developed of the Corps campgrounds, with 70 sites ($19-24), a boat ramp, a playground, and a hiking trail. All sites are lakefront.

Day-Use Areas

Other places to put a boat in on the lake or get some exercise include **Below Dam South Carolina Recreation Area** (877/444-6777, www.sas.usace.army.mil/lakes/thurmond, daily 8 A.M.-8:30 P.M.), off U.S. 221 across from the visitors center, and **Clarks Hill Park** (877/444-6777, www.sas.usace.army.mil/lakes/thurmond, daily 8 A.M.-8:30 P.M., $4 per vehicle), off U.S. 221 two miles from the visitors center. Clarks Hill Park has swimming beaches. **Parksville Recreation Area** (877/444-6777, www.sas.usace.army.mil/lakes/thurmond, daily 8 A.M.-8:30 P.M., $4 per vehicle) also has swimming beaches. From the visitors center, take U.S. 221 north and turn left onto Highway 28 through Parksville.

GREENVILLE AND THE UPSTATE

Conservative in culture and worldview, the Upstate—you'll also hear it called the Upcountry—is the fastest-growing region of South Carolina. As such, it's becoming much more diverse each passing year, but the area's hospitality and small-town values remain largely intact.

In spirit, the Upstate is the other side of the pendulum of South Carolina history. Unlike the indulgent Anglican plantation culture of the coast, the Upstate traces its pedigree to the Scots-Irish "crackers" who came down from Virginia and Pennsylvania in the mid-1700s along Appalachian trails first blazed by Native American hunters. They brought with them a fiercely Calvinist sense of right and wrong, an often-stubborn self-reliance, and a deep skepticism of the motives and politics of the Lowcountry's slave-owning elite—typified by Charleston, in their eyes a sort of Sin City.

You don't read about it much in the history books, but the Upstate was the most pivotal theater of the American Revolution, in which groups of Upcountry militia and Loyalist Tories savagely battled back and forth while the uniformed regular armies in New England were at a stalemate. (Filmed entirely in South Carolina, Mel Gibson's film *The Patriot,* though much embellished, does a good job of encapsulating this turbulent period.)

By far the region's main metro area, Greenville is rapidly outpacing its reputation for conservatism. It does so through a devotion

© JIM MOREKIS

GREENVILLE

HIGHLIGHTS

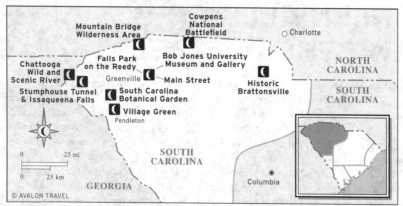

LOOK FOR **(** TO FIND RECOMMENDED SIGHTS, ACTIVITIES, DINING, AND LODGING.

(Falls Park on the Reedy: This rolling green oasis is in excellently restored downtown Greenville (page 347).

(Greenville's Main Street: A nationally renowned example of great walkable urban re-design (page 348).

(Bob Jones University Museum and Gallery: The largest single collection of religious-themed fine art in North America is housed here (page 350).

(Cowpens National Battlefield: A well-done interpretive site that commemorates a key patriot victory in the American Revolution (page 368).

(Chattooga Wild and Scenic River: Ride the white water of *Deliverance* fame or take a relaxing hike (page 377).

(Stumphouse Tunnel and Issaqueena Falls: This fun twofer features a tunnel with a unique history and a scenic waterfall (page 382).

(Mountain Bridge Wilderness Area: The wildest area of the Upstate combines Jones Gap State Park with Caesars Head State Park (page 389).

(South Carolina Botanical Garden: The state's official gardens are on the scenic campus of Clemson University (page 392).

(Pendleton Village Green: This historic hamlet has a delightful central square (page 399).

(Historic Brattonsville: Living history and educational fun for the whole family can be found at this restored Upcountry village (page 414).

to smart urban redevelopment and a forward-looking business sense that has allowed it to move beyond the old mill-based economy that long ago moved offshore.

In the northernmost part of the state, along the fringes of the Blue Ridge mountains, you'll find stunning natural beauty and plenty of outdoor recreation, all at prices much lower than in the heavily

visited havens across the border in more trendy North Carolina.

PLANNING YOUR TIME

You can spend as much or as little time in the Upstate as you want. For the full flavor, from York County over to Clemson and Pendleton, you'll need at least three days and two nights. Remember to budget time to explore

GREENVILLE

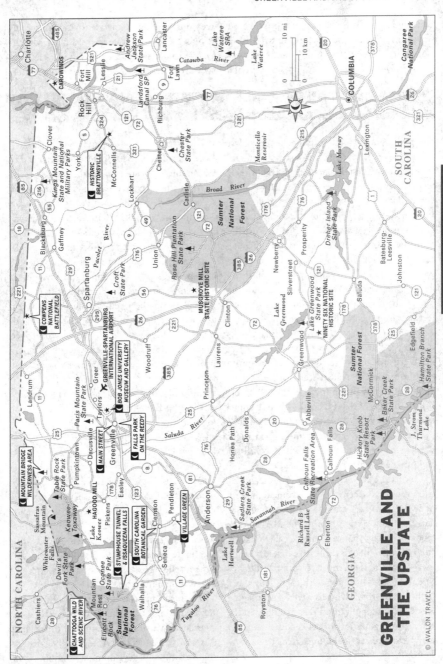

GREENVILLE AND
THE UPSTATE

© AVALON TRAVEL

Greenville's Main Street. For a more focused stay—say, one devoted to hiking or fishing along the Cherokee Foothills Scenic Highway (Hwy. 11)—a couple of nights, or perhaps even one, will do. Be aware that cabin rentals at South Carolina state parks during March-October usually require a weeklong stay, and they are often booked up to a year in advance.

Greenville

Greenville, South Carolina, might be the coolest city you've never heard of. It's a source of frustration to Greenville residents that so few of their fellow Americans—heck, even their fellow South Carolinians—are aware of the city's modern renaissance. When the rest of the country hears about Greenville at all, they complain, it's usually in media reports about its conservative religious residents, exemplified by Bob Jones University, which gained notoriety during the 2000 presidential campaign when it was discovered that the school's ban on interracial dating was still in effect (it was immediately rescinded).

There are plenty of well-scrubbed block-long megachurches here, to be sure, but the only crusade most residents of Greenville seem to be on is spreading the word that their city—inevitably pronounced in the local foothills twang as "GRUHN-vul"—is not populated by backward Bible-thumping bigots, but rather is a rapidly growing and increasingly wealthy city nestled in the scenic foothills of the Appalachians.

Once the very nexus of the American textile industry, Greenville has avoided the fate of so many former manufacturing centers, instead making a transition to the 21st-century global economy that can only be called masterful. Over 250 foreign firms have invested in the area—many of them involved with the automotive industry—bringing with them jobs and a higher standard of living as well as encouraging a certain cosmopolitanism that manifests in the city's growing number of coffeehouses and theater performances (including a free Shakespeare Festival).

HISTORY

Like much of the Upstate, modern-day Greenville is located on what used to be the heart of the Cherokee nation. The first white settler of note was Richard Pearis, who began a plantation around 1770 in what's now downtown Greenville at East Court and South Main Streets. Well regarded by his Cherokee neighbors, Pearis built up his possessions to include a trading post, stables, a dairy, and a sawmill at what's now Greenville's main visitor attraction, Falls Park on the Reedy River. Pearis would also lend his name to an important area landmark, the name of which has now morphed into Paris Mountain. Indeed, Greenville would probably be known today as Paris or even Parisville were it not for the fact that Pearis and his Cherokee friends chose the losing side during the Revolutionary War. The staunch loyalist was stripped of all his possessions by the victorious colonists, and the Cherokee had their land taken—much of it ceded to veterans as payment for service in the war.

By 1786 there was Greenville County, named after General Nathanael Greene, whose military exploits in the Carolinas helped secure the young nation's independence. By 1831 there was a village known as Greenville. And while the name is a nod to the Revolutionary War general, there has always been a certain respect for sustainability here.

The next important phase in Greenville history came in 1915, when North Carolina entrepreneur Vardry McBee moved to the area. A sort of early Walt Disney, he began buying up land and developing it, combining his

© JIM MOREKIS

Greenville's modernity can come as a surprise to some.

1917, Greenville began promoting itself as the "Textile Center of the South." After World War II, that slogan was expanded to "Textile Center of the World." In the 1960s, however, as far-sighted community and business leaders began to see the coming decline of the U.S. textile industry, Greenville began pursuing a more diversified economy, concentrating on increasing foreign investment.

SIGHTS
◖ Falls Park on the Reedy
In a fun quirk of fate, Greenville's most historic spot, the place it began, is also its coolest visitor attraction. Falls Park on the Reedy (864/232-2273, www.greatergreenville.com, daily dawn-dusk, free), a rambling, manicured, eclectic outdoor experience along the Reedy River, is where Richard Pearis, the first white settler up this way, set up his trading post and grist mill in 1768 on what was then Cherokee land.

The scenic **Reedy River Falls** themselves powered Pearis's mill and literally helped spawn the city you see today. While the Pearis Mill is long gone, you can still see some ruins of the later Vardry and McBee mills from the early 1800s on the riverbank.

You can keep up with the historic events that happened here through a series of markers, but Falls Park is more of an all-around pedestrian experience. Walk the 355-foot **Liberty Bridge**—the only curved pedestrian suspension bridge in the country—over the Reedy River falls, and see the nearby **Falls Cottage,** built by George Dryer in 1840.

Meander through the landscaped flower gardens, a legacy of an arboretum set up here by Furman University in the 1930s. Relax and have a picnic on the grassy knoll near the stage where the Upstate Shakespeare Festival is performed, or wade out into the shallow rushing waters of the Reedy River and cool your feet. Get the picture? Quite simply, Falls Park on the Reedy is a unique experience in one of the more criminally underrated cities in the United States.

transactions with a concerted marketing effort and philanthropy to local groups and churches.

The first town council made sure that trees were planted along downtown streets, and to protect the trees, citizens who tied their horses to them were fined. It was during this time that Greenville (and much of the Upstate) also became a haven for Lowcountry planters seeking to escape coastal heat and mosquito-borne malaria. One of those planters, Joel R. Poinsett, gained fame as a notable South Carolina statesman and politician. However, the world today knows him best as the namesake of the poinsettia flower. A respected botanist in his own right, Poinsett grew those flowers and many others in hothouses in the Greenville area.

Greenville saw no real action during the Civil War, but it did act as a major hospital center for the care of wounded Confederate soldiers. By the turn of the 20th century, textile mills began to thrive in the area, and by

⟨ Greenville's Main Street

To get the true feel of how revitalized and fun Greenville is these days, take a leisurely walk down historic Main Street, which in a nice reversal of the usual situation was actually narrowed from four lanes to the current cozy two. The renovated area—one of the most well-done I've seen in the country—runs roughly from the Hyatt Regency Hotel slightly downhill to the newest restored area, the West End. Along the way you will enjoy quality stores, cafés, and restaurants of all descriptions, all under a particularly well-crafted and shady tree canopy.

Buildings of note along Main Street include the old **Greenville County Courthouse** (130 S. Main St.), which served as a courthouse 1918-1950; the **Chamber of Commerce Building** (130 S. Main St.), built in 1925 and one of the first skyscrapers in Greenville; the way-cool **First National Bank Building** (102 S. Main St.), built in 1938 and Greenville's only major art deco structure; the 1898 Romanesque Revival **Stradley and Barr Dry Goods Store** (14 S. Main St.); and of course the grand old **Poinsett Hotel** (120 S. Main St.), one of Greenville's original skyscrapers, built in 1925 at the then-enormous cost of $1.5 million, now a Westin property.

Broad Margin

Fans of Frank Lloyd Wright always want to

know where his houses are, even if they usually cannot visit them. The great architect designed two in South Carolina: Auldbrass is in Yemassee, and Broad Margin (9 W. Avondale St.) is in Greenville, built in 1954. Both are privately owned. One of Wright's Usonian homes, intended to fit into the natural environment and blur the distinction between interior and exterior, Broad Margin is intended to be invisible from the street, and it pretty much is. I include the house here for your edification and well-roundedness, although your experience with it is likely to be fleeting.

Downtown Baptist Church
The tall needlelike spire of the Downtown Baptist Church (101 W. McBee Ave., 864/235-5746) announces that you'll soon be seeing the sanctuary's imposing Greek Revival exterior. Built in 1858, this was one of Greenville's premier congregations in the city's biggest denomination. Most of the congregation split for a bigger church in the 1970s, but now it's as popular as ever.

John Wesley Methodist Episcopal Church
Built at the turn of the 20th century, the cruciform Gothic Revival John Wesley Methodist Episcopal Church (101 E. Court St.) was built by an African American congregation organized after the Civil War by former "slave preacher" Reverend J. R. Rosamund. The congregation has its roots in a decision by the national Methodist Episcopal Church to send missionaries to the South after the Civil War to help educate newly freed African Americans. The congregation's first church was built on a different parcel of land donated by Alexander McBee, son of the "Father of Greenville," Vardry McBee.

Christ Episcopal Church
The first church in Greenville, organized about 1820, is Christ Episcopal Church (10 N.

Church St., 864/271-8773, www.ccgsc.org). The original parishioners were Lowcountry residents who came to the Upstate during the summer, and therefore this design is more typical of the grand Anglican churches of that region, with a notably tall 130-foot spire. The current Gothic sanctuary dates from 1852. In the churchyard is the final resting place of the "Father of Greenville," Vardry McBee.

Kilgore-Lewis House
Cotton planter Josiah Kilgore built the two-story Palladian Kilgore-Lewis House (506 Academy St.) for his daughter in 1838 as a wedding present, and it is one of the oldest structures in town. Currently the headquarters of the Greenville Council of Garden Clubs, its ostentatious style is countered by the old-school Upcountry construction of heart pine fastened with wooden pegs. Note the home's original handblown windowpanes.

On an interesting side note, this house was moved to its present location to avoid demolition. This is also where the spring that once supplied the drinking water for Greenville was located.

Whitehall
The oldest home in Greenville is Whitehall (310 W. Earl St.), built in 1813 as a summer home by the famed Henry Middleton, who also owned Middleton Place plantation in Charleston. It's now a private residence, but you can see the grandeur of the exterior, a classic example of the Barbadian-influenced Lowcountry style here in the Upcountry.

Hampton-Pinckney Historic District
Greenville boasts some fine examples of Victorian architecture, with the best clustered in the Hampton-Pinckney Historic District bounded by Butler Avenue, Asbury Avenue, and Lloyd Street; the eponymous Hampton and Pinckney Avenues are the main arteries. You might hear

this area referred to simply as "Old Money" because of its pedigree dating back to the days of city founder Vardry McBee, who built a house here along with many of his children. You'll see lots of different styles, including Italianate, Greek Revival, Queen Anne, Greek Revival, Colonial Revival, and even a few bungalows.

Shoeless Joe Jackson Museum

With memorabilia from the life and career of Greenville's favorite native son, the Shoeless Joe Jackson Museum (356 Field St., 864/235-6280, www.shoelessjoejackson.org, Sat. 10 A.M.-4 P.M. and Greenville Drive home game nights, free) suitably sits adjacent to the new Fluor Field minor-league ballpark in the historic West End. The house, formerly the home of Joe and his family, was moved to this site from 119 East Wilborn Street in spring 2008, and it currently houses a variety of photos and artifacts, all in a cozy loving setting. Parking next to the museum is free except on Greenville Drive game days.

◖ Bob Jones University Museum and Gallery

Though Bob Jones University gained national notoriety during the 2000 presidential election for its unfortunate stance on interracial dating, you have to give credit where it's due: A fair-minded person has to say that Bob Jones U. deserves national praise for the outstanding—and puzzlingly under-the-radar—collection of religious art at the Bob Jones University Museum and Gallery (1700 Wade Hampton Blvd., 864/770-1331, www.bjumg.org, Tues.-Sun. 2-5 P.M., $5 adults, $3 students, free ages 6-12). Indeed, the museum calls itself "Greenville's best-kept secret." The largest single array of such artwork in the western hemisphere, this museum contradicts the idea that Bob Jones U. is a backward collection of bigoted malcontents.

The main gallery at the museum, and the highlight for most visitors, is the Old Masters collection, focusing primarily on baroque and Renaissance work from northern Europe and Italy. It includes work by Botticelli, Rubens, and Anthony van Dyck, but don't overlook the often stunning works by lesser-known artists such as the starkly beautiful *Crucifix* by the 14th-century Italian painter Francesco di Vannuccio.

Other collections include the Egyptian and Holy Land artifacts of the Bowens Collection and the wholly unique *The Progress of Revealed Religion* series by 18th-century English artist Benjamin West. West almost single-handedly rekindled religious art in the Anglican Church, which previously disdained visual representations because of their supposedly Roman Catholic tendencies.

Note the unusually truncated hours of the gallery—it's open only three hours each afternoon Tuesday-Sunday—and plan accordingly. There's a much smaller downtown satellite, the **Museum and Gallery at Heritage Green** (Buncombe St., 864/770-1331, www.bjumg. org, Tues.-Sat. 10 A.M.-5 P.M., Sun. 2-5 P.M., $5 adults, $4 students, free under age 12). Get a combo ticket ($8 adults, $4.50 students and children) to see both collections the same day.

Greenville County Museum of Art

The Greenville County Museum of Art (420 College St., 864/271-7570, www.greenvillemuseum.org, Tues.-Wed. and Fri.-Sat. 11 A.M.-5 P.M., Thurs. 11 A.M.-8 P.M., Sun. 1-5 P.M., free) is located in a nice space on the "Heritage Green" downtown at the corner of Academy and College Streets. The feather in their cap is the resident collection, always on display, of 32 of what Andrew Wyeth himself called his best watercolors. They also have an eclectic collection of American contemporary artists such as Josef Albers, Jasper Johns, Andy Warhol, Edward Hopper, and Romare Bearden.

Upcountry History Museum

Also at Heritage Green is a much newer facility, the Upcountry History Museum (540

THE STORY OF SHOELESS JOE

With the possible exception of another controversial man with the same surname—civil rights leader Jesse Jackson—Greenville's most famous native son is Joseph Jefferson "Shoeless Joe" Jackson, one of a handful of baseball players whose name is mentioned in the same breath as Babe Ruth (who eagerly took hitting tips from the South Carolinian, in fact). Baseball purists remember him for the deceptive grace of his powerful natural swing and his claim on the third-highest career batting average at .356. But to much of the general public, he's best known for his role in the Black Sox gambling scandal, which he seems to have actually had little to do with.

Born in next-door Pickens County in 1888—though some scholars think it was actually a year earlier—Jackson began working in a textile mill while still a young child, and as a result had no formal education. In those days each mill fielded its own team, and "textile ball" was a popular local pastime for mill workers and area spectators alike. Jackson soon became a standout on the Brandon Mill nine, gaining his nickname when, during a game in nearby Anderson, he took the batter's box in his socks because his new cleats were aggravating a bad blister. After he then swatted a triple, a frustrated fan of the opposing team called Jackson a "shoeless son of a gun," and the name stuck—along with an unfortunate image of a clueless Southern bumpkin.

In 1908 Jackson went on to play minor league ball for the Greenville Spinners. He was soon signed for a short stint with the Philadelphia Athletics, an unproductive relationship that soon had him moonlighting around the South Atlantic League with the Savannah minor-league team. Settling into life in the big leagues, he went on to a five-year run with the Cleveland Indians, chalking up a .408 batting average his rookie season. The gangly left-fielder signed with the Chicago White Sox in 1915, and he still holds the career triples and batting average records for that team.

Jackson's aw-shucks persona would come back to haunt him during the 1919 Black Sox scandal, when the White Sox were accused of throwing that year's World Series. Although he had by far the best performance of both teams during the series, his output dipped notably in the games the White Sox lost. The Chicago papers had a field day savaging the Southerner when under oath he admitted he'd participated. Modern scholarship has shown, however, that an unscrupulous lawyer manipulated him into making the admission. Years later, his teammates admitted he was at none of the meetings where the fix was discussed.

While the jury acquitted Jackson, baseball commissioner Kenesaw Mountain Landis banned him from the sport anyway. A hang-dog Jackson returned to the familiar South, opening up a successful dry-cleaning business back in Savannah. He also quietly managed and played on several Georgia semipro and "outlaw" teams. He eventually moved back to Greenville with his wife in 1933, continuing to play and manage. For the rest of his life Jackson would proclaim his innocence, though he fatalistically accepted his tarnished place in history. While working at a Greenville liquor store he owned late in life, none other than the great Ty Cobb and sportswriter Grantland Rice came in. According to Rice, after Cobb paid for his bottle he asked Jackson, "Don't you know me, Joe?" Jackson said, "Sure, I know you, Ty, but I wasn't sure you wanted to speak to me. A lot of them don't."

Jackson died of a heart attack in 1951 and is buried in Woodlawn Memorial Park in Greenville, section 5, plot 333. You can find a striking bronze statue of Shoeless Joe in downtown Greenville in the West End on Main Street. The **Shoeless Joe Jackson Museum** (356 Field St., 864/235-6280, www.shoelessjoejackson. org, Sat. 10 A.M.-4 P.M. and Greenville Drive home game nights) is adjacent to the new ballpark in the historic West End. Once the Jackson family home, the structure was moved from 119 East Wilborn Street to this location. Another effort to honor him is the dedication of **Shoeless Joe Jackson Memorial Park** (406 West Ave., 864/288-6470, daily dawn-dusk, free), farther out on the West End on the site of an old ball field where the man himself once played.

Today, Jackson's legacy is in a bit of a renaissance, and you can find out more about the advocacy effort to get him into the Baseball Hall of Fame at www.blackbetsy.com, a website bearing the nickname of his favorite bat.

Buncombe St., 864/467-3100, www.upcountryhistory.org, Tues.-Sat. 10 A.M.-5 P.M., Sun. 1-5 P.M., $5 adults, $3 ages 4-12, free under age 4). With its interactive exhibits, this is a great way for the whole family to pick up on some of the little-known but compelling history of the Upstate's settlement and economic development.

Greenville Zoo

This is a far cry from the expansive nationally renowned facility at Columbia's Riverbanks Zoo and Garden, so if you've already been there, don't expect to be wowed. Nonetheless,

the smallish Greenville Zoo (150 Cleveland Park Dr., 864/467-4300, www.greenvillezoo. com, daily 10 A.M.-4:30 P.M., $6 adults, $3 children, free under age 4) is good for an hour or so of fun if you're in the downtown area, and of course the kids will enjoy it immensely. Comprising 10 acres tucked into verdant Cleveland Park, with well-done landscaping, the Greenville Zoo's selection of wildlife is sort of a "greatest hits" compilation, with the key attractions being lions, elephants, giraffes, orangutans, leopards, and cute red pandas.

Roper Mountain Science Center

The eclectic Roper Mountain Science Center (402 Roper Mt. Rd., 864/355-8900, www. ropermountain.org, hours vary, free) offers a planetarium, nature trails, a pioneer farm, and an amphitheater. A big draw for area schools, your area of interest is likely to be the "Starry Night" programs in the planetarium (Fri. 7:30-10 P.M.), with shows at 7:30 P.M. and 8:30 P.M.; the rest of the time you can look through the telescope.

The facility is also open to the public on the second Saturday of each month approximately 9 A.M.-1 P.M. You can visit the gardens and grounds (Mon.-Fri. 8:30 A.M.-5 P.M.), which include a pretty good arboretum. Bikes are not allowed on the trails.

American Legion War Museum

Devoted to chronicling in a serious fashion the area's military contributions, mostly from the Spanish-American War onward, the small volunteer-run American Legion War Museum (430 N. Main St., 864/271-2000, www.americanlegion3warmuseum.com, Sat. 10 A.M.-5 P.M., Sun. 1-5 P.M., free) features displays of uniforms, weapons, and memorabilia from area military units. It's a research facility as well, with the service record books for all South Carolinians who served during World War II.

GREENVILLE

ALBERT EINSTEIN IN GREENVILLE

Plain-spun, Baptist-dominated Greenville would seem an odd place for a world-renowned nuclear physicist, but the Upstate did indeed host the great scientist for a time in the early 1940s while he served on the board of directors for nearby Black Mountain College in North Carolina.

Einstein often came to Greenville to visit his son from his first marriage, Hans Albert, busy doing landmark research of his own (in his case on hydraulics) at Clemson University's Agricultural Experiment Station.

But the story gets even more unlikely. A cousin of Albert's—also named Hans, a coincidence that has led to much misinformation on the Internet—moved to Greenville in the early 1940s on a student exchange program. Once there, he attended Furman University. Looking in the Greenville phone book for other Einsteins on his arrival, he saw Hans Albert's name listed. Over time, the three Einsteins—Albert, Hans Albert, and Hans—would spend social time together.

Now in private hands, Hans's house—Albert's son Hans, that is—can be found at 9 West Avondale Street in Greenville's historic district.

TOURS

Carriage rides are available downtown (864/369-1411, Fri.-Sat. 6-11 P.M.). For more detailed guided tours, check out **Greenville History Tours** (864/567-3940, www.greenvillehistorytours.com, $12, culinary tour $39), which offers several options.

Bicycle rental and guided bike tours are available from **Reedy Rides** (864/419-2944), or try an even closer-to-the-pavement downtown experience with **Reedy River Rickshaw** (864/373-1222).

ENTERTAINMENT AND EVENTS
Nightlife

For a city so strongly associated with Southern Baptist conservatism, there's actually quite a lively nightlife scene in Greenville. Last call in Greenville is a lusty 2 A.M., later than one might imagine for this once dry county.

Since native son Edwin McCain's heyday in the late 1990s, there has been no Greenville music "scene" per se, but the center of live music is undoubtedly **The Handlebar** (304 E. Stone Ave., 864/233-6173, www.handlebar-online.com, ticket prices vary), a little ways north of downtown. Subtitled "A Listening Room," the Handlebar markets itself specifically as an intimate space that's friendly for musicians and audiences alike. You never know what you're going to get: Neo-pop, Afro pop, heavy metal, and gypsy jazz, you'll find it here.

In the restored West End across from Falls Park is **Chicora Alley** (608 S. Main St., 864/232-4100, www.chicoraalley.com, Tues.-Sat. 5 P.M.-2 A.M., Sun.-Mon. 5 P.M.-midnight), a great place to grab a bite, have a brew, and listen to reggae or jazz. It's one of the main places for local 20-somethings to hang out, and it can get pretty packed on a weekend night or football-viewing day.

In the same neighborhood is another popular hangout, **Blue Ridge Brewing Company** (217 N. Main St., 864/232-4677, www.blueridgebrewing.com, daily 11 A.M.-2 A.M., entrées $10-20), featuring handcrafted beers by on-site brew master Jay Simpson such as the Kurli Blonde, the Colonel Paris Pale Ale (named after the city's founder), and The Rainbow Trout ESB.

There are several other popular hops-oriented hangouts along the same lines in the area: **Liberty Tap Room** (941 S. Main St., 864/770-7777, www.libertytaproom.com, daily 4 P.M.-2 A.M.) is part of the T-Bonz regional food and beverage chain and has its own line of handcrafted beers. **Barley's Tap Room** (25 W. Washington St., 864/232-3706, www.barleystaproom.com) offers great music several nights a week with no cover charge. While Barley's isn't a true microbrewery, its massive selection of beers on tap easily makes up for that.

Carolina Ale House (113 S. Main St., 864/351-0521, www.carolinaalehouse.com) has a full food menu and a rooftop bar, a signature of this regional chain. The nearby **Nose Dive** (116 S. Main St., 864/373-7300, www.thenosedive.com, Thurs.-Sat. 11 A.M.-11 P.M., Mon.-Wed. 11 A.M.-10 P.M.) is a fun gastropub.

For those with a more swanky taste in libation, try the **Blu Martini Bar and Nightclub** (1 College St., 864/242-5743, Tues.-Fri. 5 P.M.-2 A.M., Sat. 7 P.M.-2 A.M., cover charges vary) or **The Art Bar on Main** (18 S. Main St., 864/991-8278, www.theartbaronmain.com), which offers a range of Prohibition cocktails in addition to craft beers.

For a truly unique experience, check out the dinner-and-improv scene at **Café and Then Some** (101 College St., 864/232-2287, www.cafeats.com, dinner seatings Wed.-Sat. 6:30 P.M., 7 P.M., and 7:30 P.M., show only seatings Wed.-Sat. 7:45 P.M., shows $15, entrées $12-20). For an incredible 30 years running, Café has brought combined sketch comedy with good food. Husband-and-wife owners Bill and Susan Smith—he's "Bubba" onstage—join in the fun as performers themselves.

If you're more in the mood for a straight-up Irish pub, try **Connolly's** (24 E. Court St., 864/467-0300) just off Main Street. Though a far cry from the legendary Manhattan locations with the same name, the Greenville version is a great place to beat the heat and enjoy a pint.

Performing Arts

One might not rank the **Greenville Symphony Orchestra** (GSO, 200 S. Main St., 864/232-0344, www.greenvillesymphony.org) among the world's greatest ensembles, but it is an impressive group nonetheless and is the city's performing arts crown jewel. The GSO is actually one of the Southeast's oldest orchestras, with roots going back to 1948, when a group of volunteer musicians began playing at Furman University. The GSO now plays most of its concerts at the modern and beautiful Peace Center Concert Hall on the banks of the Reedy River. A chamber orchestra series usually plays at the adjacent Gunter Theatre.

The only professional dance troupe in the Upstate is the **Carolina Ballet Theatre** (872 Woodruff Rd., 864/421-0940, www.carolinaballet.org), which performs an intriguing variety of dance, from modern to classical—and a December *Nutcracker*, of course—at the Peace Center downtown. **Greenville Ballet** (105 Woodruff Industrial Lane, 864/234-5677, www.greenvilleballet.com) also puts on the requisite holiday *Nutcracker* performance in December.

The prime exponent of the dramatic arts in Greenville is the **Warehouse Theatre** (37 Augusta St., 864/235-6948, www.warehousetheatre.com), a professional company that stages the annual three-month Upstate Shakespeare Festival May-July. They put on their regular season shows, a mix of chestnuts and more adventurous pieces, in a space in a renovated warehouse in the historic West End. Another key group is **Centre Stage–South Carolina!** (501 River St., 864/233-6733, www.centrestage.org), complete with exclamation point, a professional troupe that performs a solid season of classics in a large space downtown.

While the liberal arts **Furman University**

(3300 Poinsett Hwy., 864/294-2000, www.furman.edu) is an all-undergraduate institution that grants no advanced degrees, its music program is still pretty decent. They offer a well-received series of free summer concerts, "Music by the Lake," in a charming outdoor amphitheater on campus. Shows generally begin on Thursday evenings at 7:30 P.M.

VENUES

Because of the size of its metro area and its strategic location near several interstate highways, Greenville brings in a surprisingly high caliber of big-name acts. Most of these perform at the huge **Bi-Lo Center** (650 N. Academy St., 864/467-0008, www.bilocenter.com), a 15,000-seat arena named after a regional grocery chain (here in NASCAR country, no one gripes about corporate naming rights). It's located right off I-385 near downtown Greenville.

The wonderfully named **Peace Center** (3300 S. Main St., 864/467-3000, www.peacecenter.org) is actually named after the influential local Peace family, who made a large donation to help build the facility in the late 1980s in a then-rundown area of town. Perhaps the first really big neighborhood renovation project in Greenville, the Peace Center overlooks the Reedy River in the heart of downtown at the corner of Main and Broad Streets. It features a variety of different spaces, including the 2,100-seat Peace Concert Hall, the intimate 427-seat Gunter Theatre, and the 1,100-seat outdoor DowBrands Amphitheatre. Larkin's hosts several open-air jazz events throughout the year.

The city's main expo space is the **Carolina First Center** (1 Exhibition Dr., 864/233-2562, www.palmettoexp.com), formerly known as the Palmetto Expo Center. This massive space encompasses over 300,000 square feet.

Festivals and Events

Greenville takes full advantage of its generally

wonderful weather, relatively cool in the summer for a Southern city and bearable enough during the winter. Note how many of the following festivals take place outdoors, and how many are free.

WINTER

Other cities have huge Christmas tree lighting ceremonies or parades with Santa Claus. But as is fitting in a city with a founder named Poinsett, Greenville's version is the annual **Poinsettia Parade** (Main St., 864/467-4350, www.greatergreenville.com, free), a fun event the first Saturday in December marking the start of the holiday season. Floats trundle down Main Street bedecked with poinsettias and other holiday vegetation. And yes, Saint Nick makes an appearance or two.

In January comes the **South Carolina International Auto Show** (Carolina First Center, 1 Exposition Ave., 864/233-2562, www.motortrendautoshows.com, $8 adults, $5 children, free under age 7), one of several high-profile annual events tapping into the region's automotive industry. See new car and truck models, exotics, and hybrids, often well before the general public gets a peek.

Greenville's name becomes quite apt in March, when several St. Patrick's Day-themed events happen. On the Sunday before St. Patrick's Day comes the **Irish Cultural Festival** (Falls Park, South Main St., 864/370-2272, www.irishcaraclub.com, free), a.k.a. "Return to the Green," sponsored by the local social organization, The Irish Cara Club and showcasing Celtic culture, music, and food. On the weekend nearest St. Patrick's Day itself comes the **St. Patrick's Day Walk** (864/288-4937, free), a fun family event that leaves from St. Mary's Church, includes City Hall, and finishes up at Piazza Bergamo.

SPRING

In April comes perhaps the city's most unique large public event, the **Artisphere International Arts Festival** (various venues, 864/271-9398, www.artisphere.us, admission varies), held in the historic West End area, which is rapidly being restored. Greenville's answer to Charleston's Spoleto features some perhaps surprisingly cutting-edge art in the outdoor "Artist's Row," music, and theater performances. Many events are free, but some indoor performances are ticketed. As is typical of most South Carolina festivals, there are plenty of activities for children.

Visitors with a green thumb—or those just yearning for one—will enjoy the **Piedmont Plant and Flower Festival** (1354 Rutherford Rd., 864/244-4023, free), which takes place over a weekend in early May at the Greenville State Farmers Market. One of three massive statewide events of its kind, the Plant and Flower Festival is *very* popular, drawing people from all over the Upstate to acquire new seeds and varieties of plants as well as fresh fruit and vegetables, which they can be seen wheeling off to their pickup trucks in large wagons (bring your own wheels, or there are wagons you can use on-site). Expert gardeners are on hand to give advice and spread some of the collective greenness of their thumbs on to you.

SUMMER

My favorite Greenville event—and perhaps the most surprising one to outsiders who assume the city is populated by clueless hayseeds—is the summer-long **Upstate Shakespeare Festival** (Falls Park, S. Main St., 864/787-4016, www.upstateshakespearefestival.org, performances May-Aug. Thurs.-Sun. 7 P.M., free). A project of the local Warehouse Theatre, a professional troupe, the festival brings two complete productions by the Bard downtown, separated by a period classic by another well-known playwright. The setting is the rolling Falls Park, where the audience lolls around on the grass, enjoys a bottle of wine and a picnic dinner, and takes in the show in the gradually cooling air of a fine Upstate evening. Did I mention it's free?

© JIM MOREKIS

The annual Upstate Shakespeare Festival is held in Falls Park.

The popular **Greek Festival** (St. George Greek Orthodox Church, 406 N. Academy St., 864/233-8531, free) takes place on a Thursday-Saturday in May. The fare is typical of any Greek Festival throughout the nation, with the usual assortment of Greek music and dancers in traditional garb. It takes place mostly outside in the courtyard between the beautiful neoclassical cathedral and its parish center.

The Scots have their time in June with Greenville's **Scottish Games and Highland Festival** (3300 Poinsett Hwy., 864/268-3550, www.greenvillegames.org, $15 adults, $5 children, free under age 6), held on the Furman University campus. It's a two-day event with a ceilidh (pronounced "KAY-lee"), or party, with music on Friday night, followed by various competitions and performances Saturday. While much of the action centers on the usual Scottish obsession with burly men throwing heavy objects around, a special treat at this event is the Border Collie Invitational Tournament, in which the canines and their handlers perform a variety of athletic maneuvers.

Each Father's Day week in June comes an especially distinctive Upstate event with roots in upstate New York, the **Chautauqua Festival** (Faris Rd., 864/244-1499, http://greenvillechautauqua.org, free), held on the campus of Greenville Technical College. Its pedigree goes back to the first such event, an outdoor Methodist education program in New York in the 1920s, which eventually gave rise to the Lyceum Movement, the forerunner of modern American adult education. Greenville's edition began in 1999, and nearby Asheville, North Carolina, also holds a similar event. It's hard to describe, really: Part teach-in, part free-for-all discussion, Chautauqua focuses on a special topic each year for in-depth exploration. No conclusions are reached, with the goal instead being a full and complete discussion. The 2008 edition was subtitled "They Came to America" and featured interactive shows about Winston

Churchill, Golda Meir, and the Marquis de Lafayette.

The biggest fireworks display in fireworks-mad South Carolina happens in Greenville at the **AT&T Red, White, and Blue Festival** (Main St., 864/770-1331, www.mainstevents.com, free) each July 4.

FALL

After a hiatus during August's blistering heat, the city wakes up again in September, starting with the weekend-long **Southern Exposure** (various venues, 864/233-5663, www.southernexposure-greenville.com, admission varies), a food, wine, and music event featuring some of Greenville's best chefs. The festival is organized in part by the platinum-selling singer, songwriter, and South Carolina native Edwin McCain.

A fun outdoor fall event is September's **Art in the Park Festival** (South Main St., 864/232-4433, www.upstatevisualarts.org, free). About 20,000 people come to the renovated West End to browse booths featuring art by well over 100 regional artists. An enclosed Beer and Wine Garden offers libations.

A popular fall event is the weekend-long **St. Francis Fall for Greenville** (Main St., 864/235-5525, www.mainstevents.com, free) in October, featuring music on four outdoor stages downtown and food by many of the region's best restaurants. Fun competitions include a waiters' race, a bartender "mix-off," and ice carving. It can get annoying having to buy tickets to make food and drink purchases, but the event is well-organized and geared toward families. If you're 21 or over and want to drink alcohol, you must buy a wristband ($1).

As one of the centers of auto production in the United States, Greenville hosting the annual **Euro Auto Festival** (104 Lakecrest Dr., 864/242-0761, www.euroautofestival.com, $5) is something of a no-brainer. The weekend-long event is held each October on the grounds of the BMW Zentrum, a state-of-the-art display facility sponsored by the German automaker and located just outside Greenville on I-85 on the way to Spartanburg. The Euro Festival, with all proceeds going to the American Red Cross, generally concentrates on a different European country or maker each year, with the 2012 edition focusing on the cars of the Mercedes-Benz brand. Highlights include the Saturday "Car Corral" auto show and a road rally on Sunday.

SHOPPING

For all practical purposes, shopping in Greenville comes in two forms: on Main Street and off. Don't neglect the restored West End section of Main Street.

Main Street

The most unique shopping experience on Main Street is at the **Mast General Store** (111 N. Main St., 864/235-1883, Mon.-Thurs. 10 A.M.-6 P.M., Fri.-Sat. 10 A.M.-9 P.M., Sun. noon-5 P.M.), a branch of a North Carolina-based regional chain. This hard-to-define and sprawling store, restored to a 1920s vibe, has camping gear, outdoor clothing, preppy clothes, local books, maps, gifts, and an entire candy section in the back.

Despite its bland name, the **Clothing Warehouse** (123 N. Main St., 864/467-1238, www.theclothingwarehouse.com, Mon.-Wed. 11 A.M.-8 P.M., Thurs.-Sat. 11 A.M.-9 P.M., Sun. 11 A.M.-7 P.M.), a branch of a popular Southern chain, is the hippest vintage clothing and shoe store in town, with a great selection from various eras.

Paying homage to one of the area's largest employers is **Michelin on Main** (550 S. Main St., 864/241-4450), which contains every kind of Michelin-branded thing you can imagine. The funky **Christopher Park Gallery** (608-A S. Main St., 864/232-6744, www.chicken-manart.com) in the West End has a variety of outsider paintings and sculptures and locally crafted jewelry. On the other end of Main is

GREENVILLE

the **Mary Praytor Gallery** (26 S. Main St., 864/235-1800, www.themarypraytorgallery. com, Tues.-Sat. 10 A.M.-5 P.M.), which features eclectic folk art and contemporary paintings from regional artists.

Into beading? Try **The Beaded Frog** (241 N. Main St., 864/235-2323, www.beadedfrog. com, Tues.-Wed. and Fri.-Sat. 11 A.M.-5:30 P.M., Thurs. 11 A.M.-8 P.M., Sun. 1-5 P.M.), a locally owned store with every type of bead you could imagine. A unique store just for Fido is **The Barkery Bistro** (118 N. Main St., 864/236-1503, http://thebarkerybistro.myshopify.com, Mon.-Sat. 10 A.M.7 P.M.), which sells a variety of fresh gourmet treats, gadgets, jewelry (!) and clothing for your pup.

Take the kids to **O.P. Taylor's** (117 N. Main St., 864/467-1984, www.optaylors.com, Mon.-Sat. 10 A.M.-6 P.M., Sun. 1-5 P.M.), a fine toy store with a variety of European toys, Thomas the Tank Engine gear, and games. As military surplus stores go, **Greenville Army Store** (660 S. Main St., 864/232-3168, www.greenvillearmystore.com, Mon.-Sat. 9:30 A.M.-5:30 P.M.) is outstanding—which makes sense when one considers it's been in business for half a century and served many generations of martial Upstaters.

Unique Stores

There aren't many indie record stores left in the United States, but a great one is still thriving at **Horizon Records** (2-A W. Stone Ave., 864/235-7922, http://blog.horizonrecords.net), catering to true music enthusiasts since 1975 with a variety of new and used product on CD, DVD, and vinyl. Owner Gene Berger and his eclectic helpful staff often host some fairly high-profile musicians for workshops and in-house concerts; check the website for details.

There aren't too many bicycle shops that cater specifically to female riders, but you'll find that at **Pedal Chic** (651-B S. Main St., 864/242-2442, http://shop.pedalchic.com). Owner Robin Bylenga sells and rents bikes as well as offers a range of cute but practical women's bicycle clothing.

Malls and Markets

The main mall in the area is **Haywood Mall** (700 Haywood Rd., 864/288-0511, www. simon.com, Mon.-Thurs. 10 A.M.-9 P.M., Fri.-Sat. 10 A.M.-9:30 P.M., Sun. 12:30-6 P.M.), whose anchor stores are Belk, Dillard's, J. C. Penney, Macy's, and Sears. They're at the intersection of I-385 North and Haywood Road near the airport.

On Court Street between Main and Fall Streets, April-October each Saturday, you'll find the **Saturday Market** (864/467-5780, 7 A.M.-noon), a showcase of local growers and their goods.

SPORTS AND RECREATION

While most serious outdoor activity in the Upstate is in the region to the north, there are still plenty of delightful recreation opportunities in and around Greenville, especially for families with children.

Parks

Rustic it isn't, but any discussion of parks in Greenville must begin with the scenic and convenient **Falls Park on the Reedy** (601 S. Main St., 864/467-4350, www.fallspark.com, daily 24 hours, free). Whether it's for a picnic, bird-watching, or a stroll on the riverside trail network, it's a great place downtown to relax, exercise, get some sun, or simply just enjoy the greenery.

Often simply called "city park," another great park within Greenville proper is **Cleveland Park** (E. Washington St. and Cleveland Park Dr., www.greatergreenville.com, daily dawn-dusk, free). Lovers of ball sports will enjoy the tennis, volleyball, and softball facilities at this 126-acre green space, while in-town hikers will enjoy the simple trail areas. And, of course, Cleveland Park hosts the Greenville Zoo.

More valuable for its history than its recreational opportunities, we can't forget **Shoeless**

Joe Jackson Memorial Park (406 West Ave., 864/288-6470). The old stomping grounds of the mill team that Shoeless Joe played on, the field was recently renamed and partially restored by the city in honor of its most revered native son. Get here from downtown by taking Academy Street west, which turns into Easley Bridge Road. Look for West Avenue across from a church, and take a right directly to the ballpark.

My favorite park in the Greenville area, and one of South Carolina's coolest state parks (and that's saying a lot), is **Paris Mountain State Park** (2401 State Park Rd., 864/244-5565, www.southcarolinaparks.com, daily 8 A.M.-sunset, $2 adults, free under age 16). This is yet another of the 16 state parks built by the Civilian Conservation Corps in the mid-1930s, with many of the sturdily built, evocative structures typical of that effort. This is a great taste of what's in store at some of the parks higher up in the mountains, but with charming accessibility, both in terms of distance from Greenville and ease of transit, that sets it apart from some of the Upstate's harder-to-reach spots. To get to Paris Mountain State Park, take the North Pleasantburg Drive/Highway 291 exit from I-385. Go north on Piney Mountain Road, take a right onto State Park Road, and continue on to the park entrance.

Lake Conestee Nature Park (864/380-5233, www.conesteepark.com, daily dawn-dusk, free) is 300 acres of woodland on the Reedy River a few miles south of downtown Greenville. In the future it will be the southern terminus of the Greenville County Greenways system, and currently it has a two-mile nature trail, a mile-long paved wheelchair-accessible trail, and a 650-foot wetlands boardwalk with an observation tower. To get here, take I-85 exit 46A south of Greenville. Turn right on Augusta Road, then take a left on Old Augusta Road, and then a left again on Henderson Avenue.

Hiking and Biking

For an easy but fun experience closer to town, get on the **Reedy River Corridor Trail,** essentially a connector route for several Greenville parks, including Cleveland Park, Falls Park, and Linky Stone Park. You can access it at any of those parks, but most visitors will find Falls Park to be the easiest entry point.

Still under construction is a multiuse **Rails to Trails** path along the Reedy River, paved for bicyclists and runners. It runs along the Reedy River and is easily accessed at Falls Park.

Bicyclists should try the **Timmons Park Mountain Bike Trail,** a short (only two miles) but fun ride along a creek and through the 27-acre Timmons Park as well as one mile of nearby Cleveland Park. Take Laurens Road and then make a right onto East North Street. After about one mile, turn left onto Blackburn Street, which takes you to the park.

Water Park

Discovery Island Waterpark (417 Baldwin Rd., Simpsonville, 844/963-4345, www.gcrd.org/discoveryisland, Mon. 10 A.M.-8 P.M., Tues.-Sat. 10 A.M.-6 P.M., Sun. 1-6 P.M., $8 48 inches tall and over, $7 under 48 inches tall) offers a variety of kid-friendly splash-and-swim rides just outside town. Take Standing Springs Road from I-385 exit 30.

Spectator Sports

If you ask the typical Greenville resident what is the most important sports event in the area, they'll almost certainly say Clemson University football. But technically speaking, a more pertinent spectator pastime in Greenville comes courtesy of the **Greenville Drive** (945 S. Main St., 864/240-4528, www.greenvilledrive.com, box seats $8), an affiliate of the Boston Red Sox playing in the South Atlantic League. Despite their drab name—an obvious homage to the city's automotive industry—they play in the delightful new retro-style Fluor Field in the historic West End, built in 2005 as a nearly exact facsimile of Boston's own Fenway Park, complete with its own short-porch "Green Monster" left field wall. While the level of play might not always be up to snuff, a day at Fluor Field is always a great way to spend a few hours with the family. It's affordable too, with tickets ranging from $5 for a lawn space on the third-base line up to the grand sum of $8 for a box seat.

Other spectator sports activity in Greenville tends to center on athletics at **Furman University** (3300 Poinsett Hwy., 864/294-2150, http://furmanpaladins.cstv.com, ticket prices vary). The Paladins play football in the Southern Conference and are the only private school to have won the NCAA Division I-AA national championship, which they did in 1988. They play home games in Paladin Stadium on campus. Another notable Paladin squad is the soccer team, consistently one of the best in the country. They play on campus in a specifically soccer-oriented stadium, the 3,000-seat Eugene Stone III Stadium (soccer legend Pele was present at its grand opening in 1995).

ACCOMMODATIONS

Visitors to Greenville will be pleasantly surprised at the low rates for lodging compared to other American metropolitan areas, a surprise made even more pleasant by the generally high standards.

Under $150

The best accommodation value in Greenville, the **Drury Inn and Suites** (10 Carolina Point Pkwy., 800/378-7946, www.druryhotels.com, $96-175) doesn't offer a location smack-dab in the middle of downtown, but it's still pretty close to all the action on Main Street. With excellent facilities, classy decor, prompt, attentive service, and most rooms under $150, the very-new Drury Inn rises well above most chain-hotel experiences. It even offers a breakfast that's a cut above most.

For a luxurious stay that's only a short drive (less than 10 minutes) into the city center or to the airport, try the **Crowne Plaza Greenville** (851 Congaree Rd., 864/297-6300, www.crowneplaza.com, $125-180). Like most Crowne Plazas, this is considered a resort property and thus has very spacious public areas. Whether you need that or not, the guest rooms are very pleasant and modern. As an added plus, Greenville's only Ruth's Chris Steakhouse is on-site. While the larger suites are above this price range, a standard room is usually under $150.

It's not downtown either, but the **Hilton Greenville** (45 W. Orchard Park Dr., www.hilton.com, 864/232-4747, $110-150) offers a clean, newly renovated, entirely smoke-free building. Another great value, the prices are far below what you'd expect for the amenities and service.

The best and most popular B&B in town is ◖**Pettigru Place** (302 Pettigru St., 864/242-4529, www.pettigruplace.com, $115-195), and not only because of its proximity to scenic Cleveland Park and being a 20-minute walk from Main Street's activity. While the exterior won't knock your socks off in the way that a Charleston B&B can, Pettigru's five guest rooms are decorated tastefully along particular themes. For example, the safari-inspired Brass Giraffe is the most romantic suite, while the larger Rosamunde is both romantic and sumptuous. The prices are right too; three of the guest rooms can be had for under $150, and one—the Chantilly—can occasionally be had for around $100.

$150-300

The only four-diamond hotel in Greenville and easily its most pedigreed, the ◖**Westin Poinsett** (120 South Main St., 864/421-9700, www.starwoodhotels.com, $185-245) isn't for those who insist on a brand-new building. This is a historic inn built in 1925, and the elegantly simple guest rooms and decor reflect this. The staff is professional and friendly, and you can't beat the location—right on top of the old town center on bustling Main Street. Parking is a surprising value too for those accustomed to the often extortionate rates charged in other city centers.

The **Hampton Inn and Suites Greenville Downtown** (171 Riverplace, 864/271-8700, www.hamptoninnandsuitesgreenville.com, $165) offers the typically high standards of that chain, except more so here, in a well-designed and almost striking new building. That said, the biggest draw is the happy paradox that is the incredible location—one block from Main Street's Falls Park but with prices that say "airport." As with the Westin Poinsett, stay here and you will be able to walk to most any attraction in Greenville.

Anchoring the east end of Main Street's revitalization is the **Hyatt Regency Greenville** (220 N. Main St., 864/235-1234, www.greenvillehyatt.com, $159-259), which is somewhat dated in its monolithic style, typical of the chain. Still, it's a Hyatt, and you couldn't really ask for a better location. As with almost all lodging in the Upstate, you will find the price surprisingly low for what you get. When people downtown talk about going "up near the Hyatt," this is what they're referencing.

Camping
For camping in Greenville, go no farther than **Paris Mountain State Park** (2401 State Park Rd., 864/244-5565, www.southcarolinaparks.com, daily 8 A.M.-sunset, $2 adults, free under age 16), an absolutely charming Civilian Conservation Corps-built state park, and one of the best in the state's already great state park system. There are 39 sites, 13 of which are dedicated tent sites ($14-15). There are also five primitive sites ($10-12) on the North Lake trail.

To get to Paris Mountain State Park, take the North Pleasantburg Drive/Highway 291 exit from I-385. Go north on Piney Mountain Road, take a right onto State Park Road, and continue on to the park entrance.

FOOD
Barbecue
Don't be put off by the nondescript exterior and small dining room at ◖**Henry's Smokehouse** (240 Wade Hampton Blvd., 864/232-7774, www.henryssmokehouse.com, call for hours, $4-10). This is one of the best, if not the best, Upstate barbecue joints and a true Greenville tradition, even though they have taken on some trappings of Midlands 'cue cooking, offering a mustard-based sauce. Cooked in proper style—over an open wood fire—its pulled pork, taken from the lean butt cut, is melt-in-your-mouth perfect. If the mustard sauce is too acquired a taste for you, they also offer the indigenous upcountry tomato-based sauce as well.

Just about as good as Henry's is **Smokin' Stokes** (1622 Augusta St., 864/242-9716, www.smokinstokes.com, call for hours, $7-10), a similarly humble location offering a lot of taste for the buck. They offer a selection of sauces on the side, but their signature is a sauce made from Cheerwine, a regional cherry-flavored soda. As with most authentic 'cue joints in the South, it's a good idea to call ahead to double-check their hours.

Classic Southern
Like its older sister location in Charleston, ◖**High Cotton** (550 S. Main St., 864/335-4200, www.mavericksouthernkitchens.com, daily 5:30-10 P.M., Sun. jazz brunch 10 A.M.-2 P.M., $20-40) deals in robust, nononsense takes on Southern and American classics. This isn't high-concept cooking, but a combined emphasis on fresh ingredients, a rotating and vibrant menu, and bold taste palettes makes it an extraordinary dining experience. Meats and game are a particular specialty, whether it's a painstaking recipe like the venison osso buco or a deceptively simple one like

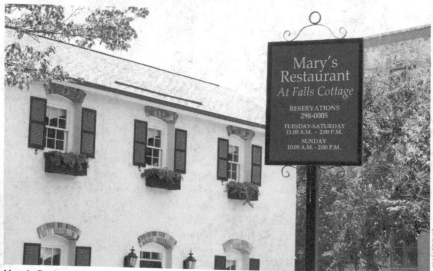

Mary's Restaurant at Falls Cottage, next to Falls Park

the local free-range chicken with whipped potatoes. Reservations are recommended.

The word *quaint* seems to be applied quite often to dining at **Mary's Restaurant at Falls Cottage** (615 S. Main St., 864/298-0005, www.fallscottage.com, Tues.-Sat. 11 A.M.-2 P.M., Sun. 10 A.M.-2 P.M., prix fixe dinner $22-33), and rightly so for an experience in this daintily restored little cottage scenically overlooking Falls Park. Breakfast buffet, lunches, and brunches are popular here, and the dinner menu is a range of prix fixe offerings such as "The West End" (Waldorf salad, roast pork loin, sweet potato casserole, veggies, rolls, and tea or coffee). Reservations are strongly recommended.

Coffee, Tea, and Sweets

The java trend has hit Greenville big time, and while there is indeed a Starbucks on Main Street, there are some excellent indie coffeehouses in the restored downtown area as well. If you're walking near Falls Park on the Reedy, take a coffee and snack break at **Spill the Beans** (531 S. Main St., 864/242-6355, http://stbdowntown.com, Mon.-Sat. 6:30 A.M.-11 P.M., Sun. 1:30-9:30 P.M.) right at the entrance to the park. Besides a great selection of coffees, they have the best fresh, hot (and huge!) waffles in town and good yogurt and smoothie offerings.

For truth in advertising, you can't beat **Coffee Underground** (1 E. Coffee St., 864/298-0494, www.coffeeunderground.biz, Mon.-Thurs. 7 A.M.-11 P.M., Fri. 7 A.M.-midnight, 8 A.M.-midnight, Sun. 8 A.M.-10 P.M.), literally located underground and on Coffee Street. Walk down the stairs below ground level at the intersection of Main and Coffee Streets to enter this spacious bistro and art gallery atmosphere. They have a nice brunch menu in addition to breakfast and snack goodies.

Down in the restored West End of Main Street you'll find **Coffee To a Tea** (1 Augusta St., 864/373-9836, http://coffeetoatea.com, Mon.-Fri. 7 A.M.-5 P.M., Sat. 8 A.M.-3 P.M.), which, in addition to its hot beverages, is known for its decadent cakes and other sweet treats.

Mediterranean

You might not expect to find a great Lebanese place in the Upstate, but **The Pita House** (495 S. Pleasantburg Dr., 864/271-9895, $5-8) is just that. It's not fancy, but you come for the food—we're talking perfect falafel, hummus, and baba ghanoush made by experts from family recipes.

One of Greenville's best Italian restaurants is **Portofino's** (3795 E. North St., 864/268-9432, Mon.-Thurs. 5-9:30 P.M., Fri.-Sat. 5-10:30 P.M., $8-15), a refreshingly unpretentious home-style place where the portions are huge and they aren't afraid to use a lot of garlic.

New Southern

Housed in an old cigar factory across from the Westin Poinsett downtown, **Devereaux's** (25 E. Court St., 864/241-3030, www.devereauxsdining.com, Tues.-Sun. from 6 P.M., $20-40) is the kind of place where out-of-town executives or locals looking for a special night out dine. You can go one of three ways: either the usual à la carte selections from their menu, such as a bourbon pork loin or a seared black grouper; the five-course tasting menu ($75 pp, wine flights $25) by Chef Steven Devereaux Greene, which can include anything from sashimi to a short stack of gourmet pancakes; or the 10-course Chef's Ultimate Tasting Menu (price varies).

A somewhat trendier foodie pick, however, is **C** American Grocery (732 S. Main St., 864/232-7665, www.americangr.com, Tues.-Sat. 6-10 P.M., $15-25), which is not a grocery store at all but an upscale advocate for *very* locally sourced organic and all-natural meats and produce, all featured in a menu that changes not only seasonally but daily under the practiced and enthusiastic eye of Spartanburg native chef Joe Clarke.

Southwestern

One of Greenville's favorite nightspots, **Chicora Alley** (608 S. Main St., 864/232-4100, www.chicoraalley.com, lunch daily 11:30 A.M.-2:30 P.M., dinner Tues.-Sat. 5 P.M.-2 A.M., Sun.-Mon. 5 P.M.-midnight, $5-15) is also one of its favorite restaurants, with a small but tasty menu of burritos, quesadillas, and Caribbean fare. Expect a casual but raucous experience.

INFORMATION AND SERVICES

The main visitors center in Greenville is the **Greenville Downtown Visitor Center** (206 S. Main St., 864/233-0461, www.greenvillecvb.com, Mon.-Fri. 8:30 A.M.-5 P.M.). Another one close by is the **Greenville Convention and Visitors Bureau** (631 S. Main St., 864/421-0000, www.greenvillecvb.com, Mon.-Fri. 8:30 A.M.-5 P.M.), which has brochures and maps only.

The newspaper of record is the *Greenville News* (www.greenvilleonline.com). As of this writing, the city has no free independent weekly, but Furman University has a student paper, *The Paladin* (www.thefurmanpaladin.com).

There is one main **police station** (4 McGee St., 864/271-5333, www.greenvillepd.com) in Greenville. The most convenient **U.S. Post Office** (600 W. Washington St., 864/282-8313, www.usps.com, Mon.-Fri. 7:30 A.M.-6 P.M.) is located downtown.

There are two excellent hospital facilities in Greenville. There's the huge **Greenville Hospital System University Medical Center** (www.ghs.org), a nonprofit with five campuses, the main one being **Greenville Memorial Hospital** (701 Grove Rd., 864/455-7000). There's also **Bon Secours St. Francis Health System** (www.stfrancishealth.org), which has a location downtown (1 St. Francis Dr., 864/255-1000) and a location on the eastside (125 Commonwealth Dr., 864/675-4000).

GETTING THERE AND AROUND
By Air

This rapidly growing metro area is served by the **Greenville-Spartanburg International Airport** (GSP, www.gspairport.com), the busiest in the state, at I-85 exit 57. Airlines here include American, Delta, Northwest, United, and U.S. Airways.

By Train

Trains stop at the **Greenville Amtrak Station** (1120 W. Washington St., 864/255-4221, www. amtrak.com), with daily service in each direction on the New Orleans-New York *Crescent*.

By Car

The main routes into Greenville are I-85 as well as I-185, which enters the city from the west side and becomes Mills Avenue, and then shortly becomes Church Street. From there, most attractions of interest are to the west (on your left) as you drive into town. Signage is generally excellent in Greenville.

A spur off I-85 called I-385 enters Greenville from the east and runs by the airport. Keep in mind, however, that this is a toll road. There really is no need to use it unless you are coming

in and out of the airport. Laurens Road (U.S. 276) on the other side of the airport leads into town in virtually the same place.

By Bus

Greenlink (864/467-5000, www.ridegreenlink. com) is an all-biodiesel fleet with various routes throughout Greenville County. Each ride is $1.25 and transfers are $0.50. Children under age 6 ride free.

Parking

Finding a space is becoming increasingly more difficult in downtown Greenville, but overall the situation is much better than in many other growing cities. Find a map of the city's many good parking garages at www.greatergreenville. com. The main and largest garage downtown is the **Poinsett Garage** (25 W. McBee Ave., $6 per day), adjacent to the Westin Poinsett Hotel and Poinsett Plaza right downtown. It has over 800 spaces.

Spartanburg

A half hour's drive from Greenville, it's tempting to think of Spartanburg as a miniature version of the same thing. They're quite often mentioned literally in the same breath, as when people speak of the Greenville-Spartanburg metro area. The two are linked not only by geography but demographics as well, sharing a history as onetime textile centers and emphasizing traditional values. But Spartanburg definitely has a vibe all its own. Not as enveloped in new construction as Greenville or as thick with newer residents, it retains its small-town attitude while hosting a growing contingent of progressive thinkers. Also, Spartanburg has a larger African American population than is typical in the Upstate and thus is without Greenville's notable lily-white aspect.

Because of its melting-pot nature,

Spartanburg's musical contributions have been more interesting to the world at large. The late legendary gospel great Ira Tucker was from here, as is the Southern rock group Marshall Tucker Band (no relation to Ira, and no, there's not actually anyone in the band named Marshall Tucker). Other musical Spartanburg natives include seminal Nashville session guitarist Hank Chapman (Elvis Presley's "Little Sister," the Everlys "When Will I Be Loved") and, of course, the great bluesman Pink Johnson, the real-life inspiration for the name of classic rock group Pink Floyd.

HISTORY

Like Greenville, Spartanburg was once part of one big rich hunting ground for Native American people. During the dominance of the Creek Nation,

Spanish explorer Juan Pardo, sent from the coast to claim the inland area for Spain, came through in 1567 and etched his name on "The Pardo Stone," now in a local museum. Later, the Cherokee and the Catawba people would be the dominant groups. In 1753, a treaty with the Cherokee opened up the area to white settlement, with the frontier being the modern Greenville County border.

During its time under the British crown, the area was heavily Loyalist in its politics, but redcoat heavy-handedness soon soured the locals on the benefits of being royal subjects. As the focal point of British General Cornwallis's "Southern Strategy," this part of the Upstate became a cauldron of violence, by some counts hosting more engagements than any other part of the country.

One of the Revolutionary War's key engagements took place at nearby Cowpens, where a combined force of colonial militia and Continental Army soldiers soundly defeated a British contingent of redcoats and Loyalists. Spartanburg resident Kate Barry entered legend as South Carolina's own version of Paul Revere, warning local commanders of the approach of the British in time for them to prepare for their eventually victorious battle.

The town didn't get its modern name until 1785, when it was named for the local Spartan Rifles militia regiment. Though Spartanburg saw little real action during the Civil War, it did provide several thousand troops to the Confederate effort as well as several African American regiments who fought for the Union.

In the nineteenth century, with a break during the Civil War, Spartanburg, along with Greenville, grew in importance as major textile centers. It was during this time that Spartanburg got its nickname, "Hub City." While local Chamber of Commerce types today are quick to link the nickname to the big BMW plant just outside of town, in truth the name comes from the fact that Spartanburg was a major railroad hub during the days of King Cotton. While it's still home to one large textile concern, the Milliken Corporation, Spartanburg today has made the same transition to a global economy as much of the Upstate, with a continuing emphasis on restoring the historic downtown area.

SIGHTS
Morgan Square
The best place to start your explorations in Spartanburg is downtown at Morgan Square (daily 24 hours), the center of the city's efforts to transform into a model of pedestrian-friendly downtown redevelopment. Nicely restored in an effort begun in 2005 to upgrade the downtown area, Morgan Square also has history as the site of the original village and courthouse. The square is typical of many central plazas in mountain towns of Spartanburg's age and includes early 1900s-style Main Street America buildings, facades restored, and a picturesque fountain.

Nearby is another throwback to Spartanburg's rail heyday, the **Magnolia Street Train Depot** (Magnolia St. and Morgan Ave.). This historic building, once the main local depot, now hosts not only the local Amtrak station but the Visitors Bureau and the Hub City Farmer's Market (Sat. 8 A.M.-noon).

Seay House
Vernacular architecture buffs will enjoy viewing the oldest building still standing in Spartanburg, the Seay House (106 Darby Rd., 864/596-3501, by appointment the third weekend of the month Apr.-Oct., Sat. 11 A.M.-5 P.M., Sun. 2-5 P.M., donation), built by farmer Kinsman Seay around 1800. Although several rooms were added in the Victorian period, the structure still centers on the original homestead-style log cabin, much of which is still visible. Be aware that the Seay House is in a somewhat sketchy neighborhood. Take Crescent Drive off John B. White Boulevard, and then a left onto Darby Road.

© JIM MOREKIS

renovated Morgan Square in downtown Spartanburg

Hatcher Garden and Woodland Preserve

Set in what was once a cotton field, the altogether delightful Hatcher Garden and Woodland Preserve (832 John B. White Sr. Blvd., 864/574-7724, www.hatchergarden.org, daily dawn-dusk, free) was the labor of love of Harold and Josephine Hatcher, who in 1969 began planting over 10,000 trees and flower bushes to realize their vision of a community garden. Now an expertly and lovingly tended 10-acre public garden, the site boasts gorgeous flower displays, little ponds, and tastefully arranged viewing platforms.

Perhaps more than any other civic garden in the state, Hatcher Garden makes full use of the gently rolling topography, with the peaceful look and Zen feel of a Japanese garden. Another thing that makes Hatcher Garden so cool is that unlike so many attractions in the Deep South, it was not made possible by the disposable income of wealthy planters but by the modest funds and sweat equity of a couple of humble retirees.

Walnut Grove Plantation

The most notable historic structure in the Spartanburg area is the Walnut Grove Plantation (1200 Otts Shoals Rd., Roebuck, 864/576-6546, Apr.-Oct. Tues.-Sat. 11 A.M.-5 P.M., Sun. 2-5 P.M., Nov.-Mar. Sat. 11 A.M.-5 P.M., Sun. 2-5 P.M., $6 adults, $3 children, free under age 6), outside of town in little Roebuck and lovingly maintained by the Spartanburg County Historical Society. It was built in 1765 on land granted by King George III to the family of planter Charles Moore; the most famous resident was their daughter Margaret Kathryn "Kate" Moore (later Barry), the local heroine who warned of the approach of the British on the eve of the pivotal Battle of Cowpens. About 500 yards west of the main house is the Moore family cemetery. All told, the grounds are the final resting place of about 150 people,

© JIM MOREKIS

Hatcher Garden and Woodland Preserve

including soldiers killed in battle and slaves who worked on the plantation over the years.

A fairly unique aspect of Walnut Grove—probably attributable to the relative lack of action and attendant Union vengeance in the Upstate during the Civil War—is the survival of several outbuildings, mostly log structures such as a kitchen, a blacksmith shop, a wheat house, a barn, and a smokehouse dating from 1765, perhaps the oldest testament to South Carolina's abiding love for barbecue. Inside the main house, an elegantly simple Georgian structure, are furnishings typical of the King Cotton era of the early 1800s.

BMW Zentrum

Although it's technically located in Greer, right next door, Spartanburg tends to claim the BMW Zentrum (1400 Hwy. 101 S., Greer, 888/868-7269, Mon.-Fri. 9:30 A.M.-5:30 P.M., free admission, guided factory tours $5 adults, $3.50 students) as its own. Currently the only place

outside Germany where BMWs are manufactured—specifically the X3, X5, X6, Z4, M Roadster, and M Coupe—the Zentrum is an interesting hybrid exhibit combining a factory and a museum.

There are two basic experiences: the sleek, crescent-shaped Zentrum Museum, where you'll explore the history of the Bavarian Motor Works, see some fine historical autos and motorcycles, and witness some experimental models; and the BMW factory, where guided tours take you inside the intriguing high-tech process whereby these modern machines are made. No high heels or open-toe shoes on factory tours, and you have to be 12 or older to take part.

On the factory tour, don't expect a hot, dimly lit place where hordes of wretches are bathed in sparks. Cars are mostly made by robots these days, in a bright, nearly sterile environment that's closer to an operating room than a sweatshop. Of course, when you get tired, hungry, and ready for souvenirs, there's a well-done gift shop and Euro-style café, both open during regular museum hours.

You can't miss the Zentrum—it's between Greenville and Spartanburg right on I-85. Take exit 60 and follow the signs.

Spartanburg Museum of Art

The aggressively local Spartanburg Museum of Art (200 E. St. John St., 864/948-5364, www. spartanburgartmuseum.org, Tues.-Wed. and Fri.-Sat. 10 A.M.-5 P.M., Thurs. 10 A.M.-8 P.M., $5 adults, $3 students and ages 4-17, free under age 4, first Thurs. of the month free) began with the acquisition of *The Girl with Red Hair* by Robert Henri in 1907. Since then, the Museum has acquired over 400 pieces of art and sculpture for its permanent collection, which mostly focuses on regional artists. It's housed in the big Chapman Cultural Center downtown.

Spartanburg Regional Museum of History

In the same building as the Museum of Art is the Spartanburg Regional Museum of History (200 E. St. John St., 864/596-3501, Tues.-Wed. and Fri.-Sat. 10 A.M.-5 P.M., Thurs. 10 A.M.-8 P.M., Sun. 1-5 P.M., $5 adults, $3 students and ages 4-17, free under age 4, first Thurs. of the month free), run by the Spartanburg County Historical Association. Perhaps the single most historically important item in the collection is the Pardo Stone, a boulder supposedly bearing graffiti from the first Spanish explorer to come through the Upstate, Juan Pardo. Otherwise, exhibits tend to concentrate on the textile industry and the military camps of Croft and Wadsworth, the former of which is now a state park. It's housed in the big Chapman Cultural Center downtown.

Susan Jacobs Arboretum

The Upstate is Clemson Tiger Country, but the University of South Carolina does have a campus in Spartanburg. Within it you will find the relaxing 12-acre Susan Jacobs Arboretum (800 University Way, 864/503-5235, www. uscupstate.edu). Situated on the north end of campus, it's located along a meandering stream and features indigenous plant life.

Hollywild Animal Park

The closest thing to a zoo in Spartanburg is Hollywild Animal Park (2325 Hampton Rd., Inman, 864/472-2038, Apr. 1-Labor Day Mon.-Fri. 9 A.M.-4 P.M., Sat. 9 A.M.-7 P.M., Sun. 11 A.M.-6 P.M., $10 adults, $8 children). As the name indicates, Hollywild's claim to fame is giving a home to animals that have "retired" from service in films and TV. Because of this, you won't find a wide range of species, as you might in a bona fide zoo. Rather, the emphasis is on cutesy, cuddly animals like goats and deer, many of which kids can pet (an exception is the Bengal tiger and assorted cubs). A guided Safari Ride through the grounds is included in the admission price.

Hollywild is just east of Spartanburg in Inman. Take U.S. 176 into Inman and take a left onto Highway 292. Turn right onto New Cut Road and then left onto Holly Springs Road. Take a left onto Hampton Road, and the park is one mile ahead on the right.

◖ Cowpens National Battlefield

In historical terms the most significant sight in the Spartanburg area is Cowpens National Battlefield (4001 Chesnee Hwy., 864/461-2828, www.nps.gov/cowp, daily 9 A.M.-5 P.M., free), which commemorates one of the key victories over the British in the Revolutionary War.

Fought literally in an old cattle pasture, hence the name, the once-dreaded British cavalry colonel Banastre Tarleton was driven from the field by a combined force of General Daniel Morgan's continentals and local militia (Morgan is memorialized with a park bearing his name in nearby downtown Spartanburg).

© JIM MOREKIS

GREENVILLE

Cowpens National Battlefield

From that point on, the British remained on the defensive for the rest of the war.

In addition to seeing the battlefield and learning about the history of the period in the interpretive center, the other big attraction at Cowpens is the trails, some of which have historic significance. The 1.3-mile **Battlefield Trail** includes exhibits, the 1856 Washington Light Infantry Monument, and the Green River Road, along which the battle was fought.

If you want to stay in your car, take the 3.8-mile **Auto Loop Road,** which includes exhibits and parking areas with short trails to the Green River Road, an 1818 log cabin, and a picnic area. Also at Cowpens you'll find a trailhead for the **Overmountain Victory National Historic Trail** (864/936-3477, www.nps.gov/ovvi), which begins at nearby Kings Mountain, North Carolina, and goes all the way to Virginia, marking the key inland engagements of the southern theater of battle in the Revolutionary War.

April-October you can take advantage of free one-hour guided walks of the battlefield

(Sat. 9:30 A.M., Sun. 1:30 P.M.). Each year on the weekend closest to January 17, the anniversary of the battle, the park celebrates with various demonstrations of period weaponry and a cool living-history encampment. There's also a nice fireworks celebration around July 4—fitting because this site played such a big role in securing independence in the first place.

Poinsett Bridge

The oldest bridge in the state is the beautiful little 14-foot Poinsett Bridge (Callahan Mountain Rd., Lyman), built around 1820 by Joel T. Poinsett, city father of Greenville and the man for whom the poinsettia is named. Get there by taking U.S. 25 north past its intersection with Highway 11 and turn right onto Old Highway 25. Take a right onto Callahan Road.

The Peachoid

The town of Gaffney, just east of Spartanburg, is primarily known for two things: being the

HOW SOUTH CAROLINA SAVED AMERICA

To read most history books, you'd think the Revolutionary War took place almost entirely in Boston. But South Carolina was the location of the conflict's fiercest fighting, suffering the most men killed of all 13 colonies. Savage and personal, the fighting here usually involved not uniformed regulars but Patriot and Tory militia, many of whom knew each other from peacetime life. The established rules of war were often disrespected—or ignored entirely—by both sides.

In a span of 90 days, Upstate South Carolina hosted two of the most important Patriot victories of the war, Kings Mountain and Cowpens. Ironically, in previous months the colony also hosted two of the worst defeats of the war, the fall of Charleston and the rout at Camden. All four battles were intimately related.

The decisive British wins at Charleston and Camden had the intended effect: With Patriot sentiments at their lowest ebb, many new Tory militiamen joined the redcoat ranks. But every action has an equal and opposite reaction—in this case, the renewed determination of the backcountry's independent-minded Scots-Irish colonists, who had no intention of submitting to more years of heavy-handed British occupation.

Sent to pacify them, British Major Patrick Ferguson led 1,000 Tory militiamen to a stronghold at the base of Kings Mountain on the border of the Carolinas. On October 7, 1780, an equal number of Appalachian militiamen assaulted the position using tactics they'd learned fighting Indians. Rather than marching as a unit and shooting en masse as a European army would, each militiaman fired at will as he attacked, hiding behind rocks to reload. Another trick the colonists learned from the Indians was the demoralizing effect of a high-pitched whoop as they attacked.

The battle seesawed for an hour. The end came when Ferguson, attempting to rally his men, was riddled with eight bullets. As the Tory line collapsed, colonists initially sounded the cry "Tarleton's Quarter!," an ironic reference to the brutal British colonel Banastre Tarleton, infamous for murdering prisoners. But cooler heads prevailed, and 700 Loyalists were taken prisoner.

By January 1781 many Kings Mountain veterans had joined General Daniel Morgan, who chose a large cattle-grazing area—literally, the "cow pens"—outside modern-day Spartanburg to make a stand. Learning from the debacle at Camden, Morgan picked a wide-open battlefield with no place for potentially panicking militiamen to run and hide. To further bolster the colonists, he posted regular Continental Army troops behind them.

With enough time to prepare, Morgan was confident his troops could hold up against the dreaded Tarleton and his forces, on their way to the Cowpens to avenge the loss at Kings Mountain. Morgan's plan was simple: A line of sharpshooters would fire first, retreating behind the second rank of militiamen, who would then fire two volleys under the command of Andrew "Wizard Owl" Pickens. The first and second ranks would then fall behind a combined line of Continental regulars and Georgia and Virginia militiamen, who would then start shooting. Meanwhile, a cavalry detachment behind the lines waited to exploit any opening in Tarleton's lines.

It worked to perfection. Thinking the retreating militiamen were panicking as at Camden, Tarleton's men advanced into a firestorm of bullets, and the assault withered almost as soon as it started. A desperate and failed attempt by the British to outflank the Patriot line was the catalyst for the coup de grâce. Sending militiamen out on both wings, Morgan surrounded the British in a classic double envelopment, studied by military leaders to this day.

In a very real way, Cowpens led directly to American victory in the war. With the exception of his stronghold at Charleston, Cornwallis wrote off South Carolina and moved his troops into North Carolina instead. A series of engagements led to his retreat up the Virginia coast to Yorktown, where, bottled up by Washington's army and the French fleet, he was forced to surrender.

You can visit both battle sites today, at **Kings Mountain National Military Park** (2625 Park Rd., 803/222-3209, www.nps.gov/kimo, Labor Day-Memorial Day daily 9 A.M.-5 P.M., Memorial Day-Labor Day daily 9 A.M.-6 P.M., free) near Blacksburg and **Cowpens National Battlefield** (4001 Chesnee Hwy., 864/461-2828, www.nps.gov/cowp, daily 9 A.M.-5 P.M., free) near Gaffney.

GREENVILLE

birthplace of actress Andie MacDowell and hosting the "Peachoid," a million-gallon water tower just off I-85.

The tower was specifically built in the 1980s to portray the area's cash crop, in an effort to spread the word that South Carolina is actually a larger producer of peaches than the Peach State itself, Georgia. However, you'll often hear locals call it something else: the "Big Butt," an allusion to the Peachoid's alarming resemblance to the naked human posterior.

Gaffney celebrates its just-peachy heritage every year in the annual **South Carolina Peach Festival** (www.scpeachfestival.org, free) happening each July and featuring music, barbecue, a parade, the crowning of the Peach Queen, and, of course, lots of peaches and peach-related baked goods.

ENTERTAINMENT AND EVENTS
Nightlife
On Morgan Square you can't miss the popular, cavernous **Delaney's Irish Pub** (117 W. Main St., 864/583-3100, Mon.-Sat. 11 A.M.-2 A.M., Sun. 3 P.M.-2 A.M.). They have a great selection of beer on tap and in the bottle as well as a very good menu of pub food.

Dating from 1938, the **Nu-Way Restaurant and Lounge** (373 E. Kennedy St., 864/582-9685) is Spartanburg's version of every town's loveable old dive. This is the place to go for that ironically hip night out on the town.

Performing Arts
Some vibrant stuff goes on downtown is at the **Hub-Bub** (149 S. Daniel Morgan Ave., Suite 2, 864/582-0056, www.hub-bub.com, admission varies). Housed in a former Nash Rambler dealership, Hub-Bub hosts over 100 evenings a year of concerts, film, art exhibits, plays, and workshops, almost all of it with a decidedly countercultural edge for this conservative area.

Activity centers on the Showroom Gallery (Mon.-Fri. 10 A.M.-5 P.M.) and Performance Hall, a nod to the building's (and Spartanburg's) automotive roots. Some events

© JIM MOREKIS

Spartanburg cherishes its musical tradition.

charge admission, but it's never exorbitant. For a fun look behind the scenes, check out the blog at http://hubbubblog.wordpress.com.

The very definition of a "multiuse" venue, the beautiful new **Chapman Cultural Center** (200 E. St. John St., 864/542-2787, www.chapmanculturalcenter.org, admission varies) next to Barnet Park has a 500-seat theater that hosts performances by several local theater groups as well as Ballet Spartanburg. It also houses the city's two main museums, the Spartanburg County Museum of Art and the Spartanburg Regional History Museum.

The city does have its own orchestral ensemble, the **Spartanburg Philharmonic Orchestra** (SPO, 864/948-9020, www.spartanburgphilharmonic.com, $25 adults, $15 students) under the direction of Sarah Ioannides, who also conducts the El Paso Symphony Orchestra. The SPO has its roots in a music program begun at Converse College, a local women's college, in the late 1800s. In fact, most performances are still on the Converse campus, at Twichell Auditorium.

Converse College occasionally provides performances by students and faculty from its well-regarded **Carroll McDaniel Petrie School of Music** (www.converse.edu, 864/596-9021, free). Most of these concerts happen at Daniel Recital Hall on campus. Not to be outdone, **Wofford College** (429 N. Church St., 864/597-4000, www.wofford.edu) brings in a great Chamber Music Series (free) in the fall and spring. A guitar-oriented Troubadour series (free) is a nod to the school's relationship with Carl Sandburg, who besides being a great poet was also quite the guitarist as well. Faculty and students of the Wofford music department play concerts throughout the academic year.

Dance fans can check out **Ballet Spartanburg** (200 E. St. John St., 864/583-0339, www.balletspartanburg.com, $25 adults, $15 students). They perform mostly in the Chapman Cultural Center downtown, but do an annual *Nutcracker*

($27 adults, $17 students) at the Twichell Auditorium on the Converse College campus.

Outside in Morgan Square downtown, you can hear **Jazz on the Square** (www.cityofspartanburg.org, Apr.-May and Sept.-Oct. Fri. 6-8 P.M., free), in which regional jazz performers play.

Festivals and Events

Each March on St. Patrick's Day weekend comes the **Shamrocks on the Square** (www.cityofspartanburg.org, free) celebration downtown at historic Morgan Square. There's live Celtic music, face-painting, food, and, of course, green beer.

In October the city celebrates the **Spartanburg International Festival** (www.cityofspartanburg.org, 11 A.M.-6 P.M., free), which generally happens on a Saturday in Barnet Park. You can get a "passport" stamped as you travel through different areas representing the culture, art, music, and food of about 60 different countries. Local Chamber of Commerce types have jumped on this festival as a way to highlight the large number of foreign firms—over 100 at last count—who have opened U.S. offices in Spartanburg.

SHOPPING

My favorite shop in Spartanburg is the nonprofit **Hub City Bookshop** (186 W. Main St., 864/577-9349, www.hubcity.org, Mon.-Thurs. 10 A.M.-7 P.M., Fri.-Sat. 10 A.M.-9 P.M.), which has a great selection of new and used tomes and also serves as the central meeting point for the Hub City Writers Project and houses the Hub City Press. They also host frequent readings and meet-ups. All profits go to fund creative writing projects and outreach in Spartanburg. There's also an attached coffee shop.

There are a couple of cute boutiques on Morgan Square: **Diva's on Main** (131 W. Main St., 864/591-2033) and **Two Doors Down** (100 E. Main St., 864/582-0850). For vintage stuff, try **Beehive Resale Shop** (135

W. Main St., 864/582-6712, Tues. and Fri. 10 A.M.-5 P.M., Wed.-Thurs. 10 A.M.-6 P.M., Sat. 10 A.M.-2 P.M.).

The best farmers market in town is the **Hub City Farmers Market** (298 Magnolia St., 864/595-1422, www.spartanburgnutrition-council.org, June-Nov. Sat. 8 A.M.-noon). A smaller version happens Wednesday 3-6 P.M. at the same location. The focus is on the charming stands of local farmers, such as the "Cream of the Crop Co-op" and the "Share Croppers."

But the biggest shopping draw in Spartanburg—indeed, they say it's the largest mall in the state—is the combined **Westgate Mall** (205 W. Blackstock Rd., 864/574-0263, www.westgate-mall.com, Mon.-Sat. 10 A.M.-9 P.M., Sun. noon-6 P.M.) and **Westgate Crossing** (660 Spartan Blvd., 864/587-0884) complex off I-26. The two adjacent entities comprise over 150 stores, including five anchor department stores.

SPORTS AND RECREATION
Hiking and Biking

Spartanburg is becoming a mecca of sorts for bicyclists. The city is the launching point for the **Assault on Mt. Mitchell** (www.free-wheelers.info) each May, an amateur race over 100 miles long taking participants from Spartanburg to Mt. Mitchell, North Carolina, highest point east of the Mississippi River.

You can contact the **Foothills Cyclists** (www.foothillscyclists.com) to participate in their frequent group rides. If you didn't bring a bike on your trip, relax—borrow one for free from **Partner for Active Living** (864/598-9638, www.active-living.org).

The still-expanding state-wide **Palmetto Trail** (www.palmettoconservation.org) has several sections in Spartanburg, the most popular of which is the **Mary Black Foundation Rail Trail,** a rails-to-trails project on the east side of town. One end is at Country Club Street, the other at Henry Street.

The **Chinquapin Greenway** is a wooded segment on Graham Road; get there by taking I-85 Business exit 73. Another completed Palmetto Trail segment is at the **South Carolina School for the Deaf and Blind** off Holmes Boulevard; it is designed for the mobility-impaired.

The main recreation area close to Spartanburg is **Croft State Natural Area** (450 Croft State Park Rd., 864/585-1283, www.southcarolinaparks.com, daily 7 A.M.-9 P.M., $2 adults, free under age 16), which offers 12 miles of biking and hiking trails within its massive acreage, once a U.S. Army training ground. As the Palmetto Trail nears completion, a section is expected to join Croft with the rest of the trail.

Another relaxing walk is at **Hatcher Garden and Woodland Preserve** (832 John B. White Sr. Blvd., 864/574-7724, www.hatchergarden.org, daily dawn-dusk, free) on the west side of town.

Golf

Spartanburg is not a hotbed of quality courses, but the fairly new **Woodfin Ridge Course** (215 S. Woodfin Ridge Dr., Inman, 864/578-0023, www.woodfinridge.com, $40-50), built around Lake Bowen near the town of Inman outside Spartanburg, is a good one. Set in a golf community, it's open to the public and is known for copious water challenges.

Another good 18-hole course nearby is the Gary Player-designed **River Falls Plantation** (100 Player Blvd., Duncan, 864/433-9192, www.riverfallsgolf.com, $42-52).

Fishing

Spartanburg is inland, but there's some decent fishing on the two lakes at **Croft State Park** (450 Croft State Park Rd., 864/585-1283, www.southcarolinaparks.com, daily 7 A.M.-9 P.M., $2 adults, free under age 16), including bass, bream, and crappie. You'll need a valid South Carolina fishing license, available at www.dnr.sc.gov or at any tackle shop. You can rent a non-motorized boat at Croft ($20 per day).

GREENVILLE

Spectator Sports

Spartanburg's "home team" is actually an National Football League team based in Charlotte, North Carolina, the **Carolina Panthers** (864/594-5050, www.teamspartanburgsc.com, free), who hold their training camp on the Wofford College campus in Spartanburg. The practice sessions in July are free and open to the public, attracting quite a crowd.

With the departure of the city's minor-league baseball team, spectator sports focus on **Wofford College** (864/597-4000, http://athletics.wofford.edu). The Terriers teams compete in football, basketball, baseball, and more.

ACCOMMODATIONS
Under $150

The first and still best-regarded B&B in Spartanburg is the award-winning **◖ Inn on Main** (319 E. Main St., 864/585-5001, www.innonmain-spartanburg.com, $95-155). Located in a historic 1904 building right on the main drag, Inn on Main offers six distinctive, exquisitely furnished suites that wouldn't be out of place in one of the classic B&Bs in Charleston or Beaufort (and at about half the price). The beds alone, some of which are genuine antiques, will wow you. Of course, you get the requisite full Southern breakfast served in a clubby setting typical of the inn's common areas. Keep in mind they discourage kids under age 12.

Along similar lines, but farther out of town, is the circa-1902 **Walnut Lane Inn** (110 Ridge Rd., Lyman, 864/949-7230, www.walnutlaneinn.com, $139-155). Its five guest rooms, while sporting period furnishings, are a little more Victorian in style than the Inn on Main's more classic interiors. A big plus is the verdant expanse of its five-acre semirural setting, beautifully rife with species of the inn's eponymous tree. To get to the Walnut Lane Inn, take Spartanburg's Main Street west (it becomes U.S. 29). Go about three miles to Highway 292, turn left into Lyman, and take a left on Ridge Road.

As far as hotels in Spartanburg, your best bet is the **Spartanburg Marriott at Renaissance Park** (299 N. Church St., 864/596-1211, www.spartanburgmarriott.com, $109-179). This spacious (240 rooms) new facility is smoke-free and offers the usual hip design of Marriotts these days, with the big plus of being within walking distance of the downtown area's shopping and dining opportunities. The only downside is that, like most Marriotts, you will find yourself paying for small amenities that are free at other chains.

For a true budget stay, go straight to the **Sleep Inn** (501 S. Blackstock Rd., 864/595-4040, www.sleepinn.com, $60) just off I-26. It's surprisingly well-run for a budget chain, and it's a straight shot down John White Boulevard into downtown.

Camping

Croft State Natural Area (450 Croft State Park Rd., 864/585-1283, www.southcarolinaparks.com, daily 7 A.M.-9 P.M., $2 adults, free under age 16) has 50 sites ($12-13) with electricity and water. A private RV-oriented campground is **Cunningham RV Park** (600 Campground Rd., 864/576-1973) at I-26 exit 17.

FOOD
Asian

A good Thai place is right downtown on Morgan Square, **Lime Leaf** (101 E. Main St., 864/542-2171, www.limeleaf101.com, Mon.-Fri. 11:30 A.M.-3 P.M. and 5-10 P.M., Sat. 5-11 P.M., $9-15). For a sushi fix, check out **Wasabi** (1529 John B. White Sr. Blvd., 864/576-8998, Tues.-Sat. 11:30 A.M.-2:30 P.M. and 5-10 P.M., $5-10).

Breakfast and Brunch

Good 24-hour all-day-breakfast diners are becoming a thing of the past, but **Papa's Breakfast Nook** (191 E. Saint John St., 864/582-6655, daily 24-hours, $5-8) in Spartanburg is the real

© JIM MOREKIS

the legendary Beacon Drive-In

thing. The pancakes and omelets are delicious, and don't miss the home fries.

Downtown, try **Cafe on Morgan Square** (137 Main St., 864/585-8506, Mon.-Sat. 7 A.M.-9 P.M., $7), which has good sandwiches and sweet treats.

Classic Southern

No visit to Spartanburg is complete without a visit to the **Beacon Drive-In** (255 John B. White Blvd., 864/585-9387, www.beacondrivein.com, Mon.-Sat. 6:30 A.M.-10 P.M., $5-7), one of those joints that's a destination in itself. As is the case with many surviving greasy-spoon type places with a certain retro allure, the media-driven hype now surrounding the Beacon doesn't quite match up to the food, which is really very simple when you get down to it. But you can't deny the Beacon's authentic atmosphere, nor the fervor of its dedicated employees, some of whom have worked here for decades, nor the sincerity of its signs congratulating local high school teams on recent successes, nor the Beacon's very real impact on local history and lore (the street on which it sits is named for the longtime owner). The signature offering is the Chili Cheese A-Plenty, which sounds like a chili dog but is actually a burger topped with chili and cheese ("A-Plenty" means you get a huge mound of fries and onion rings tossed on top). Other offerings include chicken (fried), fish (ditto), and barbecue (but of course). While the food is frankly overrated, I can say that the Beacon's sweet tea—they claim to be the single largest seller of the distinctive Southern drink in the world—is fantastic.

Once considered the best barbecue place in Spartanburg, **Wade's Restaurant** (1000 N. Pine St., 864/582-3800, www.eatatwades.com, Mon.-Sat. 10:45 A.M.-8:30 P.M., Sun. 10:45 A.M.-3 P.M., $6-9) has gradually branched out and now deals out all kinds of Southern comfort food, meat-and-two style, including collard greens, fried chicken, and dinner rolls. Wednesday nights are big here, so if you don't like waiting in line, be forewarned.

Coffee, Tea, and Sweets

The most happening coffee and sweet-treat shop in town is (**The Coffee Bar** (188-A W. Main St., 864/582-1227, www.), located in the historic Masonic Temple downtown and directly adjacent to the Hub City Bookshop and the nonprofit goings-on there. This is the home of Little River Coffee Roasters, and the java is predictably fresh and delicious. The little bake shop in the back cooks up some tasty goodies.

Pizza

There's a continuing rivalry over who has the best pizza in Spartanburg: **Venus Pie Pizza** (400 E. Main St., 864/582-4200, Mon.-Tues. 11:30 A.M.-9 P.M., Wed. 11:30 A.M.-9:30 P.M., Thurs.-Fri. 11:30 A.M.-10:30 P.M., Sat. 11:30 A.M.-10 P.M., $6-12) or **The Mellow Mushroom** (464 E. Main St., 864/582-5495, Mon.-Thurs. 11 A.M.-10 P.M., Fri.-Sat. 11 A.M.-midnight, Sun. noon-9 P.M., $7-14) down the block. The former is a totally local venture, while the latter is a regional chain.

INFORMATION AND SERVICES

The **Spartanburg Convention and Visitors Bureau** (298 Magnolia St., 864/594-5052, www.visitspartanburg.com) is located downtown. The newspaper of record is the *Spartanburg Herald-Journal* (www.goupstate.com). There's also the smaller *Spartan Weekly News* (www.spartanweeklyonline.com).

The **Spartanburg Public Safety Department** (145 W. Broad St., 864/596-2035) has a station downtown. The main **post office** (250 S. Church St., 864/585-0301, Mon.-Fri. 7:30 A.M.-5:30 P.M., Sat. 8:30 A.M.-1 P.M.) location is also downtown. Medical care is provided by the main campus of the **Spartanburg Regional Healthcare System** (101 E. Wood St., 864/560-6000, www.srhs.com).

GETTING THERE AND AROUND

While Spartanburg does have its own small municipal airport, **Spartanburg Downtown Memorial Airport** (SPA, 500 Ammons Rd., 864/574-8552, www.cityofspartanburg.org), most visitors fly into the area at the much larger **Greenville-Spartanburg International Airport** (GSP, 2000 GSP Dr., 864/877-7426, www.gspairport.com), a short distance west of town along I-85. Another option is **Charlotte-Douglas International Airport** (CLT, 5501 Josh Birmingham Pkwy., 704/359-4000, www.clt.com) in nearby North Carolina.

Amtrak (290 Magnolia St., 800/872-7245, www.amtrak.com) has a station downtown, with daily service in each direction on the New Orleans-New York *Crescent*. There's also a **Greyhound bus station** (100 N. Liberty St., www.greyhound.com).

Public transportation by bus in Spartanburg is offered by **Spartanburg Area Regional Transit Agency (SPARTA)** (100 N. Liberty St., 864/562-4287, www.spartabus.com). Fares run $1.25 per trip, and eight interlocking routes take you all over town, including the mall area.

Bicycling is big in Spartanburg. Contact the **Foothills Cyclists** (www.foothillscyclists.com) to participate in their group rides. If you don't have a bike of your own, you can borrow one for free from **Partner for Active Living** (864/598-9638, www.active-living.org, refundable deposit $15).

Along the Blue Ridge

While the Tar Heel State to the north has a higher profile for mountain recreation—with higher prices to match—South Carolina is an important gateway to enjoy the Blue Ridge Mountains, the southernmost portion of the great and ancient Appalachian Mountain chain.

While the landscape is not as stark as north of the border, the Blue Ridge in South Carolina has the dual advantages of being both more easily accessible and much less expensive than the increasingly upscale area of the North Carolina mountains.

One unique aspect of the South Carolina mountain region is a natural feature called the **Blue Ridge Escarpment,** or "Blue Wall," a steep and scenic wall of rock marking the abrupt end of the Blue Ridge Mountains and the beginning of the piedmont region. This sudden contrast in regions is one reason there are so many great waterfalls up here.

To fully enjoy this part of the Palmetto State, I recommend camping or renting a cabin at any one of the state and county parks, especially any of the Civilian Conservation Corps-built parks. However, if that doesn't quite float your boat—or if you want a slightly cozier place to rest your head—there are several options. But the best meals I've had up here have been the ones I ate around a campfire.

☾ CHATTOOGA WILD AND SCENIC RIVER

If you've seen the 1972 film *Deliverance,* then you've seen the Chattooga River (U.S. 76, www.rivers.gov, daily dawn-dusk, free), the South's best white-water rafting locale (in the movie it bore the fictional name Cahulawassee). If you remember that the film had a lot to do with the state of Georgia and are wondering why this listing is in a book on South Carolina, don't be confused. The Chattooga River actually forms part of the Georgia-South Carolina border during its run from its origin at the base of Whiteside Mountain in North Carolina to its end at Lake Tugaloo in South Carolina.

If you're white-water rafting, you'll likely be putting in farther upstream, but the easiest way to get to the Chattooga River is to take U.S. 76 until just before the Chattooga River Bridge into Georgia. On the east side of the road on the Carolina side is a sizeable parking area, unfortunately with subpar restroom facilities. You can cross the river and park in Georgia if you'd like, but there's a $2 parking fee there, and far fewer parking spaces; in addition, the river trail is not as good as the one in South Carolina.

What greets you after a short walk down to the river is a sight straight out of a primordial era. Because of the river's federal Wild and Scenic designation, given in the 1970s, there is no development or damming along a sizeable portion of its length. It lies between two large national forests: Sumter in South Carolina and the Chattahoochee in Georgia. The banks are so lush with ferns that you might expect a dinosaur to show up any minute and begin munching on them.

At this point the Chattooga River forms the **Bull Sluice Falls,** a picturesque and popular thrill-seeking point for rafters and kayakers at the very end of Section III of the river, with a 14-foot drop when the river's at full level (Bull

Sluice also had a starring role in *Deliverance*). But you don't have to be a rafter or thrill-seeker to enjoy the Chattooga. Unless the water is particularly high the season you go, you can make your way gingerly out on the rocks and find shallow pools away from the white water. If you're in your swimsuit, you can relax in the water and even swim a short way—just be aware of the strong downstream current in the middle of the river.

Occasionally one of the baby trout might give you a playful nip when you're out in the water, but they don't cause any real harm. Bull Sluice is a popular free place for area families to come enjoy a dip in the cool water among the roaring sounds of the sluice. On a sunny weekend day, bring your bathing suit and towel, just like a day at the beach.

White-Water Rafting

White-water rafting in the Upstate basically means the Chattooga River, a Wild and Scenic River running from Whiteside Mountain in North Carolina along the Georgia-South Carolina border and ending at Lake Tugaloo in South Carolina. The Chattooga offers a wide range of experiences, from simple tubing to family-friendly rafting and some truly frightening Class V rapids.

For recreational purposes, the Chattooga River is divided into four sections: Section I is primarily for anglers and is mostly off-limits to boating. Section II begins at Highway 28 and ends at Earl's Ford, where there's a 0.25-mile hike to reach vehicles. This is a great little seven-mile run for families, tubers, and novice rafters, with only a single Class III rapid at Big Shoals. The real action begins at Section III, a 14-mile run from Earl's Ford to the U.S. 76 bridge, with a 0.25-mile walk to put in. Beginning with Warwoman Rapid, you'll get a lot of Class II, III, and IV rapids, including the final Class IV-V rapid at Bull Sluice, which concludes Section III. In all, Section III takes

GREENVILLE

DELIVERANCE SYNDROME

© JIM MOREKIS

white water on the Chattooga River

Before the 1972 film *Deliverance* brought the Chattooga River to the nation's consciousness, less than 1,000 people a year went down the white-water rapids of the largely unknown waterway up in the corner where Georgia and the Carolinas meet. The year after the film's release, that number skyrocketed to 21,000 people a year.

Along with the dramatically increased traffic came an increase in foolhardiness and needless risk-taking, as rafters—many with little or no experience on the water—tried to emulate the crashing, adrenaline-filled rides from the movie. In the four years after the film's release, 24 people lost their lives on the river in displays of what came to be known as "*Deliverance* syndrome." Today, the prevalence of professional

raft trip guides means that even though up to 100,000 people a year raft the river these days, a lot fewer are getting hurt.

While a casual glance would infer that the river being granted official Wild and Scenic River status in 1974 had something to do with *Deliverance*, that's just coincidence. As early as 1969—a year before James Dickey's novel of the same name was published—a congressional task force was studying the Chattooga for possible inclusion on the list. The river had to meet several criteria: it had to be "free flowing" long enough to provide a "meaningful experience"; it had to have enough volume to "allow full enjoyment of water-related activities"; its environment had to be "outstandingly remarkable"; the river had to be "generally inaccessible" and "essentially primitive"; and its waters had to be unpolluted.

The Wild and Scenic designation in 1974 by the full Congress came none too soon. (Technically speaking, 39.8 miles of the Chattooga have "wild" status, 2.5 miles "scenic" status, and 14.6 miles are "recreational," for a total of 56.9 miles.) During its deliberations, the task force discovered that from 1935 to 1969 there were no less than four serious proposals to dam and impound the river for hydroelectric power—the fate of so many of South Carolina's once free-flowing Upstate rivers. While two main proponents of hydroelectric power in the region—Georgia Power and the U.S. Army Corps of Engineers—cited environmental reasons in their support for the Wild and Scenic River designation, the likely truth is that it would simply have been too expensive to build hydroelectric facilities on the Chattooga.

But all's well that ends well, and a ride down the Chattooga—either in a white-water raft or on a relaxing tube ride—is considered one of the must-do outdoor activities in the entire Southeast.

6-8 hours from beginning to end. The most challenging ride is Section IV, from the U.S. 76 bridge to the river's conclusion at Lake Tugaloo. It's a short but exciting five-mile run with a whole bunch of Class III and IV rapids, especially in the crazy Five Falls section.

The main professional rafting tour company on the river is **Nantahala Outdoor Center** (888/905-7238, www.noc.com, prices vary). They run tours on several rivers in the region, including several packages on Sections III and IV of the Chattooga, some with lunch included. If you have kids ages 8-17, they offer a tour on Section III (Section IV is for ages 18 and over only due to its extreme rapids). Expect to pay at least $85 pp, more during the summer high season. While walk-ins are welcome, I recommend reserving your trip in advance. A nice plus is that they take your picture while you raft as a souvenir.

To get to Nantahala's put-in location on the Chattooga River, take U.S. 76 west out of Westminster. Go 15 miles and turn right onto Chattooga Ridge Road. About three miles later you'll find Nantahala's place on the right. If you go into Georgia, you've gone too far. If you're coming from Walhalla and Highway 28, go north to Mountain Rest and take a left on Chattooga Ridge Road for six miles.

Another popular Chattooga rafting guide is **Wildwater Rafting** (800/451-9972, www.wildwaterrafting.com, prices vary). They run a similar series of guided tours on Sections III and IV, as well as a kid-friendly "mini trip" on Section III. To get to their put-in location, take U.S. 76 out of Westminster about 14 miles and take a right on Academy Road. Wildwater Rafting is about a mile along on the left. As with Nantahala Outdoor Center, reservations are strongly encouraged.

The prime independent outfitter for the Chattooga and environs is **Chattooga Whitewater Outfitters** (14239 U.S. 76, Long Creek, 864/647-9083, www.chattooga-whitewatershop.com). They offer most any equipment you might find yourself needing, as well as an in-house pizza restaurant where you can load up on carbs.

Hiking

Bull Sluice isn't the only way to enjoy the Chattooga River. The South Carolina side features the southern trailhead of the well-maintained 15-mile **Chattooga River Trail,** actually an old Cherokee path, which is accessible from the parking area.

For an even more primitive experience, hike to the river from within the wild **Ellicott Rock Wilderness Area** (803/561-4000, www.fs.fed.us), which has portions in South Carolina, North Carolina, and Georgia and contains the northern terminus of the Chattooga River Trail.

Food

If you find yourself craving some serious carbs after a day of white-water rafting on the Chattooga, check out **Humble Pie** (14239 U.S. 76, Long Creek, 864/647-9083, www.chattoogawhitewatershop.com, Tues.-Sun. 3-10 P.M.), within and owned by Chattooga Whitewater Outfitters. A 14-inch pizza with all the fixin's (the Bull's Sluice Supreme) will only cost you about $15, and you can wash it down with a decent selection of domestic and international beers.

ELLICOTT ROCK WILDERNESS AREA

With roots in a scenic area designated in the 1960s, one of the oldest trails in the Southeast is the Ellicott Rock Wilderness Area (864/638-9568, www.fs.fed.us/r8/fms/forest/recreation/ellicottrock.shtml, daily, free), which has acreage in three states. It takes you through the Chattooga River gorge in the Sumter National Forest, with about half the trail in North Carolina and a small portion in Georgia. Ellicott Rock itself, once inaccurately considered the meeting point of the three states, is actually in North Carolina. You can reach it on one of the trails in the wilderness area.

Get here by taking Road 708 (Burrells Ford Rd.) west of Highway 107. There's a parking area near the Burrells Ford campground, and it's a short hike to the Chattooga River.

Hiking

As the name indicates, this setting is not suitable for those overly enamored with creature comforts. But with bug spray in hand, sturdy shoes, and a poncho (you are near the highest rainfall area in the United States up here), you will encounter steep cliffs, an amazing variety of old-growth tree specimens, and an absolute inundation of beautiful wildflowers, as well as likely encounters with local fauna.

Also, just outside the wilderness area on the South Carolina side near the Burrell's Ford Campground are two nice waterfalls, Spoon Auger Falls and King's Creek Falls. Order a free map of the entire Ellicott Wilderness Area on the website.

Camping

The true nature lover (or the obsessively frugal) can camp for free in the wilderness area at a site of their choosing. But there are a few important rules: no camping or fires within 50 feet of the Chattooga River or a trail; you have to pack all your trash out; and the maximum stay is two weeks.

Since the Chattooga River became designated a Wild and Scenic River, you can no longer drive your car all the way into **Burrell's Ford Campground** in the Sumter National Forest, a longtime favorite in the extreme northwest corner of the state. But if you don't mind hiking a short distance, you'll be happy to be away from the RV crowd. As you'd expect, this is a no-frills campground, with a hand-pumped well and minimal toilet facilities.

CHAU RAM COUNTY PARK

One of the most accessible and least-known resources in the northwest corner of South Carolina is Chau Ram County Park (Westminster, 864/647-9286, www.oconeesc.com, daily dawn-dusk, parking $2 per vehicle), just off U.S. 76. Located at the confluence of the Chauga River and Ramsay Creek—hence the park's name—Chau Ram is a great base of operation for those looking to spend some time on the Wild and Scenic Chattooga River.

The actual site is pretty cool too, with a very accessible 40-foot waterfall and a long suspension footbridge as well as miniature golf, tennis, and horseshoes. You can stay at Chau Ram at one of 28 RV or tent sites ($20), which are strictly first-come, first-serve. Alcohol is strictly prohibited. Get here by taking U.S. 76 north from Westminster.

OCONEE STATE PARK

One of the gems of the Civilian Conservation Corps era in South Carolina, Oconee State Park (624 State Park Rd., Mountain Rest, 864/638-5353, www.southcarolinaparks.com, during daylight saving time daily 7 A.M.-9 P.M., other seasons Sun.-Thurs. 7 A.M.-7 P.M., Fri.-Sat. 7 A.M.-9 P.M., $2 adults, free under age 16), a few miles north of Walhalla, is also one of the Upstate's most popular campgrounds. Its two lakes are picturesque, with paddleboat and johnboat rentals available ($10 per day). There's a very good network of trails on-site, including the beginning of the Foothills Trail. About an hour in, you'll come across Hidden Falls, a nice waterfall and one of nearly 50 in the Upstate.

Hiking

The most comprehensive hiking experience in the Upstate is the **Foothills Trail,** a 76-mile-long corridor stretching across the upper portion of South Carolina from Oconee State Park in the west to Table Rock State Park to the east. Perhaps the most underrated major trail in the

© SOPHIA MOREKIS

fishing on the lake at Oconee State Park

Southeast—and possibly the country—the Foothills Trail provides a wealth of Blue Ridge scenery, including several beautiful waterfalls and copious displays of South Carolina's famous wildflowers. It's no Appalachian Trail, but it's still pretty awesome and similarly rustic—with the added benefit of not being anywhere nearly as crowded as that more popular route.

Horseback Riding

The hilly but not severe topography in this portion of South Carolina makes it ideal for horseback recreation. If you find yourself rolling through the northwestern section of the state near Oconee State Park, a great place to rent an hour or two of horseback time is at **Chattooga Ridge Stables** (230 Beulah Land Dr., Mountain Rest, 864/638-5754, $20 per hour). They will take you on one of their beautiful mounts through their farm, which includes streams, woods, meadows, and some nice views of the Blue Ridge. Get there by taking Highway 28 north. Several miles before you get to Oconee State Park, go west on

Whetstone Road for five miles, and look for the first pasture after the bridge on the right. Call ahead to reserve a time.

Camping

A great family campground, Oconee State Park has a modest little miniature golf course and even square dancing on Friday nights. However, the layout of the campground is rather cramped, which means tent campers will find themselves on a gravel site packed in among wall-to-wall RVs and their attendant odors and sounds.

If you're tent camping, avoid the main campground like the plague and go to one of the rustic sites ($10-18) near the south end of the park (10 are in the woods, and another 5 are a farther down on the lake). There's no water or electricity, and you have to pack your stuff in a couple of hundred yards from the parking area, but it's worth it. The woods are dense and relaxing, the sites themselves are spacious and spread out, and best of all, the hum of the cicadas in the trees at night will drown out any hubbub from the main campground.

If you can secure a reservation far enough in advance, the rental cabins ($60-94)—13 on the lake and 6 in the woods—are also a nice experience, especially for a family or larger group, though you'll hardly be roughing it. Featuring the exquisite log-and-stone architecture common to the 1930s Civilian Conservation Corps parks, the cabins are, in South Carolina camping tradition, pretty plush and completely furnished on the inside.

Overall, Oconee State Park is a great base of operations for any in-depth exploration of the northwest corner of South Carolina's scenic waterfalls and wild rivers.

◀ STUMPHOUSE TUNNEL AND ISSAQUEENA FALLS

This combo free attraction, a neat place to bring the family, is overseen by the nearby town of Walhalla as part of a conservation agreement among the town, local landowners, and a few

nonprofit groups. You'll find it clearly marked on the east side of Highway 28 several miles north of Walhalla. If you're up this way checking out the Chattooga River, there's no reason not to stop by.

The Stumphouse Tunnel (864/638-4343, daily 8 A.M.-5 P.M., free) is a cool (literally) and possibly slightly frightening experience that kids will either really enjoy or be really petrified of. You won't know until you get them here, so it's worth checking out.

In the early 1800s somebody hatched a plan to run a railroad from Charleston to the Midwest, to be known as the Blue Ridge Rail Line. The line was built from Charleston to nearby Pendleton, but one big problem remained: Stumphouse Mountain was in the way. Residing in a hastily formed rough-and-rowdy burg called, suitably enough, Tunneltown, 1,500 workers managed to dig about 1,600 feet of the planned mile-long tunnel through the mountain when funds ran out. Then the Civil War started, and thus ended the Blue Ridge Line.

The 25-foot-high tunnel stayed empty until

Stumphouse Tunnel, near Walhalla

© JIM MOREKIS

the 1940s, when Clemson University professor Paul Miller discovered that the tunnel's interior stayed a consistent 56°F with 85 percent humidity year-round, making it a perfect natural cooler to store and age the signature Clemson blue cheese. The school in fact aged its cheese in the Stumphouse Tunnel for years until they were able to duplicate those conditions on campus.

Today, a walk in the tunnel—about 500 feet of it is still open—is like a scary, albeit very low-budget, thrill ride. Your first thrill comes as you walk up to the yawning tunnel entrance and the cool damp air hits you as if someone just opened a huge refrigerator. Sometimes you'll clearly see a layer of fog hanging over the entrance, adding to the somewhat spooky atmosphere of the place. Take your flashlight if you go inside because once you're a few feet in, there is no light at all. As you walk along, occasionally point your beam up into the roof of the tunnel; occasionally you'll see bats as well as the remnants of an old lighting system. If you're brave enough, you'll eventually come to a brick doorway, behind which is another couple of hundred feet of even darker tunnel before it's finally closed off.

A short walking distance from Stumphouse Tunnel is another charming attraction, Issaqueena Falls (864/638-4343, daily 8 A.M.-5 P.M., free). It's a popular place to visit and admire the water's forceful path down over the rocks, many of which you can climb out on if you're feeling adventurous (be warned: the rock gets very slippery in places). Keep in mind that if you hear someone say it's a "short five-minute hike" to the falls, they're talking about the short hike to the overlook station. If you want to go down Stumphouse Mountain and start climbing on the rocks within the falls, that can be a very strenuous hike of a good bit longer than five minutes. Near the little footbridge to the falls, you'll see a sign for the Blue Ridge Rail Line Trail, a hiking path that follows the route of the old rail bed.

OCONEE STATION STATE HISTORIC SITE

Not to be confused with nearby Oconee State Park, Oconee Station State Historic Site (500 Oconee Station Rd., 864/638-0079, www.southcarolinaparks.com, daily 9 A.M.-6 P.M., free) is a much smaller park with no camping facilities, geared toward the enjoyment of two historic sites within it as well as a popular and easily accessible waterfall.

The main structure is **Oconee Station** (Sat.-Sun. 1-5 P.M., free), a reconstructed late-1700s blockhouse (fort), used to defend what was then the frontier against Cherokee and other Native American attacks. The other structure is the **William Richards House** (Sat.-Sun. 1-5 P.M., free), built in 1805 by the Irish settler of that name and used as a trading post.

Get here by taking Highway 11 (Cherokee Foothills Scenic Byway) north of West Union and Walhalla a few miles and following the signs.

Hiking

Oconee Station makes up for the short length of its hiking trail system—less than two miles—with the beautiful **Station Cove Falls,** a 60-foot cascade about one mile along the interpretive trail. The trail is considered a must-see for wildflower enthusiasts, who particularly enjoy the displays on the trail in the spring and fall. Other activities include fishing in the pond (state fishing license required), and a frontier encampment, courtesy of reenactors, in mid-October.

WALHALLA AND VICINITY
Oconee Heritage Center

If you're interested in the history of northwestern South Carolina and find yourself passing through the cute town of Walhalla, check out the Oconee Heritage Center (123 Brown Square Dr., 864/638-2224, www.oconeeheritagecenter.org, Tues. and Thurs.-Fri. noon-5 P.M., Sat. 10 A.M.-3 P.M., free). It has a series of exhibits detailing the history of

GREENVILLE

THE LEGEND OF ISSAQUEENA FALLS

Issaqueena Falls

Oconee County lore says that sometime in the late 1700s, Cherokee maiden Issaqueena fell in love with an English trader named Allan Francis. When the local Cherokee planned an attack on an English outpost, Issaqueena got on her pony and took a 96-mile ride to warn them, which fittingly ended at the English fort at Ninety Six. She stayed by her man, beginning a family with him back at Stumphouse Mountain where she had grown up.

But one day a group of Cherokee staged a kidnapping attempt on Issaqueena. She ran from them, but they eventually caught up with her at the 200-foot waterfall at the base of the mountain. Legend has it that Issaqueena pretended to fling herself to her death over the falls but actually hid under a ledge until her pursuers left. Another version has it that she hid under the falls because the Cherokee supposedly thought evil spirits dwelled in waterfalls.

So is the story true? In the frontier memoirs of Ann Matthews, we read about an Indian woman: Because she "disliked very much to think that the white women who had been so good to her in giving her clothes and bread and butter in trading parties would be killed, she became determined to let them know their danger, she started after night, when all was still, and walked 96 miles in twenty-four hours spreading news as she went." Other accounts confirm this story. Some recent scholars, however, doubt her existence at all, citing a curious abundance of highly romantic and elaborately embellished tales from the Victorian era about comely Indian maidens falling in love with white settlers.

If she did exist, however, perhaps the best clue to Issaqueena's psychology has as much to do with lineage as with love. Legend says that Issaqueena was actually one of the Choctaw people kidnapped by the Cherokee, and her given name at birth was Cateechee.

© JIM MOREKIS

the area from prehistory through the present. A small gift shop has stuff like coffee mugs, books, and folk art.

Walhalla Fish Hatchery

The only trout hatchery in the state, the Walhalla Fish Hatchery (198 Fish Hatchery Rd., Mountain Rest, 864/638-2866, www.dnr. sc.gov, daily 8 A.M.-4 P.M., free) was created by the Civilian Conservation Corps in the 1930s. In the mid-1990s ownership transferred from the feds to the South Carolina Department of Natural Resources, who currently use its natural bounty to stock the Upstate's public lakes, to the tune of about 500,000 trout per year.

Interestingly, only the brook trout is native to the state. The more popular rainbow trout is from the western United States, and brown trout are originally from Europe. The Walhalla Fish Hatchery raises all three species. While visiting, you can see the trout behind a glass display case and learn more about this species, so vital to the recreation-based economy of the state. The best time to visit is in the fall, when you can see more of the trouts' interesting life cycle. You can also fish at an adjacent creek.

Accommodations

If you're in Oconee County, check out the nice **Walhalla Liberty Lodge Bed and Breakfast** (105 Liberty Lane, 864/638-8239, www.walhallalibertylodge.com, $95-105), just off the main drag in the little town of Walhalla. The 1884 main house is a two-story heart-pine beauty with wraparound porches. Its five suites are all themed, from Oriental to Ladybug, and a big plus is the restaurant, the **Willow Room** (Thurs.-Sat. 5-9 P.M., Sun. 11 A.M.-2 P.M., $15-25), also open to nonguests.

In Westminster, off U.S. 76, you'll find the splendid **Magnolia Manor Bed and Breakfast** (207 Westminster Hwy., 864/647-8559, www.magnoliamanorbb.com, $99-125). While they do a strong business in weddings and other private functions, they offer eight suites in the Victorian mansion to the public, varying in size and decor but all in excellent taste. There's even an indoor swimming pool.

Food

The premier eatery in Walhalla is **The Steak House Cafeteria** (316 E. Main St., 864/638-3311, lunch and dinner Tues.-Sun., $10-15) on that little town's main drag. Don't miss the fried chicken. The barbecue is good as well, but either way, save some room for their signature Snickers Pie.

As unlikely as the name may sound in the flag-waving ultrapatriotic Upstate, **Yousef's Kitchen** (1109 E. Main St., Westminster, 864/647-6947, Mon.-Sat. 10 A.M.-9 P.M., Sun. 11 A.M.-3 P.M., $5-10) is actually quite a popular place—one of the more popular in the northwest corner of the state. Unassuming like Mr. Yousef himself, this small-town diner,

sporting the somewhat cryptic nonspecific motto "Home Cooking," offers a range of comfort fare with an eclectic Middle Eastern flair.

DEVIL'S FORK STATE PARK

Don't be put off by the name—Devil's Fork State Park (161 Holcombe Circle, 864/944-2639, www.southcarolinaparks.com, spring-summer daily 7 A.M.-9 P.M., winter Sat.-Thurs. 7 A.M.-6 P.M., Fri. 7 A.M.-8 P.M., $2 adults, free under age 16) is one of the easier and more picturesque modern, non-Civilian Conservation Corps South Carolina state parks. Its claim to fame is being the only public access to Lake Jocassee, which despite its artificial nature is pretty picturesque. As you might expect, this park, with four boat ramps, is popular with boaters and anglers (Jocassee is the only lake in South Carolina offering both trophy trout and smallmouth bass).

Fishing

The best fishing up here is on the 7,500-acre Lake Jocassee, and the best way to get out on Jocassee is at Devil's Fork State Park. There are four boat ramps, and you can rent a fishing boat with trolling motor (half day $75, full day $125) at the nearby **Jocassee Outdoor Center** (516 Jocassee Lake Rd., Salem, 864/944-9016, www.jocasseeoutdoorcenter.com). Charter a more serious fishing trip with **Jocassee Charters** (864/350-9056, www.jocasseecharters.com, half day $225, each extra hour $35), whose specialty is trolling for brown and rainbow trout.

Fish in Lake Jocassee include brown trout, rainbow trout, white bass, smallmouth bass, largemouth bass, bluegill, and black crappie. You might have to go deeper than usual to get to some of these, especially the trout, sometimes down to 85 feet. You need a valid state fishing license (www.dnr.sc.gov).

Hiking

This is a decent hiking park as well, with the

© JIM MOREKIS

Keowee-Toxaway State Natural Area

two-mile **Bear Trail** through the hardwood forest as well as a wildflower lover's delight, the **Oconee Bell Trail,** named for a very rare species of wildflower said to live only in this area.

Camping

Devil's Fork is lakefront life at its best, with 20 modern "villas" in true luxurious South Carolina style—15 two-bed, one-bath cabins ($85-140) and five three-bed, two-bath cabins ($110-172), all fully furnished with the creature comforts. There's a catch, though: As with most South Carolina state parks, there's a weeklong minimum cabin stay Labor Day-Memorial Day and a two-night minimum stay the rest of the year.

Campers have a choice of two campgrounds: the main campground, with 59 paved sites ($18-20) with water and electricity, and a dedicated tent site with 25 tent pads ($14-15) without water or electricity. There's a short walk-in to the tent area. I strongly urge tent campers to rough it and use the dedicated tent area.

Accommodations

If you're near Lake Jocassee and Salem, South Carolina, try **Sunrise Farm Bed and Breakfast** (325 Sunrise Dr., Salem, 864/944-0121, www.bbonline.com/sc/sunrisefarm). Set on an old cotton plantation, the Victorian main house offers three gorgeous suites ($108-195) as well as a garden cottage ($158-183) and the restored corncrib ($140-163).

KEOWEE-TOXAWAY STATE NATURAL AREA

At the halfway point between the two ends of the Cherokee Foothills Scenic Byway (Hwy. 11) lies Keowee-Toxaway State Natural Area (108 Residence Dr., Sunset, 864/868-2605, www. southcarolinaparks.com, during daylight saving time daily 7 A.M.-9 P.M., other seasons Sat.-Thurs. 9 A.M.-6 P.M., Fri. 9 A.M.-8 P.M., free). This is one of the state's newer and smaller campgrounds, built in the 1970s on 1,000 acres of land donated by Duke Power, which is also responsible for the existence of Lake Keowee, on which the site resides and under which are the remains of an ancient Cherokee town.

When crossing the lake on Highway 11 you'll see a sign saying "Keowee River," which was actually submerged during the formation of the lake. Duke Power is also responsible for the massive nuclear power plant dominating one end of Lake Keowee. I'll let you decide for yourself whether this will cramp your sense of fun and relaxation.

While you're here, or even if you're just driving by, don't miss the **Cherokee Heritage Interpretive Center** (daily 11 A.M.-noon and 4-5 P.M., free) on-site. There's a modest museum explaining the natural and human history of the area, including the inundation of the ancient village of Keowee, now under the waters of the artificial lake of the same name. But most interesting are the four kiosks arranged on a nice walking trail (not wheelchair accessible). Each kiosk details some aspect of the story of the Cherokee people in South Carolina. While the story ends with the tragic chapter of the Trail of Tears, you'll come away with a new appreciation for the majesty and culture of the Cherokee, whom 19th-century settlers considered one of the "Five Civilized Tribes," as well as for the extreme danger and tribulation involved in settling this area of South Carolina.

Even if you're not going to stay at Keowee-Toxaway, because of the free admission to both the park and the Interpretive Center, I heartily suggest making a stop here if you pass by. Indulge yourself and your family in this underreported yet vitally important aspect of American history.

Fishing

The main angling locale is **Lake Keowee,** accessible at Keowee-Toxaway State Natural Area. This is another place where the fish run deep, in Keowee's case, especially the bass. Rent good-quality boats (around $300 per day) at **Lake Keowee Marina** (864/882-2047, www.lakekeoweemarina.com).

Camping and Cabins

Keowee-Toxaway is what the rangers call a "weekend park," which means it fills up fast on Friday nights. Conversely, if you stay here during the week, you'll sometimes have the park almost to yourself. Because of its relative newness, you'll find none of the picturesque buildings typical of the 1930s Civilian Conservation Corps-era state parks. However, the facilities are still well-appointed and tasteful. A big plus in this RV-happy state is the existence of a separate campground for tent campers, its elevated pads spaced well apart and totally away from the RV area.

There's only one cabin available ($115-144), with three bedrooms and housing up to 10 people. There are pull-through RV sites ($12-14) with electricity and water, and 10 dedicated tent sites ($8-10). At the end of the site's nice and moderately strenuous Raven Rock Trail are 10 trail-side tent sites ($7-9, reservation required) on the lake.

TABLE ROCK STATE PARK

A very popular state park with the casual RV crowd as well as with serious hikers is Table Rock State Park (158 E. Ellison Lane, 864/878-9813, www.southcarolinaparks.com, during Daylight Saving Time Sun.-Thurs. 7 A.M.-7 P.M., Fri.-Sat. 7 A.M.-9 P.M., other seasons Sun.-Thurs. 7 A.M.-9 P.M., Fri.-Sat. 7 A.M.-10 P.M., $2 adults, free under age 16), just off Highway 11, the Cherokee Foothills Scenic Byway. With two lakes, well-appointed cabins, tent and RV sites, and some exceptional examples of Civilian Conservation Corps handiwork, there is plenty to do and see. But perhaps the key element is Table Rock itself, dominating the northern sky-scape and compelling hikers like a large magnet. Serving as the eastern

GREENVILLE

WATERFALLS OF THE UPSTATE

Because of South Carolina's location on the Blue Ridge Escarpment—the so-called "Blue Wall" marking the sudden end of the Appalachians—it contains dozens of waterfalls, from grand to humble. While there are plenty of brochures and websites out there guiding you to the locations of South Carolina's waterfalls, keep in mind that some falls are significantly more difficult to get to than others, especially if there has been a recent rain to turn the old logging roads into muck. Also remember that some of the more remote falls require strenuous, if enjoyable, hikes.

Here is a sampling of some of the more accessible falls in the Upstate. For more info, go to www.alleneasler.com/waterfalls.html or www.sctrails.net.

· At 420 feet, **Raven Cliff Falls** are the highest in South Carolina, and by some measures, the highest in the eastern United States. Get here by way of a fairly easy 4.4-mile round-trip hike out of Caesars Head State Park in the Mountain Bridge Wilderness Area. There's a parking area off U.S. 276.

· Table Rock State Park has several smaller falls on its network of trails, with most on the two-mile **Carrick Creek** loop.

· **Issaqueena Falls** just north of Walhalla on Highway 28 comes with its own legend of a love-struck Cherokee princess. The parking area is near the head of the falls, and there's a nice trail down the falls with a scenic overlook.

· **Spoon Auger Falls** up near the Chattooga River in the northwest corner of the state has a 40-foot drop. It's a short hike out of the Burrells Ford Campground parking area. To get here from Walhalla, take Highway 107 north 17 miles to Forest Service Road 708 (Burrells Ford Rd.). The parking lot is three miles ahead.

· The comically misnamed **Hidden Falls** are easily found within Oconee State Park. Get to this 40-foot cascade by taking the two-mile yellow-blazed Hidden Falls Trail.

· Just up the road on Highway 11 are the 60-foot **Station Cove Falls,** easily found on a short trail within the Oconee Station State Historic Site.

· The picturesque 30-foot **Reedy Branch Falls** are very easy to get to. From Westminster, take U.S. 76 about 15 miles north and look for a pull-off on the left after you pass Chattooga Ridge Road on the right. The falls are about a 300-yard walk from the road.

· Perhaps the easiest cascade to find—and one of the more enjoyable—is 30-foot **Chau-Ram Falls** in Oconee County's Chau-Ram County Park. (The name derives from the Chauga River and Ramsey Creek.) Drive west of Westminster on U.S. 76 for about three miles; the park entrance is on the left. Unlike most local waterfalls, this one has a nice campground nearby.

trailhead for the 76-mile-long Foothills Trail, the park provides access to several strenuous but ultimately rewarding journeys.

Hiking

Designated as a National Historic Trail, the hiking path system at Table Rock—which features a lot of smaller waterfalls of the type abundant in this portion of the state—does offer something of a difficulty scale. There are three ways to get up Table Rock, the shortest of which, the 1.8-mile **Carrick Creek Trail,** is best for families with smaller children.

The 6.8-mile **Table Rock Trail** takes you to the top of the park's eponymous mountain. The last portion, however, is challenging indeed, and you will need your hands to help you get up the stone steps that have been chiseled out of the rock to ease your way.

Finally, there's the 7.2-mile **Pinnacle Rock Trail,** which takes you to the top of that mountain—the tallest one that is entirely within South Carolina (Sassafras Mountain is taller but is partially in North Carolina). This is a very long, challenging, and not especially well-marked trail that is recommended only for those who've done some intense hiking before.

A cool aspect of the hiking trails at Table Rock is how all three intersect at some points, allowing you to mix and match. In any case, remember to take lots of water on any of these hikes.

Fishing and Boating

Anglers will be pleased by the 67-acre Lake Oolenoy, which allows private boats and has a public ramp, and the smaller Pinnacle Lake, where you can rent nonmotorized and motorized fishing boats ($15-25 per day). A valid South Carolina fishing license is required to fish on both. Canoe enthusiasts can inexpensively rent one at Lake Oolenoy.

Camping and Cabins

The park's 15 "villas" are typical of South Carolina state park cabins: rustic on the outside, nicely furnished and comfortable on the inside, with a full kitchen. One villa is handicap accessible. Cabins go for $60-120 depending on size and season. There's a weeklong minimum stay in the high season and a two-day minimum stay otherwise. Book early, because these cabins are usually booked well in advance.

Tent and RV campers can choose from the main 69-site campground near the main entrance ($19-25) or a 25-site area near a picnic ground ($19-25). Because of the preponderance of RV campers in both areas, I recommend that serious tent campers bypass both and go for the walk-in tent-only area near Lake Oolenoy (central water, no electricity, $9-17).

Accommodations

Just off the Cherokee Foothills Scenic Highway is **The Inn at Table Rock** (117 Hiawatha Tr., 864/878-0078, www.theinnattablerock.com, $129-179). This six-room historic Victorian offers a bucolic, sumptuous setting on four acres, with some nice views of Table Rock and the Blue Ridge to the north. Keep in mind they discourage guests under age 18.

◖ MOUNTAIN BRIDGE WILDERNESS AREA

By far the most wild and wooly nature experience in the Upstate is at Mountain Bridge Wilderness Area (8155 Geer Hwy./U.S. 276, Cleveland, 864/836-6115, www.southcarolinaparks.com, spring-summer daily 9 A.M.-9 P.M., fall-winter daily 9 A.M.-6 P.M., $2 adults, free under age 16) just shy of the border with North Carolina. Technically speaking, this site actually comprises two well-known parks, **Caesars Head State Park** and **Jones Gap State Park,** but these are very atypical South Carolina state parks, so don't be fooled by the designation.

There are no plush mountain villas or RV-friendly campgrounds. That's why it's in a wilderness area—this is a place to truly enjoy nature up close and personal. The only way to stay here is truly primitive camping—no water, no tent pad, no electricity, and certainly no showers or restrooms nearby. On the Middle Saluda River through the area, anglers find some great trout fishing; a valid state fishing license is required (www.dnr.sc.gov).

Hiking

The focal point of the area is the hike to Caesars Head, a fancifully shaped 3,622-foot-tall rock outcropping along the Blue Ridge Escarpment. The other major landmark—besides the stark Escarpment—is the 420-foot **Raven Cliff Falls,** one of the most stunning cataracts in the state. It greets you at the end of a strenuous two-mile hike, with a suspension bridge available for your scenic vertigo-inducing pleasure.

There are over a dozen other marked trails to enjoy in the area, most joined by connector trails. A spur of the Foothills Trail goes through the area as well.

Camping

Campers will find 24 primitive trail-side sites ($8-20), 18 of which have fire rings and 6 of which allow no fires. You must have a permit in advance to camp in the Mountain Bridge Wilderness; call 866/345-7275 or go to the website.

A good private campground just south of the Caesars Head and Mountain Bridge Wilderness Areas is **Pleasant Ridge County Park** (4232 Hwy. 11, Cleveland, 864/836-6589, www.gcrd.org, daily 9 A.M.-dusk, day-use free). There are tent sites ($20), a large cabin ($250 per weekend) and a smaller cabin ($175 per weekend), a walking trail, and a lake for fishing and swimming.

LANDRUM

Minutes from the North Carolina border, Landrum is increasingly taking on more of the trappings of the typical tourist mountain town, with a more picturesquely restored downtown than is typical in this part of South Carolina.

Campbell's Covered Bridge

The only remaining covered bridge in South Carolina is Campbell's Covered Bridge (Campbell's Bridge Rd.). Built in 1909, the 38-foot-long, 12-foot-wide span now only handles foot traffic over a charming little stream. To get here, take U.S. 25 north from Travelers Rest to Highway 414 through little Tigerville. Turn right onto Pleasant Hill Road, and make a right onto Campbell's Bridge Road.

Foothills Equestrian Nature Center

The nearby town of Landrum is the nearest thing Upstate South Carolina has to one of the more posh mountain towns of North Carolina. In fact, just over the border outside Landrum in the Tar Heel State is the Foothills Equestrian Nature Center (3381 Hunting Country Rd., Tryon, NC, 828/859-9021, www.fence.org, daily dawn-dusk, free), a sprawling equestrian and educational complex that combines

services for members with free access for the general public.

While the center's six miles of trails are only open to members for horseback riding, the public can ride in any of the frequent special events, or simply hike the trails at their leisure (one trail joins the Palmetto Trail). A lot of area schoolchildren from both Carolinas come to walk the scenic grounds and learn about the indigenous wildlife and habitat.

Blue Wall Passage, Palmetto Trail

Parts of this segment of the statewide Palmetto Trail (www.palmettoconservation. org) are strenuous and not for amateurs, but it is known as one of the best hikes in the state. Ending at the 3,000-foot elevation of Vaughn's Gap, the 14-mile trek includes some stunning vistas of the piedmont as the Blue Ridge Mountains open up. The steepest portion is through the Blue Wall Preserve, managed by the Nature Conservancy. There are two sections, one beginning at the Foothills Equestrian Nature Center and the other from Lake Lanier on to Vaughn's Gap.

Accommodations

Perhaps the best B&B in the Blue Ridge area of South Carolina is ◖ **The Red Horse Inn** (45 Winstons Chase Court, 864/895-4968, www.theredhorseinn.com, $175-300) in Landrum. Decorated in the now-familiar Victorian style typical of many Southern B&Bs, the Red Horse is a particularly tasteful example of the genre. There are a lot of lodgings to choose from at this sprawling estate, including six suites in the main house and six cottages nearby on the grounds. All offer the same access to amenities and public areas.

GETTING AROUND

Getting around is quite easy. The main route is Highway 11, the Cherokee Foothills Scenic

Byway, running roughly east-west along the base of the Blue Ridge. Other key routes are U.S. 76 in the northwest corner, which takes you from Westminster up to the Chattooga River and into Georgia; Highway 28, which links Highway 11 and U.S. 76 through the cute town of Walhalla; and U.S. 276, a spur from Highway 11 to the Caesars Head area.

Clemson and Vicinity

The fast-growing area around Lake Hartwell is lively and rich in history and recreation. While not the largest city, Clemson is the clear spiritual center of this area, largely due to the iconic presence of Clemson University.

Economically, the area is something of a microcosm for the whole state. Clemson is quite stable due to the university presence. Historic Pendleton seems frozen in time, totally dependent on tourism. Seneca has seen hard times and is only just now coming out of them. Bustling Anderson doesn't get much attention from the world at large but is growing by leaps and bounds.

When not busy donning orange and obsessively following Clemson's athletic teams, the locals like to fish and boat on Lake Hartwell, an artificial reservoir with plenty of easy access points.

CLEMSON

There's no mistaking you're in Clemson when you hit College Avenue and see the big orange paw prints leading the way to campus. Like any great American college town, the home of the Clemson University Tigers is vocally proud of their local sports teams and has few boundaries in terms of letting everyone know it. If you're the type to scoff at the Southern passion for college football—or if you're a fan of their archrival, the University of South Carolina—you might not enjoy Clemson very much. Also, if you don't like the color orange: There's lots of orange here. But if you enjoy friendly and picturesque Southern towns with a good bit of history and that sense of youthful optimism that's always present in a college town, do spend some time here.

Unlike most cities in the South, Clemson's pedigree is of relatively recent vintage. It is as inextricably a part of the history of Clemson University as those orange tiger paws adorning everything from license plates to toilet seats. Philadelphia native Thomas Green Clemson married well, as we say down here. He was betrothed to Anna Maria Calhoun, the daughter of powerful South Carolina statesman John Calhoun. Together they lived in the Calhoun family's Fort Hill Plantation through the worst days of the Civil War. After the South's defeat, Clemson, a mining engineer by trade, was struck by the breakdown of the region's agrarian economy and crushing sense of despair. "Conditions are wretched in the extreme," he wrote with alarm, "people are quitting the land." He decided that the South's youth needed to have an avenue of instruction for a new way of agriculture, saying, "The only hope we have for the advancement of agriculture is through the sciences, and yet there is not one single institution on this continent where a proper scientific education can be obtained." Putting his money where his mouth was, Clemson willed Fort Hill Plantation's 814 acres as the site of a new school where such advanced farming and husbandry techniques would be taught, along with a then-hefty $80,000 endowment. The founder died in April 1888, and his plan for a "people's university" went into motion with the establishment of Clemson Agricultural College, an all-male military style institute, the following year. In 1955 the school went coed, and with that change lost its military underpinnings. In 1964 it was renamed Clemson University, and today it has nearly

GREENVILLE

© JIM MOREKIS

South Carolina Botanical Garden

20,000 undergraduates and an expanding research and graduate presence as well.

Outside Clemson are several other areas worth visiting: charming little Pendleton, with its historic homes and antique shops; Seneca and its restored Ram Cat Alley; Anderson, third-largest city in the Upstate; and Lake Hartwell, a major recreational destination.

Sights

With the key exception of the Old Stone Church, the following attractions are all on the Clemson University campus, which welcomes visitors. Catch a campus tour at the **Clemson University Visitors Center** (109 Daniel Dr., 864/656-4789, www.clemson.edu) most days at 9:45 A.M. and 1:45 P.M.

JOHN C. CALHOUN HOME

The ancestral home of the great South Carolina statesman and subsequently his daughter and Thomas Clemson, the John C. Calhoun Home (101 Fort Hill St., 864/656-2475,

www.clemson.edu, Mon.-Sat. 10 A.M.-noon and 1-4:30 P.M., Sun. 2-4:30 P.M., $5 adults, $2 ages 6-12, free under age 6) is the spiritual center of Clemson. Also known as Fort Hill, the Greek Revival mansion, a National Historic Landmark, is essentially all that remains of the original plantation of that name.

Inside you'll find Calhoun's office and a reconstructed kitchen. Interestingly, the mansion wasn't originally built for the Calhouns but for the pastor of the Old Stone Church in nearby Pendleton. When Calhoun acquired the house in 1825, he added 10 rooms to the four-room building.

◖ SOUTH CAROLINA BOTANICAL GARDEN

The official botanical garden of the Palmetto State since 1992, the South Carolina Botanical Garden (150 Discovery Lane, 864/656-3405, www.clemson.edu, daily dawn-dusk, free) takes up the entire southeastern tip of the Clemson campus and is a delightful place to stroll, relax, and take in the aromas of the tens of thousands of types of plants, flowers, and herbs planted on the site's 300 acres. (Although I'm a nonsmoker, I particularly like the heady, sweet smell of tobacco leaves that sometimes hits you just as you enter the grounds from the parking lot.)

The garden has its pedigree in a camellia garden planted in 1958 next to what was John C. Calhoun's Fort Hill plantation. There are 70 acres of display gardens, including the impressive camellia garden, a dwarf conifer garden, a hosta garden, and a butterfly garden. A 40-acre arboretum and nearly 100 acres of woodlands with walking trails completes the outdoor package. The best times to visit are spring and fall; in the summer there are significantly fewer flowering plants, and the heat can be stifling.

On the grounds is the **Fran Hanson Discovery Center** (864/656-3405, Mon.-Sat. 10 A.M.-4 P.M., closed home football Sat., free), which contains several interactive educational exhibits, a nice little art gallery, and, of course, a gift shop. The first thing most visitors see, however, is the **Heritage Garden,** an attractively done stone entrance way and trellised walkway. Panels on the low circular wall around the main entrance detail, in an often humorous manner, what daily life was like for cadets at Clemson during its stint as a military school from 1893 to 1955.

In addition, the garden grounds contain several additional attractions you shouldn't miss. Within the grounds of the Botanical Garden is the **Bob Campbell Geology Museum** (140 Discovery Lane, 864/656-4600, http://virtual. clemson.edu/groups/geomuseum, Wed.-Sat. 10 A.M.-5 P.M., Sun. 1-5 P.M., closed home football Sat., $3 adults, $2 children), which has its roots in a small rock collection in the Clemson geology department. Caretaker Betty Newton gradually solicited donations and built the collection into the nucleus of what's on display now. The museum is named after Robert S. "Bob" Campbell, a local rock quarry owner who passed on a large collection of gemstones, minerals, and

fossils to Clemson. A donation from Campbell in 1996 also helped build the current structure. Every third Saturday of the month you can get in for free. Inside you'll find a large and beautiful collection of rocks and minerals from all over the region and the world, both shiny and rough. A cute highlight is "Clemson's oldest tiger," actually a skeletal replica of an ancient *Smilodon,* or saber-toothed cat, which roamed the Upstate in primordial days.

Sometimes called the Huguenot House, the fabulously old **Hanover House** (South Carolina Botanical Garden, 864/656-2475, www.clemson. edu, Sat. 10 A.M.-noon and 1-5 P.M., Sun. 2-5 P.M., free) is on the grounds of the South Carolina Botanical Garden. A relic of the French Huguenot presence in the Lowcountry, this charming cypress-built house—said to be the only surviving example of French Huguenot architecture in the United States—was moved to the Upstate in 1941 from an area set to be inundated by the artificial lakes in the Santee Cooper region. Originally on the east side of the Clemson campus, it was later moved yet again to its current location. Built in 1716 by Paul de St. Julien, the house was later home to several generations of the famous Ravenel family, also of French Huguenot descent and a constant presence in South Carolina history. The interior is simple, compact, and well kept. Look for the family's French bible in the drawing room. Keep in mind that most of the furnishings are later donations, because the house was looted and abandoned for many years.

Finally, on the grounds of the Botanical Garden you'll find the **Hunt Cabin** (www. clemson.edu, free), a restored 1826 upcountry log cabin in the garden's Pioneer Complex. Like the Hanover House, the Hunt Cabin was moved here from elsewhere. Charles Hunt Jr. married Martha Dalton in 1825. As a wedding present, Martha's father gave her new husband 2,300 acres of land near Seneca. When the cabin was set to be demolished, the Clemson class of 1915 bought it for $35 and moved it to

© JIM MOREKIS

the famous Esso Club

campus in 1955. While we know for sure that General Andrew Pickens spent several nights in the Hunt home while visiting the family, we're less sure about another guest: Local lore has it that General William Sherman spent a night in the cabin during the Civil War.

OLD STONE CHURCH

With roots in a Presbyterian church built on the same site in 1789, the present Old Stone Church (101 Stone Circle, 864/654-2061, Sun. 8 A.M.-6 P.M., free) was built in 1797 with fieldstone by Revolutionary War hero John Rusk, who is buried with his wife in the adjacent historic cemetery. But perhaps the most famous soul laid to rest here is General Andrew Pickens, one of the key early movers and shakers in the Upstate. The building is as simple as its name indicates, both inside and out. The interior is dominated by the pulpit and wooden pews.

The Old Stone Church is technically within the city limits of Clemson, but geographically it

is right between Clemson and Pendleton. Take U.S. 76 east from Clemson, and take a right on Stone Church Road. Stone Circle is immediately on the right.

Entertainment and Events

Like everything else in Clemson, local entertainment here moves with the ebb and flow of student life—especially during football season.

NIGHTLIFE

The most famous college bar in Clemson—indeed, one of the most famous in the country—is **The Esso Club** (129 Old Greenville Hwy., 864/654-5120, www.theessoclub.com), on the northwestern edge of campus. As the name indicates, it's in an old gas station, built in 1933 on what was then the main road to Atlanta. Sometime in the 1940s, beer began to be sold on-site, in addition to bait, tackle, fishing licenses, and gasoline. By the mid-1950s the station was known as the only place in Clemson you could go in, sit down, and have a beer. It was during that time that folks started calling it "The Esso Club." You could actually fill up your car until the mid-1980s, when it became a full-time bar and tavern. Attention from Georgia columnist and sportswriter Lewis Grizzard and a visit from CBS broadcaster Brent Musberger helped put the Esso Club on the national map. Now a 75-year-old institution, the Esso Club and its wood-panel interiors underwent a major restoration in 2004, but it retains that old college-dive sensibility, albeit with big-screen TVs and a decent kitchen. Often there are good regional college rock and alternative country bands playing on the porch outside.

The other key watering hole in town is the **Tiger Town Tavern** (368 College Ave., 864/654-5901, www.tigertowntavern.com), a.k.a. Triple T's, which traces its pedigree to 1977, when it took over the Red Carpet Lounge after a controversial shooting occurred there. For 20 years it was basically a pool hall, but in the mid-1990s it got a facelift and an actual kitchen. However, it has retained its "drunken tiger" logo. Upstairs is Top of Tiger Town Tavern, a "private club"—meaning for a few bucks a year its members can drink there on Sunday. You can too if you come as a current member's guest and pony up.

Next to the Triple T's is **356** (366 College Ave., 864/653-1356). Yeah, the name and the address don't match—apparently it's a long story. This is the closest Clemson comes to having a swank artsy bar space.

Nick's Tavern and Deli (107 Sloan St., 864/654-4890) is one of the oldest bars in Clemson, opened by Nick Vatakis and Milton Antonakos in 1976, in the former home of another beloved institution, Pat Belew's Gold Nugget. (If you look closely, you'll see the original lettering on the back of the current sign—Nick and Milt just turned the sign around.) The original founders have long since sold their interest,

but they are still friends of the establishment. One of the rules of the house is, "All employees asking to be excused because of serious illness or death in the family, please notify the office before 11 A.M. on the day of the game."

Next door to Nick's is another downscale bar with a lot of local history and very few frills, the **Sloan Street Tap-Room** (109 Sloan St., 864/654-7210), which has ownership ties to legendary Clemson football coach Frank Howard.

CINEMA

Movie buffs should check out **The Astro III Theatre** (430 College Ave., 864/654-1670) downtown. It doesn't screen first-run flicks, but the price is right at about $2.

FESTIVALS AND EVENTS

For those of a literary or theatrical bent, there's the well-regarded **Clemson Shakespeare Festival** (864/656-7787, www.clemson.edu, $20 adults, $10 students), a project under the auspices of the Clemson University English Department that happens each winter at the Brooks Center for the Performing Arts on campus. In addition to the main stage performance—the 2008 "election year" edition was *Julius Caesar*—there are colloquiums and film screenings, which are generally free. Don't expect an amateurish student production; because the performances are generally by well-respected touring companies, the caliber of the stage shows is generally very high indeed.

Bringing in about 5,000 folks a night, **Clemsonfest** (275 YMCA Circle, Seneca, 864/654-1200, www.cityofclemson.org, free) happens every Independence Day week and brings the entire Clemson, Seneca, and Anderson town and university community together along the shores of Lake Hartwell at the Foothills Area YMCA for fireworks, food, and music in a block-party atmosphere.

By far the most quirky festival in Clemson—and actually the biggest music festival in the

GREENVILLE

Upstate—is **Spittoono** (www.spittoono. org, free), held on a late-August weekend at the National Guard Armory (U.S. 76 and Pendleton Rd.). Yes, the name is a play on Charleston's far more genteel Spoleto Festival. Founded by the "Redneck Performing Arts Association" based at the Esso Club, Spittoono features a wide variety of regional rock bands. Funds raised by beer and merchandise sales go back to local charities.

Shopping

The best and cutest shops in Clemson are clustered along College Avenue. Just start walking and you'll find something you'll like. At the corner of College and Clemson Avenues is a third-generation Clemson tradition, **Judge Keller's Store** (307 College Ave., 864/654-6446). Technically a "dry goods" store in the old tradition, creaking wooden floors and all, this is actually a great place to get any Clemson Tiger merchandise. A nice jewelry store is **The Beaded Tiger** (518 College Ave., 864/624-9240). Clemson students get their

textbooks at the **Barnes & Noble** (Palmetto Blvd. and McMillan Ave., 864/656-2050, Mon.-Thurs. 8 A.M.-6 P.M., Fri. 8 A.M.-5 P.M., Sat. 11 A.M.-4 P.M., Sun. 1:30-5 P.M.) inside the Hendrix Student Center on campus, but it's also another good place to shop for orange-and-white Tiger merch.

Sports and Recreation
SPECTATOR SPORTS

Clemson University plays about seven Saturday home football games during the regular season, August-November. During this time, everything in town focuses on the game, to the exclusion of all else except basic bodily functions. Many attractions in town are closed on home football Saturdays. The games are played in **Clemson Memorial Stadium** (Centennial Blvd., 864/656-2118, http://clemsontigers. cstv.com), a.k.a. "Death Valley," at the western edge of campus. You can buy advance tickets to a Clemson University home game at the school's official ticket site (http://clemsontigers. cstv.com) or by calling the school directly at

© JIM MOREKIS

Clemson Memorial Stadium, also known as "Death Valley," is the home of the Clemson Tigers.

800/253-6766. Of course, you don't need tickets to enjoy the tailgate parties.

Big games, such as with archrival South Carolina, sell out immediately. If the school is sold out of tickets, your option is with online brokers such as www.stubhub.com or www. ticketcity.com, or perhaps waiting outside the stadium and finding someone hawking tickets there. Prices always vary depending on the game and the seating area.

A few caveats: Do not even think about parking illegally during a home football game. Also, don't bring the following into Memorial Stadium: umbrellas, folding chairs, chaise longues, food and beverage containers, alcoholic beverages, thermos jugs, and ice chests.

GOLF

Golfers will enjoy the **John E. Walker Sr. Golf Course** (864/656-0236, www.clemson.edu, call for green fees), an 18-hole Nathan DeVictor-designed course that is the stomping grounds of the Clemson University golf team, who were national champs in 2003. The course is fully open to the public as well as students and alumni, but you must have a reserved tee time to play. It's particularly known for its last five holes along Lake Hartwell, including the "Tiger's Paw" 17th.

Accommodations

There are several nice places to stay in Clemson, but don't stay near Tiger Boulevard unless you enjoy the sound of trains—there are busy railroad tracks that cut through town in that area. Also keep in mind that rates here skyrocket on home-game weekends.

Not near the train tracks and right next to the campus's Walker Golf Course—and like that facility, completely open to the public—is the **James F. Martin Inn** (100 Madren Center Dr., 864/654-9020, www.clemson.edu, $100). Many of its 89 guest rooms overlook Lake Hartwell. There's an outdoor pool, tennis courts, Wi-Fi, and included continental breakfast.

A wholly unique lodging just outside town is the **Clemson Outdoor Lab** (864/646-7502, www.clemson.edu, $69-129), a combination retreat, conference center, and summer camp for students young and old with special needs. Cabins are available for those not in large groups. To get here from Clemson, take U.S. 76/Highway 28 east toward Anderson for four miles. Take a right onto West Queen Street when you see the sign for the Outdoor Lab. The entrance is three miles ahead on the left.

The circa-1837 **Sleepy Hollow Bed and Breakfast** (220 Issaqueena Trail, 864/207-1540, www.sleepyhollow.ws, $100-175) is reportedly the site of the first introduction of Percheron horses and Jersey cows to South Carolina, in addition to what's purported to be the state's largest white oak tree out back. Its four guest rooms currently reflect the Victorian era of life here. A full breakfast is offered on weekends and a continental breakfast during the week.

Back on Tiger Boulevard, your best bet is probably the **Hampton Inn Clemson** (851 Tiger Blvd., 864/653-7744, www.hamptoninn.com, $104-124), a clean, safe, and relatively inexpensive stay. While it's on the western end of town closer to Lake Hartwell, it's not too far from everything of interest in town and on campus.

Food

Whatever you do in Clemson, don't miss a stop by the Hendrix Student Center on campus, where you'll find ◖ **'55 Exchange** (864/656-2155, www.clemson.edu/icecream, Aug.-May Mon.-Fri. 11:30 A.M.-6 P.M., Sat.-Sun. 1-6 P.M., June-July Mon.-Thurs. 11:30 A.M.-8 P.M., Fri. 11:30 A.M.-6 P.M., Sat.-Sun. 1-6 P.M., $4-10). They have what I believe to be the best ice cream and milk shakes on the planet, courtesy of the Clemson University Dairy Sciences Department. Totally open to the public, this little corner shop—named for the Clemson graduating class that funded its opening—features rich, robust ice cream in the old style, served in a multitude of equally fresh and tasty cones and edible cups. Pick from the bins of ice cream at the counter, or consult the "Tiger Slab" recipe book, filled with dozens of signature recipes by longtime customers and students. You can also buy wheels of the famous Clemson Blue Cheese, also a product of Dairy Sciences. The only bummer is that they're closed for winter break, when the students are gone.

Housed in a former frat house, the **Mellow Mushroom** (189 Old Greenville Hwy., 864/624-1226, $10-15) serves a variety of pizzas, calzones, and salads as well as pitchers of beer. Service is slow, but people don't come here to eat and run—it's a place to savor the college town atmosphere.

Another favorite student hangout—not only for the prices but for the flavor—is **(Super Taco** (1019 Tiger Blvd., 864/654-6474, $3-10). A clear cut above your usual Mexican food joint, Super Taco offers a variety of fresh, quick, tasty items like burritos, quesadillas, and, of course, the eponymous tacos, all in a clean if not flashy atmosphere.

The original location is in nearby Anderson, but **Skin Thrashers** (129 Anderson Hwy., 864/654-4422, $2-5) in Clemson serves the same fresh beer-boiled little chili-cheese hot dogs. You can't eat just one.

Considered the finest of fine dining in Clemson, **Pixie & Bill's** (1058 Tiger Blvd., 864/654-1210, www.tigergourmet.com, lunch Mon.-Fri. 11:30 A.M.-1:30 P.M., dinner Mon.-Sat. 5:30-9:30 P.M., $18-26) is a favorite of students and visiting alumni alike. It ain't cheap, but any meat dish is good, especially the signature prime rib au jus. Seafood lovers should try their unique "seafood cakes," essentially crab cakes buttressed with scallops and shrimp.

Getting Around

Clemson is essentially bounded by Tiger Boulevard (U.S. 76/123) to the north and Pearman Boulevard (Perimeter Rd.) to the south. The town's western border is the northern finger of Lake Hartwell. Pendleton and Anderson are a short drive to the east.

The university campus, where the vast majority of sights are in Clemson, is freely accessible to the public, with College Avenue being the main, but not only, entry point for cars.

A nice touch is the free public **Clemson Area Transit** (www.catbus.com, free) system. A variety of routes take you all around the area, including to Seneca and Pendleton. Though not designed for visitors per se, it's still a great resource. And yes, it's totally free for everyone, student or not.

If you want to get around by car, there are metered parking spots for visitors on campus, or you can go by the **Clemson University Visitors Center** (109 Daniel Dr., 864/656-4789, www.clemson.edu, Mon.-Fri. 8 A.M.-4:30 P.M., Sat. 9 A.M.-4:30 P.M., Sun. 1-4:30 P.M.) and get a visitor parking pass.

PENDLETON

Right next door to Clemson and basically contiguous with it, the significantly older Pendleton is one of the most impossibly cute small towns you'll ever see. "Cute" might be the wrong word, considering its well-preserved historical pedigree, so significant that the entire town is essentially its own historic district. But "small" is definitely the case, considering an afternoon is all it will take to soak in everything it has to offer.

As with so much of the Upstate area, Pendleton is located on what was once Cherokee land. The Cherokee, unfortunately for them, backed the wrong horse in the Revolution, supporting the British and the local Tories. Shortly after American independence, the Cherokee were removed from the region, which was named Pendleton County, and later named the Pendleton District—an informal designation that remains to this day, although the original boundaries of the district

© JIM MOREKIS

historic Farmers Society Hall on Pendleton's Village Green

have been split into three counties: Anderson, Oconee, and Pickens (Pendleton is now in Anderson County).

The town was founded in 1790, one of the first in the Upstate. Pendleton's origin came over a century after Charleston's founding, but you'll find this Upstate town oddly familiar if you've been to that great Lowcountry city: Most of the finer buildings in Pendleton, sometimes called the "Charleston of the Mountains," were built by Lowcountry planters who kept summer homes here to escape the malaria-carrying mosquitoes of the coast. The dominant species of mosquito in the Upcountry at that time could fly no farther than 10-12 feet off the ground—hence the raised second-floor porches on these grand homes.

Sights
◖ VILLAGE GREEN

Pendleton's main claim to fame is its central Village Green (125 E. Queen St., 864/646-3782,

www.pendleton-district.org). Now surrounded by cute shops and cafés, it's the center of the area of Pendleton that's on the National Register of Historic Places—over 50 buildings in town date from before 1850. The focal point is the circa-1828 **Farmers Society Hall** (255 Old Depot Rd., 864/646-8161) in the center of the Green. Built on the site of the old courthouse, it is the oldest farmers hall in continuous use in the nation. Perhaps oddly, it currently houses a restaurant. So what is a farmers hall? It was a place in a town or county seat where farmers could gather to effectively lobby their local leaders, just as they do today in Congress and state legislatures. The most famous lobbying effort here happened in the second-floor meeting room, where Thomas Clemson successfully argued for the establishment of an agricultural university on his estate. This farmers hall is a particularly fine and compact example of the genre, with its four-column Greek Revival portico.

On the other end of the green from the Farmers Hall is the old **Guard House** (Mon.-Fri. 9 A.M.-4:30 P.M.), once the town police headquarters and now a combined visitors center and magistrate's office. Just off the Green and now the home of the Pendleton tourism office, the circa-1850 **Hunter's Store** (East Queen St.) was once one of the main mercantile stores in the entire Upstate. Now it hosts the **Pendleton District Historical, Recreational, and Tourism Commission** (864/646-3782, Mon.-Fri. 9 A.M.-4:30 P.M., Sat. 10 A.M.-3 P.M.). The nearby historic wooden warehouse, a stirring example of vernacular architecture, was built 30 years later and features a "captain's walk" porch.

ST. PAUL'S EPISCOPAL CHURCH

The second-oldest church in the Upstate, the simple but stately St. Paul's Episcopal Church (328 East Queen St., 864/646-3782) features a historic 1848 pipe organ. Its churchyard is the final resting place for many important figures in Upstate history.

PENDLETON DISTRICT AGRICULTURAL MUSEUM

To get a taste of what life was like in the days of King Cotton, visit the Pendleton District Agricultural Museum (U.S. 76, 864/646-3782, www.pendleton-district.org, by appointment, free), which contains exhibits not only on the European farming history of the area but also Cherokee agriculture. A grim highlight is the first boll weevil found in South Carolina, harbinger of the collapse of the regional cotton economy at the end of the 1800s.

ASHTABULA

The Upstate always surprises with its impressive antebellum homes, so far from Charleston but comparable in so many ways. The phenomenon is partly due to the fact that so many Lowcountry planters built summer homes up this way. A particularly fine example is three miles outside Pendleton: Ashtabula (444 Hwy. 88, 864/646-7249, www.pendletonhistoricfoundation.org, Apr.-Oct., hours vary, $5 adults, $2 children), pronounced "ash-ta-BYEW-la," was built in the 1820s by Charleston's well-connected Lewis Ladson Gibbes. He was a descendant of the first English settler in South Carolina, Dr. Henry Woodward, and married Maria Henrietta Drayton, daughter of Dr. Charles Drayton of Drayton Hall fame, and Esther Middleton, of the magnificent Middleton Place and sister of Arthur Middleton, who signed the Declaration of Independence. Ashtabula only stayed in the Gibbes family for a couple of decades and then was bought and sold several times; at one point it was the first licensed tavern in the Upstate. The house survived the Civil War despite a chilling visit from some of Stoneman's Raiders, a U.S. Cavalry regiment notorious for its aggressive role in the aftermath of that conflict.

Today, a preservation effort provides a good look at the place during its tenure under some of the early pre-Civil War owners. Some of the lovely furnishings actually predate the home's construction, the rationale being that a family at that time would bring previously owned furnishings into such a grand home. The house occasionally offers Victorian Tea on the piazza (veranda), followed by a costumed guided tour; call for dates and prices. The real highlight, however, is the popular **Christmas at Ashtabula Candlelight Tour** (864/646-3782, $6 adults, $3 ages 5-10) the first weekend of December.

WOODBURN PLANTATION

Another magnificent home with deep historical roots is Woodburn Plantation (328 U.S. 76, 864/646-7249, www.pendletonhistoricfoundation.org, Apr.-Oct., hours vary, $5 adults, $2 children). Like Ashtabula, it is a very short drive from Pendleton, although on the other side of town. And like Ashtabula, this four-story house with high ceilings, spacious verandas, and great cross-ventilation was owned as a summer home by Lowcountry planter and statesman Charles Cotesworth Pinckney, cousin of the Charles Pinckney who was nicknamed "Constitution Charlie" for his key but largely unsung role in crafting the U.S. Constitution. Pinckney was a rare breed: a Southern aristocrat abolitionist. This farm was the birthplace of noted African American activist Jane Edna Hunter, who founded the Phyllis Wheatley Society.

The home passed among several other prominent families over the years, serving as an outpost for some prominent Charleston refugees during the Civil War. By the Great Depression, no single owner was able to keep up the estate, and in the 1950s it was given to Clemson College (now Clemson University). In 1966, the school in turn deeded the house to the Pendleton Historic Foundation, with 6.25 acres of land.

Outbuildings you can visit here include a cabin and an 1810 cookhouse. Outside the main house, notice the Greek key designs in the window and door moldings, echoed by

Federal star designs on the interior moldings. The house sports no less than nine fireplaces.

HISTORIC TOURS

Try **Historic Pendleton District Tours** (125 E. Queen St., 864/646-3782), inside the historic Hunter's Store building, which also houses the **Pendleton District Historical, Recreational, and Tourism Commission** (864/646-3782, Mon.-Fri. 9 A.M.-4:30 P.M., Sat. 10 A.M.-3 P.M.); they can hook you up with materials to take your own self-guided tour.

Shopping

Antiques buffs will find themselves in heaven in Pendleton, with several good stores ringing the Village Green. Keep in mind that store hours are not always religiously observed.

The best is **Past Times** (165 S. Mechanic St., 864/654-5985, Tues.-Sat. 11 A.M.-5 P.M.), which boasts the largest collection of vintage Edgefield pottery in the nation. Owner Von McCaskill is very nice—as is his resident cat, Lucy—and he will fill you in on the whys and wherefores of this increasingly in-demand folk art form. His store features plenty of other hard-to-find retro items too, from vintage tools and utensils to old dairy and medicine bottles.

Colonial and Shaker furniture is the specialty of **The Renaissance Man** (130 S. Mechanic St., 864/646-8862), where you'll find hutches and cabinetry galore. Specializing in a different regional art form, **Mountain Made** (102 Exchange St., 864/646-8836, Mon.-Sat. 10:30 A.M.-5:30 P.M., Sun. 12:30-4 P.M.) focuses on the arts and crafts of southern Appalachia.

For a change of pace, try **Sturee Tribal Village** (128 Exchange St., 864/646-2900), which deals in regional Native American handicrafts, although the store is owned by an astute collector from Afghanistan.

Accommodations

The premier bed-and-breakfast in Pendleton is the seven-room ◖ **Liberty Hall Inn** (621 S. Mechanic St., 864/646-7500, $159), a historical plantation home with large wraparound verandas and 14-foot ceilings typical of the style. While the breakfast is fantastic, lunch and dinner are served at an on-site restaurant, the Cafe at Liberty Hall Inn.

For a slightly more rustic ambience, try the **Rocky Retreat Bed and Breakfast** (1000 Milwee Creek Rd., 864/225-3494), another historic plantation home with two guest rooms on the upstairs floor and a large two-bedroom suite on the first floor. The home is actually called the Boone-Douthit House, and the original farm was called Rocky Retreat, once possibly used for silkworm culture. The full breakfast is served in an arts and crafts-style dining room with heart-pine floors.

Food

Because of the proximity of Clemson and Anderson, many of Pendleton's 3,000 or so residents often go there to get a bite. Here are a few choices inside town limits.

The simply but accurately named **Just More Barbecue** (1410 Cherry St., 864/646-3674, www.justbarbecue.com, Fri.-Sat. 5-9 P.M., $12 buffet) does things right: The meat is cooked over a wood fire and served with South Carolina mustard-based sauce. And like any authentic barbecue joint, it's only open on weekends.

For a really nice meal in Pendleton, the recommended stop is at ◖ **Brandini's Cuisine at Liberty Hall Inn** (621 S. Mechanic St., 864/646-7500, lunch Tues.-Sat. 11 A.M.-2 P.M., dinner Tues.-Sat. 5-9 P.M., Sun. brunch 11 A.M.-2 P.M., dinner entrées $18-30), formerly the Cafe at Liberty Hall Inn. Chef Victor offers Italian specialties like chicken parmagiana, osso buco and veal marsala as well as more American-style dishes such as Atlantic salmon and bourbon New York strip.

Of course, if you want to eat within the historic Farmers Hall, step inside and have a seat

GREENVILLE

Seneca's restored Ram Cat Alley

at **1826 on the Green** (864/646-5500, lunch Tues.-Sat. 11:30 A.M.-1:30 P.M., dinner Thurs.-Sat. 5:30-8:30 P.M., $12-23), operated by the former chef at the Cafe at Liberty Hall Inn.

SENECA

Named for the old Cherokee town of Isunigu, which the English settlers morphed into Seneca, this relatively young city was founded in 1873. But in short order Seneca became the very image of the classic South Carolina mill town—only all the mills are now closed. However, Seneca has profited from a particularly well-done renovation of a one-block area of historic downtown, Ram Cat Alley.

Sights

SENECA HISTORIC DISTRICT

The Seneca Historic District was listed on the National Register of Historic Places in 1974 and features homes from the late 1800s along with three historic churches. Here are a few highlights.

Dating from 1917, the imposing **Seneca Presbyterian Church and Chapter House** (S. 1st St. and Oak St.) is a good example of straightforward classicism and high-period Presbyterian Church architecture. Named for a notable small business-owning family of the time, the circa-1906 **Lunney Museum** (211 S. 1st St., Thurs.-Sun. 1-5 P.M., free) contains some interesting exhibits detailing life in and around Seneca.

On the next block you'll find the ornate **Marett-James House** (301 S. 1st St.), now a private residence. Built in 1898 by a member of the locally famous Gignilliat family of merchants, who basically put Seneca on the map, the seven gables of this house make it unique and romantic indeed.

Right across the street is the **Miss Sue Gignilliat House** (300 S. 1st St.), a private residence and another good example of Victorian architecture. In virtually original condition except for the color, it boasts stained glass panels over the front door and some of the windows.

RAM CAT ALLEY

The Ram Cat Alley Historic District (www.ramcatalleysc.com) is a much newer creature, only becoming listed on the National Register of Historic Places in 2000 after renovation began in the mid-1990s. Basically confined to a single block of what was once part of Main Street and a portion of North Townville Street, it comprises 21 formerly commercial buildings dating from 1880 to 1930. This is where the vast bulk of the action is for visitors, with lots of shops and cafés.

DUKE ENERGY'S WORLD OF ENERGY

Suitably located at the Oconee Nuclear Station outside town on Lake Hartwell, the World of Energy (7812 Rochester Hwy., 800/777-1004, www.duke-energy.com, Mon.-Fri. 9 A.M.-5 P.M., Sat.-Sun. noon-5 P.M., free) is essentially a PR project of the huge regional utility Duke Energy to convince people that the nearby power plant is perfectly safe and contributes greatly to the betterment of the entire area. While most of the exhibits border on cheesy, there is an interesting interactive exhibit where you (or more likely, your kids) can pretend to be an atom in a fission chamber of the type used in the big reactors of the nuclear plant.

Shopping

The bulk of shopping, as with most visitor-friendly things in Seneca, is in Ram Cat Alley. **The Purple Sunflower** (125 Ram Cat Alley, 864/886-8222), as the name indicates, offers a lot of garden items along with some antiques and neat folk art. **Patina on the Alley** (114 Ram Cat Alley, 864/888-1110, Mon.-Sat. 11 A.M.-6 P.M.) is an eclectic mix of art, gifts, cards, and stationery items.

Accommodations

Seneca is not a hotbed of quaint lodging. The best hotel for the price is the **Best Western Executive Suites** (511 U.S. 123 Bypass, 864/886-9646, www.bestwesternsouthcarolina.com), which has good rooms in high season for under $100. Although it caters to the business crowd, it offers a lot for any traveler, including a good complimentary breakfast and free passes to the nearby Gold's Gym.

Food

Because of Seneca's proximity to Clemson and Anderson, locals think nothing of popping into those cities to get a bite to eat. Here are some notable spots within Seneca itself.

The aptly named **Spot on the Alley** (122 Ram Cat Alley, 864/985-0102, www.thespot.us, Mon.-Thurs. 11:30 A.M.-1 A.M., Fri.-Sat. 11:30 A.M.-2 A.M., $8) was a "private club" not too long ago, meaning that for a nominal fee you could become a member and be served alcohol on Sunday. Because of the increase in foot traffic on Ram Cat Alley, however, they've opened their doors to the general public. This relaxed sports bar and restaurant is a good place to go to chill out and have one of their excellent and amazingly inexpensive burgers (a six-ounce burger for $5), or go in at night for a Guinness or Harp on tap.

Despite its subtitle, "eclectic dining," **Circa 1930** (112 Ram Cat Alley, 864/888-1933, www.circa1930eclecticdining.com, $6-10) is actually just a good sandwich and salad place offering a selection of sandwiches with a pasta-salad side and some quality meal-type salads.

ANDERSON

The third-largest city in the Upstate, Anderson is a sort of miniature Greenville, with a similarly tastefully restored Main Street and a similar sense of optimism. It also boasts what claims to be the single most visited place in the state, the kitschy, sprawling Jockey Lot and Farmers Market.

Named for Revolutionary War hero Robert Anderson, the Anderson area was originally

© JIM MOREKIS/SCULPTURE BY ZAN WALLS

statue of William Whitner, the man who electrified Anderson, the Electric City

part of the great Cherokee homeland until the land was ceded in a 1777 treaty. As with almost all of the Upstate, its original settlers were Scots-Irish farmers from the Virginia and Pennsylvania colonies. In time, Anderson, like the rest of the area, jumped on the cotton band-wagon and became a major textile mill center.

Anderson's nickname, "The Electric City"—an unlikely moniker for such a laid-back lo-cale—refers not to any sense of urban vibrancy (although that is growing) but to a particular historical episode. Local engineer William Whitner found a way to send electricity from a waterwheel north of town to all the county's textile mills. This meant that Anderson was the first city in the United States to have modern hydroelectric power. Today, Anderson remembers Whitner in several place names, including a major street downtown.

The title of "most famous Anderson native" is a tie between two other men: James "Radio" Kennedy, eccentric subject of the 2003 Cuba Gooding Jr. movie *Radio;* and Jim Rice, Boston Red Sox great and Major League Baseball Hall-of-Famer.

Orientation

The important thing to remember about Anderson is that the main entrance route from Clemson, U.S. 76/Clemson Boulevard, heads straight into downtown, where it splits off into Highway 28, which is also Main Street. As with most South Carolina cities of decent size, Anderson has a clearly defined downtown center unfortunately surrounded by a gauntlet of retail sprawl. Don't be too overwhelmed by the retail sprawl on U.S. 76 coming into town from Clemson; it soon gives way to something more manageable.

A good first stop is the **Visitors Center** (110 Federal St., 877/282-4650, Mon.-Fri. 8 A.M.-5 P.M., Sat. 9 A.M.-2 P.M.) in the warehouse section of the Anderson County Arts Center downtown off Main Street, where you can find brochures and tips, including a walking-tour guide.

Sights
COURTHOUSE SQUARE
The centerpiece of the excellently restored old Main Street section of downtown Anderson is the square in front of the very modern-looking county courthouse. For whatever reason, the building's modern architecture works quite well in the context of the restored Main Street fa-cades and pedestrian-friendly layout.

Every Southern town has one, but Anderson's **Confederate Monument,** on the square right in front of the courthouse, is a particularly fine example. So who's portrayed in the statue? This life-size modernist sculpture is a portrayal of William Whitner, who put the "electric" in "Electric City." Close by is **Old Reformer,** a cannon dating from 1764. Brought from Charleston in 1814 to help protect the town during the War of 1812, it gave a celebra-tory boom when news of the signing of the Ordinance of Secession in 1860 hit Anderson. It was also fired after each Confederate victory.

ANDERSON COUNTY MUSEUM
For a more in-depth look at area history, check out the little Anderson County Museum (202 E. Greenville St., 864/260-4737, Tues. 10 A.M.-7 P.M., Wed.-Sat. 10 A.M.-4 P.M.), which has an old balloon gondola, a nod to Anderson's role in the history of ballooning.

ANDERSON COUNTY ARTS CENTER
Housed in a magnificent former Carnegie li-brary in the middle of Main Street's bustle, the Anderson County Arts Center (110 Federal St., 864/222-2787, www.andersonarts.org, Mon.-Fri. 9:30 A.M.-5:30 P.M.) features exhibitions, readings, and other events throughout the year. They recently sponsored a "Fish Out of Water, Hooked on the Arts" public art display, in which 32 colorfully decorated fiberglass sculptures of largemouth bass were erected all around the downtown area. The "Warehouse" addition right behind the Carnegie portion

© JIM MOREKIS

Jockey Lot and Farmers Market, north of Anderson

houses a small visitors center (Mon.-Thurs. 8 A.M.-5 P.M., Fri. 8 A.M.-4:30 P.M., Sat. 10 A.M.-2 P.M.).

ANDERSON CITY FIRE DEPARTMENT MUSEUM

Kids and firefighting buffs will enjoy the Fire Department Museum (400 S. McDuffie St., 864/231-2256, Mon.-Fri. 9 A.M.-5 P.M., free), which is within the main city firefighting complex (if you'd like a tour of the fire station, you can usually just ask, and someone will take you around). The museum's collection of historic fire trucks includes a horse-drawn wagon from the 1800s and the city's first motorized fire truck, a 1911 model.

JOCKEY LOT AND FARMERS MARKET

Need a T-shirt that says "Jesus was nailed for my sins"? How about a NASCAR handbag? Some used gospel CDs? Karate movies on VHS? Fresh grapefruit by the basket? Over-the-counter medicines for a buck? A new puppy? You'll find it all and then some in the dollar-store-run-wild atmosphere of the sprawling Jockey Lot and Farmers Market (4530 U.S. 29, Belton, 864/224-2027, www.jockeylot. com, Sat. 7 A.M.-5 P.M., Sun. 8 A.M.-5 P.M., free), which claims to be South Carolina's single most-visited attraction and the South's biggest flea market. *Attraction* really isn't the word, however, because this is hardly intended for tourists; it's mostly for the benefit of budget shoppers from around the Upstate, who jam the sheds and roam the display tables of this huge complex between Anderson and Greenville on U.S. 29. Table after table of merchandise, ranging from personal junk to odd lots of cheap Chinese-made stuff, spread before you like a vast discount smorgasbord. Honestly, the sheer bulk of the offerings can be overwhelming.

I suggest just walking slowly through the

place, soaking in the rustic vibe and smiling and talking with people as you pass. If you're really meant to buy something here, it will jump out at you. Otherwise, frankly, most of this stuff, you can live without. For the visitor, this is more an experience than a shopping trip. As you enter, you will probably see some folks walking out with a cute little puppy in their arms. A highlight for many Jockey Lot shoppers is "puppy row" or "dog alley," an area where you can pick out puppies, generally pedigreed, for prices ranging $20-250.

The Jockey Lot is a good distance north of Anderson on U.S. 29. From downtown Anderson, take East River Street out of the area and follow the signs for U.S. 29. Just when you think you've gone too far, you'll see the Jockey Lot on the right. You cannot miss it.

RADIO KENNEDY STATUE

Anderson native James Robert "Radio" Kennedy, nicknamed for his habit of always carrying an old-fashioned transistor radio, is memorialized in this statue (2600 Hwy. 81) outside of the football stadium at T. L. Hanna High School. Kennedy has been a fixture at Yellow Jacket football practices there since 1963, and his life was the subject of the 2003 film *Radio* starring Cuba Gooding Jr. and Ed Harris. Once located downtown, the statue is now outside the grounds of the high school. Get here by taking East Greenville Street outside town, where it becomes Highway 81.

Entertainment and Events
PERFORMING ARTS

The prime artistic exponent in town is the **Greater Anderson Musical Arts Consortium** (864/231-6147, www.gamac.org), an umbrella nonprofit that brings together the Anderson Symphony Orchestra and an associated choral group and chamber ensemble for various performances throughout the year. Many performances are held on the campus of Anderson

University (316 Boulevard, www.andersonuniversity.edu). A 2,000-student private school, Anderson University is affiliated with the Baptist Convention and hosts plenty of visual and performing arts events of its own at the expansive, nicely done **Rainey Fine Arts Center** (864/231-2080, www.andersonuniversity.edu).

FESTIVALS AND EVENTS

The highlight of the annual calendar is the Labor Day **Balloons Over Anderson** (3027 MLK Jr. Blvd., www.balloonsoveranderson.org, free) at the Civic Center, which typically features nearly 100 old-fashioned hot-air balloons, live music, and plenty of activities and food.

Fall brings the **Anderson Chili Cook-off,** a fairly self-explanatory—but very fun—event on Main Street in late October or early November pitting local restaurants and chefs against each other to see who can best cook this Tex-Mex standard. Your $4 ticket gets you a four-ounce taste of each competition entry. Everything else, including adult beverages, is à la carte.

Shopping

The **Anderson County Farmers Market** (Tues. and Thurs. 10 A.M.-2 P.M., Sat. 7 A.M.-2 P.M.) is a fun stop right downtown on Main Street. Load up on veggies, fruit, and assorted goodies.

For a more pedestrian shopping experience, there's always the **Anderson Mall** (3131 Main St., 864/225-3195, www.simon.com, Mon.-Sat. 10 A.M.-9 P.M., Sun. 12:30-6 P.M.), on the main drag, U.S. 76.

Food

The sprawl on U.S. 76/Clemson Boulevard into Anderson is chockablock with every conceivable brand of chain restaurant. Here are a few notable all-local spots instead.

Anderson's premier contribution to cuisine is ◖ **Skin Thrashers** (3420 Clemson Blvd., 864/226-4588, www.skinshotdogs.com, Tues.-Sat. 11 A.M.-6:50 P.M., $5), specializing in some of the most delectable hot dogs in the world. The decor couldn't be simpler—a smallish diner in a strip mall off crowded U.S. 76. Load up on several of the tasty little beer-soaked dogs and wash 'em down with an ice-cold Coke—served in a bottle, no less.

Another local tradition—since 1965—is **Little Pigs Barbecue** (1401 N. Main St., 864/226-7388, Tues.-Thurs. 11 A.M.-8 P.M., Fri.-Sat. 11 A.M.-9 P.M., $5-8). Also in a strip mall and also with a diner atmosphere, Little Pig serves huge mouthwatering barbecue sandwiches, cooked old-school over a wood fire. They choose to buck the trend toward Midlands mustard-based sauce, however, opting instead for a vinegar-based sauce more typical of the Upstate. Ordering is a little confusing at first; just walk right up to whatever window is open and someone will take your order, pass you your plate, and ring you up right there.

When in downtown Anderson, I get my coffee kicks from **E City Java** (208 S. Main St., 864/222-0990, Mon.-Thurs. 7:30 A.M.-10 P.M., Fri. 7:30 A.M.-11:30 P.M., Sat. 8:30 A.M.-11:30 P.M.). They have a tasteful, cozy sitting area with solid old-fashioned furniture and excellent free Wi-Fi coverage. Oh, yeah, the coffee's great too.

LAKE HARTWELL

Built by the U.S. Army Corps of Engineers between 1955 and 1963 as part of a massive hydropower and navigation project, Lake Hartwell forms part of the Georgia-South Carolina border and is contained by the Hartwell Dam's actions on the Savannah River, seven miles below where the Tugaloo and Seneca Rivers join. (The Corps manages two other lakes in South Carolina, Richard B. Russell Lake and J. Strom Thurmond Lake, formerly Clarks Hill Reservoir.) Although not as big as Lake Thurmond, the 56,000-acre Lake Hartwell seems to have a more diverse variety of access points. Approximately 50 miles

long, it has 962 miles of shoreline. With a depth in some points of 180 feet, it's also a particularly fertile fishing area.

Parks and Recreation Areas

A popular base to explore the lake, with 14 miles of shoreline, is **Lake Hartwell State Recreation Area** (866/345-7275, www.southcarolinaparks. com, daily dawn-dusk, $2 adults, free under age 16). In addition, the state of South Carolina runs a whole slew of day-use recreation areas along Hartwell, all with easy water access. Some offer more amenities than others, and all have public boat ramps, but not all are free.

Asbury Recreation Area (daily 6 A.M.-10 P.M., free) is near Anderson. To get here, take Whitehall Road out of Anderson, take a right on Centerville Road, and then a left onto Asbury Road. **Broyles Recreation Area** (daily 6 A.M.-10 P.M., $4 per vehicle) is perhaps the plushest of these state-run areas. Take I-85 exit 11, get onto Highway 24, and take a right onto Hattons Ford Road. **Fair Play Recreation Area** (daily 6 A.M.-10 P.M., $4 per vehicle) also has extended amenities, like a playground and a swimming beach. Take I-85 exit 2 and make an immediate left; the area is at the end of that road. From Townville, South Carolina, **Friendship Recreation Area** (boat ramp year-round daily 6 A.M.-10 P.M., park May-Oct. 1 daily 6 A.M.-10 P.M., boat launch $3) can be reached by taking Highway 24 west and following the signs.

Lawrence Bridge Recreation Area (daily 6 A.M.-10 P.M., boat launch $3) is a no-frills site in Oconee County. Take U.S. 76 north of Clemson and take a right on Old Clemson Highway. Then take a right onto Clemson Bridge Road and follow the signs. **Mullins Ford Recreation Area** (daily 6 A.M.-10 P.M., free) is off of U.S. 123 just inside the Georgia-South Carolina border; take a right on Tabor Road. **Richland Creek Access** (daily 6 A.M.-10 P.M., boat launch $3) is in Anderson County. Turn off Highway 187 onto Providence Church Road and follow the signs. A large and well-equipped site is **River Forks Recreation Area** (boat ramp year-round daily 6 A.M.-10 P.M., park May-Oct. 1 daily 6 A.M.-10 P.M., $4 per vehicle). In Anderson County, take Highway 187 to old Robert's Church Road and follow the signs.

Another popular spot with playgrounds and swim beaches is **Singing Pines Recreation Area** (boat ramp year-round daily 10 A.M.-6 P.M., park May-Oct. 1 daily 10 A.M.-6 P.M., $4 per vehicle). It's off U.S. 29 just inside the Georgia-South Carolina border. Another family-friendly spot is **Twelve Mile Recreation Area** (boat ramp year-round daily 10 A.M.-6 P.M., park May-Oct. 1 daily 10 A.M.-6 P.M., $4 per vehicle) in Pickens County near Clemson. From U.S. 123, turn onto Highway 132 and follow the signs. **Twin Lakes Recreation Area** (boat ramp year-round daily 6 A.M.-10 P.M., park May-Oct. 1 daily 6 A.M.-10 P.M., $4 per vehicle) is near Clemson. Take I-85 exit 14 and head north on Highway 187 to Pendleton. When you pass the Clemson Research Center, take a left onto Fant's Grove Road.

In addition, the city of Anderson runs the **Darwin H. Wright Park** (864/231-2235), which has a boat ramp, a playground, a fishing pier, and restroom facilities. Paddlers will enjoy the **Keowee Trail Park** (864/653-2030), which has similar amenities.

Boating, Kayaking, and Canoeing

Besides the public landings at the parks and recreation areas above, there are 13 municipal public landings on the South Carolina side of Lake Hartwell, and over twice as many as on the Georgia side. Amenities are limited. For a full list, go to www.sas.usace.army.mil/lakes/hartwell/hartnoncounty.htm.

Full-service marinas on the lake that have restaurants include **Big Water Marina** (864/226-3339, www.bigwatermarina.com), **Clemson Marina** (864/653-8100, www.

clemsonmarina.com), and **Portman Marina** (864/287-3211, www.portmanmarina.com).

Fishing

Lake Hartwell is big on fishing, specifically bream, crappie, catfish, and all kinds of bass. To take a crack yourself, you need a South Carolina or Georgia fishing license, available for just a few bucks at almost any bait-and-tackle shop or convenience store.

Don't fish at boat ramps or off bridges. Otherwise you can fish just about anywhere on Hartwell, from a boat or at any of the parks and recreation areas. Fishing piers are located at the Singing Pines Recreation Area and Darwin H. Wright Park, both in Anderson County. In addition, some bank fishing areas have been installed, which are built-up brush piles that attract fish; most are identified with a sign.

Camping

Lake Hartwell State Recreation Area (866/345-7275, www.southcarolinaparks.com, daily dawn-dusk, $2 adults, free under age 16) is probably the coolest place to camp, offering a pair of one-room "camper cabins" with no running water that occupy a feasible middle ground between tenting and the more expensive cabin rentals you'll find at most South Carolina state parks. There are also 115 paved sites with water and electricity ($16-19) as well as 13 tent sites ($13). Of course, there's a boat ramp too. To get to the park, take I-85 exit 1 onto Highway 11 toward Walhalla and look for the signs.

In addition, there are four Army Corps of Engineers-managed campgrounds on the South Carolina side of Lake Hartwell, with hundreds of campsites among them. Alcohol is prohibited at all of them. **Coneross Campground** (May-Sept. daily 7 A.M.-10 P.M., $14-22) is on the north end of Lake Hartwell. It has 106 mostly shaded sites, 12 of which are primitive. There's a boat ramp, a playground, a small beach, showers, and restrooms. To get here, take I-85 exit

11 onto Highway 24. A little past Townville, take a right onto Coneross Creek Road. **Oconee Point Campground** (May-Sept. daily 7 A.M.-10 P.M., $22) is also on the northern end of the lake near Clemson. It has the same amenities as Coneross but is smaller, with 60 sites. Take I-85 exit 11 onto Highway 24. A little past Townville, take a right onto Coneross Creek Road, and then go south on Friendship Road. **Springfield Campground** (May 1-Oct. 31 daily 7 A.M.-10 P.M., $22) is closer to Anderson and has typical amenities and 79 sites, almost all of which are right on the water. Get here by taking I-85 exit 11 until you reach Providence Church Road, and follow the signs from there. Because it's the closest site to Clemson, **Twin Lakes Campground** (May 1-Nov. 30 daily 7 A.M.-10 P.M., $20-22) is one of the most popular Hartwell campgrounds. It has 102 sites, all with full hookups and the usual amenities. Get here by taking I-85 exit 14 and going north on Highway 187 to Pendleton. When you pass the Clemson Research Center, take a left onto Fant's Grove Road and follow the signs.

A notable private campground on the lake is **Lake Hartwell Camping and Cabins** (400 Ponderosa Point, Townville, 864/287-3223, www.camplakehartwell.com). There are 120 sites ($21-25), half with full hookups and half with water and electricity only. There are also seven fully equipped cabins ($80) that sleep 4-6 people, and one smaller "rustic" cabin ($70) that sleeps three. Keep in mind not all the cabins are right on the lake, so ask beforehand.

Ninety Six District

In the early 1700s, this region—or in colonial parlance, "district"—was named after the key trading post on the edge of what was then the rugged frontier. Ninety Six was thought, erroneously, to be 96 miles from the nearest big Cherokee settlement in Keowee. While it's considered part of the Upstate, the vibe here is a little different. The landscape is rolling and more lush than the typical Upstate hill country. You start to see the beginnings of the thoroughbred country immediately to the south. The Upstate's often-frenetic growth has largely passed this region by as well, and things are slower and more relaxed.

ABBEVILLE
Founded in 1758 by a group of French Huguenots—who named it after their city back in the old country—pretty little Abbeville has about 6,000 people. French roots aside, I'm not sure why Abbeville reminds me so much of a Western town. Perhaps it's the wide, open town square, with a layout and surrounding facades so similar to Taos, New Mexico; or maybe it's Abbeville's popularity with Harley riders, a common sight passing through this rolling scenic portion of South Carolina seemingly tailor-made for riding.

But make no mistake, Abbeville is all Southern. In fact, it saw both the birth and the death of the Confederacy. In November 1860, on Secession Hill, the first meeting to discuss South Carolina's departure from the union was held. Five years later, Jefferson Davis dissolved the Confederacy in the grand Burt-Stark Mansion just off the town square. As if that weren't enough, Abbeville is also the birthplace of the polarizing statesman John C. Calhoun, author of the state's rights movement and the doctrines of nullification and secession. Today, that legacy is very much remembered. You see it in the occasional rebel battle flag hoisted in someone's window; in the name of Jefferson Davis Park just north of downtown; and certainly in the offerings of the Southern Patriot bookstore, with its row of Confederate flags over the awning.

© JIM MOREKIS

the Abbeville Opera House

There's also a distinct Mennonite presence in Abbeville, evinced in two Mennonite-run restaurants and the private Cold Springs Mennonite School.

Sights

ABBEVILLE OPERA HOUSE

The town's main claim to fame these days is the 1908 Abbeville Opera House (Town Square, 864/366-2157, www.theabbevilleoperahouse.com), a compact and elegant gem of a building from the heyday of traveling theater. In the early 1900s Abbeville was a key stop on the road-show circuit, hosting popular musicals, plays, and vaudeville shows. The Opera House survived a transition to a movie theater in the 1940s, and then to a playhouse in the 1950s. Now fully and beautifully restored, it still hosts plenty of stage productions, attracting about 30,000 spectators through the course of a typical year.

Right next door to the Opera House, in front of the adjacent courthouse, is a monument to Thomas Howie, the "Major of Saint-Lô." Howie

was a hero of the Normandy invasion during World War II and was killed in France trying to take the town of Saint-Lô. A famous photograph shows his flag-draped coffin on the rubble of the Saint-Lô Cathedral. Now buried in St. Laurent Cemetery, his childhood home is a block off the town square on Pinckney Street, with a marker right outside. Howie was reportedly an inspiration for Tom Hanks's character, John Miller, in the Steven Spielberg film *Saving Private Ryan*.

BURT-STARK MANSION

Abbeville's other key attraction is the Burt-Stark Mansion (400 N. Main St., 864/366-0166, www.burt-stark.com, Fri.-Sat. 1:30-4:30 P.M., $10), where President Jefferson Davis uttered the simple words, "All is indeed lost," and committed the last official act of his office—dissolving the Confederacy. This grand 1830s mansion dominating the northern approach to town is furnished with period pieces and includes a facsimile 1820s kitchen. Admission includes an hour-long tour.

TRINITY EPISCOPAL CHURCH

Tucked off the town square is the graceful, simply evocative Trinity Episcopal Church (Church St., daily 9 A.M.-5 P.M., free), now in a state of romantic decay. The elegantly constructed Gothic sanctuary was completed less than a month before the meeting on Secession Hill that would change Abbeville's fortunes forever. During the Civil War, when most of Abbeville's menfolk took up arms, the congregation consisted of women and children, many of them refugees from Charleston and the Lowcountry.

Now listed on the National Register of Historic Places, Trinity is looking better after a series of renovations. Outside, you can't miss the 125-foot spire or the nice salmon-colored stucco exterior. When inside, note the beautiful pews and stained glass windows. The chancel window, originally made in England and delivered to Charleston by a blockade-runner, was transported here in the middle of the Civil War.

Shopping

A nice thing about Abbeville is that many shops around the town square stay open late on play nights at the Opera House.

Antiquing is big in Abbeville. Good shops on the square are **Dust and Rust Antiques** (102 E. Pickens St., 864/366-6565, Mon.-Sat. 10 A.M.-5 P.M.), **Mama's Memories** (118 Court Square, 864/366-0260, Wed.-Thurs. 11 A.M.-5 P.M., Fri.-Sat. 11 A.M.-7 P.M.), and **Abbey's Alley** (113 Washington St., 864/366-3636, Wed.-Thurs. 9 A.M.-6 P.M., Fri.-Sat. 9 A.M.-9 P.M.).

In other shopping, **Southern Patriot Shoppe** (107 N. Main St., 864/366-2395, Mon.-Sat. 10 A.M.-6 P.M.) is devoted to Civil War history from a distinctly pro-Southern stance.

Accommodations and Food

The best-known lodging in town is on the town square, the historic **Belmont Inn** (104 E. Pickens St., 864/459-9625, www.belmontinn. net). The Belmont actually began life in 1903 as the Eureka, catering to traveling salespeople in the textile trade. Closed in the 1970s, it reopened as a 25-room hotel in the 1980s. The guest rooms are smallish but fairly well-furnished, and you have access not only to a nice tavern but to the hotel's Heritage Dining Room ($10-20), specializing in classic Southern and American dishes. They offer some attractive combo packages with play tickets at the Opera House directly across the street.

There are two Mennonite-run restaurants in town, **Yoder's Dutch Kitchen** (809 E. Greenwood St., 864/366-5556, Wed.-Sat. 11 A.M.-2:30 P.M. and Fri.-Sat. 5-8:30 P.M., $5-10) and **Dutch Oven** (108 N. Main St., 864/366-5513, www.dutchovenrestaurant.com, breakfast Tues. and Sat. 6:30-10:30 A.M., lunch Mon.-Fri. 10:30 A.M.-2:30 P.M., dinner Thurs.-Fri. 4:30-8:30 P.M., $5-10). Both are excellent and affordable, although the menu tends more toward simple Southern favorites.

If that doesn't float your boat, there's a great Mexican place right on the town square, **Maria's** (125 Court Square, 864/366-6394, daily 10 A.M.-10 P.M., $5-10) that serves a mean chile poblano.

GREENWOOD

As its bucolic name hints, Greenwood is a safe, relaxing, pleasant place that has done a good job revitalizing its central downtown area (actually called "uptown" here). Its main claim to fame is hosting the annual **South Carolina Festival of Flowers** (864/223-8411), held each June at venues all over town.

Greenwood is somewhat unusual among South Carolina towns in that it has no real central square. What it does have is an almost unbelievably wide Main Street—about 300 feet wide, the result of hosting an old rail line.

Sights

EMERALD TRIANGLE

The marketing term used for the restored (and in places oddly modernist) uptown area is the Emerald Triangle (www.emeraldtriangle.sc).

This is where you'll find the little **Greenwood Museum** (106 Main St., 864/229-7093, Wed.-Sat. 10 A.M.-5 P.M., $5 adults, $2 children) and the adjacent **Greenwood Community Theatre** (110 Main St., 864/229-5704).

A few doors down is the decommissioned 25,000-square-foot Federal Building, now the fully restored site of the **Greenwood Arts Center** (120 Main St., 864/388-7800), which hosts numerous exhibits in its gallery space. The **Greenwood Regional Tourism and Visitors Bureau** (120 Main St., 864/953-2466, www.visitgreenwoodsc.com, Mon.-Fri. 8:30 A.M.-5:30 P.M., Sat. 9:30 A.M.-1:30 P.M.) is also here.

RAILROAD HISTORICAL CENTER

Set in an old home off the main drag at the southernmost portion of the Emerald Triangle, the Railroad Historical Center (415 Main St., 864/229-7093, www.emeraldtriangle.sc, Apr.-Oct. Sat. 10 A.M.-4 P.M. and by appointment, $5 adults, $2 children) commemorates the Upstate's role in the railroad industry. The main attraction is the collection of rail cars, including a massive locomotive visible from the highway.

PARK SEED COMPANY

Greenwood's most famous attraction is the Park Seed Company (3507 Cokesbury Rd., 800/213-0076, www.parkseed.com), which, since its founding in the early 1900s in Pennsylvania, shortly thereafter moving to Greenwood, has grown to become one of the largest seed houses around. While most of its business is done online these days, the retail selection is comprehensive.

The attached **Park Garden Center** (Mon.-Sat. 9 A.M.-5 P.M., free) is an attraction in itself, with lots of gorgeous and well-maintained trial gardens, at their peak May-July.

Get to Park Seed by taking Highway 254 north of Greenwood about three miles.

EMERALD FARM

The Emerald Farm (409 Emerald Farm Rd., 864/223-2247, www.emeraldfarm.com,

Tues.-Sat. 9 A.M.-5 P.M., free), on 75 beautiful acres on the edge of town, is a fun place for the whole family. Organic goods available for purchase, including homemade goat milk soap.

NINETY SIX NATIONAL HISTORIC SITE

Virtually from the time of its founding in the mid-1700s, the trading post called Ninety Six—in the mistaken belief that it was 96 miles from the great Cherokee town at Keowee—was a center of conflict. In 1760, the Cherokees attacked it twice. During the American Revolution in 1775, it was the site of the first land engagement south of New England. A few years later in 1781, General Nathanael Greene and 1,000 Continental troops staged a long, unsuccessful siege of the British-held fortress here. It is this chapter of history that is recalled at the 1,000-acre Ninety Six National Historic Site (1103 Hwy. 248, 864/543-4068, www.nps.gov/nisi, daily dawn-dusk, visitors center daily 9 A.M.-5 P.M., free), south of the modern-day town of Ninety Six, which is east of Greenwood.

The center of the battle occurred at the Star Fort, site of many bloody frontal assaults. The redoubt is well preserved, and archaeological discoveries continue. The old site of the town of Ninety Six is also on the grounds, along with a neat re-creation of an old-time watering hole, the Black Swan Tavern.

This is a particularly diverse park, with lots of nature to go along with the important history. There's a one-mile interpretive historical trail, which begins and ends at the visitors center parking lot. There are also several nature trails, including a portion of the old Cherokee trail; get a map of them all from the visitors center. There's even a pond at the back of the property where you can do some fishing, during limited times of the year; call ahead or check the website. In addition, rangers lead tours year-round; check the bulletin board at the visitors center.

CALHOUN FALLS STATE RECREATION AREA

There are no falls anymore at Calhoun Falls State Recreation Area (46 Maintenance Shop Rd., 864/447-8267, www.southcarolinaparks. com, daily dawn-dusk, $2 adults, free under age 16) since they were submerged with the damming of this leg of the Savannah River to form 26,000-acre Lake Russell. But this is a nice location with great access to this lesser-developed reservoir.

There's a marina on-site as well as a boat ramp. With a valid state fishing license you can fish all around the lake, including from the central pier. There are three campgrounds on-site as well, two of which are RV-oriented ($19-22) and one designated tent campground ($14-16).

Old English District

Chamber of Commerce types have given this area across the top of the state the tourist-friendly moniker "Old English District." The ancestral home of President Andrew Jackson, this region exemplifies the hardscrabble home-spun values of that president, who was typical of the stubborn and self-reliant Scots-Irish homestead farmers who originally settled the region. So why "Old English"? In the early days of the Revolution, this area was considered safe ground for British soldiers and settlers due to the Loyalist sentiments of most of the local population, who had no great love for the aristocratic slave-owning elite of Charleston and the Lowcountry. All that changed due to the heavy-handed occupation by the redcoats, who soon found themselves harried by the colonial army and local Tories. With Loyalists in much shorter supply than promised, the British soon found themselves on the run, especially after key defeats at Cowpens outside Spartanburg and at Kings Mountain on the modern North Carolina-South Carolina border.

Today, the Old English District still retains a lot of colonial sensibility, in contrast to the more Civil War-oriented sites in other areas of South Carolina. Its cachet has been helped along immensely by the above-noted proactive effort to market the region as a specific destination.

Be aware that the massive growth of Charlotte, North Carolina, just over the border to the north, has turned some Old English District towns—chief among them Rock Hill—into rapidly developing bedroom communities of that economic titan on I-77. While there is no shortage of box-type chain lodging in the area, I suggest staying at one of the inexpensive historic B&Bs or simply camping.

KINGS MOUNTAIN NATIONAL MILITARY PARK

Nestled against the North Carolina border (the actual town of Kings Mountain is in the Tar Heel State) is Kings Mountain National Military Park (2625 Park Rd., 803/222-3209, www.nps.gov/kimo, Labor Day-Memorial Day daily 9 A.M.-5 P.M., Memorial Day-Labor Day daily 9 A.M.-6 P.M., free). The site marks the battle of October 7, 1780, when American militia defeated a band of Loyalists under British major Patrick Ferguson. While the Patriots clearly carried the day, only later did it become clear that the Battle of Kings Mountain was the turning point in the Revolutionary War, after which the British never again gained the offensive.

Kings Mountain is the end point of the **Overmountain Victory National Historic Trail** (864/936-3477, www.nps.gov/ovvi), marking the route of the victorious militia forces through the Carolinas. It's important to note that this is a federal site, therefore no battle reenactments are allowed.

Historical aspects of the park include a half-hour film, exhibits, and a 1.5-mile self-guided battlefield tour along the Patriot lines up to the Loyalist position on the crest of the battle's central hill. The trail passes several monuments, including the grave of Major Ferguson, a casualty of the battle. In addition to being historic, the trails are also quite scenic.

Not to be confused with the nearby Kings Mountain State Park, campers can spend the night within the National Military Park only at the Garner Creek campsite, intended for a single large party. No reservations are taken, but you must get a permit (free) at the park's visitors center. Oh, and another catch: It's a three-mile hike in to the campsite.

KINGS MOUNTAIN STATE PARK

Not to be confused with the adjacent National Military Park of the same name, Kings Mountain State Park (1277 Park Rd., Blacksburg, 803/222-3209, www.southcarolinaparks.com, during daylight saving time daily 7 A.M.-8 P.M., other seasons daily 8 A.M.-6 P.M., $2 adults, free under age 16) offers plenty to do amid the picturesque setting of one of the classic South Carolina state parks built in the 1930s by the Civilian Conservation Corps. There are miles of good trails, two fishing lakes with boat rentals ($20 per day), and a living-history farm replicating the look, feel, and livestock of a typical piedmont farm in the early 1800s.

For the horse lover, there are 20 miles of equestrian trails that connect to the National Military Park. The state park has 15 equestrian campsites ($12)—but bring your own horse. For regular campers, the park has a whopping 115 RV and gravel tent sites with electricity and water ($16-18) and 10 primitive campsites with no water or electricity ($12-13).

◖ HISTORIC BRATTONSVILLE

Near the town of McConnells, Historic Brattonsville (1444 Brattonsville Rd., 803/684-2327, www.chmuseums.org, Mon.-Sat. 10 A.M.-5 P.M., Sun. 1-5 P.M., $6 adults, $3 ages

Historic Brattonsville

© JIM MOREKIS

4-17, free under age 4) includes the site of the Revolutionary War Battle of Huck's Defeat, a pivotal victory of Patriot militia over the Tories. But the chief allure of this 775-acre site is the impressive grouping of more than 30 well-restored historic structures (although not all are open to the public), including the circa-1840 visitors center, a reconstruction of a backwoods log cabin, and a mid-1800s milk barn and hog pen.

The crown jewel is the 1766 **William Bratton House,** probably the oldest building in this part of the state and where some scenes in Mel Gibson's *The Patriot* were filmed. (After a few minutes wandering the grounds, you'll wonder why more movies aren't filmed here.) An archetypal figure of this region, William Bratton was a Presbyterian, judge, sheriff, and state legislator with eight children who was also a hard-fighting colonel in the militia that fought on this site.

Every year on the second Saturday of July, authentically uniformed and equipped reenactors commemorate the Battle of Huck's Defeat, which took place on July 12, 1780, and is sometimes known as the Battle of Williamson's Plantation. Loyalist forces under Captain Christian Huck, who had a famously low regard for the Scots-Irish settlers of the region, were sent to corner Colonel Bratton when they got intelligence that he'd gone back home to supervise the wheat harvest. They arrived at the Bratton home only to find Bratton's wife, Martha, whom they threatened with a reaping hook if she wouldn't give up the location of her husband.

According to lore, Martha Bratton was saved from harm by the intervention of a Loyalist officer named John Adamson. She repaid his kindness by promptly sending out a slave to warn her husband of the British presence. Captain Huck arrived and set up shop in the neighboring home of James Williamson. While he slept inside, his combined force of British cavalry and New York Loyalists was attacked and enveloped at dawn by Bratton's returning militia. Huck lost 35 men and was himself killed instantly by a militiaman's lethal shot. The Patriots lost just one man. The entire battle took about 10 minutes.

The chief highlight of Brattonsville for most visitors, however, is the year-round series of living history reenactments (year-round Sat. 10 A.M.-4 P.M.), featuring knowledgeable guides in period garb. Simply put, there's plenty of history for the history buff, plenty of beauty for the nature lover (including several nature trails), and plenty of room for the kids to blow off some steam. There's even a very good, if somewhat pricey, gift shop.

ROCK HILL AND VICINITY
York

In the 1940s an Ivy League grad student did his thesis on the mill culture of a Southern county, which he called "Kent County" to preserve the anonymity of his subjects. The actual place he studied was York County, South Carolina, and the resulting research became somewhat renowned in sociological circles.

York County is pretty big, but its county seat, York, is small. It has seen better days but is currently making a sincere if uneven effort to get onto the tourism radar screen.

Located in what was originally the Yorkville Female Academy, the **McCelvey Center** (212 E. Jefferson St.) is a Smithsonian-sponsored component of the state's Culture & Heritage Museums. Today it hosts the **Historical Center of York County** (803/684-3948, www.chmuseums.org, Mon.-Sat. 10 A.M.-4 P.M., free) as well as a 560-seat theater, home to occasional musical performances. Among the Historical Center's databases are collections of Confederate veterans and African Americans in the American Revolution. Saturday mornings often see 45-minute programs highlighting aspects of the archival material. Another important facet of the McCelvey Center is the **Southern Revolutionary War Institute**

(803/684-3948), devoted to the study of the ridiculously underreported Southern theater of the American Revolution.

If you're hungry or thirsty when in York, go no further than **The Coal Yard Restaurant and Lounge** (105 Garner St., 803/684-9653, Wed.-Sat. 4 P.M.-midnight, $6-25), a fun place with good American cuisine.

Museum of York County

On the outskirts of Rock Hill is another of the Culture & Heritage Museums, the Museum of York County (4621 Mt. Gallant Rd., 803/329-2121, http://chmuseums.org, Tues.-Sat. 10 A.M.-5 P.M., Sun. 1-5 P.M., $5 adults, $3 students, free under age 5). Permanent exhibits include an extensive natural history of the piedmont region, while rotating exhibits tend to focus on cultural aspects such as the story of a slave, known to history only as Kessie, who lived and worked on the Bratton plantation.

Possibly of more interest to kids will be the **Settlemyre Planetarium** (www.chmuseums. org, showtimes vary, $5 adults, $3 ages 4-17, free under age 4), which displays the night sky on the darkened interior of its large dome. Shows are generally Saturday at 11 A.M., 2 P.M., and 3 P.M. and Sunday at 2 P.M. and 3 P.M., but check the website for details.

Getting here can be tricky. Take Liberty Street (Hwy. 161) east of York, veering left to stay on Highway 161 (at that point called Old York Rd.). Continue past the intersection with Highway 274 (Hands Mill Rd.), and the museum is two miles ahead on the right.

Downtown Rock Hill

Technically the fourth-largest city in South Carolina, Rock Hill is essentially a satellite of Charlotte, North Carolina, to the north. Compared to many other cities in the state, there's not much history here and relatively few attractions, although the downtown area is well restored.

The city's main historic claim to fame is the "Friendship Nine," a group of African

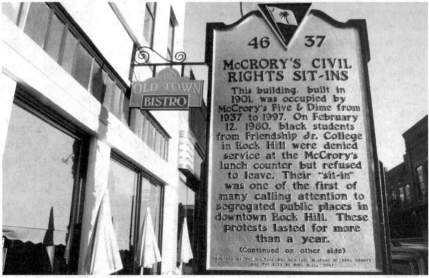

Rock Hill's historic Old Town Bistro

© JIM MOREKIS

Americans—eight of whom were students at Friendship Junior College in town—who staged a nonviolent "counter strike" in February 1961 to protest segregation. Their actions were simple: They took seats at the whites-only counter at the downtown McCrory's and asked to be served. Also known as the "Rock Hill Nine," the men deliberately chose a 30-day jail sentence as part of a new "jail, no bail" strategy by civil rights leaders. Activists throughout the South adopted the technique, which relied on courage—which they had in abundance—rather than scarce funding to keep the civil rights movement alive.

While McCrory's is no more, the historic spot on Main Street is now the home of ◖ **Old Town Bistro** (135 E. Main St., 803/327-9222, www.rholdtownbistro.com, Mon.-Fri. 10:30 A.M.-10 P.M., Sat.-Sun. 7 A.M.-10 P.M., $6-10), a cute diner-style restaurant based on the old McCrory's layout, including the counter. The Greek owners offer some cuisine of their home country, including a great gyro and even the famous frappé iced-coffee drink that's all the rage around the Mediterranean. While enjoying your tasty meal you can read displays on the exploits of the Friendship Nine.

A short distance out of downtown is the scenic wooded campus of **Winthrop University** (701 Oakland Ave., 803/323-2211, www.winthrop.edu). A historic district in its own right, the campus is quite attractive, with the signature Tillman Hall building the most notable structure, often used as a symbol of Rock Hill.

For a nice place to stay in Rock Hill, try **The Book and the Spindle** (626 Oakland Ave., 803/328-1913, $75-95). Its four suites are in a classy brick Georgian home overlooking the campus of Winthrop University, and it's a short walk from Rock Hill's little historic district.

Rock Hill Blackjacks Heritage Preserve

One of the last remaining prairie habitats in South Carolina, the Rock Hill Blackjacks Heritage Preserve (803/734-3886, www.dnr.sc.gov, daily dawn-dusk, free) gets its name from the blackjack oaks that predominate here, forming what's technically known as a montmorillonite forest. The wildflower displays are particularly nice. There are no facilities, and bow hunting does go on in the fall.

To get here from downtown Rock Hill, take Main Street east to Albright Road. Take a right and then a left onto Blackmon Street. The Preserve's parking area is ahead on the left.

Carowinds

On a totally separate note is Carowinds (Ave. of the Carolinas, 800/888-4386, www.carowinds.com, summer daily, spring and fall Sat.-Sun., hours vary, admission varies). If you need a break from history, this is surely the place: a theme park that prides itself not on reenactments but on a whole bunch of outstanding roller-coaster rides sprinkled with a number of well-known pop-culture figures, arranged in a series of subparks within the massive central Carowinds complex on the North Carolina-South Carolina border.

Young kids will enjoy **Nickelodeon Central,** which features their favorite TV characters in 20 different attractions. There's also a Scooby-Doo Haunted House. Teens will enjoy the dozen or so serious **roller coasters** at Carowinds. Rides like the Hurler, Thunder Road, and the skydiving/hang gliding combo ride Xtreme Skyflyer are not for the faint-of-heart and are designed specifically to scare you.

In summer, visitors of all ages will enjoy the **Boomerang Bay** water park. There are tube slides galore, tons of Aussie-themed water rides, and a heated lagoon complete with cabana rentals. Boomerang Bay is only open in the summer, and even then the hours are fairly erratic; consult the website closely for details. I suggest checking the website for all operating hours, as they vary with the season and the month.

GREENVILLE

Carowinds regularly hosts large concerts tending heavily toward popular country-western acts and contemporary Christian groups; consult the website for the latest schedule.

There are several ways to get into Carowinds. The best deal is the three-day online advance general admission ticket ($36 adults, $20 children). To spread your visit over two days, the best option is the "pay once, visit twice" ticket ($52 all ages). Another interesting option is to take advantage of "twilight" admission, after 4 P.M. ($26 all ages).

There's even a campground, the **Carowinds Camp Wilderness Resort,** an upscale place with air-conditioned cabins, pull-through RV sites, Wi-Fi access, and a free shuttle to the theme park.

Carowinds is about 15 minutes north of Rock Hill and about the same distance south of Charlotte, North Carolina. Take I-77 to exit 90.

Anne Springs Close Greenway

Just south of the North Carolina border is the Anne Springs Close Greenway (803/548-7252, www.leroysprings.com, daily dawn-dusk, $3), a 35-mile network of trails through over 2,000 acres of very nice piedmont habitat. There are separate trails for cyclists and horseback riders. Each April, Earth Day brings a festive event with food, wildlife exhibits, and Native American demonstrations. They also offer guided horse rides; call or go to the website for details. Take U.S. 21 north out of Fort Mill.

Catawba Reservation

Although the Upstate is better known for its Cherokee heritage, the Catawba people actually have a large reservation—by East Coast standards, anyway—just outside Rock Hill. The history of the Catawba in the area dates quite far back, but they didn't receive official federal status until 1993, which was 33 years after the last speaker of the old Catawba language had died.

The main attraction on the 640-acre reservation, home to about 300 people, is the

Catawba Cultural Center (1536 Tom Steven Rd., 803/328-2427, www.ccppcrafts.com), the best place to explore the fascinating and unique world of Catawba pottery. Unlike other pottery traditions, the Catawba don't use a pottery wheel or glazes. They use favorite objects or whatever is at hand to shape the clay, which is dug from the banks of the Catawba River, as it has been for hundreds of years.

The Cultural Center, housed in what used to be the reservation's elementary school, has exhibits and a cute gift shop with crafts, books, and, of course, some Catawba pottery. There's also an herb garden and a nature trail that follows the path of an old wagon trail along the Catawba River.

ANDREW JACKSON STATE PARK

While it's not one of the charming South Carolina state parks built during the Depression—this one dates from the 1950s and is much smaller in scale—Andrew Jackson State Park (196 Andrew Jackson Park Rd., 803/285-3344, www.southcarolinaparks.com, during daylight saving time daily 9 A.M.-9 P.M., other seasons daily 8 A.M.-6 P.M., $2 adults, free under age 16) is worth visiting. It's devoted not only to the great outdoors but also to the 7th president of the United States, born near this site.

There is a museum detailing Jackson's boyhood, with occasional living-history reenactments. There's also a replica of an 18th-century one-room schoolhouse and an amphitheater, which occasionally hosts musical performances. Don't miss the equestrian statue of Jackson sculpted by Anna Hyatt Huntington, who's also responsible for many of the sculptures at Myrtle Beach's Brookgreen Gardens.

The park has five pull-through RV campsites and 20 gravel sites for RVs and tents ($12-13) with electricity and water. You can fish at the 18-acre lake at the park, either from the bank, the pier, or by renting a little johnboat ($12 per day).

Get here by taking I-77 exit 77 onto

Highway 5 east to U.S. 521 north. The park is a 0.5 miles ahead, nine miles north of Lancaster.

LANDSFORD CANAL STATE PARK

The popular Landsford Canal State Park (2051 Park Dr., Catawba, 803/789-5800, www.southcarolinaparks.com, daily 9 A.M.-6 P.M., $2 adults, free under age 16) chronicles the time when an active canal system made the Catawba River commercially navigable, from 1820 to 1835. You can see the remains of several canal locks and the old lockkeeper's quarters, furnished with interpretive exhibits.

Landsford does have one very unique natural offering: This area is home to the largest population of Rocky Shoals spider lilies in the world. The plant blooms spectacularly in late May-early June. There are two trails on-site, the self-explanatory Canal Trail and the Nature Trail along the river, which thoughtfully includes a viewing deck from which you can see the spider lilies.

LAKE WATEREE STATE RECREATION AREA

Located on scenic Desportes Island, the popular Lake Wateree State Recreation Area (881 State Park Rd., 803/482-6401, www.southcarolinaparks.com, daily 6 A.M.-10 P.M., $2 adults, free under age 16) near Winnsboro offers some great angling opportunities. There's a tackle shop on-site and a public boat ramp, not to mention 72 campsites ($16-19).

MUSGROVE MILL STATE HISTORIC SITE

In August 1780, north of the modern-day town of Clinton, a force of Patriot militia—mostly Georgians and "Overmountain Men" from Tennessee—clashed with a larger body of Tories under the command of Major Patrick Ferguson. The militia got the best of the Loyalists in the largely hand-to-hand combat that followed, but news of the disastrous defeat

at Camden—which actually happened three days earlier—put a damper on their plans to pursue the shattered Loyalist force further.

You can learn more about the battle at the Musgrove Mill State Historic Site (398 State Park Rd., 864/938-0100, www.southcarolinaparks.com, daily 9 A.M.-6 P.M., free), which has a good interpretive center (Mon.-Fri. 1-5 P.M., Sat.-Sun. 10 A.M.-5 P.M.). At the site you can also put your kayak in on the Enoree River; the folks at the interpretive center can give you good info on that. Unusually for a place this far away from the Blue Ridge, there's a nice little waterfall with full access and a scenic overlook. The site is a few miles off I-26 on Highway 56.

ROSE HILL PLANTATION STATE PARK

Just south of Union at the edge of the Sumter National Forest is Rose Hill Plantation State Park (2677 Sardis Rd., 864/427-5966, www.southcarolinaparks.com, daily 9 A.M.-6 P.M., free), the former homestead of the "Secession Governor," William H. Gist, who pushed for South Carolina to take the irrevocable step toward war soon after the election of Abraham Lincoln. The central attraction is the magnificent home along with its outbuildings and beautiful gardens. A tour of the house ($4 adults, $3 ages 6-16) runs every hour on the hour 1-4 P.M. You can also take a nice nature trail down to the Tyger River.

If you're not coming directly from Union—in which case it's just a quick drive south on Sardis Road—Rose Hill is a little tricky to get to: Take I-26 exit 44 onto Highway 49 toward Union. Continue through Cross Anchor to Cross Keys and veer right onto Old Buncombe Road. After five miles, take a left onto Galilee Church Road to the front gate. You'll see the Gist family cemetery on the left as you approach.

UNION

The nearby town of Union—named not for an excess of federalist sentiment but for the old

Union Church erected in 1765—was one of the first areas of the state settled by Scots-Irish from Virginia and Pennsylvania. The key site downtown is the **Union County Courthouse** on Main Street, with a grand Robert Mills-designed jail next door.

A great place to stay in downtown Union is the ◖ **Inn at Merridun** (100 Merridun Place, 864/427-7052, www.merridun.com, $109-115). The five-room inn has garnered a reputation for excellent friendly service in an authentic antebellum setting—the 1855 home is on the National Register of Historic Places—with a fantastic Southern breakfast to boot. That said, don't expect a bright and shiny bauble—this is essentially still a historic home, not a museum, and not every physical aspect is perfect. A couple of the smaller guest rooms can be had for $99.

INFORMATION AND SERVICES

The main clearinghouse for information is the **Old English District Visitor Center** (201 N. Main St., Richburg, 803/789-7076, www.sctravel.net). In Rock Hill and York County, check out the **Rock Hill/York County Convention and Visitors Bureau** (452 S. Anderson Rd., Rock Hill, 803/329-5200, www.visityorkcounty.com).

The largest newspaper serving the region is the *Charlotte Observer* (www.charlotteobserver.com) in North Carolina. Other papers include the *Rock Hill Herald* (www.heraldonline.com) and the *Lancaster News* (www.thelancasternews.com).

Medical centers in the region include **Chesterfield General Hospital** (711 Chesterfield Hwy., Cheraw, 843/537-7881, www.chesterfieldgeneral.com) and **Piedmont Medical Center** (222 S. Herlong Ave., Rock Hill, 803/329-1234, www.piedmontmedicalcenter.com).

GETTING THERE AND AROUND

Two major airports border the region: **Greenville-Spartanburg International Airport** (GSP, 864/877-7426, www.gspairport.com), along I-85 between Greenville and Spartanburg, and **Charlotte Douglas International Airport** (CLT, 704/359-4910, www.charmeck.org), over the border in North Carolina.

Like most of South Carolina, the Old English District is particularly well-served by the interstate highway system. The main artery is the north-south I-77 from the North Carolina border to Columbia. The region's southern boundaries are I-26 to the southwest and I-20 to the southeast.

BACKGROUND

The Land

GEOGRAPHY

The story of South Carolina's geography begins with the Appalachian Mountain chain. It's in Appalachia where so much of the coast's freshwater—in the form of rain—comes together and flows southeast—in the form of rivers—to the Atlantic Ocean. A feature called the **Blue Ridge Escarpment,** or Blue Wall, demarcates the mountains, and its steep face is responsible for most of the many waterfalls in the state.

Moving east, the next level down from the Appalachians is the **piedmont** region (in South Carolina often called simply the Upstate). The piedmont is a rolling, hilly area, the eroded remains of an ancient mountain chain now long gone.

At the piedmont's eastern edge is the **fall line,** so named because it's there where rivers make a drop toward the sea, generally becoming navigable. This slight but noticeable change in elevation—which actually marked the shoreline about 60 million years ago—not only encouraged trade but has provided water power for mills for hundreds of years. Many inland cities of the region, like Columbia, trace their origin and commercial success to their strategic location on the fall line.

© JIM MOREKIS

© JIM MOREKIS

The Edisto River is the longest blackwater river in the world.

Around the fall line zone in the **Upper Coastal Plain** you can sometimes spot **sand hills,** usually only a few feet in elevation, generally thought to be the vestigial remains of primordial sand dunes and offshore sandbars. Well beyond the fall line and the sometimes nearly invisible sand hills lies the **lower coastal plain,** gradually built up over a 150-million-year span by sedimentary runoff from the Appalachian Mountains, which were then as high or even higher than the modern-day Himalayas.

The coastal plain was sea bottom for much of the earth's history, and in some eroded areas you can see dramatic proof of this in prehistoric shells, shark teeth, fossilized whale bones, and oyster beds, often many miles inland. In some places, calcium from these ancient shells has provided a lush home for distinct groups of unique plants, called **disjuncts.**

At various times over the last 50 million years, the coastal plain has submerged, surfaced, and submerged again. At the height of the last major ice age, when global sea levels were very low, the east coast of North America extended out nearly 100 miles farther than the present shoreline. (We now call this former coastal region the **continental shelf.**) The Coastal Plain has been in roughly its current form for about the last 15,000 years.

Rivers

Visitors from drier climates are sometimes shocked to see how huge the rivers can get in the South, wide and voluminous as they saunter to the sea, their seemingly slow speed belying the massive power they contain. South Carolina's big **alluvial,** or sediment-bearing, rivers originate in the region of the Appalachian mountain chain.

The **blackwater river** is a particularly interesting Southern phenomenon, duplicated elsewhere only in South America and one example each in New York and Michigan. While alluvial rivers generally originate in highlands and carry with them a large amount of sediment, blackwater rivers—the Edisto River being the chief example—tend to originate in low-lying areas and move slowly toward the sea, carrying with them very little sediment. Their dark tea color comes from the tannic acid of decaying vegetation all along the banks, washed out by the slow, inexorable movement of the river toward the sea. While I don't necessarily recommend drinking it, despite its dirty color, blackwater is for the most part remarkably clean and hygienic.

Carolina Bays

An interesting regional feature of the state is the **Carolina bay,** an elliptical depression rich with biodiversity, thousands of which are found all along the coast from Delaware to Florida. While at least 500,000 have been identified, new laser-based imaging technology is enabling the discovery of thousands more, previously unnoticed.

Though not all Carolina bays are in the

Carolinas, many are, and that's where they were first documented. They're called "bays" not for the water within them—indeed, many hold little or no water at all—but for the proliferation of bay trees often found inside. Carolina bays can be substantially older than the surrounding terrain, with many well over 25,000 years old. Native Americans referred to the distinctive wetland habitat within a Carolina Bay as a pocosin.

Theories abound as to their origin. One has it that they're the result of wave action from when the entire area was underwater in primordial times. The most popular, if unproven, theory is that they are the result of a massive meteor shower in prehistoric times. Certainly their similar orientation, roughly northwest-southeast, makes this intuitively possible as an impact pattern. Further bolstering this theory is the fact that most Carolina bays are surrounded by sand rims, which tend to be thicker on the southeast edge.

An old theory, once discredited but now gaining new credence, is that Carolina bays are the result of a disintegrating comet that exploded on entry into the earth's atmosphere somewhere over the Great Lakes. Apparently, if you extend the axes of all the Carolina Bays, that's where they converge. This theory takes on an ominous edge when one realizes that the same comet is also blamed for a mass extinction of prehistoric animals such as the mammoth.

The Intracoastal Waterway

You'll often see its acronym, ICW, on signs—and sadly you'll probably hear the locals mispronounce it "intercoastal"—but the casual visitor might actually find the Intracoastal Waterway difficult to spot. Relying on a natural network of interconnected estuaries and channels, combined with artificial **cuts,** the ICW often blends in rather subtly with the already extensive network of creeks and rivers in the area.

Mandated by Congress in 1919 and maintained by the U.S. Army Corps of Engineers, the Atlantic portion of the ICW runs from Key West to Boston and carries recreational and barge traffic away from the perils of offshore currents and weather. Even if they don't use it specifically, kayakers and boaters often find themselves on it at some point during their nautical adventures.

Estuaries

Most biologists will tell you that the coastal plain is where things get interesting. The place where a river interfaces with the ocean is called an estuary, and it's perhaps the most interesting place of all. Estuaries are heavily tidal in nature (indeed, the word derives from *aestus,* Latin for tide), and feature brackish water and heavy silt content.

South Carolina typically has about a 6-8-foot tidal range, and the coastal ecosystem depends on this steady ebb and flow for life itself. At high tide, shellfish open and feed. At low tide, they literally clam up, keeping saltwater inside their shells until the next tide comes.

Waterbirds and small mammals feed on shellfish and other animals at low tide, when their prey is exposed. High tide brings an influx of fish and nutrients from the sea, in turn drawing predators like dolphins, who often come into tidal creeks to feed.

It's the estuaries that form the most compelling and beautiful sanctuaries for the area's incredibly rich diversity of animal species. Many estuaries are contiguous with those of other rivers; Charleston Harbor, formed by the confluence of the Ashley and Cooper Rivers, is an excellent example of that phenomenon.

Salt Marsh

All this water action in both directions—freshwater coming from inland, saltwater encroaching from the Atlantic—results in the phenomenon of the salt marsh, the single most recognizable and iconic geographic feature of the South Carolina coast, also known simply as "wetlands."

(Freshwater marshes are rarer, Florida's Everglades being perhaps the premier example.)

Far more than just a transitional zone between land and water, marshes are also nature's nursery. Plant and animal life in marshes tends not only to be diverse but to encompass multitudes. You may not see its denizens easily, but on close inspection you'll find the marsh absolutely teeming with creatures. Visually, the main identifying feature of a salt marsh is its distinctive reedlike marsh grasses, adapted to survive in brackish water. Like estuaries, marshes and all life in them are heavily influenced by the tides, which bring in nutrients.

The marsh has also played a key role in human history as well, for it was here where the massive rice and indigo plantations grew their signature crops, aided by the natural ebb and flow of the tides. While most wetlands you see look quite undisturbed, very little of it could be called pristine.

In the heyday of the rice plantations, much of the entire coastal salt marsh was crisscrossed by the canal-and-dike system of the paddy fields. You can still see evidence almost everywhere in the area if you look hard enough (the best time to look is right after takeoff or before landing in an airplane, since many approaches to regional airports take you over wetlands). Any time you see a low, straight ridge running through a marsh, that's likely the eroded overgrown remnant of an old rice field dike. Kayakers occasionally find old wooden water gates, or "trunks," on their paddles.

In the Lowcountry, you'll often hear the term **pluff mud.** This refers to the area's distinctive variety of soft, dark mud in the salt marsh, which often has an equally distinctive odor that locals love but some visitors have a hard time getting used to. Extraordinarily rich in nutrients, pluff mud helped make rice a successful crop in the marshes of the Lowcountry.

In addition to their huge role as wildlife incubators and sanctuaries, wetlands are also one of the most important natural protectors of the health of the coastal region. They serve as natural filters, cleansing runoff from the land of toxins and pollutants before it hits the ocean. They also help humans by serving as natural hurricane barriers, their porous nature helping to ease the brunt of the damaging storm surge.

Beaches and Barrier Islands

The beaches of South Carolina are almost all situated on barrier islands, long islands parallel to the shoreline and separated from the mainland by a sheltered body of water. Because they're formed by the deposit of sediment by offshore currents, they change shape over the years, with the general pattern of deposit going from north to south (meaning the northern end will begin eroding first). Most of the barrier islands are geologically quite young, only having formed within the last 25,000 years or so. Natural erosion by currents and by storms, combined with the accelerating effects of dredging for local port activity, has quickened the decline of many barrier islands. Many beaches in the area are subject to a mitigation of erosion called **beach renourishment,** which generally involves redistributing dredged material closely offshore so that it will wash up on and around the beach.

As the name indicates, barrier islands are another of nature's safeguards against hurricane damage. Historically, the barrier islands have borne the vast bulk of the damage done by hurricanes in the region. Sullivan's Island near Charleston was submerged by 1989's Hurricane Hugo. Like the marshes, barrier islands also help protect the mainland by absorbing the brunt of the storm's wind and surging water.

Wiregrass and Longleaf Ecosystems

In prehistoric times, most of South Carolina's upper coastal plain was covered by what's known as a wiregrass or longleaf pine ecosystem. Wiregrass (*Aristida stricta*) is a foot-tall species of hardy grass that often coexists with forests of longleaf pine (*Pinus palustris*), a relative of the slash pine now used as a cash crop throughout the South. The longleaf pine is fire-dependent, meaning it only reproduces after wildfire—usually started by lightning—releases its seed cones.

Wiregrass savanna and old-growth forests of longleaf pine once covered about 100 million acres, most of the Southeast. Within about 200 years, however, settlers had deforested the region. Currently only a few good examples remain in South Carolina, especially the Carolina Sandhills National Wildlife Refuge, Lynchburg Savanna Heritage Preserve, and Longleaf Pine Heritage Preserve.

Contrary to Hollywood portrayals, no one ever needed a machete to tear their way through an old-growth forest. Because the high, thick tree canopy allows little but wiregrass to grow on the forest floor, Native Americans and early settlers could walk through these primordial forests with ease.

CLIMATE

One word comes to mind when one thinks about Southern climate: *hot.* That's the first word that occurs to Southerners as well, but virtually every survey of why residents are attracted to the area puts the climate at the top of the list. Go figure. How hot is hot? The average high for July, the region's hottest month, in Charleston is about 89°F. While that's nothing compared to Tucson or Death Valley, coupled with the region's notoriously high humidity it can have an altogether miserable effect.

Technically South Carolina has a **humid subtropical** climate. During summer, the famous high-pressure system called the **Bermuda High** settles over the entire southeastern United States, its rotating winds pushing aside most weather coming from the west. This can bring drought as well as a certain sameness that afflicts the area. Heat aside, there's no doubt that

one of the most difficult things for a nonnative to adjust to in the South is the humidity. The average annual humidity in Charleston is about 55 percent in the afternoons and a whopping 85 percent in the mornings. The most humid months are August and September. There is no real antidote to humidity—other than air conditioning, that is—though many film crews and other outside workers swear by the use of Sea Breeze astringent. If you and your traveling partner can deal with the strong minty odor, dampen a hand towel with the astringent, drape it across the back of your neck, and go about your business. Don't assume that because it's humid you shouldn't drink fluids. Just as in any hot climate, you should drink lots of water if you're going to be out in the Southern heat.

If you're on the South Carolina coast, you'll no doubt grow to love the steady ocean breeze during the day. But at night you may notice the wind changing direction and coming from inland. That's caused by the land cooling at night and the wind rushing toward the warmer water offshore. This shift in wind current is mostly responsible for that sometimes awe-inspiring, sometimes just plain scary phenomenon of a typical Southern **thunderstorm.** Seemingly within the space of a few minutes on a particularly hot and still summer day, the afternoon is taken over by a rapidly moving stacked storm cloud called a **thunderhead,** which soon bursts open and pours an unbelievable amount of rain on whatever is unlucky enough to be beneath it, along with frequent huge lightning strikes. Then, almost as quickly as it came on, the storm subsides, and the sun comes back out again as if nothing had happened. August-September is by far the rainiest time, with averages well over six inches for each of these months. July is also quite wet, with over five inches on average.

Winters are pretty mild but can seem much colder than they actually are because of the dampness in the air. The coldest month is

January, with a high of about 58°F for the month and an average low of 42°F. You're highly unlikely to encounter snow in the area, and if you do, it will likely only be skimpy flurries that a resident of the Great Lakes region wouldn't even notice as snow. But don't let this lull you into a false sense of security. If such a tiny flurry were to hit, be aware that most people down here have no clue how to drive in rough weather and will not be prepared for even such a small amount of snowfall. Visitors from snow country are often surprised by how completely a Southern city will shut down when that rare few inches of snow hits.

Hurricanes

The major weather phenomenon for residents and visitors alike is the mighty hurricane. These massive storms, with counterclockwise-rotating bands of clouds and winds pushing 200 mph, are an ever-present danger to the southeast coast June-November, with the most serious danger period around Labor Day. As most everyone is aware from the horrific and well-documented damage from such killer storms as Hugo, Andrew, and Katrina, hurricanes are not to be trifled with. Old-fashioned drunken "hurricane parties" are a thing of the past for the most part, as the images of cataclysmic destruction everyone has seen on TV have long since eliminated any lingering romanticism about riding out the storm.

Tornadoes—especially those that come in the "back door" through the Gulf of Mexico and overland—are a very present danger with hurricanes. As hurricanes die out over the land, they can spawn literally dozens of tornadoes, which in many cases prove more destructive than the hurricanes that spawned them.

Local TV, websites, and print media can be counted on to give more than ample warning in the event a hurricane is approaching the area during your visit. Whatever you do, do not discount the warnings; it's not worth it. If the locals are preparing to leave, you should too.

Typically, when a storm is likely to hit the area, there will first be a suggested evacuation. But if authorities determine there's an overwhelming likelihood of imminent hurricane damage, they will issue a **mandatory evacuation order.** What this means in practice is that if you do choose to stay behind, you cannot count on any type of emergency services or help.

Generally speaking, the most lethal element of a hurricane is not the wind but the **storm surge,** the wall of ocean water that the winds drive in front of them onto the coast. During 1989's Hurricane Hugo, Charleston's Battery was inundated with a storm surge of over 12 feet, with an amazing 20 feet reported farther north at Cape Romain.

ENVIRONMENTAL ISSUES

The coast of South Carolina in particular is currently experiencing a double whammy, environmentally speaking: Not only are its distinctive wetlands extraordinarily sensitive to human interference, this is one of the most rapidly developing parts of the country. New and often poorly planned subdivisions and resort communities are popping up all over the place. Vastly increased port activity is also taking a devastating toll on the salt marsh and surrounding barrier islands. Combine all that with the South's often skeptical attitude toward environmental activism and you have a recipe for potential ecological disaster.

Thankfully, there are some bright spots. More and more communities are seeing the value of responsible planning and not greenlighting every new development sight unseen. Land trusts and other conservation organizations are growing in size, number, funding, and influence. The large number of marine biologists in these areas at various research and educational institutions means there's a wealth of education and talent available in advising local governments and citizens on how best to conserve the area's natural beauty.

Hilton Head Island is a longtime trendsetter for sustainable development, dating back to the insistence of its original residential developer, Charles Fraser, that the Sea Pines development interfere as little as possible with the island's ecosystem. But in South Carolina, the city of Charleston and Charleston County are leading the pack on environmental issues right now—perhaps because its wealth and comparatively large size mean it has so much more to lose if things go badly. Planners estimate that the Charleston area will have to accommodate about 250,000 new residents over the next 25 years, and there's a clear consensus locally that the time to act is now. One concrete step Charleston County has taken is devoting part of a new transportation sales tax to its new comprehensive greenbelt plan to help responsibly guide the next 25 years of development here. It calls for at least $12 million to go to preserving rural green space and nearly $2 million to conserve remaining urban green space.

Marsh Dieback

The dominant species of marsh grass, *Spartina alterniflora* (pronounced "spar-TINE-uh") and *Juncus roemerianus* thrive in the typically brackish water of the coastal marsh estuaries, their structural presence helping to stem erosion of banks and dunes. While drought and blight have taken their toll on the grass, increased coastal development and continued channel deepening have also led to a steady creep of ocean saltwater farther and farther into remaining marsh stands.

The Paper Industry

Early in the 20th century, the Southeast's abundance of cheap undeveloped land and plentiful free water led to the establishment of massive pine tree farms to feed coastal pulp and paper mills. Chances are that if you used a paper grocery bag recently, it was made in a paper mill in the South. But in addition to making a whole lot of paper bags and providing lots of employment for residents through the decades, the paper industry also gave the area lots of air and water pollution, stressed local water supplies (it takes a lot of water to make paper from trees), and took away natural species diversity from the area by devoting so much acreage to a single crop, pine trees.

Currently the domestic paper industry is reeling from competition from cheaper Asian lumber stocks and paper mills. As a result, an interesting—and not altogether welcome—phenomenon has been the wholesale entry of Southeastern paper companies into the real estate business. Discovering they can make a whole lot more money selling or developing tree farms for residential lots than making paper bags, pulp and paper companies are helping to drive overdevelopment in the region by encouraging development on their land rather than infill development closer to urban areas. So, in the long run, the demise of the paper industry in the South may not prove to be the net advantage to the environment that was anticipated.

Aquifers

Unlike parts of the western United States, where individuals can enforce private property rights to water, the South has generally held that the region's water is a publicly held resource. The upside of this is that everybody has equal claim to drinking water without regard to status or income or how long they've lived here. The downside is that industry also has the same free claim to the water that citizens do—and they use a heck of a lot of it.

Currently most of South Carolina gets its water from aquifers, which are basically huge underground caverns made of limestone. Receiving **groundwater** drip by drip, century after century, from rainfall farther inland, the aquifers essentially act as massive sterile warehouses for freshwater, accessible through wells. The aquifers have human benefit only if their water remains fresh. Once saltwater from the ocean begins intruding into an aquifer, it doesn't take much to render all of it unfit for human consumption—forever. What keeps that freshwater fresh is natural water pressure, keeping the ocean at bay. But nearly a century ago, paper mills began pumping millions and millions of gallons of water out of coastal aquifers. Combined with the dramatic rise in coastal residential development and a continuing push to deepen existing shipping channels, the natural water pressure of the aquifers has decreased, leading to measurable saltwater intrusion at several points under the coast.

Currently, the state and local governments are increasing their reliance on **surface water** (treated water from rivers and creeks) to relieve the strain on the underground aquifer system. But it's too soon to tell if that has contained the threat from saltwater intrusion.

Nuclear Energy

South Carolina has four nuclear power plants, in the Greenville, Hartsville, and Jenkinsville areas, and in York County. They are major job providers and are likely to remain a major driver of the state economy well into the future.

Looming upstream of the entire area is the massive Cold War-era nuclear bomb plant called Savannah River Site, near Aiken. Groundwater in the area has already shown measurable amounts of radioactivity from the site, and activists have long warned of potential catastrophe from its aging infrastructure. Most activity there is now limited to environmental cleanup.

Air Pollution

Despite growing awareness of the issue, air pollution is still a big problem in the coastal region. Paper mills still operate, putting out their distinctive rotten-eggs odor, and auto emissions standards are notoriously lax in South Carolina. The biggest culprit, though, are coal-powered electric plants, which are the norm throughout the region and which continue to pour large amounts of toxins into the atmosphere.

Flora and Fauna

FLORA

The most iconic plant life of the coastal region is the **Southern live oak** (*Quercus virginiana*). Named because of its evergreen nature, a live oak is technically any one of a number of evergreens in the *Quercus* genus, many of which grow in South Carolina, but in local practice the name almost always refers to the Southern live oak. Capable of living over 1,000 years and possessing wood of legendary resilience, the Southern live oak is one of nature's most magnificent creations. The timber value of live oaks has been well known since the earliest days of the American shipbuilding industry—when the oak dominated the entire coast inland of the marsh—but their value as a canopy tree has finally been widely recognized by local and state governments.

Fittingly, the other iconic plant life of the coastal region grows on the branches of the live oak. Contrary to popular opinion, **Spanish moss** (*Tillandsia usneoides*) is neither Spanish nor moss. It's an air plant, a wholly indigenous cousin to the pineapple. Also contrary to folklore, Spanish moss is not a parasite nor does it harbor parasites while living on an oak tree—although it can after it has already fallen to the ground. Also growing on the bark of a live oak, especially right after a rain shower, is the **resurrection fern** (*Polypodium polypodioides*), which can stay dormant for amazingly long periods of time, only to spring back to life with the introduction of a little water. You can find live oak, Spanish moss, and resurrection fern anywhere in the **maritime forest** ecosystem of

Longleaf pine once covered most of the Southeast.

flowering shrub of the *Rhododendron* genus. Over 10,000 varieties have been cultivated through the centuries, with quite a wide range of them on display during blooming season, March-April, on the South Carolina coast (slightly earlier farther south, slightly later farther north). The area's other great floral display comes from the **camellia** (*Camellia japonica*), a large, cold-hardy evergreen shrub that generally blooms in late winter (Jan.-Mar.). An import from Asia, the southeastern coast's camellias are close cousins to *Camellia sinensis,* also an import and the plant from which tea is made. Other colorful ornamentals of the area include the ancient and beautiful **Southern magnolia** (*Magnolia grandiflora*), a native plant with distinctive large white flowers that evolved before the advent of bees; and the **flowering dogwood** (*Cornus florida*), which, despite its very hard wood—great for daggers, hence its original name "dagwood"—is actually quite fragile. An ornamental imported from Asia that has now become quite obnoxious in its aggressive invasiveness is the **mimosa** (*Albizia julibrissin*), which blooms March-August.

coastal South Carolina, a zone generally behind the **interdune meadows,** which is itself right behind the beach zone.

Far and away South Carolina's most important commercial tree is the pine, used for paper, lumber, and turpentine. Rarely seen in the wild today due to tree farming, the dominant species is now the **slash pine** (*Pinus elliottii*), often seen in long rows on either side of rural highways. Before the introduction of large-scale monoculture tree farming, however, a rich variety of native pines flourished in the **upland forest** inland from the maritime forest, including **longleaf** (*Pinus palustris*) and **loblolly** (*Pinus taeda*) pines. Longleaf forest covered nearly 100 million acres of the southeastern coastal plain when the Europeans arrived; within 300 years most of it would be cut down or harvested.

Right up there with live oaks and Spanish moss in terms of instant recognition would have to be the colorful, ubiquitous **azalea,** a

Moving into watery areas, you'll find the remarkable **bald cypress** (*Taxodium distichum*), a flood-resistant conifer recognizable by its tufted top, its great height (up to 130 feet), and its distinctive "knees," parts of the root that project above the waterline and which are believed to help stabilize the tree in lowland areas. Much prized for its beautiful pest-resistant wood, great stands of ancient cypress once dominated the marsh along the coast; sadly, overharvesting and destruction of wetlands has made the magnificent sight of this ancient, dignified species much less common. The acres of **smooth cordgrass** for which the Golden Isles are named are plants of the *Spartina alterniflora* species. (A cultivated cousin, *Spartina anglica,* is considered invasive.) Besides its simple natural beauty, *Spartina* is also a key food source for marsh denizens. Playing a key environmental role on the coast are **sea oats** (*Uniola paniculata*). This wispy, fast-growing perennial grass anchors sand dunes and hence is a protected species (it's a misdemeanor to pick them).

South Carolina isn't called the "Palmetto State" for nothing. Palm varieties are not as common up here as in Florida, but you'll definitely encounter several types along the coast. The **cabbage palm** (*Sabal palmetto*), for which South Carolina is named, is the largest variety, up to 50-60 feet tall. Its "heart of palm" is an edible delicacy, which coastal Native Americans boiled in bear fat as porridge. In dunes and sand hills you'll find clumps of the low-lying **saw palmetto** (*Serenoa repens*). The **bush palmetto** (*Sabal minor*) has distinctive fan-shaped branches. The common **Spanish bayonet** (*Yucca aloifolia*) looks like a palm, but it's actually a member of the agave family.

FAUNA
On Land

Perhaps the most iconic land animal—or semi-land animal, anyway—of South Carolina is the legendary **American alligator** (*Alligator mississippiensis*), the only species of crocodilian native to the area. Contrary to their fierce reputation, locals know these massive reptiles, 6-12 feet long as adults, to be quite shy. If you come in the colder months, you won't see them at all, since alligators require an outdoor temperature over 70°F to become active and feed (indeed, the appearance of alligators was once a well-known symbol of spring in the area). Often all you'll see is a couple of eyebrow ridges sticking out of the water, and a gator lying still in a shallow creek can easily be mistaken for a floating log. But should you see one or more gators basking in the sun—a favorite activity on warm days for these cold-blooded creatures—it's best to admire them from afar. A mother alligator, in particular, will destroy anything that comes near her nest. Despite the alligator's short, stubby legs, they run amazingly fast on land—faster than you, in fact.

If you're driving on a country road at night, be on the lookout for **white-tailed deer** (*Odocoileus virginianus*), which, besides being quite beautiful, also pose a serious road hazard. Because coastal development has dramatically reduced the habitat—and therefore the numbers—of their natural predators, deer are very plentiful throughout the area, and as you read this they are hard at work devouring vast tracts of valuable vegetation. No one wants to hurt poor little Bambi, but the truth is that area hunters perform a valuable service by culling the local deer population, which is in no danger of extinction anytime soon.

South Carolina hosts large populations of playful **river otter** (*Lontra canadensis*). Not to be confused with the larger sea otters off the West Coast, these fast-swimming members of the weasel family inhabit inland waterways and marshy areas, with dominant males sometimes ranging as much as 50 miles within a single waterway. As strict carnivores, usually of fish, otters are a key indicator of the health of their ecosystem. If they're thriving, water and habitat quality are likely to be pretty high. If they're not, something's going badly wrong.

While you're unlikely to encounter an otter, if you're camping, you might easily run into the **raccoon** (*Procyon lotor*), an exceedingly intelligent and crafty relative of the bear, sharing that larger animal's resourcefulness in stealing your food. Though nocturnal, raccoons will feed whenever food is available. Raccoons can grow so accustomed to the human presence as to almost consider themselves part of the family, but resist the temptation to get close to them. Rabies is prevalent in the raccoon population, and you should always, always keep your distance.

Another common campsite nuisance, the **opossum** (*Didelphis virginiana*) is a shy, primitive creature that is much more easily discouraged. North America's only marsupial, an opossum's usual "defense" against predators is to play dead. That said, however, they have an

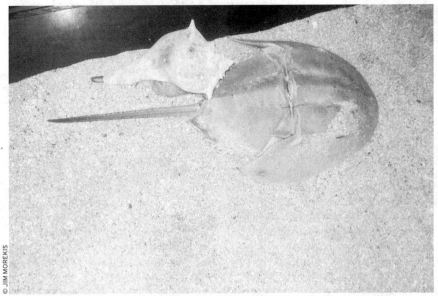

© JIM MOREKIS

The horseshoe crab has remained essentially unchanged in tens of millions of years.

immunity to snake venom and often feed on the reptiles, even the most poisonous ones.

Opossums are native to the area, but another similarly slow-witted, slow-moving creature is not: the **nine-banded armadillo** (*Dasypus novemcinctus*). In centuries past, these armor-plated insect-eaters were mostly confined to Mexico, but they are gradually working their way northward. Obsessive diggers, armadillos cause quite a bit of damage to crops and gardens. Sometimes jokingly called "possum on the half shell," armadillos, like opossums, are frequent roadkill on South Carolina highways.

While you're highly unlikely to actually see a **red fox** (*Vulpes vulpes*), you might very well see their distinctive footprints in the mud of a marsh at low tide. These nocturnal hunters, a nonnative species introduced by European settlers, range the coast seeking mice, squirrels, and rabbits.

Once fairly common in South Carolina, the **black bear** (*Ursus americanus*) has suffered from hunting and habitat destruction and is extremely rare in the state.

In the Water

Humankind's aquatic cousin, the **Atlantic bottle-nosed dolphin** (*Tursiops truncatus*) is a well-known and frequent visitor to the coast, coming far upstream into creeks and rivers to feed. Children, adults, and experienced sailors alike all delight in encounters with the mammals, sociable creatures who travel in family units. When not occupied with feeding or mating activities—both of which can get surprisingly rowdy—dolphins show great curiosity about human visitors to their habitat. They will gather near boats, surfacing often with the distinctive chuffing sound of air coming from their blowholes. Occasionally they'll even lift their heads out of the water to have a look at you; consider yourself lucky indeed to have such a close encounter. Don't be fooled by their cuteness, however. Dolphins live life with gusto and aren't scared of much. They're voracious eaters of fish, amorous and energetic lovers, and will take on an encroaching shark in a heartbeat.

Another beloved part-time marine creature of

the barrier islands of the coast is the **loggerhead turtle** (*Caretta caretta*). Though the species prefers to stay well offshore the rest of the year, females weighing up to 300 pounds come out of the sea each May-July to dig a shallow hole in the dunes and lay over 100 leathery eggs, returning to the ocean and leaving the eggs to hatch on their own after two months. Interestingly, the mothers prefer to nest at the same spot on the same island year after year. After hatching, the baby turtles then make a dramatic, extremely dangerous (and extremely slow) trek to the safety of the waves, at the mercy of various predators. A series of dedicated research and conservation efforts are working hard to protect the loggerheads' traditional nursery grounds to ensure the survival of this fascinating, loveable, and threatened species. Cape Island within the Cape Romain National Wildlife Refuge accounts for about a quarter of all loggerhead nests in South Carolina and is the leading nesting site north of Florida. Other key sites include Kiawah, Edisto, and Hilton Head Islands.

Of course, the coastal waters and rivers are chockablock with fish. The most abundant and sought-after recreational species in the area is the **spotted sea trout** (*Cynoscion nebulosus*), followed by the **red drum** (*Sciaenops ocellatus*). Local anglers also pursue many varieties of **bass, bream, sheepshead,** and **crappie.** It may sound strange to some accustomed to considering it a "trash" fish, but many types of **catfish** are not only plentiful here but are a common and well-regarded food source. Many species of **flounder** inhabit the silty bottoms of estuaries all along the coast. Farther offshore are game and sport fish like **marlin, swordfish, shark, grouper,** and **tuna.**

Each March, anglers jockey for position on coastal rivers for the yearly running of the **American shad** (*Alosa sapidissima*) upstream to spawn. This large (up to eight pounds) catfish-like species is a regional delicacy as a seasonal entrée as well as for its tasty roe. There's a catch limit of eight shad per person per season. One of the more interesting fish species in the area is the endangered **shortnose sturgeon** (*Acipenser brevirostrum*). A fantastically ancient species that has evolved little in hundreds of millions of years, this small freshwater fish is known to exist in the estuaries of the ACE Basin. Traveling upriver to spawn in the winter, the sturgeons remain around the mouths of waterways the rest of the year, venturing near the ocean only sparingly.

Crustaceans and shellfish have been a key food staple in the area for thousands of years, with the massive shell middens of the coast being testament to Native Americans' healthy appetite for them. The beds of the local variant, the **eastern oyster** (*Crassostrea virginica*), aren't what they used to be due to overharvesting, water pollution, and disruption of habitat. In truth, these days most local restaurants import the little filter-feeders from the Gulf of Mexico. Oysters spawn May-August, hence the old folk wisdom about eating oysters only in months with the letter "r" so as not to disrupt the breeding cycle.

Each year April-January, shrimp boats up and down the southeastern coast trawl for **shrimp,** most commercially viable in two local species, the white shrimp (*Litopenaeus setiferus*), and the brown shrimp (*Farfantepenaeus aztecus*). Shrimp are the most popular seafood item in the United States and account for bringing hundreds of millions of dollars in revenue into the coastal economy. While consumption won't slow down anytime soon, the South Carolina shrimping industry is facing serious threats, both from species decline due to pollution and overfishing and from competition from shrimp farms and the Asian shrimp industry.

Another important commercial crop is the **blue crab** (*Callinectes sapidus*), the species used in such Lowcountry delicacies as crab cakes. You'll often see floating markers bobbing up and down in rivers throughout the region.

These signal the presence directly below of a crab trap, often of an amateur crabber. A true living link to primordial times, the alien-looking **horseshoe crab** (*Limulus polyphemus*) is frequently found on beaches of the coast during the spring mating season (it lives in deeper water the rest of the year). More closely related to scorpions and spiders than crabs, the horseshoe has evolved hardly a lick in hundreds of millions of years. Any trip to a local salt marsh at low tide will likely uncover hundreds of **fiddler crabs** (*Uca pugilator* and *Uca pugnax*), so-named for the way the males wave their single enlarged claws in the air to attract mates. (Their other, smaller claw is the one they actually eat with.) The fiddlers make distinctive burrows in the pluff mud for sanctuary during high tide, recognizable by the little balls of sediment at the entrances (the crabs spit out the balls after sifting through the sand for food).

One charming beach inhabitant, the **sand dollar** (*Mellita quinquiesperforata*), has seen its numbers decline drastically due to being entirely too charming for its own good. Beachcombers are now asked to enjoy these flat little cousins to the sea urchin in their natural habitat and to refrain from taking them home. Besides, they start to smell bad when they dry out. The **sea nettle** (*Chrysaora quinquecirrha*), a less-than-charming beach inhabitant, is a jellyfish that stings thousands of people on the coast each year (although only for those with severe allergies are the stings potentially life-threatening). Stinging their prey before transporting it into their waiting mouths, the jellyfish also sting when disturbed or frightened. Most often, people are stung by stepping on the bodies of jellyfish washed up on the sand. If you're stung by a jellyfish, don't panic. You'll probably experience a stinging rash for about half an hour. Locals say applying a little baking soda or vinegar helps cut the sting. (Some also swear fresh urine will do the trick, and I pass that tip along to you purely in the interest of thoroughness.)

In the Air

When enjoying the marshlands of the coast, consider yourself fortunate to see an endangered **wood stork** (*Mycteria americana*), although their numbers are on the increase. The only storks to breed in North America, these graceful long-lived birds (routinely living over 10 years) are usually seen on a low flight path across the marsh, although at some birding spots beginning in late summer you can find them at a **roost,** sometimes numbering over 100 birds. Resting at high tide, they fan out over the marsh to feed at low tide on foot. Old-timers sometimes call them "Spanish buzzards" or simply "the preacher." Often confused with the wood stork is the gorgeous **white ibis** (*Eudocimus albus*), distinguishable by its orange bill and black wingtips. Like the wood stork, the ibis is a communal bird that roosts in colonies. Other similar-looking coastal denizens are the white-feathered **great egret** (*Ardea alba*) and **snowy egret** (*Egretta thula*), the former distinguishable by its yellow bill and the latter by its black bill and the tuft of plumes on the back of its head. Egrets are in the same family as herons. The most magnificent is the **great blue heron** (*Ardea herodias*). Despite their imposing height—up to four feet tall—these waders are shy. Often you hear them rather than see them, a loud shriek of alarm that echoes over the marsh. So how to tell the difference between all these wading birds at a glance? It's actually easiest when they're in flight. Egrets and herons fly with their necks tucked in, while storks and ibis fly with their necks extended.

Dozens of species of shorebirds comb the beaches, including **sandpipers, plovers,** and the wonderful and rare **American oystercatcher** (*Haematopus palliatus*), instantly recognizable for its prancing walk, dark brown back, stark white underside, and long bright-orange bill.

Gulls and **terns** also hang out wherever there's water. They can frequently be seen swarming around incoming shrimp boats, attracted by the catch of little crustaceans.

The chief raptor of the salt marsh is the fish-eating **osprey** (*Pandion haliaetus*). These large grayish birds of prey are similar to eagles but are adapted to a maritime environment, with a reversible outer toe on each talon (the better for catching wriggly fish) and closable nostrils so they can dive into the water after prey. Very common all along the coast, they like to build big nests on top of buoys and channel markers in addition to trees. The **bald eagle** (*Haliaeetus leucocephalus*) is making a comeback in the area thanks to increased federal regulation and better education of trigger-happy locals. Of course, as we all should have learned in school, the bald eagle is not actually bald but has a head adorned with white feathers. Like the osprey, they prefer fish, but unlike the osprey will settle for rodents and rabbits.

Inland among the pines you'll find the most common area woodpecker, the huge **pileated woodpecker** (*Dryocopus pileatus*) with its huge crest. Less common is the smaller, more subtly marked **red-cockaded woodpecker** (*Picoides borealis*). Once common in the vast primordial pine forests of the Southeast, the species is now endangered, its last real refuge being the big tracts of relatively undisturbed land on military bases and national wildlife refuges.

Insects

Down here they say that God invented bugs to keep the Yankees from completely taking over the South. And insects are probably the most unpleasant fact of life in the southeastern coastal region. The list of annoying indigenous insects must begin with the infamous **sand gnat** (*Culicoides furens*), scourge of the lowlands. This tiny and persistent nuisance, a member of the midge family, lacks the precision of the mosquito with its long proboscis. No, the sand gnat is more torture master than surgeon, brutally gouging and digging away its victim's skin until it hits a source of blood. Most prevalent in the spring and fall, the sand gnat is drawn to its prey by the carbon dioxide trail of its breath. While long sleeves and long pants are one way to keep gnats at bay, that causes its own discomfort because of the region's heat and humidity. The only real antidote to the sand gnat's assault—other than never breathing—is the Avon skin-care product Skin So Soft, which has taken on a new and wholly unplanned life as the South's favorite antignat lotion. Grow to like the scent, because the more of this stuff you lather on, the better. In calmer moments grow to appreciate the great contribution sand gnats make to the salt marsh ecosystem—as food for many species of birds and bats.

Running a close second to the sand gnat are the over three dozen species of highly aggressive **mosquito,** which breeds anywhere a few drops of water lie stagnant. Not surprisingly, massive populations blossom in the rainiest months, in late spring and late summer. Like the gnat, the mosquito—the biters are always female—homes in on its victim by trailing the plume of carbon dioxide exhaled in the breath. More than just a biting nuisance, mosquitoes are now carrying West Nile disease, signaling a possibly dire threat to public health. Local governments in the region pour millions of dollars of taxpayer money into massive pesticide spraying programs from helicopters, planes, and trucks. While that certainly helps stem the tide, it by no means eliminates the mosquito population. This is just as well, because like the sand gnat, the mosquito is an important food source for many species, including bats and dragonflies. Alas, Skin So Soft has little effect on the mosquito. Try over-the-counter sprays, anything smelling of citronella, and wearing long sleeves and long pants when weather permits.

But undoubtedly the most viscerally loathed of all pests on the Lowcountry and Georgia coasts is the so-called "palmetto bug," or **American cockroach** (*Periplaneta americana*). These black, shiny, and sometimes grotesquely massive insects—up to two inches long—are living fossils, virtually unchanged over hundreds of millions of years. And perfectly adapted as they are to life in and among wet, decaying vegetation, they're unlikely to change a bit in 100 million more years. While they spend most of their time crawling around, usually under rotting leaves and tree bark, the American cockroach can indeed fly—sort of. There are few more hilarious sights than a room full of people frantically trying to dodge a palmetto bug that has just clumsily launched itself off a high point on the wall. Because the cockroach doesn't know any better than you do where it's going, it can be a particularly bracing event—though the insect does not bite and poses few real health hazards.

Popular regional use of the term *palmetto bug* undoubtedly has its roots in a desire for polite Southern society to avoid using the ugly word *roach* and its connotations of filth and unclean environments. But the colloquialism actually has a basis in reality. Contrary to what anyone tells you, the natural habitat of the American cockroach—unlike its kitchen-dwelling, much-smaller cousin the German cockroach—is outdoors, often up in trees. They only come inside human dwellings when it's especially hot, especially cold, or especially dry outside. Like you, the palmetto bug is easily driven indoors by extreme temperatures and by thirst. Other than visiting the Southeast during the winter, when the roaches go dormant, there's no convenient antidote for their presence. The best way to keep them out of your life is to stay away from decaying vegetation and keep doors and windows closed on especially hot nights.

History

BEFORE THE EUROPEANS

Based on studies of artifacts found throughout the state, anthropologists know that the first humans arrived in South Carolina at least 13,000 years ago, at the tail end of the last ice age. However, a still-controversial archaeological dig in the state, the Topper Site on the Savannah River near Allendale, has found artifacts that some scientists say are about 50,000 years old.

In any case, during this **Paleo-Indian Period,** sea levels were over 200 feet lower than present levels, and large mammals such as woolly mammoths, horses, and camels were hunted for food and skins. However, rapidly increasing temperatures, rising sea levels, and efficient hunting techniques combined to quickly kill off these large mammals, relics of the Pleistocene Era, ushering in the **Archaic Period** in what's now the southeastern United States. Still hunter-gatherers, Archaic Period

Indians began turning to small game such as deer, bears, and turkeys, supplemented with fruit and nuts. The latter part of the Archaic era saw more habitation on the coasts, with an increasing reliance on fish and shellfish. It's during this time that the great **shell middens** of the Georgia and South Carolina coasts trace their origins. Basically serving as trash heaps for discarded oyster shells, as the middens grew in size they also took on a ceremonial status, often being used as sites for important rituals and meetings. Such sites are often called **shell rings,** and the largest yet found was over nine feet high and 300 feet in diameter. Hilton Head Island, for example, has two remaining shell rings. Using ground-penetrating radar, archaeologists are finding more and more Archaic Period shell middens and rings all the time.

The introduction of agriculture and improved pottery techniques about 3,000 years ago led to the **Woodland Period** of Native American settlement. Extended clan groups were much less migratory, establishing year-round communities of up to 50 people, who began the practice of clearing land to grow crops. The ancient shell middens of their ancestors were not abandoned, however, and were continually added onto. Native Americans had been cremating or burying their dead for years, a practice which eventually gave rise to the construction of the first **mounds** during the Woodland Period. Essentially built-up earthworks sometimes marked with spiritual symbols, often in the form of animal shapes, mounds not only contained the remains of the deceased but items like pottery to accompany the deceased into the afterlife.

Increased agriculture led to increased population, and with that population growth came competition over resources and a more formal notion of warfare. This period, about A.D. 800-1600, is termed the **Mississippian Period.** It was the Mississippians who would be the first Native Americans in what's now the continental United States to encounter European explorers and settlers after Columbus. The Native Americans who would later be called **Creek Indians** were the direct descendants of the Mississippians in lineage, language, and lifestyle. Described by later European accounts as a tall, proud people, the Mississippians often wore elaborate body art and, like the indigenous inhabitants of Central and South America, used the practice of **head shaping,** whereby an infant's skull was deliberately deformed into an elongated shape by tying the baby's head to a board for about a year. By about A.D. 1400, change came to the Mississippian culture for reasons that are still not completely understood. In some areas, large chiefdoms began splintering into smaller subgroups in an intriguing echo of the medieval feudal system going on concurrently in Europe. In other areas, however, the rise of a handful of more powerful

chiefs subsumed smaller communities under their influence. In either case, the result was the same: The landscape of the Southeast became less peopled as many of the old villages, built around huge central mounds, were abandoned, some suddenly. As tensions increased, the contested land became more and more dangerous for the poorly armed or poorly connected. Indeed, at the time of the Europeans' arrival, much of the coastal area was more thinly inhabited than it had been for many decades.

THE SPANISH ARRIVE

The first known contact by Europeans on the southeastern coast came in 1521, roughly concurrent with Cortés's conquest of Mexico. A party of Spanish slavers ventured into what's now Port Royal Sound from Santo Domingo in the Caribbean. Naming the area Santa Elena, they kidnapped a few Indian slaves and left, ranging as far north as the Cape Fear River in present-day North Carolina, and by some accounts even farther up the coast.

The first serious exploration of the coast came in 1526, when Lucas Vázquez de Ayllón and about 600 colonists made landfall at Winyah Bay near present-day Georgetown. They didn't stay long, however, immediately moving down the coast and trying to set down roots in the St. Catherine's Sound area of modern-day Liberty County, Georgia. That colony—called San Miguel de Gualdape—was the first European colony in North America (the continent's oldest continuously occupied settlement, St. Augustine, Florida, wasn't founded until 1565). The colony also brought with it the seed of a future nation's dissolution: slaves from Africa. San Miguel lasted only six weeks due to political tension and a slave uprising.

Hernando De Soto's infamous expedition of 1539-1543 began in Florida and went through southwest Georgia before crossing the Savannah River somewhere near modern-day North Augusta, South Carolina. He immediately came in contact with emissaries from the Cofitachequi empire of Mississippian Indians. The powerful Cofitachequi empire was the culmination of years of consolidation among regional nations. They had attained a high level of sophistication and military and economic prowess, with the rule of their eponymous queen, Cofitachequi, recognized for about 250 miles in every direction—in other words, over almost all of what is now South Carolina. When De Soto and his men arrived near the Cofitachequi capital, near modern-day Camden, he was met on the shores of the Wateree River by Queen Cofitachequi herself. She had heard the tales of De Soto's previous atrocities against Native American villages who refused to aid him in his quest for gold, and she was savvy enough to receive him diplomatically. According to a Spanish account, the queen "was a young girl of fine bearing, and she spoke to the governor quite gracefully and at her ease," carried on a platform covered with pillows.

While De Soto found no fabled cities of gold, he was impressed by the quality and quantity of the Cofitachequi great homes and the copper and pearls they had amassed. In true conquistador fashion, De Soto decided to take the queen hostage to guarantee his safe passage through the rest of her empire. The queen proved smarter than her captor, however. During their journey across South Carolina, at one point she excused herself into the woods to attend to bodily functions. She immediately vanished, heading back to her people.

Long after his departure and eventual death from fever in Alabama, De Soto's legacy was felt throughout the Southeast in the form of various diseases for which the indigenous Mississippian people had no immunity whatsoever: smallpox, typhus, influenza, measles, yellow fever, whooping cough, diphtheria, tuberculosis, and bubonic plague. While the barbaric cruelties of the Spanish certainly took their toll, far more damaging were these deadly diseases to a population totally unprepared for them. As the viruses they introduced ran rampant, the Europeans themselves stayed away from this area for several decades after the ignominious end of De Soto's quest. During that quarter-century, the once-proud Mississippian culture, ravaged by disease, disintegrated into a shadow of its former greatness.

The French Misadventure

The Spanish presence in South Carolina was briefly threatened by the ill-fated establishment of Charlesfort in 1562 by French Huguenots under Jean Ribault. Part of a covert effort by the Protestant French admiral Coligny to send Huguenot colonizing missions around the globe, Ribault's crew of 150 first explored the mouth of the St. Johns River near present-day Jacksonville, Florida, before heading north to Port Royal Sound and present-day Parris Island, South Carolina.

After establishing Charlesfort, Ribault returned to France for supplies. In his absence, religious war had broken out in his home country. Ribault sought sanctuary in England but was clapped in irons anyway. Meanwhile, most of Charlesfort's colonists grew so demoralized they joined another French expedition led by René Laudonnière at Fort Caroline on the St. Johns River. The remaining 27 built a ship to sail from Charlesfort back to France; 20 of them survived the journey, which was cut short in the English Channel when they had to be rescued.

Ribault himself was dispatched to reinforce Fort Caroline, but was headed off by a contingent from the new fortified Spanish settlement at St. Augustine. The fate of the French presence on the southeast coast was sealed when not only did the Spanish take Fort Caroline but a storm destroyed Ribault's reinforcing fleet. Ribault and all survivors were killed as soon as they struggled ashore. To keep the French away for good and cement Spain's hold on this northernmost part of their province of La Florida, the Spanish built the fort of Santa Elena directly on top of Charlesfort. Both layers are currently being excavated and studied today on Parris Island, near a golf course on the U.S. Marine camp.

Juan Pardo's Expedition

The next serious Spanish expedition into South Carolina began on the coast in 1566, when Juan Pardo set out from Santa Elena on Parris Island. Pardo and his party of 125 soldiers were on a mission to explore the hinterland and scout a location for a road to the main Spanish silver mines in Mexico. Inland, he encountered the Cofitachequi nation, much diminished since De Soto's time. Because they had set out without pack animals and serious supplies of their own, the Spanish obtained most of their food from local Indians, whether by request or by force. At all Indian villages he encountered, Pardo delivered the traditional *requerimiento,* a formal notification of the jurisdiction of the Spanish crown and the primacy of Christianity.

Before heading into present-day North Carolina and into Appalachia, Pardo stopped for a time near modern Spartanburg, South Carolina. A rock supposedly bearing an inscription of Pardo's name was overturned by a local farmer and is currently in the Spartanburg County Museum.

The Mission Era

With Spanish dominance of the region ensured for the near future, the lengthy mission era began. It's rarely mentioned as a key part of U.S. history, but the Spanish missionary presence in Florida and on the Georgia coast was longer and more comprehensive than its much more widely known counterpart in California. While the purpose of the missions was to convert as many Indians as possible to Christianity, they also served to further consolidate Spanish political control. It was a dicey proposition, as technically the mission friars served at the pleasure of the local chiefs. But the more savvy of the chiefs soon learned that cooperating with

the militarily powerful Spanish—with the friars came soldiers—led to more influence and more supplies. Frequently it was the chiefs themselves who urged for more expansion of the Franciscan missions.

The looming invasion threat to St. Augustine from English adventurer and privateer Sir Francis Drake was a harbinger of trouble to come, as was a Guale uprising in 1597. The Spanish consolidated their positions near St. Augustine, and Santa Elena was abandoned. As Spanish power waned, in 1629 Charles I of England laid formal claim to what is now the Carolinas, Georgia, and much of Florida, but made no effort to colonize the area. By 1706 the Spanish mission effort in the Southeast had fully retreated to Florida. In an interesting postscript, 89 Native Americans—the sole surviving descendants of Spain's southeastern missions—evacuated to Cuba with the final Spanish exodus from Florida in 1763.

ENTER THE ENGLISH

South Carolina is a product of the **English Restoration,** when the monarchy returned to power after the grim 11-year tenure of Oliver Cromwell, who had defeated Royalist forces in the English Civil War. The attitudes of the Restoration era—expansionist, confident, mercantile—is key to understanding the character of South Carolina even today. Historians dispute exactly how close-minded Cromwell was, but there's no debating the puritanical tone of his reign as British head of state. Theater was banned, as was most music, except for hymns. Hair was close-cropped, and dress was extremely conservative. Most disturbing of all for the holiday-loving English, the observation of Christmas and Easter was strongly discouraged because of their supposedly pagan origins.

Enter Charles II, son of the beheaded Charles I. His ascent to the throne in 1660 signaled a release of all the pent-up creativity and energy of the British people, stagnant under

Cromwell's repression. The arts returned to their previous importance. Foreign policy became aggressive and expansionist. Capitalists again sought profit. Fashion made a comeback, and dandy dress and long hair for both men and women were all the rage. This, then, is the backdrop for the first English settlement of what is now South Carolina. The first expedition was by a Barbadian colonist, William Hilton, in 1663. While he didn't establish a new colony, he did leave behind his name on the most notable geographic feature he saw—Hilton Head Island.

In 1665 King Charles II gave a charter to eight **Lords Proprietors** to establish a colony, generously to be named Carolina after the monarch himself. (One of the Proprietors, Lord Ashley Cooper, would see not one but both rivers in the Charleston area named after him.) Remarkably, none of the Proprietors ever set foot in the colony they established for their own profit. Before their colony was even established, the Proprietors themselves set the stage for the vast human disaster that would eventually befall it. They encouraged slavery by promising that each colonist would receive 20 acres of land for every black male slave and 10 acres for every black female slave brought to the colony within the first year.

In 1666 explorer Robert Sandford officially claimed Carolina for the king, in a ceremony on modern-day Seabrook or Wadmalaw Island. The Proprietors then sent out a fleet of three ships from England, only one of which, the *Carolina,* would make it the whole way. After stops in the thriving English colonies of Barbados and Bermuda, the ship landed in Port Royal. They were greeted without violence, but the fact that the local indigenous people spoke Spanish led the colonists to conclude that perhaps the site was too close for comfort to Spain's sphere of influence. A Kiawah chief, eager for allies against the fierce, slave-trading Westo people, invited the colonists north to

settle instead. So the colonists—148 of them, including three African slaves—moved 80 miles up the coast and in 1670 pitched camp on the Ashley River at a place they dubbed Albemarle Point after one of their lost ships. Living within the palisades of the camp, the colonists farmed 10-acre plots outside the walls for sustenance. The Native Americans of the area were of the large and influential Cusabo people of the Creek Nation, and are sometimes even today known as the Settlement Indians. Subgroups of the Cusabo whose names live on today in South Carolina geography were the Kiawah, Edisto, Wando, Stono, and Ashepoo.

A few years later some colonists from Barbados, which was beginning to suffer the effects of overpopulation, joined the Carolinians. The Barbadian influence, with an emphasis on large-scale slave labor and a caste system, would have an indelible imprint on the colony. Indeed, within a generation a majority of settlers in the new colony would be African slaves. By 1680, however, Albemarle Point was feeling growing pains as well, and the Proprietors ordered the site moved to Oyster Point at the confluence of the Ashley and Cooper Rivers (the present-day Battery). Within a year Albemarle Point was abandoned, and the walls of Charles Towne were built a few hundred yards up from Oyster Point on the banks of the Cooper River.

The original Anglican settlers were quickly joined by various **Dissenters,** among them French Huguenots, Quakers, Congregationalists, and Jews. A group of Scottish Presbyterians established the short-lived Stuart Town near Port Royal in 1684. Recognizing this diversity, the colony in 1697 granted religious liberty to all "except Papists," meaning Roman Catholics. The Anglicans attempted a crackdown on Dissenters in 1704, but two years later Queen Anne stepped in and ensured religious freedom for all Carolinians (again with the exception of Roman Catholics, who wouldn't be a factor in the colony until after the American Revolution).

The English settlements quickly gained root as the burgeoning deerskin trade increased exponentially. Traders upriver, using an ancient network of trails, worked with local Native Americans, mostly Cherokees, to exploit the massive numbers of deer in the American interior. The deerskin trade had a deleterious effect on the indigenous population, as men were gone from their villages much longer than in previous times, when hunting trips had been for sustenance only. By the mid-1700s, the deer population had been so overharvested that the Cherokees had trouble feeding themselves. This led to the need to purchase or barter for food from the English, a dependency that would lead inexorably to violence in years to come.

But before that conflict would come, other scores had to be settled.

The Yamasee War

Within 20 years the English presence had expanded throughout the Lowcountry to include Port Royal and Beaufort. Charles Towne became a thriving commercial center, dealing in deerskins with traders in the interior and with foreign concerns from England to South America. Its success was not without a backlash, as the local Yamasee people became increasingly disgruntled at the settlers' growing monopolies on deerskin and the slave trade. Slavery was a sad and common fact of life from the earliest days of European settlement in the region. Indians were the most frequent early victims, with not only white settlers taking slaves from among them but the Indians themselves conducting slaving raids on each other, often selling hostages to eager colonists.

As rumors of war spread, on Good Friday, 1715, a delegation of six white Carolinians went to the Yamasee village of Pocataligo to address some of the Yamasee's grievances in the hopes of forestalling violence. Their effort was in vain, however, as Yamasee warriors murdered four of them in their sleep, the remaining two escaping to sound the alarm. The treacherous attack signaled the beginning of the two-year Yamasee War, which would claim the lives of nearly 10 percent of the colony's population and an unknown number of Native Americans—making it one of the bloodiest conflicts in American history. Energized and ready for war, the Yamasee attacked Charles Town itself and killed about 90 of the 100 or so white traders in the interior, effectively ending commerce in the area. As Charles Towne began to swell with refugees from the hinterland, water and supplies ran low, and the colony was in peril.

After an initially poor performance by the Carolina militia, a professional army—including armed African slaves—was raised. Well trained and well led, the new army more than held its own despite being outnumbered. A key alliance with local Cherokees was all the advantage the colonists needed to turn the tide for good. While the Cherokee never received the overt military backing from the settlers that they sought, they did garner enough supplies and influence to convince their Creek rivals, the Yamasee, to begin the peace process. The war-weary settlers, eager to get back to life and to business, were eager to negotiate with them, offering goods as a sign of their earnest intent. By 1717 the Yamasee threat had subsided, and trade in the region began flourishing anew.

No sooner had the Yamasee War ended, however, when a new threat emerged: the dread pirate Edward Teach, a.k.a. Blackbeard. Entering Charleston harbor in May 1718 with his flagship *Queen Anne's Revenge* and three other vessels, he promptly plundered five ships and began a full-scale blockade of the entire settlement. He took a number of prominent citizens hostage before finally departing northward.

Slavery Expands

While it was the Spanish who introduced slavery to the New World—of Indians as well as of Africans—it was the English-speaking settlers who dramatically expanded the institution.

HENRY WOODWARD, COLONIAL INDIANA JONES

He's virtually unsung in the history books, and there are no movies made about him, but Dr. Henry Woodward, the first English settler in South Carolina, lived a life that is the stuff of novels and screenplays. Educated in medicine in London, Woodward first tried his hand in the colony of Barbados. But Barbados, crowded and run by an elite, was no place for a young man with a sense of adventure but no contacts in the sugar industry. Still in his teens, Woodward left Barbados in Captain Robert Sandford's 1664 expedition to Carolina. Landing in the Cape Fear region, Sandford's cohort made its way down to Port Royal Sound to contact the Cusabo Indians. In 1666, in what is perhaps the New World's first "cultural-exchange program," Woodward volunteered to stay behind while the rest of the expedition returned to England with a Native American named Shadoo.

Woodward learned the local language and established political relations with surrounding Native American groups, actions for which the Lords Proprietors granted him temporary "formall possession of the whole Country to hold as Tennant att Will." The Spanish had different plans, however. They came and kidnapped the young Englishman, taking him to what turned out to be a very permissive state of house arrest at the Spanish stronghold of St. Augustine in Florida. Surprising the Spanish with his request—in Latin, no less—to convert to Catholicism, Woodward was popular and well-treated. An excellent student of the Catechism, Woodward became a favorite of the Spanish governor and was even promoted to official surgeon. During that time, he studied Spanish government, commerce, and culture, with the same diligence with which he studied the Indians a year earlier. In 1668, Woodward was "rescued" by English privateers—pirates, really—under the command of Robert Searle, who'd come to sack St. Augustine. Woodward's sojourn with the pirates would last two years, during which he was kept on board as ship's surgeon. Was the pirate raid a coincidence? Or, as some scholars suggest, was Woodward really one of history's greatest spies? We will probably never know.

Incredibly, the plot thickens. In another coincidence, in 1670 Woodward was rescued when the pirates shipwrecked on the Caribbean island of Nevis. His rescuers were none other than the settlers on their way to found Charles Towne. On landfall, Woodward asserted his previous experience in the area to direct the colonists away from Port Royal to an area of less Spanish influence. That same year he began a series of expeditions to contact indigenous people in the Carolina interior—the first non-Spanish European to set foot in the area. Using economic espionage gained from the Spanish, Woodward's goal was to jumpstart the trade in deerskins that would be the bulwark of the Charles Towne colony. Woodward's unlikely 1674 alliance with the aggressive Westo people was instrumental in this burgeoning trade. As if all this weren't enough, in 1680 Woodward, now with property of his own on Johns Island, would introduce local farmers to a certain strange crop recently imported from Madagascar: rice.

Woodward made enemies, however, of settlers who were envious of his growing affluence and suspicious of his friendship with the Westo. His outspoken disgust with the spread of Indian slavery brought a charge against him of undermining the interests of the crown. But Woodward, by now a celebrity of sorts, returned to England to plead his case directly to the Lords Proprietors. They not only pardoned him but made him their official Indian agent—with a 20 percent share of the profits. Woodward would never again see the land of his birth. He returned to the American colonies to trek inland, making alliances with groups of Creek Indians in Spanish-held territory. Hounded by Spanish troops, Woodward fell ill of a fever somewhere in the Savannah River valley. He made it to Charleston and safety but never fully recovered and died around 1690—after living the kind of life you usually only see in the movies.

For the English colonists, the Blackbeard episode was the final straw. Already disgusted by the lack of support from the Lords Proprietors during the Yamasee War, the humiliation of the pirate blockade was too much to take. So to almost universal agreement in the colony, the settlers threw off the rule of the Proprietors and strenuously lobbied in 1719 to become a crown colony, an effort that came to final fruition in 1729.

While this outward-looking and energetic place—whose name would morph into Charlestown, and then simply Charleston—was originally built on the backs of merchants, with the introduction of the rice and indigo crops in the early 1700s it would increasingly be built on the backs of slaves. For all the wealth gained through the planting of indigo, rice, and cotton seeds, another seed was sown by the Lowcountry plantation culture. The area's total dependence on slave labor would soon lead to a disastrous war, a conflict signaled for decades to those smart enough to read the signs. By this time Charleston was firmly established as the key American port for the importation of African slaves, accounting for about 40 percent of the trade. As a result, the black population of the coast outnumbered the white population by more than three to one. The very real fear of violent slave uprisings had great influence over not only politics but day-to-day affairs.

These fears were eventually realized in the great **Stono Rebellion** on September 9, 1739. Twenty African American slaves led by an Angolan known only as Jemmy met near the Stono River near Charleston. Marching with a banner that read "Liberty," they seized guns with the plan of marching all the way to Spanish Florida and sanctuary in the wilderness. On the way they burned seven plantations and killed 20 more whites. A militia eventually caught up with them, killing 44 escaped slaves and losing 20 of their own. The prisoners were decapitated and had their heads spiked on every milepost between the spot of that final

battle and Charleston. The result was not only a 10-year moratorium on slave importation into Charleston, but a severe crackdown on the education of slaves—a move that would have damaging implications for generations to come.

Spain Vanquished

In 1729, Carolina was divided into north and south. In 1731, a colony to be known as Georgia, after the new English king, was carved out of the southern part of the Carolina land grant specifically to provide a military buffer to protect Carolina. A young English general, aristocrat, and humanitarian named James Edward Oglethorpe gathered together a group of Trustees—similar to Carolina's Lords Proprietors—to take advantage of that grant. Like Carolina, the Georgia colony also emphasized religious freedom. While to modern ears Charleston's antipathy toward "papists" and Oglethorpe's original ban of Roman Catholics from Georgia might seem incompatible with this goal, the reason was a coldly pragmatic one for the time: England's two main global rivals, France and Spain, were both staunchly Catholic countries.

In 1742 Oglethorpe defeated a Spanish force on St. Simons Island, Georgia, in the **Battle of Bloody Marsh.** That clash marked the end of Spanish overtures on England's colonies in America. With first the French and then the Spanish effectively shut off from the American East Coast, the stage was set for an internal battle between England and its burgeoning colonies across the Atlantic.

The Coming of the "Crackers"

In the mid-1700s, Scots-Irish settlers from Pennsylvania and Virginia came down the **Great Wagon Road** along the Appalachians to enter upstate South Carolina in great numbers. Although many of these independent farmers owned slaves, generally they were far less sympathetic to slavery than coastal residents, and certainly much less dependent on it. Calvinist in religion and self-reliant in outlook, these "crackers"—called that either because of the sound of their whips as they drove their wagons or from the Gaelic word *craic,* meaning to boast—grew to become a formidable political force in South Carolina.

The interior began filling up with Scottish, Irish, German, and Swiss settlers. Their subsequent demands for political representation led to tension with the coastal inhabitants, typically depicted through the years as an Upcountry versus Lowcountry competition.

In later years the Scots-Irish of the Upstate would go on to contribute two of South Carolina's most prominent figures, Andrew Jackson and John C. Calhoun. Ironically, the men would find themselves on opposing sides of the nation-shattering question of secession.

The Cherokee War

By 1750 the Cherokees of the Upstate were the most numerous and important Native American allies of English settlers in South Carolina. However, tired of being ripped off by white traders against whom they had little recourse, the Cherokees grew increasingly embittered, their morale further shattered by a particularly devastating outbreak of the plague. They began to play the English against the French to the west, who were generally more ethical in their relations with indigenous population. Isolated violence by the Cherokees against English settlers—much of which was subsumed within what's now known as the French and Indian War—was also on the upswing.

An attack on some white settlers in 1759 convinced South Carolina Governor James Lyttleton to put his foot down. He demanded that the Cherokees surrender those responsible, knowing full well that they had no centralized governmental authority capable of doing so. When the Cherokees cobbled together a delegation to Charleston to negotiate, Lyttleton promptly had the Indian emissaries taken hostage and held at Fort Prince George on the Keowee River (the site is now submerged under the reservoir of Lake Keowee). However, the Cherokee answered subterfuge with subterfuge. They invited the fort's commander, Lieutenant William Coytmore, outside the walls under a flag of truce to bargain for the hostages' release. They then ambushed Coytmore and his unarmed men, killing the lieutenant. The English furiously responded by immediately murdering all 22 hostages within the fort.

Thus all-out war came to the Upstate, between the Cherokees and the English, their former allies. Violence flared throughout the colony. A war party massacred 50 settlers near present-day Abbeville. An Indian assault on the outpost at Ninety Six was barely repulsed. An entire surrendered garrison, marching from Tennessee to Fort Prince George, was murdered. While the first phase of the Cherokee War favored the Cherokees—accustomed as they were to guerrilla tactics—the tide would soon turn. Ever-larger deployments of regular British Army troops were dispatched to Cherokee land, both to protect settlers as well as to sack and burn Cherokee towns wholesale.

In a foreshadowing of the total war which General William Sherman would later unleash on the South, in 1761 a massive British force under General James Grant burned fields and crops throughout the Midlands and Upcountry, depriving the Cherokee of sustenance for the winter ahead. In September 1761, the Cherokees signed a peace treaty with the colony, ceding most of its eastern lands. The Cherokees would later embark on a disastrous alliance with the crown during the American Revolution, but for the time being they were neutralized, and South Carolina settlers could focus on a larger, much more powerful enemy: the crown. The brutal lessons learned fighting the Cherokees would come in handy.

REVOLUTION AND A NEW NATION

It's a persistent but inaccurate myth that the affluent elite on the southeastern coast were reluctant to break ties with England. While the Lowcountry's cultural and economic ties to England were certainly strong, the **Stamp Act** and the **Townshend Acts** combined to turn public sentiment against the mother country there as elsewhere in the colonies. South Carolinian planters like Christopher Gadsden, Henry Laurens, John Rutledge, and Arthur Middleton were early leaders in the movement for independence.

At war's outbreak, the British failed to take Charleston—fourth-largest city in the colonies—in June 1776. The episode gave South Carolina its "Palmetto State" moniker when redcoat cannonballs bounced off the palm tree-lined walls of Fort Moultrie on Sullivan's Island. The British under General Sir Henry Clinton successfully took the city, however, in 1780, holding it until 1782. The area's two major cities were captured—Savannah fell to the British in 1778—but the war raged on in the surrounding area. Indeed, throughout the Carolinas the fighting was as vicious as anything yet seen on the North American continent. With over 130 known military engagements occurring in South Carolina, that colony sacrificed more combatants during the war than any other.

The struggle became a guerrilla war of colonists versus the British as well as a civil war between Patriots and Loyalists, or **Tories.** Committing what would today undoubtedly be called war crimes, the British routinely burned homes, churches, and fields, and killed recalcitrant civilians. In response, Patriots of the Lowcountry formed a group of deadly guerrilla soldiers under legendary leaders such as Francis Marion, "the Swamp Fox," and Thomas Sumter, "the Gamecock." Using unorthodox tactics perfected in years of backcountry Indian fighting, the Patriots of the Carolinas attacked the British in daring hit-and-run raids staged from the swamps and marshes and from the hills and forests.

Although the British originally assumed they would be supportive of the crown, Upstate Carolinians were swayed by the resurgence of violence by the Cherokees, newly allied with the British. The savagery of the repeated frontier massacres—some of which, it must be said, were encouraged by the British—hardened the Upcountry settlers against redcoat and Indian alike. Some of them, such as Andrew Jackson, would take their anti-Indian prejudice to extremes.

In all, the Scots-Irish of the Upstate would play a key role—some historians say *the* key role—in turning the tide of the American Revolution. South Carolina militiamen would defeat Loyalist forces in two pivotal battles of the war, at Cowpens and Kings Mountain. The unexpected show of patriotism from Upcountry settlers put a dagger in Lord Cornwallis's ill-fated Southern Strategy and led inevitably to the British retreat through North Carolina to Yorktown, Virginia, and ignominy.

In all, four South Carolinians signed the Declaration of Independence: Thomas Heyward Jr., Thomas Lynch Jr., Arthur Middleton, and Edward Rutledge.

The Cotton Boom

True to form, the new nation wasted no time in asserting its economic strength. Rice planters from Georgetown north of Charleston on down to the Altamaha River in Georgia built on their already impressive wealth, becoming the new nation's richest men by far—with fortunes built on the backs of the slaves working in their fields.

Charleston was still by far the largest, most powerful, and most influential city in the Southeast. While most Lowcountry planters spent the warmer months away from the mosquito- and malaria-infested coast, Charleston's elite grew so fond of their little peninsula that they took to living in their "summer homes" year-round, becoming absentee landlords of their various plantations. As a result of this affluent, somewhat hedonistic atmosphere, Charleston became an early arts and cultural center for the whole country.

In 1786, a new crop was introduced that would only enhance the financial clout of the coastal region: cotton. A former loyalist colonel, Roger Kelsal, sent some seed from Anguilla in the West Indies to his friend James Spaulding, owner of a plantation on St. Simons Island, Georgia. This crop, soon to be known as **Sea Island cotton** and considered the best in the world, would supplant rice as the crop of choice for coastal plantations. Plantations on Hilton Head, Edisto, Daufuskie, and Kiawah Islands would make the shift to this more profitable product and amass even greater fortunes for their owners. With the boom in cotton, there needed to be a better way to get that cash crop to market quickly. In 1827, the South Carolina Canal and Rail Road Company was chartered to build a line that would expedite cotton trade from the Upcountry down to the port of Charleston. The resulting 137-mile Charleston-Hamburg line, begun in 1833, was at the time the longest railroad in the world.

Secession

Much of the lead-in to the Civil War focused on whether slavery would be allowed in the newest U.S. territories in the West, but there's no doubt that all figurative roads eventually led to South Carolina. During Andrew Jackson's presidency in the 1820s, his vice president, South Carolina's John C. Calhoun, became a thorn in Jackson's side with his aggressive advocacy for the concept of **nullification,** which Jackson strenuously rejected. In a nutshell, Calhoun said that if a state decided that the federal government wasn't treating it fairly—in this case with regard to tariffs that were hurting

the cotton trade in the Palmetto State—it could simply nullify the federal law, superseding it with law of its own.

As the abolition movement gained steam and tensions over slavery rose, South Carolina congressman Preston Brooks took things to the next level. On May 22, 1856, he beat fellow senator Charles Sumner of Massachusetts nearly to death with his walking cane on the Senate floor. Sumner had just given a speech criticizing pro-slavery forces—including a relative of Brooks—and called slavery "a harlot." (In a show of support, South Carolinians sent Brooks dozens of new canes to replace the one he broke over Sumner's head.)

In 1860, the national convention of the Democratic Party, then the dominant force in U.S. politics, was held in—where else?—Charleston. Rancor over slavery and state's rights was so high that they couldn't agree on a single candidate to run to replace President James Buchanan. Reconvening in Maryland, the party split along sectional lines, with the Northern wing backing Stephen A. Douglas. The Southern wing, fervently desiring secession, deliberately chose its own candidate, John Breckenridge, in order to split the Democratic vote and throw the election to Republican Abraham Lincoln, an outspoken opponent of the expansion of slavery. During that so-called **Secession Winter** before Lincoln took office, seven states seceded from the union, first among them the Palmetto State, followed by Mississippi, Florida, Alabama, Georgia, Louisiana, and Texas.

A UNION DISSOLVED

Five days after South Carolina's secession on December 21, 1860, U.S. Army Major Robert Anderson moved his garrison from Fort Moultrie in Charleston harbor to nearby Fort Sumter. Over the next few months and into the spring, Anderson would ignore many calls to surrender, and Confederate forces would

OLD HICKORY'S LEGACY

Although many histories of Andrew Jackson, seventh president of the United States, say he was born in North Carolina, don't tell that to South Carolinians. They're sure Old Hickory is one of their own. If you don't believe them, get into your time machine and ask Andrew Jackson himself. He always insisted he was born in a log house in South Carolina a couple of miles from the border with the Tar Heel State.

In any case, we know that Old Hickory was born in what's called the Waxhaws region, straddling the border of the Carolinas roughly in the area of modern-day Charlotte and its suburbs to the south. Like much of the Upstate, the area was generally immune to the charms of the Lowcountry planters, whom they thought of as a pampered elite. While owning slaves was certainly a part of the entire state's economy, it was noticeably less important in the Upstate.

This sensitivity to the needs and basic dignity of the common man would go on to inform Jackson's time in the White House. Prior to Jackson's presidency, only white male landowners could vote in the United States. Setting the stage for gradually increasing suffrage gains—such as for African American men, and later for all women—Jackson changed the system so that owning land was not a requirement to vote.

Jackson had noticeably less populist sympathy for Native Americans, however. As a product of the rough Carolina frontier, the site of generations of savage wars between settlers and local indigenous people, he grew up with a strong bias against the region's original inhabitants. This enmity would see its awful height in the Trail of Tears, a direct result of Jackson's Indian Removal Act of 1830. The most famous—and possibly apocryphal—example of Jackson's literal "my way or the highway" approach came in 1831, when the Supreme Court, under Chief Justice John Marshall, ruled against the state of Georgia's action to take Cherokee land. In response, Jackson supposedly said, "John Marshall has made his decision—now let him enforce it."

Another development that didn't necessarily have such sanguine results was his introduction of the patronage system, in other words, "to the victor go the spoils." Before Jackson, civil servants kept their jobs regardless of which team was in the White House. Afterward, bureaucrats became political appointees. While today patronage is generally thought of as leading to corruption and cronyism, at the time Jackson intended it as an antidote to what he saw as a creeping aristocracy in the government and another example of the venal self-centered nature of the Lowcountry planter elite.

One of Jackson's key philosophies, a sharp distrust of banks, did not survive his time in office. Although he fought strenuously against the undue influence of the banking industry on the American body politic, no one could say he was successful in light of their power today.

Learn more about Old Hickory when you're in the state of his birth (according to the man himself, anyway) by visiting **Andrew Jackson State Park** (196 Andrew Jackson Park Rd., 803/285-3344, www.southcarolinaparks.com, during daylight saving time daily 9 A.M.-9 P.M., other seasons daily 8 A.M.-6 P.M., $2 adults, free under age 15).

---

prevent any Union resupply or reinforcement. Shortly before dawn on April 12, 1861, Confederate batteries around Charleston—ironically none of which were at the Battery itself—opened fire on Fort Sumter for 34 straight hours, until Anderson surrendered on April 13.

In a classic example of why you should always be careful what you wish for, the secessionists had been too clever by half in pushing for Lincoln. Far from prodding the North to sue for peace, the fall of Fort Sumter instead caused the remaining states in the union to rally around the previously unpopular tall man from Illinois. Lincoln's skillful—some would say cunning—management of the Fort Sumter standoff meant that from then on out, the South would bear history's blame for initiating the conflict that would claim over half a million American lives.

After Fort Sumter, the remaining four states

of the Confederacy—Arkansas, Tennessee, North Carolina, and Virginia—seceded. The Old Dominion was the real prize for the secessionists, as Virginia had the South's only ironworks and by far the largest manufacturing base.

War on the Coast

In November 1861, a massive Union invasion armada landed in Port Royal Sound in South Carolina, effectively taking the entire Lowcountry and Sea Islands out of the war. Charleston, however, did host two battles in the conflict. The **Battle of Secessionville** came in June 1862, when a Union force attempting to take Charleston was repulsed on James Island with heavy casualties. The next battle, an unsuccessful Union landing on Morris Island in July 1863, was immortalized by the movie *Glory*.

The 54th Massachusetts Regiment, an African American unit with white commanders, performed so gallantly in its failed assault on the Confederate Battery Wagner that it inspired the North and was cited by abolitionists as further proof that African Americans should be given freedom and full citizenship rights. Another invasion attempt on Charleston would not come, but it was besieged and bombarded for nearly two years (devastation made even worse by a massive fire, unrelated to the shelling, that destroyed much of the city in 1861).

In other towns, white Southerners evacuated the coastal cities and plantations for the hinterland, leaving behind only slaves to fend for themselves. In many coastal areas, African Americans and Union garrison troops settled into an awkward but peaceful coexistence.

In Savannah, to the south, General William Sherman concluded his **March to the Sea** in 1864, famously giving the city to Lincoln as a Christmas present. While staunch Confederates, city fathers were wise enough to know what would happen to their accumulated wealth and fine homes should they be foolhardy enough to resist Sherman's army of war-hardened veterans, most of them farm boys from the Midwest with a pronounced distaste for the "peculiar institution" of slavery.

Aftermath

The only military uncertainty left was in how badly Charleston, the "cradle of secession," would suffer for its sins. Historians and local wags have long debated why Sherman spared Charleston, the hated epicenter of the Civil War. Did he fall in love with the city during his brief posting there as a young lieutenant? Did he literally fall in love there, with one of its legendarily beautiful and delicate local belles? We may never know for sure, but it's likely that the Lowcountry's marshy, mucky terrain simply made it too difficult to move large numbers of men and supplies from Savannah to Charleston proper. So Sherman turned his terrifying battle-hardened army inland toward the state capital, Columbia, which would not be so lucky. Most of Charleston's once-great plantation homes were also put to the torch.

For the African American population of South Carolina, however, it was not a time of sadness but the great Day of Jubilee. Soon after the Confederate surrender, black Charlestonians held one of the largest parades the city has ever seen, with one of the floats being a coffin bearing the sign "Slavery is dead."

As for the place where it all began, a plucky Confederate garrison remained underground at Fort Sumter throughout the war, as the walls above them were literally pounded into dust by the long Union siege. The garrison quietly left the fort under cover of night on February 17, 1865. Major Robert Anderson, who surrendered the fort at war's beginning, returned to Sumter in April 1865 to raise the same flag he'd lowered exactly four years earlier. Three thousand African Americans attended the ceremonies, including the son of Denmark Vesey. Later that same night, Abraham Lincoln was assassinated in Washington DC.

Reconstruction

A case could be made that slavery need not have led the United States into Civil War. The U.S. government had banned the importation of slaves long before, in 1808. The great powers of Europe would soon ban slavery altogether (Spain in 1811, France in 1826, and Britain in 1833). Visiting foreign dignitaries in the mid-1800s were often shocked to find the practice in full swing in the American South. Even Brazil, the world center of slavery, where four out of every 10 slaves taken from Africa were brought (less than 5 percent came to the United States), would ban slavery in 1888. Still, the die was cast, the war was fought, and everyone had to deal with the aftermath.

For a brief time, Sherman's benevolent dictatorship on the coast held promise for an orderly postwar future. In 1865 he issued his sweeping "40 acres and a mule" order seeking dramatic economic restitution for coastal Georgia's free blacks. Politics reared its ugly head in the wake of Lincoln's assassination, however, and the order was rescinded, ushering in the chaotic Reconstruction era, echoes of which linger to this day. Nonetheless, that period of time in the South Carolina and Georgia Sea Islands served as an important incubator of sorts for the indigenous African American culture of the coast—called Gullah in South Carolina and Geechee in Georgia. Largely left to their own devices, these insulated farming and oystering communities held to their old folkways, many of which exist today.

Even as the trade in cotton and naval stores resumed to even greater heights than before, urban life and racial tension became more and more problematic. Urban populations swelled as freed blacks from all over the depressed countryside rushed into the cities. As one of them, his name lost to history, famously said: "Freedom was freer in Charleston." It was during this time that some gains were made by African Americans, albeit with little support from the white population. Largely under duress, the University of South Carolina became the first Southern university to grant degrees to black students. The historically black, Methodist-affiliated Claflin College in Orangeburg was founded in 1869. While the coast and urban areas saw more opportunities for African Americans, tension remained high in the countryside. The Edgefield District along the Savannah River, in particular, saw long periods of standoff between heavily armed black and white militias.

Largely with the support of those white militia groups, in 1876 the old guard of the Democratic Party returned to power in South Carolina with the election of former Confederate General Wade Hampton III to the governor's office. Supported by a violent paramilitary group called the Red Shirts, Hampton used his charisma and considerable personal reputation to attempt to restore South Carolina to its antebellum glory—and undo Reconstruction in the process.

"Pitchfork" Ben

The natural antipathy between the Lowcountry and the Upstate came to a head with the Populist movement of the 1890s. While the movement itself was short-lived, the empowerment it gave to South Carolina's long-ignored poor white farmers marked a permanent shift. A direct impact was the establishment of the agriculturally oriented Clemson College (later Clemson University) in 1889 specifically to counter the influence of the University of South Carolina in Columbia, which was perceived by some as an elite institution. The white farmers' standing became immeasurably enhanced by the new state constitution of 1895. With new poll taxes and literacy tests designed to dramatically hinder black voting, the constitution effectively ushered in the Jim Crow era in South Carolina.

The man behind the new charter was

Benjamin Ryan Tillman of Trenton, South Carolina, who posed as the friend of the rural white South Carolinian but was essentially a career politician. He was also an extreme and unrepentant racist, as evidenced by this inflammatory quote, one of many like it:

> We of the South have never recognized the right of the negro to govern white men, and we never will. We have never believed him to be the equal of the white man, and we will not submit to his gratifying his lust on our wives and daughters without lynching him.

Tillman quickly rose in the newly nascent state Democratic Party and went on to become a U.S. senator from 1895 to 1918. Not only the main spokesman for the state's white backlash after the Civil War, he also ensured the supremacy of the Upstate in most internecine political battles, a legacy that lives on, more or less, to this day.

RENAISSANCE AND DEPRESSION

While the aftermath of the Civil War was painful, it was by no means bereft of activity or profit. The reunification of the states marked the coming of the Industrial Revolution, and in many quarters of the South, the cotton, lumber, and naval stores industries not only recovered but exceeded antebellum levels. A classic South Carolina example was in Horry County, where the town of Conway exploded as a commercial center for the area logging industry. By 1901 the first modest resort had been built on nearby Myrtle Beach, and the area rapidly became an important vacation area—a role it serves to this day.

The textile industry ramped up as well, and the Upstate became the new world center of the trade—gaining a certain amount of regional revenge by taking business from the once-dominant New England textile industry. For some parts of South Carolina, it was specifically an influx of Northern money after Reconstruction

that heralded a mini boom. The classic example of this is in Aiken, where the heralded Winter Colony was responsible for much of the affluent, equestrian culture that reigns there even now.

The **Spanish-American War** of 1898 was a major turning point for the South. For most Southerners, it was the first time since the Civil War that they were enthusiastically patriotic about being Americans. The southeastern coast felt this in particular, as it was a staging area for the invasion of Cuba. Charlestonians cheered the exploits of their namesake heavy cruiser the USS *Charleston,* which played a key role in forcing the Spanish surrender of Guam.

Bernard Baruch, a South Carolinian, Wall Street financial wizard, and presidential adviser would make many Americans more familiar with the state's natural beauty. After his acquisition of the old Hobcaw Barony near Georgetown in 1905, he hosted many a world leader there, including President Franklin D. Roosevelt and British Prime Minister Winston Churchill.

Charleston would elect its first Irish American mayor, John Grace, in 1911. Though it wouldn't open until 1929, the first Cooper River Bridge joining Charleston with Mount Pleasant was the child of the Grace administration, which is credited today for modernizing the Holy City's infrastructure (as well as tolerating high levels of vice during Prohibition) and making possible much of the civic gains to follow.

A major change that came during this time is rarely remarked on in history books: This was when South Carolina became a majority white state for the first time since the early colonial days. With thousands of African Americans leaving for more tolerant pastures and more economic opportunity in the North and the West—a move known as the **Great Migration**—the demographics of the state changed accordingly.

The arrival of the tiny but devastating boll weevil all but wiped out the cotton trade on the coast after the turn of the 20th century, forcing the economy to diversify. Naval stores and lumbering were the order of the day at the advent of **World War I,** the patriotic effort of which did wonders in repairing the wounds of the Civil War, still vivid in many local memories.

A major legacy of World War I that still greatly influences life in the Lowcountry is the Marine Corps Recruiting Depot Parris Island, which began life as a small Marine camp in 1919.

The Roaring '20s

In the boom period following World War I, Charleston entered the world stage and made some of its most significant cultural contributions to American life. The dance called the Charleston, originated on the streets of the Holy City and popularized in New York, would sweep the world. The Jenkins Orphanage Band, often credited with the dance, traveled the world, even playing at President Taft's inauguration.

In the visual arts, the Charleston Renaissance took off, specifically intended to introduce the Holy City to a wider audience. Key work included the Asian-influenced work of self-taught painter Alice Ravenel Huger Smith and the etchings of Elizabeth O'Neill Verner. Edward Hopper was a visitor to Charleston during that time and produced several noted watercolors. The Gibbes Art Gallery, now the Gibbes Museum of Art, opened in 1905.

Recognizing the cultural importance of the city and its history, in 1920 socialite Susan Pringle Frost and other concerned Charlestonians formed the Preservation Society of Charleston, the oldest community-based historic preservation organization in the country.

In 1924, lauded Charleston author DuBose Heyward wrote the locally set novel *Porgy.* With Heyward's cooperation, the book would soon be turned into the first American opera, *Porgy and Bess,* by George Gershwin, who labored over the composition in a cottage on Folly Beach. Ironically, *Porgy and Bess,* which premiered with an African American cast in New York in 1935, wouldn't be performed in its actual setting until 1970 because of segregation laws.

And in a foreshadowing of a future tourist boom, the Pine Lakes golf course opened in Myrtle Beach in 1927, the first on the Grand Strand.

A NEW DEAL

Alas, the good times didn't last. The Great Depression hit the South hard, but since wages and industry were already behind the national average, the economic damage wasn't as bad as elsewhere in the country. As elsewhere in the South and indeed across the country, public works programs in President Franklin D. Roosevelt's New Deal helped not only to keep locals employed but contributed greatly to the cultural and archaeological record of the area. The Public Works of Art Project stimulated the visual arts. The Works Progress Administration renovated the old Dock Street Theatre in Charleston, and theatrical productions once again graced that historic stage. You can still enjoy the network of state parks built in South Carolina by the Civilian Conservation Corps.

The New Deal also left its mark on South Carolina in the form of numerous hydroelectric projects, which involved the damming of rivers and the flooding of thousands of acres of land, much of it inhabited. Lakes Marion, Moultrie, Hartwell, Russell, and Thurmond are all artificial byproducts of these massive engineering projects. Used for recreation today, they played a vital role in the electrification of rural South Carolina and in the huge war effort that was soon to come.

WORLD WAR II AND THE MODERN ERA

With the attack on Pearl Harbor and the coming of World War II, life in the United States and in South Carolina would never be the same. Military funding and facilities swarmed the area, and populations and long-depressed living standards rose as a result. Here are some key developments:

- The Charleston Navy Yard became the city's largest employer, and the population soared as workers crowded in.
- Fort Jackson near Columbia became one of the U.S. Army's largest infantry training grounds, and Colonel Jimmy Doolittle's famed Tokyo Raiders trained for their daring missions over Lake Murray.
- Camp Croft near Spartanburg opened, training 250,000 infantrymen during the war.
- Down in Walterboro, the Tuskegee Airmen, a highly decorated group of African American fighter pilots, trained for their missions escorting bombing raids over Germany. Walterboro also hosted a large German POW camp.
- The Marine Corp Recruiting Depot Parris Island expanded massively, training nearly 250,000 recruits 1941-1945.
- The entire 1944 graduating class of the Citadel in Charleston was inducted into the armed forces—possibly the only time an entire class was drafted at once.

The Postwar Boom

Up in Aiken, the construction of the sprawling Savannah River Site hydrogen-bomb plant in the early 1950s forced the relocation of thousands of citizens, mostly low-income African Americans. Although environmentally problematic, the site has continued to provide many jobs to the area.

Myrtle Beach and the Grand Strand were already the breeding ground of that unique South Carolina dance called the shag. The postwar era marked the shag's heyday, as carefree young South Carolinians flocked to beachfront pavilions to enjoy this indigenous form of music, sort of a white variation on the regional black rhythm and blues of the time.

The postwar U.S. infatuation with the automobile—and its troublesome child, the suburb—brought exponential growth to the great cities of the coast. The first bridge to Hilton Head Island was built in 1956, leading to the first of many resort developments, Sea Pines, in 1961. On many outlying islands, electricity came for the first time. With rising coastal populations came pressure to demolish more and more fine old buildings to put parking lots and high-rises in their place. A backlash grew among the cities' elites, aghast at the destruction of so much history. The immediate postwar era brought about the formation of both the Historic Charleston Foundation, which began the financially and politically difficult work of protecting historic districts from the wrecking ball of "progress." They weren't always successful, but the work of these organizations—mostly older women from the upper crust—laid the foundation for the successful coastal tourist industry to come, as well as preserving important American history for the ages.

Civil Rights

Contrary to popular opinion, the civil rights era wasn't just a blip in the 1960s. The gains of that decade were the fruits of efforts begun decades earlier. Many of the efforts involved efforts to expand black suffrage. Though African Americans had secured the nominal right to vote years before, primary contests were not under the jurisdiction of federal law. As a result, Democratic Party primary elections—the de facto general elections because of that party's total dominance in the South at the time—were effectively closed to African American voters. In Charleston, the Democratic primary was opened to African Americans for the first time in 1947.

In 1960 the Charleston Municipal Golf Course voluntarily integrated to avoid a court battle. Lunch counter sit-ins happened all over South Carolina, including the episode of the "Friendship Nine" in Rock Hill. Martin Luther King Jr. visited South Carolina in the late 1960s, speaking in Charleston in 1967 and helping reestablish the Penn Center on St. Helena Island as not only a cultural center but a center of political activism as well.

The hundred-day strike of hospital workers at the Medical University of South Carolina in 1969—right after King's assassination—got national attention and was the culmination of Charleston's struggle for civil rights. By the end of the 1960s, the city council of Charleston had elected its first black alderman, and the next phase in local history began.

The South Carolinian most closely associated with the civil rights era is the Reverend Jesse Jackson. Although the Greenville native has operated out of Chicago for most of his career, his early work with Martin Luther King in the South put an indelible stamp on the struggle for civil rights.

While South Carolina avoided much of the large-scale violence that plagued many other parts of the country during the civil rights era, there was one exception. A drive to peacefully integrate a whites-only bowling alley in Orangeburg turned violent one February night in 1968 when a crowd of African Americans confronted local police. When police opened fire with buckshot, three men were killed and nearly 30 wounded in what would be known as the "Orangeburg Massacre."

Both major universities in the state integrated without major incident in 1963: first Clemson University (then Clemson College) followed rapidly by the University of South Carolina. Only eight years after the University of South Carolina integrated, an African American was elected student body president.

A Coast Reborn

While the story of the South Carolina coastal boom actually begins in the 1950s with Charles Fraser's development of Sea Pines Plantation on Hilton Head—forever changing that barrier island—the decade of the 1970s was pivotal to the future success of the South Carolina coast.

In Charleston, the historic tenure of Mayor Joe Riley began in 1975, and as of this writing he is still in that office. The Irish American has broken precedents and forged key alliances, reviving not only the local economy but tamping down age-old racial tensions. Beginning with downtown's Charleston Place, Riley embarked on a series of high-profile public works projects to reinvigorate the then-moribund Charleston historic area. King Street would soon follow. Tourism in the Holy City increased 60 percent 1970-1976.

The coast's combination of beautiful scenery and cheap labor proved irresistible to the movie and TV industry, which began filming many series and movies in the area in the 1970s, which continues to this day. Beaufort in particular would emerge from its stately slumber as the star of several popular films, including *The Great Santini* and *The Big Chill*. Of course, Myrtle Beach had been a leisure getaway for generations, but with the 1980s and the building of the Barefoot Landing retail and lodging development—followed by many others like it—the Grand Strand entered the first tier of American tourist destinations, where it remains.

Charleston received its first major challenge since the Civil War in 1989 when Hurricane Hugo slammed into the South Carolina coast just north of town. The Holy City, including many of its most historic locations, was massively damaged, with hardly a tree left standing. In a testament to the toughness beneath Charleston's genteel veneer, the city not only rebounded but came back stronger. In perhaps typically mercantile fashion, Charlestonians used the devastation of Hugo as a reason to introduce a new round of residential construction to the entire area, particularly the surrounding islands.

The most recent phenomenon on the coast has been the exponential increase in golf and retirement communities in the Beaufort-Bluffton area. The largest development, Sun City, has brought thousands of retirees to a habitat that is not naturally able to support this level of human density. Despite a recent emphasis on more environmentally friendly development, it remains to be seen whether local and state planners and elected officials will have the wisdom to regulate the more land- and water-intensive projects.

Change Comes to the Upstate

Greenville was still calling itself the "Textile Capital of the World" as late as 1980, but the mill culture of the Upstate had largely disintegrated by the 1950s, victim of the car culture and increased opportunity elsewhere. By the 1970s the industry was further threatened by international competition.

By the dawn of the 1990s, however, the Upstate was well positioned to attract foreign capital to fill the void left by the almost complete annihilation of the textile industry. In 1988, European tire maker Michelin ushered in this new era by locating a manufacturing facility near Greenville. In 1992, German auto manufacturer BMW announced its North American factory would be based in Spartanburg County. Today, the Upstate hosts literally hundreds of foreign firms, and the resulting influx of both money and transplants from other regions and countries has brought rapid socioeconomic change to the region, the most visible being Greenville's Main Street, once an unsightly four-lane affair, now shrunk to a pedestrian-friendly two lanes and augmented with cozy shops, restaurants, and hotels.

Conservatism and Controversy

South Carolina's movement into the future, while inexorable, has been slow and fraught with missteps, most of them related to the state's long embrace of political and social conservatism. The most notable example was the controversy in the late 1990s over the display of the Confederate battle flag over the State House in Columbia, the last Southern capitol to continue a practice begun as a protest of integration in the 1960s. Facing a vast boycott of the entire state by the National Collegiate Athletic Association, including a threat to remove the

lucrative Final Four basketball tournament, the state relented—sort of. While moving the flag might seem like a no-brainer—indeed, the business community was strongly supportive of the move—no state politician wanted to be the one to risk the ire of conservative white "heritage"-minded voters, not an insignificant voting bloc in South Carolina. After a dramatic debate in the legislature that was quite emotional on both sides, a compromise solution was found in 2000 that left neither side satisfied. The rebel banner was moved to a different location on the State House grounds—no longer flying along with Old Glory, to be sure, but quite literally front and center, where it stands to this day off Gervais Street.

A more ironically humorous episode involving the State House came in 2003, when the inscription on the statue of archconservative U.S. Senator Strom Thurmond was changed to acknowledge the former segregationist's illegitimate children by an African American mistress. A truly unfortunate controversy ensued during the presidential election campaign of 2000, when an appearance by then-candidate George W. Bush at Bob Jones University in Greenville brought out the news that the school's longtime ban on interracial dating was still in effect. President Bob Jones III immediately rescinded the ban.

A lesser echo took place in Greenville during the 2008 election campaign, when a Catholic bishop in Greenville stated that any parishioner who voted for Barack Obama was not eligible for Communion, supposedly because of the Democrat's pro-choice position on the abortion issue. Although the Vatican quickly invalidated the bishop's ill-timed policy, it was another embarrassment for the state.

Not all the controversies have had to do with race, however. The once all-male Citadel in Charleston is still struggling with the issue of gender following a 1990s court decision requiring them to open their doors to female applicants. In 1994 Shannon Faulker became the first female to enter Citadel day classes. Her physical unreadiness and relentless hazing by fellow students combined to force her departure shortly thereafter. In 1996 another four women enrolled, and two left because they were harassed in a similar fashion. The first female graduate—who was also the daughter of the college commandant—got her degree in 1999. Today, female day-students at the Citadel are more common (night graduate courses have been coed for quite a while). But episodes of sexual harassment are still alleged to be more common than on typical campuses.

Government and Economy

GOVERNMENT

For many decades, the South was completely dominated by the Democratic Party. Originally the party of slavery, segregation, and Jim Crow, the Democratic Party began attracting Southern African American voters in the 1930s with the election of Franklin D. Roosevelt. The allegiance of black voters was further cemented in the Truman, Kennedy, and Johnson administrations. The region would remain solidly Democratic until a backlash against the civil rights movement of the 1960s drove many white Southerners, ironically enough, into the party of Lincoln, the Republicans. This added racial element, so confounding to Americans from other parts of the country, remains just as potent today.

The default mode in the South is that white voters are massively Republican and black voters massively Democratic. Since South Carolina is 69 percent white, there is an overwhelming Republican dominance. The GOP currently controls the governor's mansion and both houses of the state legislature. However, the coastal areas and parts of the Midlands, with their large, predominantly Democratic African American populations, function somewhat separately from this realignment. For instance, in 2008 John McCain easily won South Carolina's eight electoral votes with 54 percent of the vote, but in Charleston County, Barack Obama received 54 percent of the vote. In Orangeburg County, Obama received nearly 70 percent.

But don't make the mistake of assuming that local African Americans are particularly liberal because of their voting habits. Deeply religious and traditional in background and upbringing, African Americans in South Carolina are among the most socially conservative people in the region, even if their choice of political party does not always reflect that.

South Carolina's presidential primary is the first in the South, and as such carries more than its share of influence. The brutal 2000 Republican primary made the career of George W. Bush as he bested John McCain and went on to the nomination. Barack Obama's massive 2008 victory in the state Democratic primary ended all hopes for Hillary Clinton in capturing a decent-size share of the African American vote in her quest for the party's nomination.

In addition to its constitutionally mandated pair of U.S. Senators, South Carolina currently sends six representatives to the U.S. House of Representatives, although that number could change based on 2010 census data.

ECONOMY

Even before the recent economic downturn, South Carolina had experienced a century's worth of profound changes in economy and business. The rice-growing industry moved offshore in the late 1800s, and the center of the cotton trade moved to the Gulf states in the early 1900s. That left timber as the main cash crop all up and down the coast, specifically huge pine tree farms to feed the pulp and paper business. For most of the 20th century, the largest employers along the coast were massive sulfur-spewing paper mills that had as big an effect on the local environment as on its economy. But even that is changing as Asian competition is driving paper companies to sell off their tracts for real estate development—from an environmental perspective, not necessarily a more welcome scenario.

In the Upstate, the story has been the declining manufacturing base of the old textile industry. However, despite frequent media portrayals, the truth is that many towns and cities in the Upstate—Greenville in particular—have made a deft transition into the global economy.

Since World War II, the U.S. Department of Defense has been a major employer and economic driver in the South overall, and South Carolina is certainly no exception. Despite the closure of the Charleston Naval Yard in the mid-1990s, the grounds now host the East Coast headquarters of the Space and Naval Warfare Systems Center (SPAWAR), which provides high-tech engineering solutions for the Navy. Charleston also retains a large military presence in the Charleston Air Force Base near North Charleston, which hosts two airlift wings and employs about 6,000 people.

Myrtle Beach went through a similarly anxious state of events in the mid-1990s with the closure of Myrtle Beach Air Force Base. As with Charleston, the local economy appears to have weathered the worst effects of the closure. Farther down the coast, Beaufort is home to the Naval Hospital Beaufort as well as the Marine Corps Air Station Beaufort and its six squadrons of FA-18 Hornets. On nearby Parris Island is the legendary Marine Corps Recruit Depot Parris Island, which puts all new Marine recruits from east of the Mississippi River through rigorous basic training. Major military facilities inland include the sprawling Fort Jackson complex outside Columbia and Shaw Air Force Base in Sumter.

Of course, tourism is also an important factor in the local economies of the area, particularly in seasonal resort-oriented areas like Hilton Head, Myrtle Beach, Kiawah, and Seabrook Islands. Charleston also has a well-honed tourism infrastructure, bringing at least $5 billion per year into the local economy; it is routinely voted one of the top three American cities to visit.

Another huge economic development on the coast has been the exponential growth of the Charleston seaport. From the 1990s on, the quickened pace of globalization has brought enormous investment, volume, and expansion to area port facilities. Charleston's port experienced record volumes in 2006-2007, although the subsequent economic downturn has hurt business.

As a statistical snapshot, the median income of South Carolina is $39,326 per year, ranked 39th among the states.

People and Culture

Contrary to how the state is portrayed in the media, South Carolina is hardly exclusive to natives with thick flowery accents who still obsess over the Civil War and eat grits three meals a day. As you will quickly discover, the entire coastal area and much of the Upstate is becoming heavily populated with transplants from other parts of the country. In some of these places you can actually go quite a long time without hearing even one of those Scarlett O'Hara accents.

Some of this is due to the region's increasing attractiveness to professionals and artists, drawn by the temperate climate, natural beauty, and business-friendly environment. Part of it is due to its increasing attractiveness to retirees, most of them from the frigid Northeast. Indeed, in some places, chief among them Hilton Head, the most common accent is a New York or New Jersey one, and a Southern accent is rare.

In any case, don't make the common mistake of assuming you're coming to a place where footwear is optional and electricity is a recent development (although it's true that many of the islands didn't get electricity until the 1950s and 1960s). Because so much new construction has gone on in the South in the last 25 years or so, you might find some aspects of the infrastructure—specifically the roads and the electrical utilities—actually superior to where you came from.

POPULATION

The 2010 U.S. Census put South Carolina's population at 4,679,230. Population statistics for individual cities are quite misleading because of South Carolina's notoriously strict annexation laws, which make it nearly impossible for a city to annex growing suburbs. For example, while the cities of Greenville and Spartanburg are listed as having populations of approximately 58,000 and 37,000, respectively, in practice this is grossly inaccurate; the combined Greenville-Spartanburg area actually has well over one million residents. The city of Anderson technically has only about 27,000 residents, but Anderson County has over 200,000.

In rough order of rank, the largest official metropolitan areas in South Carolina are Columbia (767,000), Charleston, North Charleston, and Summerville (664,000), Greenville, Mauldin, and Easley (636,000), Myrtle Beach, North Myrtle Beach, and Conway (329,000), Florence (200,000), and Hilton Head and Beaufort (170,000).

Racial Makeup

Its legacy as the center of the U.S. slave trade and plantation culture means that South Carolina continues to have a large African American population, about 28 percent of the total. The coast has a higher percentage, with Charleston at about 31 percent African American and Georgetown about 40 percent. Portions of the Midlands are heavily African American as well; Orangeburg, for example, is 60 percent black. The Upstate has the lowest proportion of African Americans. Seneca, for example, is only 8 percent black; Spartanburg and nearby Gaffney have the highest proportions in the Upstate, at about 20 percent.

One unfortunate legacy of South Carolina's history is the residual existence of a certain amount of de facto segregation. Visitors are often shocked to see how some residential areas even today still break sharply on racial lines—as do schools, with most public schools mostly black and most private schools overwhelmingly white. However, despite persistent media portrayals, overt racism is extremely rare in the areas covered in this book. In remote areas an interracial couple might get some disapproving looks, but in any urban area, hardly anyone will bat an eye.

OFFBEAT FESTIVALS

South Carolina's lack of dominant metropolitan areas—its biggest city, Columbia, isn't really that big—means that its original patchwork of small communities is more or less intact. And, of course, the whole state's got that Southern Gothic thing going for it. This translates into the fact that nearly every town seems to have its own trademark festival or event. In some cases the festivals celebrate important local crops or products, sometimes long after said crops and products have faded into irrelevance. In other cases the events have grown out of a more basic desire to jump-start tourism. In any case, laugh all you want, but many of them are quite well-attended and successful. Here is but a partial list of South Carolina's many offbeat local festivals.

- Beaufort Water Festival, Beaufort
- Canadian-American Days, Myrtle Beach
- Chitlin' Strut, Salley
- Come-See-Me Festival, Rock Hill
- Flopeye Fish Festival, Great Falls
- Fried Green Tomato Festival, Beech Island
- Iris Festival, Sumter
- Lobster Races, Aiken
- Mighty Moo Festival, Cowpens
- National Shag Dance Championships, Myrtle Beach
- Okra Strut, Irmo
- Orangeburg Festival of Roses
- Peach Festival, Gaffney
- Puddin' Swamp Festival, Turbeville
- Soft Shell Crab Festival, Port Royal
- Spittoono, Clemson
- Turkey Strut and Chicken Pickin' Festival, Cross Anchor
- Watermelon Festival, Hampton
- World Grits Festival, St. George

No discussion of offbeat festivals in the Palmetto State is complete without a long mention of the beauty pageant **Miss South Carolina** (rotating venues, 864/843-9090, http://misssouthcarolina.com, $30-40 per night, $125 combo tickets for both pageants). Held each July—the most recent was in North Charleston, although the preceding several were in Spartanburg—this event is where every Miss South Carolina and Miss South Carolina Teen is crowned. The latter title has gained pop culture notoriety in the wake of Caitlin Upton's unfortunate YouTube-topping performance at the 2007 Miss Teen USA pageant, in which she referenced "U.S. Americans" and "the Iraq," among other malapropisms.

This is a great place to soak in the Southern beauty pageant culture in all its maudlin glory: the smiles, the tears, the talent competition, the wearing of high heels with bikinis. Local papers throughout South Carolina report the ongoing results of the multiday competition as the *Washington Post* might report on a key vote in Congress. One thing you won't find at this pageant is the stereotypical "big hair" and caked-on makeup of legend. Pageants like this one have become major breeding grounds for future modeling and showbiz stars—Vanessa Minnillo is a former Miss South Carolina Teen—and the contestants' hairstyles and makeup are state-of-the-art (though certainly nowhere close to edgy).

The Hispanic population, as elsewhere in the United States, is growing rapidly, but statistics can be misleading. Although Hispanic populations are growing at a triple-digit clip in the region, they still remain only about 5 percent of South Carolina's total population. Bilingual signage is becoming more common but is still quite rare.

RELIGION
The Coast

The Lowcountry, and Charleston in particular, is unusual in the Deep South for its wide variety of religious faiths. While South Carolina remains overwhelmingly Protestant—over 80 percent of all Christians in the state are members of some Protestant denomination, chief among them Southern Baptist and Methodist—the coast's cosmopolitan polyglot history has made it a real melting pot of faiths.

The Lowcountry was originally dominated by the Episcopal Church (known as the Anglican Church in other countries), but from early on it was also a haven for those of other faiths. Various types of Protestant groups soon arrived, including French Huguenots and Congregationalists. Owing to vestigial prejudice from the European realpolitik of the founding era, the Roman Catholic presence in South Carolina was late in arriving, but once it came, it was there to stay, especially on the coast.

Most unusually of all for the Deep South, Charleston had a large Jewish population that was a key participant in the city from the very first days of settlement. Sephardic Jews, primarily of Portuguese descent, were among the first settlers. One of them, Judah Benjamin, spent a lot of time in the Carolinas and became the Confederacy's secretary of state. Indeed, up to about 1830, South Carolina had the largest Jewish population of any state in the union.

The Midlands

Because of the large numbers of German and Swiss settlers that came to the Midlands, the region has more of a Lutheran quality today. There is even a notable Mennonite presence, particularly in Blackville and Abbeville.

The Upstate

The Upstate was first settled by Presbyterians, hard-shell Baptists, and various Christian fundamentalists. Their collective attitude was much more sternly moralistic, and this conservatism has colored the region's sensibilities to this day. The Greenville area in particular is a hotbed of fundamentalism, with the archconservative Bob Jones University the premier example. Sprawling, well-attended **megachurches** dot the region and are increasingly the focal point of religious activity—to the dismay of the pastors of smaller, older churches.

And, of course, who could forget the tragicomic reign of televangelists Jim and Tammy Faye Bakker? Though both Midwesterners, their now-defunct religious empire, Heritage USA in Fort Mill, South Carolina, became a byword for kitsch and corruption.

MANNERS

The prevalence and importance of good manners is the main thing to keep in mind about the South. While it's tempting for folks from more outwardly assertive parts of the world to take this as a sign of weakness, that would be a major mistake. Bottom line: Good manners will take you a long way here. Southerners use manners, courtesy, and chivalry as a system of social interaction with one goal above all: to maintain the established order during times of stress. A relic from a time of extreme class stratification, etiquette and chivalry are ways to make sure that the elites are never threatened—and, on the other hand, that even those on the lowest rungs of society are afforded at least a basic amount of dignity. But as a practical matter, it's also true that Southerners of all classes, races, and backgrounds rely on the observation of manners as a way to sum up people quickly. To any Southerner, regardless of class or race, your use or neglect of basic manners and proper respect indicates how seriously they should take you—not in a socioeconomic sense, but in the big picture overall.

The typical Southern sense of humor—equal parts irony, self-deprecation, and good-natured teasing—is part of the code. Southerners are loath to criticize another individual directly, so often they'll instead take the opportunity to make an ironic joke. Self-deprecating humor is also much more common in the South than in other areas of the country. Because of this, you're also expected to be able to take a joke yourself without being too sensitive.

LOCAL FOOD

- **Blenheim Ginger Ale:** Generally pronounced "BLEN-um," this heady and addictive retro-style brew is still obtainable at country roadside stores throughout the state. Even if they don't have a beat-up Blenheim sign out front, feel free to inquire inside.

- **Boiled peanuts:** Usually pronounced "ball peanuts" and sold from roadside stands, this soft, salty, mouthwatering treat—usually served in plastic grocery bags—is just the ticket on a hot South Carolina day.

- **Chick-fil-A:** This Atlanta-based chain, which you'll often find inside South Carolina malls, boasts a signature pressure-cooked chicken sandwich. Enjoy them only Monday-Saturday, though—the owners are devout Christians and give all their employees Sunday off to observe the Sabbath.

- **Coca-Cola:** In local patois it's "Coke-Cola." In any case, never call it "pop"—in South Carolina that's not a soft drink, it's the sound a firecracker makes.

- **Duke's:** It seems almost every little town in the state has a barbecue place called Duke's. At one time most of them had a pedigree descending from the Earl Duke dynasty of Orangeburg, but these days many are independently owned.

- **Iced tea:** Down here it's just "ice tea," or even just "tea," and the default mode is sweet to extremely sweet. If you want it unsweetened, or "unsweet," you'll have to ask. You'll usually get a lemon wedge in any case.

- **Piggly Wiggly:** Based in Memphis, Tennessee, "the Pig" is the supermarket of choice for much of South Carolina, especially in semirural areas.

Etiquette

As we've seen, it's rude here to inquire about personal finances, along with the usual no-go areas of religion and politics. Here are some other specific etiquette tips:

- **Basics:** Be liberal with "please" and "thank you," or conversely, "no thank you" if you want to decline a request or offering.

- **Eye contact:** With the exception of very elderly African Americans, eye contact is not only accepted in the South, it's encouraged. In fact, to avoid eye contact in the South means you're likely a shady character with something to hide.

- **Handshake:** Men should always shake hands with a *very* firm, confident grip and appropriate eye contact. It's OK for women to offer a handshake in professional circles, but otherwise not required.

- **Chivalry:** When men open doors for women here—and they will—it is not thought of as a patronizing gesture but as a sign of respect.

Accept graciously and walk through the door. Also, if a female of any age or appearance drops an object on the floor, don't be surprised if several nearby males jump to pick it up. This is considered appropriate behavior and not at all unusual.

- **The elderly:** Senior citizens—or really anyone obviously older than you—should be called "sir" or "ma'am." Again, this is not a patronizing gesture in the South but is considered a sign of respect. Also, in any situation where you're dealing with someone in the service industry, addressing them as "sir" or "ma'am" regardless of their age will get you far.

- **Bodily contact:** Interestingly, though public displays of affection by romantic couples are generally frowned upon here, Southerners are otherwise pretty touchy-feely once they get to know you. Full-on body hugs are rare, but Southerners who are well acquainted often say hello or goodbye with a small hug.

- **Driving:** With the exception of the interstate perimeter highways around the larger cities, drivers in the South are generally less aggressive than in other regions. Cutting sharply in front of someone in traffic is taken as a personal offense. If you need to cut in front of someone, poke the nose of your car a little bit in that direction and wait for a car to slow down and wave you in front. Don't forget to wave back as a thank-you. Similarly, using a car horn can also be taken as a personal affront, so use your horn sparingly, if at all. In rural areas, don't be surprised to see the driver of an oncoming car offer a little wave. This is an old custom, sadly dying out. Just give a little wave back; they're trying to be friendly.

THE GUN CULTURE

One of the most misunderstood aspects of the South is the value the region places on the personal possession of firearms. No doubt, the 2nd Amendment to the U.S. Constitution ("A well regulated Militia, being necessary to the security of a free State, the right of the people to keep and bear Arms, shall not be infringed") is well known here and fiercely protected, at the governmental and at the grassroots levels. But while guns are indeed more casually accepted in everyday life in the South, the reason for this has less to do with personal safety than with the rural background of the region and its long history of hunting. If you're traveling on a back road and you see a pickup truck with a gun rack in the back containing one or more rifles or shotguns, this is not intended to be menacing or intimidating. Chances are the driver is a hunter, nothing more.

State laws do tend to be significantly more accommodating of gun owners here than in much of the rest of the country. It is legal to carry a concealed handgun in South Carolina with the proper permit, and you need no permit at all to possess a weapon for self-defense. However, there are regulations regarding how a handgun must be conveyed in automobiles.

South Carolina now has a so-called "stand your ground" law, whereby if you're in imminent lethal danger, you do not first have to try to run away before resorting to deadly force to defend yourself.

ESSENTIALS

Getting There and Around

BY AIR

There are six key airports serving South Carolina. **Charleston International Airport** (CHS, 5500 International Blvd., 843/767-1100, www.chs-airport.com) is served by AirTran (www.airtran.com), American (www.aa.com), Delta (www.delta.com), Northwest (www.nwa.com), United (www.ual.com), and US Airways (www.usairways.com). This is a primary gateway to the entire coast.

Columbia Metropolitan Airport (CAE, 3000 Aviation Way, 803/822-5000, www.columbiaairport.com) is served by American (www.aa.com), Delta (www.delta.com), Northwest (www.nwa.com), Spirit (www.spiritair.com), United (www.ual.com), and US Airways (www.usairways.com). It's a good access point for the center of the state.

Greenville-Spartanburg International Airport (GSP, 2000 GSP Dr., 864/877-7426, www.gspairport.com) is served by Allegiant (www.allegiantair.com), American Eagle (www.aa.com), Delta (www.delta.com), Northwest (www.nwa.com), United (www.ual.com), and US Airways (www.usairways.com) and is a good point of entry for the upper half of the state.

© JIM MOREKIS

Myrtle Beach International Airport (MYR, 1100 Jetport Rd., 843/448-1589, www.flymyrtlebeach.com) is served by Delta (www.delta.com), Myrtle Beach Direct Air (www.mbdirectair.com), Northwest (www.nwa.com), Spirit (www.spiritair.com), United (www.ual.com), and US Airways (www.usairways.com). Because of the lack of interstate highway coverage in this area, the Myrtle Beach airport is best used only if Myrtle Beach is your primary destination.

Savannah/Hilton Head International Airport (SAV, 400 Airways Ave., 912/964-0514, www.savannahairport.com), off I-95 in Savannah, Georgia, is served by AirTran (www.airtran.com), American Eagle (www.aa.com), Delta (www.delta.com), Northwest Airlink (www.nwa.com), United (www.ual.com), and US Airways (www.airways.com). Although it is located in Georgia, because of its location near the extreme southern tip of South Carolina, this airport is perhaps the best access point to enjoy the lower portion of the South Carolina coast, and definitely Hilton Head.

Charlotte-Douglas International Airport (CLT, 5501 Josh Birmingham Pkwy., 704/359-4000, www.clt.com) is served by Air Canada (www.aircanada.com), AirTran (www.airtran.com), American (www.aa.com), Delta (www.delta.com), JetBlue (www.jetblue.com), Lufthansa (www.lufthansa.com), Northwest (www.nwa.com), United (www.ual.com), and US Airways (www.usairways.com). This is by far the busiest airport of the bunch. Its location just across the North Carolina border and on I-77 makes it a fairly convenient point of entry unless your goal is to head for the coast.

While some may be tempted to fly into Atlanta's Hartsfield-Jackson International Airport because of the sheer number of flights into that facility—the world's busiest airport—I strongly advise against it because of the massive congestion in the Atlanta area and because it's really not that close to South Carolina.

BY CAR

South Carolina is extremely well-served by the U.S. interstate highway system. The main interstate arteries into the region are the north-south I-95, I-77, and I-85, and the east-west I-20 and I-26. Charleston has a perimeter interstate, I-526 (the Mark Clark Expressway). Columbia's perimeter is I-126. Greenville has two, I-185 and I-386; Spartanburg's is I-585.

Keep in mind that despite being heavily traveled, the Myrtle Beach area is not served by any interstate highway. A common landmark road through the coastal region is U.S. 17, which used to be known as the Coastal Highway and currently goes by a number of local incarnations as it winds its way along the coast.

Unfortunately, the stories you've heard about speed traps in small South Carolina towns are correct. Always strictly obey the speed limit, and if you're pulled over, always deal with the police respectfully and truthfully, whether or not you agree with their judgment.

Winter driving in South Carolina is generally easy, since it rarely snows here. During periods of heavy rainfall, however, unpaved roads can become quite muddy. Should you be unlucky enough to be on the coast during a mandatory hurricane evacuation, be aware that some roads, especially interstate highways, will become one-way westbound for all lanes to streamline the evacuation. In any case, always follow all law enforcement directions. For updates on planned slowdowns due to construction projects, go to www.dot.state.sc.us/getting/roadcondition.shtml.

South Carolina's copious network of interstate highways offers numerous **rest stops.** They are often a very welcome sight, since the state's heavily rural nature means services can be hard to come by on the road. The following is a list of rest areas.

- I-95: Mile markers 5 (northbound near the Georgia border), 17 (Ridgeland, no facilities), 47 (south of Walterboro), 99 (Santee), 139 (south of Florence), 171 (north of Florence), and 195 (southbound at the North Carolina border).

- I-26: Mile markers 63 (north of Newberry), 123 (south of Columbia), 150 (eastbound at Orangeburg), 152 (westbound at Orangeburg), 202 (westbound at Summerville), and 204 (eastbound at Summerville).
- I-85: Mile markers 17 (northbound at Anderson), 24 (southbound at Anderson), and 89 (Gaffney).
- I-20: Mile marker 93 (Camden).
- I-77: Mile marker 66 (south of Rock Hill).

While all rest stops are clean, safe, and well-equipped, remember there is no gasoline sold at any of them.

Car Rentals

Unless you're going to hunker down in one city, you will need auto transportation to enjoy South Carolina. Renting a car is easy and fairly inexpensive as long as you play by the rules, which are simple. You need either a valid driver's license from any U.S. state or a valid International Driving Permit from your home country, and you must be at least 25 years old.

If you do not either purchase insurance coverage from the rental company or already have insurance coverage through the credit card you rent the car with, you will be 100 percent responsible for any damage caused to the car during your rental period. While purchasing insurance at the time of rental is by no means mandatory, it might be worth the extra expense just to have that peace of mind.

Key rental car companies include **Hertz** (www.hertz.com), **Avis** (www.avis.com), **Thrifty** (www.thrifty.com), **Enterprise** (www.enterprise.com), and **Budget** (www.budget.com). Some rental car locations are in the cities, but the vast majority of outlets are at airports, so plan accordingly. The airport locations have the bonus of generally being open for longer hours than their in-town counterparts.

BY TRAIN

Passenger rail service in the car-dominated United States is far behind that in other developed nations, both in quantity and quality. Many towns and cities in South Carolina are served by the national rail system, **Amtrak** (www.amtrak.com), which is pretty good, if erratic at times—though it certainly pales in comparison with European rail transit.

With the notable exception of the Grand Strand, South Carolina is well-served by Amtrak. You'll find stations in Camden, Charleston, Clemson, Columbia, Florence, Greenville, and Spartanburg. The closest Amtrak station to the Beaufort/Hilton Head area is in Yemassee.

BY BUS

South Carolina is well-served by the privately owned bus company **Greyhound** (www.greyhound.com), which has stops throughout the state, including Aiken, Anderson, Beaufort, Camden, Charleston, Columbia, Florence, Georgetown, Greenville, Myrtle Beach, Orangeburg, Spartanburg, Sumter, and Walterboro. While rates are reasonable and the vehicles are high-quality, this is by far the slowest possible way to travel around the state, as buses stop frequently and sometimes for lengthy periods of time.

BY BOAT

One of the coolest things about the South Carolina coast is the prevalence of the Intracoastal Waterway, a combined artificial and natural sheltered seaway from Miami to Maine. Many boaters enjoy touring the coast by simply meandering up or down the Intracoastal, putting in at marinas along the way.

Recreation

STATE PARKS AND NATURAL AREAS

South Carolina has one of the best state park systems in the United States, with a total of 46 parks and natural areas. Seventeen of the parks were built by the Civilian Conservation Corps during FDR's New Deal and boast distinctive, rustic, and well-made architecture. While primitive camping is available in South Carolina, the general preference here is for plusher surroundings more conducive to a family vacation. Many state parks offer fully equipped rental cabins with modern amenities that rival a hotel's. Generally speaking, such facilities tend to sell out early, so make reservations as soon as you can. Keep in mind that during the high season (Mar.-Nov.) there are minimum rental requirements. While I encourage camping in South Carolina, be aware that the closer you are to the Appalachian Mountains, the higher the rainfall. Be prepared to camp wet if you're camping in the Upstate near the Blue Ridge. Dogs are allowed in state parks, but they must be leashed at all times.

While admission and lodging expenses are very reasonable at South Carolina state parks, long-term visitors can save money on frequent visits by purchasing a **State Park Passport** ($50), which covers a full year of admission from the date of purchase. You currently can't get them online but must charge by phone (803/734-0156). For info and reservations call 866/345-7275 or go to www.southcarolinaparks.com.

NATIONAL WILDLIFE REFUGES

There are seven federally administered National Wildlife Refuges (NWR) in the South Carolina region:

- **ACE Basin NWR** (www.fws.gov/acebasin)
- **Cape Romain NWR** (www.fws.gov/caperomain)
- **Carolina Sandhills NWR** (www.fws.gov/carolinasandhills)
- **Pinckney NWR** (www.fws.gov/pinckneyisland)
- **Santee NWR** (www.fws.gov/santee)
- **Savannah NWR** (www.fws.gov/savannah)
- **Waccamaw NWR** (www.fws.gov/waccamaw)

Admission is generally free. Access is limited to daytime hours (sunrise-sunset). Keep in mind that some hunting is allowed on some refuges.

ZOOS AND AQUARIUMS

There are plenty of opportunities for kids and nature lovers to learn about and enjoy animals up close and personal in the Palmetto State. Chief among them are the **Riverbanks Zoo and Garden** (www.riverbanks.org) in Columbia and the **South Carolina Aquarium** (www.scaquarium.org) in Charleston.

On a smaller scale is **Charles Towne Landing** (www.charlestowne.org) in Charleston, the **Greenville Zoo** in Greenville, **Alligator Adventure** (www.alligatoradventure.com) and **T.I.G.E.R.S.** (www.tigerfriends.com), both in Myrtle Beach.

BEACHES

Some of the best beaches in the country are in the region covered in this book. While the upscale amenities aren't always there and they aren't very surfer-friendly, the area's beaches are outstanding for anyone looking for a relaxing scenic getaway.

By law, beaches in the United States are fully accessible to the public up to the high-tide mark during daylight hours, even if the beach fronts are private property and even if the only means of public access is by boat.

It is a misdemeanor to disturb sea oats, those wispy, waving, wheat-like plants among the dunes. Their root system is vital to keeping the beach intact. Also never disturb a turtle nesting area, whether it is marked or not.

The barrier islands of the Palmetto State have seen more private development than their Georgia counterparts. Some Carolina islands, like Kiawah, Fripp, and Seabrook, are not even accessible unless you are a guest at their affiliated resorts. This means that if you're not a guest, the only way to visit the beaches there is by boat, which I really don't advise.

The Grand Strand, of course, has many miles of beach, from North Myrtle Beach on down to Huntington Beach State Park. Charleston-area beaches include **Folly Beach, Sullivan's Island,** and **Isle of Palms.** Moving down the coast, some delightful beaches are at **Edisto Island** and **Hunting Island,** which both feature state parks with lodging.

Hilton Head Island has about 12 miles of beautiful family-friendly beaches, and while most of the island is devoted to private golf resorts, the beaches remain accessible to the general public with parking at four points: Driessen Beach Park, Coligny Beach Park, Alder Lane Beach Access, and Burkes Beach Road.

KAYAKING AND CANOEING

In the Grand Strand, you can enjoy kayaking on the Waccamaw River and Winyah Bay. Some key kayaking and canoeing areas in the Charleston area are Cape Romain National Wildlife Refuge, Shem Creek, Isle of Palms, Charleston Harbor, and the Stono River.

Farther south in the Lowcountry are the Ashepoo, Combahee, and Edisto blackwater rivers, which combine to form the ACE Basin. Next is Port Royal Sound near Beaufort. The Hilton Head-Bluffton area has good kayaking opportunities at Hilton Head's Calibogue Creek and Bluffton's May River.

Inland, some great kayaking opportunities can be found at many state parks and natural areas, including Congaree National Park and Woods Bay State Natural Area. You can also kayak or canoe on any of the great artificial reservoirs that dot inland South Carolina, including Lake Jocassee, Lake Hartwell, and Lake Marion.

FISHING AND BOATING

In coastal South Carolina, because of the large number of islands and wide area of salt marsh, life on the water is largely inseparable from life on the land. Fishing and boating are very common pursuits, and fish species include spotted sea trout, channel bass, flounder, grouper, mackerel, sailfish, whiting, shark, amberjack, and tarpon.

Freshwater fishing on the many artificial lakes in South Carolina is a huge business and a major driver of the state's economy. You'll find largemouth bass, bream, catfish, and crappie, among many more. Key freshwater fishing locations are Lakes Jocassee and Keowee in the Upstate; the "freshwater coast" along the Savannah River and Lakes Hartwell, Russell, and Thurmond; and the twin lakes of the Santee Cooper region, Marion and Moultrie.

It's easy to fish on piers, lakes, and streams, but if you're over age 16, you need to get a nonresident fishing license from the state. A nonresident seven-day license is $11. Go to www.dnr.sc.gov for more information or to purchase a license online.

The most popular places for **casual anglers** are the various public piers throughout the area. There are public fishing piers at North Myrtle Beach, Folly Beach, Edisto Beach State Park, and Hunting Island State Park. Two nice little public docks are at the North Charleston Riverfront Park on the grounds of the old Charleston Navy Yard and the Bluffton public landing on the May River. Many anglers cast off from abandoned bridges unless signage dictates otherwise, and fishing charters and marinas are common throughout the region.

GOLF

The first golf club in the United States was formed in Charleston, and South Carolina as a whole is one of the world's golf meccas. There is a great variety of facilities, from tony courses like the Pete Dye-designed Ocean Course at the **Kiawah Island Golf Resort** or **Harbour Town** on Sea Pines Plantation in Hilton Head, to the more **budget-conscious courses** in the Santee Cooper region, Myrtle Beach, and North Myrtle Beach.

Don't be shy about pursuing golf packages that combine lodging with links access. South Carolina, especially the coastal area, is currently suffering from something of a glut of golf courses, and you can find some great deals online.

Tips for Travelers

WOMEN TRAVELING ALONE

Women should take the same precautions they would take anywhere else. Many women traveling to this region have to adjust to the prevalence of traditional chivalry. In the South, if a man opens a door for you, it's considered a sign of respect, not condescension.

Another adjustment is the possible assumption that two or three women who go to a bar or tavern together might be there to invite male companionship. This misunderstanding can happen anywhere, but in some parts of the South it might be slightly more prevalent.

While small towns in South Carolina are generally very friendly and law-abiding, some are more economically depressed than others and hence prone to more crime. Always take commonsense precautions no matter how bucolic the setting may be.

TRAVELERS WITH DISABILITIES

While the vast majority of attractions and accommodations make every effort to comply with federal law regarding those with disabilities, as they're obliged to do, the historic nature of this region means that some structures simply cannot be retrofitted for maximum accessibility. This is something you'll need to find out on a case-by-case basis, so call ahead. The sites in this book administered by the National Park Service (Charles Pinckney National Historic Site, Fort Sumter, and Fort Moultrie) are as wheelchair-accessible as possible.

GAY AND LESBIAN TRAVELERS

While South Carolina would never be called a gay-friendly state, don't believe everything you hear. Charleston and Columbia, in particular, are quite accepting, and gay and lesbian travelers shouldn't expect anything untoward to happen. Because of its general religious conservatism, the Upstate could be considered the least gay-friendly part of the state.

In small towns all over South Carolina, the best approach is to simply observe dominant Southern mores for anyone, gay or straight. In a nutshell, that means keep public displays of affection and politics to a minimum. Southerners in general have a low opinion of anyone who flagrantly espouses a viewpoint too obviously or loudly.

SENIOR TRAVELERS

Both because of the large proportion of retirees in the region and because of the South's traditional respect for the elderly, the area is quite friendly to senior citizens. Many accommodations and attractions offer a senior discount, which can add up over the course of a trip. Always inquire *before* making a reservation, however, as check-in time is sometimes too late.

TRAVELING WITH PETS

While the United States is very pet-friendly, that friendliness rarely extends to restaurants and other indoor locations. More and more accommodations are allowing pet owners to bring pets, often for an added fee, but please inquire *before* you arrive. In any case, keep your dog on a leash at all times. Some beaches in the area permit dog-walking at certain times of the year, but as a general rule, keep dogs off beaches unless you see signage saying otherwise.

Health and Safety

CRIME

While crime rates are indeed above national averages in much of South Carolina, especially in inner-city areas, incidents of crime in the more heavily touristed areas are no more common than anywhere else. In fact, these areas might be safer because of the amount of foot traffic and police attention.

By far the most common crime against visitors is simple theft, primarily from cars. (Pickpocketing, thankfully, is quite rare in the United States). Always lock your car doors. Conversely, only leave them unlocked if you're absolutely comfortable living without whatever's inside at the time. As a general rule, I try to lock valuables—such as CDs, a recent purchase, or my wife's purse—in the trunk. (Just make sure the "valet" button, allowing the trunk to be opened from the driver's area, is disabled.)

Should someone corner you and demand your wallet or purse, just give it to them. Unfortunately, the old advice to scream as loud as you can is no longer the deterrent it once was, and in fact may hasten aggressive action by the robber.

A very important general rule to remember is not to pull over for cars you do not recognize as law enforcement, no matter how urgently you might be asked to do so. This is not a common occurrence, but a possibility you should be aware of. A real police officer will know the correct steps to take to identify him or herself. If you find yourself having to guess, then do the safe thing and refuse to stop.

If you are the victim of a crime, *always call the police.* Law enforcement wants more information, not less, and at the very least you'll have an incident report in case you need to make an insurance claim for lost or stolen property.

Remember that in the United States as elsewhere, no good can come from a heated argument with a police officer. The place to prove a police officer wrong is in a court of law, perhaps with an attorney by your side, not at the scene.

For emergencies, always call 911.

AUTO ACCIDENTS

If you're in an auto accident, you're bound by law to wait for police to respond. Failure to do so can result in a "leaving the scene of an accident" charge, or worse. In the old days, cars in accidents had to be left exactly where they came to rest until police gave permission to move or tow them. However, South Carolina has recently loosened regulations so that if a car is blocking traffic as a result of an accident, the driver is allowed to move it enough to allow traffic to flow again. That is, if the car can be moved safely. If not, you're not required to move it out of the way.

Since it's illegal to drive without auto insurance, I'll assume you have some. And because you're insured, the best course of action in a minor accident, where injuries are unlikely, is to patiently wait for the police and give them your side of the story. In my experience, police react negatively to people who are too quick to start making accusations against other people. After that, let the insurance companies deal with it. That's what they're paid for.

If you suspect any injuries, call 911 immediately.

ILLEGAL DRUGS

Marijuana, heroin, methamphetamine, and cocaine and all its derivatives are illegal in the United States with only a very few select exceptions, none of which apply to the areas covered by this book. The use of ecstasy and similar mood-elevators is also illegal. The penalties for illegal drug possession and use in South Carolina are *extremely severe.* Just stay away from them entirely.

ALCOHOL

The drinking age in the United States is 21. Most restaurants that serve alcoholic beverages allow those under 21 inside. Generally speaking, if only those over 21 are allowed inside, you will be greeted at the door by someone asking to see identification. These people are often poorly trained, and anything other than a state driver's license may confuse them, so be forewarned.

Drunk driving is a problem on U.S. highways, and South Carolina is no exception. Always drive defensively, especially late at night, and obey all posted speed limits and road signs—and never assume the other driver will do the same. You may never drive with an open alcoholic beverage in the car, even if it belongs to a passenger.

As far as retail purchase goes, generally speaking in South Carolina you may only buy beer and wine on Sunday when it is allowed by local municipal law, but not hard liquor. Closing times at bars vary by municipality. As a general rule, the closer you are to the coast, the more lax the attitude is toward drinking.

GETTING SICK

Unlike most developed nations, the United States has no comprehensive national health care system (there are programs for the elderly and the poor). Visitors from other countries who need nonemergency medical attention are best served by going to freestanding medical clinics. The level of care is typically very good, but unfortunately you'll be paying out of pocket for the service.

For emergencies, however, do not hesitate to go to the closest hospital emergency room, where the level of care is generally also quite good, especially for trauma. Worry about payment later; emergency rooms in the United States are required to take true emergency cases whether or not the patient can pay for services.

Pharmaceuticals

Unlike in many other countries, antibiotics are available in the United States only on a prescription basis and are not available over the counter. Most cold, flu, and allergy remedies are available over the counter. While homeopathic remedies are gaining popularity in the United States, they are nowhere near as prevalent as in Europe.

Drugs with the active ingredient ephedrine are available in the United States without a prescription, but their purchase is now tightly regulated to cut down on the use of these products to make the illegal drug methamphetamine.

NOT GETTING SICK
Vaccinations

As of this writing, there are no vaccination requirements to enter the United States. Contact your embassy before coming to confirm this before arrival, however.

In the autumn, at the beginning of flu season, preventive influenza vaccinations, simply called "flu shots," often become available at easily accessible locations like clinics, health departments, and even supermarkets.

Humidity, Heat, and Sun

There is only one way to fight the South's high heat and humidity, and that's to drink lots of fluids. A surprising number of people each year refuse to take this advice and find themselves in various states of dehydration, some of which can land you in a hospital. Remember: If you're thirsty, you're already suffering from dehydration. The thing to do is keep drinking fluids before you're thirsty, as a preventative action rather than a reaction.

Always use sunscreen, even on a cloudy day. If you do get a sunburn, get a pain relief product with aloe vera as an active ingredient. On extraordinarily sunny and hot summer days, don't even go outside between the hours of 10 A.M. and 2 P.M.

HAZARDS
Insects

Because of the recent increase in the mosquito-borne West Nile virus, the most important step to take in staying healthy in the Lowcountry and Georgia coast—especially if you have small children—is to keep mosquito bites to a minimum. Do this with a combination of mosquito repellent and long sleeves and long pants, if possible. Not every mosquito bite will give you the virus; in fact, chances are quite slim that one will. But don't take the chance if you don't have to.

The second major step in avoiding insect nastiness is to steer clear of **fire ants,** whose large gray or brown-dirt nests are quite common in this area. They attack instantly and in great numbers, with little or no provocation. They don't just bite; they inject you with poison from their stingers. In short, fire ants are not to be trifled with. While the only real remedy is the preventative one of never coming in contact with them, should you find yourself being bitten by fire ants, the first thing to do is to stay calm. Take off your shoes and socks and get as many of the ants off you as you can. Unless you've had a truly large number of bites—in which case you should seek medical help immediately—the best thing to do next is wash the area to get any venom off, and then disinfect with alcohol if you have any handy. Then a topical treatment such as calamine lotion or hydrocortisone is advised. A fire ant bite will leave a red pustule that lasts about a week. Try your best not to scratch it so that it won't get infected.

Outdoor activity, especially in woodsy, undeveloped areas, may bring you in contact with another unpleasant indigenous creature, the tiny but obnoxious **chigger,** sometimes called the redbug. The bite of a chigger can't be felt, but the enzymes it leaves behind can lead to a very itchy little red spot. Contrary to folklore, putting fingernail polish on the itchy bite will not "suffocate" the chigger, because by this point the chigger itself is long gone. All you can do is get some topical itch or pain relief and go on with your life. The itching will eventually subside.

For **bee stings,** the best approach for those who aren't allergic to them is to immediately pull the stinger out, perhaps by scraping a credit card over the bite, and apply ice if possible. A topical treatment such as hydrocortisone or calamine lotion is advised. In my experience, the old folk remedy of tearing apart a cigarette and putting the tobacco leaves directly on the sting does indeed cut the pain. But that's not a medical opinion, so do with it what you will. A minor allergic reaction can be quelled by using an over-the-counter antihistamine. If the victim is severely allergic to bee stings, go to a hospital or call 911 for an ambulance.

Threats in the Water

While enjoying area beaches, a lot of visitors become inordinately worried about **shark attacks.** Every couple of summers there's a lot of hysteria about this, but the truth is that you're much more likely to slip and fall in a bathroom than you are even to come close to being bitten by a shark in these shallow Atlantic waters.

A far more common fate for area swimmers is to get stung by a **jellyfish,** or sea nettle. They can sting you in the water, but most often beachcombers are stung by stepping on beached jellyfish stranded on the sand by the tide. If you get stung, don't panic; wash the area with saltwater, not freshwater, and apply vinegar or baking soda.

Lightning

The southeastern United States is home to vicious, fast-moving thunderstorms, often with an amazing amount of electrical activity. Death by lightning strike occurs often in this region and is something that should be taken quite seriously. The general rule of thumb is that if you're in the water, whether at the beach or in a swimming pool, and hear thunder, get out of the water immediately until the storm passes. If you're on dry land and see lightning flash a distance away, that's your cue to seek safety indoors. Whatever you do, do not play sports outside when lightning threatens.

Information and Services

MONEY

Automated Teller Machines (ATMs) are available in all urban areas covered in this guide. Be aware that if the ATM is not owned by your bank, not only will that ATM likely charge you a service fee, but your bank may charge you one as well. While ATMs have made traveler's checks less essential, traveler's checks do have the important advantage of accessibility, as some rural and less-developed areas covered in this guide have few or no ATMs. You can purchase traveler's checks at just about any bank.

Establishments in the United States only accept the national currency, the U.S. dollar. To exchange foreign money, go to any bank.

Generally, establishments that accept credit cards will feature stickers on the front entrance with the logo of the particular cards they accept, although this is not a legal requirement. The use of debit cards has dramatically increased in the United States. Most retail establishments and many fast-food chains are now accepting them. Make sure you get a receipt whenever you use a credit card or a debit card.

Tipping

Unlike many other countries, service workers in the United States depend on tips for the bulk of their income. In restaurants and bars, the usual tip is 15 percent of the pretax portion of the bill for acceptable service, 20 percent (or more) for excellent service. For large parties, usually six or more, a 15-18 percent gratuity is automatically added to the bill.

It's also customary to tip bellboys about $2 per bag when they assist you at check-in and checkout of your hotel; some sources recommend a minimum of $5.

For taxi drivers, 15 percent is customary as long as the cab is clean, smoke-free, and you were treated with respect and taken to your destination with a minimum of fuss.

INTERNET ACCESS

Visitors from Europe and Asia are likely to be disappointed at the quality of Internet access in the United States, particularly the area covered in this book. Fiber-optic lines are still a rarity, and while many hotels and B&Bs now offer in-room Internet access—some charge, some don't, so make sure to ask ahead—the quality and speed of the connection might prove poor.

Wireless (Wi-Fi) networks also are less than impressive, although that situation continues to improve on a daily basis in coffeehouses, hotels, and airports. Unfortunately, many hot spots in private establishments are for rental only.

PHONES

Generally speaking, the United States is behind Europe and much of Asia in terms of cell phone technology. Unlike Europe, where "pay-as-you-go" refills are easy to find, most American cell phone users pay for monthly plans through a handful of providers. Still, you should have no problem with cell phone coverage in urban areas. Where it gets much less dependable is in rural areas and on beaches. Bottom line: Don't depend on having cell service everywhere you go. As with a regular landline, any time you face an emergency, call 911 on your cell phone.

All phone numbers in the United States are seven digits preceded by a three-digit area code. You may have to dial a 1 before a phone number if it's a long-distance call, even within the same area code.

RESOURCES

Suggested Reading

NONFICTION

Edgar, Walter. *South Carolina: A History*. Columbia: University of South Carolina Press, 1998. An engaging tome written by the state's most beloved historian and public radio personality.

Ferling, John E. *Almost a Miracle: The American Victory in the War of Independence*. New York: Oxford University Press, 2007. Not only perhaps the best single volume detailing the military aspects of the Revolutionary War, but absolutely indispensable for learning about South Carolina's key role in it. In a dramatic departure from most New England-focused books of this genre, fully half of *Almost a Miracle* is devoted to an in-depth look at the Southern theater of the conflict.

Grosvenor, Vertamae. *Vibration Cooking: The Travel Notes of a Geechee Girl*. New York: Ballantine, 1992. This Hampton County, South Carolina, native and popular National Public Radio commentator delivers an offbeat travelogue and cookbook.

Hudson, Charles M. *The Southeastern Indians*. Knoxville, TN: University of Tennessee Press, 1976. Although written decades ago, this seminal work by the noted University of Georgia anthropologist remains the definitive work on the life, culture, art, and religion of the Native Americans of the Southeast region.

Klein, Maury. *Days of Defiance: Sumter, Secession, and the Coming of the Civil War*. New York: Vintage, 1999. A gripping and vivid account of the lead-up to war, with Charleston as the focal point.

Robinson, Sally Ann. *Gullah Home Cooking the Daufuskie Island Way*. Chapel Hill, NC: University of North Carolina Press, 2007. Subtitled *Smokin' Joe Butter Beans, Ol' 'Fuskie Fried Crab Rice, Sticky-Bush Blackberry Dumpling, and Other Sea Island Favorites*, this cookbook by a native Daufuskie Islander features a foreword by Pat Conroy.

Rogers, George C. Jr. *Charleston in the Age of the Pinckneys*. Columbia: University of South Carolina Press, 1980. This 1969 history is a classic of the genre.

Rosen, Robert. *A Short History of Charleston*. Columbia: University of South Carolina Press, 1997. Quite simply the most concise, readable, and entertaining history of the Holy City I've found.

Stokes, Thomas L. *The Savannah*. Marietta, GA: Cherokee Publishing, 2007. This reissued classic is for those interested in a broader historical view of the key regional waterway that forms the western border of South Carolina. Its chapters on Henry Woodward, Hernando

De Soto, and Benjamin "Pitchfork" Tillman are particularly well done. It features original sketches by Lamar Dodd, founder of the University of Georgia art school.

Todd, Leonard. *Carolina Clay: The Life and Legend of the Slave Potter Dave.* New York: W. W. Norton, 2008. A fascinating exploration of the world of the largely anonymous African American artisans who created the now-hot genre known as Edgefield Pottery. We know the story of one of them, the man simply known as Dave, because he was literate enough to sign his name to his amazing works—an extremely unusual (and dangerous) act for the time.

Vernon, Amelia Wallace. *African Americans at Mars Bluff.* Columbia: University of South Carolina Press, 1995. An engaging look at the author's ancestral African American community of Mars Bluff outside Florence, where individual families grow rice on small plots using the old methods.

Woodward, C. Vann, ed. *Mary Chesnut's Civil War.* New Haven, CT: Yale University Press, 1981. The Pulitzer Prize-winning classic compilation of the sardonically funny and quietly heartbreaking letters of Charleston's Mary Chesnut during the Civil War.

FICTION

Caldwell, Erskine. *God's Little Acre.* Athens, GA: University of Georgia Press, 1995. Scandalous in its time for its graphic sexuality, Caldwell's best-selling novel chronicles socioeconomic decay in the mill towns of South Carolina and Georgia during the Great Depression.

Conroy, Pat. *The Lords of Discipline.* New York: Bantam, 1985. For all practical purposes set at the Citadel, this novel takes you behind the scenes of the notoriously insular Charleston military college.

Conroy, Pat. *The Water is Wide.* New York: Bantam, 1987. Immortal account of Conroy's time teaching African American children in a two-room schoolhouse on "Yamacraw" (actually Daufuskie) Island.

Frank, Dorothea Benton. *Sullivan's Island.* New York: Berkley, 2004. This South Carolina native's debut novel, and still probably her best, chronicles the journey of a Charleston woman through the breakup of her marriage to eventual redemption.

Jakes, John. *Charleston.* New York: Signet, 2003. Historical fiction dealing with exploits in and around the Holy City in the years up to the American Revolution.

Kidd, Sue Monk. *The Secret Life of Bees.* New York: Penguin, 2003. Set in South Carolina in the 1960s, this best-seller delves into the role of race in the regional psyche. It gained critical acclaim due to the unusual fact that the author, a white woman, features many African American female characters.

Kinsella, W. P. *Shoeless Joe.* New York: Houghton Mifflin, 1982. Magical realist novel about a man who hears a voice telling him to "build it and they will come" and constructs a baseball diamond in an Iowa cornfield. Later adapted into the hit film *Field of Dreams* starring Kevin Costner and—with a totally out-of-place New York accent—Ray Liotta as Greenville native "Shoeless" Joe Jackson.

Poe, Edgar Allan. *The Gold Bug.* London: Hesperus Press, 2007. Inspired by his stint there with the U.S. Army, the great American author set this classic short story on Sullivan's Island, South Carolina, near Charleston.

Internet Resources

RECREATION

Dozier's Waterway Guide
www.waterwayguide.com

A serious boater's guide to stops on the Intracoastal Waterway, this site features a lot of solid navigational information.

South Carolina Department of Natural Resources
www.dnr.sc.gov

More than just a compendium of license and fee information—although there's certainly plenty of that—this site features a lot of practical advice on how best to enjoy South Carolina's great outdoors, whether you're an angler, a kayaker, a bird-watcher, a hiker, or a biker.

South Carolina State Parks
www.southcarolinaparks.com

This site offers vital historical and visitor information for South Carolina's excellent, underrated network of state park sites, including camping reservations.

U.S. Forest Service
www.fs.fed.us

Much of South Carolina is covered with National Forest, and this federal site contains extensive recreational tips and information.

NATURE AND ENVIRONMENT

Francis Beidler Forest Blog
http://beidlerforest.blogspot.com

This site features an informative blog by a nature expert with Francis Beidler Forest, a jointly owned conservation venture of the South Carolina Audubon Society and the Nature Conservancy.

Go Green Charleston
www.gogreencharleston.org

The latest environmental and sustainable-living news in Charleston, this site features a lot of practical and fun visitor information and links.

South Carolina Waterfalls
www.alleneasler.com/waterfalls.html

Allen Easler's site provides a loving look at the waterfalls of the Palmetto State, along with great photos.

FOOD

Charleston City Paper
www.charlestoncitypaper.com

In addition to providing up-to-date news and entertainment listings for Charleston, this is also where to find the latest foodie and nightlife news.

HISTORY AND BACKGROUND

Charleston Wiki Project
www.charlestonwiki.org

This Wikipedia site is just for Charleston, from a resident's point of view.

South Carolina Information Highway
www.sciway.net

An eclectic cornucopia of interesting South Carolina history and assorted background facts makes for an interesting Internet portal into all things Palmetto State.

South Carolina National Heritage Corridor
www.sc-heritagecorridor.org

This trek covers 14 historically important counties, from the mountains to the coast. The site also features plenty of downloadable brochures.

VISITOR INFORMATION
Charleston Convention and Visitors Bureau
www.charlestoncvb.com
This very professional and user-friendly tourism site is perhaps the best and most practical Internet portal for visitors to Charleston.

Citytrex.com
www.citytrex.com
Professionally produced downloadable MP3 walking tours covering Charleston and Beaufort are available at this site.

Index

List of Maps

www.moon.com

DESTINATIONS | ACTIVITIES | BLOGS | MAPS | BOOKS

MOON.COM is ready to help plan your next trip! Filled with fresh trip ideas and strategies, author interviews, informative travel blogs, a detailed map library, and descriptions of all the Moon guidebooks, Moon.com is all you need to get out and explore the world—or even places in your own backyard. While at Moon.com, sign up for our monthly e-newsletter for updates on new releases, travel tips, and expert advice from our on-the-go Moon authors. As always, when you travel with Moon, expect an experience that is uncommon and truly unique.

KEEP UP WITH MOON ON FACEBOOK AND TWITTER
JOIN THE MOON PHOTO GROUP ON FLICKR

MAP SYMBOLS

≡≡≡	Expressway	**(**	Highlight	✗	Airfield	⚓	Golf Course
⋯⋯	Primary Road	○	City/Town	✗	Airport	**P**	Parking Area
⋯⋯	Secondary Road	◉	State Capital	▲	Mountain	▲	Archaeological Site
- - - -	Unpaved Road	⊛	National Capital	✛	Unique Natural Feature	♠	Church
- - - -	Trail	★	Point of Interest			🛢	Gas Station
⋯⋯⋯	Ferry	•	Accommodation	⟋	Waterfall		Glacier
⋯⋯	Railroad	▾	Restaurant/Bar	▲	Park		Mangrove
≡≡≡	Pedestrian Walkway	▪	Other Location	**🛑**	Trailhead		Reef
⊞⊞⊞	Stairs	Λ	Campground	⛷	Skiing Area		Swamp

CONVERSION TABLES

°C = (°F - 32) / 1.8
°F = (°C x 1.8) + 32
1 inch = 2.54 centimeters (cm)
1 foot = 0.304 meters (m)
1 yard = 0.914 meters
1 mile = 1.6093 kilometers (km)
1 km = 0.6214 miles
1 fathom = 1.8288 m
1 chain = 20.1168 m
1 furlong = 201.168 m
1 acre = 0.4047 hectares
1 sq km = 100 hectares
1 sq mile = 2.59 square km
1 ounce = 28.35 grams
1 pound = 0.4536 kilograms
1 short ton = 0.90718 metric ton
1 short ton = 2,000 pounds
1 long ton = 1.016 metric tons
1 long ton = 2,240 pounds
1 metric ton = 1,000 kilograms
1 quart = 0.94635 liters
1 US gallon = 3.7854 liters
1 Imperial gallon = 4.5459 liters
1 nautical mile = 1.852 km

MOON SOUTH CAROLINA

Avalon Travel
a member of the Perseus Books Group
1700 Fourth Street
Berkeley, CA 94710, USA
www.moon.com

Editor and Series Manager: Kathryn Ettinger
Copy Editor: Christopher Church
Graphics Coordinator: Tabitha Lahr
Production Coordinator: Tabitha Lahr
Cover Designer: Tabitha Lahr
Map Editor: Kat Bennett
Cartographers: June Thammasnong, Chris Henrick
Indexer: Greg Jewett

ISBN-13: 978-1-61238-342-2
ISSN: 1543-4893

Printing History
1st Edition – 1999
5th Edition – January 2013
5 4 3 2 1

KEEPING CURRENT

If you have a favorite gem you'd like to see included in the next edition, or see anything that needs updating, clarification, or correction, please drop us a line. Send your comments via email to feedback@moon.com, or use the address above.